SINGING TO THE PLANTS

STEPHAN V. BEYER

SINGING TO THE PLANTS

A GUIDE TO MESTIZO SHAMANISM IN THE UPPER AMAZON

UNIVERSITY OF NEW MEXICO PRESS / ALBUQUERQUE

Printed in the United States of America

First paperbound printing, 2010
Paperbound ISBN: 978-0-8263-4730-5

All photographs © Ayahuasca SpiritQuest, Howard Lawler.
Design by Carrie House, HOUSEdesign llc

Library of Congress Cataloging-in-Publication Data
Beyer, Stephan V., 1943–
Singing to the plants : a guide to mestizo shamanism
in the upper Amazon / Stephan Beyer.
p. cm.
Includes bibliographical references and index.
ISBN 978-0-8263-4729-9 (cloth : alk. paper)
1. Shamanism—Peru—Maynas Region. 2. Healing—Peru—Maynas Region. 3. Human-plant relationships—Peru—Maynas Region. 4. Plants—Religious aspects—Peru—Maynas Region. 5. Ayahuasca ceremony—Peru—Maynas Region. 6. Ethnobotany—Peru—Maynas Region. 7. Maynas Region (Peru) —Religious life and customs. 8. Maynas Region (Peru) —Social life and customs. I. Title.
GN564.P4B49 2009
581.6'30985—dc22
2009021509

The plant comes and talks to you, it teaches you to sing.

—DON SOLÓN TELLO LOZANO

What good do you think my remedies would be if I didn't sing to them?

—DON MANUEL CÓRDOVA RÍOS

I have become an artist in the music of plants.

—DON JUAN FLORES SALAZAR

CONTENTS

ACKNOWLEDGMENTS

This work has grown out of seven trips to the Amazon, first to study jungle survival and then, gradually, to become absorbed, both personally and academically, in Amazonian spirituality. I have had the great good fortune to have studied with four mestizo shamans—don Antonio Barrera Banda, don Rómulo Magin, doña María Luisa Tuesta Flores, and don Roberto Acho Jurama. I am particularly indebted to doña María and don Roberto, who generously answered my questions, guided my visions, worked on the ache in my knee, protected me from sorcery, and taught me more than I have any right to know. Don Roberto is my treasured *maestro ayahuasquero*.

My contacts with mestizo healers were arranged by my friend Howard Lawler, a herpetologist by training and a longtime resident of the Amazon, who has shared with me his remarkable ethnobotanical knowledge and has been a cultural and linguistic translator, friend, confidant, generous resource, trusted guide and adviser, and brother on the medicine path. He has generously shared with me his remarkable library of digital images of Amazonian plants, and allowed me to reproduce those and other of his photographs in this book. For all of that—as for so much else—I am forever in his debt.

I am grateful too to the kind people at the October Gallery in London, especially Danielle Nunez and its director Chili Hawes, who helped provide the cover illustration painted by visionary artist don Francisco Montes Shuña. The gallery is a leading pioneer of the *transvangarde* or transcultural avant-garde, a sponsor of traditional and indigenous artists, and dedicated to the appreciation of cutting-edge contemporary art from cultures around the planet.

Of course, there is my large, boisterous, loving, warm, supportive, curious, critical, outspoken family, who connect me to all things most deeply human, bind me to the tragic and glorious cycles of life, and make me whole.

And this one, finally, is for Miriam. At last there is a neat symmetry between my books and my children, and Miriam's spirit goes together with my newest adventure.

INTRODUCTION

There are several reasons why a book on the mestizo shamanism of the Upper Amazon is worth writing at this time. Mestizo shamanism occupies an exceptional place among the shamanisms of the Upper Amazon, assimilating key features of indigenous shamanisms, and at the same time adapting and transforming them. There is today considerable interest in shamanism in general, and in Upper Amazonian shamanism in particular, especially its use of plant hallucinogens; yet there is currently no readily accessible text giving general consideration to the unique features of Amazonian shamanism and its relationship to shamanisms elsewhere in the world.

Moreover, many key texts, such as Luis Eduardo Luna's 1986 dissertation, are out of print and almost impossible to find; and many important studies are in foreign languages, especially French, such as the work of Alfred Métraux and Jean-Pierre Chaumeil. The beautiful and informative book *Ayahuasca Visions*, the combined work of mestizo visionary artist Pablo Amaringo and anthropologist Luis Eduardo Luna, is organized as a commentary on a series of paintings and thus, despite an extensive index, is not well organized for overall information. And much information, of course, is buried in specialist ethnographies of Amazonian peoples intended for a professional rather than general audience.

We now know much more about shamanism than when Mircea Eliade published his famous overview in 1951. There is now a wider range of excellent ethnographies, including many of Amazonian peoples; debates within the field have sharpened an awareness of many of the assumptions that underlay the fieldwork of many decades ago. Indeed, we now know, too, much more about ethnobotany, hallucinations, and the actions of such substances as dimethyltryptamine. It is time to try to put some of this together.

There was a time when I was deeply interested in wilderness survival. I was filled with machismo; drop me in the desert naked with a knife, I said, and I will eat lizards and survive. I undertook training in mountain, desert, and especially jungle survival, which took me on a number of trips to the Upper

FIGURE 1. The ayahuasca vine.

Amazon, both for training and to study indigenous survival techniques. One of these trips, with wilderness survival expert Ron Hood, to study the jungle survival skills of the last of the head-hunting Shapra and Candoshi Indians, became an award-winning survival training film.[1]

But, as I learned more and more about the ways in which indigenous people survive—indeed, flourish—in the wilderness, it became increasingly clear to me that wilderness survival includes a significant *spiritual* component—the maintenance of right relationships both with human persons and with the other-than-human persons who fill the indigenous world. Thus I began to explore wilderness spirituality, to learn ways to live in harmony with the natural world, striving, like indigenous people, to be in right relationship with the plant and animal spirits of the wilderness. I undertook numerous four-day and four-night solo vision fasts in Death Valley, the Pecos Wilderness, and the Gila Wilderness of New Mexico. I began to work with ayahuasca and other sacred plants in the Upper Amazon, peyote in ceremonies of the Native American Church, and *huachuma* in Andean mesa rituals.

So, too, this book is a result of my own need to make sense of the mestizo shamanism of the Upper Amazon, to place it in context, to understand why and how it works, to think through what it *means*, and what it has meant for me.

Here is a story. I am drinking ayahuasca. Suddenly I find myself standing in the entry hallway of a large house in the suburbs, facing the front door. The floor of the hallway is tiled, like many places in the ayahuasca world. There is a large staircase behind me, leading to the second floor; there are large ceramic pots on either side of the entrance way. I open the front door and look out at a typical suburban street—cars parked at the curb, traffic going by, a front lawn, trees along the curb. Standing at the door is a dark woman, perhaps in her forties, her raven hair piled on her head, thin and elegant, beautiful, dressed in a red shift with a black diamond pattern. She silently holds out her right hand to me. On her hand is a white cylinder, about three inches long, part of the stem of a plant, which she is offering to me.

I was concerned about this vision, because the red and black dress might indicate that the dark woman was a *bruja*, a sorceress. But don Roberto, my maestro ayahuasquero, and doña María, my plant teacher, both immediately and unhesitatingly identified her as *maricahua*, whom they also call *toé negro*, the black datura. They told me that this plant is ingested by splitting the stem and eating a piece of the white inner pith, about three inches long. The lady in my vision was handing me just such a piece of the plant, a part of herself.

Ayahuasca teaches many things—what is wrong or broken in a life, what medicine to take for healing. It teaches us to *see through* the everyday, to see that the world is meaningful and magical; it opens the door to wonder and surprise. I need to open my front door, look out onto a bland suburban street, and see standing there the Dark Lady, the black datura—thin and dark, raven hair piled on her head, elegant and beautiful, silently holding out to me a stem of maricahua—and follow her into her dark and luminous world.

PART I

SHAMANIC HEALING

CHAPTER 1

TWO HEALERS OF THE UPPER AMAZON

This book is based on two remarkable healers of the Upper Amazon—my teachers don Roberto Acho Jurama and doña María Luisa Tuesta Flores. The purpose of the book is to try to understand who they are and what they do, by placing them in a series of overlapping contexts—as healers, as shamans, as dwellers in the spiritual world of the Upper Amazon, as traditional practitioners in a modern world, as innovators, as cultural syncretists, and as individuals.

DON ROBERTO

Don Roberto Acho Jurama lives much of the time in the port town of Masusa, at the mouth of the Rio Itayo, in the Mainas district, not far from Iquitos. Like many mestizos, he often leaves the city for extended periods to return to his jungle village and tend his *chacra*, his garden, cleared from the jungle every few years by slashing and burning. In Masusa, don Roberto's thatched wooden house is at the end of a dirt street, alternately dusty and muddy; the house can be easily recognized by the pink and purple jaguar painted on its front wall.

Don Roberto holds healing ceremonies at his house on Tuesday and Friday evenings, the same days as other mestizo healers; he is also on call at almost any time for brief healings. The number of participants at his ceremonies varies from a few to a dozen or so. He also performs healing ceremonies, often with doña María when she was alive, for ayahuasca tourists, in a large tourist lodge in the jungle about two hours by boat from Iquitos. These ceremonies are open as well to any local person who wants to attend; thus the number

FIGURE 2. Don Roberto.

of participants—including local Bora, Yagua, and Huitoto Indians, as well as mestizos—can often be greater than at don Roberto's own private ceremonies. He is, in many ways, an Amazon traditionalist, certainly as compared to doña María. He cures by shaking his leaf-bundle rattle, blowing tobacco smoke, and sucking from the body of his patient the magic darts that have caused the illness—*shacapar*, *soplar*, and *chupar*, the foundational triad of Amazonian shamanism. Thus, much of what he does as a healer is recognizably similar to shamanic practices found among indigenous peoples throughout the Upper Amazon.

He is, as doña María described him, *flaquito*, wiry, compact, "like iron," she said; he is thin because he keeps *la dieta*, the sacred diet. Don Roberto has an intense gaze and a quick smile; he is serious about his work, but not serious about himself. As doña María put it, he is a *buen médico*, a good doctor, "who learned everything from ayahuasca."

Don Roberto was born on June 10, 1946, in the town of Lamas in the province of San Martín—the same town in which doña María was born, and a traditional home of powerful shamans. His father, José Acho Flores, was a carpenter and also a *banco tabaquero*—a healer of the very highest level who achieved visions and contacted the spirits through drinking infusions of potent tobacco. He had three brothers, all of whom had died by the time I met him; his father too was dead, while his mother was alive in the town of Punchana.

Roberto went to school through the seventh grade. His uncle, don José Acho Aguilar, was an *ayahuasquero*, and Roberto became an apprentice to his uncle at the age of fourteen. He became a shaman, he says, because, when he first drank ayahuasca, he *saw things*, which he enjoyed, and he wanted to learn more. Interestingly, neither don Roberto nor doña María reported that an illness or other crisis led them to become shamans. Doña María was, apparently, born with her visionary gift, which manifested itself when she was a young girl; don Roberto apprenticed himself out of curiosity, and discovered his talents as he grew in skill.

At the age of sixteen, Roberto began to work by himself. As his teacher got older, Roberto explains, his *fuerza*, power, diminished, and so he transferred his power to Roberto. That is why it is so important to Roberto for his son Carlos to follow in his footsteps; when Roberto's power starts to decline, he can transfer it to his son. During his apprenticeship, Roberto learned to *dominar la medicina*, master the medicine; he learned many plants, learned how to prepare ayahuasca, learned how to conduct the ceremony. After two years, his uncle said, "You are ready to work with ayahuasca by yourself." Such a two-year apprenticeship was considered very quick.

Roberto's uncle was his only teacher. To master the ayahuasca path, Roberto says, one must find the right maestro ayahuasquero and never change. "Some teachers don't know much," he warned me. "Some don't teach all they know, or have ulterior motives."

Roberto currently works as a carpenter, making furniture and boats, and only part time as a shaman; you cannot earn a living these days as a shaman, he says. Don Roberto had lived, unmarried, for some time with a woman who died while still childless; later he married Eliana Salinas, the mother of his eight children. The second youngest child is Carlos, don Roberto's pride and joy, who is studying with his father to become a shaman. Roberto is teaching his son in just the way he himself had been taught by his uncle. He took over his son's training when he discovered that Carlos was being deceived by another teacher with whom he was drinking ayahuasca: "The medicine was not staying in him."

Don Roberto and Eliana moved from Roberto's jungle chacra to the town of Punchana, where they lived for eighteen years, although, like many urbanizing mestizos, they continued to spend a good part of the year in the jungle. They lived in the town so that their children could attend secondary school, which don Roberto could afford, since he earned a good living as a carpenter.

Don Roberto is my maestro ayahuasquero, my teacher on the ayahuasca path. He was never as loquacious as doña María; but it is his phlegm that I carry in my chest, which has transformed me and turned me in directions I would never have guessed. He taught me how, on my own path, to be a healer. *Don't set a price,* he said: *Never turn away the poor. Do your healing. Trust the medicine.*

DOÑA MARÍA

Don Roberto constructs his life as essentially *eventless*, linear, uninterrupted by dramatic life-changing events. He apprenticed with his uncle; he learned how to heal from the plants; he goes on healing and teaching. Doña María, on the other hand, viewed her life as having had three dramatic *turning points*—her *coronación*, initiation, as a healer, during an extended dream; the first magical attack against her and her subsequent ayahuasca apprenticeship with don Roberto; and the second attack, launched against her by a shaman we will here call don X, which ultimately, after the passage of several years, proved fatal.

This story is worth telling for several reasons. Doña María's eclecticism and syncretism are in fact not unusual among mestizo shamans. Indeed, her early work as an *oracionista*, prayer healer, contained a number of practices found in more traditional mestizo shamanism, just as her later work as an *ayahuasquera* contained elements of her earlier work, influenced by both folk Catholicism and traditional Hispanic medicine. Her life vividly illustrates the risks and joys of being a healer in the Upper Amazon.

Psychologist and novelist Ágnes Hankiss discusses the way in which, in the narration of a life history, certain episodes are endowed with symbolic significance that in effect turns them into myths. She says that this is a never-ending process, for the adult constantly selects new models or strategies of life, by which the old is transmuted into material useful for the new—the new self and the new situation. Everyone attempts, "in one way or another, to build up his or her own ontology."[1] Daphne Patai, reflecting on her experience interviewing sixty women in Brazil, writes that "the very act of telling one's life story involves the imposition of structure on experience. In the midst of this structure, a subject emerges who tends to be represented as constant over time."[2] The women she interviewed, she says, "were telling me a truth, which reveals what was important *for them*."[3]

The same is true for doña María's story. When she was my teacher, she mythologized her past, centering on her three turning points, all of which validated her career as a healer and practitioner of *pura blancura*, the pure white path. Doña María was not a simple person, and certainly not a saint; she was genuinely warm, giving of her knowledge, impatient, dramatizing, complaining, generous, fussy, proud, unassuming, earthy, demanding, motherly. She lived as a healer in the disorderly landscape of the soul.

Childhood and Initiation

She was born on September 15, 1940, in the town of Lamas in the province of San Martín. Don Roberto came from the same town, although María did not meet him until many years later. Her father was a fisherman as well as a tabaquero, drinking infusions of tobacco to induce visions; he also possessed, as we will see, two *piedras encantas*, magical stones, one of which was a *demonio*, an evil spirit. María had three brothers and three sisters. Two of her brothers were killed—one murdered in a pathetic drunken robbery, the other robbed and murdered on a boat, struck on the head by a paddle and dumped, either dead or unconscious, into the water. María knew what happened, she told me, because she had seen both murders in her visions.

Doña María began her healing career as an oracionista, a prayer healer. Her youth was filled with dreams and visions of angels and the Virgin Mary. She delighted in working with children; when she retrieved the soul of a child, lost through sudden fright, the soul would appear to her as an angel. She did not drink ayahuasca until she was twenty-five, when, injured in a magical attack by a vengeful sorcerer, she first apprenticed herself to don Roberto, already at that time a well-known ayahuasquero. Toward the end of her life, she frequently joined don Roberto in his healing ceremonies for the tourist lodge. She did not herself perform regular Tuesday and Friday ceremonies; she would go—as she always had—wherever her healing powers were needed.

She remembered her early childhood as made idyllic by her visions and dreams. When she was seven years old, she had her first dream of the Virgin Mary—María called her *hermana virgen*, sister virgin—who began to teach her how to heal with plants. From that time on, she frequently had dreams in which either the Virgin Mary or an angel appeared to her. The Virgin would appear as a young and very beautiful woman; show her the healing plants, especially those for protection against *malignos*, evil spirits of the dead; and teach her the plants to cure specific diseases. The angel would appear and tell her where in the area there was a child who was sick and needed her help. She then went to the house of the child and told the family what plant would cure the illness and how to prepare it. In one dream, she was told that she must heal one hundred babies of *mal de ojo*, the evil eye; and she understood that her work was to be the healing of children.

María told me of one dream from this period of her life, which remained especially vivid. She was very tired, she recalled, and went to bed early. She dreamt that many people, adults and children, came and embraced her, showed her many plants, walked with her in the mountains and on the beaches. She played with these people in a beautiful river, and saw the *sirenas*, the mermaids, with their long hair, and the beautiful and seductive *yacuruna*, the water people, who live in cities beneath the water. Every day, she said, she had dreams like this and became happy and unafraid of any animal or insect.

During this time, too, she frequently made up *oraciones*, prayer songs, which she sang while walking to and from school. The other children, she said, liked to hear her sing her prayer songs. Even at this time, she called these songs her *icaros*—the term used not for prayers but for the sacred songs of mestizo shamans. She also discovered that she could foretell the future; she told me a story of how, when she was young, on a sunny day, she warned her mother to return early from gathering beans in her swidden garden in the jungle because, as she correctly foresaw, a fearsome thunderstorm was coming.

This is the paradisal portion of doña María's narrative. She told not only of her innocence and spiritual happiness but also of her turning away from evil. She could have been a *gran bruja*, a great sorceress, she said; the evil spirit in one of her father's magic stones gave her eight chances to turn toward sorcery, and each time she refused.

When María was nine, her father ran away with a *brasilera*, a woman from Brazil. It is remarkable how frequently Peruvian men are said to run off with Brazilian women—so remarkable, in fact, that I have come to believe that the term *brasilera* is not meant literally, but is used as a generic pejorative term for the type of woman who runs off with a married man. His sudden departure left María, her mother, and her brothers and sisters all destitute; around this time, too, perhaps due to the departure of the father, the family moved from Lamas to Iquitos, where they lived a hand-to-mouth existence. At the same time, María's dreams and visions were increasing in frequency and intensity. She was frequently told by angels where there were sick children who needed healing, and she was able to help her family with the offerings she received from grateful families.

When she turned eighteen, doña María had the dream that was to influence her entire life—what she called her coronación, her crowning or initiation. She told me each episode in the dream in precise detail, although the episodes differed somewhat in different retellings. She was lifted up in her mosquito net by the Virgin Mary and carried to the earthly paradise, where she was greeted by thousands of white-robed angels, holding beautiful brightly lit candles, lifting up their hands and saying *amén* in a single voice.

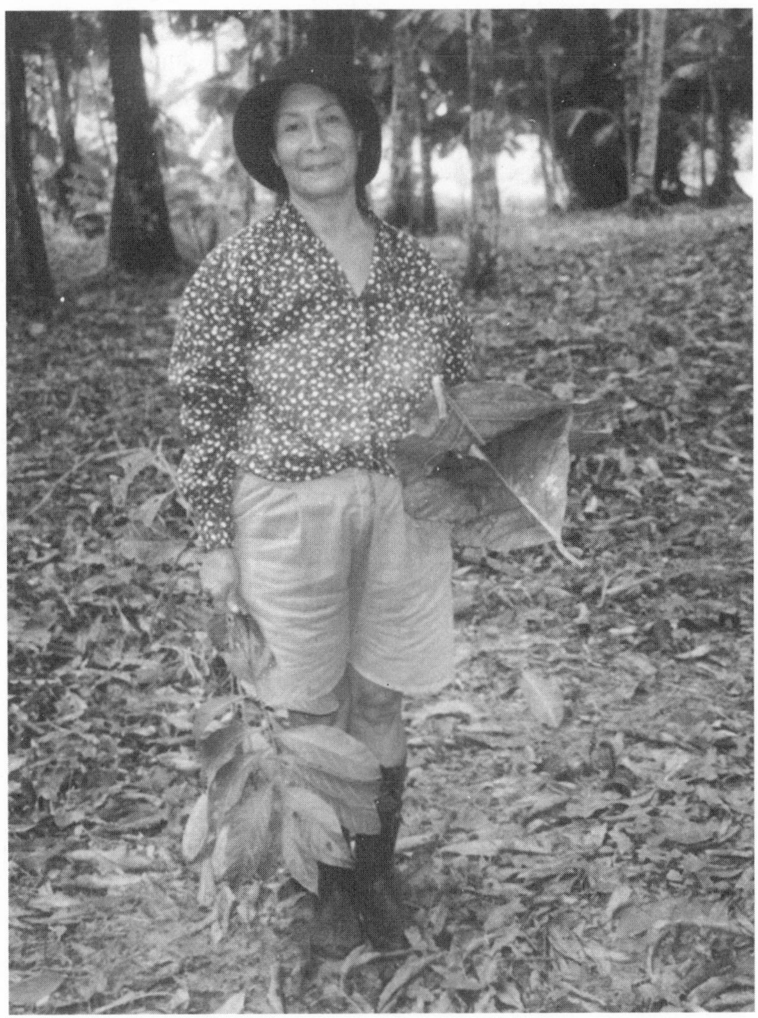

FIGURE 3. Doña María gathering plants.

Here she had numerous marvelous encounters—with magic stones, who sang to her in welcome; with the suffering souls of aborted babies; with the souls of the dead. They came to a great spiritual hospital where people greeted her, saying, "We've been waiting for you. We are going to crown you because you are a spiritual doctor." She was taken to a room where she was dressed in white clothing, white shoes, and a surgical mask, and her hands were washed with fragrant perfume. "You were brought here because you are a doctor for the earth," she was told. "Tonight you will begin your work here and on earth." She observed operations performed by the heavenly doctors, and was taken to a huge spiritual pharmacy filled with plant medicines of all kinds. Again she was told, "Welcome, *doctora*. Tonight you are going to receive the spiritual medicine." And everything that María saw and learned in the pharmacy she remembered when she awoke.

Finally, María and the Virgin came to two forking paths. One path was filled with beautiful, fragrant, inviting flowers and led into the green valley; the other path was filled with spiny and thorny plants and led to the rocky and barren mountains. "Now choose a path," the Virgin Mary said. "Will it be flowers or mountains?" María decided to take the path to the mountains, on which she saw many plants she recognized from the earth, as well as many that were new to her. The woman gave her a hug and kissed her forehead. "It is the better path you have taken," she said. María and the woman held hands and prayed. María felt emotion through her whole body and began to tremble. "Do not be afraid," the woman said; and María saw that the rocky path was in fact a precious highway, leading far away. "As far as you have come," the woman said, "you have a long way to go. As of this day, you have the *corona de medicina*, the crown of medicine"; and the woman placed a brilliant shining crown on María's head. From the time of this initiation dream, doña María told me, she understood that she was no longer to heal only children, but adults as well.

Ayahuasqueras

There are very few women shamans in the Amazon and certainly few among the mestizos.[1] Doña María said that she had encountered very little prejudice because she was an ayahuasquera. There were some shamans who said that she should not be a healer, but, in her typical way, she said that those were all stupid people with no fuerza, shamanic power, anyway.

Still, her vocation is rare. Rosa Amelia Giove Nakazawa, a physician at the Takiwasi center who treats addictions with traditional Amazonian medicine, reports that, in twelve years of investigation, she has known only two women who heal with ayahuasca. One is an elderly Quechua-speaking woman from Lamas, who lives in isolation, feared in her village as a bruja, sorceress; the other is well known in Iquitos but has fewer patients than the male ayahuasqueros, despite the fact that their methods are similar.[2]

I know of just two female mestizo shamans—doña María and doña Norma Aguila Panduro Navarro, who, until her recent death, performed healing ceremonies at Estrella Ayahuasca, her Centro de Investigaciones de la Ayahuasca y Otras Plantas Medicinales between Iquitos and Nauta.[3]

One of the reasons for the scarcity of ayahuasqueras is a concern, widespread in the Upper Amazon, about menstruation; the Shuar are perhaps unique in making no distinction regarding ayahuasca use based on sex.[4] Doña María told me that the plant spirits—who dislike the smells of human sex, semen, and menstrual blood—will not go near a woman who is menstruating. The presence of a menstruating woman at an ayahuasca ceremony, she said, will disturb the shaman's concentration and impair the visions of everyone present. Such a participant can drink ayahuasca, but she will not receive the full benefit of the drink. Blowing tobacco smoke on the menstruating woman—all over her body, beginning from the crown of her head down to the soles of her feet—may mitigate but does not eliminate the problem. For the same reason, doña María said, a female shaman cannot work while menstruating,

Such prohibitions are common in the Upper Amazon. Among the Piro, a menstruating woman—or even one who has recently had sex—should not participate in an ayahuasca ceremony.[5] Don José Curitima Sangama, a Cocama shaman, says that for the ayahuasca vine to grow properly, it must not be seen by a woman, especially a woman who is menstruating, or has not slept well because she was drunk. "If those women see the ayahuasca," he says, "the plant becomes resentful and neither grows nor twines upright. It folds over and is damaged."[6] For the same reason, don Enrique Lopez says that anyone undertaking la dieta must avoid women who are menstruating, or who have made love the previous night.[7] Menstruating women must even avoid touching or crossing over fishing equipment or canoes, lest they bring bad luck.[8]

There is less consensus regarding the effects of ayahuasca on a pregnant woman. Doña María told me that drinking ayahuasca while pregnant gives fuerza, power, to the developing child.[9] The same belief is found among the Shuar: some women express the belief that a child is born stronger if it receives the beneficial effects of ayahuasca while still in the womb.[10] Elsewhere, because of fear of spontaneous abortion, women do not drink ayahuasca at all.[11] The Piro agree; ayahuasca, they say, causes a pregnant woman to miscarry.[12]

Some of these attitudes may be slowly changing, at least in some urban centers, in large part due to the effect of ayahuasca tourism. Female tourists who have come great distances at considerable expense to attend an ayahuasca ceremony object strongly to being excluded because they are menstruating. There are also an increasing number of ayahuasca retreats for women-only tourist groups, and an increasing demand for female ayahuasqueras to accommodate female tourists.

NOTES

1. On Amazonian women healers generally, see Giove, 2001; Zavala, 2001. For a comprehensive review of gendered shamanism among the Shuar, by a woman anthropologist who is herself an initiated Shuar shaman, see Perruchon, 2003.
2. Giove, 2001, p. 37.
3. Brief accounts of three female healers in the Iquitos area are given in Dobkin de Ríos & Rumrrill, 2008, pp. 95–98, 109–110.
4. Perruchon, 2003, pp. 222–223.
5. Gow, 2001, p. 138.
6. Quoted in Dobkin de Ríos & Rumrrill, 2008, p. 61.
7. Quoted in Cloudsley & Charing, 2007.
8. Hiraoka, 1995, p. 213.
9. See also Giove, 2001, p. 39.
10. Perruchon, 2003, p. 223.
11. For example, Siskind, 1973a, p. 136.
12. Gow, 2001, p. 138.

The Meeting with Don Roberto

At the age of twenty-five, María was attacked by an angry and envious sorcerer, one of whose victims she had healed with her prayer songs. She was struck by his magic darts, one in her throat and two in her chest, which penetrated so deeply that she could not talk and could scarcely breathe.

Doña María spoke frequently about other people's *envidia*, envy, at her successes as a healer, and their unwillingness to share with her. There are three sins that characterize most adults, she said—envidia; *egoísmo*, selfishness; and *ambición de la plata*, greed. When she calls the spirit of an adult, she told me, the spirit feels like a wind; but when she calls the lost soul of a child, it appears as an angel, because children are innocent of these sins.

She frequently compared her own openhandedness with the selfishness of other shamans, who do not want to reveal their icaros, their magic songs. "I'm not selfish," doña María said. "I sing loud because I'm not afraid to let people know what I know." She frequently spoke of her own practice as pura blancura, pure whiteness, compared with the black or—even worse—red magic practiced by other, less disciplined shamans. Her attack by this *brujo* was the result of his envy and resentment; her later attack by don X, as we will see, was the result of his resentment and greed.

During this first magical attack, she went to the cemetery and prayed, cried out to all the *almas olvidadas*, the lost and despised souls, to help her find a shaman to remove the darts that had been shot into her body. Around three o'clock in the afternoon, a friend came to María's house; María could barely speak to her, because of the darts that had been shot into her throat. The friend offered to take María to meet a shaman she knew—a man named don Roberto.

It was Sunday when she came to don Roberto's house. When she knocked on the door, Don Roberto opened it and said, "Welcome, sister. I have been waiting for you." He continued: "Sister, I knew you were coming. Your body is fine, you are strong, you know much about the spirits, but you lack defense. Ayahuasca will give you defense." He told María how he had just cured a woman of sorcery, inflicted on her by the use of a *manshaco*, a wood stork. Then he sucked out the three darts. He gave one of the darts to María, putting it safely into her body through her corona, the crown of her head. He said, "Sister, this one is for you. I will keep the others."

Don Roberto told her, "Sister, you are very strong, but you do not yet know ayahuasca. If you come to me on Tuesday"—Tuesday and Friday nights are the traditional times for ayahuasca healing ceremonies—"I will introduce you." On Tuesday she drank ayahuasca with don Roberto, had a very powerful purge, and started on the ayahuasca path as his apprentice, along with five men and four other women who were already working under his direction. "Now you will work with ayahuasca in addition to what you are doing," don Roberto told her, "and you will move forward."

Doña María worked with don Roberto for ten years, until she was thirty-five years old, learning ayahuasca. This was a time, she said, of *pura medicina,* pura blancura, only medicine, only whiteness; *nada de rojo, nada de negro,* no red or black magic. After these ten years, don Roberto decided to return to his chacra in the jungle; but even when they were separated, doña María said, they continued to call upon each other from afar for help in their work.

The Attack by Don X

In the late 1990s, doña María was employed from time to time to do healing ceremonies for ayahuasca tourists at a lodge about two hours by boat from Iquitos. There she worked alongside a well-known ayahuasquero whom we will here call don X.

As we will discuss, accusations of sorcery are not infrequent in the Upper Amazon, and can have serious consequences. Although I knew don X personally—indeed, I was living with him in his jungle *tambo* during part of this period—the constraints imposed by the relationship of *confianza* I had with doña María and her friends prevented me from asking him for his side of the allegations against him. Hence his anonymity.

Now, don X had a son whom he had trained as an ayahuasquero, and who was able to pick up occasional employment at the lodge when doña María was unable to attend. According to doña María and her friends, don X decided that if doña María could be eliminated, the way would be open for his son to take her place in the relatively lucrative business of healing gringo tourists. So don X attacked doña María with *virotes,* magic darts, sending them deep into her chest and throat, causing her to suffer a serious stroke.

The attack took place at the tourist lodge, at night, when doña María was sleeping. She tried to get out of bed to urinate, but, when she got up, she fell to the floor, partially paralyzed, unable to move. She cried for help. One worker came, but he was not strong enough to move her; eventually, with the help of the gringo owner, she was lifted back onto the bed. "She was just like deadweight," the owner later told me. "It was all I could do to get her up to her bed myself."

Doña María spent the next six weeks in the hospital, slowly recovering from her stroke. She had originally resisted hospitalization, because she believed that the injections she would be given there would kill her. She felt herself to be lost. "Where will I find help?" she thought. Throughout this period, she heard a wicked mocking brujo laugh—the voice, she realized, of don X.

When she returned home, she was cared for by a Cocoma Indian shaman named Luis Culquiton, who was able to remove a few of the virotes, and who took care of her for six months. Don Roberto, her maestro ayahuasquero, had gone away to his chacra, his swidden garden in his village, but sent her medicine from afar. Although she recovered slowly from her stroke, she was unable to drink ayahuasca. She was thus cut off from the very sources of her protection; indeed, part of the cleverness of the attack was to separate her from her protectors by making it hard for her to drink ayahuasca.

The problem was that María continued to work with don X. She did not tell anyone that she had recognized his mocking laugh. Don X, as brujos do, allegedly concealed his malevolence under the guise of concern and sympathy. The virotes in her throat kept María from being able to sing at the healing ceremonies. "See, she can't sing," said don X to the gringo owner. "She is still too weak. You need to bring in my son."

Finally, after six months, don Roberto returned and sucked out the remaining virotes, but María continued to be weak. After her stroke, she said, her brain was "blank," and all the power she had received from ayahuasca was taken from her. She lost her visions, she could not drink ayahuasca—yet, she said, her spiritual power remained, because that came from Jesucristo and Hermana Virgen. "Whatever happens," she told me, "you must keep going forward, never give up."

Slowly, she began to drink ayahuasca again. As she drank more and more, she began to recover some of her powers. Yet, at the same time, she continued to work with don X, who actively suppressed her ayahuasca visions with his secret songs. Indeed, one of the ways a sorcerer attacks another shaman is by using an icaro to darken the vision of the victim. I do not know why María continued to work alongside her attacker—perhaps concern over accusing a well-known ayahuasquero, although, over time, she let the identity of her attacker be known; perhaps bravado, a demonstration of her own fuerza; perhaps—and this seems to me most likely—a demonstration of the forbearance she prized as part of her practice of pura blancura, the pure white path.

In July 2006, doña María died of complications resulting from the stroke. She continued her healing work, especially with children, to the end.

Doña María often shook her head in dismay at my questions, my blockheaded inability to absorb the immense plant knowledge she offered to me.

What I needed to learn I would learn, over time, from the plants themselves, she said; the way for me to learn was to "continue on, and all will be shown to you." This was typical doña María. When I would say I couldn't learn any more, she would scold me. *Study, study, study*, she would tell me. *Follow, follow, follow.*

CHAPTER 2
THE AYAHUASCA CEREMONY

PRELIMINARIES

It is getting dark, and the room is lit only by a few candles. People are beginning to gather. They talk quietly in small groups or lie in mute and solitary suffering on the floor. People tell jokes and exchange stories; they talk about their neighbors, about hunting conditions, about encounters with strange beings in the jungle. Some of them will drink ayahuasca, and some will not; some will drink for vision, and some for cleansing. Some drink in order to see the face of the envious and resentful enemy who has made them ill, or the one who has caused their business plans to fail, or the one with whom their spouse is secretly sleeping. Some drink to find lost objects, or see distant relatives, or find the answer to a question. Some may use *la medicina* as a purgative, a way to cleanse themselves. All are here for don Roberto to heal them.

Except for me. I am here not to be healed but, rather, to *learn the medicine.* I am here to be the student of *el doctor, la planta maestra, la diosa*, ayahuasca, the teacher, the goddess; to take the plant into my body, to give myself over to the teacher, to become the *aprendiz* of the plant, while under the powerful protection of don Roberto's magical songs, his icaros. I have been following la dieta, the diet—no salt, no sugar, no sex, eating only plantains and *pescaditos*, little fish. I have drunk ayahuasca with don Roberto before, and with other mestizo healers around Iquitos—doña María, don Rómulo, don Antonio. I am nervous about the vomiting. I wonder what I will see tonight; I wonder if I will see anything.

Don Roberto comes into the room and moves from person to person, joking, smiling, asking about mutual acquaintances, gathering information, talking about matters of local interest, getting the stories of the sick. Some people laugh at a joke, feel the brief light of his full attention on them and

Learning the Medicine

When I lived with don Rómulo Magin in his jungle hut, we drank ayahuasca together, sometimes with his son don Winister, also a shaman, as often as I could stand it. The goal of the sessions was not healing but, rather, for don Rómulo to guide my visions with his songs, make sure I kept the prescribed dietary prohibitions, and protect me from sorcerers who might resent my presence. None of my teachers was concerned that I myself might not become a healer; it is not uncommon among mestizo shamans to follow the ayahuasca path as a personal quest for learning and understanding.[1] Indeed, mestizo shamans may periodically gather just to share their visions, trade magical knowledge, and renew their strength.[2]

NOTES

1. See Luna, 1986c, p. 51.
2. Luna, 1986c, p. 142; Luna & Amaringo, 1993, p. 43 n. 69.

their problems. He spends some time talking informally with each person who has come for healing, and often with accompanying family members, quietly gathering information about the patient's problems, relationships, and attitudes. In addition, as himself a member of the community, don Roberto often has a shrewd idea of the tensions, stresses, and sicknesses with which the patient may be involved. There are about twenty people present. Everyone is given a seat and a plastic bucket, filled with a few inches of water, to vomit in.

THE MESA

Don Roberto leaves and then returns, dressed for the ceremony. He is now wearing a white shirt painted with Shipibo Indian designs, a crown of feathers, and beads. He smiles, makes a joke, and then spreads a piece of Shipibo cloth on the ground, to form his *mesa*, table.[1] On the cloth he places his ceremonial instruments:

- a bottle containing the hallucinogenic ayahuasca that will be drunk during the ceremony;
- a gourd cup from which the ayahuasca will be drunk;
- a bottle of *camalonga*, a mixture of the seeds of the yellow oleander, white onion, camphor, and distilled fermented sugarcane juice, which he may drink during the ceremony;

- bottles of sweet-smelling ethanol-based cologne—almost always commercially prepared *agua de florida*, but also including *colonia de rosas* and *agua de kananga*—which he will use to anoint the participants and which he also may drink during the ceremony;
- *mapacho*, tobacco, in the form of thick round cigarettes hand-rolled in white paper, distinguished from *finos*, thinner and considerably weaker commercial cigarettes;
- his *shacapa*, a bundle of leaves from the shacapa bush, tied together at the stem with fibers from the *chambira* or fiber palm, which he shakes as a rattle during the ceremony; and
- his *piedritas encantadas*, magical stones, which he may use during the ceremony to help locate and drain the area of sickness in the patient's body.

PROTECTION

Don Roberto then goes around the room, putting agua de florida in cross patterns on the forehead, chest, and back of each participant; whistling a special icaro of protection called an *arcana*; and blowing mapacho smoke into the crown of the head and over the entire body of each participant. Don Roberto usually sings the same protective icaro at each ceremony. The song has no special name; don Roberto simply calls it *la arcana*.

The goal is to cleanse and protect, on several levels. The arcana calls in the protective *genios*, the spirits of thorny plants and fierce animals, and the spirits of birds—hawks, owls, trumpeters, screamers, macaws—which are used in sorcery and thus the ones who best protect against it. Moreover, the good spirits like—and evil spirits hate—the strong sweet smell of agua de florida and mapacho, which thus both cleanse and protect the body of the participant. The goal, as don Roberto puts it, is to erect a wall of protection "a thousand feet high and a thousand feet below the earth."

PREPARING THE AYAHUASCA

Don Roberto sits quietly on a low bench behind his mesa, lights another mapacho cigarette, picks up the bottle of ayahuasca, and blows mapacho smoke over the liquid. He begins to whistle a tune—a soft breathy whistle, hardly more than a whisper—as he opens the bottle of ayahuasca and blows tobacco smoke into it. The ayahuasca, don Roberto says, tells him—in the resonating

FIGURE 4. Don Roberto blowing tobacco smoke over the ayahuasca.

sound of his breath whistling in the bottle—which icaro he should sing, and he "follows the medicine." The initially almost tuneless whistling takes on musical shape, becomes a softly whistled tune, and becomes the whispered words of an icaro, which may be different at different ceremonies.

When the icaro is finished, he whispers into the bottle the names of everyone present, adding ". . . and all the other brothers and sisters" if there are people present whose names he does not know or remember. Finally, he whistles softly once more into the bottle, the breathy whistle fading into his whispered song, his *icaro de ayahuasca*. He is *jalando la medicina*, calling in the medicine, summoning the spirit of ayahuasca.

DRINKING THE AYAHUASCA

The participants who will drink are called up, one by one, to stand before don Roberto, who fills the small cup from the altar with ayahuasca, singing over it, blowing tobacco smoke on it. The medicine itself tells don Roberto how much to pour for each participant; after he pours the appropriate amount into the cup, he blows mapacho smoke over the liquid. One by one, they take the pungent, oily, nauseating, and profoundly emetic ayahuasca; swallow it down quickly, asking the medicine for the healing or revelation that is desired; hand back the cup, and return to their places.

I come up to the mesa. I am among the last to drink, an honor. Don Roberto hands me the cup of ayahuasca—particularly full tonight, I note with dismay. Every molecule of my body rebels against drinking this vile liquid. I swallow it down as quickly as I can. It is one of the worst things I have ever tasted; it coats my teeth and tongue. I am grateful to return to my seat and smoke more mapacho.

Don Roberto drinks the ayahuasca last, singing over the cup. All light has gone from the sky. Someone blows out the candles, and everyone sits in the growing dark. Don Roberto sings icaros, rhythmically shaking his shacapa, calling in the spirits of the plants. After a while, the first gagging and vomiting sounds are heard in the dark room. Many participants are smoking mapacho; every few seconds the darkness is pierced by the glowing end of a cigarette. The room is filled with the smells of tobacco smoke and agua de florida, the one rich and deep, the other high and sweet, like musical tones.

CALLING IN THE PLANT SPIRITS

Now, while the ayahuasca is taking effect, don Roberto calls in all the remaining genios, the spirits of the plants, of whom ayahuasca is the *jefe*, chief. He sings the icaros of the plants—separate special icaros for some plants, often a single long icaro that lists dozens of plants and their healing powers, sometimes as many as a half-dozen icaros in a row. Here he is calling in the spirits of *all* the plants—like having the whole hospital staff present, he has told me—so that the appropriate plant spirit is immediately available if needed to heal a particular participant. Other shamans say the same: the shaman should convene as many spirits as possible, so that all may contribute to making the healing most effective;[2] don Juan Flores Salazar, an Asháninka shaman, sometimes jokingly refers to this as "the parade."[3] These icaros are often repeated from ceremony to ceremony; many in the audience—those who regularly attend don Roberto's healing ceremonies—know the melodies, and at least some of the words, and sing along. The icaros sung during the individual healings are more likely to be specialized, unknown to the audience.

CALLING IN THE DOCTORS

Here too there descend from the sky what don Roberto calls the *doctores extraterrestreales*, the extraterrestrial doctors. Such celestial spirits appear common to the healing ceremonies of many mestizo shamans; often they are from distant planets or galaxies, or are the spirits of deceased healers, *maestros de la medicina*. Don Rómulo Magin calls them jefes, chiefs; they descend from the sky dressed like Peruvian military officers. Don Emilio Andrade Gomez calls them *doctores* or *doctorcitos*; they may be Indian shamans or the spirits of doctors that come from other parts of the world, such as England, America, China, Japan, Spain, or Chile.[4] To Elvis Luna, a mestizo shaman and painter from Pucallpa, they are brilliant celestial beings that appear like angels. To don Roberto, they appear as dark-skinned people, Indians, almost naked, wearing only short skirts that cover their genitals; doña María calls them *marcianos*, Martians.

They speak, but not in human language. Rather, they speak in sounds: doña María says they speak in computer language, *beep boop beep beep boop beep beep*; don Roberto says they sound like *ping ping dan dan*. These are the spirits who help provide the diagnosis; they look at the patient and tell don Roberto where the problem lies, where to suck, what songs to sing, what healing plants to call; they also help him to heal, by blowing on the patients and waving their hands over them. "Treatment begins with the calling of spirits," says don Juan Flores Salazar, "the studying of what plants are required."[5]

SMALL HEALINGS

It is full dark. The frogs have started calling from the trees. There is one that sounds surprisingly like the ringing of a cell phone. Outside the hut, the jungle is breathing in the darkness—the river flowing, the wind in the palm trees, the delicate susurration of the shacapa, the syncopated singing of the magical icaros. I am beginning to feel really nauseous. *Oh boy, here it comes*, I think.

Once all the healing spirits have assembled in response to don Roberto's icaros, he begins the treatment of individual patients. He walks around the room, stopping before individuals, checking whether they are *mareado*, hallucinating. He approaches some of the patients, stands in front of them, and does relatively quick healings. He draws crosses on their palms and foreheads with agua de florida, sings icaros, and rattles his shacapa leaves, touching the bundle to their head and torso. He bends over and blows tobacco smoke into their bodies through the crowns of their heads, each with a soft voiceless sound—*pshooo*. . . .

Meanwhile, I am vomiting. Among mestizos, vomiting is accepted as natural and healthy; indeed, for many participants in this healing session, it is the vomiting, not the visions, that is the primary goal. But, to a North American like me, vomiting is a painful loss of control, a humiliating admission of weakness, often resisted, done in private; my embarrassed attempts to silence the sounds of my vomiting result in strangled retching, horrible sounds. In the context of ayahuasca, at least for those on the ayahuasca path, the giving up of control to the doctores, the plant teachers, is a lesson in itself, one I have still to learn.

BIG HEALINGS

Then the most serious healing begins. The patients requiring special attention are called up to the front, walking by themselves or helped forward by friends and relatives. One by one, the most seriously sick first, they sit or lie in front of the room, before the cloth where don Roberto has laid out his implements. Sometimes he asks them, "Where does it hurt? What is your problem?" Then he sings over them, shaking his shacapa, touching it to the places where they claim affliction. The patient is touched, prodded, as don Roberto seeks out the place where the illness is lodged in the form of a magic dart; then he blows tobacco smoke on the place, rubs it to loosen the affliction from the flesh in which it is embedded.

Then he ceases his singing and begins making extraordinary and dramatic sounds of belching, sucking, gagging, and spitting. He is drawing up his *mariri*, his magical and protective phlegm, to make sure that what he sucks from the body of his patient cannot harm him; then he loudly and vigorously sucks out the affliction, the magic dart, the putrid flesh or stinging insect, the magically projected scorpion or razor blade. He gags audibly at its vicious power and noisily spits it out on the ground. I watch don Roberto do his work—a synesthetic cacophony of perfumes, tobacco smoke, whispering, whistling, blowing, singing, sucking, gagging, the insistent shaking of the shacapa leaves, the internal turmoil, the inchoate visions. When the healing is done, don Roberto blows mapacho smoke into the patient through the crown of the head, over the place from which the sickness was sucked, and over the patient's entire body, cleansing and protecting both inside and out.

It is the medicine that tells don Roberto which icaros to sing, what healing plants are needed. He hears this as a voice speaking clearly and distinctly in his ear. "Suck in this place," he told me the voice says. "Blow mapacho smoke in that place. Use this icaro." The appropriate plant spirit steps forward and says, "Use me!" Don Roberto gave me an example of what he had heard during a healing ceremony the night before; he put his mouth right next to my ear and said, with startling clarity, "This patient has a serious sickness, pain in her womb. Tomorrow prepare medicine made from *catahua* and *patiquina*."

The same is true for doña María. "When you are in ayahuasca," she says, "the spirits come forth to do the healing." Just as with don Roberto, all the plant spirits attend doña María's healings, and, for each patient, the correct medicine steps forward and speaks into her ear in a clear voice, telling her what icaro to sing and what plant medicines to prescribe. She understands what they say, although they speak to her in Quechua, a language she does not know.

I am watching all this go on, with great lucidity, weak from vomiting, my legs like rubber. I am watching the preliminary effects of ayahuasca—lights, swirling galaxies, interlocking patterns, Van Gogh skies, fleeting images, floating and disembodied eyes. Suddenly, I am no longer in the jungle hut. Instead, I am walking down a street in an urban setting, with no one around, near a vacant lot with a chain-link fence, garbage scattered around. I come upon a vendor with a wooden cart—two large wheels behind, two small wheels in front, a handle to push it with—who has necklaces for sale, hanging from wooden pegs, of the inexpensive kind that are tossed to the crowd at Mardi Gras in New Orleans. I buy one and see a small girl, maybe five or six years old, standing on the sidewalk. She is blond, *muy gringa*, dressed in a pale blue satin party dress, as if she is on her way to a birthday party. In fact, she is wearing a crown on her head, which looks like a cardboard crown covered with gold foil, which I take to be a sort of party costume. I hand her the necklace as a gift, and she stands there very still, like a statue, holding the rosary—that is how I think of it now—raised in her right hand, the golden crown on her head, covered in light on the broken sidewalk.

She is, don Roberto tells me later, ayahuasca, the goddess, speaking to me. She has come to me before when I have drunk ayahuasca, in the form of a teenage Indian girl, in shorts and a white T-shirt, with long straight black hair and the most dazzling smile I have ever seen. I do not know why, but the spirits of the plants come to me as women.

ENDING

The ceremony continues through the night, as individual patients come forward. The icaros continue, rhythmic, syncopated, repetitive; there are breaks in the ceremony, during which don Roberto sings an icaro by himself, or the participants sit quietly or go outside for some fresh air. I go outside, into the jungle, breathing deeply, listening to the river, listening to the frogs.

Patients are called forward, rubbed, sung over, touched with the rhythmic shacapa, in some cases their bodies sucked and their gagging illness spit away. Hours pass, and the pace slows; people are nodding off. The ceremony does not so much end as fade away, like my nausea and visions. I am weak and tired, wrung out, wired. *I can't take much more of this*, I think, knowing that I will take much more of this. The call of vision is very strong. Why did la diosa come to me? What did she try to say? Did I listen for her song?

Doña María typically sings a concluding icaro thanking the spirits and sending them away; but, for don Roberto, the spirits simply fade away with the passing of his own *mareación*. Don Roberto relaxes, smiles, and slumps slightly, exhausted, once again informal, making a joke, talking about the ceremony.

CHAPTER 3
SHAMANIC PERFORMANCE

THE SHAMAN AS PERFORMER
Drama and Plot

The first thing we can notice about don Roberto's ayahuasca healing ceremony is that it is a *performance.* This should not be a surprise. Look at the healing performance of a typical American doctor—the white coat, the surgical scrubs, the stethoscope casually draped around the neck, the serious demeanor, the studied frown, the authoritative issuing of what are called *orders,* all conveying the authority of the healer and the risk and mastery of the healing process; then the patient waiting in a separate area, the name publicly called, the patient stripped and dressed in special healing clothes, the sudden appearance of the doctor, wearing a healing costume, at the door of the separate room. Indeed, as medical anthropologists Carol Laderman and Marina Roseman put it, "All medical encounters, no matter how mundane, are dramatic episodes."[1]

Don Roberto creates his healing performance with music, movement, props, plots, comedy, poetry, and dialogue.[2] Like all shamans, he is audience-oriented; his performance is designed to engage and affect audiences.[3] Historian Ronald Hutton puts it this way: all shamans are performing artists. If shamanism is partly a craft and partly a spiritual vocation, he writes, it is also an aspect of theater, and often a spectacularly successful one.[4] Indeed, performance artist Guillermo Gómez-Peña says that, throughout the years, he and his friends have become regular audience members of brujos or shamans. "Being performance artists ourselves," he says, "we view them as colleagues."[5]

But don Roberto's performance is not mere spectacle. It is also high drama. The healing ceremony is staged as a battle; the episodes of cure develop a plot with the same revelatory structure as myth. The shaman struggles with and for and through the patient's body in order to find the disease and cast it out. *The drama is to go into the patient's body and carry away the disease.*[6] It is the descent into the underworld, the perilous journey, the struggle against other-than-human enemies waged by a person along with other-than-human allies, ultimate confrontation, victory, triumphant return carrying a trophy—the illness, the magic dart, the envy and resentment, the disruption in the social fabric, sucked out of the body of the victim and spit, gagging, onto the ground.

Risk and Mastery

If don Roberto's healing ceremony is a performance, it makes sense to turn to an expert on theater for insight. Richard Schechner, founder of the Performance Studies Department at New York University, has proposed a form of nonmimetic theatrical work he calls an *actual*. Nonmimetic performance features a performer, in his or her own identity, doing something appreciated for its own sake. Actuals thus include sports events, stunts, circus acts, acrobatics, speeches, lectures, and some kinds of performance art. As Schechner says, "The idea of danger is exploited by the circus; that of excellence is the kernel of athletics. The combination of risk and mastery is asked of the performer of actuals."[7]

Indeed, *risk and mastery* constitute the essence of the shamanic performance. The risk is in the confrontation, especially, with the powers of sorcery that have caused the suffering being treated; the participants cannot know whether or when a more powerful sorcerer will turn upon the healer, especially a healer who has appeared to be initially successful and thus is an affront to the sorcerer.

Performer, Audience, Participants

Writing as a theatrical theorist, Schechner sees the force of any performance in the very specific relationship between performers and those for whom the performance exists.[8] Spectators are well aware of the quality and artistry of a performance, and can sense the precise moment when a performance takes off, when a presence is manifest, when something has *happened*. When the performers have touched or moved the audience, then a collective theatrical collaboration is born.[9] Many participant observers recall being swept up in the intensity of a ritual performance; in fact, anthropologist Victor Turner has famously used the term *communitas* for that which is induced by a well-performed ritual.[10]

The shaman's task is to constitute all the participants into an active presence with which a dynamic relation can be created. The shaman keeps the

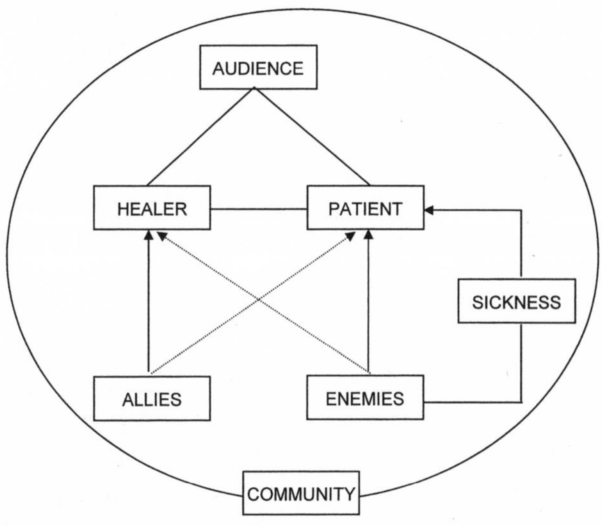

FIGURE 5. The field of the shamanic performance.

audience active and interested by providing enigmatic commands and riddles, mysteries that engage the audience. Because life is at stake—both the patient's and the shaman's—the risks are high, and much depends, not on the meaning of symbols, but on the performative competence of the shaman. In such rituals, risk becomes a measure of the importance and value attached to the performance. When a life is at stake, the healing ceremony must be challenging; otherwise the life is undervalued.[11]

Figure 5 provides a much simplified map of the dramatic field within which don Roberto's healing performance takes place. There is, first of all, a one-to-one relationship between the shaman and the patient—the shaman as entrepreneur and the patient as consumer. This relationship is itself related to an *audience*, present not as neutral or even interested bystanders but as a kind of Greek chorus.[12] Members of the audience both stand apart from and participate in the dramatic action. They assist, comment, criticize, participate, and evaluate; they move in and out of the action; sometimes they occupy the foreground and sometimes the background. They may sing along with the icaros, comment on the action, or ask the shaman questions in the course of the treatment.[13] They are critics of the shamanic performance, a source of future clients, and friends and enemies of the shaman and patient. They are deeply implicated in the struggle; their own lives hang on the outcome, on whether the shaman's power is sufficient to overcome the divisive evils that have manifested themselves in the body of the sufferer. One of them may even be the secret inflictor of the very harm the shaman now seeks to cure.

But, even if not physically present, the enemy—the inflictor, the sorcerer, the envious one—is a presence within the dramatic field. The spirits and powers that the enemy uses to curse are a reflection of the spirits and powers that the shaman uses to heal. The tools are the same; sorcerer and healer contest each other with the same weapons. The enemy of the patient—or the sorcerer engaged by the enemy of the patient—is the enemy of the healer as well. Victory in this battle invites retaliation in another; the humiliated sorcerer will seek revenge against the healer. And here the moral ambiguity of the healer becomes manifest, choosing whether to defend or attack, protect or harm, add the extracted magic darts of the sorcerer to the healer's own protective power or turn them back, counterattacking, to sicken or destroy.

The spirits are also active participants in the drama. The healer has built a relationship with them during years of interaction and now, in the drama of healing, seeks to enlist their aid as allies of the patient. The strength of the shaman lies in the strength of these relationships. Yet the allies of the healer are ambiguous, necessary and feared, sharing the same ambiguity as the healer—agents of good, possessors of menacing powers, jealous, potentially arbitrary, capable of abandoning the healer to solitary defeat.

As much as the healer's allies and the powers of the enemy, the sickness itself is a presence at the shamanic drama. As historian of religion Lawrence Sullivan puts it, shamanic medicine involves personal engagement with the forces of sickness that afflict the patient; the healer steps into the path of the attacking spirit in order to do battle with it.[14] The medicine of the healer fights the sickness with the weapons and the cunning of the sickness itself: the same plants that are used to harm can be used to dispel the harm; the magical phlegm of the healer protects against the *flemosidad*, the phlegmosity, of the illness. The disease, as Schechner puts it, is an embodiment of the community's curses, hatreds, and aggressions; the sickness is "whatever the community dislikes, fears, holds to be taboo, resists, resents, cannot face."[15] The sickness, the community, healer and patient, ally and enemy, are all bound together in a great and uncertain struggle, a battle between trust and resentment that mirrors the struggle of the entire community.

From this point of view, drama permeates the performance—the healer as ambiguous hero, maintaining doubtful alliances, facing an enemy of unknown powers, threatened with retaliation, exposed to the noxious gagging sickness, relying, ultimately, on skill and strength and knowledge, the outcome always in doubt.

Healing is often, in our culture, attributed in greater or lesser part to inherent personal qualities of the healer. The book *Healers on Healing* compiles a number of candidates—empathy; nonpossessive warmth and personal genuineness; compassion and intentionality; trust, faith, love, and humility; and "simple presence."[16] None of the pieces in the collection specifies an ability as a performer.

We will have occasion to discuss the social ambiguity of the shaman—that shamans may be considered treacherous, unstable, and touchy, and thus be suspect, feared, and distrusted.[17] I myself would hesitate before characterizing shamans generally—even just the small group of shamans I have known—as empathetic, warm, compassionate, loving, and humble. But they are all performers. Not all in the same way, of course; don Roberto is dramatic, forceful, flamboyant; doña María is warm, solid, comforting; don Antonio is sly, sensual, funny; don Rómulo is professional, impassive, controlled. Shamanism, writes anthropologist Stephen Hugh-Jones, is like acting or playing music—received knowledge and training combined with originality, skill, and performance. To know what you are saying and doing, you must learn from others; but to be any good, you must add something of yourself.[18] Such stylistic differences can be seen between don Roberto's practice of *chupando*, sucking, placing his mouth directly on the body of a patient—noisy, dramatic, flamboyant—and doña María's equivalent practice of *jalando*, pulling, drawing out the illness or intrusion from a distance—quiet, altogether more dignified, more ladylike.

Not only does each shaman have an individual performing *style*, but the style may vary from performance to performance. Every shaman is an individual performer, writes historian Ronald Hutton, "with a personal mode of operation which could be varied to suit each occasion." Hutton cites pioneering ethnographer Sergei Mikhailovich Shirokogoroff, who said, "In almost every shamanizing, there is something new."[19]

Shamanic performance is a skill, and skills are, at least in part, learned. There are tricks to shamanizing—conjuring, sleight of hand, poetry, gravitas, all aspects of the performing art. Laderman and Roseman ask a series of compelling questions: What kinds of skills are necessary for a performer-healer to command in order to be accepted in that role? What is involved in the performative creation of presence, verisimilitude, and social effectiveness? How is spirit presence created and convincingly sustained?[20] We must be careful here to avoid a dichotomy between true inspiration and pure performance—the sort of facile distinction expressed by anthropologist Andrew Strathern when he says, "Indeed, it is difficult . . . to be sure that we are dealing with an altered state of consciousness as against a dramatic performance."[21] Rather, as anthropologist Laurel Kendall has demonstrated in her account of the training of Chini, a Korean shaman, a healing performer cannot naively assume that the spirits will move her tongue for her: "She was repeatedly prompted in performative business that would transform the passive stuff of visions, inference, and intuition into an active spiritual presence."[22]

Don Roberto's son Carlos, of whom don Roberto is immensely proud, is training to be a shaman like his father. Now in his early twenties, he attends all his father's healing sessions, sitting at his father's side, wearing, like his father, a white shirt with Shipibo designs, observing, singing along, helping. Carlos does healings of his own, under his father's eye, singing his own icaros, shaking his bunch of shacapa leaves, blowing tobacco into the crown of the head. He does this now the way his father does, yet slowly and hesitantly developing a style of his own.

CONJURING AND PERFORMANCE

Is don Roberto a fraud? He *says* he sucks things out of the body; he *performs* sucking things out of the body; yet, obviously, the skin is not broken, *what* he sucks out is not clearly visible, mixed with phlegm, charged with power, dangerous to examine too closely. And the belching, the gagging, the retching, the slurping, the spitting—isn't that just *show*, performance, a sort of sleight of hand, drawing attention away from the fact that he is doing, really, nothing?

Dramatizing

Part of what is going on is simply effective drama. The !Kung shaman, too, pulls illness out of the patient's body, accompanied by sounds intended to convey the risk and seriousness of the process:

> The pain involved in the boiling of the healers' *num* (spiritual energy), in the putting of that *num* into the one being healed, in the drawing of the other's sickness into their own body, and in the violent shaking of that sickness out from their body is acknowledged by the healers by crying, wailing, moaning, and shrieking. They punctuate and accent their healing with these sometimes ear-shattering sounds. As their breath comes with more difficulty, until they are rasping and gasping,

> the healers howl the characteristic *kowhedili* shriek, which sounds something like "*Xsi—i! Kow-ha-di-di-di-di!*" Some say the shriek forcibly expels the sickness from a spot on the top of the healers' spine. Others say the shriek marks the painful process of shaking the sickness out from the healers' hands.[23]

For both the mestizo and the !Kung shaman, the noises *dramatize* both the risk and the mastery of the shamanic performance. Don Roberto's loud, liquid burping sounds indicate that he is drawing his mariri, transmogrified phlegm, up into his throat, where it will protect him from the darts, the sickness, the rotten putrid matter that he will be sucking from the patient. His slurping and sucking sounds dramatize the struggle to draw the sickness out. His gagging and spitting indicate the horrid nature of the sickness and his own strength in overcoming its nauseating power and expelling it from his body. The noises dramatize his struggle with the sickness, his own risk in handling the dangers assailing the patient, his mastery, his victory. The noises—visceral, corporeal—symbolize the triumph of the shaman's mouth over sickness and misfortune.

Sleight of Hand

We can approach this question by thinking about sleight of hand. Early anthropologist Martin Gusinde reports the following performance by a shaman in Tierra del Fuego: "He put a few pebbles in the palm of his hand, concentrated on them, and suddenly the pebbles vanished."[24] Can anyone with even a rudimentary knowledge of sleight of hand believe that this *wasn't* a conjuring trick?

One Siberian shaman showed eighteenth-century researcher Johann Gmelin how he pushed arrows through his ceremonial coat, piercing a bladder filled with blood to give the impression that the arrow had run through his body.[25] Other feats have puzzled anthropologists unschooled in conjuring. Russian anthropologist Waldemar Bogoras watched a Central Alaskan shaman, in broad daylight, wring out a fist-sized stone so that a stream of small pebbles fell from it and piled up on a drum placed below, while the original rock remained intact. Bogoras was convinced that it was a conjuring trick, but he could not figure out how it was done, especially as the shaman was stripped to the waist.[26] Such performances demonstrate why shamanism is, in such large measure, *a skill to be learned*.

Of course, some shamans are more skilled than others. Anthropologist and ethnobotanist Weston La Barre tells the story of Lone Bear of the Kiowa, who was so clumsy a shaman that he could be seen fumbling red clay from his pouch and chewing it in his mouth, later to be spit out as his own blood.[27] Some sleight of hand requires some investigation to unravel. In 1986, anthropologist Philip Singer made a film of Filipino "psychic surgeon" Reverend Philip S. Malicdan, who claimed to be able to open a patient's body with his bare hands, remove pathological material, and close the wound. Present at the filming were a professional magician, an audiovisual specialist, and a pathologist, who came to the unanimous conclusion that the psychic surgery was a fraud.[28]

Singer, remarking on the psychic surgery that he had filmed, concluded that psychic surgery is "cultural behavior learned by its practitioners, just as it represents cultural behavior by those patients, Philippine and Western, who accept it as a gift of the spirit." In this context, psychic surgery is adapted shamanism. Psychic surgeons, Singer says, have simply made a transition from traditional shamanism—extracting leaves, seeds, worms, or hair from the body—to a simulacrum of Western scientific medicine—extracting blood, tissue, tumors, or organs.[29] While this is a cogent analysis, it does not move our own inquiry forward; under this view, a fraudulent shamanism had simply become a fraudulent psychic surgery.

Skeptical Shamans

There have, of course, been shamans who were skeptical of their own practice, and their stories are of interest. The Winnebago Crashing Thunder, for example, longed all his life to be a member of the Medicine Dance, who could be shot and brought back to life.[30] During his initiation, he says, "I was shown how to fall down and lie quivering on the ground and how to appear dead. I was very much disappointed for I had had a far more exalted idea of the shooting. 'Why, it amounts to nothing,' I thought. 'I have been deceived. They only do this to make money.' . . . Now throughout the ceremony I felt all the time that we were merely deceiving the spectators."[31]

Claude Lévi-Strauss retells a fragment of the autobiography of a Kwakiutl Indian from the Vancouver region of Canada, originally obtained by Franz Boas, which tells a more subtle story. Quesalid began as a skeptic, eager to discover and expose the tricks of the shamans. To that end, he began to associate with the shamans until one of them offered to make him a member of their group. His story recounts his lessons in shamanizing—a curriculum that included pantomime, conjuring, and empirical knowledge; the art of simulating fainting and nervous fits; the learning of sacred songs; the technique for inducing vomiting; rather precise notions of auscultation and obstetrics;

and the use of spies to listen to private conversations and secretly convey to the shaman bits of information concerning the origins and symptoms of the ills suffered by different people. Most important, he learned how to hide a little tuft of down in a corner of his mouth, bite his tongue or make his gums bleed, throw up the bloodied fluff at the proper moment, and present it to the patient and audience as the sickness, extracted as a result of his sucking and manipulations.

One day he was summoned to the hut of a sick person who had dreamed that Quesalid was to be his healer. To Quesalid's surprise, this first healing was a success. Quesalid was puzzled that the healing was successful; it must be, he reasoned, because the sick person "believed strongly in his dream about me."

Not only did Quesalid discover that his conjuring *worked*, he found that his conjuring worked *better* than that of shamans with less dramatic skill. While visiting the neighboring Koskimo Indians, he saw that their shamans, instead of spitting out the sickness in the form of a "bloody worm," as he did, merely spit some saliva into their hands and claimed that it was the sickness. He requested and received permission to try his own method in a case where theirs had failed; the sick woman declared herself cured. Quesalid was troubled. The Koskimo shamans were even less honest than he was. At least he gave his clients some value—the sickness in its repulsive and tangible form. The others did nothing.

Meanwhile, the Koskimo shamans were discredited and ashamed before their people. They arranged a meeting with Quesalid and discussed their theory of illness with him. Sickness takes the form of a person, they said; when the soul of that person is extracted, its body disappears inside the shaman. What is there to show? When Quesalid performs, how does "the sickness stick to his hand"? Quesalid refused to say. He maintained his silence even when the Koskimo shamans sent him their allegedly virgin daughters to try to seduce him and discover his secret.

When Quesalid returned home, he was challenged to another healing contest by an elder shaman of a neighboring clan. This shaman healed by placing the invisible sickness into his headring or his rattle, which would then, by the power of the illness, remain suspended in midair. Once again, Quesalid, with his trick of the bloody worm, healed where the elder shaman could not. Again, the old shaman, ashamed and despairing, sent his daughter to beg Quesalid for an interview. "It won't be bad what we say to each other, friend," the elder said, "only I wish you to try and save my life for me, so that I may not die of shame, for I am a plaything of our people on account of what you did last night. I pray you to have mercy and tell me what stuck on the palm of your hand last night. Was it the true sickness or was it only made up? For I beg you have mercy and tell me about the way you did it so that I can imitate you. Pity me, friend."

In exchange for this information, the elder explained his own sleight of hand—a nail driven at right angles into the headring and rattle, which he held between his fingers to make the objects look as if they were floating in the air. He was a fraud; he admitted to being "covetous for the property of the sick men." Once again, Quesalid remained silent. That night, the elder shaman disappeared with his entire family, to return a year later, both himself and his daughter gone mad. Three years later, he died.

So Quesalid pursued his career. He continued to heal, using the trick of the bloody fluff, defending his technique against those of rival shamans. "Only one shaman was seen by me," he said, "who sucked at a sick man and I never found out whether he was a real shaman or only made up. Only for this reason I believe that he is a shaman; he does not allow those who are well to pay him. I truly never once saw him laugh."[32]

At the end of Lévi-Strauss's account, Quesalid had come to recognize that, despite the fraudulent nature of shamanic healing, it was still magical and effective. And so he continued to practice his healing. This conclusion may reflect Lévi-Strauss's own conviction that, from the shaman's point of view, magical power is identified with effectiveness, which does not depend on honesty or even purity of intention.[33] I am not so sure. Quesalid was a complex and intelligent person; he was far from being a cynical fraud. I do not think that his healing was independent of his intention—certainly not, if his intention was to heal.

Shamanic Defenses

At the same time, there are shamans who defend the authenticity of their practices. The "shaking tent" is a ritual widespread among indigenous peoples of North America, during which a shaman is tightly bound within a darkened lodge; the structure shakes violently; the shaman—and sometimes the audience as well—converses with spirits who speak and sing; and the shaman, when light is restored, is revealed to be unbound and sitting comfortably, apparently untied by the spirits.[34]

As professional magician Eugene Burger has pointed out, Native American shamans performing the shaking tent ritual had long been aware of the skepticism of traders and missionaries and of their assumption that the shaman was responsible for both the shaking of the lodge and the voices of the spirits. Therefore, it is interesting to hear the comments of shamans who had been converted to Christianity. The performers were unanimous in denying trickery. One said:

> I have become a Christian, I am old, I am sick, I cannot live much longer, and I can do no other than speak the truth. Believe me, I did not deceive you at that time. I did not move the lodge. It was shaken by the power of the spirits. Nor did I speak with a double tongue. I only repeated to you what the spirits said to me. I heard their voices. The top of the lodge was filled with them, and before me the sky and wide lands lay expanded. I could see a great distance around me, and believed I could recognize the most distant objects.[35]

Other shamans as well have argued for the authenticity of their performance. The healer don Antonio, of the Otomi Indians of Mexico, worked with anthropologist James Dow. His healing performance is strikingly similar to that of don Roberto:

> The patient uncovers the part of the body where pain or discomfort is felt. The shaman massages the area to work the object loose. He may first magically draw up the object from deep inside the body to just below the surface with a crystal. Then he places his mouth on the skin of the patient and sucks against it strongly. He clears his throat forcefully and then spits a substance into a cone of paper. . . . He chews tobacco in his mouth and sucks so hard that there is some blood mixed into the mass of mucus and tobacco shreds that he spits out. The substance he spits out is so loathsome and the retching sounds he makes are so unpleasant that I have seen no patients examine what is in the paper cone when invited. Most are content to take his word about what it is.

Dow comments, dismissively, that "obviously the skin is not broken and he doesn't really do it. This is a magical procedure the effect of which is to reduce pain and discomfort by psychological suggestion." To don Antonio, however, there is no cognitive dissonance in the fact that the object sucked from the body into his mouth does not actually pierce the patient's skin:

> When I suck objects I spit them out into a paper cone, because the stuff is so rotten. Sorcerers implant cow meat, pig meat, sardine meat, chicken meat, or whatever meat there is. They implant it, and so these

> bits of meat are cooked inside the body of their victims by the heat of the blood. So when you're about to suck out this stuff, you won't be able to stand its foulness. So this is why you use cigarettes. . . . At the moment that the illness is about to surface in the body, put a piece of cigarette in your mouth. If a piece of flesh is coming up, its rottenness will not be able to resist. Spit it out. . . . With this you pull it up. Pull it up with a crystal. This you'll have. But, the thing will not pop out on the surface of the skin. It's inside the flesh. It's below the surface, and then it comes up into your mouth.[36]

The Cultural Context

Neville Drury opens his book on shamanism by talking about Iban shaman Manang Bungai, who used monkey blood to fake a shamanic battle with an incubus. Drury claims that this is not "true shamanism," which is "characterized by access to other realms of consciousness."[37] But, apart from the unseemliness of an outsider anthropologist acting as neocolonial arbiter of the authenticity of someone else's tradition, it is worth pointing out that Manang is not a fake on his own terms or in the eyes of the culture in which he practices. The use of monkey blood in his shamanic performance requires a more subtle analysis than a simple European dichotomy into the authentic and the fake.

One theory we may call the *trophy view*. Anthropologist Marvin Harris, for example, writes that such conjuring has a persuasive healing purpose, producing the evidence needed for achieving a therapeutic effect, "although from the shaman's point of view the real business of curing involved the removal of intangible spirit-world realities."[38] Michael Harner distinguishes between the *spiritual essence* of an illness, which may appear, in the "shamanic state of consciousness," to be, say, a spider, and its *manifestation*, in the physical plane, as a "plant power object"—some twigs, say, which the shaman may hide in the mouth and then display to the patient and audience, who are in the "ordinary state of consciousness," as evidence of the extraction.[39] Lawrence Sullivan says that shamans "must make available to the naked eye what they see in their clairvoyant penetration of the spirit domain. By means of miraculous performances and shamanic miracle plays, the audience is able to see reality reflexively, the way shamans see it." Dramatic curing performances "provide for the public what ecstasy offers the shaman: a visible encounter with the forces at work on other planes of existence."[40]

This theory has been applied to shamanic performance in the Amazon. Anthropologist Philippe Descola recounts that an Achuar shaman told him that old pieces of glass, which he had spit into his palm as the pathogenic objects sucked from his patient, had actually been secreted earlier in his mouth. The shaman did this, Descola says, in order to avoid explaining to the patient that he had taken the *real* pathogenic objects, the darts he had sucked out, and blown them into his own wrist, for use against his own enemies.[41]

But I am not persuaded of the trophy view. It is based on what we can call a two-realm assumption—that there is a spirit world separate from this world, that there is a shamanic state of consciousness opposed to an ordinary state of consciousness. Like the dichotomy between curing and healing, the trophy theory assumes that the sucking shaman removes nothing really . . . well, *real*, an assumption based in a naive metaphysical dualism. Achuar patients are hardly unaware of what shamans do with the darts they have sucked out from them. Both don Antonio, an Otomi Indian from Mexico, and don Augustin Rivas, a mestizo shaman from Pucallpa, talk about physical *stuff*—rotten meat, a metallic object, thick choking phlegm—that appears in their mouths when they suck.[42]

Many shamans simply deny this dichotomy. Anthropologist Marie Perruchon, who is married to a Shuar husband and is herself an initiated *uwíshin*, shaman, puts it this way: ayahuasca "is a plant which has the effect that when you drink it, it allows you to see what otherwise is invisible, and it attracts the spirits. It is not that the ayahuasca takes one to another world, otherwise unreachable; it just opens one's eyes to what is normally hidden. There is only one world, which is shared by all beings, humans, spirits, and animals."[43]

Let us turn again to the shaking tent ritual. Anthropologist Weston La Barre offers a simple explanation. "How does the shaman make the séance tent shake?" he asks. "By the same naturalistic means the séance medium makes the table tip."[44] Professional magician Eugene Burger is more subtle. There are many ways that a professional conjurer could approach such ceremonies, including discussion of the numerous ways in which the effect could be achieved. Burger, however, makes two important points. First, he notes the numerous tales of the shaking of heavy and stable structures—a lodge with a double row of forty poles set close together, a lodge of sixty poles—with the inference being that such structures would be too solid to be shaken by human effort. There are also tales of frail old men in a lodge that shook for hours, shamans operating in full view, tents shaking while the shaman remained entirely outside, three lodges shaking at once. The point, he says, is that the audience was quite aware of the potential for trickery; otherwise, they would not have told such stories.

Second, there were criteria for distinguishing between fake and genuine performers. An old man confided: "Once when I was a boy I made a lodge and shook it myself. I was trying to do what I had seen done. My father stopped me immediately. He said something bad would happen to me if I played with things like that."[45] The tent-shaking ceremony could be done only if authorized by the appropriate dreams on how to build the lodge and how to call the spirits; failure to have the dreams, or failure to follow the dream instructions, meant failure in the long run and even illness or death. Burger remarks, tellingly, "But members of the community tried to duplicate the phenomena anyway. Some showed off, and some never had the dreams in the first place. Who were the imposters and charlatans? Those who had not had, and had not followed, the dream. Concern for sincerity was acute. But it was not a concern about the method of shaking the lodge, or about prowess with the method, but concern about vision and discipline."[46]

The problem, of course, is the importation of our own cultural attitudes toward conjuring into our appreciation of the conjuring other. That cultural attitude is not simply that conjuring is bad because it is somehow *false*. The attitude is that conjuring is *about* what Burger calls "the adventures of the props in the performer's hands"—strange adventures that happen to objects.[47]

We tend to see shamanic conjuring as *about* vanishing pebbles, bloody fluff, and retching and gagging, while that is not what it is about at all. "In the earliest conjuring performances," Burger writes, "magicians would probably have thought they had *failed* if people had complimented them on their skill and technique. These early conjurers seem to have believed that skill and technique were to be invisible, so that the *mystery* was the center of focus." In modern magical performances, on the other hand, the effects "do not point beyond themselves to an audience member's actual life in the world; nor do they point to a larger magical universe beyond the boundaries of the performance."[48]

HEALING CEREMONY AS ART FORM

The healing ceremony is intended to communicate the mystery of healing and the risk and mastery of the healing performer. Shamanic healing rituals in particular are designed to use a "multiplicity of communicative channels"—costumes, props, music, conjuring, poetry, movement, plots, suspense, stagecraft, dialogue.[49] The ceremony, like other compositions in art, dance, and music, does not constitute a single message sent intact to receivers; it relies instead on the spectators to *make* meaning of the performance.

We should not assume, just because we have our own cultural bias toward linear verbal interactions between healers and patients, that emplotment by a healer is necessarily either verbal or linear. Healing ceremonies do not restore order or resolve contradictions; healing performances manipulate spiritual and social power in part by *withholding* denotative meaning from some of the participants. It is, I think, this *mystery* that is at the heart of the shamanic performance. Don Roberto's ceremony is rife with uncertainty, ambiguity, and obscurity, filled with apparently meaningless elements, with communicative indeterminacy. His icaros are in secret incomprehensible languages, whistled, whispered; his interactions with the spirits are hidden; his power is dangerous and ambiguous.

The fact is that some stories are not told so much as acted, embodied, played. Healing actions acquire the formal and artistic qualities of the narrative—drama, suspense, risk, adventure, surprise, plot, a sense of the whole, and especially a sense that *something significant is happening*.[50] The healing ceremony of a mestizo shaman such as don Roberto is just such a narrative; it has a quality of vividness and heightened experience that sets the healing apart from the merely routine. To the sufferer, participation in the ceremony is not *mere* experience, forgettable and dull; rather, it is *an* experience, an extraordinary event, fixed in memory as a singular time.[51] In don Roberto's healing, with its active touching and sucking, its sounds and whispers, its penetrating smells and intestinal heavings, its *drama*, the body becomes the place in which the meaning of the sickness is revealed.

CHAPTER 4
THE SHAMANIC LANDSCAPE

THE SPIRITUAL SHAMAN

Anthropologist Michael Brown, who has studied the shamanism of the Aguaruna, an Amazonian people of northeastern Peru, tells how his friends in Santa Fe, New Mexico, have expressed to him their admiration for the beauty of the shamanic tradition, the ability of shamans to "get in touch with their inner healing power," and the superiority of spiritual treatments over the impersonal medical practices of our own society.[1] This spiritual view of shamanism is expressed in several key themes—healing, personal growth, empowerment, community, compassion; it sees shamanism as a set of techniques for self-realization, alternative healing, personal fulfillment, and success. Indeed, an anthology of contemporary writings on shamanism declares itself to be about "healing, personal growth, and empowerment."[2]

We can, very briefly, lay some of these beliefs alongside the Amazonian ethnographic evidence. Shamans, we read, work in harmony in an egoless way.[3] Yet the visionary paintings of Pablo Amaringo, based on his years of experience as a mestizo shaman, show recurring images of attack sorcery, dark shamanism, in which "evil shamans try to kill the person who is counteracting their evil doings by throwing magical darts, stealing the soul of their victims, or sending animals to bring harm."[4] We are told that true shamans do not even claim to be shamans; they are humble, identify only as servants of the sacred, and put the interests of others before their own.[5] Yet Shuar shamans brag about their experience and power and find it morally appropriate to put themselves and their families first.[6] Warao shamans, similarly, gain status and reputation by demonstrating their skills and talents.[7] In other cases, as among the Desana, shamans are indeed silent about their knowledge and power, but only in order to avoid magical attacks by envious sorcerers.[8] Again, we are told that shamans find their calling through "a spontaneous initiatory crisis conducive to profound healing and psychospiritual transformation . . . an experience of psychological death and rebirth followed by ascent into supernal realms."[9] Yet many mestizo ayahuasqueros "have learned their trade much as one would learn to become a car mechanic or doctor."[10] Among the Aguaruna and Canelos Quichua, shamanic power may be purchased for money or trade goods.[11]

Such descriptions of the benevolence and spirituality of shamans have little to do with the real world of shamanic practice, a world filled—like real human life—with danger, uncertainty, envy, betrayal, and loss. Doña María was twice stricken, the second time fatally, by magical attacks launched against her by envious and resentful sorcerers. Two shamans with whom I had close relationships turned, apparently for reasons of greed and envy, on two other friends of mine, one a shaman, filling their bodies with magical darts: shaman A attacked my friend B, who was healed by shaman C, who in turn attacked shaman D because he believed that shaman D was being favored by my friend B. That is the true landscape of shamanism—the landscape of suffering, passion, and mess.

SPIRIT AND SOUL

Psychologist James Hillman distinguishes between two basic orientations to the world, which he calls spirit and soul. *Spirit*, he says, is detached, objective, intense, absolute, abstract, pure, metaphysical, clear, unitary, eternal, and heavenly. *Soul*, on the other hand, is mortal, earthly, low, troubled, sorrowful, vulnerable, melancholy, weak, dependent, and profound.[12] Spirit means fire and height, the center of things; soul means water and depth, peripheries, borderlands. Spirit seeks to transcend earth and body, dirt and disease, entanglements and complications, perplexity and despair.[13] But soul "is always in the thick of things: in the repressed, in the shadow, in the messes of life, in illness, and in the pain and confusion of love."[14]

Spirit "seeks to escape or transcend the pleasures and demands of ordinary earthly life."[15] Spiritual transcendence, writes Hillman, "is more important than the world and the beauty of the world: the trees, the animals, the people, the buildings, the culture." Spirit seeks "an imageless white liberation."[16] What Hillman calls *spirit*, Martin Buber calls, simply, *religion*—as he puts it, "exception, extraction, exaltation, ecstasy." But the mystery instead dwells *here*, he says, "where everything happens as it happens," in the possibility of dialogue.[17] Philosopher Emmanuel Levinas puts this idea in theological terms: "Going towards God is meaningless," he says, "unless seen in terms of my primary going towards the other person."[18]

The transcendent orientation of spirit can be a way of escaping the messy demands of soul—a process that psychotherapist John Welwood, in a much-copied phrase, has called *spiritual bypass*.[19] Buddhist meditation teacher Jack Kornfield puts the idea this way: "Many students have used meditation not only to discover inner realms and find inner balance but also to escape. Because we are afraid of the world, afraid of living fully, afraid of relationships, afraid of work, or afraid of some aspect of what it means to be alive in the physical body, we run to meditation."[20]

THE SHAMAN AND SOUL

It is soul, not spirit, that is the true landscape of shamanism. Shamans deal with sickness, envy, malice, betrayal, loss, conflict, failure, bad luck, hatred, despair, and death—including their own. The *purpose* of the shaman is to dwell in the valley of the soul—to heal what has been broken in the body and the community. Graham Harvey, a scholar of indigenous religions, puts it about as pithily as it can be put: "Salmon ceremonies and salmon respecting," he says, "are about eating salmon, not about communing with symbols of transcendence."[21]

Eliade, Wasson, and the Mushrooms

Historian of religions Mircea Eliade famously viewed shamans as essentially characterized by celestial ascent, ecstasy, soul flight, and out-of-body journeys to the spirit realm.[22] His widely cited treatise on shamanism is filled with references to the sky, to ascent, to the vertical rather than the horizontal. He sees the sacred in the transcendent, the vertical plane, the center as opposed to the peripheries of things;[23] it is thus at the center, he says, at the tent pole, the mountain, the world axis, that the shaman communicates with the sky, ascends through the central opening, ascends the sacred mountain, and ascends to the sky.[24] Eliade is willing to denigrate as decadent or aberrant any shamanism in which the ascent to the sky plays an insufficiently important role.[25] Shamanism among the Tungus people today, he says—that is, in the 1930s, when Shirokogoroff produced his famous studies—cannot be considered shamanism in its classic form, because, among other things, of "the small role played by the ascent to the sky."[26] Eliade's description of shamanism thus emphasizes both the center of things and the upward journey—almost paradigmatically as spirit rather than soul.

In 1955, banker R. Gordon Wasson, an amateur connoisseur of mushrooms, was introduced by the Mazatec shaman María Sabina to the ancient *teonanácatl*—the *Psilocybe* mushroom, called *'nti-ši-tho* in Mazatec, Little-One-Who-Springs-Forth. María Sabina called them her *saint children*. Wasson was deeply impressed by his mushroom experience. He speaks of ecstasy, the flight of the soul from the body, entering other planes of existence, floating into the Divine Presence, awe and reverence, gentleness and love, the presence of the ineffable, the presence of the Ultimate, extinction in the divine radiance. He writes that the mushroom freed his soul to soar with the speed of thought through time and space. The mushroom, he says, allowed him to know God.[27]

Wasson's description falls effortlessly into the language of ecstasy, awe, soul flight, the Divine Presence, the knowledge of God—the same stock of European concepts from which Eliade drew. But María Sabina herself could not understand any of this. She says: "It's true that Wasson and his friends were the first foreigners who came to our town in search of the *saint children* and that they didn't take them because they suffered from any illness. Their reason was that they came to find God."

And none of it, of course, had anything to do with the indigenous uses of the mushroom, whose purpose was to cure sick people by, among other things, making them vomit.[28] She adds: "Before Wasson nobody took the mushrooms only to find God. They were always taken for the sick to get well."[29] To find God, Sabina—like all good Catholics—went to Mass.[30]

When Sabina ingested the mushrooms, the mushroom spirits would show her the cause of the sickness—for example, through soul loss, malevolent spirits, or human sorcerers: "The sickness comes out if the sick vomit. They vomit the sickness. They vomit because the mushrooms want them to. If the sick don't vomit, I vomit. I vomit for them and in that way the malady is expelled."[31] And she would then be able to cure the patient through the power of her singing. Sometimes the spirits told her that the patient could not be cured.[32]

Wasson had clearly come to Mexico anticipating a religious or mystical experience, and now he had one.[33] Indeed, he had been less than forthright about his motives. He knew that the mushroom ceremonies were for curing sickness or finding lost objects, and he told Sabina—as well as other Mazatec healers—that he was concerned about the whereabouts and well-being of his son. He later admitted that this was a deception in order to gain access to the ceremonies.[34]

Like Wasson, the influx of North Americans who followed him to Sabina's village were not seeking the cure of sickness; they were seeking enlightenment. Sabina could not understand why well-fed and apparently healthy foreigners were seeking her mushrooms. These people certainly did not look sick to her:[35] "Some of these young people sought me out for me to stay up with the *Little-One-Who-Springs-Forth*. 'We come in search of God,' they said. It was difficult for me to explain to them that the vigils weren't done from the simple desire to find God, but were done with the sole purpose of curing the sicknesses that our people suffer from."[36] She laments: "But from the moment the foreigners arrived to search for God, the *saint children* lost their purity. They lost their force; the foreigners spoiled them. From now on they won't be any good. There's no remedy for it."[37]

While Wasson was climbing the mountain of spirit, seeing Sabina as a saint-like figure, a spiritual psychopomp, "religion incarnate," María Sabina dwelled steadfastly in the valley of soul, healing the sick, vomiting for them, expelling their sickness, living her own difficult and messy life—until Wasson's spiritual bypass destroyed the power of her mushrooms.[38]

Ayahuasca and the Body

Moreover, ayahuasca shamanism is irreducibly physical. The body is the instrument of power and understanding—power stored in the chest as phlegm, understanding achieved through ingestion. The shaman learns the plants by taking them into the body, where they teach the songs that leave the body as sound and smoke. An ayahuasca healing session enacts the physical materiality of the human body—nausea, vomiting, diarrhea, sucking, gagging, belching, blowing, coughing up, spitting out; perfume, tobacco smoke, rattling, whispering, whistling, blowing, singing, the taste of tobacco and ayahuasca, the imagery and ritual of the body, conflict, mess.

Similarly, in the ayahuasca ceremony substances traverse body boundaries, reminding us of our penetrable and leaky borders. Excrement and vomit are ejected, magical darts are sucked out through the skin, internal substances are spit out through the mouth, magical phlegm is transferred from shaman to disciple, tobacco smoke is blown into the body through the crown of the head—the body exaggerated, vast excretions, ferocious corporeality. Reminders of the darker side of human existence constantly lurk in the margins of shamanic performance—dangerous ambiguity, broken boundaries, ambivalence, transgression, disorder.

THE SOCIAL AMBIGUITY OF THE SHAMAN

The territory occupied by the shaman is suffering, hope, failure, envy, spite, and malice. We are stricken by the resentment of others; we are betrayed by those we have trusted; our successes are stalked by illness and death. In this landscape, the shaman occupies a position of dangerous power and ambiguous marginality. Native American writer Gerald Vizenor says that "shamans can be treacherous, unstable, and touchy."[39] The idea is the same in the Amazon: the shaman is "ambiguous, suspicious, . . . fundamentally distrusted," says one anthropologist;[40] "dangerous, disquieting," says another.[41] "Once one is known as a shaman," writes anthropologist Marie Perruchon, herself an initiated Shuar shaman, "trust is forever gone."[42] Even shamans do not trust each other. As one mestizo shaman puts it, "The only shaman you can really trust is yourself."[43]

People see that the shaman can heal, which means that the shaman can also kill.[44] Social anthropologist Stephen Hugh-Jones points specifically to the ambivalent nature of the shaman in Amazonia; shamans may use their power for good or evil.[45] Anthropologist Mary Douglas calls this the *theory of the unity of knowledge*—that those who can cure can kill.[46] Among the Napo Runa of Amazonian Ecuador, for example, to proclaim oneself a *yachac*, possessor of *yachay*, shaman, is to endanger not only one's life but the lives of one's family. Shamans are thought to have the power to harm as well as to heal, doing the former sometimes through their mere anger. Because most sicknesses and deaths are thought to be caused by the ill will or anger of a shaman, to reveal oneself is to risk being associated with and attacked for the tragedies of others.[47]

In the Amazon, the power of the shaman to heal *is the same as* the power to harm. As pioneering ethnographer Alfred Métraux points out, the shaman is able "to draw magic substances from his body in order to heal or to harm. In many cases, the power that infuses a shaman's being and resides in his body is identical with poison capable of killing."[48] The same theme is repeated throughout the Amazon. Among the Desana of the Upper Río Negro, the Yagua of eastern Peru, and the Aguaruna of the Río Marañon, shamans and sorcerers, curing and killing, come from the same source.[49] Healing and sorcery are two aspects of the same process. "A particular plant," says don

Javier Arévalo Shahuano, a Shipibo shaman, "has a spirit which can either heal or kill."[50]

Anthropologist Steven Rubenstein, speaking of Shuar shamanism, puts it this way: "One cannot help others unless one works within the same framework that hurts others. The power to kill and to cure is the same because it is embodied in the same instrument"—the *tsentsak*, the shaman's magic darts.[51] As one Shuar puts it, "There are bad shamans and there are good shamans, but they are all bad."[52]

The very nature of shamanic power is believed to invite malfeasance on the part of the healer. Shamans have the power to call the spirits, the Sharanahua say, and no one can be sure if they call them for good or evil; shamans enjoy killing.[53] Indeed, increasing power often goes hand in hand with increasing ambivalence: more powerful shamans may be better healers but are also potentially more dangerous.[54] This ambivalence has been described either as sociopolitical—shamans should kill their enemies in other groups and heal their friends in their own group—or as the product of apprenticeship—shamans who master their emotions and aggressive desires use their powers to heal, and others who fail to exercise self-control become sorcerers.[55] It is in fact much easier—requiring less time and suffering—to become a sorcerer than a healer.[56]

Outbreaks of sickness have often been the occasion for one village to attack another whose shaman is deemed responsible. Early Spanish incursions into the Amazon, bringing epidemics in their wake, may in fact have caused an increase in interethnic warfare.[57] A raid by one Achuar village on another, occasioned by high fevers in both, and blamed by each on the shaman in the other, was recounted as recently as 1996.[58]

Until recently, little attention was paid to dark shamanism—what has also been called *assault sorcery*—or to the centrality and importance of dark shamanism to the overall spiritual and cosmological ideas of Amazonian peoples in general.[59] There is an ambiguity inherent in shamanic practice, where the dangerous work of healing and sorcery intersect. Because shamans possess spirit darts, and with them the power to kill, the boundary between sorcerer and shaman is indistinct.[60] Social anthropologist Carlos Fausto characterizes Amazonian shamanism as *predatory animism*, where some people can enter into relationships with other-than-human persons, which permit them to cure, to fertilize, and to kill. Shamanism, he says, "thrives on ambivalence."[61]

This ambivalence is nowhere more clear than among the Shipibo, who clearly state that the healing act itself ineluctably causes harm—that to remove the sickness from one person is to cast it upon another who lacks the power to repel it. Since the illness-causing substance cannot be destroyed, the shaman, in curing one, always harms another.[62] In the same way, Yagua shamans toss extracted sickness-causing darts toward the sun, where they reach the subterranean realms of the people-without-an-anus, causing considerable harm. Even more, the harm multiplies. In reprisal, the shamans of the people-without-an-anus fling balls of earth at the Yagua, on which their children sometimes choke.[63] Similarly, in return for successful hunting, the Tukano shaman must pay a fee—the lives of living people, who are sent to serve the Master of Animals. The shaman drinks ayahuasca and sees these victims in the form of birds sitting on the rafters of the spirit's house. The lives are those of people who live far away; when shamans learn that people have died in some other place, they know that the debt has been paid.[64]

In the Amazon, the dark and the light, killing and curing, are at once antagonistic and complementary; shamanic healers and shamanic killers represent interlocking cultural tendencies, and their battleground is the flesh of the sick, the ambiguous heart of the shaman, the valley of the soul. Thus, the shaman's power is granted grudgingly by a society that both needs and fears it. As Brown reports, in the Alto Río Mayo, if one asks, "Do you have an ishiwín, a shaman, in your community?" the reply is likely to be, "No, we get along well here. We have no problems."[65]

THE DANGERS OF BEING A SHAMAN

It is, in fact, *dangerous*—and I mean physically dangerous—to be a shaman, for four reasons. First, since all shamans are themselves potential sorcerers, and have the ability to kill if they desire, they are prime suspects when there are deaths suggestive of sorcery, especially the deaths of their own patients. Second, since the shaman can identify sorcerers, and such sorcerers may be marked for death because of this accusation, the shaman inevitably has enemies. Third, the spirits with whom the shaman works can be dangerous, fickle, jealous, and unpredictable, and they may abandon the shaman without warning. And, fourth, a successful shaman invites envidia, and other shamans will attack out of jealousy and resentment.

Accusations of Sorcery

"Sorcerers are still murdered in the Upper Peruvian Amazon," writes Françoise Barbira Freedman. Two Lamista suspects were recently killed in revenge, shot dead at night: "'People got tired of their evil doings,' I was told."[66] Shuar shaman Alejandro Tsakimp describes the murder of an uwíshin, shaman, named Tséremp, who boasted of his power to kill and was suspected in the illness of a relative:

> Then we went to see where they killed him—they killed him in his own bed! Everything was shot up! And my uncle, my father's own brother, Pedro, had cut Tséremp in the chest with a machete. The shotgun hadn't killed Tséremp, so Pedro cut until the machete penetrated the heart.
>
> Tséremp was a powerful uwíshin, Alejandro concludes, but he fell because of the many bad things he had done.[67]

In 1978, anthropologist Jean-Pierre Chaumeil did a survey of Yagua shamans in eastern Peru, including which shamans had died during the preceding decade. All eleven deceased shamans reportedly had been killed, either by other shamans, using sorcery, or by villagers, in reprisal for sorcery of their own. Yagua shamans, he writes, are often blamed for the suffering of others, and may be attacked at any time by the relatives of a victim or by a rival shaman. The shaman must constantly be on guard to prevent and to be instantly aware of this type of attack.[68]

When I was among the Shapra Indians, about 800 kilometers up the Chapuli River in the highland jungle border area between Peru and Ecuador, I was told that the community no longer had shamans—we used the Spanish word *chamán*—but, rather, now sought out *médicos*, doctors, because of the destructive blood feuds that resulted from failed healings, subsequent accusation of sorcery, and bloody interminable headhunting vendettas between the families of patient and shaman. The same thing has happened among the Yawanahua, where pepper and tobacco powder have fallen into disuse because of their association with sorcery; in one village, a community meeting was organized by the old and new village heads, where a collective agreement was made not to practice sorcery anymore.[69]

Among the Shuar, when a person in the neighborhood falls ill, the shamans are the first to be blamed.[70] Moreover, because shamans control spirit darts, people fear that shamans may be tempted to use the cover of healing as an opportunity to bewitch their own clients for personal reasons. The clients therefore expect results; and, if such results are not forthcoming, the shaman may be suspected of sorcery, and punished for it.[71]

And failures occur, accidents happen, patients die. On April 25, 2003, in Ontario, Canada, an Ecuadorian Shuar shaman named Juan Uyunkar pled guilty in the death of a seventy-one-year-old woman who had died during a three-day ayahuasca healing ceremony. In addition to the ayahuasca, participants had been given infusions of tobacco to drink, and tobacco enemas if they wished, in order to help induce vomiting and purgation. An autopsy concluded that the woman had died of nicotine poisoning. Uyunkar was originally charged with eight offenses, including criminal negligence causing death; he pled guilty to reduced charges of administering a noxious substance and trafficking in ayahuasca, a controlled substance, the charges carrying a maximum penalty of two years in prison. On April 26, 2003, an Ontario judge, seeking to balance "the conflicting principles between the spiritual and the temporal," sentenced Uyunkar to twelve months of house arrest and 150 hours of community service, and forbade him from conducting any further ayahuasca rituals.[72]

This is exactly the sort of adverse event that could happen in any shaman's practice, but in traditional shamanic cultures the outcome could have included the murder of the shaman by outraged relatives of the patient, convinced that ill will and sorcery were involved. If the shaman declines to treat people, if the shaman is reluctant to work hard at healing, *if too many patients die*, the question arises: Is the shaman really a sorcerer? Is the shaman pursuing sorcery under the guise of healing?[73]

The Amazonian shaman is thus, in the words of anthropologist Pierre Clastres, a person of "uncertain destiny"—a holder of prestige, but at the same time responsible in advance for the group's sorrows, and held accountable for every extraordinary occurrence.[74]

Every shaman, then, is in a precarious position. As anthropologist Steven Rubenstein reports among the Shuar, when the veteran shaman Tséremp would not—or could not—heal Chúmpi's son, Chúmpi concluded that Tséremp was a killer—a conclusion that led finally to the murder of the shaman, described above. And when Alejandro Tsakimp, as a novice shaman, was asked to perform a healing, Tsakimp could not refuse; although he was terrified of failing, Rubenstein writes, he was more afraid of saying no.[75] Similarly, among the Desana of the Upper Río Negro, a shaman will never propose to attempt to heal a sick person, lest the shaman be suspected of intending harm—indeed, will not claim to know what the illness is or how to cure it, even to the extent of letting the sick person die. If asked, however, the shaman cannot refuse, and then, after the curing session, will explain in some detail exactly what was done and used to heal the sickness—again, to protect against suspicions of sorcery in case the sickness gets worse.[76] As shamans get older and their occasional therapeutic failures accumulate, they find themselves increasingly vulnerable to suspicions of no longer being willing to heal or of causing sicknesses themselves.[77]

Thus, shamans need explanations for their failures to cure. Among the Cashinahua, sickness may be caused by a sorcerer materializing the *muka*, the bitter shamanic substance, within the sorcerer's body and shooting it as an invisible dart into the victim. The healing shaman can see this substance and suck it out of the victim's body, but only if it has not yet spread out, in which case the victim's death, the shaman will explain, was inevitable.[78] In the same way, a Cubeo shaman cannot cure where the darts are simply too numerous.[79] The Sharanahua believe that the Culina are particularly powerful shamans, who kill by throwing the *dori* that is inside their bodies. If enough dori is thrown, the sickness can be cured only by a Culina shaman; the Sharanahua shaman is helpless.[80]

The Revenge of Sorcerers

The shaman's role is not limited to healing; the shaman also identifies the enemy shaman who caused the illness.[81] This identification is conveyed to the shaman as visionary information supplied by ayahuasca. Achuar shamans, for example, can see the pathogenic darts in the patient's body connected by very long silvery threads to the one who sent them. But naming that person creates a mortal enemy, and Achuar shamans may decline to do so, or require high payment, commensurate with the risk.[82]

Indeed, the person the shaman names as the sorcerer runs a real risk of being killed.[83] Michael Brown worked with an Aguaruna shaman named Yankush. When a respected elder died suddenly of unknown causes, Yankush came under extraordinary pressure to identify the sorcerer responsible. From an ayahuasca vision he concluded that the sorcerer was a young man from a distant region who happened to be visiting a nearby village. The young man was killed within a few days. Because Yankush was widely known to have named the sorcerer, he became the likely victim of a reprisal raid by members of the murdered man's family. "Yankush's willingness to accept this risk in order to protect his community from future acts of sorcery," Brown writes, "was a source of his social prestige, but it was also a burden. I rarely saw him leave his house without a loaded shotgun."[84] Such a dilemma is profound. Failure to identify another as the responsible sorcerer is to bring suspicion on oneself.

Fickle Spirits

The spirits can be fickle; ayahuasca, doña María warned me, is *muy celosa*, very jealous. The spirits hate the smells of human sex, menstrual blood, and semen; they may abandon the shaman for many reasons or no reason at all. Shamans can be made "worthless," "drunk-like," reduced to a sorry state through the loss of their power in spirit attacks, a fate greatly feared among mestizo shamans. There is no tenure in shamanism; spirit helpers are imponderable and can desert powerful shamans from one day to the next.[85]

Envious Competitors

Rivalry, jealousy, and mutual accusations of sorcery are integral features of shamanism;[86] a shaman must always be on guard against the evil attacks of vengeful foes.[87] The shaman lives in a world filled with danger. Shamans envy other shamans who are more successful, have more clients, and heal more sickness; shamans seek revenge on other shamans who have thwarted their attacks or attacked their friends. Sorcerers will attempt to destroy their competition, and, if they cannot kill the shaman, they will concentrate on the more vulnerable members of the shaman's family.[88] One Colombian woman recalls the days of the great shamans: "They could become tigers and parrots. They could fly. Now they are finished. They ate one another. They fought each other. They were consumed with envy. They would turn into a tiger to eat the whole family of their enemy."[89]

Indeed, even admitting that one is a shaman opens the door to such attacks; despite economic or social benefits of the shaman role, many prefer to conceal their gift and remain hidden, at least until they are sufficiently powerful to resist attack.[90] To declare oneself a shaman is in itself a boast of one's powers. And every healing is potentially a contest between shamans, defense and attack, revenge, turning magical darts back upon the one who sent them. A shaman is at constant risk of being killed by other more powerful shamans.

CHAPTER 5
LEARNING THE PLANTS

THE IMPORTANCE OF THE DIET

To learn the plants—the term used is *dominar*, master—means to create a *relationship* with the plant spirits, by taking them into the body, listening to them speak in the language of plants, and receiving their gifts of power and song. To win their love, to learn to sing to them in their own language, shamans must first show that they are strong and faithful, worthy of trust. To do this, they must go into the *monte*, the wilderness, away from other people, and follow la dieta, the restricted diet. Indeed, some plants, such as catahua and *pucalupuna*, want to deal only with the strongest and most self-controlled of humans, those willing to undertake a *dieta fuerte*, a lengthy and rigorous diet. Other humans they kill.

The restricted diet is the key to a relationship with the plants. Apprentice shamans learn the plants by dieting with them, ingesting them, studying their effects, awaiting the appearance of the plant spirit in a vision or dream to be taught their uses and their songs. La dieta is vital during apprenticeship; and shamans continue to observe la dieta from time to time throughout their careers, when treating difficult patients, when preparing certain medicines, to revitalize their shamanic power, or to learn new plants. According to don Guillermo Arévalo, a Shipibo shaman, such ongoing diets throughout one's lifetime are the sign of a real shaman.[1]

The plant spirits reveal themselves, their uses, and their icaros, sacred songs, only to one who follows la dieta. Don Roberto insists on periodic—and often lengthy—*dietas* for his apprentices. Don Roberto is a good example: during his apprenticeship, he dieted for ten days before drinking ayahuasca for the first time, fifteen days before drinking it for the second time, and twenty days before drinking it for the third time. While on la dieta, he could have no salt, no sugar, and no sex. He could eat *plátanos*, plantains, grilled in their skins, and pescaditos, little fish, all without salt; he could drink a little lemon juice in water, but nothing sweet; he could eat no rice. He drank the ayahuasca in the monte, the jungle, alone with his maestro and three other apprentices. Some shamans, such as don Agustin Rivas, have their apprentices drink the latex of *ojé*, which causes a violent purge, before beginning the diet.[2]

THE SMELL OF THE JUNGLE

The term *monte* occurs frequently in mestizo shamanism. It generally refers both to mountains and to woodlands; in the Amazon, it is, technically, the term used to differentiate the highland jungle from the *várzea*, the annually flooded lowland forest. But to the mestizos, the term means—as one regional dictionary puts it—*despoblado*, unpopulated, deserted, and thus dangerous, solitary, and frightening.[3]

Since the plant spirits are very sensitive to smells, dwelling in the jungle allows one to acquire *olor a monte*, the smell of the jungle, the smell of other-than-human persons, while abstinence eliminates the smells of human sex.[4] Pablo Amaringo says that human beings just smell bad to the spirits generally, and only a long diet will purify one from this bad smell.[5] Grandfather Alonso Andi, a Napo Runa, speaks of hunting: "From so much walking . . . the body acquires the smell of the forest; man becomes the forest and animals don't flee."[6]

The same is true of the spirits. César Calvo notes that those following la dieta may dress in special ancient *cushmas*, never washed: "The cushmas blend into the stink and the colors of the deep jungle, so that animals and souls aren't made restless by the smell of man."[7] To *become the forest* makes one acceptable to the spirits of the plants.

Don Leoncio Garcia, a Shipibo shaman, makes this point with a story. Once there was a man, he says, who learned so much from ayahuasca that he kept on drinking it, singing day and night. His two sons tried to feed him, but, when they tried to pick him up, they found that he had become rooted to the ground. When the sons returned a month later, they saw that ayahuasca vines were growing from their father's fingers; when they returned once again they saw that the vines had tangled all about him; and, finally, they returned to find that their father had merged completely into the jungle.[8]

It is certainly possible to diet alone; but apprentices generally diet under the tutelage of their maestro ayahuasquero, who keeps them to the diet, and protects them and modulates their visions with magic song. But much of the

Cushma

The temperature in the jungle remains pretty steady at around 85 degrees, and the relative humidity at about 90 percent. You can certainly walk around the jungle naked without discomfort, at least from the weather. Still, the jungle is pretty much filled with insects and sharp objects, and many indigenous people wear clothing of one sort or another. In the Upper Amazon, the traditional dress of a number of indigenous peoples—the Machiguenga, Asháninka, Yine, Conibo, Cashibo—is the cushma.

A cushma—the word is Quechua—is a woven cotton tunic, rather like a large poncho, sewn together from armpits to feet, sometimes tied with a belt around the waist. Cotton for cushmas may be cultivated in the garden, or wild cotton may be gathered in the jungle; the cotton is spun into fine thread and woven into cloth—a demanding and time-consuming process, which is one reason why indigenous people acquire ready-made European-style clothing whenever possible.[1] A cushma may also be made out of factory-woven cloth, although hand-woven cushmas are more prestigious.[2]

A cushma is made by weaving a strip of cloth about half a yard wide and about four times the length of the finished product. This cloth is them cut in half, and the two halves are sewn together lengthwise, except for a foot-long head opening in the middle; and the sides are sewn up except for a small opening at the top for the arms. A woman's cushma usually has the head opening crosswise rather than lengthwise; the head opening in a woman's cushma is also wider, to allow for breast-feeding.[3]

The cushma can be worn white or can be dyed in stripes or other patterns.[4] Among the Asháninka, a man's cushma always has vertical stripes, and a woman's has horizontal; when an Asháninka cushma becomes worn, it is often dyed reddish brown, and the process may be repeated until it is almost black.[5] Shipibo men may wear cushmas covered with the intricate, labyrinthine ayahuasca-inspired designs for which the Shipibo are famous. Shipibo women wear distinctive brightly colored blouses, and short skirts often covered with the same designs.

The cushma is a pretty comfortable garment, made from local materials. Like so many comfortable and sustainable things in the Amazon, it is disappearing.

NOTES

1. Johnson, 2003, p. 83.
2. Hvalkof, 2004, p. 49.
3. Hvalkof, 2004, p. 49.
4. Farabee, 1922, pp. 9–10.
5. Hvalkof, 2004, p. 49.

time is spent in solitude, alone in a small tambo, an open thatched shelter they have built themselves, in which they stay throughout the diet, with not much to do. Days of drinking ayahuasca alternate with days on which they go out into the jungle, learning to identify, gather, and prepare the plants.

It is probably worth noting that many mestizo shamans are skilled *mitayeros*, hunters and fishers, in large part, I think, because of months of sitting

Tambo

All *ribereño* houses are built on pretty much the same principles—a thatched house on stilts, built entirely of jungle materials, which may range in size from a small temporary hunting shelter, just large enough to sleep one or a few people, to an elaborate structure able to house an extended family. Some of these houses are relatively isolated; some—connected together by dirt paths through the jungle or clustered about a central square—form *caseríos*, villages, with a soccer field, perhaps a cement schoolhouse and community center, and even a clinic or a small bodega for goods brought upriver by motorized canoe.

Both the thatched roof and the raised flooring are supported by upright posts made of durable hardwoods such as *huacapú*, *icoja*, and *tahuari*. These hardwoods have acquired symbolic meaning in mestizo shamanism and plant medicine: their bark is used in medicines to enhance male potency, and is added to the ayahuasca drink to support those who drink it, just as these trees support the ayahuasca vine.

The roof is thatched with *irapay* palm leaves, whose stems are looped and knotted on poles of *pona* wood to form long sheaves, called *crisneja*, that are then tied in an overlapping pattern onto the rafters with strips of *atadijo* bark—the same bark that is used to bind the long cylindrical bundles of cured tobacco sold in the market. The peak of the roof is covered with *yarina* palm leaves, and the springy floor—it bounces when you walk on it, which can be disconcerting at first—is made from slats cut from the trunk of the *huacrapona* palm. Ethnobotanist James Duke estimates that as many as twenty different species of plants may be used in the construction of a single dwelling.

There is usually a single primary room, where people sleep under mosquito nets, either on the floor or in hammocks; bedding and nets are rolled up during the day. There may be a separate storeroom or a separate sleeping room for the older members of the household. Supplies and equipment are also kept up in the rafters that support the thatched roof. The kitchen is often separated from the main house, at ground level, or connected with the main house by an elevated walkway, with a thatched roof for cooking when it rains. A notched tree trunk provides steps to the main room; there may be a railing around the front of the elevated room, forming a porch, from which residents talk to passersby.

There are few latrines. Many people go out into the jungle to defecate, or squat in the water at the edge of the river; many houses on stilts on the river's edge have tiny rooms with a hole in the floor directly over the water. I have seen people bathe and wash dishes downstream from where they defecate. Even when ventilated concrete latrines have been constructed, they are often not well maintained and, when full, abandoned. Many larger riverboats have a small screened room sticking out over the water with a hole in the floor. Clean potable water remains a significant need in many ribereño communities.[1]

NOTE

1. See generally Chibnik, 1994, pp. 46, 72. On construction materials, see Duke & Vasquez, 1994, pp. 3–5; on potable water issues, see Aguiar, Rosenfeld, Stevens, Thanasombat, & Masud, 2007.

quietly and observing the jungle during la dieta. The very blandness of the diet sharpens the senses. The network of almost invisible paths that interlace the jungle is thought to have been created by the great and powerful shamans of the past.

That is how the plants teach you—sitting quietly in the jungle, with no place to go, listening for their song.

THE RESTRICTED DIET

Food Restrictions

The term *dieta*, diet, and the corresponding verb *dietar*, is more comprehensive than suggested by its English equivalent. The term encompasses not only food restrictions but also sexual abstinence, social isolation, and dwelling, by oneself, in the monte. The diet may be more or less elaborated by different shamans.[9] Beyond salt, sugar, and sex, most often prohibited is oil or fat. César Calvo says that ayahuasca has four requirements—no salt, no sugar, no fats, no sex.[10] Pork is often prohibited as well, although the flesh of some wild animals—such as the *huangana* (white-lipped peccary), *sajino* (collared peccary), or *sachavaca* (common tapir)—may be permitted or prohibited, depending on the teacher. Don Agustin Rivas Vasquez, a mestizo shaman from Tamshiyacu, ate only rice, plantains, mushrooms, and a toothless fish called *boquichico*, which itself eats only water plants; he ate no fruits, vegetables, salt, or spices.[11] Another apprentice had to abstain from salt, sugar, spices, pork, lemon, and sex; sugar, said his teacher, makes one timid and fearful.[12] Don Emilio Andrade Gómez, a mestizo healer, had to abstain from pork, sweets, salt, pepper, and sex, because his stomach was very dirty—"full of the essence of all sorts of species, like garlic, and pepper, and also of pork and other things." Only by following la dieta would he learn to see.[13]

Additional prohibitions may include avoiding the sun by staying indoors, avoiding being seen by strangers, and not eating spicy food.[14] Pablo Amaringo says that the dieter must avoid the sun, salt, sweets, garlic, liquor, and pig fat while also abstaining from sex or socializing with anyone who is sexually active.[15] Cocama shaman don Juan Curico says that one must first eliminate salt, then sugar, then fried food, then sex, and then exposure to sun.[16]

A six-month diet is usually considered the minimum; diets may last a year or longer.[17] It is said that to become a *banco*, a supreme shaman, one must diet for more than forty years.[18] This does not mean that the diet is continuous, but, rather, refers to a lifetime of periodic diets, to refresh one's energy and to learn new plants. During this time, too, new or additional plants may appear, in dreams or intuitions or intentions or visions, with instructions on how to diet with them, as when my beautiful Dark Lady, the spirit of maricahua, the black datura, held out to me, in an ayahuasca vision, a split piece of the stem of the maricahua plant.

The idea of a special diet for shamans and their apprentices is widespread throughout the Amazon. For example, Shuar shaman Alejandro Tsakimp, when an apprentice, could eat small chickens and little fish but not tapir, armadillo, or guinea pig.[19] Ashéninka apprentices eat no meat or chilies, drink no alcohol, and abstain from sex. They must eat only vegetables, particularly fried manioc, as well as toothless fish such as catfish.[20] Shipibo apprentices must not eat salt, herbs, spices, and certain fish and animals; they must not let themselves be seen or spoken to and must be sexually abstinent.[21]

Shaman apprentices among the Tukano must abstain from sex and live on nothing but manioc and water, giving up fish, broiled game flesh, and pineapples. Apprentices are expected to become thin.[22] Yagua apprentices too must abstain from sex and observe a strict diet before and for several days after drinking ayahuasca, in order, they say, to prolong the vision. Greasy or rotten food is prohibited, but the apprentice may eat plantains braised in their skin, mashed boiled plantain, and two or three small fish. Anything with a strong taste is prohibited. Apprentices are also separated from their family, living for several months in an isolated place, learning the plants and their preparation.[23] Alonso Andi, a Napo Runa elder, says that apprentices "must not sleep with their wives, eat red pepper, salt, or hot manioc. They have to keep on fasting for several days and eat what sick people eat, such as little birds, but no other type of food."[24]

Maricahua

The term *maricahua* is usually identified as an alternative name for *toé* or *floripondio*, referring to any of several *Brugmansia* species, particularly *B. suaveolens*.[1] The term *toé negro* is usually identified as referring to a plant in an entirely different genus, *Teliostachya lanceolata*.[2] Doña María and don Roberto instead identify maricahua with toé negro, and distinguish this plant from toé, which in this context they call *toé blanco*.

NOTES

1. Duke & Vasquez, 1994, p. 33; López Vinatea, 2000, pp. 37–38; Schultes & Raffauf, 1990, p. 421.
2. Duke & Vasquez, 1994, p. 167; López Vinatea, 2000, pp. 71; McKenna, Luna, & Towers, 1995, p. 356; Rengifo, 2001, pp. 71, 142; Schultes & Raffauf, 1990, pp. 47–48.

Sexual Abstinence

Both sexual abstinence and food restriction relate to the fact that the plant spirits are, as I was frequently told, muy celosa, very jealous, and demand the full attention and commitment—including the sexual commitment—of those who would work with them. Just as, in human relations, to break the bonds of confianza, trust, mutuality, intimacy, is to invite magical retaliation, those who break the diet, who spurn the spirits, who are *unfaithful*, may be subject to fearful punishment. "I have to be pure," says don Javier Arévalo Shahuano, a Shipibo shaman, "so as to be a receptacle of the spirit of the medicine."[25]

One problem with sexual abstinence during la dieta is that a man who is keeping the diet becomes sexually very attractive, and may be pursued by sexually active women.[26] Shipibo shaman don Enrique Lopez says that these women are "the test that the plants give us. It has happened to me twice, a woman comes just when you are working and wants to make love."[27] I must confess that this has not been my personal experience.

Still, it is often recommended that one following the diet have contact, where necessary, as when being brought food, only with premenstrual girls or postmenopausal women.[28] Don Enrique Lopez says, "It is important to avoid women who are menstruating, or who have made love the previous night; that is bad with the plants. It clashes, like a mirror smashing; it makes you ill or goes against you."[29]

Thus, during his training, Shuar shaman Alejandro Tsakimp had to remain separate from his wife for eight months. Sex would be very dangerous, he was told, because the power of the tsentsak, darts, his teacher gave him "would leave me if I had sex with a woman."[30] Cocama shaman don Juan Curico explains the prohibition in medical terms—that ejaculation bothers the functioning of the brain, weakens the mind, and interferes with the effect of the medicine.[31] Shipibo shaman don Guillermo Arévalo says the same thing—that sex is debilitating, and that the plants, instead of being a medicine when ingested, become toxic. And then he adds: "Under these circumstances, it is said that the plant becomes jealous of the human lover and can make you ill or kill you. That is why the shaman goes into the forest. There is no temptation there."[32] Don Enrique Lopez says that, if you are not sexually abstinent, if you give in just once, "you will fall ill, go mad, fall into the water, or die. These are the tremendous problems of being a shaman."[33] Typically, don Roberto and doña María express this understanding in terms of odors: while the spirits love the sweet smells of tobacco and cologne, they hate the smells of menstrual blood, semen, and human sexual intercourse.

BREAKING THE DIET

As simple as the diet seems, it is hard to keep. Food without salt or sugar is bland and boring; I have tried to live on just fish and plantains, and, believe me, the craving for salt or sugar can become intense. Commenting on a similar diet among Achuar apprentice shamans, limited to plantains, boiled palm hearts, and small fish, anthropologist Philippe Descola calls it "dauntingly dull."[34]

La dieta is a form of self-imposed discipline, self-control, *suffering*, which makes the apprentice or shaman worthy of the love of the plants. In order to be a shaman, one Napo Runa elder says, "one has to suffer much with all this fasting."[35] Novelist Mario Vargas Llosa has one of his characters describe the process of becoming a Machiguenga shaman: "You will have to be born again. Pass all the tests. Purify yourself, have hallucinations, and above all suffer. It is hard to achieve wisdom."[36] Alonso Andi compares the restricted diet to a university, where "the body and the mind suffer while learning, and learning never ends."[37]

Breaking the diet can, it is said, have terrible consequences. Shipibo shaman Guillermo Arévalo says that sex during la dieta can produce *cutipa*.[38] The verb *cutipar* apparently comes from the Quechua *kutichiy*, return, give back;[39] it is commonly used to mean to plant yuca, manioc, in the same garden from which yuca has been taken—that is, to give back to the garden what was taken from it.[40] Thus, the term *cutipar* also means to give back in the sense of revenge or retaliation—to infect, contaminate, use sorcery;[41] one who is the victim of sorcery is said to be *cutipado*.[42]

This is what happens when people *quiebran la dieta*, break the diet: the plant with which they were dieting takes revenge, often by marking the body of the unfaithful one in various ways, with stains, bumps, protuberances, or red splotches all over the body.[43] For example, Shuar shaman Alejandro Tsakimp was told not to eat pork, because "it could cause bumps to appear on your skin and they won't heal, and your nose could rot from leprosy."[44]

Even more, shamans who master their desires may use their powers to heal; those who break the diet, by their lack of self-control, become brujos, sorcerers, followers of the easy path. Secoya shaman Fernando Payaguaje, speaking of the restricted diet kept when drinking *yagé*, says: "Some people drink yagé only to the point of reaching the power to practice witchcraft; with these crafts they can kill people. A much greater effort and consumption of yagé is required to reach the highest level, where one gains access to the visions and power of healing. To become a sorcerer is easy and fast."[45] As anthropologist Françoise Barbira Freedman puts it, shamans who master their emotions and aggressive desires use their powers to heal; apprentices who break the rules of their ascetic training become weak, and therefore become sorcerers.[46] As we will see, similar self-control is necessary after the new shaman has been initiated.

LEARNING THE PLANTS

But to learn the plants, you do not just diet; you *diet with a plant*—that is, ingest the plant, take it into your body, let it teach you from within while you keep loyal to it. Depending on the maestro, there are several ways to learn a plant while keeping the restricted diet. The plant may be ingested just once, or just a few times, at the start of the diet period, which is usually a few weeks to a month, or may be taken every day during that period.[47] The plant may be boiled into the ayahuasca drink, and the plant spirit may then appear during the ayahuasca vision, or in a subsequent dream; or the plant may be ingested by itself, and the plant spirit may then appear when subsequently drinking ayahuasca, or in a dream, vision, stream of thought, insight, melody, snatches of song, or vague stirrings of intention. Certain plants seem traditionally to be taken alone for the purposes of dieting rather than mixed with ayahuasca—mapacho and toé, as we might expect, since they are as sacred and powerful as ayahuasca itself, and also catahua, *mucura*, *chiricsanango*, *suelda con suelda*, *raya balsa*, *ajo sacha*, and ojé.[48]

Some masters prescribe at least an initial sequence of plants for their apprentices. Don Roberto begins, of course, with ayahuasca; then his disciples work to master four medicines—toé, maricahua, camalonga, and *piedras encantadas*, magic stones. After that, the key plants include chiricsanango, *chullachaqui caspi*, *machimango*, *ishpingo caspi*, *chuchuhuasi*, and *ayahuma*. And the apprentice diets with the plants who call.

Whether ingested alone or with ayahuasca, the goal of the diet is to maintain an ongoing connection and dialogue with the plant; to allow the plant to interact with the body, often in subtle ways; and to wait for its spirit to appear, as the spirit wishes, to teach and give counsel. The effect of the most powerful plants may be instantaneous, but the effect of others may be gradual: the plants become your body and give you the power to heal; they become—through this lengthy, dreamlike, silent, sacred process—your allies. You learn the plants in plant time, not in human time.

One does not generally diet a second time with a particular plant—don Agustin Rivas says that would be like going to university and taking the same course twice—but some shamans may diet again with a plant for a longer period of time or drink the plant again if the visions or effects are weak.[49]

Amazonian shamans conceptualize this process as *learning with the body*. Don Casimiro Izurieta Cevallas puts it this way: "Through the diet, the body takes on the gift of learning."[50] But we would be wrong to think of this plant knowledge as being merely cognitive, like learning a recipe. To diet with a plant is to devote one's attention to the plant, to form a bond with it, to establish a relationship with it—an *intimate* relationship, taking the plant into your body, creating mutual love and trust.

All these plants are called doctores, teachers, healers; these are the *vegetales que enseñan*, plants who teach. They are not necessarily psychoactive; each healing and protective plant is a *teacher of its own secrets*, of how it may be used as medicine. Learning the plants is learning to *listen to the plants*, who speak a language of *puro sonido*, pure sound, and learning to sing to them in their own language. And once you have learned to listen to the plants, the more easily you can learn each additional plant—what sicknesses it can heal, what song will summon it, what medicines it enters into, how it should be prepared.

This, too, is how the shamans study the properties of new plants, and the way they expand the native pharmacopoeia.[51] Don Fidel Mosombite, a practitioner from Pucallpa, told anthropologist Luis Eduardo Luna that he had taken a *mejoral*, aspirin, to study it under the effects of ayahuasca, and that he had discovered that it contained an "essence of plants," which is why it worked.[52] Don Santiago Murayari, wondering whether he could use the psychoactive mushroom *Psilocybe cubensis* for medicine, said that he intended to mix it with ayahuasca in order to study it.[53] Such plants are often medicinal, without psychoactive effects of their own; it is in this category that we find the most diverse substances added to ayahuasca.

We must remember that the plant spirits are powerful and unpredictable; the relationship between shaman and plant is complex, paradoxical, multilayered, embodied in a recurrent phrase in doña María's songs, *doctorcito poderoso*, powerful little doctor—the diminutive indicating warmth and familial affection, the adjective acknowledging power. The shaman "masters" the plant by taking the plant inside the body, letting the plant teach its mysteries, giving the self over to the power of the plant. There is a complex reciprocal interpersonal relationship between shaman and other-than-human person—fear, awe, passion, surrender, friendship, and love. The shaman is the *aprendiz*, apprentice, of the plant; in return the plant *teaches*, and teaches by *showing*—the verb *enseñar* means both.

There are spirits in things other than plants. The term *doctor* in fact embraces more than plants, and includes such substances as agua de florida cologne, camphor, the commercial mouthwash Timolina, the disinfectant Creolina, and magic stones.[54] *Perfumero* Artidoro Aro Cardenas dieted with agua de florida, Timolina, and camalonga.[55] By putting a few drops of perfume in the ayahuasca drink, it is possible to learn *huarmi icaros* to attract women. It is possible to diet with flint, or steel, by putting the material in water for several days and then drinking the water. It is even possible to diet with gasoline, by inhaling it rather than by drinking it. Each of the substances has a spirit, which will appear and teach its magic song—the *icaro de pedernal*, song of flint, which is used by sorcerers to destroy with fire; or the *icaro de acero*, song of steel, which makes the body strong enough to resist wind and rain.[56] Piedras encantadas, magic stones, may also be kept in water or in a cold aqueous infusion of tobacco, and the liquid may be drunk, to gain their trust and power.

CHAPTER 6
SOUNDS

ICAROS

One of the most striking features of Amazonian mestizo shamanism is the icaro, the magic song, whispered, whistled, and sung. The term *icaro* may come from the Quechua verb *ikaray*, blow smoke for healing, or perhaps from the Shipibo term *ikarra*, shaman song.[1] The icaro is given to the shaman by the spirits of the plants and animals, and the shaman uses it to call the spirits for healing, protection, or attack, and for many other purposes as well—to control the visions of another person who has drunk ayahuasca, work love magic, call the spirits of dead shamans, control the weather, ward off snakes, visit distant planets, or work sorcery.[2] As one mestizo shaman puts it, you cannot enter the world of spirits while remaining silent.[3]

Communication between the shaman and the plants through the icaro is two-way. Francisco Montes Shuña says that the icaro is the language of the plant. "If you have dieted with the plant and have not learned its icaro," he says, "then you know nothing." The icaro is the language by which the shaman communicates with the plant, and through the icaro the plant will reply.[4]

In possessing these songs, the mestizo shaman is not different from shamans found among indigenous peoples throughout the Amazon, for whom songs are a key element of the healing ritual.[5] Anthropologist Jean Matteson Langdon considers the South American shaman to be distinguished from the ordinary person in three ways that constitute the shaman's power—the visionary experience, the acquisition of spirit allies, and the acquisition of songs.[6] Among the Araweté, "the most frequent and important activity of a shaman is chanting."[7] Anthropologist Graham Townsley puts it this way: "What Yaminahua shamans do, above everything else, is sing."[8]

The importance of the song is virtually universal in shamanism. Poet Gary

Snyder says that the shaman *gives song to dreams.*[9] The shaman, he says, "speaks for wild animals, the spirits of plants, the spirits of mountains, of watersheds. He or she sings for them. They sing through him."[10] Jerome Rothenberg, poet and pioneer of ethnopoetics, calls the shaman the *protopoet.*[11] For these poets, the shaman is the healer who sings.[12]

LEARNING TO SING

It is universally said that each shaman learns his or her own icaros from the spirits themselves; the poet César Calvo calls them "untransferable magic songs."[13] But there are exceptions. First, icaros can be learned from one's maestro ayahuasquero.[14] Doña María told me that I should first learn the icaros of don Roberto, my teacher; as time passed, and I dieted with the plants, I would learn icaros of my own. And icaros can be learned from other shamans. There are many stories of shamans traveling long distances to learn specific icaros. Anthropologist Françoise Barbira Freedman reports that one of the Lamista shamans with whom she worked went to the Ucayali to learn an *icaro del kapukiri.*[15] Anthropologist Peter Gow tells of how Artemio Fasabi Gordon, son of a well-known Piro shaman, don Mauricio Roberto Fasabi, would visit Gow repeatedly to listen to a recording of an icaro from another village, so that he could learn to sing it when he drank ayahuasca.[16] I was told the same thing—that when I was back home, I should listen to the recordings I had made of don Roberto, my maestro ayahuasquero.

Some shamans even visit other shamans incognito in order to steal their icaros. That is why many shamans mumble their songs, or sing in many different languages; the goal is to make their songs hard to learn, to keep them from being stolen.[17] Doña María frequently compared her own openhandedness with the selfishness of other shamans, who do not want to reveal their

Kapukiri

Pablo Amaringo explains *kapukiri* as a kind of dark brown vapor, which results from the decomposition of living beings and which rises up and collects in the atmosphere. The kapukiri of certain trees—the pucalupuna, *ajosquiro*, *catahua negra*, and *huairacaspi*—is poisonous and causes sicknesses specific to that tree. Sorcerers use this kapukiri to cause harm, and an icaro del kapukiri can be used to counteract the poison.[1]

NOTE

1. Luna & Amaringo, 1993, pp. 106–107.

icaros. "I'm not selfish," doña María said to me. "I sing loud because I'm not afraid to let people know what I know."

But one's own icaros most frequently come while dieting with the plants and other substances, in ayahuasca visions, in dreams, in the unheard rhythms of one's own heart. It is a process that people find hard to describe, especially when the songs are in strange or incomprehensible languages. It has something to do, I think, with solitude. "While you are alone with the sounds of the jungle and its animals," says Cocama shaman don Juan Curico, "it is a real concert, a choir, that is the silence of the jungle."[18]

The icaros arrive in various ways. Don Solón Tello Lozano, a mestizo shaman in Iquitos, says, simply, "The plant talks to you, it teaches you to sing."[19] One may hear the icaro as if sung by someone else, or one may hear it inwardly. Both words and melody may come together, or first one and then the other. One may hear only the words and then complete the melody oneself. Don Agustin Rivas says that he would make a song for each plant he dieted with as its power entered him, with the melodies coming first and the words added later; indeed, the lyrics of some of his icaros were written by Faustino Espinosa, a professor of Quechua.[20] Sometimes, as with don Francisco Montes Shuña, a spirit whistles and sings the melody of the icaro in a dream.[21] Sometimes there is simply an overwhelming urge to sing, and the song and melody come out by themselves.

Three days after Pablo Amaringo had undergone a healing, he was astonished to find himself singing, perfectly, the icaros he had heard there, including the words. "I sang many icaros," he says, "as if the song were in my ears and on my tongue."[22] The third time doña María drank ayahuasca, the spirit of ayahuasca entered into her, and she began to sing loudly. El doctor ayahuasca was in her body, she says, singing to her, and ayahuasca appeared to her as two genios, spirits, one male and one female, who stood on either side of her—a woman dressed in beautiful clothing, wearing jewelry made of *huayruro* beads, "everything of the *selva*, the jungle," and an ugly man, with bad teeth. Everyone in the room became very quiet, she says, as she sang her new icaro de ayahuasca.

USES OF ICAROS

There are thousands of icaros, and shamans assert their prestige depending on how many they have in their repertoire; an experienced shaman will have scores of icaros, perhaps more than a hundred. The uses of these songs are as varied as the needs of shamans. When the icaro arrives, one may know its use immediately, or its use may become clear as one continues to sing it. There are icaros for calling, for protection, for learning, for exchanging knowledge, and for healing. There are icaros to stun a snake,[23] cure snakebite,[24] make a distant loved one return home,[25] make a person into a good hunter,[26] call the soul back to the body,[27] give strength to the ayahuasca drink,[28] enhance the ayahuasca visions,[29] bless the participants in a healing ceremony,[30] protect from lightning and thunder,[31] protect before sex,[32] cure *mal aire*,[33] make a sorcerer fall asleep,[34] drive away *chullachaquis*,[35] call in the great boas,[36] ease childbirth,[37] call the protective spirits of the water,[38] swallow darts extracted from snakes and scorpions,[39] call the spirits of mapacho, ajo sacha, chiricsanango, and the magic stones,[40] cleanse the body,[41] make the body strong enough to resist wind and rain,[42] protect against sorcery,[43] call the spirit of a dead shaman,[44] attract the *paiche* fish,[45] visit distant planets,[46] call the rainbow,[47] see the problems from which the patient suffers,[48] cause to vomit and faint,[49] cause destruction by fire,[50] kill.[51]

Sometimes the connection between song and purpose is highly metaphorical. Don Emilio Andrade, for example, has an *icaro del ninacuru*, the song of the *ninacuru*, an insect whose eyes are said to resemble the headlights of a car. By singing this song, he can project lights out of his eyes and locate a person who has been abducted by the yacuruna, the people of the waters. Again, the toucan is said to sing a sad and beautiful song in the evening to attract females. By singing the *icaro de la pinsha*, song of the toucan, one can similarly make a woman cry and win her love.[52] Cocama shaman don José Curitima Sangama will sing a song invoking a stone to strengthen a weak patient, or invoking a condor or peccary for one with a weak stomach, since these are animals who can eat rotten things and never have stomach problems.[53] Don Daniel Morlaconcha, a skilled ayahuasquero, gave doña María an icaro that calls the sajino, the collared peccary, and the *boa negra*, the black boa; it tells of a *colpa*, a small lake in the jungle where all the animals come to drink and bathe in harmony. The purpose is to attract clients.

Thus, icaros can be used for just about any purpose, any contingency encountered by a shaman. But three primary functions are to call spirits, to "cure" objects and endow them with magical power, and to modulate the visions induced by ayahuasca.

Calling

Icaros may be used to call the spirit of a plant or animal; the icaro is taught to the shaman by the particular plant or animal as a means of calling it for healing, protection, or attack. Such icaros call both healing and protective spirits; a protective icaro is often called an arcana or an *icaro arcana*. We will discuss arcanas when we talk about protective spirits and defense against sorcery.

Even the spirit of a human being can be called by an icaro. The shaman uses the appropriate song to summon a lost or stolen soul, or to call the soul of a man or woman for purposes of *pusanguería*, love magic. "With one of those icaros, Maestro Ximu made me come with his calling," writes poet César Calvo. "He made me come as if I were a protective spirit."[54] A powerful shaman can even call the souls of sorcerers. Pascual Pichiri was the grandfather of Pablo Amaringo the artist; when Amaringo was stricken by a Shipibo sorcerer, Pichiri cried out, "You will see how I will send your own virote back to you! But don't think that I am doing that because I am a brujo myself, but only because you deserve a lesson! Don't you know that there is no brujo capable of doing any harm to me?" Then Pichiri summoned before him the spirits of one brujo and then another, until the second one admitted his guilt and asked for forgiveness.[55]

Curing

The verb *icarar* means to sing or whistle an icaro over a person, object, or preparation to give it power;[56] water over which an icaro has been sung or whistled and tobacco smoke has been blown, for example, is called *agua icarada*.[57] Another term for the same process is *curar*, cure; that which has been sung over is said to be *curado*, cured, in the sense that fish or cement is cured, made ready for use. "To cure any object," says poet César Calvo, "is to provide it with powers, to give it strengths, to endow it with purposes previously ignored by the object, which would not have been placed there originally by habits or from birth."[58] And again: "That is why we work so hard at fasting, and why we are so careful about curing plants, stone or water or wood plants, charging them with suitable powers, gathering from the air the suitable icaros, and giving power to those remedies."[59] Manuel Córdova Ríos, a mestizo shaman, puts it this way: "What good do you think my remedies would be if I didn't sing to them?"[60]

A shaman can cure objects of just about any sort—a seed necklace, a bracelet of snakeskin, a wristlet made from the labia of a dolphin, a ring, a lock of hair, a handkerchief. Most important is a medicine; the shaman sings the icaro of the spirits that infuse the healing mixture. The song is what Calvo calls the *charge*; the object, the medicine, operates, he says, "according to the intensity and intention of the charge, to grant life, love, youth, forgetfulness, sexual plenitude, evil spells, or death. The same object, once cured, is capable of resuscitating, healing, making sick, or killing, according to the length of the fast and the direction of the charge."[61]

Pablo Amaringo gives several examples of healing with a variety of cured medicines. In one case, a patient's eyes had been harmed by a sorcerer shining a magic flashlight at him. The shaman cured this person by giving him a drink of water over which he had sung icaros and blown tobacco smoke.[62] Similarly, a menstruating woman had left her wet underwear in a canoe by the riverside; a boa had excreted something living into her underwear and thus implanted the larvae of boas into her womb. The shaman treated her by taking a fruit of the *huito*, cutting it in half, and scraping some into warm water for the woman to eat. He prepared this medicine—in fact, considered an abortifacient—"by singing many icaros, blowing on it, and putting in it arcanas." The icaros called all the spirits that would cause the medicine to work—the great serpent *corimachaco*, the multicolored rainbow, the precious stones, the mud of the waters, the laughing falcon, and the tiger; with his icaro he summoned the spirits of the *pucunucho*, pepper, and of the *rocoto*, hairy pepper—both hot pepper plants with which to stun the boa who, with its own spirit helpers, was supporting the pregnancy.[63]

Anthropologist Luis Eduardo Luna tells of how don Williams Vásquez deals with difficult childbirth, singing icaros of slimy fish, demulcent and mucilaginous trees, the slippery boa, and the ray, which can give birth in any position. He sings these songs over a glass of water, which is given to the woman to drink.[64] And again: A man had been poisoned by a woman he had spurned by being given the blood of a black dog. Pablo Amaringo, directed by a spirit who gave him instructions in a dream, put some leaves of *lengua sacha* in a bowl of water, and added three drops of camphor water, three drops of perfume, and three drops of Timolina; he sang an icaro, blew on the medicine, and then gave it to the young man to drink from the same side of the bowl that Amaringo blew on.[65]

A common way to create *pusangas*, love charms, is by blowing on an object—soap, perfume, cloth—which is then given, now imbued with power, to the person one desires, causing the person to fall madly in love. A shaman can also blow on a photograph of the one desired.[66] A shaman once blew his icaros into some perfume, a drop of which was then put on each of several sculptures don Agustin Rivas had made and which he was exhibiting in Lima. "This is for you to sell your art work," the shaman said. Don Agustin sold nearly all his sculptures, while other artists sold nothing.[67]

Such cured objects can be used for countersorcery as well. Don Emilio

Andrade fills a dried toad with tobacco, patiquina, and camphor; sings over it; and places it in the house of a person persecuted by sorcery, to catch the magic darts directed at the owner.[68]

Controlling Visions

Icaros also have the ability to modulate the effects of ayahuasca and other psychoactive plants, both for the shaman who is singing the icaro and for a patient or apprentice to whom the shaman has given the medicine. Songs can *subir mareación*, bring on the vision, or *llamar mareación*, call the vision; they can also *sacar mareación*, take away the vision.[69] The latter can be used benevolently, in order to alleviate frightening visions in a patient, or malevolently, as when don X used his magic to take away doña María's ayahuasca visions. A shaman more powerful than the attacking sorcerer can then use countericaros to restore the visions.[70]

Songs can also modulate the contents of the visions of a patient or apprentice.[71] When doña María tired of my incessant questions, she would tell me, "I will show you," which meant that I should expect my next ayahuasca visions to give me the answers I was looking for. César Calvo, in his novel about the life of Manuel Cordova Ríos, tells how the shaman Ximu controlled the visions of his young apprentice, "calibrating the hallucinogenic apparitions in the mind of the young man. . . . The slightest gesture of the old man developed in his consciousness the caresses of an order. Whatever Ximu thought was seen and heard by the boy. They understood each other through flashes of lightning and through shadows, amid slow visions and colors, and Ximu began to confide his patience and his strength."[72]

NAMES OF ICAROS

It is important to note that most icaros do not have names; when don Roberto or doña María spoke about their icaros, they would often, instead of providing a name, whistle or sing a bit of the melody. Some *appear* to have names—for example, don Roberto will speak of, say, the *icaro de bellaquillo*, where the *bellaquillo* is the spirit of the camalonga, yellow oleander; but there may be many icaros of that particular plant spirit, each belonging to a different singer.

When required to give an icaro a name by a gringo investigator with a tape recorder, a shaman will use such names as *icaro para espantar brujería*, song to scare away sorcery; *arcana para defensa*, protection for defense; *icaro para botar malos*, song to expel evil; *icaro de la medicina*, song of the medicine; or *icaro para la curación*, song for healing. Every shaman, for example, has an icaro de ayahuasca taught by the plant, and a huarmi icaro, woman icaro, for use in love magic, but all are different, and each is unique to the particular shaman.

ICAROS AS MUSIC

Icaros are a distinct musical genre; a mestizo icaro is instantly recognizable. In addition, there is a difference between icaros and oraciones, prayer songs, of the sort doña María produced as a child and continued to produce, even though, as a child, she called these songs her icaros. In fact, there are rival shamans, I am told, who claim that the songs she sang during her healings are not icaros at all but, rather, oraciones, because of their musical style. And, indeed, there is a discernible difference between doña María's icaros and those of don Roberto. Don Roberto's rhythms contain many backbeats, with one or two syllables per beat, and few syllables stretched out over more than one beat; doña María's syllables, in contrast, tended to spread out over several beats, and the emphasized syllables in each word tended to fall on the beat rather than off it. Her tunes were sweeter and more melodious, and her rhythm was less syncopated and staccato than those in the icaros of other more traditional mestizo shamans; she used fewer vocables and other unintelligible words attributed to Quechua, tribal languages, or the speech of animals but, rather, primarily words in intelligible Spanish. Some of her loveliest songs, like the *oración de picaflores*, prayer of the hummingbirds, were for her *baños de flores*, flower baths and other *limpias*, cleansing baths. It is worth adding that, while don Roberto whistles his arcanas, the icaros of protection at the start of an ayahuasca healing ceremony, doña María would sing them. One of her principal arcanas, songs of protection, was the *avemaría*, the Ave Maria.

It may be worth mentioning that many icaros have such Latin-inflected rhythms that one may wonder about the influence of popular Peruvian music, especially the form known as *chicha*, and its variety called *cumbia amazónica*, which can be heard even deep in the jungle on transistor radios or on CDs carried upriver by canoe. I remember don Rómulo Magin playing an ancient radio for me, barely bringing in the scratchy music of a station in Colombia. The music was infectiously lively, and I asked him what it was. *La música de la selva*, he told me, grinning. Jungle music.

Just as mestizo shamans modulate their singing voice in the direction of whispering, breathiness, and whistling, some indigenous shamans sing in a penetrating falsetto. For the Shipibo, this voice is what the shaman hears when the spirit is teaching its song; the spirit sounds sometimes like a choir, sometimes like a single voice, neither male nor female.[73] Yagua apprentices undertake special steps to achieve a high-pitched sound, scraping their tongues with the sharp edge of the *samatu* seashell and doing exercises to maintain their voices as long as possible at a high pitch, at the limits of audibility. The higher the pitch, they say, the harder it is for another shaman to steal the song and its power to call the spirit.[74]

ICAROS AND IMPROVISATION

Any particular icaro provides a structure within which the singer can improvise; the extent of improvisation varies from singer to singer. At the most basic level, many icaros are *pattern songs*: the lyrics do not vary from verse to verse or line to line except for a section in which replaceable words or phrases can be inserted. Many of doña María's songs are of this type: she repeats the lyrics, except where she inserts the name of the plant she is calling, along with a standardized description of its powers: "Come, come, patiquina, protection from sorcery, protection from witchcraft, help my brothers and sisters. . . . Come, come, *cariñito*, protection from sorcery, protection from witchcraft, help my brothers and sisters." Such pattern songs can go on for fifteen or twenty minutes at the beginning of an ayahuasca healing session, naming and calling scores of plant spirits.

Moreover, there are several reasons to believe that there is more improvisation in the singing of icaros generally—even those that are not pattern songs—than might first appear. First, from time to time a line will run several beats too long; in other words, an extemporized line turns out not to fit the meter of the song. Second, the icaros contain a number of *filler words*, which the singer will use to pad out extemporized lines that turn out to be too short, sometimes using vocables, such as *nonay nonay nonay*, and sometimes inserting ordinary words in Spanish; doña María is fond of the word *reina*, queen, for this purpose. Third, the icaros are often built up of words with similar metrical properties, making improvisation easier; doña María, again, is fond of four-syllable words such as *medicina*, *doctorcito*, *poderoso*, *picaflores*, and *ayudarle*, which she uses constantly and with whose metrical properties she is familiar.

On occasion, when two healers are working together, they will sing simultaneously, each singing his or her own icaro. When I was living with don Rómulo Magin, I had several ayahuasca sessions in which don Rómulo was assisted by his adult son, don Winister, who had learned to be an ayahuasquero from his father, having drunk his first ayahuasca when he was eight

Jungle Music

Cumbia is a popular music of Colombia, especially along the northern Caribbean coast. A form of cumbia is also found in Peru, called *chicha,* named after the popular fermented drink, usually made of maize. Peruvian chicha took Colombian cumbia rhythms and instrumentation and added the Andean elements of popular *huayño* music;[1] and in turn chicha spun off two variants—*tecnocumbia*, which added synthesizers and other electronica to the mix, and cumbia amazónica—jungle music.[2]

Cumbia amazónica developed in the 1960s in the larger Upper Amazonian towns such as Iquitos, Moyobamba, and Pucallpa, where the accordions of chicha were replaced by cheap, loud, portable garage-band instruments such as Farfisa organs and big-reverb guitars, and local bands played cumbias amazónicas for oil workers—what one commentator has called "eastern Peruvian wild west Amazon mining town jump up music."[3] They sang about partying, oil prospecting, and jungle life, often with wry tongue-in-cheek humor: "My grandfather has died *ayayay*, drinking liquor *ayayay*, my grandfather has died *ayayay*, drinking fermented manioc *ayayay*." Their sense of their music's regional and ethnic roots was encapsulated in the phrase *poder verde*, green power.

Two long-surviving groups, Juaneco y su Combo and Los Mirlos, are primarily associated with this music. The original Juaneco y su Combo was formed in 1966 in Pucallpa. It consisted of singer Wilindoro Cacique; guitarist Noé Fachín, called El brujo because, it was said, his melodies came to him during ayahuasca visions; and saxophonist Juan Wong Paredes, leader and principal composer, the original Juaneco.[4] When Paredes's son Juan Wong Popolizio took over the band, he traded in his accordion for a Farfisa organ.[5]

The group put on their first public concert in Iquitos in 1967. The concert spawned legends—that the crowd was so large the army had to be called in; that the venue was too small, and the band played out in the street; that Fachín's guitar was so erotically charged that rioting broke out. Half of the group, including Fachín, died in 1976 in a plane crash. Wong died in 2004, but the group continues under the leadership of Mao Wong Lopez, the founder's grandson. The only survivor of the original trio, Wilindoro Cacique, lives in a taxi garage in Pucallpa and does occasional all-night gigs under the name Wilindoro y la Leyenda Viva de Juaneco, Wilindoro and the living legend of Juaneco.[6]

Most distinctive about Juaneco y Su Combo was their adoption of the symbols of indigenous Amazonia. While band members were mostly poor mestizos, their pride in local tradition led them to wear Shipibo cushmas and feather coronas onstage. "They think of it as their culture, even though they are not Shipibo," says Olivier Conan, a New York musician who has been key to their revival. "It is a very important part of their whole music."[7] Their song lyrics also embraced distinctively Amazonian themes and legends—"Vacilando con ayahuasca," floating with ayahuasca; "Mujer hilandera," Woman Spinning; "El llanto de Ayaimama," The Weeping of the Potoo Bird.[8]

Los Mirlos was founded in 1973 by Jorge Rodríguez Grández, who enlisted two of his brothers and a cousin to form the group. Many of their songs—"Sonido amazónico" (Amazonian Sound), "El milagro verde" (The Green Miracle), "Muchachita del oriente" (Jungle Girl), "Fiesta en la selva" (Party in the Jungle)—refer to the area of Moyobambo, in the *departamento* of San Martín, where Rodríguez was born, although he moved to Lima when he was very young. Guitarist Danny Johnson gave the band a darker sound—music critic Francisco Melgar Wong calls his guitar work "sinuous and reptilian"—which differentiated the group from its more cheerful contemporaries.[9] Rodriguez has been outspoken about his regional roots. "I have spoken to my jungle," he has said, "to all immigrants from Peru."[10]

Both these groups have had a remarkable revival beginning in the 1990s, as their countercultural style appealed to a new generation of young people in Lima. Despite its recent embrace by the middle class, chicha remains an outsider music—an expression of migrants, nostalgia for home, hope for a better life.[11] It is, above all, party music, a concept operationalized by the ubiquitous scantily clad callipygian *bailarinas* who dance onstage while the band plays. The term *chicha*, very much like the term *hip-hop* in the United States, has come to refer to a broad range of *limeño* underclass culture, including cheap architecture, tabloid newspapers, and outdoor concerts and dance parties in venues, such as empty parking lots, called *chichodromos*.[12]

Cumbia amazónica brought an indigenous world to the attention of those who had previously been only dimly aware of it. Juaneco y Su Combo and Los Mirlos achieved their primary success in the mid-1970s, the time of the Amazon oil boom. Prior to that period, the axis of Peruvian indigenous discourse had run between Lima and Cuzco and thus between Spanish and Inca culture. Indeed, the term *indigenismo* traditionally had little to do with indigenous peoples of the jungle; it was, instead, an identification that the upper-class light-brown *trigueño* elite in Cuzco made of *themselves* in connection with their own purported Inca heritage.[13] Jungle Indians were *chunchos*, not worth thinking about.

Although there undoubtedly have been culturally exploitative currents in cumbia amazónica, it was, in fact, revelatory. As we will discuss, there had long been a profound social divide between urbanized mestizos and indigenous peoples of the jungle. But, according to music critic Ricardo León Almenara, when Juaneco y su Combo began to appear in Shipibo cushmas, it seemed for the first time that there might be *something* in common between the two worlds, if only a species of good-time jump-up bar music; and for the first time, says anthropologist César Ramos, mestizos and Shipibos would drink beer from the same glass at a festival.[14]

NOTES

1. Cánepa, 2008, p. 38.
2. For a collection of early chicha on CD, including classic cumbia amazónica tracks, see Conan, 2007.
3. Camp, 2008; Gehr, 2008.
4. Almenara, 2008.
5. World Music News Wire, 2008.
6. Almenara, 2008; Gehr, 2008.
7. World Music News Wire, 2008.
8. Almenara, 2008; Wong, 2007; Yerba Mala, 2008.
9. Wong, 2007; Yerba Mala, 2008.
10. Quoted in Romero, 2002, pp. 227–228.
11. Cánepa, 2008, p. 38.
12. Bardales, 2008a, 2008b; Gehr, 2008.
13. De la Cadena, 2001, p. 5.
14. Almenara, 2008; Ramos, 2004

years old. Both would sing together, but different icaros; because their icaros had such similar rhythmic and even melodic structures, the two icaros sung together sounded like a round, but they were sufficiently different to produce a decidedly eerie effect.[75] Shipibo shamans, who have traditionally sung without rhythmic accompaniment, also from time to time do the same thing.[76]

STRANGE LANGUAGES

Abstraction from conceptual meaning is a key feature of mestizo shamanic music. The most powerful icaros, such as the protective arcanas, are vocally refined into *silbando*, breathy and almost inaudible whistles. Thus, when learning icaros, doña María told me, I should first *hum* the melody, or whistle it in the breathy whispering whistle of silbando; only then should I learn the words, for the words are much less important than the melody. Another shaman has told his apprentices not to be overly concerned with trying to memorize the words; singing the icaros from the heart with the correct resonance and vibration is more important.[77]

Here there is a relationship between sound and phlegm, made explicit in the use of the term *mariri*, raised and purified phlegm, as a synonym for *icaro*.[78] Just as the shaman's magical phlegm, stored in the chest, is raised and rarefied into mariri in the throat in order to protect against magical attack—becoming intangible, less physical, just like air, as don Roberto puts it—in the same way, the more abstract, less conceptual, less overtly intelligible the icaro, the more powerful it is. Both mariri, purified phlegm, and icaro, purified song, ultimately converge upon the same condition—that of *puro sonido*, pure sound, which is the language of the plants.

I think this is something like what poet César Calvo is getting at in this mysterious passage: "He revealed to me magical songs, which some call icaros. . . . And he showed me something more precious: how to gather the musics that live in the air, repeat them without moving my lips, to sing in silence 'with the memory of the heart,' as he used to say."[79]

Just as the extraterrestrial doctors speak in computer language, and spirits speak in Inca, and shamans know the language of animals, greater power inheres in language refined away from ordinary meanings. Many mestizo shamans, for example, study indigenous languages and mix their words—sometimes haphazardly—into their songs.[80] Poet Jerome Rothenberg says that such mysterious special languages fall into several types: purely invented sounds, distortions of ordinary words and syntax, ancient words emptied of their long-since-forgotten meanings, and words borrowed from other languages and likewise emptied. And they may be explained as spirit language, animal language, or ancestral language;[81] to which we may add tribal language, or a *lenguaje especial*, special language, the language of nature, or the *lengua mística*, mystical language, of the spirits, which is different from—but somehow includes—all human languages.[82]

It is a mystery, this ability to understand a language you do not know—Quechua, for example, or Martian. Alonso del Río, a musician as well as an ayahuasquero, who apprenticed for three years with the renowned Shipibo shaman don Benito Arévalo, explains it this way: "This is something which an English person, or a Peruvian born in Lima, can experience just as an Amazonian person. Because you can do it without speaking in a native dialect, it doesn't go through the mind but between one spirit and another."[83] Anthropologist Janet Siskind reports that when she drank ayahuasca with the Sharanahua, she believed that she could understand the words of every song, even those that were metaphorical.[84]

The spirits use clearly audible speech to diagnose and prescribe, as we will see; they speak directly into the shaman's ear, telling what is wrong, what icaros to sing, where to suck out the sickness or malignant darts. Sometimes they speak in *castellano*, Spanish, and sometimes they speak in *idioma*, tribal languages. Speaking with the spirits is just like a conversation with a human, says don Juan Curico, but with this difference: you understand them no matter what language you speak yourself.[85] Thus, doña María's spirits speak to her in Inca—that is, Quechua—which is perfectly comprehensible to her, although she herself speaks no Quechua. Both doña María and don Roberto, at the start of each healing ceremony, are attended by outer space spirits who speak in computer language; doña María says they speak like this: *beep boop beep beep boop beep beep*; don Roberto says they sound like *ping ping dan dan*. Amazonian mestizo shamans also know the languages of birds and animals. Don Rómulo Magin, for example, is fluent in the language of *búhos*, owls; their language, I am told, sounds like this: *oootutututu kakakaka hahahahaha*.

Thus, icaros, the songs that are taught by these spirits of plants and animals, range from ordinary Spanish through non-Spanish but human language such as Quechua or Shipibo; purported languages of indigenous people and unknown archaic tongues; the languages of animals, birds, and computers; pure vocables; whispered sounds; whistling; and breathy whistling. One mestizo shaman has said that whistling is a form of communication with the plants, an aspect of true shamanism, the power to see within with clarity, the path of clear vision.[86] And the shaman, when blowing tobacco smoke, makes a blowing sound, an almost silent and untranscribable *pshoo*, which is the shaman's most refined and abstract sound, beyond even silbando, the breathy and unintelligible whistling of the sacred songs. *Soplando*, blowing, which can both kill and cure, is the most powerful song of all.

Again, there are analogies in neighboring indigenous cultures. Among the Yaminahua, songs—sung under the influence of ayahuasca—are a shaman's most highly prized possessions. Such songs are made up of *twisted language*—metaphoric circumlocutions or unusual words for common things, held to be in archaic speech or the language of neighboring peoples. The word for a shaman's song is *koshuiti*, given an onomatopoetic etymology from the sound *kosh-kosh-kosh*—the sound of blowing tobacco into the crown of the patient's head. Similarly, witchcraft songs are called *shooiti*, from the sound *shoo-shoo-shoo*—the powerful, prolonged breath of the sorcerer blowing away the victim's soul.[87]

Shuar and Achuar *anent*, magical songs, similarly employ deliberate distortion—very high or low pitch, word deformation, semantic ambiguity. One researcher speaks of their "idiosyncratic creativity" and notes that even Achuar listeners are often unable to grasp what the singer of a given anent is referring to. The singers say that these songs are in a foreign language—the language of the Napo Runa or the language of the Cocoma—or are in the language of their tsentsak, magic darts, and their *pasuk*, spirit helpers.[88] Indeed, Shuar shamans who have learned from the well-respected Canelos Quichua often whistle instead of sing.[89] In the Venezuelan Amazon, sorcerers—naked, with their bodies painted black, wandering at night through forests and towns, seeking out their enemies in order to destroy them—are called both *dañeros*, harmers, and *pitadores*, whistlers.[90]

While living among the Suyá of Amazonian Brazil, ethnomusicologist Anthony Seeger was frequently asked to sing "Rain, rain go away, come again some other day" when towering dark thunderclouds threatened to interrupt some enjoyable activity. He had, he says, some surprisingly successful performances.[91] Equally important, the invocation was sung in English, a strange and mysterious language.

THE LEAF-BUNDLE RATTLE

Two rhythmic instruments are used in shamanic performance in the Upper Amazon—the shacapa, the leaf-bundle rattle, and the maraca, the seed-filled gourd rattle. Whether shacapa or maraca, rattles are the shaman's most important tool—the equivalent of the shaman's drum elsewhere.[92] Anthropologist Lawrence Sullivan, in his work on the history of religion in South

America, calls them the paradigm of sacred sound, the epitome of the link between sacred sound and shamanic power;[93] ethnographer Alfred Métraux describes them as the most sacred object among the tropical tribes of South America;[94] anthropologist Jean-Pierre Chaumeil says that, among the Yagua, the rattle is the voice of the spirits.[95] Among the Araweté of eastern Amazonia, there are two emblems of shamanism—tobacco and the rattle.[96]

Mestizos use the shacapa exclusively. Other Amazonian peoples use leaf-bundle rattles as well—for example, the Aguaruna, who use a rattle of *sampi* leaves; the Shuar, who shake a bunch of *shinku* leaves; the Canelos Quichua, who use a leaf bundle called *shingui shingu panga*; the Achuar, who use a bundle of *shinki-shinki* leaves; the Yagua, who use a rattle of *chacapa* leaves; and the Akawaio, who in fact abandoned the seed-filled gourd maraca in the mid-1950s in favor of "shaman's leaves."[97] Quechua speakers often use the term *huairachina*, wind-maker, for the leaf-bundle rattle, which creates a *supai huaira*, a spirit wind.[98] Hugh-Jones reproduces an illustration from a health booklet published in Tukanoan by the Colombian government that shows Tukanos, holding crosses, lined up for the healing of tuberculosis before a shaman shaking two leaf bundles.[99]

The shacapa used by mestizo shamans is a bundle of leaves from the shacapa bush tied together at the stem with fibers from the chambira, fiber palm. Mestizo shamans reportedly also make leaf-bundle rattles from *carricillo*, *albaca* or wild basil, and achiote or annatto.[100] In any case, don Roberto was very specific about the plant he wanted for his shacapa when I would go with him to find the leaves.

The shacapa has a unique sound—"a cross between birds flying, rattles, and wind in the trees," says one commentator.[101] It is considered, along with sucking and blowing, a tool for healing; as doña María used to put it, in her typical way, "My shacapa is my *pistola*." Thus, some songs, such as calling in the spirit of ayahuasca at the start of a ceremony, are performed without rhythmic accompaniment, while healings are all performed with the shacapa. The healing effect of the shacapa is described in different ways: it is used to *ventear el mal*, blow away the sickness with its breeze; it makes the body *sellado*, sealed, or *cerrado*, closed, to resist further attacks; it brings on visions during an ayahuasca ceremony.[102]

The word has become an Amazonian Spanish verb—*shacapar*, heal by rattling. When don Roberto initiated doña María, already a plant healer, into ayahuasca shamanism, two of the key things she learned were shacapar, healing and protecting with the leaf-bundle rattle, and soplar, healing and protecting by blowing mapacho, tobacco. Indeed, blowing, rattling, and singing are synergistic modes of sound; elsewhere in the Amazon, too, tobacco, rattle, and song are mythologically interconnected. Among the Makiritare of the Orinoco Valley in Venezuela, Nadeiumadi, a messenger or emanation of Wanadi, the heavenly creator, dreamed his mother into existence: "He gave birth to her dreaming, with tobacco smoke, with the song of his maraca, singing and nothing else."[103]

The Tukano shaman carries a rattle adorned with feathers. With this rattle, the shaman attracts all things, the stones and splinters within the body of the sick, and with the sound of the rattle orders them to depart.[104] Among the Desana, the sound produced by the gourd rattle shaken by the shaman is said to echo the sound made by the thorns and splinters that the shaman carries hidden in his forearm. The rattle is a prolongation of the shaman's arm; when he shakes the rattle, these thorns and splinters are shaken toward the victim.[105]

There is thus a homology between the sound of the Desana rattle and the phlegm of the mestizo shaman: both are the vehicles for the thorns and darts with which the victim may be harmed, the medium within which the projective power of the shaman is stored. It is the same with the mestizo shaman: the refined whispering, whistling, blowing, and rattling of the most powerful music are the same as the air-like presence of mariri, the most refined form of phlegm. Among the mestizo shamans, the wordless rhythmic rustle of the shacapa—like the breathy whistle of the song or the almost silent whispered blowing of tobacco smoke—approaches pure sound.

THE SPECTRUM OF MAGICAL SOUND

There is a continuum of sound from the concrete, verbal, and intelligible at one end to the abstract, sonic, and unintelligible at the other. The continuum begins with intelligible lyrics in castellano, Spanish, and progresses through non-Spanish but human language such as Quechua; purported languages of indigenous people and unknown archaic tongues; the languages of animals, birds, and computers; pure vocables; whispered sounds; whistling; breathy whistling; the silent *pshoo* of the blowing of tobacco smoke; and the susurration of the shacapa. The rarefaction of sound parallels the rarefaction of the shaman's phlegm, from gross physical *flema* in the chest to abstract protective air-like mariri in the throat. The more rarefied the sound, the further it departs from the materiality of intelligible words, the closer it comes to the state of mariri, the most rarefied phlegm in the sound-producing throat of the shaman. Both converge in a state of puro sonido, pure sound, which is the language of the plants.

Cultural critics Jeremy Gilbert and Ewan Pearson point out that music can be understood either as possessing or producing *meanings*, or as producing *effects* that cannot be explained in terms of meaning—that "music can affect us in ways that are not dependent on understanding something, or manipulating verbal concepts, or being able to represent accurately those experiences through language." Music has a metaphysical dimension; where music affects the body, the distinction between *outside*—where the music comes from—and *inside*—where the music is felt—is radically called into question.[106] Musicologist John Shepherd therefore describes music as a site of exchange, a shifting boundary between the outer and the inner.[107]

Here sound differs from vision. The eye and its gaze have long been the primary trope of European thought—what cultural theorist Luce Irigaray calls "the predominance of the visual, and of the discrimination and individualization of form."[108] This discourse privileges the visual as the purest and most important form of sense experience.[109] Vision encourages projection into the world, occupation and control of the source of experience; whereas sound "encourages a sense of the world as received, as being revelatory rather than incarnate."[110]

But the visual is a relatively less important part of the ribereño cognitive set. When I studied jungle survival with mestizo instructor Gerineldo Moises Chavez, I was struck by how little emphasis he placed on animal tracking. Instead, the mestizos have a great ability to recognize and imitate the *sounds* of the animals, along with an intimate knowledge of their habits and likely locations. On one level, of course, mestizos do not emphasize tracking when they hunt because the thin jungle soil simply does not take tracks well, and rain regularly washes away both tracks and sign in any event. But there may be more. Two anthropologists—Peter Gow, speaking of western Amazonia, and Alfred Gell, speaking of New Guinea—emphasize the *spatial boundedness* of rain forest life. As Gow puts it,

> It is hard to see Amazonia as landscape, in the sense this term has for people from temperate climes. The land does not recede away from a point of observation to a distant horizon, for everywhere vegetation occludes the view. In the forest, sight penetrates only a short distance into the mass of trees. Along the big rivers, you can see further, but even here there is no distant blue horizon. The sky starts abruptly from behind the screen of forest.[111]

To travel in the jungle, Gow says, "is to pass through an endless succession of small enclosed spaces."[112] Gell speaks the same way of New Guinea. "I spent fourteen months," he writes, "in visual surroundings limited to tens of metres. . . . To this day, I do not know what Umeda village looks like from a distance."[113] Gell proposes that such a primary forest environment imposes an organization of sensibility that emphasizes both hearing and smell over vision.[114] In the Amazon, the Aguaruna group and classify trees by how they smell rather than by what they look like.[115]

Thus, hunting in dense forest "places a premium on hearing as the main sensory modality for detecting objects and events at a distance, where they are invariably out of sight."[116] Gell also notes the large class of vocal "sound effects" with which the Umeda punctuate and illustrate their stories—a phenomenon I had noted among the mestizos, and had puzzled over, until I read Gell's article.[117] The mestizo shaman inhabits a sound world in which *sound itself* is meaningful and powerful beyond words.

SOUND AND AYAHUASCA

When we reflect on the range of words and sounds spoken by the spirits of plants and animals, and the reflections of those words and sounds in the songs the spirits teach, it is worth remembering the auditory effects of ayahuasca. Ayahuasca drinkers often hear inchoate sounds—the sound of flowing water, loud rushing sounds, the sound of wind rushing, the sound of rushing water, the roar of rain or waterfall.[118] These sounds may then become *meaningful* in a variety of ways—the sound of people singing, sorrowful songs, people speaking in unknown languages, the voice of a recently deceased friend, Native American chanting, a brass band.[119] In psychopharmacologist Rick Strassman's dimethyltryptamine (DMT) experiments, which we will discuss later, auditory hallucinations were noted in more than half the subjects, and were described as high-pitched, whining, chattering, crinkling, or crunching.[120] These sounds may then become meaningful as well. Users of DMT report hearing "alien music" and "alien languages," which may or may not be comprehensible;[121] Terence McKenna speaks of hearing "a language of alien meaning that is conveying alien information."[122]

CHAPTER 7
PHLEGM AND DARTS

NURTURING PHLEGM

Throughout the Upper Amazon, shamanic power is conceptualized as a physical substance—often a sticky saliva- or phlegm-like substance—that is stored within the shaman's body, usually in the chest or stomach, or sometimes permeating the shaman's flesh.[1] This substance is used both for attack and for defense. The virtually universal method of inflicting magical harm in the Upper Amazon is to project this substance into the body of the victim—either the substance itself or pathogenic projectiles the shaman keeps embedded within it. Chiquitano shamans, for example, kill their enemies by injecting them with a black substance they keep in their stomachs at all times.[2] The virtually universal method of healing such an intrusion is for the healing shaman to suck it out and dispose of it, protected from its contamination by a defense made of the same substance.

Mestizo shamans use a number of terms for this shamanic phlegm. Most common is the ordinary Spanish word *flema*, which refers to the phlegm at its most corporeal, stored in the shaman's chest; it is in this phlegm that the shaman, whether healer or sorcerer, stores the virotes, magic darts, used for both attack and defense; in the phlegm of the sorcerer are also toads, scorpions, snakes, and insects—all sorts of stinging, biting, and poisonous creatures. The same substance is also called *llausa* and *yachay*. The former is the ordinary Quechua term for phlegm; the latter is the Quechua word for knowledge. The term *yachay* derives from the verb *yacha*, know, and refers specifically to ritual knowledge. The Lamista term for shaman is *yachak*, owner of yachay;[3] similarly, the Napo Runa and Canelos Quichua term for shaman is *yachaj*, one who knows.[4]

This flema must be distinguished from mariri, which is phlegm rarefied, raised from the chest into the throat, becoming like air, don Roberto says—immaterial, vibratory, and protective. Don Roberto's raising of the magical phlegm from his chest into his throat as mariri is accompanied by dramatic burps and belches. It is this mariri that extracts the magic darts, the sickness, and the other evils in the patient's body, and at the same time protects the shaman from the sickness and sorcery the shaman sucks out.

The phlegm is the materialization of the shaman's fuerza, power, which grows and diminishes with the growth and decrease of the phlegm.[5] As fuerza, the phlegm can become more material and manifest as darts, insects, stones, and crystals; and it may become more rarefied, raised from chest to throat, and become mariri. As ethnologist Alfred Métraux notes, "The magical substance, the pathogenic objects, and the spirit allies constitute three aspects of the same magical power."[6]

Phlegm grows as a result of smoking mapacho and drinking ayahuasca. Within months of beginning his training with his uncle, don Roberto's phlegm grew in his chest. He would notice, when smoking mapacho, that he would burp up mariri, the refined form of phlegm; when flema becomes mariri, when it moves from chest to throat, don Roberto says, it is just like air, one does not really feel it. The flema is received from the maestro ayahuasquero, "like planting a seed in your chest." Nurturing one's flema is like raising a plant until it is the proper size and then maintaining it. "Flema makes you fearless," don Roberto says. Fearlessness is a constant theme in relation to phlegm. When you have this protection, doña María told me, there is no need to fear anyone; the medicine grants a *corazón de acero*, a heart of steel.

Here we can see a close correspondence between icaro and phlegm. Both range from the grossly physical and intelligible to the rarefied, refined, airlike; converge in the act of *blowing*, which can both cure and kill; and unite in the magical mouth of the shaman, which contains the power and wisdom of the plant spirits. As we have seen, the term *mariri* can be used as a synonym for *icaro*.[7] Both icaro and mariri, sound and power, aspire to the condition of puro sonido, pure sound, which is the immaterial and wordless language of the plants.

MATERIALIZED POWER IN THE AMAZON

Sometimes the shamanic substance permeates the shaman's body, and becomes a pathogenic object—a dart or stone—only when projected into a victim. The substance is often described as poisonous or bitter or caustic. Culina shamans keep a substance called dori in their bodies, which permeates their flesh, where it is formless and insubstantial; yet, outside the shaman's body, it resembles a small stone. Different colors of stone represent different types of dori. This substance is caustic and dangerous; it would be poisonous to its possessor if it were not acquired in the context of ritual training. Dori gives the shaman the power to heal, but its poisonous property makes it also the shaman's weapon, which can be hurled into the body of a victim, where it becomes a stone that grows until it kills, unless sucked out by another shaman.[8]

Among the Siona, drinking ayahuasca causes a substance called *dau* to grow inside the drinker; when sufficient dau has been accumulated, the person has the power to cure and to harm. As with the Culina dori, the Siona dau is dispersed throughout the shaman's body; but, when projected outside, it may take the form of a dart, or a stone, or a snake's tooth, or a rotting substance, or a black butterfly.[9]

Most often the shamanic substance is localized in the chest or stomach, and the pathogenic objects are embedded within it. Among the Shuar, the substance is called tsentsak, and the term refers equally to the substance and to its contents—spirit helpers in the form of darts, which are at the same time jaguars, monkeys, or giant butterflies. This tsentsak is a living substance that functions both for attack, in the form of darts, and for defense, to protect from the darts of others. Shuar shamans keep their tsentsak in their stomach, so that the darts can be vomited up at will.[10] Among the Shipibo-Conibo, the shaman's power substance is called *quenyon*—a sticky substance, sometimes a paste or dough—and it is materialized in phlegm, which the shaman keeps in his or her chest.[11]

Among the Achuar, each type of tsentsak, magic dart, exists in its own *maen*, mother-saliva, a sticky substance in which it develops as a fetus does in its amniotic fluid, and which a shaman can draw up from his chest into his mouth when he needs to. An apprentice shaman will spend a lot of time mastering the regurgitation of tsentsak saliva that the master has injected into him mixed with manioc beer and tobacco.[12]

Aguaruna shamans also possess tsentsak darts, which are held in the shaman's upper torso, embedded in a saliva-like substance called *kaag*, and which they propel into the bodies of their victims to cause illness; healing shamans use their own tsentsak to find and remove the darts of sorcerers.[13]

VIROTES

Very often the shaman's pathogenic projectiles, embedded in the phlegm, are conceptualized as a kind of dart, which mestizo shamans call a *virote*.

Originally the term denoted a crossbow bolt, brought to South America by the conquistadors; the Spanish term was then applied to the darts shot by Indians with a blowgun. These darts were made primarily from two sources—from the spines of any of the spiny *Bactris* or *Astrocaryum* palms or from any of several *Euterpe* palms, whose very hard wood is used to make both bows and arrows.[14] My jungle survival instructor, Gerineldo Moises Chavez, whittled a usable dart from the wood of a *Euterpe* palm with his machete in about a minute.

Both *Euterpe* and *Bactris* species are known as *chonta*, and the term *chonta* is often used as a synonym for *virote*.[15] The verb *chontear* means to cast magic darts at a victim;[16] a *chontero* is a sorcerer who inflicts harm with magic darts. The Shuar term *uwíshin*, shaman, may derive from *uwí*, the spiny *Bactris* palm, which they also know as chonta. Thus the Shuar use the term *chonta* as a synonym for *tsentsak*, magic dart, and the Napo Quichua use the term *chontapala* as a synonym for *biruti*, from the Spanish *virote*.[17] *Euterpe* and *Bactris* species, too, are a primary source of edible palm hearts, also generically called *chonta*, which make a delicious salad.

The intrusion of such darts causes acute and painful sickness, which can kill within a few days.[18] To understand the power of the virote, we can turn to poet César Calvo, who writes that it is a "very small poisoned dart, capable of abandoning and resuming its material shape in order to traverse any distance; any time; any wall, shield, or protection; to nail itself in enemy flesh and to reach the target selected by the sorcerer who gave it form and then animated that form, endowing it with destiny and transcendence."[19]

But these pathogenic projectiles can also be—varying in different cultures and under different circumstances—the thorns of spiny palm trees, tufts of hair, tiny stones, quartz crystals, pieces of cotton, fur, insects, beetles, scorpions, snake fangs, stingray stings, monkey hair, the beaks of certain birds, porcupine quills, bats, toads, snakes, gnawing grubs, monkey teeth, sharp-pointed bones, a piece of a knife, a bead, stinging caterpillars, crystal arrows, or razor blades.[20] A Cashinahua claimed to have seen the muka, the bitter shamanic substance, within the body of a shaman—a small ball of poison, a small piece of a knife, a small wood splinter, a bead.[21] A painting by Pablo Amaringo shows the phlegm of two sorcerers—a Shipibo chontero, who inflicts harm with darts made from the thorns of spiny palms, the fangs of snakes, the beaks of birds, and porcupine quills; and a Cocama sorcerer, whose mariri contains snakes, scorpions, bats, rays, and toads, which he sends to inflict harm.[22]

The projectiles are also in some sense autonomous, alive, spirits, sometimes with their own needs and desires, including a need for nourishment, often supplied by tobacco, or a need to consume human flesh. As we will see, a crucial part of shamanic initiation is learning to control the aggressive desires of one's own darts.

PROJECTING THE DART

Among mestizos and a number of indigenous peoples, pathogenic projectiles are taken from the phlegm and shot into the victim by blowing with the mouth, either with or without tobacco smoke. Other sorcerers may project them through their arms and out an opening in their hands;[23] or they may be carried by an animal or bird controlled by the sorcerer, given in food or drink, or left on the ground to be stepped on.[24] Among the Shuar, darts that enter the body by being stepped on are believed to cause a fatal, often cancerous, sickness.[25] Yagua shamans keep their darts in their stomach—some claim to have as many as a thousand—and project them by rubbing their arm and shoulder progressively toward their hand; the dart is extracted by blowing with tobacco smoke, propelled with the aid of magic gloves, and carried to its destination by the spirit allies.[26]

DARTS AND COMMERCE

These darts can be traded or bought and sold. Aguaruna shamans may give their darts as a gift or sell them for money or trade goods.[27] Canelos Quichua shamans also sell their spirit darts, which include such substances as spiny palm splinters, small frogs, living hair, small snakes, stinging caterpillars, spiders, *machaca* moths, blood-sucking insects, bees, stinging ants, stones, and "sentient scissors and Gillette razor blades."[28] After buyer and seller have both drunk ayahuasca, the shaman coughs up the dart from his stomach. It moves around in the shaman's hand, proving its genuineness to the purchaser, and the purchaser takes it, swallows it, and then keeps it—along with all the other spirit helpers he has acquired—in his stomach.[29] Similarly, shamans from different ethnic groups will trade or purchase darts: a Quichua shaman will visit an Achuar shaman in order to exchange darts,[30] or a Shuar will travel to a Canelos Quichua shaman in order to buy them.[31] The language of commerce is found in the spirit world as well. Yagua darts are impregnated with a poison the shaman purchases from the iguana spirit at the celestial lake.[32] Don Rodrigo Andi, a Canelos Quichua shaman, carries a shield of medicine he bought in a spirit drugstore on the Napo River.[33]

PHLEGM AS DEFENSE

The darts, and their slimy or sticky carrier, are defensive as well as offensive; they prevent enemy darts from entering the body or absorb them, acquire their power, or project them back to the one who sent them. The mariri extracts the magic darts, the sickness, and the other evils in the patient's body, and at the same time protects the shaman from the sickness and sorcery being sucked out. The same darts that are used in attack sorcery are most effective in protection against attack. The Canelos Quichua shaman keeps, in his stomach and chest, sharp dangerous objects called *tsintsaca*—or sometimes *supai biruti*, spirit virotes—that can be brought up into the throat as a *lurira*, a shield, to protect the shaman from the pathogenic objects sucked from the patient. The shaman sucks out these intrusive objects, noisily and sometimes violently, and holds them in his mouth, rolling them around. The shaman's own darts, brought up into the throat, examine the darts the shaman has sucked, diagnose their source, and take away their power, adding it to the shaman's own. The shaman then disposes of the evil darts by blowing them outward into a tree or stump or rock, where they stay, or by projecting them at an enemy.[34]

The Shuar shaman keeps tsentsak, magic darts, in his chest, nurtured by tobacco juice; when he is ready to suck, the shaman regurgitates two tsentsak into the sides of his throat and mouth. He holds one in the front and one in the back of his mouth: the dart in front absorbs the tsentsak he has sucked out of the patient; the dart in back blocks the throat if the first dart fails. If the tsentsak did not block the entry of the tsentsak sucked from the patient, the sickness would pass into the shaman's stomach and kill him. The sickness dart, dissolved into the shaman's dart, is vomited out and displayed to the patient.[35] Among the Achuar, too, drinking tobacco juice forms what anthropologist Philippe Descola calls a "viscous carapace" within the shaman's mouth and throat. This substance prevents the darts sucked out of the patient's body from slipping into the shaman's own chest and stomach, where they can do great damage.[36]

Don Francisco Montes Shuña says that the phlegm is so important a protection that it must be nourished by swallowing tobacco smoke every four hours, even during the night. Indeed, if the mariri is not fed with tobacco smoke, it may come out of the shaman's mouth of its own accord, where an enemy sorcerer can cut it off, with fatal results.[37]

Because the mariri in his throat protects don Roberto from ingesting the darts and other evil objects he sucks out—the sorcerer's phlegm, the insects and scorpions and toads—the remainder, after spitting out the sickness, becomes flema in his mouth, dissolves into the mariri in his throat, and is swallowed, to be added to his own store of phlegm and thus his fuerza, shamanic power. When the sorcerer sends the virotes, the sorcerer laughs a vindictive laugh; when the shaman acquires the sorcerer's dart, don Roberto told me, the shaman gets to laugh.

Many shamans take these evils and direct them back to the sorcerer who sent them, to cause the sorcerer harm. Both don Roberto and doña María disclaimed any interest in sending back the darts or other pathogenic projectiles to harm the sorcerer from whom they came; that would be inconsistent with their practice of pura blancura, the pure white path. Indeed, don Roberto claims—with what candor I do not know—that he does not even know how to project magic darts back into an enemy shaman. This is not unusual; very few mestizo shamans will admit knowing how to cause harm, presumably as a way of avoiding the accusation of being a sorcerer.[38] Instead, don Roberto uses the materials of the magical attack to increase his own power, his ability to withstand attacks directed—as they inevitably are—against himself. Doña María, however, left some ambiguity. "We are gentle people," she once told me, giving me one of her looks. "But sometimes we show our claws."

SOURCES OF PHLEGM

The shaman's phlegm may be received from either of two sources. An apprentice may receive phlegm from the mouth of the maestro ayahuasquero; or phlegm may be received from the plant spirits themselves, by drinking ayahuasca, smoking mapacho, and ingesting substances with strong sweet smells. Doña María had nourished her phlegm—and thus the fuerza, power, of her oraciones, prayers—for years before meeting don Roberto and drinking ayahuasca or smoking mapacho. She had done this by drinking commercial cologne, mouthwash, camphor dissolved in alcohol, and yellow oleander seeds dissolved in alcohol with white onion.

The maestro ayahuasquero can also transfer some of his or her own phlegm—and the fuerza it manifests—into the apprentice, as part of the apprentice's coronación, crowning or initiation, by regurgitating the phlegm and putting it into the apprentice's body. The mariri can be transferred to the apprentice through the corona, through the mouth, or both; the stream of mariri entering the apprentice is often envisioned as a shining stream of light or as a great snake. Other shamans maintain that it is a dangerous practice to give phlegm to an apprentice who might break the dieta, with disastrous repercussions for the master; these shamans say that they received their phlegm directly from the spirits.[39] We turn to this process of initiation in the next chapter.

CHAPTER 8
INITIATION

MOTIVES AND QUALITIES

People become shamans in the Upper Amazon for many reasons. Among the Shuar, a primary motive is revenge for earlier harms, or the desire to protect oneself and one's family from attacks by enemy shamans.[1] An Achuar told anthropologist Philippe Descola why he had become an uwíshin, a shaman:

> I decided to become an uwíshin after my marriage. My father-in-law had died from a spell, followed by my brother-in-law. Then my son died too, while still a suckling babe. A bad uwíshin had sent tsentsak into the breasts of my wife Najari, and the baby died very quickly from suckling at the tsentsak. What could I do? . . . Do you really think that I should have waited for us all to be exterminated? So off I went to Sharian so that I too could learn.[2]

Other motives include a wish to heal one's family, obtain prestige and influence, and gain economic advantages.[3] Among the Aguaruna and Canelos Quichua, shamanic power may be purchased for money or trade goods.[4]

Among mestizo shamans, a typical story tells of finding a healing vocation when being healed by another. At the age of fifteen, for example, don Francisco Montes Shuña got an incurable pain in his heart. When he drank ayahuasca for the first time, he saw that he had been accidentally hit by the virote, magic dart, of a sorcerer. The shaman then cut him open, took out his heart, healed it, and put it back with the ability to cure. After that, don Francisco went to the Campa tribe and met don Pasqual Yumpiri, who became his maestro ayahuasquero.[5]

Don José Coral Moré first took ayahuasca because of a great pain in his stomach; the twentieth time he drank, spirits he calls *murayas* appeared, removed the dart, and stayed with him thereafter. Don Celso Rojas suffered from an intractable infection in his leg, which the doctors wanted to amputate; he drank ayahuasca and undertook la dieta for three years, whereupon a bird appeared, ate the maggots that had been infecting his leg, and disappeared into the ayahuasca pot. After that, the spirits of the plants began to appear in his visions and teach him medicine.[6]

These stories are often not particularly dramatic. The future shaman drinks ayahuasca, as often from curiosity as from sickness; a spirit will appear in the ayahuasca vision, offer an icaro, magical song, and prescribe a dieta of a particular sort and duration. There seem to be few cases of what has been called *shamanic illness*. Rather, the sicknesses are quite ordinary—unexplained pains and infections, caused by darts, undoubtedly, and in one case inadvertently, sent by a sorcerer.

Indeed, doña María simply appears to have been born with a visionary gift. When she was seven years old, she had her first dream of the Virgin Mary—María calls her hermana virgen, sister virgin—who began to teach her how to heal with plants. From that time on, she frequently had dreams in which either the Virgin Mary or an angel appeared to her. The Virgin would appear as a young and very beautiful woman, show her the healing plants, especially those for protection against malignos, evil spirits, and teach her the plants to cure specific diseases. The angel would appear and tell her where in the area there was a child who was sick and who needed her help. She then went to the house of the child and told the family what plant would cure the illness and how to prepare it. In one dream, she was told that she must heal one hundred babies of mal de ojo, the evil eye.

Don Roberto apprenticed with his uncle, José Acho Aguilar, an ayahuasquero, at the age of fourteen. He became a shaman, he says, because, when he first drank ayahuasca, he *saw things*, which he enjoyed, and he wanted to learn more. Interestingly, neither don Roberto nor doña María reports that an illness or other crisis led them to become shamans.

According to Shuar shaman Alejandro Tsakím Suánua, to become a shaman one must have a desire to be strong; one must be decisive, courageous, and determined.[7] Tukano shamans, says anthropologist Gerardo Reichel-Dolmatoff, are driven by curiosity, always interested in animals and plants, the weather, the stars, sicknesses—anything, he says, that to others is unpredictable.[8] And, as we note repeatedly, self-control is critical to becoming a healer, although less self-control is required to be a sorcerer; to be a sorcerer is to give oneself over to aggression, lust, and vengeance. The Amazonian shamans I have known have been characterized, I believe, not only by courage and self-control but also by intellectual curiosity and, often, a flair for performance. They have all been highly regarded as mitayeros, competent hunters and fishers, unlikely to get lost; indeed, a term often used for great shamans of the past is *trailmakers*.

RECEIVING THE MASTER'S PHLEGM

The shamanic coronación, initiation, consists, in part, of the master shaman transferring magical phlegm through his or her mouth to the apprentice: the mouth of the master shaman regurgitates mariri, which is ingested by the mouth of the apprentice. During an ayahuasca ceremony with don Roberto, he gave me a portion of his phlegm, for me to keep and nurture in my chest while I was gone and to protect me from attacks by wicked or jealous sorcerers. This was my coronación in the ayahuasca path; receiving the llausa of the maestro ayahuasquero, he said, is reserved for those who are "learning the medicine."

First he put his llausa or flema, phlegm, into my body through my corona, the crown of my head. Then he shook his shacapa rattle all over my body, protecting and preparing my body to hold the medicine. He brought his phlegm up from his chest with a series of dramatic burps and belches; then he placed his mouth over mine and transferred into my mouth a slippery cohesive globule about a half inch in diameter, which I swallowed. This llausa went into my chest, he said, to join the llausa he had put in through my corona. He told me that I must smoke mapacho every day to keep the llausa in place, to nurture this seed he had planted inside me; in the same way, a Shuar shaman must drink tobacco juice every few hours, to nurture the tsentsak, magic darts, given by the master shaman, and keep them fed so that they will not leave him.[9] Giving me his phlegm, don Roberto said, was like planting grass; it was up to me to keep it fertile. "Now," he said, "you will have the medicine for the rest of your life."

In addition to his phlegm, don Roberto gave me two of his spirit animals for my protection—the *otorongo*, the tawny jaguar, and the *yanapuma*, the black jaguar. Just as I must nurture my phlegm by smoking mapacho, I should maintain my connection with the jungle spirit protectors by continuing to drink ayahuasca. As we will see, when doña María was attacked by don X, part of the attack was to separate her from her protectors by making it hard for her to drink ayahuasca.

Doña María elaborated on the nature of this gift. Now that I have mariri, she said, I will be able to feel a pulsation on my body where I am about to be attacked. This *pálpito*—the word means both a physical throb and a psychological hunch—is a warning to me. If I have this feeling, for example, before a meeting, I will know that a person there has bad intentions toward me. If someone at the meeting does not shake hands with me—if the person just waves and says hello or touches the *back* of my hand—then I know the person is a brujo. Sorcerers, doña María told me, will not shake my hand, for then they would be revealed to my touch.

To nurture the seed don Roberto planted in my chest, and to build up my own store of magical and protective phlegm, I should be smoking mapacho every day. I should be drinking ayahuasca under the direction of a maestro ayahuasquero, but doña María and don Roberto understand that it is difficult to do that in North America. The longer I am away from the medicine, however, the more sickness and evil of all kinds will build up in my body; when I return—as has happened before after a long absence—I can anticipate a truly spectacular *purga*. I should be learning icaros, sacred songs—first those of my own maestro ayahuasquero, many of which I have recorded on tape, and then, eventually, my own, which the plants will teach me. Doña María told me to first *hum* the melody or to whistle it in the breathy whispering whistle called silbando; the words are less important than the melody. Any time I sing their icaros, doña María and don Roberto will be by my side. Many times when she goes to sleep, María walks far in her dreams; she will come and sit by my side, and I will fear nothing and nobody, she said, for the medicine grants a corazón de acero, a heart of steel.

INITIATION IN THE UPPER AMAZON

Similar conceptions occur throughout the Upper Amazon. One of Luna's shamans told how his teacher, after having blown tobacco smoke into both his apprentice's nostrils using a toucan beak, regurgitated his yachay into a little bowl and gave it to his apprentice to drink, together with tobacco juice.[10] When a Siona shaman teaches an apprentice his visions and songs, he imparts some of his dau to him.[11]

For the Shipibo-Conibo, quenyon, the shaman's power substance, is a sticky paste-like phlegm in which are embedded small arrows or the thorns of spiny palms. The master shaman passes this phlegm to an apprentice by swallowing a large amount of tobacco smoke and bringing up the phlegm from his chest to his mouth, from which the apprentice sucks it out, nightly, for a week. The phlegm accumulates first in the apprentice's stomach, where it is believed to be harmful; to make it rise to the chest and remain there, the apprentice drinks tobacco water and swallows tobacco smoke. If the phlegm rises to the mouth, the apprentice must swallow it again, in order to ensure that the phlegm does not leave the body through the mouth or other orifice.[12]

Similarly, among the Shuar, the master shaman vomits tsentsak, magic darts, in the form of a brilliant substance. The master shakes the shinku leaf rattle over the apprentice's head and body, singing to the tsentsak, makes profound throat-clearing noises, and spits out the phlegm on the palms and the backs of the apprentice's hands, and then on the chest, head, and finally the mouth; it is then swallowed—painfully—by the apprentice.[13] Shuar shaman Alejandro Tsakimp describes his initiation by his aunt, Maria Chúmpa, whom he approached "to study how it is to be a shaman of the woman's way": "The shamanism of my aunt Maria was different from that of Segundo and Lorenzo because they blew on the crown of my head, and they gave me the ayahuasca to concentrate. But my aunt gave me phlegm, like this, taking out her *chuntak*. She made me put it in my mouth and swallow it."[14]

Among the Iquitos, the materialized power of the shaman is described as a ball of leaves inside the body, which can be transmitted by a bird or passed mouth to mouth from the master shaman to the apprentice.[15]

The Achuar apprentice drinks ayahuasca and inhales tobacco juice with the master shaman, who then blows darts into the apprentice's head and shoulders and between the fingers, and then puts his saliva into the apprentice's mouth, speaking the names of the different kinds: "Take the saliva of the anaconda! Take the saliva of the rainbow! Take the saliva of iron!"—all of which the apprentice must swallow and not vomit. A shaman recalls his initiation: "My stomach heaved and all the saliva rose into my mouth. I almost spat everything out, but managed to swallow it down."[16]

Anthropologist Marie Perruchon tells an interesting story about her own initiation as a Shuar uwíshin. She was, she says, quite concerned about swallowing the phlegm of her master, Carlos Jempekat, who was also her brother-in-law; she thought that this—combined with the emetic effect of ayahuasca—would cause her to throw up the phlegm immediately. Apparently Carlos sensed her hesitation; at her initiation, he blew the tsentsak into the crown of her head, rather than giving them to her through her mouth. Both methods seem to have been acceptable; receiving shamanic power by blowing is attributed to Canelos Quichua shamans, whom the Shuar hold in high esteem. Carlos Jempekat said that tsentsak received in phlegm are less liable to leave the body accidentally than those received *en aire*, by blowing: "Sometimes it is enough to stumble," he said, "and, whoops, the tsentsak leave."[17] It is also possible to receive tsentsak in a dream, instead of receiving them from a shaman.[18]

A Tukano apprentice receives the darts—the sharp thorns of a spiny palm—through the skin on the inside of the left forearm. The teacher presses upon these thorns with a cylinder of white quartz, with the handle of the gourd rattle, and finally with his clenched fist, through which he blows to make the splinters enter the arm, into which they disappear. These darts can then be projected at an enemy with a violent movement of the arm; they are placed in the left arm so that they are not hurled inadvertently during a fight or quarrel. The shaman also places darts on the apprentice's tongue, and blows them into the apprentice's body through his fist, so that the apprentice can then safely suck the sickness from a patient's body.[19]

THE INITIATION DIET

In order to allow the tsentsak to mature and keep them from leaving the body, the Shuar apprentice must undertake a severe diet—only green plantains for the first week, remaining in bed without coughing or speaking loudly, with one hand always covering the mouth. The apprentice also drinks tobacco juice night and day to feed the darts. After a week the apprentice may get out of bed and take a bath, but must stay inside the house or in shady spots in the courtyard for the next few weeks. The apprentice is also allowed to eat some vegetables, fruits, and domestic chicken. The idea is to avoid anything—animal fat, spices, laughing, coughing, shouting, sex—that may heat the body and drive out the darts. Ideally, these restrictions are kept for about a year, during which time they are slowly relaxed, one at a time. The apprentice may not touch anyone else; even the chickens the apprentice eats have to be sexually inactive.[20]

The Achuar initiate has to stay at home for at least a month, without moving, drinking tobacco water every day, without sex, so that the darts can get used to their new host.[21] The same is true for the newly initiated Tukano shaman. For several weeks or months, he may not eat meat, or fat grubs, or peppers—only certain fish, manioc, and thin soups. Even the preparation of such foods near the house is prohibited. And sexual abstinence continues; he must have no sex and must avoid contact with menstruating women. The new shaman must avoid any loud or shrill or sudden noises, which would drown out the voices of the spirits.[22]

SELF-CONTROL

There is a theme woven through the shamanisms of the Upper Amazon—that human beings in general, and shamans in particular, have powerful urges to harm other humans. The difference between a healer and a sorcerer is that the former is able to bring these urges under control, while the latter either cannot or does not want to.

Thus, what distinguishes a healer from a sorcerer is self-control. This self-control must be exercised specifically in two areas—first, in keeping to la dieta, the restricted diet; and, second, in resisting the urge to use the magical darts acquired at initiation for frivolous or selfish purposes. Shamans who master their desires may use their powers to heal; those who give in to desire, by their lack of self-control, become sorcerers, followers of the easy path.[23]

As with la dieta, a significant part of the initiation process is for the new shaman to demonstrate the self-control that separates healers from sorcerers. Self-control is manifested in resisting the immediate urge to use newly acquired powers to cause harm. Among the Shuar, there is a sentiment that becoming a shaman—acquiring tsentsak, darts—creates an irresistible desire to do harm, that "the tsentsak make you do bad things." Shuar shamans dispute this. While the tsentsak indeed tempt one to harm, the desire can be resisted; those who "study with the aim to cure" become healers.[24]

Shuar shaman Alejandro Tsakím Suánua describes one of these temptations as the urge to try out the new darts on an animal—"a dog or a bird, anything that has blood." Once one does that, once one "starts doing harm, killing animals, one cannot cure" but, rather, becomes a *maliciador*, sorcerer.[25] Similarly, the Desana believe that sorcery is very dangerous, apt to rebound on its practitioner, and to be used only for revenge on a sorcerer who has killed a family member. It is the untrained person, the novice, who causes sickness—who lacks the self-control imposed by the shamanic initiation, who experiments with evil spells, who uses them carelessly and irresponsibly, just to see if they work.[26]

This self-control is often expressed in terms of regurgitation and reingestion of shamanic power. After a month of apprenticeship, a tsentsak comes out of the Shuar apprentice's mouth. The apprentice must resist the temptation to use this tsentsak to harm his enemies; in order to become a healing shaman, the apprentice must swallow what he himself has regurgitated.[27] Among the Canelos Quichua, the master coughs up spirit helpers in the form of darts, which the apprentice swallows. Here, too, the darts come out of the apprentice's body and tempt him to use them against his enemies; again, the apprentice must avoid the temptation and reswallow the darts, for only in this way can he become a healing shaman.[28]

This self-control is also sometimes put in terms of turning down gifts from the spirits. The spirits of the plants may offer the apprentice great powers and gifts that can cause harm. If the apprentice is weak and accepts them, he will become a sorcerer. Such gifts might include phlegm that is red, or bones, or thorns, or razor blades. Only later will the spirits present him with other and greater gifts—the gifts of healing and of love magic.[29]

And sometimes self-control develops through the moral intervention of the healing plants themselves. Shipibo shaman don Javier Arévalo Shahuano decided to become a shaman at the age of twenty, when his father was killed by a virote, magic dart, sent by an envious sorcerer. "I wanted to learn in order to take vengeance," he says. It was only during his apprenticeship that he learned self-control. "Bit by bit, through taking the very plants I had intended to use for revenge," he says, "the spirits told me it was wrong to kill and my heart softened."[30]

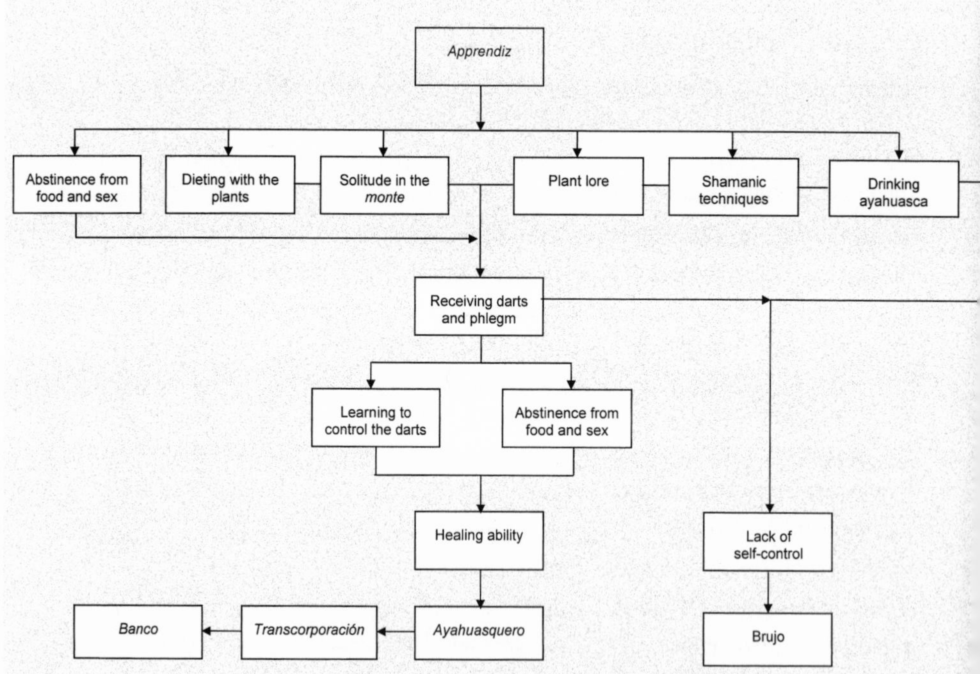

FIGURE 6. The path of the ayahuasquero.

Self-control is, therefore, central. It is difficult to control lust and abstain from sorcery; even experienced shamans must work hard to maintain control over their powers, which are often conceptualized as having their own volitions.[31] The pathogenic objects that are kept within the shaman's body, often embedded in some saliva- or phlegm-like substance, are also in some sense spirits—autonomous, alive, with their own needs and desires, including a need for nourishment, often supplied by tobacco, and often a need to kill.

The tsentsak, magic darts, kept within the chest of a Shuar shaman, want to kill; it is difficult to resist the urges of the darts.[32] The darts acquired by an Achuar shaman, having once caused sickness, have acquired a taste for human flesh. They seek to escape the shaman's control and go hunting on their own.[33] The magic darts can control the actions of a shaman who does not have sufficient self-control, and it requires hard work to use them for healing rather than attack. In this way, the pathogenic objects hidden within the shaman's body enact the Amazonian belief in innate human aggressiveness. To be a healer is to keep this powerful force in check with great effort.

DREAM INITIATIONS

It is worth noting that a number of mestizo shamans report having had initiatory dreams that announced—or confirmed—their healing vocation. Strikingly, these dreams tend to share certain themes—a journey, often to a spiritual hospital; initiation by a powerful woman, such as the Virgin Mary or the queen of the hospital; the gift of healing or shamanic tools, flowers and a shining crown; and the prediction of great strength or healing ability.

Doña María's Dream

One day in September 1958, just around her eighteenth birthday, María drank a tea made from *hierba luisa*, lemon grass; went to bed early, about four o'clock in the afternoon; and had a dream that was to influence her entire life—what she calls her coronación, her crowning or initiation. By this time, she had already been healing children for ten years with oraciones, prayer songs, and plant remedies taught her in dreams by the Virgin Mary. The account of the dream is lengthy and complex, made up of a number of separable episodes; I have heard the dream told twice, and, although the two versions had considerable overlap, each telling contained episodes that were missing from the other. There is little doubt that María had a compelling dream at this time, which served to confirm her on her chosen healing path; but there is also,

How I Became a Sorcerer

We have discussed the idea, widely held in the Upper Amazon, that human beings in general, and shamans in particular, have powerful urges to harm other humans, and that the difference between a healer and a sorcerer comes down to a matter of self-control. On that there hangs a story.

A while ago, I was sitting in a training seminar, and I was angry with the facilitator, a man I greatly respect and admire. I was angry for foolish and childish reasons; I felt that I was not being paid enough attention.

Suddenly, without any apparent intention on my part, a spider flew out of my mouth—a large, black, hairy spider, about three inches across. The spider flew from my mouth to the face of the seminar facilitator, where it grasped and clung to his cheek, eventually melting into his face. I was taken aback by this. Damn, I said; I didn't realize I was that angry. And that would have been the end of it, except that, at the next day's session, the distraught facilitator announced that he had been told that his wife's breast cancer, thought to be in remission, had recurred.

Now, was there any connection between my spider and his wife's illness? Of course not. The spider touched him, not his wife. And the recurrence must have taken place before the spider left my mouth; certainly sorcery cannot be temporally retroactive. Of course there was no connection. Yet what I carry away from this experience is still a sense of guilt. I did not cause the harm; I could not have caused the harm. But what happened was a loss of control—my momentary anger, my ego, my envidia, the worst part of me leaping from my mouth in the form of a spider, just like the spiders and scorpions that are projected, in the Upper Amazon, from the phlegm of a brujo, a sorcerer.

From this inconsequential incident, I have learned three things.

First, there really is no going back. Once you walk through the door into the realm of the spirits, you cannot return to any prior state of innocence. Once you begin la dieta, once you drink ayahuasca, once you begin to form relations of confianza with the healing plants, the world becomes a more dangerous place. When you have begun to realize the porosity of reality; when the world has become magical, filled with wonders, filled with the spirits, filled with meaning; when you have begun to see what was there all along but was invisible to you—then you must accept that your childish anger is, right here and now, as it always was, an ugly spider leaping from your lips, capable of causing great harm.

People in the Upper Amazon consider the darts and other pathogenic objects in a shaman's phlegm to be autonomous, alive, spirits, sometimes with their own needs and desires, including a desire to kill. I now believe that is profoundly true. Our egos are as tricky and autonomous as magical darts. Our envidia, our foolish willingness to destroy relationships of confianza with others, seems to flair up at the slightest provocation. The popular image of the sorcerer in the Upper Amazon reflects this truth: the figure of the evil sorcerer embodies resentment, greed, selfishness, constriction. Just like my ego.

And that is why self-control is mandatory. Since that inconsequential incident, I have been tempted to try it again—just, you know, to see if it works, just to express my anger, just to be—somehow—powerful. And I cannot do it, ever again.

Mosquitero

The fact that doña María was carried to heaven in her *mosquitero*, mosquito net, has significant symbolic resonance in the Upper Amazon. In crowded households, the impenetrable cotton mosquito net is a refuge of privacy.[1] Mestizo communities have even refused free insecticide-impregnated nets because they were insufficiently opaque. "The whole world will be able to see us," they objected.[2]

Even more, shamans of the highest order work secretly within their woven mosquiteros—as pioneering ethnographer Robert H. Lowie says, "in complete darkness under a mosquito net."[3] The ability to enter a mosquito net and disappear, or to converse under the mosquito net with the most powerful spirits, is one of the things—along with becoming a jaguar—that distinguishes the Shipibo *meraya* shaman from the lesser *onanya*.[4] The mosquito net within which the meraya retreats after drinking ayahuasca is called a *bachi*, egg.[5]

Don Francisco Montes Shuña says that the *banco*—the highest rank of shaman—enters a mosquito net in the middle of the house, lying facedown, while all the disciples remain outside. Then the spirits come to the banco from below to talk to him and to speak through him.[6] Pablo Amaringo has painted a picture of a banco lying beneath his mosquito net while three spiritual beings—a wise old king and two princes—descend and sit on his body. The shaman is here the *banco*, the bench, for the sprits descending into the mosquitero. Others wait outside the mosquito net to hear these spirits speak through the shaman's mouth.[7]

A mestizo who heard doña María's dream would understand, from the mosquito net reference, that she was experiencing an initiation of a very high order.

NOTES

1. For example, see Lagrou, 2000, pp. 153, 159.
2. Harvey et al., 2008.
3. Lowie, 1948, p. 49.
4. Ministerio de Salud del Perú, 2002, p. 106; Tournon, 1991.
5. Roe, 2004, p. 272.
6. Sammarco & Palazzolo, 2002.
7. Luna & Amaringo, 1993, p. 100.

I believe, good reason to think that the dream episodes she narrates are a composite of congruent dreams she has had over a period of time.

María dreamed that a beautiful young woman came and sat by her side. "Today we are going to go upward," the woman said, "and see everything that is happening on earth." María and the woman went into María's mosquito net, which carried them up into the clouds to a beautiful green meadow. This was paradise, filled with angels—men and women, adults, children, and babies—wearing brilliant white robes and crowns of sweet-smelling flowers. All the angels started to pray the Ave Maria and the Paternoster, holding hands and dancing in a circle around her. As María marveled at the sight, the young woman told her she was in *paraíso terrenal*, the earthly paradise. There were thousands of angels, holding beautiful brightly lit candles, holding up their hands and saying amén in a single voice.

María and the young woman walked on, and they came to a mountain from which clear crystal water was falling. In the water were *piedritas*, magical stones of all kinds, large and small, *encantadas*, enchanted, which began to sing to her, "Welcome, welcome, *maestra*, doctora." But the young woman warned María not to stop and pick up the stones or lower her head.

The two kept on walking and praying, until they arrived at a very large and beautiful house, inside of which were the spirits of the *abortos*, babies who had never been born, babies of all races, black and white. The souls of these babies were being boiled in a large kettle, and the young woman explained that they had to remain there for a certain number of years of penance. They continued on, passing more magical stones, still hearing the cries of the abortos. "From here on," the young woman said, "you may not turn around." All along the path were stones, and among the stones were millions of babies.

They came to a cemetery where there were many wooden houses. The houses were being built by dead people, who cried out to her, "Blessings, sister! Blessings, sister!" María knew some of these dead people; one was a mayor from her town, who had committed suicide. The dead were held by chains around their ankles, for penance.

The two went on walking and saw two women. María remembered one of them, who had died when María was fourteen. María tried to speak to her, and the woman invited them into her house, but María's guide told her not to approach, because María was not yet ready to be there.

They came to the house of María's grandmother, who also invited them in. Inside, María saw all sorts of healing plants. María asked her grandmother for something to drink; her grandmother gave her *chicha morado*, a dark purple drink made of fermented maize. María hesitated to drink it, thinking it was the blood of the dead. "Do not think that," said the young woman, "for here there is no blood." So María drank it, but doubted; the young woman said, "No, this is not a place for doubt," and they prayed three times.

Finally, they came to a beautiful paved highway where there was a great hospital in which surgical operations were performed. A jeep drove by, containing four men elegantly dressed in pure white. The woman said, "Lie down here," so María lay down until the jeep had passed by. "Who are these people?" María asked. "They are the doctors at the hospital," she was told, "who are going to do an operation." They walked on to the hospital and stood at the door praying. People inside the hospital said, "We've been waiting for you. We are going to crown you because you are a spiritual doctor." María said, "But I don't know anything about doing operations." The door to the hospital opened with a creaking sound—*ehrrrrrrr*, said doña María, demonstrating—and the hospital was filled with brilliant white light, filled with thousands of doctors, all dressed in white surgical scrubs, all prepared for the operation, saying to her, "Welcome, doctora. Tonight you are going to receive the spiritual medicine."

María was taken to a room where she was dressed in white clothing, white shoes, and a surgical mask, and her hands were washed with fragrant perfume. She expressed doubts that she could go through with this. "You were brought here because you are a doctor for the earth," she was told. "Tonight you will begin your work here and on earth." She felt *poder*, *fuerza*, *luz*—divine power, shamanic force, light.

Then all the doctors disinfected their hands, took needles and sutures for surgery, and performed their operations on their patients—operations on their eyes, ears, hearts, and minds. Each doctor worked to heal a specific disease; when the operations were completed, all the patients who had been operated on returned to their rooms.

"Now we are going to the *botica*, pharmacy," she was told, "to see the many plants that are medicines." The pharmacy was huge, with plant medicines of all kinds—bark, stems, leaves, prepared in various ways—a *botica espiritual*, spiritual pharmacy. And the woman showed María which plants were good for which diseases. "Everything you see here," she told María, "is medicine for the earth." And everything that María saw and learned in the pharmacy she remembered when she awoke.

Finally, María and the woman came to two forking paths. One path was filled with beautiful, fragrant, inviting flowers and led into the green valley; the other path was filled with spiny and thorny plants like *uña de gato*, cat's claw, and led to the rocky and barren mountains. "Now choose a path," the woman told María. "Will it be flowers or mountains?"

María decided to take the path to the mountains, on which she saw many plants she recognized from the earth, as well as many that were new to her; she wanted, she said, to see what was there. The woman—whom María now understood to be the Virgin Mary—gave her a hug and kissed her forehead. "It is the better path you have taken," she said. María and the woman held hands and began to pray. María felt emotion through her whole body and began to tremble. "Do not be afraid," the woman said; and María saw that the rocky path was in fact a *carretera preciosa*, a precious highway, leading far away. "As far as you have come," the woman said, "you have a long way to go. As of this day, you have the corona de medicina, the crown of medicine," and the woman placed a brilliant shining crown on María's head. "After this," the woman said, "you are going to heal and know very important people." Which, doña María added, turned out to be true. From the time of this initiation dream, doña María understood that she was no longer to heal only children but adults as well.

Pablo Amaringo's Vision

Pablo Amaringo was similarly initiated during an ayahuasca vision. Beautiful women carrying baskets full of sweet-smelling flowers, white and pink, came to him and crowned him; they gave him the mantle of a king, a wide belt, beautiful shoes, a scepter, books, swords, an elegant throne, and animal protectors—wolves, a bear, a tiger, a panther, an eagle, and worms. He did not understand what they were doing, but he felt like a king. The queens gave him the flowers, kissed him, and said, "Now we are coming to be with you, so that you will be very strong. You will have guardians to your right and left."

Later he understood that the white flowers symbolized the medicine he was to practice, and the pink flowers symbolized the defenses he was to use. There were no red or black flowers, which represent sorcery. About a month later, directed by a woman who appeared to him in a dream, he did his first healing.[34]

Francisco Montes Shuña's Dream

Don Francisco Montes Shuña had a dream in which he was initiated as a perfumero. He was shown a hospital "where all the operations were performed psychically." He looked for the queen of the hospital and found her at the eighth door he opened. Behind this door was a garden in which people were working with flowers and scents. When the queen arrived, everyone recognized her; she invited Montes to enter, embraced him, and took him to a long table on which were placed many bottles of fragrance. She explained the contents of each one and said of the last: "This is yours. With this you will become a great *curandero*."[35]

CHAPTER 9

SUCKING AND BLOWING

As we have discussed, the power of the mestizo shaman is stored in the physical form of phlegm in the shaman's chest. But the gateway of the shaman's power is the shaman's *mouth*, out of which the shaman's power passes in the form of singing, whistling, whispering, and blowing, and into which the shaman sucks out the sickness, the sorcery, and the magic darts that cause the patient's suffering.

All across the Amazon, *blowing* and *sucking* are the primary and complementary means of manifesting the magical power of the mouth. In the Upper Río Negro region, the Desana shaman "effects cures by means of blowing tobacco smoke . . . and sucking out pathogenic objects from the body and spitting them away."[1] At the other end of the Amazon, in the Middle Xingu of Brazil, the Araweté shaman fumigates with tobacco and sucks out pathogenic substances.[2] The Yagua shaman in eastern Peru and the Tukano shaman in Colombia both blow tobacco smoke over an afflicted body part and suck out darts and other intrusive pathogens.[3]

SUCKING

Not all sucking is physical. I was taught that there are three ways through which the shaman's mouth can draw out intrusive objects, sickness, darts, and magical harm from the patient's body—by sucking with the lips directly on the skin, by using one's cupped hands to make a tube through which the sickness can be drawn out, and by pulling with the mouth from a distance. As opposed to chupando, sucking, working at a distance is called jalando, pulling. A shaman may use different techniques under different circumstances. Don Agustin Rivas used jalando—which he calls "pulling the illness from a distance"—when he sucked AIDS from the forehead of an AIDS patient.[4]

The sucking or pulling removes the *haire*, air, and the *flemocidades*, "phlegmosities," of the sickness. The shaman is protected by his or her own flema, phlegm, stored in the chest and raised into the throat as mariri, phlegm rarefied, like air, vibratory and protective. The phlegm of the healer contests with the phlegm of the sickness, the phlegm of the sorcerer, filled with darts and scorpions.

As the shaman sucks, the sickness comes out into the mouth—sometimes like cold air, sometimes like a metallic object, sometimes as rotten meat, darts, toads, scorpions, insects, or razor blades. In fact, doña María warned me, what comes out of the patient's body may have a sweet taste, tempting one to swallow—a temptation clearly to be resisted. The healer then spits out what is bad and keeps what will increase the healer's own power. Often what is sucked out is so vile that the shaman gags and retches dramatically before spitting it onto the ground. If the object sucked or pulled from the patient is a powerful pathogenic object like a dart, it enters the mariri to become part of the shaman's own dart collection; or, if the healer wishes, the dart caught in the mariri can be projected back onto the one who sent it—the sorcerer, the sorcerer's client.

Thus, the key to don Roberto's healing is his chupando, sucking, like other shamans, throughout North and South America, who suck out sickness from the suffering body. Healing by sucking is widely distributed among the indigenous people of the Amazon.[5] The Machigengua shaman sucks out pathogenic objects—thorns, leaves, bones, spines—and shows them to the audience; the blood he sucks out is said to be black.[6] The Tukano shaman lays a magic stone on the place where the thorn or splinter or monkey fur has entered the body, puts his fist on the stone, thumb up, and sucks through that to remove the object, which he spits out onto the palm of his hand and shows the patient before throwing it away.[7]

The Toba shaman sucks out little stones, sticks, or worms.[8] Anthropologist Phillipe Descola describes an Achuar shaman sucking out and revealing "half a dozen pieces of glass, opaque with age."[9] Among the Aguaruna and the Shuar what is sucked out is said to be darts.[10] The Yagua shaman sucks out darts and then vomits them at a special place called *pánjo*, place of healing. The shaman there spits up a thread of saliva that, as it hardens, takes on the appearance of a dart. This is kept to be shown to the relatives of the sick person, who keep their distance, since the dart is charged with electricity, like lightning.[11]

The practice of sucking out sickness is old in the Amazon. A report of the Tupinambá dating to 1613 gives this account: "I see the shaman at work, sucking up the patient's illness, as hard as he can, into his mouth and throat, pretending to hold them full and distended and then quickly spitting outside the enclosed space. He spits with great force, making a noise like a pistol shot and says that it is the illness which he has sucked."[12]

Similarly, in North America, the Chippewa Indians make use of a "sucking doctor."[13] Anthropologist John Lee Maddox listed many Native American peoples among whom the doctor sucks the affected part and exhibits some foreign body. He describes how the Californian Karok doctor sucks the patient and then vomits up a frog, and how the Cumana suck disease from the patient and then vomit a hard black ball.[14] Extraction by suction among the Paiute is described by anthropologist Beatrice Whiting: "Sucking is part of nearly every ceremony. The doctor often sucks out some foreign object and thus effects a cure. He spits the object out of his mouth and shows it to the people. He then mixes it with dirt in his hands, rubs his hands together, and the object disappears. Sometimes he vomits the object into a pan of earth to make it disappear."[15]

There are different styles of sucking as well. Some draw up their phlegm into their throat silently; others, such as don Roberto, make dramatic sounds of belching or burping. Don Agustin Rivas remembers, as a child, laughing with his sister about the gurgling sounds that don Pancho Oroma made when healing their mother.[16] Doña María, although she was taught chupando by don Roberto, had previously used jalando, pulling, and she continued to use that same technique throughout her life. Some shamans suck gently; don Roberto sucks vigorously, placing his mouth full on the place where he has detected an embedded pathogenic object and drawing the skin fully into his mouth. As in all aspects of his shamanic performance, the patient knows that serious chupando is taking place.

Don Agustin Rivas tells of what it was like to suck a pathogenic object out of the brain of a patient. He drank ayahuasca to locate the object—it looked like a leaf with a serrated edge, he says—and then drank more ayahuasca to help raise his phlegm. He vomited this phlegm onto the patient's head and then sucked it back into his mouth, along with *something* not a leaf but, rather, similar to a clock battery, which he could feel with his tongue—round, cold, making a clicking noise between his teeth. This pathogenic object he swallowed; but ten minutes later he vomited it onto the ground, feeling it click against his teeth. He searched for the object in the small puddle of vomit, but, though he could feel it there, he could see nothing.[17] Otomi healer don Antonio sucks out rotten meat.[18] Peter Gorman, a student of don Julio Jerena, describes an experience of sucking out objects like balls of thick phlegm; when one slipped down his throat, he immediately began to vomit and choke.[19]

Here is another account, from the patient's side. The patient is Pablo Amaringo, and the shaman is don Pascual Pichiri:

> He then took his pipe, swallowed the smoke, and began to wake up his mariri. When the mariri was in his mouth, he came towards me and began to suck the place where the virote was nested. He barely touched my skin. After some time, the virote came out, he broke its tip with his teeth, and showed it to me: it was a thorn of cumaceba, thin like a needle. "Now let's take out the yausa," he said. When he finished, I felt a tremendous relief. I felt no pain, and the fever was gone.[20]

Sucking out a disease is risky, dramatic, and unpredictable. To suck out a sickness means committing to deal with something that is disgusting and dangerous. It is also a direct and personal challenge to the sorcerer who sent the sickness, and thus risks creating a powerful enemy. No wonder some shamans keep silent about their knowledge and abilities.

BLOWING

Blowing is a common Amazonian means of both healing and harming; blowing, singing, and whistling—the movement of breath out into the world, the projection of sound—are all modes that may be used for both attack and defense, and the less conceptual, the more abstract and refined the sound, the less tied to mere human intelligibility, the more powerful it is. The Wai distinguish two kinds of blowing, which have in common that they are used to kill an enemy by sending a fluidlike substance into the victim; the death of a person is almost always considered to be due to magical blowing by an enemy, and revenge blowing by a relative is considered an obligation of honor.[21] Among the Yagua, to use sorcery is called *to blow*; one says *I will cast a curse on you* by saying *I will blow on you*.[22] Similarly, among the Piro, whenever a death or serious illness is mentioned, the question is quickly asked, *Who blew?*[23] The Canelos Quichua word *shitana* means both sorcery and blowing—"a dangerous blowing of unseen tangibility."[24] To learn to blow, among the Shuar, means to become a shaman.[25] How powerful is blowing? In 1896, before attacking a Pangoa River settlement, an Asháninka shaman told his warriors to blow against the white man's bullets, which would turn them into leaves.[26]

Among the Akawaio, ritual blowing, *taling*, used to sicken or harm a person, is performed by blowing tobacco smoke on an object that is then thrown in the direction of the victim. The spirit of the object enters into the victim and makes the victim sick. The most powerful sickening objects are spirit stones—quartz crystals, possessed by shamans, which contain powerful spirits.[27]

But blowing—especially the blowing of tobacco—can be creative and life giving as well. In Ywalapíti myths, a demiurge named Kwamuty transforms large logs into living beings by blowing tobacco smoke on them. Among the Xingu, in the important female initiation rite, the girls are transformed into human beings by being blown on with tobacco smoke.[28] A Tukano creation myth has the creator, Yepá Huaké, give life to humans by blowing on them; when humans decline to bathe in the waters of immortality, thus becoming mortal, he compensates them by giving them shamans, who will also blow on them when they become sick.[29] Among the Machiguenga, the shaman's breath is charged with sacred energy that is enhanced by tobacco smoke.[30] The Yagua shaman summons his spirit allies by blowing tobacco smoke, and sends them forth and directs them by blowing smoke. Blowing tobacco smoke allows the extraction of darts by heating them, like a ripening abscess; blowing smoke drives out evil from the bodies of the sick; blowing smoke on an object reveals its true nature.[31] Ethnologist Alfred Métraux puts it somewhat differently. Breath and smoke are together the healing power of the Amazonian shaman, he says; it is the tobacco smoke that *materializes* the breath.[32]

The mestizo shaman's blowing sound—an almost silent and untranscribable *pshoo*—is the most refined and abstract sound of the shaman, beyond even silbando, the breathy and unintelligible whistling of the icaros, like the rustling of the leaf-bundle shacapa. Blowing tobacco smoke over the patient, or into the patient through the patient's corona, crown, combines the protective effect of mapacho with the power of the shaman's mouth. Tobacco, blown over and into the body, protects it *como una camisa de acero*, like a steel shirt.[33]

Shamans may blow strong sweet substances other than tobacco smoke. Some blow *aguardiente* over a patient's body, to cleanse and cure, or agua de florida, or the mouthwash Timolina—even the disinfectant Creolina.[34] Don

Agustin Rivas says, "I'd blow a fine spray, very powerfully and very fast, upwards from their feet."[35] Pablo Amaringo tells of a female shaman who sweetened her breath by drinking a mixture of chopped tobacco, perfume, camphor, aguardiente, hot pepper, lemon, and salt, together with a little arsenic; then she began to sing, and to blow forcefully here and there with her perfumed breath.[36]

THE PHENOMENOLOGY OF THE MOUTH

Throughout the Amazon, sucking and blowing—the power of the mouth to draw out sickness and to blow tobacco smoke—constitute the defining features of the shaman's art. Chupando, sucking, and soplando, blowing, were two key features that differentiated don Roberto's practice from doña María's when she first came to him as an apprentice. In a Guayaki myth, the creator, Inapirikuli, called into being the first two *pajé*, shamans. The first spoke the proper words over food so that humans could consume food without dying; the second sucked objects out of the body—bones, hair, stones, and tiny bits of wood—in order to make healthy life possible.[37] The name of the second shaman was Mariri. The pair of first shamans instantiate the two modes of contact between the sacred mouth and the world: the first demonstrates speaking, singing, blowing, regurgitating—movement *outward*; and the second demonstrates sucking—movement *inward*. Both defeat death.

This twofold symbolism of the mouth is reinforced in shamanic initiations in which the apprentice first regurgitates and then reswallows the magical darts that have been received from the master.[38] The darts coming out of the mouth are a temptation to blow, to project outward, to use the darts for destruction; the darts swallowed back into mouth are an exercise in self-control, mastery of shamanic power, becoming a healing shaman.

Sucking, swallowing, and regurgitating are part of the shaman's physical spirituality—a corporeal spirituality of bodily boundaries transgressed. The shaman's mouth is transformative and curative, a synecdoche for the function of shamanic healing itself.[39] Just as the shaman's mouth takes in sickness, magic darts, evil of all sorts, and spits it out—just as the shaman's mouth takes in the power of sorcery and incorporates it and then regurgitates it into the corona or mouth of the apprentice—the shaman's mouth incorporates the sociospiritual illness of the sufferer and renders it harmless, yet retains, with all the ambiguity of the shaman, the possibility of projecting it once more—as song, as dart, as blowing—into the body politic.

Healing and protection come together in the shaman's mouth, the contact point between sickness and healing; the mouth sucks in sickness, blows out tobacco smoke, and regurgitates phlegm and magic darts. Life and death move in and out through the sucking, blowing, gagging, regurgitating mouth.

CHAPTER 10
SPIRITS

THINKING ABOUT THE SPIRITS

Mestizo shamans in the Upper Amazon maintain relationships with two types of spirits—the spirits of the healing plants, who appear almost invariably in human form; and the protective spirits, often powerful animals, birds, or human beings, or the spirits of certain plants such as the spiny palms. The animals and plants that protect the healer are the same as those that carry out the destructive will of the sorcerer.

And, of course, the visionary world is filled with other-than-human persons of all sorts—visitors from other planets and galaxies in shining spaceships, denizens of vast sparkling cities, the beings who live in the deep jungle and beneath the dark waters, great teachers and healers of the past and future, silent denizens of infinite labyrinths of crystal rooms. I have seen dark-robed and faceless beings gathered to support me in my nausea, tall thin dark-skinned men in white shirts and white pants with black suspenders flitting on unknown errands among the participants at a ceremony, vast lines of Peruvian schoolgirls in blue and white uniforms ascending and descending a stairway by a radiant swimming pool.

The healing plants are doctores, teachers and healers; these are the vegetales que enseñan, the plants who teach. What they teach are their own secrets—what sicknesses of body or soul they heal, how to summon them with their songs, and how to prepare and apply them. Several different terms are used to designate the spirits of plants and animals. Don Roberto and doña María generally used the term *genio*, genius or nature; shamans also speak of the plant's *madre*, mother; its *espíritu*, spirit; and even its *imán*, magnet. Don Rómulo Magin spoke to me of the plant's *matriz*, its womb, and thus its matrix, its archetype.

Informally, we generally translate all these terms simply as the *spirit* of the plant. In addition, we call the wide variety of protective birds and animals and plants that mestizo shamans have something like *protective spirits*. Yet, as Graham Harvey points out, those who are willing to argue endlessly about the meaning and applicability of the term *shaman* often refer to spirits as if everyone knows what the word means—as if, he says, "the word were self-evidently universally understood, and the beings universally experienced."[1]

So, what do we know about these spirits?

In many ways, spirits act very much like imaginary objects. First, spirits lack the *sensory coherence* of real things. That is, primarily, spirits cannot be touched, unlike real things, though they can often be heard and occasionally smelled; although, in fairness, perhaps I should add that I have *felt* spirits—for example, rubbing my head—but never been able to *touch* them. Second, spirits are, unlike real things, *not public*. Other people, in the same place at the same time, do not see the same spirit objects or persons I see. This point can be disputed by claims to the contrary, or by a claim that shamans, at least, can perceive the ayahuasca visions of others; but, as far as I know, these claims have not been well tested. Third, the *behavior* of spirits is unusual; spirits appear and disappear suddenly and unpredictably, fade away gradually, and transform themselves in ways inconsistent with the generally recognized behavior of real things. Fourth, the *appearance* of spirits may be significantly different from that of real objects and people. For example, the spirit of the ayahuma tree often appears as a person without a head, contrary to the normal appearance of real people, at least living ones. And the spirit of a particular plant may appear in a different form at different times—for example, as male or female, old or young, with one or several heads—unlike real objects and people, who are generally fairly consistent in appearance from meeting to meeting.

On the other hand, spirits have many of the qualities of people—self-awareness, understanding, personal identity, volition, speech, memory. They are autonomous; they come and go as they wish; they may unilaterally initiate or terminate a relationship with a human. They can provide information or insight that the recipient finds surprising or previously unknown. They may have relatively consistent personalities—helpful, harmful, callous, malicious, indifferent, or tricky, just like human persons. Relationships with spirits may be comforting, demanding, dangerous, and exhausting, just as with human persons. As a result of such relationships, other-than-human persons may provide information, insight, power, vision, healing, protection, songs, and ceremonies. The receipt of such gifts entails reciprocal obligations, just as with human persons. The shaman's relationship with such spirits is the core of Amazonian animism.

ANIMISM

Animism is the view that human beings on the earth live—whether they know it or not—in community with persons who are not human beings. These other-than-human persons may include animals, plants, trees, rocks, clouds, thunder, and stars. The phrase *other-than-human persons* was coined by anthropologist Irving Hallowell to describe the world of the Ojibwe, in which humans, animals, fish, birds, and plants—and some rocks, trees, and storms—are all relational, intentional, conscious, and communicative beings.[2] Ethnographer Thomas Blackburn reached similar conclusions for the Chumash, whose cosmos, he said, is composed of an "interacting community of sentient creatures."[3] Cultural ecologist David Abram speaks of "the intuition that every form one perceives . . . is an *experiencing* form, an entity with its own predilections and sensations."[4]

Persons are recognized in a variety of ways, including whether they can be talked with, whether gifts can be exchanged with them, and whether they can be engaged in a cultural system of respect and reciprocity. Human persons can give gifts to stone persons, who can receive those gifts and give their own gifts to human persons in return—a dream, say, or a song. Animism is what anthropologist Nurit Bird-David has called a *relational epistemology*.[5] Anthropologist Enrique Salmón, himself a Tarahumara, calls this a *kincentric ecology*—"an awareness that life in any environment is viable only when humans view the life surrounding them as kin."[6] When indigenous cultures speak of *spirits*, says David Abram, what they are really referring to are "those modes of intelligence or awareness that do not possess a human form"—that is, precisely, other-than-human persons.[7]

This use of the term *animism* differs sufficiently from its earlier use that the term *neoanimism* is sometimes used instead. The term *animism* was first used by nineteenth-century anthropologist Edward Tylor to define the essence of religion as "the belief in spirits"—that is, as a *category mistake* made by young children and primitives who project life onto inanimate objects, at least until they reach a more advanced stage of development.[8]

The more recent view, on the other hand, does not see animism as a set of beliefs so much as a way of *engaging with the world*. This engagement is based on relationships, within which humans are not separate from the world or distinct from other beings in any meaningful way. Indeed, for some humans—certain clans, for example—the mutual relationship with a particular other-than-human person, sometimes called a *totem*, from the Ojibwe word *dodem*, can provide a significant focus for social and ritual life. The new animism, Harvey says, "contests modernist preconceptions and invites the widening of relational engagements generated and enhanced by gift exchanges and other forms of mutuality."[9]

This engagement is often reflected in animist mythology, in which other-than-human persons were created before humans, at one time spoke with humans in a mutually intelligible language, and, indeed, appeared in the form of humans. When asked to define the term *myth*, anthropologist Claude Lévi-Strauss once said that it is "a story about the time when humans and animals did not yet distinguish themselves from each other."[10] Anthropologist Eduardo Viveiros de Castro says that a virtually universal notion in indigenous thought in both North and South America "is that of an original state of non-differentiation between humans and animals."[11]

Thus, in the Amazon, plants and animals are ascribed the status of persons, who may differ corporeally from human persons but, like them, possess intentionality and agency.[12] Indeed, other-than-human persons are believed to *see themselves* in human form, and thus to be self-aware of their own personhood. Among the Ashéninka, for example, a white-lipped peccary is held to perceive its own herd as a foraging human tribe, its wallow as a human village, and the wild root it eats as cultivated manioc. A peccary sees a human hunter as a jaguar; a jaguar sees its human prey as a peccary, and sees other jaguars as humans.[13] Similarly, among the Machiguenga, a human sees him- or herself as a human; but "the moon, the snake, the jaguar and the mother of smallpox see him or her as a tapir or a peccary that they kill."[14] These percepts extend to all aspects of culture: animals see their fur, feathers, claws, and beaks as body decorations and cultural instruments, and their social system as organized in the same way as human institutions.[15] In a series of influential articles, Viveiros de Castro has called this theory of the world *perspectivism*, and has explicitly tied it to theories of animism.[16]

In the Amazon, this idea is almost always associated with another—that the visible form of every species is an envelope, a form of clothing, that conceals an internal human form visible only to other members of the same species, or to a shaman.[17] This clothing is changeable and removable;[18] in the Amazon, not only do shamans become jaguars, but also humans and animals constantly shift into each other, in what anthropologist Peter Rivière has called a "highly transformational world."[19] But, interestingly, humans put on animal clothes and turn into animals, and animals take off animal clothes and turn into humans; but animals never put on human clothes.[20] *All beings are human*—which is just how they see themselves. "The common condition of humans and animals," says Viveiros de Castro, "is humanity, not animality."[21] As

Piro shaman don Mauricio Roberto Fasabi says of the *kachpero*, the strangler fig: "We see the kachpero as a tree, but that is a lie, the kachpero is a person. We just see it as a tree. When we take ayahuasca, we see it as people."[22]

This is the animist matrix of the Amazonian shaman—as Viveiros de Castro puts it, an "intentioned universe."[23] Shamans—including don Roberto and doña María—develop relationships with powerful beings, even in the form of stones. This animism is not necessarily benign; social anthropologist Carlos Fausto calls it *predatory animism*. "Subjectivity is attributed to human and nonhuman entities," he writes, "with whom some people are capable of interacting verbally and establishing relationships of adoption or alliance, which permit them to act upon the world in order to cure, to fertilize, and to kill."[24] It is in this context, too, that we should look at the claim the people in the Amazon believe that shamans turn into jaguars; rather, jaguars, beneath their jaguar clothing, are already shamans. The ferocity of the jaguar is not due to its being an animal, but due to its being a human.[25]

IMAGINAL BEINGS

Of course, shamanic spirits are not the only anomalous nonphysical autonomous beings; we encounter what Terence McKenna has called *alien intelligences* elsewhere as well.[26] Later we will discuss what I call *visionary experiences*—hallucinations, waking dreams, apparitions, lucid dreams, false awakenings—which have in common, among other things, that they frequently involve interactions with apparently autonomous others. Psychologist Carl Jung developed a technique, which he called *active imagination*, for deliberately invoking such visionary experiences, by which one can become aware of and interact with what he called *imaginal beings* embedded in visionary worlds.[27] What is notable about these beings is how clearly they seem to be precisely *other-than-human persons*, strikingly similar to plant and animal spirits. These beings, Jung says, know things and possess insights unknown to the person encountering them; they "can say things that I do not know and do not intend."[28] The encounter is a dialogue—a conversation between me and something else that is not-me—"exactly as if a dialogue were taking place between two human beings."[29] These persons possess autonomy, independent knowledge, and the ability to form relationships—"like animals in the forest," says Jung, "or people in a room, or birds in the air."[30] They "have a life of their own."[31]

Jungian analysts have had much to say about these imaginal beings, and much of what they have said applies to spirits encountered in other contexts as well. James Hillman says that this "living being other than myself . . . becomes a *psychopompos*, a guide with a soul having its own inherent limitation and necessity."[32] When we actively confront these other-than-human persons, respond to them with our own objections, awe, and arguments, then, as analysts Ann and Barry Ulanov state, we "come to the breath-stopping realization of just how independent of our conscious control such images are. They have a life of their own. They push at us. They talk back."[33] They are, says Hillman, "valid psychological subjects with wills and feelings like ours but not reducible to ours."[34]

ONTOLOGY

Interestingly, hallucinations in other contexts do not immediately appear to raise metaphysical questions like those raised by the extraordinary experiences of people—such as shamans and ayahuasqueros—studied by anthropologists. When a patient with Charles Bonnet syndrome, for example, sees a monkey sitting in his neurologist's lap, neither patient nor doctor spends much time discussing its ontological status.[35] Among anthropologists, on the other hand, the metaphysical question is usually phrased dichotomously as whether the spirits spoken of by anthropological others are or are not *real*.

Classical animism says that there are no spirits; they are a *mistake*, a misattribution, the trope of *personification*—what anthropologist Michael Winkelman more politely calls a "metaphoric symbolic attribution" of humanlike mental qualities to unknown and natural phenomena, including "gods, spirits, and nonhuman entities, particularly animals."[36]

On the other hand, some anthropologists, sometimes based on their own anomalous experiences, contend that spirits are, instead, *real*—what Edith Turner calls *spirit stuff*.[37] Felicitas Goodman, for example, maintains that spirits are real beings who seek communication with humans;[38] Richard Shweder proposes the reality of malevolent ancestral spirits.[39] Jenny Blain specifically protests against turning spirits into "culturally defined aspects of one's own personality, not external agents." Such reductionism is, she says, "part of the individualization and psychologizing of perception that pervades Western academic discourses of the rational, unitary self."[40]

But I think that the encounter with other-than-human autonomous personalities, whether spirits or visionary beings, should be taken as subverting dichotomous ontologies that categorize such beings as either real or unreal. Both positions assume that there is only one way to be real, and that is to be a *thing*, a sort of stuff, like a chair or table, and that anything else is not real—

only imagination, *only* a hallucination. Such dichotomous metaphysics takes as normative a particular set of experiences characterized by sensory coherence, predictability, and consistency. Experiences that are not normative by these criteria are treated in one of two ways: they are dismissed as mistakes, illusions, or misattributions; or else they are *normalized*, reified, turned into *stuff*, into gaseous fauna.

PERSONIFYING

Hillman takes a very different approach. He does not reify the imaginal; rather, he mythologizes reality. He calls this *soul-making*. The act of soul-making is imagining, the crafting of images: "Soul-making is also described as imaging, that is, seeing or hearing by means of an imagining which sees through an event to its image. Imaging means releasing events from their literal understanding into a mythical appreciation. Soul-making, in this sense, is equated with de-literalizing—that psychological attitude which suspiciously disallows the naïve and given level of events in order to search out their shadowy, metaphorical significances for soul."[41] The human adventure, Hillman says, "is a wandering through the vale of the world for the sake of making soul."[42] "*Soul is imagination*," he says, "a cavernous treasury . . . a confusion and richness. . . . The cooking vessel of the soul takes in everything, everything can become soul; and by taking into its imagination any and all events, psychic space grows."[43] And soul is "the imaginative possibility in our natures, the experiencing through reflective speculation, dream, image, and fantasy—that

Magical Realism

If we want to capture the visionary world of the shaman, we can turn in part to the literary mode often called *magical realism*. Deeply embedded within the resurgent literature of South America, *el realismo magical, lo real maravilloso americano*, is characterized by a detailed realism into which there erupts—in a way often experienced as unremarkable—the magical world of the spirits. As literary critic David Mikics says, magical realism "projects a mesmerizing uncertainty suggesting that ordinary life may also be the scene of the extraordinary."[1]

This idea is often expressed in terms of "exploring—and transgressing—boundaries."[2] In an interview with Miguel Fernandez-Braso in 1969, Nobel Prize–winning author Gabriel García Márquez said, of his own magical realist writings, "My most important problem was to destroy the line of demarcation that separates what seems real from what seems fantastic. Because in the world that I was endeavoring to evoke, that barrier does not exist."[3]

Yet García Márquez describes himself as a *realist* writer, "because I believe that in Latin America everything is possible, everything is real."[4] Thus, in the fictional town of Macondo, Remedios the beauty rises to heaven with her sister-in-law's sheets. No reason is given, and her sister-in-law, Fernanda, does not wonder how this could happen. She accepts it without surprise, and only regrets that she has lost her sheets. Doña María was similarly lifted to heaven inside her mosquito net to be initiated by the Virgin Mary. For her, too, this was marvelous and unsurprising.

Thus the visionary world does what literary critic Theo L. D'Haen calls "decentering privileged centers."[5] Magical realist texts—and thus the visionary world itself—are *ontologically subversive*.[6] The magically realist world subverts the privileged ontological center that dichotomously divides experience into the real and the unreal.

Magical realism is often said to occur in places that postmodernist literary critics have called *the zone*:[7] "The propensity of magical realist texts to admit a plurality of worlds means that they often situate themselves on liminal territory between or among those worlds—in phenomenal and spiritual regions where transformation, metamorphosis, dissolution are common, where magic is a branch of naturalism."[8] William S. Burroughs put it this way in a letter to Allen Ginsberg in 1955: "The meaning of Interzone, its space time location is at a point where three-dimensional fact merges into dream, and dreams erupt into the real world. In Interzone dreams can kill . . . and solid objects and persons can be as unreal as dreams."[9]

This zone is the world of the shaman—the vision, the apparition, the lucid dream, seeing through the ordinary to the miraculous luminescence of the spirits, perceiving the omnipresent pure sound of the singing plants.

NOTES

1. Mikics, 1995, p. 372.
2. Zamora & Faris, 1995, p. 5.
3. Doody, 1997, p. 470.
4. Bowers, 2004, p. 92.
5. D'Haen, 1995, p. 191.
6. Zamora & Faris, 1995, p. 6.
7. McHale, 1987, p. 44.
8. Zamora & Faris, 1995, p. 6.
9. Miles, 2002, p. 99.

mode which recognizes *all* realities as primarily symbolic or metaphorical."[44] The question of soul-making is this: "What does this event, this thing, this moment move in my soul?"[45]

Hillman calls this *seeing through*—the ability of the imagination's eye to see through the literal to the metaphorical.[46] Re-visioning is deliteralizing or metaphorizing reality. The purpose of analysis is not to make the unconscious conscious, or to make id into ego, or to make ego into self; the purpose is to make the literal metaphorical, to make the real imaginal. The objective is to enable the realization that reality is imagination—that what appears most real is in fact an image with potentially profound metaphorical implications.[47] Thus, says Hillman, soul is "the imaginative possibility in our natures . . . the mode which recognizes all realities as primarily symbolic or metaphorical."[48] "By means of the archetypal image," he writes, "natural phenomena present faces that speak to the imagining soul rather than only conceal hidden laws and probabilities and manifest their objectification."[49]

So Hillman speaks of personifying not as a category mistake but, rather, as a "basic psychological activity—the spontaneous experiencing, envisioning and speaking of the configurations of existence as psychic presences," as a mode of thought that "takes an inside event and puts it outside, at the same time making this content alive, personal, and even divine."[50] Personifying is "a way of being in the world and experiencing the world as a psychological field, where persons are given with events, so that events are experiences which touch us, move us, appeal to us"—a way of imagining things into souls.[51]

If Hillman's personifying, seeing through, soul-making, becomes a way of engaging with the world, a relational epistemology, then it is verging upon a genuine and nonreductive animism, one in which the world has become magical, filled with wonders, filled with the spirits.

THE APPEARANCE OF SPIRITS

While animal spirits almost always appear as animals, plant spirits almost always appear in human form. There are exceptions: the spirit of the uña de gato vine has appeared to doña María as a *tigrito*, a small jaguar, and the spirit of *lobosanango* as a wolf. Doña María told me that the plant spirits often appear to her first as plants, and then transform into humans.

It is worth emphasizing that the plant spirits do not always appear in the same way to different people, or even to the same person on different occasions. For example, the spirit of ayahuasca can appear as a human, either male or female, or as an anaconda. Indeed, the spirit of ayahuasca has appeared to María as two genios at the same time, one male and one female, who stood on either side of her—the woman dressed in beautiful clothing, the man ugly, with bad teeth. The spirit of the uña de gato vine has appeared to her not only as a small jaguar but also as a strong, muscular man on whose arms were claws.

I have encountered ayahuasca in the form of a little blonde girl wearing a golden crown and of a teenage Indian girl with a dazzling smile. The spirit of maricahua has been said to appear as an Indian man surrounded by little children; but the spirit came to me as a beautiful dark lady with raven hair.

Spirits may appear as either male or female on different occasions; as poet César Calvo writes, "On some days a plant is female and good for some things, and on other days the plant is male and is good for the opposite."[52]

Pablo Amaringo has painted several pictures of various plant spirits as they have appeared to him. In one ayahuasca vision, for example, the spirit of the pucalupuna tree appeared as a dark woman with cat's eyes and a gold chain around her neck; in another vision, the spirit of pucalupuna appeared as a dark man with many heads, covered with snakes, and holding a knife and a skull. Similarly, the spirit of the ajosquiro tree appeared in one vision as a very small curly-haired man wearing a red cape and red clothes, and in another as a blue-skinned man with red hair, surrounded by birds.[53]

There is sometimes a correlation between the nature of the plant and the appearance of its spirit. A striking example is the ayahuma tree. *Huma* is the ordinary Quechua word for head; thus *ayahuma* means spirit head or head of a dead person. The tree's large, hard, globular fruit falls to the ground and cracks open with a loud sound; once cracked open, the inner pulp rots and smells like decaying flesh. The spirit of the ayahuma thus often appears as a woman without a head.

Testing the Autonomy of the Spirits

Marko Rodriguez, at the Computer Science Department of the University of California at Santa Cruz, has come up with an idea to see whether the spirits seen after ingesting dimethyltryptamine (DMT)—which would include drinking ayahuasca—are autonomous, persistent, intelligent entities. The idea is to ask these entities to calculate a prime factor of a five-digit non-prime number, such as 12,233, and then tell you the answer, which you did not know, or tell the answer to someone else who has also ingested DMT either simultaneously or subsequently.[1]

While the idea is clever, it has some obvious drawbacks. First of all, you have to remember to ask the question, which may not be easy after drinking ayahuasca, when there is often a lot going on at once and it is easy to be distracted. Second, it is not clear how the spirits would respond. In fact, James Kent, the former editor of *Entheogen Review* and *Trip* magazine, has tried the experiment.[2] He asked a DMT elf for a prime factor of 23,788, and the entity reportedly presented the visual response of *undulating Twinkie on rotating lotus, squirting*, which is not obviously an answer to the question.

I am not sure whether the plant spirits know mathematics, or whether it matters. Maybe some do and some do not. Maybe even those who do still think that there are better questions to ask.

NOTES

1. Rodriguez, 2007.
2. Kent, 2007b.

There is also some internal consistency in the identification of spirits. For example, the spirits of hardwood trees often appeared to doña María as strong or large men—the spirit of the *remocaspi* tree as a very muscular man dressed as a doctor, the spirit of the machimango tree as a tall gringo man wearing a white shirt. The spirit of the *capinurí* palm, the ends of whose fallen branches look remarkably like erect penises, has appeared to her as a large heavy pale gringo, like a weight lifter, wearing the white clothes of a doctor.

The spirits of other plants often appeared to her as doctors wearing surgical scrubs—ishpingo caspi, chullachaqui caspi, *caña brava*. The bright red latex of the *sangre de grado* tree is used to treat wounds, ulcers, and skin infections; the spirit of this tree has appeared to doña María both as a man whose whole body was blood red, and as a doctor, male or female, carrying a tray of medicines.

THE OMNIPRESENCE OF THE SPIRITS

Ayahuasca lets the shaman see these spirits in their own form—the form in which they choose to appear.

I once asked don Rómulo Magin about his awareness of the spirits when not drinking ayahuasca. Don Rómulo said that he is constantly aware of being surrounded by the spirits but that he sees them roughly, vaguely; drinking ayahuasca, he said, is "like putting on glasses." Doña María agrees; ayahuasca makes the spirits *bien claro*, really clear. When don Roberto smokes mapacho and concentrates, he says, he sees the plant spirits; he sees them now because he has seen them before, when drinking ayahuasca, but he does not see them as clearly. Most important, though, he *hears* them, clearly, speaking in his ear, instructing him—heal like this, they say, suck there, sing this icaro, make such and such a medicine—just as if they were standing next to him, just as, he says, you and I are talking right now. When he drinks ayahuasca, he both hears and sees the spirits clearly. Campa *toero* Cesar Zevallos Chinchuya says the same thing: tobacco allows the healer to *speak* with the spirits; one has to drink toé to *see* or *meet* them.[54]

And, just as some shamans say that the spirits are always present but are brought into focus by ayahuasca, some say that the songs of the plant spirits are always present and that ayahuasca brings them into audibility. Don Carlos Perez Shuma says that the icaros are like radio waves: "Once you turn on the radio, you can pick them up." Or the songs are like prerecorded tapes. "It's like a tape recorder," don Carlos says. "You put it there, you turn it on, and already it starts singing. . . . You start singing along with it."[55] A Shipibo shaman made the same point. "I am not the one creating the song," he told anthropologist Angelika Gebhart-Sayer. "It passes through me as if I were a radio."[56] One Shuar shaman described his whistling as like tuning a radio, beginning with tuneless whistling, which was like moving between stations, until he could lock on and tune into a spirit and its song.[57] Sometimes this is expressed as *singing along* with the spirits. Among the Piro, the spirits sing, and the shaman joins in—the word is *gipxaleta*, accompanies—their singing.[58] Cocama shaman José Curitima Sangama uses the same term: "It's the mother of the plant who cures," he says. "She tells us which song to sing, and which music we should use to cure the patient. We accompany the mother of the plant."[59]

So we are always surrounded by the spirits and their music. We see them sometimes, at the edges of our vision. Ayahuasca teaches us to hear them. Their music is puro sonido, pure sound, the language of the plants, reflected in the silbando, the whispered singing of the shaman, and in the susurration of the shacapa, the leaf-bundle rattle. We can learn to listen for their music, wherever we are.

CHAPTER 11

PROTECTION

VULNERABILITY

Once you begin la dieta, once you drink ayahuasca and start to learn the plant teachers with your body, the world becomes a more dangerous place.

Sorcerers resentful of your presumption will shoot magical pathogenic darts into your body, or send fierce animals to attack you, or fill your body with scorpions and razor blades—especially while you are still a beginner, before you gain your full powers.[1] Even experienced shamans under the influence of ayahuasca are vulnerable to attack by envious or vengeful sorcerers. Poet César Calvo says that drinking ayahuasca makes one into "a crystal exposed to all the spirits, to the evil ones and the true ones that inhabit the air."[2] Such transparency is perilous.

This is also true when the shaman is drunk or asleep. Elder shamans may sleep surrounded by apprentices, to be protected from such attacks.[3] Very often these struggles take place in dreams; shamans who lose this dream battle may never wake up.[4] Doña María was attacked this way during her sleep, when magic darts were shot deep into her throat and chest, so that she could not sing her protective songs.

TYPES OF PROTECTION

So there is a need for constant protection. Anything that protects from an attack—animal protectors, magical birds, spiny palms, fierce Indians, suits of armor, fighter jets—is called an arcana, probably from the Quechua *arkay*, block, bar, rather than from the Latin *arcana*, secrets, or the Spanish *arcano*, mystery, secret.[5] And that is why, at the start of every healing ceremony, don Roberto, with greater or less elaboration, constructs a wall of arcana around the site—"a thousand feet high," he says, "and a thousand feet below the earth"—to protect himself, his students, and all who are in attendance.

A shaman has many means of protection from the intrusion of pathogenic objects hurled by enemy sorcerers. First among these is the shaman's mariri, the rarified phlegm that rises from the shaman's chest into the throat, nourished by ayahuasca and mapacho, and which serves to absorb the darts, the sickness, the phlegmosity, and the scorpions and toads that the shaman sucks from the patient's body, and whose power is then assimilated by the shaman or projected back upon the one who sent them.

Similarly, tobacco—the paradigmatic strong sweet smell—protects the shaman and the shaman's patients. Mapacho, tobacco, is the essential protector, warding off the pathogenic projectiles, the animal surrogates, the detestable breath or tobacco smoke of the sorcerer. This is the protection the shaman gives to patients, after extracting a dart, by blowing tobacco smoke over and into their bodies—"a pliable steel shirt," says don Emilio Andrade.[6] A shaman must constantly maintain these defenses. Don Francisco Montes Shuña says that a shaman must blow tobacco smoke in three directions—front, right, and left—every four hours, even during the night.[7] At the very least, the shaman must have songs and tobacco ready to be deployed in case of a sudden attack. Don Juan Flores Salazar tells of how his father, a shaman, forgot his tobacco bag one day when going out to heal a sickness caused by an opposing shaman, and was killed that same day by a falling tree.[8]

Shamans also acquire protective spirits, powerful plants and animals, often the same as those that carry out the destructive will of the sorcerer, since those things that are used to inflict sorcery are the things that best protect from it. Shamans accumulate a large number of these protectors, who are called in at the beginning of the ayahuasca ceremony but who also accompany the shaman, ready to leap into action if an attack is imminent. All these protective spirits are summoned or activated by singing their icaros, called icaros arcanas or just arcanas; the spirits may be given by one's teacher, or appear to one in an ayahuasca vision or a dream. Some may be kept in the shaman's chest, embedded in the magical phlegm.

Particularly valued as protector plants—because often used in sorcery—are the spiny or thorny palms, whose spines are used by brujos as their virotes, magic darts. Of these palms, used as both weapons and arcana, doña María and don Roberto refer frequently to four—the chambira, *huicungo*, *pijuayo*, and *huiririma* palms. Other spiny palms invoked for sorcery and protection—and portrayed in a painting by Pablo Amaringo—include the *inchaui*, pona, *inayuga*, and *huasaí*.[9] The term *chonta* is applied, somewhat indiscriminately, to spiny palms in the genera *Astrocaryum*, *Euterpe*, and *Bactris*.

Birds frequently function as animal protectors. Such birds are often predators, such as *gavilán*, hawks, and búhos, owls, or are notable for plumage or particularly piercing or unusual cries—for example, the manshaco, wood stork; *cushuri*, cormorant; *camungo*, horned screamer; *jabirú*, jabiru; *sharara*, anhinga; *guacamayo*, macaw; *trompetero*, trumpeter; or *chajá*, crested screamer. A sorcerer can send these birds—and other animals as well—as spies, and can talk to birds in their own language; that is why a healer must know their language. Don Rómulo Magin, for example, is fluent in the language of búhos, owls, who are powerful sorcerer birds; their language, I am told, sounds like this: *oootututututu kakakaka hahahahaha*. These same birds can be used to remove sorcery, just as the plants most closely associated with *brujería* are the plants that offer the most protection. Since brujo birds can be used to send virotes, they are powerful arcana as well.

The birds are used like this. The sorcerer talks to the bird and puts his own soul into it; then the bird carries the sorcery to the victim, shooting darts from its beak. When sorcery is conveyed by one of these birds, I was told, the victim's hair falls out, the skin roughens, and the victim begins to look like the bird. Such an attack is particularly dangerous: even if a healer succeeds in sucking out the darts projected by the bird, the sorcerer can send the bird more darts to project into the victim and keep the victim continually sick. One should be careful any time one sees one of the birds associated with such sorcery, for one might well be the target of a magical attack.[10]

Shamans acquire a wide variety of different animals to serve as protectors. Don Roberto said that he had two protectors of the earth—the boa negra, black boa, and otorongo, tawny jaguar—and two of the water—the yanapuma, black jaguar, and the yacuruna, the water people, magical and sexually seductive spirits who live in great cities below the water. At my coronación, initiation, don Roberto gave me, along with his flema, phlegm, two protective animals, one each of earth and water—two jaguars, a tawny and a black.

Usually one's first protective animals stay with one for life, with additional protectors added over time to one's armamentarium as one progresses. When I first met doña María, she asked me whether, as a *norteamericano*, I had ever seen a bear. She had seen, she said, a polar bear—or at least an *oso blanco*—in a movie on television. In fact, María had two bears, one black and one white, as protector animals. Doña María told me that the bear had become her protector before she had ever seen it on television.

One of doña María's first protective animals was the *aquila*, in this case probably the Andean condor rather than any of the various Peruvian species of eagles; in fact, when she first drank huachuma, she had a vision of an aquila. She began acquiring her protective animals when she first drank ayahuasca. During her third ceremony with don Roberto, two macaws came and sat on her shoulders, speaking to her in the Inca language; from that time on, she knew, these macaws would be her protectors. Her protectors are, she said, like "soldiers of ayahuasca." They grew in power as she smoked mapacho and drank ayahuasca, tobacco infusions, and agua de florida. Her protectors always accompanied her; she could see them there with her while we talked. Her protectors included wolves and two bears, black and white, and two forms of boa constrictor—the *boa negra*, black boa, and *boa amarilla*, yellow boa. Her protectors also included several types of bird—condors, owls, *timelitos*, and especially guacamayos, macaws.[11] So, whenever doña María started to work, the macaws came and landed on her head and shoulders, to protect her. The animals "take care of me spiritually." If someone was about to attack her, the animals would preemptively strike on her behalf—the attacker crushed by her boas and clawed by her ferocious birds.

These animal protectors can form complex protective barriers. Don Celso Rójas, when dealing with sorcery, has, among other animals, a *condorpishcu*, a little white bird with a red neck, flying about his head to warn him of an attack; a lion on his right shoulder, a black jaguar on his left, and an elephant before him; a *shushupi*, bushmaster, around his neck; and a school of piranha.[12]

Protectors may take human form as well. The protectors of don Agustin Rivas are Indians, armed with bows, arrows, and darts, wearing feathered crowns, with eyes in the back of their heads; they are, he says, cruel, vengeful, and very protective. Even though he himself has no intentions of harming anyone, his protectors punish with sickness or death anyone who threatens or hurts him.[13] Don Emilio Andrade has a large Brazilian black man armed with daggers, who follows his enemies and locks them into dark tunnels in the Andes.[14]

Protectors may be angels with swords, tree spirits with guns, or a warplane that bombs and destroys the shaman's enemies.[15] Don Luis Panduro Vasquez has songs of protection he calls *icaro de electricidad, icaro de candela, icaro cubrir con la manta*, and *icaro como un sombrero de piedra*—icaros, respectively, of electricity, of fire, to cover with a blanket, and like a hat of stone.[16] Don Juan Flores Salazar has a pair of shoes made of steel, carries two swords in sheaths on both sides of his belt, holds a sword in each hand, and wears a hat of steel on his head.[17] Among doña María's protectors were, of course, Jesucristo, Jesus Christ, and Hermana Virgen, the Virgin Mary.

There is a distinction made among various sorts of *cuerpo*, body. A *cuerpo dañado*, harmed body, is a body attacked by sickness, usually induced by sorcery; a *cuerpo sencillo*, ordinary body, is one currently unaffected by sickness but without protection; a *cuerpo preparado*, prepared body, is one protected by plants and especially by mapacho, tobacco smoke, blown over the body and into the body through the top of the head. Strongest of all, a *cuerpo sellado*, sealed body, sometimes called a *cuerpo cerrado*, closed body, is one protected by an arcana that prevents any penetration, that resists attack by sorcery.[18]

STRONG SWEET SMELLS

The plant spirits in the Amazon love strong, sharp, sweet smells. Thus, one way to acquire protection against malevolent persons and their pathogenic projectiles is to acquire such a sweet smell oneself, as opposed to the ordinary human smell, including the smell of human sex, which the spirits dislike. Shamans achieve this state, and provide it for their patients, by putting substances with sharp sweet smells either on or inside the body.

First among such substances is, of course, tobacco, which is ingested by indigenous shamans in every conceivable way, and by mestizo shamans primarily by smoking or by drinking cold infusions of tobacco leaves in water. Blowing tobacco smoke onto the body of a patient, or into the body by blowing the smoke into the top of the head, is part of the foundational triad of mestizo shamanic healing—shacapar, rattling; chupar, sucking; and soplar, blowing.

For the same reason, mestizo shamans ingest commercial cologne, mouthwash, disinfectant, and camphor. Two commercial products are particularly common—Timolina, marketed in English-speaking countries as Thymoline, a commercial alkaline mouthwash and gargle containing thyme oil, eucalyptol, menthol, and pine oil, dissolved in alcohol, similar to Listerine; and Creolina, marketed also as Creoline, Creolin, Cresyline, and similar names, a disinfectant made of cresol or cresylic acid in soft soap solution, similar to Lysol.

And they ingest camphor and its strong, sweet, pungent, and penetrating odor. Camphor is a commercially prepared resin of the camphor laurel tree, which does not grow in the Amazon. Rather, shamans purchase commercially prepared camphor at the market in two forms—small cellophane-wrapped blocks of pure camphor and *bibaporú*, Vicks VapoRub. Shamans also drink camphor dissolved in alcohol, and a drink called *camalonga*—a mixture of camphor, alcohol, white onion, and the seeds of the camalonga plant, yellow oleander.

Bibaporú

This provides my favorite example of why ethnobotanical identification can be tricky. Doña María was telling me the ingredients of *grasa de búfalo*, buffalo fat, a liniment preparation. One of the ingredients, she said, was bibaporú. I was immediately befuddled. Was it a kind of plant? No, she said. She tried to describe it; I couldn't follow. Finally, she showed it to me. It was Vick's VapoRub. Later, when I told this story to my Hispanic friends in the United States, they said, "Bibaporú? Of course! My grandmother used that for everything."

Aguardiente is, literally, *agua ardiente*, burning water. It is distilled from the fermented first squeezing of sugarcane, unlike rum, which is made from molasses, a by-product from the processing of the sugarcane into sugar. The same drink is called *cachaça* in Brazil. In Colombia, aguardiente is sometimes flavored with anise. But in the Peruvian Amazon, aguardiente is straightforward, unflavored, potent, sold in recycled bottles or by the shot in tin-roofed bars and thatched *bodegas* throughout the jungle.

Aguardiente is a commonly used solvent and vehicle. In addition to being drunk by itself by some shamans, it is used as the solvent for camalonga, camphor, and other ingredients in the camalonga drink, and for the scrapings of ajo sacha roots, chuchuhuasi bark, and huito fruit; and it is the almost universal solvent for medicinal tinctures. Some shamans use a *trago de caña* for its psychoactive effect, and some blow it over a patient's body—like tobacco smoke or agua de florida—to cleanse and cure.[19]

Shamans also drink perfume, primarily the cologne called agua de florida. There can be combinations of sweet substances: Pablo Amaringo tells of one female shaman who drank a mixture of chopped tobacco, perfume, camphor, aguardiente, hot pepper, lemon, and salt, together with a little arsenic. "Then she drank everything," Amaringo says. "Large black stains appeared all over her skin." The shaman began to sing and sing, and to blow forcefully here and there with her perfumed breath. Doña María used to drink a mixture of tobacco, camphor, camalonga seeds, and agua de florida cologne.

During the ayahuasca ceremony, don Roberto and doña María put crosses of agua de florida on the forehead, chest, and back of each participant, whistling a special arcana of protection, to seal, close, and protect the body. Some shamans blow a fine fast spray of agua de florida from their mouths over the patient for the same purpose; some blow aguardiente, or the mouthwash Timolina, or the disinfectant Creolina. There is a type of shaman in the Amazon called a perfumero, who specializes in the use of such scents to attack, to heal, and to attract.

Agua de florida was first manufactured for Victorian ladies in the nineteenth century by the firm of Murray and Lanman in New York. It is remarkable that this commercial cologne should have assumed such a central role not only in the shamanism of the Peruvian Amazon but also for magical purposes among people of African-diaspora descent in the United States and the Caribbean: bottles of agua de florida can be found equally on the mesas of Amazonian healers and on the altars of Vodou priestesses in Brooklyn.[20] Other colognes—agua de kananga, colonia de rosas—are also widely used, and may be found for sale in the herbal market in Belén in Iquitos.[21] Not every mestizo shaman uses agua de florida; anthropologist Luis Eduardo Luna says that the *vegetalistas* with whom he worked preferred the perfume Tabu.[22]

Another way of acquiring a protective sweet strong smell is by taking a limpia or baño de flores, cleansing flower bath, using strongly scented herbs, flowers, and commercially prepared perfumes. The fragrant plants used in limpias include ajo sacha, wild garlic; albaca, wild basil; *ruda*, rue; *mishquipanga*, dwarf ginger; and mucura, garlic weed, as well as other plants—especially those that are *morado*, purple or dark, such as *piñon colorado*, red piñon—which protect from sorcery. To these may be added commercially prepared perfumes and floral essences—agua de florida, *agua de rosas*, agua de kananga, *rosa de castilla*—and the thyme-scented mouthwash Timolina.

The morning after an ayahuasca ceremony, especially if I had had a strong purge, when I was still weak and shaky from the medicine, there was nothing more pleasant than for doña María to pour buckets full of cool sweet-smelling water, filled with leaves and flowers, over my head and body, while she sang some of her most beautiful oraciones to protect me from sickness and misfortune.

Agua de florida is a teacher, just like the *plantas maestras*, the plants who teach. Doña María told me that it gives very clear visions, especially visions of your enemies; it is an excellent *virotero*, sender of magic darts; and therefore it is an especially effective protection against sorcery. One can undertake a restricted diet with agua de florida just as one could with any healing or protecting plant. For thirty days, says doña María, drink a small bottle of the cologne every night before going to sleep, then sit quietly during the day, concentrating and smoking mapacho cigarettes. At the end of this time, the genio, the spirit, of agua de florida will come to you; he will appear in a dream or vision, she says, as an *hombre buen gringo*, a very European-looking man. He will have three birds with him that serve sorcerers—the cushuri, cormorant; the camungo, horned screamer; and the sharara, anhinga—and four spiny palms from which sorcerers make their virotes, magic darts—chambira, huicungo, pijuayo, and huiririma. The spirit of agua de florida will ask you, "Why have you come here? What are you seeking?" And he will offer you a choice of how to use the power of the perfume—for attack, for defense, or for healing.

Such is the power of strong sweet smells in the Upper Amazon.

CHAPTER 12

SEX

There has been very little research on sexual relations between shamans and plant spirits. Certainly the spirits can be muy celosa, very jealous, about sexual relations between shamans and human persons. Relations with the spirits may imply both sexual abstinence with humans and sexual alliance with the spirits. There are reports of erotic ayahuasca visions;[1] regular ayahuasca use apparently does nothing to abate—and, by report, may significantly enhance—sexual desire and performance. Psychologist Benny Shanon notes that ayahuasca drinkers "often detect a sensuous, even sexual flavor in whatever surrounds them," including the eroticization of plants and trees; he reports his own visions of semi-clad women dancing erotically and lasciviously.[2] Ethnobotanists Richard Schultes and Robert Raffauf remark, rather dryly, that "erotic aspects often reported may be due to the individual differences of the participants."[3] Don Agustin Rivas reports that, while following la dieta, a beautiful strange female spirit, named Yara, would appear to him at dawn, lift his mosquito net, and lie down with him. He would awake just before having sex with her.[4]

Here is an example. I was drinking ayahuasca with don Rómulo and his son, don Winister. They were both singing icaros at the same time, but different ones, producing a decidedly eerie effect. Suddenly in front of me I saw a beautiful green woman, lying back on a couch or bed; her arms and fingers were long; her body was covered in some kind of gauzy material. The moment was intense, erotically charged; I leaned forward and kissed her. Whoa! said my rational mind. Is this all right? Are you allowed to have sex with plant spirits? The embrace was arousing; I wondered what my wife would say. The woman faded away, leaving me with a feeling of relief and disappointment.

Among indigenous Amazonian peoples, there are widespread reports of sexual relations between human persons and other-than-human persons. Anthropologist Elsje Lagrou tells the story of a Cashinahua woman shaman who married the snake spirit, who came to make love to her at night, and, because of her new spirit husband, no longer had sex with her human husband. One of the signs of her alliance with the spirit world was her deformed mouth, eaten away by the spirits, people said; another was her successful healing of fever in small children.[5]

Among the Napo Runa, the *supai*, the forest spirits with whom the shaman interacts, enter into sexual relationships with humans, often long term; one shaman was taught by a *supai huarmi*, female spirit, and his wife was made pregnant by a *supai runa*, male spirit.[6] The daughter of a famous Napo Runa shaman told an interviewer, "My mother gets angry when she wants to sleep with my father. The supai huarmi gets between them and doesn't let him."[7] Napo Runa women who give birth to deformed children are said to have been impregnated by supai and, when the child dies, often become shamans.[8]

The Shuar tell stories of men who have sex with *tsunki* women, the shamanically potent underwater people, a manifestation of Tsunki, the primordial shaman, and get power from them; a female shaman has reported a vision of having sex with a male tsunki.[9] Widowed or unmarried Achuar women may—although this is rare—become shamans, and maintain exclusive sexual relationships with Tsunki.[10] Asháninka apprentice shamans suck tobacco paste until they transform into jaguars, fly through the air, and couple with the spirit of tobacco in the form of a woman, whereupon they become shamans, united with the tobacco spirit, traveling the forest as a jaguar.[11]

Who was my Green Lady? What should I have done?

CHAPTER 13

HARMING

The conditions for which a mestizo will seek the help of a curandero are not coextensive with what a North American would consider a disease. What we normally consider to be diseases are, in Amazonian mestizo culture, merely a subset of the misfortunes, the sufferings, and the intentionally inflicted harms—fever, pain, bad luck in business, bad relationships with neighbors, an unfaithful spouse, infertility, malaise, *accidia*—which are all, in some sense, sicknesses requiring cure by a healer. Just as important, these sicknesses are almost universally caused by the malevolence of other people, by jealousy, envy, and resentment, sent in the form of a dart into the suffering body, to be sucked out and healed by the mouth of the healing shaman.

DISEASE AND ILLNESS

I have used the term *sickness* with some deliberation. There is a now well-established ethnographic distinction between *disease* and *illness*.[1] Disease is biological and biochemical malfunction; illness is impaired functioning as perceived by the patient within a particular cultural context.[2] Disease is not limited to humans; we can speak, say, of a diseased apple. But, as medical anthropologist Byron Good puts it, "Disease occurs, of course, not in the body, but in life."[3] Thus the use of the term *illness* for the social, lived experience of suffering, something innately human.[4] Eric Cassell, a physician, makes a similar distinction; he uses the term *illness* to stand for what the patient feels when going to the doctor and *disease* for what the patient has on the way home from the doctor. Disease, he says, is something an organ has; illness is something a person has.[5] This distinction has been proposed for its heuristic value.

The distinction between disease, as a phenomenon seen from the perspective of the medical practitioner, and illness, as a phenomenon seen from the perspective of the sufferer, "aspires to reorient medical practices in society."[6]

Corresponding to this distinction is one between *curing* and *healing*. Curing is the successful treatment of a specific biomedical condition, such as a duodenal ulcer; healing is the *making whole* of a person seen as an integrated totality with physical, social, and spiritual dimensions.[7] Stereotypically, biomedicine cures a disease, and ethnomedicine heals an illness.[8]

But ethnomedicine—just like biomedicine—always involves a mix of curing and healing.[9] Doña María and don Roberto are as eager to cure specific diseases, such as malaria, as they are to heal sociospiritual conditions such as bad luck or soul loss; as Byron Good notes, "All medicine joins rational and deeply irrational elements, combining an attention to the material body with a concern for the moral dimensions of sickness and suffering."[10] To a cynical observer, it might appear that the partitioning of roles between the curing biomedical specialist and the healing shaman is a way of preserving the role of the shaman in the face of biomedical doubt as to whether the shaman is able to cure any disease at all.

In fact, diseases are themselves constructs that vary according to the specialty of the medical practitioner, the context, the audience, the type of condition, the personal characteristics of the doctor, and the doctor's position in the medical hierarchy.[11] Tuberculosis, for example, is often taken paradigmatically as a disease, caused by an identifiable pathogen, responsive to streptomycin; yet tuberculosis is a complex of symbolic associations and social meanings that are irreducible to a disease, from its romanticization in the nineteenth century to its resurgence in the twenty-first, in combination with that other highly symbolic complex, HIV. Is soul loss an illness or a disease? Is anorexia nervosa an illness or a disease?

That is why I propose to use the term *sickness*—an attempt to evade the culturally loaded dichotomy between *illness* and *disease*. Anthropologist and epidemiologist Robert Hahn defines sickness as "a condition of the self unwanted by its bearer."[12] That is the definition, broad enough to be useful, that I will adopt here.

TYPES OF SICKNESS

There are several overlapping ways in which mestizos categorize sickness. One category is variously labeled as *natural*, *God-given*, *a curse of God*, *a punishment of God*—just a condition of everyday life.[13] Such natural sicknesses respond to store-bought medicine, antibiotics, injections, and hospital treatment; they do not require—or do not respond to—the intervention of a shaman.

There is not a lot of agreement as to which sicknesses fall into this category. Generally, natural sicknesses include colds, sore throats, skin infections, malaria, and parasites. Shuar shaman Alejandro Tsakím Suánua refers eye problems, amoebas, infections, and cataracts to a biomedical physician;[14] mestizo shaman don Agustin Rivas refers any sickness caused by microbes or requiring surgery;[15] don Roberto refers cases of stroke or cancer. Among the Shuar, natural sicknesses include those associated with white people, such as cholera.[16]

But accidents—falls, snakebites, a tree falling on someone, a bad machete cut—are not natural.[17] And some sicknesses are noticeably odd from the outset: the symptoms begin suddenly, the pain is focused and affects a particular part of the body, the patient deteriorates rapidly, there are bad dreams, there are inscrutable changes in bodily function and affective states, and the instruments of Western medicine are unavailing.[18] Sometimes what might otherwise seem a natural sickness—whooping cough, for example—has virulence far beyond the ordinary.[19] In such a case, the sickness is not natural, but has been *inflicted by a person*—a brujo, sorcerer, or an enemy employing any of several well-known forms of folk sorcery. Such sicknesses are caused, not by microbes, but by a failure of right relationship with a human being. Alejandro Tsakím calls such sicknesses, induced by human sorcery, *wicked sicknesses*.[20] The work of the shaman is to reveal these human acts of evil against other human beings.[21]

Often the shaman has considerable input as to whether a sickness is natural or wicked. Achuar shamans claim that pathogenic projectiles have the appearance of bundles of light, while natural sicknesses appear like a bronze vapor arising from the affected organ. Most sicknesses they see are wicked, since presumably measures against natural sickness have already failed.[22] Conversely, don Dionisio Moron Ríos says that if he cannot cure a patient with traditional medicine, then he tells the patient to go buy medicine at the pharmacy—that he knows it will make the patient better, because the spirits have told him so.[23]

Sometimes wicked sicknesses overlap with biomedical diagnoses. Doña María suffered what the biomedical doctors in Iquitos called a massive stroke, from which she eventually died; yet many of her friends claimed that she was in fact the victim of virotes, magical darts, projected into her body by a specific person, a brujo, for reasons of greed and resentment. It is in this sense, perhaps, that don Agustin Rivas considers cancer, heart attacks, and ulcers to be—at least sometimes—capable of shamanic healing.[24]

CAUSES OF SICKNESS

Beliefs about sickness can be classified as *internalizing* or *externalizing*.[25] In many ways these beliefs correspond to the distinction between biomedicine and ethnomedicine. Thus, internalizing explanations focus on pathophysiological processes in the development of illness. Externalizing explanations, on the other hand, look to causes that lie outside the body—mal de ojo or the evil eye, for example, or brujería, witchcraft or sorcery, with these often, in turn, traced to social causes, such as resentment or envy. A similar distinction may be drawn between *naturalistic* and *personalistic* etiologies.[26] In naturalistic systems, illness is explained in impersonal, systemic terms—caused by an excess of the cold humor, for example, or by the intrusion of bacteria into the body. In personalistic systems, illness is due to the purposive intervention of a person, whether human or other-than-human.[27]

Amazonian mestizos frequently resort to externalizing and personalistic explanations for their sicknesses. Nor are they unusual in the Amazon in doing so.[28] Among the Xinguana of southern Amazonia in Brazil, "nothing is more firmly rooted in the mind . . . than the notion that most of his afflictions are directly due to sorcery, and that a number of persons he comes into contact with every day are witches."[29] Among the Campa, "misfortunes of various sorts, from a swollen leg to bad luck in hunting, are understood as resulting from evil spells cast by vengeful enemies."[30] According to the Desana, the majority of their sicknesses are due to exogenous aggression—either to attacks by other-than-human persons of the waters and jungle or to human malevolence.[31] In Tukano culture, "death and disease are always regarded as the consequence of evil magic exercised by an enemy,"[32] and "usually malice lies behind an individual's illness or accident."[33] For the Cubeo, "most deaths, illnesses, and misfortunes are products of human malevolence."[34] The concept of sickness that prevails among the Yagua is of exogenous pathogenesis: the sickness always comes from outside; all harm is imputed to the malevolence of another and has a supernatural source.[35] The Waiwai believe that all death results from the intentional implementation of spiritual violence and the presence of the dark shaman.[36] Among the Marubo, sorcery is held responsible for the majority of sudden and unexplained deaths.[37]

Sorcery, *evil spells*, *exogenous aggression*, *exogenous pathogenesis*, *human malevolence*, *malice, spiritual violence*—these terms are found again and again in the ethnographic literature on the sources of sickness and death in the Amazon. Anthropologist Neil Whitehead puts it clearly: "In Amazonia, death and sickness are always the consequence of the enmity and ill-will of others."[38] Reading reports of assault sorcery in the Amazon, one is struck by common themes: sickness and death are caused by human intention; sicknesses are attributed to invisible attacks and are associated with bodily invasion, putrid smells, rotting from the inside—all symbols of secret uncontrolled aggression. Throughout the Amazon, humanity is not pictured as loving but, rather, as individuals full of contradictions and ambiguities, who can, out of envy, resentment, anger, lust, or vengeance, bring suffering and misfortune to others, even those with whom they have had a relationship of love.[39]

MOTIVES OF SICKNESS

Why do people—sorcerers or the clients of sorcerers—cause other people to become sick? One of the key terms in doña María's sickness discourse is *envidia*, a word that encompasses such concepts as envy, jealousy, spite, and resentment. The word is in many ways the opposite of *confianza*, trust, mutuality, intimacy. In fact, envidia is often the result of a perceived breach of confianza; the outstanding occasion of envy and resentment is "failure to reciprocate and treason in friendship."[40] In the contemporary culture of the United States, it is considered admirable to arouse envidia in others, to be *envidiado*, envied; we live in large houses without walls to hide them, we park our large expensive cars in the driveway where our neighbors can see them. In the Upper Amazon, such behavior would be foolhardy; to be envidiado is to invite sorcery. In the Amazon, a prudent person will never boast of accomplishment or wealth so as not to arouse the envy and resentment of others.[41] When a sick person is diagnosed as suffering from sorcery, magically inflicted harm, then the root cause is likely to be envidia; someone has so envied and resented the sufferer as to invest in the services of a sorcerer.

Envidia is remarkably constant among mestizos in the Peruvian Amazon. There is great surface politeness; people address each other as *hermano*, brother, and *hermana*, sister—even *hermanito* and *hermanita*, the diminutive used as a term of endearment. There is little overt interpersonal physical violence. But there is also a subsurface wariness, a constant checking on relative status and advantage, great quickness to perceive unfairness in the position or actions of others, and a constant readiness to resort to sorcery to redress perceived imbalances. It is a world filled with hidden plots and counterplots, both real and imagined, and incessant gossip about who has cast a curse on whom—whose business failure is due to *hechicería*, a curse, purchased by a competitor, and whose marital discord is due to pusanguería, love magic, purchased by a lustful or jealous rival. Relationships of confianza are easily ruptured by suspicion, and perceived wrongs are avenged through sorcery.

This is true throughout the Upper Amazon. Prestige, status, wealth, success—however temporary or qualified—arouses envy and resentment among neighbors, relatives, and others not so lucky or successful.[42] A description of the Palmar Quiché puts it this way: "The poor man envies the rich man, and the rich man envies the richer man. Those without skills envy those who are skillful. Those who do a good job are envied by those who do not. The ugly or plain person envies the handsome one, and so forth. If a person allows his envy to fester, he may be driven to malicious extremes." As the second richest Palmar Indian told the investigators, "In all the world, there is envy."[43]

Anthropologist Bonnie Glass-Coffin, speaking of Andean shamanism in northern Peru, notes that accusations of sorcery are made most often not against strangers but, rather, against those with whom the accuser has maintained the closest and most necessary relations of confianza—almost always, she says, family members, neighbors, and friends: "And it is envy which is the principal motive for wishing harm to those who are most dear."[44] Michael Taussig has much to say about envy in the Putumayo. Sensitivity to envy is "as ever-present and as necessary as the air we breathe."[45] "One can be envious of just about anything, so it seems," he writes. "And the envious person is dangerous, so aroused by envy that she or he will try to kill through magical means."[46]

Life is perceived as a zero-sum game. To receive more than a fair share of a good is necessarily to deprive another. A loving husband or wife, a household free of rancor, a steady job, having a healthy baby—such things can arouse resentment in one who has a cheating spouse, who has just lost a job, whose baby has died. Many times, even after a man and woman have separated and are living with others, resentment is felt at the supposed happiness of the former mate, a sentiment not unknown in North America.[47]

SORCERY

Motives for harm can be many, but almost always center on envy, jealousy, and resentment—refusal to give or to lend something, competition over women, frustrated love affairs, personal rejection. The outcome of envy is brujería, sorcery; *daño*, magically inflicted harm; hechicería, the casting of a curse;

shitana, sorcery. As medical anthropologist Marlene Dobkin de Ríos affirms, case after case of sickness in the Amazon is attributed by the sufferer to evil caused by others. Either an envious person has resorted to hechicería, throwing earth from a cemetery across the threshold, for example, or dropping vulture feces mixed with water at the doorstep; or a specialist—a brujo, a sorcerer—has been hired to cause sickness, misfortune, or death through sorcery.[48]

Bad luck does not happen by chance but is the result of envy. Sickness, frustration, and difficulty are not attributed to individual responsibility or to abstract economic causes but to the resentment of relatives or neighbors.[49] Under the influence of ayahuasca, sufferers may see who has cursed them, caused the misery they endure; a visionary drama unfolds, as the sufferer watches the neighbor or relative consult a brujo, throw an evil mess across the doorstep, and laugh. Above all, I was told, the perpetrator laughs—maliciously, gleefully, vindictively.

THE SOCIAL FUNCTIONS OF SORCERY

Concern about envidia—which is the same as concern about sorcery—is an enforcer of social norms of reciprocity and generosity. To own more goods than another—especially productive resources such as shotguns, motorized boats, or motorized pumps—arouses envy and the risk of sorcery; to avoid this risk, such commodities must be lent to others when requested. The same is true for consumables such as food, which one must share when asked.[50] Fear of sorcery governs other social interactions as well. Face-to-face confrontations are rare; except for drunken brawls, there is little interpersonal violence. People are afraid to provoke sorcery, and people resort to sorcery instead of confrontation. Competition for resources perceived as scarce—power, affection, success, prestige—results in sorcery where open conflict is not sanctioned.

Amazonian sorcery is thus what James Scott, a political scientist and anthropologist, calls a "weapon of the weak," as when women in the northern Andes use sorcery and love magic as instruments of resistance to challenge male privilege.[51] That is why envy, expressed as sorcery suspicions and accusations, increases when distribution of wealth becomes more unequal. Among the Shuar, for example, a contemporary increase in accusations of sorcery apparently correlates with increasing urbanism, consumerism, and inequality in the distribution of goods.[52]

Pusanguería, love magic, is used to subvert class lines as well. Mestizo men tell stories of using love magic to seduce women of higher classes—the sort of women who refuse the offer of a Coca-Cola because they think that the man is lower class, arrogant women with long fingernails who refuse to dance with someone at a fiesta—forms of transgressive sexual discourse not unknown in our own culture.[53] Conversely, a woman can bewitch and dominate her husband—make him *manso*, tame—by mixing her menstrual blood, urine, or vaginal secretion into his coffee.[54]

And the means are always available, even in the absence of a professional sorcerer. Anyone can take, for example, two huayruro seeds, fry them in fat, and stick them with a needle while pronouncing the name of the victim, whose eyes will first burn and then burst. Or one can use a photograph of the enemy, stick the eyes ten times with a needle, and bury the picture facedown in a well-hidden place; the enemy becomes thin, dries up, and dies.[55] One can steal a piece of a woman's underwear, defecate on it, and bury it; the woman will bleed, as though menstruating, without stopping.[56] One can harm an enemy simply by spreading the victim's clothing around the base of a pucalupuna tree.[57]

People also believe that they can be made sick through ingestion of noxious substances prepared by their enemies and put surreptitiously in their food or drink—bat saliva or phlegm, the burnt bones of dead humans mixed with the entrails of water snakes, the blood of a black dog.[58] Similarly, noxious substances can be thrown across the threshold of a house—vulture feces, for example, or cemetery dirt—or buried at a threshold or along a path where the victim walks.[59] Yagua shamans keep pieces of glass, called *transparent stones*,

Huayruro

Huayruro seeds are about the size of a chickpea and are commonly drilled and threaded for beadwork in necklaces, bracelets, and earrings; they are considered to bring good luck and protect against sorcery.[1] The trees from which they come, found throughout Central and South America, have straight, cylindrical trunks, buttressed when large, and are used in construction and carpentry.[2] In the Upper Amazon, the seeds are considered to have male and female forms, which are in fact different species: the solid red *huayruro hembra*, the female seed, is *Ormosia macrocalyx*; the strikingly red and black *huayruro macho*, the male seed, is *O. amazonica*.[3]

NOTES

1. Bussmann & Sharon, 2007, p. 293.
2. Duke & Vasquez, 1994, p. 125.
3. Waymire, n.d.; photographs can be found at Smithsonian Tropical Research Institute, 2006a, 2006b.

in their stomach, which they can regurgitate and place in the beer gourds of their victims; when swallowed, the glass cuts up the body from the inside.[60]

This sort of contamination shades over easily into poisoning. Throughout the Amazon, poisoning is perceived as widely practiced. Cultivated or wild plant poisons are put into the victim's food or drink, especially at festivals.[61] The Cubeo claim a wide variety of poisoning methods—infusing poisonous plants into the victim's drink; placing poison in the victim's urine stream so that it enters through the urethra; spilling or dripping poison on the skin; inserting poison on the end of a stick into the nostrils of the sleeping victim; dropping poison onto a bench, where it enters through the victim's anus.[62] The Cashinahua are famous for their knowledge of poison.[63] A sorcerer can destroy a whole village with the smoke of a poisonous leaf burned over a fire, they say, or kill a woman by hiding poison in her skirt.[64] The great Yawanahua warrior and shaman Antonio Luis—who obtained many wives by raiding against his enemies, and was a founder of the Yawanahua people—was finally killed by a Cashinahua sorcerer who added poison to his tobacco snuff.[65]

There is also folk countersorcery. One can take skin from the heel of a sorcerer's dead victim and bury it in a hole in a pucalupuna tree, whereupon the stomach of the unknown sorcerer will swell and burst.[66] Among the Desana, relatives can take body parts of the deceased victim—hair, nail clippings, bodily excretions, facial or bodily dirt—and cook them in a pot along with pitch and peppers. As the contents boil, the sorcerer suffers stomach and abdominal pains; if the boiling continues, the sorcerer dies.[67] Note that such methods do not require visionary information of the sort provided by ayahuasca, through which one may see the identity of the sorcerer; the sickness and death are identification enough.

The interactions of envidia and brujería, envy and sorcery, can be seen as both resistance and social control. Magic is the next step beyond gossip, which turns "hard words" into an act of secret aggression that can always be disavowed. "Witchcraft," writes Scott, "is in many respects the classical resort of vulnerable subordinate groups who have little or no safe, open opportunity to challenge a form of domination that angers them. In a society that practices magic, those who perceive a lively resentment and envy directed at them from below will easily become convinced that any reverses they suffer are the result of malevolent witchcraft."[68] Anthropologist Michael Taussig, who studied shamanism and sorcery in the Colombian Putumayo, tells of one couple walking with their son at dusk past poorer neighbors in the deepening shadows, and their fears of their neighbors' envy and readiness to deploy sorcery

Pucalupuna

The pucalupuna is a very powerful plant. It is also called *lupuna colorada*, red *lupuna*—the word *puca* means red in Quechua—and must be distinguished from the white lupuna, called *lupuna blanca*, lupuna, or *kapok*.

The red lupuna is considered to be an evil tree. Its sap is believed to be poisonous. It is also called *lupuna bruja*, sorcerer tree; there is even a verb, *lupunear*, that means to inflict magical harm with the lupuna. The base of the trunk is hollow and often looks swollen; hence the belief that the tree can cause a victim's stomach to swell.[1] It is believed to harm those who approach it without the proper protection;[2] that is why poet César Calvo says that the spirit of the tree is so dangerous: "If he finds you in his territory, he makes your belly swell, and you die with destroyed intestines."[3] Pablo Amaringo says that the pucalupuna tree is possessed by a powerful magician from another dimension.[4]

In fact, the trunk is essentially a giant hollow cylinder filled with balsa-like pith; the tree also has a distinctive smooth reddish papery bark. Its evil nature affects everything it touches. One can, for example, harm an enemy simply by spreading the victim's clothing around the base of the tree.[5] One can put a bowl of tobacco juice in a hollow of the tree and leave it overnight, so that the spirit of the tree allows its poisonous sap to run into the pot, turning it into a magical poison.[6] One can also use the tree for countersorcery: take skin from the heel of a sorcerer's dead victim and bury it in a hole in the tree, whereupon the stomach of the unknown sorcerer will swell and burst.[7]

The red lupuna can also grant the power of sorcery through contact. Doña María taught me how to make a packet of tobacco, place it into a cavity in the tree, and plug the hole with clay. After eight days, I should check the tobacco; it should now be full of worms. I should then put it back into the hole in the tree, plug it up again, and wait another eight days. Then I should remove the packet, mix it with water, and drink it, if I could; this would turn me into a powerful sorcerer. Interestingly, Luna gives a similar method for putting a bowl of tobacco juice in a remocaspi as the way to follow la dieta with this tree.[8] In both cases, apparently the spirit of the tree passes into the tobacco to be ingested by the shaman.

It is because of its power that this tree is an ally of sorcerers, and that is precisely the reason why a healer should make the pucalupuna an ally as well, by ingesting it as part of la dieta in the jungle, by learning to call it for healing with its icaro, its magic song. The tree is used to inflict suffering; that makes it the best medicine for the suffering that others inflict.

NOTES

1. Luna & Amaringo, 1993, pp. 54 n. 92, 116 n. 167.
2. Luna, 1986c, p. 120.
3. Calvo, 1981/1995b, p. 211.
4. Luna & Amaringo, 1993, p. 108.
5. Duke & Vasquez, 1994, p. 47.
6. Luna, 1986c, p. 70 n. 26.
7. Chevalier, 1982, p. 378.
8. Luna, 1986c, p. 69.

against them.[69] Sorcery is a form of social control, enforcing norms of humility, lack of ostentation, and generosity.

Faced with sickness, the sick person will examine his or her relations with relatives and neighbors in order to identify in his or her recent or past conduct the signs of an enmity that could possibly explain the sorcery attack.[70] As Taussig puts it, envy is a "constantly charged scanner" of implicit social knowledge—an organizing principle for understanding misfortune, a theory of the evil inevitably flowing from perceived inequality, "the dominant signifier of perturbation in the social bond."[71]

THE FIGURE OF THE SORCERER

The figure of the evil sorcerer represents the antithesis of proper social behavior. Nobody has the courage to scold a sorcerer, people say, for he would put poison on you and you would die. If you make fun of him, he will kill you; if you are stingy with him, he will kill you; if you refuse to have sex with him, he will kill you. The sorcerer does not eat meat and does not smell any perfume. When he kills someone he spends a month without talking to anyone; he cannot touch a woman.[72] The sorcerer is in fact the type of nasty old man who would not be tolerated in any village, epitomizing solitary retentiveness and lack of reciprocity—lonely, demanding, querulous, abusive, miserly, and vengeful.

Conversely, sorcery implicitly defines what is socially appropriate, good, beautiful, disciplined, moral, and human. Sorcerers are precisely what humans ought not to be—individualistic, self-serving, and opportunistic. Sorcerers lack empathy for other humans and act for purely personal motives of jealousy, envy, resentment, and revenge. The killing of sorcerers—through countersorcery, the magical return of pathogenic darts, or vigilante justice—is a political drama, the social equivalent of the shaman sucking the magical pathogen from the body of a patient.[73] Indeed, in some Amazonian cultures, the sorcerer has ceased to be human altogether. A Baniwa poison owner is considered to be "no longer like a person" but is, rather, a monkey, one whose "only thought is to kill." A shaman sees the poison owner as having fur all over his body.[74] "These are the brujos," says Shipibo shaman don Javier Arévalo Shahuano, "who come back from the forest with eyes red like the huayruro."[75] The Cashinahua say the same: a sorcerer who has just killed has red eyes, because he is full of the blood of the victim.[76]

Sorcery is the inverse of healing. Instead of extracting harmful objects from sick bodies, the sorcerer introduces them;[77] instead of having relationships of confianza, the sorcerer is antisocial, dangerous, secretive.[78] By forcibly intruding into bodies, sorcery is a form of human predation; the sorcerer is an eater of human flesh.[79] Stories among the Sharanahua explicitly relate shamans to cannibalism. The shaman Ruapitsi, they say, ate one of his wives; so powerful was his hunger for human flesh that he cut pieces from his own thigh for food. His second wife killed him with an axe.[80]

Throughout indigenous Amazonian communities, there is often a cultural connection among attack sorcery, hunting, warfare, and predation—particularly by the jaguar, the ultimate predator.[81] Shamans are often equated with jaguars—indeed, are thought to become jaguars; "shamans and jaguars are thought to be almost identical, or at least equivalent, in their power, each in his own sphere of action, but occasionally able to exchange their roles."[82] Strikingly, the Cubeo assert that *all* jaguars—or at least many—are actually shamans. The ferocity of the jaguar is not due to its being an animal but, rather, due to its being a human.[83] Don Roberto has a pink and purple jaguar painted on the front wall of his house.

SORCERY AND GOSSIP

In some Amazonian cultures, suspicions of sorcery lead to confrontations, accusations, murder, and blood feud. But among mestizos there is seldom a public charge or confrontation or overt violence; rather, there is malicious gossip, silent countersorcery, or secret vengeance.[84] Behind the cordiality of everyday relations there is an entirely hidden world of sorcery and countersorcery, ongoing unstoppable vendettas of individuals and families and, often, their hired sorcerers and the families of the hired sorcerers—all in secret, the subject of whispered gossip and the rumors that run along the rivers.

Despite the integrative functions of sorcery, fear of sorcery—along with gossip and rumors and accusations of sorcery—can be socially disruptive. Once, among the Kulina in western Brazil, a prominent elderly man became ill with a respiratory infection just at the time he was visited by an old friend from another village. When the elderly man died, despite two days of nonstop curing rituals, his friend and guest was accused of sorcery and clubbed to death, and his body was thrown in a stream.[85]

Sorcery is *political*. It is profoundly emotional, having to do with envy, resentment, fear, and hate; when sorcery is suspected or alleged, the atmosphere becomes charged, and divisions between individuals and groups become accentuated. Sorcery accusations involve alliances, negotiations, strategies—politics.[86] Among the Arakmbut, for example, accusations of sorcery are directed at those the accusers fear or dislike, and therefore represent current lines of political cleavage. But those lines can shift. In one Arakmbut village, after the death of a prominent and respected shaman, sorcery accusations were originally directed at non-Arakmbut outsiders. But within months, the accusations turned toward persons with prestige, influence, and position in the opposite halves of the village. Such sorcery accusations within the community usually indicate that a political situation has reached a breaking point, leading to bitter recriminations, physical attacks, and even the death of an accused sorcerer. When relations break down in this way, one party usually moves away.[87]

Accusations of sorcery, suspicions of sorcery, and gossip about sorcery usually occur after something bad has happened—a death, a sickness, a business failure, a husband deserting his family. It is always misfortune that triggers accusations; whether someone is a sorcerer or not does not matter until people start seeking an explanation for misfortune. The sorcerer may be the Other—an other-than-human person, an enemy, another resident or ethnic group, or in-laws—or the sorcerer may come from within the heart of the community itself.[88] Accusations may focus on an outsider, but not necessarily. Among the Achuar, the slightest tension between groups is enough to cast suspicion on any shaman affiliated with any one of them.[89] Among the Shuar, sorcerers often come from within the group. Thus a Shuar dilemma: on the one hand, it is useful to have a shaman in the family, since one can get quick healing at reasonable cost; on the other hand, it is risky to have a shaman in the family, since a shaman is likely to harm family members with sorcery.[90]

Among Amazonian mestizos, the first to be suspected are those closest to the victim—those most susceptible to breaches of confianza, those most likely to have a grudge. Such gossip may be seen as picking on someone to *treat* as an outsider, thereby redrawing the boundaries of the community. Given the sociological and moral dimensions of shamanic powers, the tendency in fact is to look inside the local group or to a nearby household to try to discover the guilty one.[91]

When misfortune occurs, those who seek an explanation will tap into the mills of gossip; sickness especially may set gossip in motion.[92] The same envy, resentment, and jealousy can feed into sorcery, gossip of sorcery, and accusations of sorcery. The effects of sorcery can be vague—acute localized pain, malaise, misfortune. Whether this condition is diagnosed as sorcery is contextual. Anthropologist Donald Pollock, who has studied sorcery among the Kulina of western Brazil, has noted that such aches and pains are generally ignored or considered not to be sorcery; but when there has been violence between households, diagnoses of sorcery become common.[93] Thus, too, sorcery accusations can reflect institutional deficits, the lack of adequate mechanisms to mitigate disputes.[94]

SICKNESS NARRATIVES

There is frequently a pattern to gossip and accusations of sorcery: A asks B for a favor; B refuses; A seeks revenge by sorcery. Misfortune is a trigger to search one's memory for the instigating slight: Who has reason to hate me?

Here is a typical story. Don Agustin Rivas had an uncle, a policeman, who watched over the lake. One day he found an Indian fishing without a permit, so he took away the Indian's fishing spear. The Indian, unhappy about this, cast a spell on the policeman, and, as a result, little holes appeared on the policeman's buttocks, which itched unbearably.[95] Here is another: At one time Rivas ran a restaurant, and his friend William Guevara would come there to eat. But Rivas did not charge him for the food, because Guevara was a maestro, a brujo. One day Guevara ordered beer. Rivas was in a bad mood because many customers had not paid him, so he refused to give Guevara the beer. Guevara became angry and told Rivas that he would lose customers and his restaurant was going to fail. From that day, Rivas says, his business started to decline rapidly.[96]

Pablo Amaringo also tells such a sickness story. Amaringo had insulted a sorcerer by refusing to visit him in his home on the way back from the market. The sorcerer hit Amaringo with a virote. Amaringo did not notice anything at first, but he woke up in the middle of the night with terrible pain in his neck and was unable to move his head. The next morning he was trembling with fever, had hallucinations, and felt so bad that he went to see his grandfather, don Pascual Pichiri, who removed the dart.[97]

Just about everyone has similar stories. We can call this the basic mestizo sickness narrative: Someone acted superior to someone else, and look what happened. But note the pattern, and then turn it around. The policeman has a skin disease; Agustin Rivas loses business; Pablo Amaringo is stricken with pain. The question then is: What failure of reciprocity, generosity, or openhandedness caused this effect? In each case, there is an answer, and there is an agent—the Indian, the sorcerer, the shaman.

Similar stories are told throughout the Amazon. Among the Desana, a lack of respect for a powerful shaman, even a refusal to give him something he requests, may provoke him to sorcery. Epidemics of malaria or diarrhea that have devastated whole communities have been attributed to the ill will of a shaman angered by lack of respect or because a member of his own family had refused to give him something he requested.[98]

The concern runs in the other direction as well. People need to avoid becoming involved in serious disputes, quarrels, or similar situations that can lead to being accused—or suspected—of sorcery. A reputation for kindness, generosity, and cooperation decreases the chances of beings accused.[99] To stay off the list of suspects requires maintaining the bonds of confianza.

Sorcery thus has both an integrative function and a disintegrative effect. Sorcery accusations may be in part a factor in the traditional dispersed settlement and frequent splitting found in such Amazonian societies as the Shuar and Arakmbut.[100] If sorcery challenges inequality, then sorcery, accusations of sorcery, and gossip about sorcery may be one cost of a more egalitarian society.[101]

SORCERY AND THE STATE

There is little that the ordinary state apparatus can do about sorcery. Alejandro Tsakimp, a Shuar shaman, puts the thought this way: "They killed my father with witchcraft and not with a bullet. . . . With killings like this, through witchcraft, there aren't any witnesses. I can talk about all this, I can go to lawyers, but nobody will believe me."[102] There is never any tangible proof of a crime. A person killed by sorcery may be given a medical diagnosis—acute dehydration through diarrhea, for example, but such a diagnosis does not, of course, explain *why* the sickness occurred.[103] The first recourse for aggrieved family or community members is most often to retain the services of another, and hopefully more powerful, shaman. The final recourse is often the killing of the offender—what political scientist Fernando García, in his work on indigenous law among Ecuadorian Quichua, calls *muerte social*.[104] Other dispute-resolution mechanisms have traditionally been unavailable.

Government intervention faces serious obstacles in controlling a sorcerer. Accusations are often vague and unsupported by physical evidence. Magistrates in such circumstances may issue a peace bond signed by the complainants and the alleged sorcerer; then, at least, when the accusations continue, as they often do, the sorcerer can be charged with having broken the peace bond and, thus, the law.[105] The mere presence of a police garrison in a previously remote area may limit the amount of assault sorcery.[106] However, local officials may be caught in a dilemma between, on the one hand, their reluctance to give credence to sorcery accusations and, on the other, their own concern about offending a sorcerer.

There are, generally, three ways local authorities can bring a sorcerer under control. The first is to put the sorcerer in jail, even for a few days. Among the Napo Runa, for example, this is considered a terrible punishment for a shaman, for it cuts him off from his relationship with the forest spirits.[107] One such incarcerated sorcerer managed to escape the jail by cutting through a window, sought refuge in a church, and petitioned for help from federal authorities.[108]

A second sanction is to confiscate the sorcerer's magic stones. Of course, it is difficult to know whether a stone surrendered by the sorcerer, or left in an easily discoverable place in his home, is in fact the magic stone he uses in his sorcery. Still, crushing a stone in the presence of the complainants may help to calm down an explosive community situation.[109] A third—and surprising—sanction is to give the sorcerer an electric shock. It is believed that this will weaken and dispel at least part of the sorcerer's power.[110] It is understandable that local authorities are often reluctant to do this. But there can be further creativity: in one case, dating from 1942, a sorcerer was ordered, by special decree of the local political lieutenant, to believe in God. That put an end to his sorcery.[111]

More recently, community and shaman organizations have attempted to mediate such controversies. Fernando García tells of one such mediation. The accused sorcerer had originally agreed to hand over his magic stones and other shamanic tools but had failed to do so. Community members caught the alleged sorcerer, gave him electric shocks with a generator, and put him in the community jail, from which he—understandably—escaped. Finally, local authorities invited all the parties to mediate, including the accused sorcerer's elders, representatives of the Federación de Organizaciones Indígenas del Napo and a delegation from the shamans' organization Asociación de Shamanes Indígenas del Napo. They all went to the community that had allegedly been affected by the sorcerer, where the visiting shamans drank ayahuasca to determine who was telling the truth. On the basis of this consultation, they required the accused sorcerer to heal all those he had made sick, and then to hand over his magic stones.[112]

CHAPTER 14
HEALING

Doña María and don Roberto are curanderos, healers, as opposed to brujos, sorcerers. They are both very proud of this; they have not succumbed to the temptations of easy power; they have maintained their purpose and discipline. They are, for many in their community, the primary resource in cases of sickness. Additional resources, such as biomedical clinics or the regional hospital in Iquitos, are often not readily utilized, because of fear, unfamiliarity, cost, or the recognition that the sickness, such as soul loss or magical attack, may not be susceptible to cure by biomedical approaches.

Amazonian mestizos see hospitals as places where people go to die, or where the only treatment they receive is a little piece of paper, a prescription for drugs they cannot afford.[1] We should not have an overly optimistic view of biomedicine in the Amazon. The standard of care can be appalling—"amazingly awful and absurd," one anthropologist has called it.[2] If patients want sterile syringes, they have to buy them themselves at a local pharmacy and bring them to the hospital for the doctors to use. Sitting in Chachapoyas, capital of Amazonas, a friend, a native of the city, told me of her stay in the regional clinic, where supplies were so scarce that surgeons conserved their gloves by turning them inside out for use on the next patient.

DOES IT WORK?

Ayahuasquero don Juan Tangoa Paima claims that he can heal cancer, AIDS, epilepsy, heart disease, stomach and intestinal conditions, sexually transmitted diseases, depression, drug addiction, mental disorders, migraines, anxiety, and obesity—indeed, he offers the "complete and total healing of any and all afflictions."[3]

Now, these are staggering claims. If don Juan can do even a tiny part of what he claims—cure breast cancer, for example—then by all rights he should be an immensely wealthy man, teaching his techniques at major hospitals and medical schools. Of course, the term *healing* is vague. Does he mean by the word *heal* the same thing that, say, a clinical oncologist means by it?

Here is a story. I was sitting with don Roberto late one night when a canoe pulled up on the riverbank. A man half carried another up to the house, asking for help: his cousin was very sick, he said, with pains in the belly. Don Roberto performed the usual ten-minute healing: he sang icaros; he shook the shacapa, leaf-bundle rattle; he sucked at the man's belly; he blew tobacco smoke over him. I sat there thinking: What if this man has appendicitis? I asked don Roberto and the man himself if I could touch him: no fever. I gently pressed his abdomen: no rebound tenderness or guarding; no pain on the right side when pressing on the left; nothing special in the lower right quadrant. But my relief at these findings simply postponed the real question. Do I believe that don Roberto can heal acute appendicitis?

So, before addressing the thorny issue of *how* shamans such as doña María and don Roberto heal, it is worth posing a logically prior question: *Do* they heal? There are remarkably few data on this question. In particular, even moderately long-term follow-up is lacking. As anthropologist and medical doctor Gilbert Lewis puts it, "It is rare to find examples of anthropologists who record the frequency of therapeutic failures, do follow ups, or find out how many people do not bother to come back next time to the shaman."[4] Robert Desjarlais, a psychological anthropologist, points out that most research on ritual healing attempts to explain *how* it works, without demonstrating whether—and in what ways—patients actually feel better.[5]

So, how well do shamans actually cure sickness? The answer is that no one knows. To a great extent the body heals itself without intervention; most diseases are self-limiting. Other diseases, such as arthritis, can be cyclic in nature, and can appear to get better before they get worse. Another answer is a question: cured compared to what? It is difficult to devise a metric—return to work? return to premorbid functioning? return for follow-up? consumer satisfaction? We cannot even assume that people or cultures have unitary or unequivocal resolutions of suffering, or that we can recognize a culturally relevant resolution of suffering when it occurs. We do not know how long a follow-up is useful, even if we knew what we were following.

We must not forget that there is a suffering human person who seeks out the curandero for relief of pain, sickness, sorrow, or bad luck. As medical anthropologist Arthur Kleinman forcefully points out, there are two ways in which suffering may be professionally delegitimated. Physicians and psychiatrists may reify the lived experience of suffering as a *disease*, stripping it of its irreducible existential quality, moral commentary, and political performance. The misery that comes of poverty, inequality, and hopelessness is transformed and distorted into major depressive disorder or posttraumatic stress—trivialized, dehumanized, and now subject to medical authority. But, in exactly the same way, *anthropologists* may interpret suffering as the reproduction of oppressive relationships of production, the symbolization of internalized conflicts, or resistance to authority—a transformation of everyday experience, says Kleinman, "of the same order as those pathologizing reconstructions within biomedicine."[6] Such grand narratives of sociopolitical resistance eventually undermine the genuine moral claims of indigenous suffering and, as Kleinman puts it, disparage "the personal pains and distress that sick persons bring to shamans, which shamans try to cure."[7]

Sorcery is a weapon of the weak, resistance against oppression, and a way to maintain social norms of humility, faithfulness, trustworthiness, confianza, lack of ostentation, reciprocity, and generosity. At the same time, *sickness* is resistance against intolerable life situations, itself an ironic commentary on the resentment of others. As political scientist and anthropologist James Scott puts it, "To see the causes of distress as personal, as evil, as a failure of identifiable people in their own community to behave in a seemly way may well be a partial view, but it is not a wrong view. And not incidentally, it is quite possibly the only view that could, and does, serve as the basis for day-to-day resistance."[8] The sick person has a story to tell too.

Local Moral Worlds

I think it is important to focus on what Kleinman calls *local moral worlds*, resistance in microcontexts, avoiding the false sense of inevitability conveyed in a large-scale social analysis. It is in these micromoral worlds—particular, intersubjective, and constituting the lived flow of experience—that the experience of sickness is constructed. Local moral worlds, he says, are not simply reflections of macrolevel socioeconomic and political forces: "The microlevel politics of social relationships, in the setting of limited resources and life chances, underwrite processes of contesting and negotiating actions."[9]

Persuasive examples of this last can be found in Kleinman's writings on pain and resistance, where complaints of chronic pain are readily absorbed into a language of complaint about "enormous pressures and perceived injustices," authorizing "access to the moral devices of accusation and restitution"—a way to relegitimate a world that has been delegitimated by powerful others, to move from passivity in the face of suffering to an assertive central orientation. "We resist," he writes, "in the micropolitical structure, oppressive relationships."[10] This communicative subversive body remains an only partially conscious, and thereby protected, form of protest. Sickness may be many things, but it is often a refusal; the "complex, creative, somatic, and political idiom" of sickness can express itself as refusal to work, refusal to struggle under self-defeating conditions, refusal to endure, refusal to cope.[11] This resistance may extract a price that seems, to an outsider, greater than that of the original situation; but it can be a cry for those who have no other voice.[12]

Channels of Microresistance

Resistance itself takes socially prescribed forms, flows in channels laid out by medical culture. Bioethicist Carl Elliott discusses a recent sickness—the peculiar condition known as *apotemnophilia*, the compulsion to amputate one's own healthy limbs.[13] The author applies to this condition the insights of philosopher of science Ian Hacking on dissociative disorders.[14] Hacking argues that psychiatrists and other clinicians in fact helped to *create* the epidemics both of fugue in nineteenth-century Europe and of multiple personality disorder in late-twentieth-century America, simply by the way they viewed the disorders—by the kinds of questions they asked patients, the treatments they used, the diagnostic categories available to them, and the way the patients fit into these categories. Hacking calls this the *looping effect*—the fact that people are conscious of the way they are classified, and alter their behavior and self-conceptions in response to their classification.

Elliott applies this insight to apotemnophilia: once the diagnostic category exists, people begin to conceptualize and interpret their experience in those terms—just as has happened, for example, with gender identity disorder, or multiple personality disorder, or fugue or hysteria in the nineteenth century. This same insight can be applied to culture-bound syndromes as well: in a cultural setting where a particular diagnostic category exists—soul loss, say, or the intrusion of a pathogenic object—both the experience and the behavior of the sick person will be shaped by that person's understanding of the sickness. For example, when people believe that they are performing their social roles less adequately, according to their own criteria, than others in the community, the illness category of *susto*, soul loss, provides a framework within which to conceptualize their experience and seek appropriate healing.[15] The very existence of an apotemnophilia diagnostic category, the availability of Web sites and support groups, directs previously inchoate resentments into a new—now medically validated—channel.

In our culture, people suffering from general malaise and a variety of nonspecific symptoms may conceptualize their illness as, say, multiple chemical sensitivity, and will search their memory for some relevant initiating chemical exposure; similarly, people who conceptualize their illness as susto will search their memory for some relevant initiating fright. In both cases, what might otherwise be a minor and forgotten incident becomes *significant*. In both susto and multiple chemical sensitivity, perceived social and personal failures are attributed to a culturally defined sickness.

SICKNESS AS IRONY

Such forms of sickness-as-resistance are forms of *irony*. Housewives' agoraphobia, for example, can be seen as both a ritual display of and a protest against the cultural pressures and injunctions on women, especially those that demand a restrictive domestic role. By overconforming to this stereotype, a woman is able to dramatize her situation, mobilize a caring family around herself, and at the same time also restrict her husband's movements, by forcing him to stay at home and look after her.[16] The sufferer says, "You wish to constrict my life choices? Well, look at *this*." Anorexia, apotemnophilia, multiple chemical sensitivity, fibromyalgia, susto, and sorcery can all be seen, at least in part, as *ironic* embodiments of—and thus microresistance to—states conceptualized by the sufferer as forms of starvation, amputation, powerlessness, constriction, fear, and guilt.

THE SICKNESS NARRATIVE

Narrativization is a process of locating suffering in history, of placing events in a meaningful order in time. It also has the object of opening the future to a positive ending, of enabling the sufferer to imagine a means of overcoming suffering.[17] One of the central efforts in healing is to symbolize the source of suffering, to find an image around which a narrative can take place—what medical anthropologist Byron Good calls "the struggle for a name."[18] Psychologist Theodore Sarbin proposes what he calls the *narratory principle*—that human beings think, perceive, imagine, and make moral choices according to narrative structures. This narratory principle "operates to provide meaning to the often nonsystematic encounters and interactions experienced in everyday life."[19]

This process is frequently called *emplotment*, a term derived from Aristotle through philosopher Paul Ricoeur. Emplotment is an operation, a putting-in-to-the-form-of-a-plot—specifically, "the operation that draws a configuration out of a simple succession" and thus "integrates into one whole and complete story multiple and scattered events."[20] Plot is a "synthesis of the heterogeneous."[21] The unexpected or unexplained in one's life becomes meaningful when emplotted; actions are not random events, but become beginnings, middles, and ends in a story: "In other words, we understand our own lives—our own selves and our own places in the world—by interpreting our lives as if they were narratives, or, more precisely, through the work of interpreting our lives we turn them into narratives, and life understood as narrative constitutes self-understanding."[22]

Types of Narrative

Emplotment—creating a narrative—can take different forms. Literary critic and philosopher Tzvetan Todorov, discussing causality in narrative, distinguishes between *ideological* narrative and *mythological* narrative. In the former, events relate to each other as particular manifestations of a general law; in such a narrative, isolated and independent events, even performed by different characters, reveal the same rule, the same ideological organization. In medical terms, such a narrative would be a case study: the story of a sickness would illustrate the general laws that apply to sickness of that sort. On the other hand, in a mythological narrative, events enter into immediate causal relations with each other: the story of *my* sickness would trace a narrative thread from the envy of my neighbor to the magical dart embedded in my throat.[23] In linguistic terms, ideological narrative is paradigmatic, and mythological narrative is syntagmatic.

Much of therapeutic interpretation involves efforts to turn the patient's mythic narrative into an ideological account. Turning myth into ideology serves several simultaneous functions—to give a specific kind of coherence to the story, to give the healer technical control over the interpretation and continuation of the story, and to reinforce the reality of the ideology from which it draws its structure.[24] While this account is intended as a critique of biomedicine's ideological reduction of patient narratives, I think that—just as with the idea of healing and curing—*all* medicine utilizes both forms of narrative. Doña María and don Roberto, certainly, conceptualize suffering both mythologically, as a patient's unique story, and ideologically, as subsumed under cultural and, ultimately, moral paradigms of mutuality, resentment, and revenge.

Narratives of Sickness

We have previously discussed the mestizo sickness narrative. Now we can begin to discern its function. The narrative of a sick person seeks, in Ricoeur's terms, to "extract a configuration from a succession."[25] A sickness narrative describes the events of sickness along with their *meaning* for the person who experiences them; Byron Good, adopting Ricoeur's term, says that they *emplot* experience, revealing its underlying form.[26] In this usage, *plot* is the underlying structure of a story, and *emplotment* is the activity of making sense of the story.[27] For the sick person, the sickness narrative sequence may be clear, but may make no sense; it is told "from the blind complexity of the present as it is experienced."[28]

To heal, then, is to rebuild the shattered lifeworld of the sick person. As cultural anthropologist Thomas Csordas says of Navajo healing, the criterion of success is that the patient come to "understand"—that is, to contextualize life experience in terms of a particular philosophy, to change the "assumptive world" of the sufferer.[29] "The decision to seek medical consultation is a request for interpretation," says Leon Eisenberg, a cultural psychiatrist. "Patient and doctor together reconstruct the meanings of events in a shared mythopoesis."[30] Anthropologist and ethnobotanist Daniel Moerman puts it this way: "Meaning mends."[31]

Sickness implicates the subjective response of the person, and of those around the person, to being sick; but, more than just the experience, it includes the *meaning* of the experience. To say that my sickness results from a magically propelled pathogenic object is incomplete, inadequately emplotted. The narrative—or story about how and why a person became sick—may include a wide range of events, including the actions of both human and other-than-human persons, spread over a long period of time. Telling such *stories of sickness* is a way of giving meaning to the experience of sickness, placing it in the context of the lifeworld, and relating it to wider themes and values in the culture.[32]

Thus, in the Amazon, the only useful diagnosis is not of the sickness but of the identity of the person who caused it. As anthropologist Neil Whitehead has noted, this is not to say that the physiological and epidemiological bases for sickness and death are not understood; rather, the *important* questions remain even after the medical explanation has been given.[33] In Amazonian mestizo culture, this means asking the questions, Why has this happened to *me*? Why *now*? Have I done something wrong to deserve this? Has anyone caused me to be sick? Who hired the sorcerer who cast the spell? What have I done to earn the enmity of a neighbor? What societal norms against ostentation or adultery have I violated?[34]

Segundo's Story

Anthropologists Donald Joralemon and Douglas Sharon, who studied healing practice in the Peruvian Andes, present the following case, which may stand for a large number of doña María's and don Roberto's patients. Segundo came to the curandero because, as he says, "I feel very bad in my work, bored, preoccupied, bad dreams, anger against my family, with my friends, arguments with friends at work, with my closest companions."[35] He thinks it could be *maldad*, a curse, from a woman who used to be his mistress; he had a child with her, but it died. The woman made a complaint against him to the police, "and made me spend a lot of money to get out of this." She has continued to threaten him.

Segundo worked as a fare collector on a privately owned bus. He spoke at great length about the effects of envy on his life. People he knew who took the bus envied him and expected that he would grant them special favors—for example, not charge them extra for bringing on several loaded baskets. Even his friends envied him for having a job.

On one occasion, a young drunk passenger tried to grab the money Segundo had collected in fares. Segundo pushed him out of the moving bus, causing the man to fall and injure himself. Unfortunately, the young man's mother was rumored to be a bruja, a sorceress. The woman said, "Now, these problems you have, just wait, you'll see if all the time your job is going to last won't pass fifteen days." The woman apparently cast a curse on him; shortly thereafter, Segundo's boss accused him of stealing money from the fares and fired him.

This case illustrates the extent to which fear of the envy and magical aggression of others can shape a life. It also illustrates the direct linkage between envy and sorcery, whether related to adultery or economic uncertainty. Segundo was constantly vulnerable to the hostility of others—his mistress, his passengers, those he offended by his lack of mutuality. The goal is to create relationships of confianza, trust, in order to gain security and opportunity in a world of uncertainty and frustration, to enforce expectations of mutual help and favors. If every disease is an indictment, "a punishment received by the body or soul of someone who has caused damage with his body or his soul," then Segundo suffered a failure of right relationship.[36]

From the point of view of the drunken passenger's mother, Segundo was fortunate—a steady job, a position of some power over others, the ability to grant favors to his friends. From her point of view, pushing her son off the bus was an act of *social hubris*—arrogant, excessive, ostentatious, arbitrary, precisely what the threat of sorcery should have prevented. The same considerations apply to his mistress. We do not know, from Segundo's account, why she swore out a *denuncio* against him, what she thought he owed her, in what way she believed he had betrayed their relationship of confianza. The curses these women purportedly cast on Segundo were their final weapon in their battle against his male power and betrayal.

And so, what of the suffering of Segundo? His own suffering is symbolic as well, a comment on his own constrictions—social, economic, self-imposed. His exhaustion, misery, rage, and hopelessness are less individual pathologies than socially significant signs.[37] His malaise, alienation, bad luck, economic misfortune, and failed relationships are embedded in his social situation; but his sickness shifts attention to his own suffering, relegitimates his world. The healer takes his suffering seriously, but places it within the web of Segundo's own choices and relationships, his infidelity, his anger, his failures of mutuality.

Misfortune strikes Segundo repeatedly: he gets in trouble with the police; he is accused of stealing and is fired from his job; he has bad dreams; he gets in arguments with friends and companions; he suffers from boredom, discontent, preoccupation, and indolence. All of these are sicknesses and hence *indictments*. He must undertake a searching inventory of his breaches of confianza: Who has reason to hate me?

THE HEALING PERFORMANCE

Remember that sorcery is not just a culturally meaningful construction of suffering, but also the focus for remedial action: magical harms can be *healed*. As we have discussed, the field of the shamanic drama embraces not only healer and patient but audience and community as well. The community knowledge available to all the participants in the drama includes not only who has consulted with the curandero, but also who has expressed anger or resentment against the sufferer; who may have been motivated by jealousy or rivalry to consult a sorcerer; and what social injunctions against ostentation, or adultery, or lack of reciprocity the sufferer may have violated. This entire social context is part of the healing process.[38]

The shaman here has several roles—to validate the power of these weapons of the weak; to assume, at great personal risk, community conflicts as personal duels;[39] to affirm that breach of confianza, adultery, neglect, callousness, and cruelty produce their own suffering in the perpetrator; to demonstrate to the community the ways in which such breaches of social order are both embodied and healed; and to explicate suffering as a moral drama, in which the sufferers act out, in coded ways, the impossibilities of their own social positions. "We do not only diagnose the flesh of the material body," says César Calvo's fictional shaman, don Javier. "We do not limit ourselves to watching over the palpable terrain of the patient, but with equal attention we channel him in his secret blood, the timeless blood that circulates only during the night when dreams awake."[40] Anthropologist Michael Taussig talks of an ayahuasca healing session where what the patient talked about "was neither confession nor his sins, but, on the contrary, of what scared him and what his vomiting meant, namely the envidia that someone or ones had for him. It was their envy that was in him and making him heave out the slime of his insides into the frog-quavering night."[41]

EMPLOTMENT IN THE BODY

So we return to performance, to theater, to the sensory dimensions of the healing ceremony. The healing is not explanatory; it is *visceral*—synesthetic impact on the body, the gut, the skin, the eyes, the ears. We should not think of doña María and don Roberto as primitive psychiatrists. What they do has more kinship with *eleos* and *phobos*, Aristotle's pity and terror. That this links to *katharsis*—cleansing or purging—should come as no surprise. Ayahuasca is, above all, and apart from our own cultural obsession with visions, *la purga*. The shaman works through the moral themes of healing discourse not linearly but *in performance*.

When we watch doña María or don Roberto work, we see emplotment in action, resentful social relationships not thrashed out in verbal discourse but literally sucked from the body—the individual body, the body politic—in high drama, gagging, spitting, rejected, healed.

CHAPTER 15
SPIRIT POSSESSION

SUMMONING THE SPIRITS

The shaman can see things that people who are not shamans cannot. The shaman may be able to find lost objects, know where game is plentiful, discern who has cast a curse, and diagnose the location or cause of an illness. Many scholars, influenced by the work of Mircea Eliade, maintain that the characteristic activity of shamanism is soul flight—celestial ascent, ecstasy, out-of-body journeys to the spirit realm, almost always vertically, upward, toward the sky.[1] And it is true that, among some shamanic traditions, out-of-body flight is the way that shamans acquire the information that is their stock-in-trade. They travel through the air and go look.

Shamanism in the Upper Amazon is, I think, different.

As we have seen, mestizo shamans summon the protective and healing spirits to the place of ceremony by singing the appropriate icaros, and receive from them, often in strange or secret languages, information regarding the diagnosis and treatment of their patients. The locus of their interaction with the spirits is the place where the ceremony is conducted. This general rule applies even when they are retrieving a soul lost through *manchari* or a person stolen away by the spirits of the underwater realms. They do not journey in pursuit of the soul; rather, they *summon* the soul back to the body it had inhabited, or *summon* and coerce the people of the waters to bring the stolen person back to the place of ceremony, using the icaros they have learned from the plant spirits or from the water people themselves.

VISIONARY INFORMATION

Drinking ayahuasca can give visions of distant people and events. These visions can give both shaman and patient information about the location of a lost object, the health of a distant relative, the face of a secret enemy, the seducer of a spouse, or the source of a sickness. The third time she drank ayahuasca, doña María was able to see, in another house across town, people practicing a healing ceremony, and she was surprised to find herself actually sitting on the floor in don Roberto's house. Such visions encompass past and future as well: doña María saw in her visions how her brothers had died, both murdered. People may come to a healing ceremony and drink ayahuasca simply to gather such information.

Shamans get this sort of information from ayahuasca—and more. They can see what is happening on distant planets and galaxies, where in the underwater realm a kidnapped fisherman is being held captive, the mountain cave where a stolen soul is hidden, how the doctors at vast spiritual hospitals perform their surgeries. Among the Cashinahua, too, ayahuasca is taken to get information about distant places and their beings, the hiding places of game, the real intentions of opponents in conflicts, the motives of visitors, future events, and the causes of sickness.[2] The Piro shaman drinks ayahuasca to see paths, villages, cities, distant countries, and—particularly—sorcerers and their motives.[3] Famed Shuar warrior Tukup' says that it is good to kill someone who has murdered your relative or bewitched your child; but you must first go to a shaman who drinks ayahuasca to make sure you have targeted the correct person.[4]

We should not assume, based on our own cultural preferences, that this information is only or always conveyed visually. Consistent with the role of the auditory in the jungle environment, such information can be conveyed verbally. Aguaruna shamans are able to know events that are distant in space and time because their pasuk spirits bring them information from faraway places.[5] The same is true for mestizo shamans: the etiology of a patient's illness can be whispered with startling clarity, into the ear of the shaman by the plant spirits who are in attendance at the healing.

Shamans do not drink ayahuasca to heal; they drink ayahuasca to *get information*—as Cocama shaman don Juan Curico puts it, "to screen the disease and to search the treatment." Mestizo shaman don Manuel Córdova Ríos says the same thing: "Ayahuasca, it tells you how, but by itself it cures nothing directly."[6]

SPIRIT POSSESSION

Mestizo Practice

However, on unpredictable occasions during an ayahuasca healing ceremony, doña María and don Roberto may undergo what they call *transcorporación.*

When they transcorporate, they leave their body and travel to distant landscapes, other planets, great shining mountains, brightly lit cities, while their body is occupied by the spirit of some dead healer, who performs the ceremony in their stead, speaking in a voice other than theirs, changing their physical appearance. This state is clearly distinguished from that of gaining visionary information.

When don Roberto transcorporates, he goes around the world, seeing things that are happening elsewhere. It is *como volando*, like flying, he says, like being in an airplane; his *alma*, soul, sees marvels in both this world and others—incredibly tall crystal buildings; mountains, rivers, and lakes; huge hospitals, where he can observe medical procedures and operations in progress. Meanwhile, his body is occupied by a plant spirit, such as ayahuasca, or the spirit of a tree. Doña María transcorporates as well; her body is occupied by a single and specific soul—that of Oscar Rosindo Pisarro, a deceased Rosicrucian healer. In both cases, when the body is thus occupied by a spirit, an observer who is *buen mareado*, who is well under the influence of ayahuasca, can see that the body has changed in observable ways.

I have seen this phenomenon. When drinking ayahuasca with don Antonio Barrera, I observed him transcorporate, his body occupied by the spirit of an ancient, fierce, and powerful shaman. As far as I could see in the darkness, his body grew larger, darker, threatening; his voice changed to a deeper growl; the icaros he sang changed in tone and rhythm. There is apparently some theatricality involved in such displays. Don Antonio, for example, smokes mapacho as the transcorporation occurs; when the process is complete, he holds the mapacho cigarette over his head, so that its glowing tip appears, in the dark, to be held by a much taller person. There is no doubt that the effect is impressive, especially to one who is buen mareado.

The unforeseeable possibility that the shaman will transcorporate is an important reason for singing the preliminary arcanas of protection and calling in the shaman's protective spirits. When the shaman's body is unoccupied by the shaman, it is vulnerable to occupation by another; if a sorcerer steals the shaman's body and is able to prevent the shaman's return, the shaman will die. That is why it is vital that the shaman *trust* the possessing spirit to relinquish the body when the shaman returns.

The possessing spirit is thus almost always one with whom the shaman has a relationship of confianza—a great and powerful shaman of the past, a former teacher, a maestro de la medicina. Cocama shaman Juan Curico is possessed by his grandfather, don Jacinto Masullan, who provides healing guidance;[7] Napo Runa shaman Pablo Calapucha is possessed by his father, the powerful shaman Quilluma.[8] Don José Curitima Sangama, a Cocama shaman, says of the spirits of dead shamans who enter his body and speak through his mouth: "They are my teachers who show me how to heal. For that reason, I call them and they come and teach me the music."[9] Possessing spirits appear to be almost always anthropomorphic—Indian and mestizo shamans, often venerable old men or women; famous deceased Western doctors; wise men from distant countries; or beings from other planets, solar systems, and galaxies.[10]

The spirit who enters into doña María's body is a Rosicrucian who lived in Iquitos and, according to María, did many good deeds. He is buried in the general cemetery in Iquitos; many people visit his grave and leave candles and flowers there. She routinely calls on his spirit to help her heal people, speaks with him, and transcorporates his spirit; she asks him to come help her in her work, and lets him work through her, because she trusts him—as opposed, she says, to other envious and competitive shamans.

The calling of ancient shamans, old and wise, to enter into the body and help with healing appears to be not uncommon among mestizo shamans.[11] Both don José Coral and don Santiago Murayari—like don Roberto and doña María—call upon the souls of dead shamans who live "at the end of the world" or in the underwater realms.[12] These souls enter their bodies during ayahuasca healing sessions and perform the actual healing work. During the sessions, the shamans carry on long dialogues with these souls; in addition to questions of diagnosis and treatment, they will also ask these souls such awkward questions as how much to charge for the work, or about personal problems that may have arisen with their patients. The shamans speak Spanish softly and calmly, but the souls answer in a very different voice, loud and nervous, and speak in an Indian language. Indeed, several souls may enter the body of the shaman, one after the other, each with a distinct personality.[13]

There thus may be a *spectrum* of summoning and possession among mestizo shamans. At one end, there is a summoning of a spirit or spirits to the place of ceremony; at the other end, the spirit or spirits may fully occupy the body of the shaman while the shaman's spirit has departed for other realms. In the middle there is a state in which spirits and the shaman *share* the shaman's body, in which a spirit or spirits speak through the shaman's mouth in dialogue with the shaman in his or her own voice.

Indigenous Practice

Despite the mestizo practice, such possession states have reportedly been unusual in the Upper Amazon. For example, anthropologist Gerald Weiss specifically states that "Campa culture does not include a belief in spirit possession."[14] Gerardo Reichel-Dolmatoff writes of the Desana and other Tukanoan peoples in the Amazon that "the concept of spirit-possession seems to be completely lacking. . . . A *payé* is always himself; never is he seized or invaded by a spirit; he simply interprets and transmits what this spirit shows him and tells him."[15] Yet there is reason to believe that spirit possession is also found—or, in some cases, was found at one time—among indigenous peoples of the Upper Amazon.

Machiguenga shamans, for example, work by changing places with their spirit helpers—or counterparts or doubles—among the *unseen ones*, good and powerful spirits who reside at a distance and must be invoked by a shaman. Working only at night, the shaman drinks ayahuasca and climbs to the roof beams of his house; the shaman's spirit counterpart simultaneously drinks ayahuasca, and the two change places, occupying each other's bodies. The spirit counterpart sucks out the magic arrow embedded in the sufferer; the work done, the spirit flies back to the land of the unseen ones, and the shaman returns to the mortal body. It is imperative that shamans return to their bodies before dawn, or they will become so attached to the land of the unseen ones that they will stay there, and the mortal body will die. The land of the unseen ones is an actual place, lying at a great distance.[16]

Similarly, Canelos Quichua shamans are possessed by the great shaman spirits of the forest. Thus possessed, the human shaman is *bancu*—a bench or seat—for the spirit shaman, and very dangerous; for it is through the human shaman that the spirit shaman sings, and attacks, with killing projectiles, the shaman and client who harmed the patient. The human shaman is the seat of power for the powerful spirit, but here too is danger. Both human bancu and possessing spirit are in two locations at once—in the spirit realm, the jungle soil, or the lake of ice inside a rocky mountain, and also in the house where the ceremony is taking place. If the human shaman loses his contact with the place of ceremony, he will die.[17]

The Yagua shaman too leaves the body to travel across the different levels of the universe, while one or more spirits take up residence to speak and act in the absent shaman's place. This is indicated by the shaman speaking in a very high-pitched voice, which is called the "voice of the spirits."[18]

It is interesting to note that several indigenous Amazonian peoples believe that spirit possession, though no longer practiced in their group, was once the province of great and powerful shamans in the past. The Shuar believe that Canelos Quichua shamans are particularly powerful—the Shuar call them *banku*—and that they are the only shamans in the area who are able to become possessed by and act as mediums for the spirit of a deceased person, let it speak through their mouths; among the Shuar themselves, they say, such shamans no longer exist.[19] It is the same among the Shipibo: one woman, not herself a shaman, says that the meraya have now all disappeared, but that they could be possessed by the souls of dead people, who would speak through the meraya's mouth several months after their death to name the sorcerers who had killed them. There is thus reason to believe that the meraya—like the banku—was distinguished from other shamans by giving voice to the dead.[20]

Among the Achuar, when *panku*—clearly the same word as *banku* or *banco*—drink ayahuasca, they receive the souls of the dead into their bodies, and the dead speak through their mouths, "like on the radio," says the son of an Achuar panku. Such shamans are reportedly very rare today, and very powerful; they have received darts, invisible to other shamans, directly from the dead. Anthropologist Philippe Descola describes one such panku. "I come from the depths of the Tungurahua volcano," the shaman said, "to see the tsentsak hidden in your body. Nothing escapes my clairvoyance, for I am blind in the light and exist only in the darkness. I see metal tsentsak that gleam like the surface of the water. I see many tsentsak in your legs."[21]

Similarly, among the Napo Runa, a bancu shaman is the most powerful type. A bancu begins when very young and, as Grandfather Alonso Andi, not himself a shaman, expresses it, "studies and thinks for a long time."[22] The bancu is distinguished by spirit possession; he is the only shaman through whom the spirits speak directly.[23] Grandfather Alonso describes it this way: "The supai takes possession of the yachaj, and those who want to can consult him. . . . The soul created by God leaves the body and the supai comes into it. He speaks through the yachaj. . . . The yachaj looks like he's dead, and the supai talks through him." The shaman first cleanses the patient with the huairachina leaf-bundle rattle, and then the supai asks the assembled people what they want to know. They say that they have called him to heal sickness; the supai answers, "Yes, yes." These spirits live in a place called *cielosiqui*, the end of the world: "When the bancu calls them, they come right away; for him it's only a matter of calling."[24]

Anthropologist Blanca Muratorio describes such a Napo Runa ceremony. The healer was Pablo Calapucha, a powerful shaman and son of the deceased shaman Quillama, also a bancu; the patient was a sick girl with a fever. Pablo began by whistling and then singing a song calling the spirit of ayahuasca, who arrived accompanied by a powerful spirit, who took possession of Pablo and, speaking through him, greeted those present and engaged in a dialogue with the girl's mother. The spirit diagnosed the sickness, assured the mother of the child's quick recovery, and departed. Pablo then cleansed the patient with the huairachina leaf-bundle rattle, blew tobacco smoke, and sucked out the sickness. This process was repeated several times with other spirits. When the process was completed, Pablo also called the spirit of his deceased father, the powerful shaman, who then had a lengthy dialogue with his old friend, Grandfather Alonso.[25]

CONTROL AND POSSESSION

A long-standing debate about shamanism concerns the *locus of interaction* between the shaman and the other-than-human persons with whom the shaman works—between shamans who travel to the land of the spirits and shamans whose bodies are occupied and possessed by spirits. Often the debate is expressed dichotomously as a matter of *power*—between the shaman being "the master of spirits," on the one hand, and the shaman being "the instrument of the spirits," on the other.[26] Graham Harvey, a scholar of indigenous religions, points out that "there is an almost continual conflict between those who think shamans are, by definition, people who control spirits . . . and those who think shamans are, at least sometimes, controlled by spirits."[27]

I think that we should subvert this dichotomy at the outset. It is based on dualistic assumptions about power and control: either you have power over the other or the other has power over you; either you are in control or you are *out of control*. In the Amazon, the spirits—the plants—are powerful and unpredictable. The relationship between shaman and plant is complex, paradoxical, and multilayered, embodied in a recurrent phrase in doña María's songs, doctorcito poderoso, powerful little doctor, the diminutive indicating warmth and familial affection, the adjective acknowledging power. The shaman "masters" the plants—the verb for learning a plant is *dominar*—by taking the plant inside the body, letting the plant teach its mysteries, giving oneself over to the power of the plant. As doña María warned me, ayahuasca is muy celosa, very jealous. To acknowledge that the spirits can be dangerous, and then to speak, as does anthropologist Fiona Bowie, of mastering, taming, even *domesticating* them, is to gloss over the complex reciprocal interpersonal relationship between shaman and other-than-human person—fear, awe, passion, surrender, friendship, and love.[28]

The dichotomy is also subverted among the Shuar. The tsentsak, magic darts, kept within the chest of a Shuar shaman, are living spirits who can control the actions of a shaman who does not have sufficient self-control. The magic darts want to kill, and it requires hard work to keep them under control and use them for healing rather than attack. That is why it is considered to be much more difficult to be a healer than a sorcerer:[29] it is difficult to resist the urges of the darts. As some Shuar say, "The tsentsak make you do bad things."[30] Shuar shamans are thus, in a real sense, possessed, but not by the soul of a deceased human person; they are possessed by their own shamanic power, with which they are in continuous interaction.[31]

Aguaruna shamans, too, when they begin to heal, call pasuk to enter into their bodies. Pasuk are the spirits of formidable shamans who live in the forest, enter into the human shaman's chest, and tell the shaman information about the sick person. While shamans are said to control their pasuk, the extent of this control appears to be variable.[32] Similarly, the Parakanã of eastern Amazonia believe that shamans control pathogenic agents that cause sickness, called *karowara*. When animated by a shaman, karowara are tiny pointed objects; inside the victim's body, they take the concrete form of monkey teeth, some species of beetle, stingray stings, and sharp-pointed bones. Karowara have no independent volition; but they have a compulsion to eat human flesh.[33] The case is the same for the Achuar. When shamans extract darts from their patients, they store them in their wrists. Such darts, having once caused sickness, have acquired a taste for human flesh; they seek to escape the shaman's control and go hunting on their own, and must constantly be brought under control.[34] The relationship between shaman and pathogenic agent appears complex, and control is not easily defined.

SOUL STEALING

The converse of voluntary spirit possession by the shaman is the stealing of a soul. Mestizos believe that it is possible to lose one's soul, or part of one's soul, through more or less natural processes—through fright, for example. Soul loss through susto, also called manchari, is a relatively common childhood condition, treated by calling the soul to return. But one's soul may also be stolen, especially during an ayahuasca ceremony, requiring the intervention of a shamanic healer to call it back into the body. The sorcerer who steals a soul can throw it away, either into space or into tunnels under the earth, often caves in the Andes.[35] If the shaman does not succeed in recovering the hidden soul, the person will sicken and inevitably die.

The soul is restored by shacapar, soplar, and chupar—rattling, blowing tobacco smoke, and sucking—and by singing the icaros that call the soul, much like any healing. Don Roberto first blows tobacco smoke into the corona, the crown of the head, in order to clear the head for the return of the soul. He calls back the soul with icaros; he sucks from the top of the head, the pit of the stomach, and the temples.[36] The soul reenters the body through the crown of the head, doña María told me, *como un viento*, "like a wind"—except for the lost souls of children, who always appeared to doña María as angels. The shaman does not journey to retrieve the soul but, rather, summons the soul—as the shaman would a spirit—to the place where the shaman is treating the victim's physical body.[37]

Don Emilio Andrade tells of how he once called back a stolen soul. After drinking ayahuasca, he rattled his shacapa; blew tobacco smoke; and sucked from the top of the patient's head, the pit of her stomach, her temples, and her lungs. Then he began to sing the icaros that called her soul. Suddenly he saw a road and in the center of the road, a small shadow. As he sang, calling the soul, the shadow became larger; when the shadow was just six or seven meters away, he saw that it was his patient. The soul entered into her through the top of her head, and at that moment she awoke. He continued to blow tobacco smoke on her, until she was completely recovered.[38]

TRANSCORPORATION AND SHAMANISM

For a long time, largely under the influence of historian of religion Mircea Eliade, it was assumed that *soul flight* was the defining feature of shamanism.[39] We read that "the characteristic feature of shamanism is not the entry of an alien spirit into the shaman; it is the liberation of the shaman's spirit, which leaves his body and sets off on a mantic journey."[40] Or again: "The shaman's trance is thus conceived as a journey undertaken in the company of the spirits he embodies. The shaman's soul leaves his body and voyages through the invisible regions in order to meet the dead or the spirits."[41] Anthropologist Michael Harner has defined the shaman as "a person who journeys *to* the spirits, seeking them out in their own world and remaining in control during the time spent there."[42]

Yet, as I have indicated above, there seem to be *three* modes of interaction with the spirits: the shaman can travel to where the spirits are—the classic soul flight; the shaman can summon the spirits to where the shaman is; or the spirits can enter and take possession of the shaman's body. Particular cultures—or particular shamans, on particular occasions—may utilize one or more of these modes of interaction.

The earliest scholars of shamanism focused on the first and last of these, and researchers were quickly able to point out that shamans in many cultures *combine* journeying and possession in a single shamanic performance—that soul flight trance and spirit possession can alternate in one and the same person.[43] In Siberia, for example, shamanizing involves both "soul journey shamanism" and "possession shamanism," with the shaman journeying to the other world when spirits have entered his or her body and liberated the shaman's soul from its fetters.[44] Similarly, when the Greenlandic *angakkoq* travels to the spirit world, the traveling soul is sometimes replaced by a spirit, which inhabits the body of the angakkoq. As the shaman's soul is busy elsewhere, the spirit interacts with the audience.[45] Among the Kahm-Magar in the Himalayas, the shaman, in the course of the same ritual, sometimes voyages and sometimes is possessed.[46]

But what about summoning? Anthropologist Åke Hultkrantz was one of the few researchers consistently to call attention to journeying and summoning as distinct practices.[47] In many shamanic performances of divination and curing, he notes, where there is "the enlightenment of the shaman through the arrival of auxiliary spirits," the shaman's soul does not leave the body, leading Hultkrantz to infer "two distinctive experiences"—first, "the extracorporeal flight of the shaman" and, second, "on-the-spot information passed to the shaman by helping spirits."[48] Further, Anna-Leena Siikala, an expert in northern Eurasian shamanism, has pointed to evidence among Siberian shamans for all three modes—journey, possession, and summoning.[49] These three ways of working could be combined sequentially: one Evenk shaman took his spirits into himself at the opening of the performance, then questioned them, and finally flew with them.[50] The threefold pattern in Siberian shamanism has been confirmed by historian Ronald Hutton in his thorough review of the literature.[51]

Interestingly, unlike the Greenlandic angakkoq, doña María and don Roberto do not explicitly go to the land of the spirits, nor do they interact with plant or animal spirits on their journeys, in order to heal their patients. To do that, they call the spirits to the place of ceremony. Rather, when they transcorporate, they journey to *see*—distant landscapes, far galaxies, vast hospitals, convocations of shamans. They do not travel on business.

CHAPTER 16
MAGIC STONES

Significant among the shamanic tools used by mestizo shamans are *piedras*, or piedras encantadas, magic stones, sometimes called just *encantos*, charms; such stones are called *inkantos* by the Machiguenga and Shipibo.[1] In fact, doña María's father was a *tabaquero* who kept two magic stones, one male and one female, in a jar filled with a mixture of tobacco and water. When doña María was about eight years old, while her father still lived with the family, she saw him work with the stones twice. She could see the spirits of the stones: they both had very dark skin and long black hair. The male spirit of the stone had dark red eyes like huayruro seeds. His mouth was painted red, the color of sorcery—*magia roja*, red magic, the worst kind. He could stick his tongue out all the way to his chest, as is typical of sorcerers; his magical phlegm was filled with scorpions, snakes, and toads.

She told her father that one of the stones was good and one was evil. "Why are you practicing sorcery?" she asked. "It is just to defend myself from attacks by sorcerers," he told her; but after that he hid when he worked with the stones. The thought occurred to María to steal the magic stones, but she did not. If she had taken the stones, she told me, she could have become a gran bruja, a great sorceress; but it is better that she did not, for that is not where her heart was. Sorcerers, she said, "bring harm to people for nothing."

Indeed, the evil spirit of her father's magic stone gave her eight chances to turn toward sorcery, she said; the spirit told her that, if she did not take the opportunity he offered her, she would never have the chance again. But in fact, María said, she had numerous opportunities to turn toward sorcery—a temptation to which she claimed never to have yielded.

In the dream journey that constituted her coronación as a prayer healer, doña María dreamed that she passed by a stream in which piedritas, magical stones of all kinds, large and small, were singing to her: "Welcome, welcome, maestra, doctora." Doña María counts magic stones among her animal protectors, since the *imanes*, spirits, of the stones convert into black boas, yellow boas, condors, and macaws in order to protect her. Such stones are living beings, which are activated by tobacco smoke.[2]

A magic stone may—but need not—be striking in appearance, color, shape, or texture, which indicates that it is, in fact, encantada. The stone may be shaped like a person or animal, like a snake or a jaguar claw, or have an unusual color, or be visually attractive, or just be rare.[3] The stone may turn up in an unusual place or behave oddly; among the Aguaruna, a magic stone is often found in the stomach or crop of an animal as it is being cleaned.[4] The stone may speak to the shaman, or the spirit of the stone may appear in the shaman's dreams or in an ayahuasca vision. Cocama shaman don Juan Curico says that encantos are stones that with time have taken the shape of jungle animals or human body parts. He himself has stones in the shape of a snail, the head of an anaconda, the head of a crocodile, a human hand, and a human head.[5]

Crystals are particularly prized; they are, says one mestizo shaman, *luz solidificada*, solidified light, with a celestial origin.[6] Ordinary *piedra pedernal*, flint—"like a crystal, but black," doña María explained to me—may be a powerful magic stone, perhaps in part because it is not native to the Amazon. Such stones come from Lima, I was told; they are about three inches long. If you put the stone in a glass jar of water and then drink the water, doña María said, the stone takes away shame, sorrow, and anxiety.

The doctrine of signatures applies to stones as well as to plants. Don Francisco Montes Shuña says that a shaman can tell what stones have power, and what power they have, by looking at their shape and color. A stone of white marble can be an arcana, protection, because it purifies, cleanses, and protects the body; a red stone can nourish the blood; crystals give vision and clarity.[7] A stone in the shape of a human hand can take away pain from the body part on which it is placed.[8]

Magic stones will stick for several hours to the place on the body where sorcery has struck, suck out the harm—the dart, the insect, the scorpion, the phlegmosity—and then drop off. Stones can also be used to rub the place where the sickness is located, to loosen it before sucking.

Just as the shaman drinks the plants in order to master them, the shaman drinks the magic stones. The shaman leaves the stone in water for a day, observing la dieta, blowing tobacco smoke over it, telling the stone what the shaman wants to know, and finally drinking the water. The spirit of the stone will then appear in a dream and teach the shaman what the shaman seeks. The spirit of the stone can also be seen when drinking ayahuasca; the stones can be kept in a tobacco infusion, and the tobacco may be drunk. "It is something admirable," says don Juan Curico, "to share the wisdom of millions-year-old beings."[9]

Beliefs about magic stones are widespread in the Upper Amazon. Among the Waiwai, a magic stone, called *ñukwa*, appears in the mouth of the apprentice shaman during a dream; holding the stone in his mouth, the apprentice learns to sing the magic songs.[10] Similarly, Warao shamans acquire magic stones that descend into their mouths during dreams.[11] Among the Aguaruna, magic stones are generally used for a variety of purposes—hunting, seduction, planting, warfare. These stones have souls and can assume human form in dreams; they can drink blood, eat souls, and run away if not properly fed.[12] Rock crystals among the Desana are invested with complex cosmological and sexual symbolism. The stones are fed on tobacco and stored in water infusions of tobacco; these nicotine-rich infusions are drunk in order to communicate with the spirits of the stones.[13]

Tukano shamans have thunder stones, some used to cure sickness and some used as weapons against enemies. In particular, a translucent stone is held between thumb and forefinger, like a lens, to examine the body of a patient and determine the location of pathogenic intrusions, signaled by sudden reflections or shifts in translucency. This stone is then placed on the spot, and the intrusive object is sucked out through the stone.[14]

Yagua shamans keep two kinds of magic stones—small stones called *soul-stones* or *invisible stones*, which are kept safe in the stomach; and visible stones, which are kept in a bag hung around the neck. No shaman ever shows these visible stones, saying that they would then lose their power. Blowing tobacco smoke on these stones increases their size a hundredfold; when small, they may be used as weapons, just like darts; when enlarged with tobacco smoke, they became a barrier of protection. Shamans can also keep pieces of glass, called *transparent stones*, in their stomach, which they can regurgitate and place in the beer gourds of their victims; when swallowed, they cut up the body from the inside.[15]

The Machiguenga apprentice receives stones from an invisible celestial being who appears in the apprentice's ayahuasca vision. The stones must be fed regularly with tobacco smoke; when they are thus nourished, they turn into jaguars.[16] Machiguenga shamans acquire these stones—light-colored or transparent, especially quartz crystals—during initiation or from the shaman's father or other close relative. These stones are considered the body, or residence, or material manifestation of the spirits. The shaman carries the stones in a small bag and feeds the stones tobacco daily; if the shaman fails to do so, the spirits will leave the stones, and the shaman will die.[17] Canelos Quichua believe that the spirits in their magic stones are those of dead shamans.[18] If you gently blow on such a stone, you will see condensation appear on its surface; this shows that the stone "has breath," that it is a powerful shaman.[19]

CHAPTER 17

SHAMANIC HERBALISM

SHAMANS AND HERBALISTS

Mestizo shamanism of the Upper Amazon is closely associated with plant healing; indeed, anthropologist Françoise Barbira-Freedman speaks of *vegetalismo* as a syncretic mix of herbalism and shamanism.[1] In this regard it is different from other Amazonian traditions, where shamans and herbalists occupy separate social and cultural niches.

In some Amazonian cultures, knowledge of medicinal plants is widespread and used by everyone, not only by specialists—among the Ashéninka, for example, where herbal healing is especially the province of older women.[2] An Ashéninka shaman has no need to be a good herbalist; anthropologist Marc Lenaerts noted that one widely respected Ashéninka shaman could identify considerably fewer wild medicinal plants than the average adult. In fact, plant knowledge was deprecated. When Lenaerts commented on the effectiveness of a treatment, he was told, disdainfully, "Everybody knows that plant, even the children."[3]

Shuar shamans have traditionally not used or prescribed plant medicine; such knowledge is widely distributed, especially among women, and herbal remedies have usually been tried before consulting a shaman in any event.[4] Anthropologist Michael Harner, who worked with the Shuar in the 1950s and 1960s, is unequivocal: shamans, he says, never use herb remedies.[5] Aguaruna and Achuar shamans, too, are generally called in only when a patient has already failed to respond to herbal remedies or commercial medicines.[6]

In some cultures, herbal specialists are differentiated from other types of healers. The Cashinahua of the Purus River classify shamans into two groups—the *dauya*, the one with medicine, who kills and heals through the use of medicinal plants; and the *mukaya*, the one with bitterness, who heals and kills with the help of the *yuxin*, spirits, using a bitter substance called muka, which is the materialization of yuxin power.[7] Among the Shipibo-Conibo, the *raomi*, herbalist, usually female, who works with the plants alone, is distinguished from, and has lower status than, both the onanya and meraya, shamans who work with plant spirits in their healing.[8] Don Basilio Gordon, a Shipibo shaman, uses no physical plants in his healing practice. "If you know the icaro of a plant," he explains, "you don't need to use the plant."[9]

Similarly, among Arawak-speaking peoples in Guyana and the Venezuelan Amazon, there are several levels of shamanic specialization. At the lowest level is the *biníji*, who prepares medicines with plants and water, followed by the *makákana*, the blower who cures by blowing tobacco smoke; the *uyúkuli*, who cures by sucking; and the *sibunítei*, the one who cures by dreams and divination.[10]

Among the Desana, there are two types of traditional healer—the *yee*, jaguar-shaman, and the *kumu*, blower of spells. The yee derives his powers—including the ability to turn into a jaguar—from contact with spirits after ingesting hallucinogenic snuff, and cures by seeing the sickness inside the patient's body, blowing tobacco smoke, massage, and sucking out the pathogenic objects from the body and spitting them away. The kumu cures by the inaudible recitation of highly formalized therapeutic spells over a liquid the patient then drinks, or over a plant that is then rubbed onto the patient's sick body part. The liquid or plant gives the spell a material support and transfers it to the patient.[11] These disparate functions—preparing plant medicines, sucking out pathogenic objects, blowing tobacco smoke, singing icaros over medicines—are precisely those combined by the mestizo healer.

And in some cultures, such as the mestizo, the shaman is also the carrier of plant knowledge. Among the Piro and Conibo, knowledge of herbal medicine is part of the shamanic curriculum.[12] Tukano apprentice shamans learn to pick the medicinal and magical plants of the jungle—those that cure, attract game, kill enemies, or make women fall madly in love.[13] Baniwa shamans deal with *manhene* witchcraft—inflicted through secret poisonings—both by sucking out the poison, which then appears as monkey or sloth fur, and by recommending plant medicines, usually various types of root that counteract the gastric effects of the poison.[14] César Zevallos Chinchuya, a Campa shaman, uses herbal remedies that do not differ from those used by other adults in his area.[15] Moreover, among the Cashinahua, the distinction is not quite as simple as presented above: plants themselves are imbued with and vehicles of yuxin, spirit matter and energy, just as the shaman is filled with materialized yuxin power.[16]

Finally, the distinction between shaman and herbalist seems to be dissolving in some cultures, apparently under the influence of mestizo practices. Shuar shamans today, especially those who live near larger jungle population centers, increasingly incorporate Hispanic healing techniques from the mestizos—the use of Tarot cards for divination, cleansing with eggs and candles, and the use of herbs.[17] Indeed, the Asociación Tsunki, a shamans' organization within the Federación Shuar, has recently offered courses in Shuar and Achuar traditional medicine, open only to uwíshin, shamans, which have included training in gathering plants and preparing plant medicines.[18]

Conversely, some mestizo shamans disclaim the need to use actual plant preparations—strikingly, on a plant-by-plant basis. In some cases, but not in others, if one knows the plant's icaro, then there is no need to use the physical plant. For don Roberto, this is true for the spirit of the machimango, which is so powerful that using physical medicine made from the machimango tree may not be necessary; the machimango spirit can heal, where it is indicated, all by itself. Similarly, don Emilio Andrade Gómez states that if you have learned from ayahuma, "you do not have to go out to the forest to bring back its bark, because you already know its icaro."[19]

SINGING TO THE PLANTS

It may be worth drawing a distinction between the source of plant *knowledge* and the source of plant *healing*. Many indigenous peoples assert that their knowledge of plants and their uses comes from some other-than-human person who appears in a vision or dream.[20] These spirits may, as in the mestizo tradition, be the plants themselves, but not necessarily; when doña María was young, for example, it was the Virgin Mary, not the plant spirits, who appeared in her dreams, showed her the healing plants, and taught her the plants to heal specific diseases.

On the other hand, the source of plant *healing* may be the physical plant itself, or the physical plant as a substrate of magical power, or the spirit of the plant acting independently of the physical plant. Joel Swerdlow, a scientific journalist investigating plant medicine, tells a story that illustrates this point. In Madagascar, he met with a rural healer who supplied him with leaves of a plant said to be good for cancer. Tests by a Swiss pharmaceutical company showed the leaves in fact to have anticancer activity. He returned, but the healer, concerned, probably wisely, about potential theft of his secrets, refused to supply any more leaves. Swerdlow then himself acquired leaves from the same species of plant; yet these, when tested, were ineffective.[21]

To mestizo shamans such as doña María and don Roberto, there is nothing puzzling about this. Swerdlow *did not sing to the plants*, did not cure the medicine with the appropriate songs. Herbalists—and poisoners—do not sing; shamanic herbalists and sorcerers *sing*—charge the plants, cure them, call the spirits that invest themselves in the healing process. "What good do you think my remedies would be," says don Manuel Córdova Ríos, a mestizo shaman, "if I didn't sing to them?"[22]

The song may be—but is not necessarily—the icaro of the plants who are in the medicine. In curing a woman made pregnant by a boa, the shaman prepared the fruit of the huito, but then he sang—"singing many icaros, blowing on it, and putting in it arkanas"—calling the great serpent corimachaco, the multicolored rainbow, the precious stones, the mud of the waters, the laughing falcon, the tiger, and the spirits of the pucunucho pepper and the hairy rocoto pepper—both hot pepper plants with which to stun the boa who, with its own spirit helpers, was supporting the pregnancy.[23]

As poet César Calvo writes, the physical plants are simply "the visible portion of the healing."[24] The plants, in addition to being real medicines, contain madres or genios, the beings who teach.[25] Calvo says that the *mothers* of things "are the origin of their purpose and of their use for healing or for harming."[26] When we give the plants our love, we awaken their mothers, "so that they will augment the strength of the cure with their love."[27] A cure is not caused by the ingestion or topical application of an herbal medicine; rather, it results from the benevolent intervention of the mother through the intermediation of the plant.[28]

Both doña María and don Roberto—and most other mestizo shamans as well—have an encyclopedic knowledge of the preparation and use of healing plants, and frequently prepare and prescribe plants and plant mixtures for ingestion, baths, and sweat baths. But a plant is inefficacious by itself; it is the spirit of the plant who heals, and the spirit is summoned by its song.

Perhaps the best way to conceptualize this is that, for mestizo shamans, the physical plant is the *same as* the plant spirit. The physical plant is the part of the plant spirit that you can see clearly *all the time*; the plant spirit is the part of the plant you do not notice—you cannot *see*—until you have drunk ayahuasca.

Shamanic herbalists uniquely develop a personal relationship with the *entire* plant; the song, the whisper, the whistle, the rattling of the leaf bundle, is the manifestation of that relationship in sound, puro sonido, the language of the plants. Biomedical practitioners—or contemporary herbalists who see plants as useful collocations of molecules—lack such a relationship; and they rely for healing on the mercy of a part of the plant with whom they have no relationship at all.

CHAPTER 18
PLANT MEDICINE

PLANT KNOWLEDGE

Among ribereños in the Upper Amazon, there is a body of traditional lore regarding both the uses and the administration of a relatively large number of Amazonian medicinal plants. My jungle survival instructor, Gerineldo Moises Chavez, who made no claims at all to being a healer, knew dozens of jungle plant remedies, including insect repellants, treatments for insect bites, snakebite cures, and antiseptics.

Most ribereños know, for example, that the latex of the sangre de grado tree can be used to stanch wounds and stop bleeding, both internally and externally; that an infusion of the leaves, bark, or roots of chiricsanango can be used to treat fever; that chuchuhuasi is a male potency enhancer; that the latex of the ojé tree is an emetic; and that a drink or poultice made from *jergón sacha* can be used to treat snakebite.

Several compendia of such lore have been published, containing scores of plant descriptions, which organize plant knowledge widely distributed among ribereños.[1] While mestizo shamans claim to have learned the uses and administration of their medicinal plants from the plant spirits themselves, it is also true that their uses of the plants are, in most cases, consistent with widespread folk knowledge about the plants.

Doña María, for example, was familiar with hundreds of plants, their indication, their preparation, and their application. Walking with her in the jungle was like walking with a plant encyclopedia. She was constantly pointing to the plants by name, giving their uses and their various methods of preparation and application. This knowledge came almost entirely from her own experience—that is, she said, from what the plants themselves had taught her—and from studying with other plant healers.

Doña María was, for all practical purposes, illiterate; for example, she was unable to read a menu at a restaurant in Iquitos. I spent an afternoon with her going page by page through the 105 plants described in the text *Plantas medicinales de uso popular en la Amazonía Peruana.*[2] She could begin to sound out the popular names of plants in the text until she could match the name with the plant illustrated on the same page and then complete the name of the plant from memory. Where the name listed in the text was unfamiliar to her, she had difficulty sounding it out. But once she had identified the plant, primarily from the illustration, she would give me a lengthy discourse on its qualities, preparation, and medicinal uses.

There were two striking features of this exercise. First, doña María knew every plant in the book. Second, the descriptions she gave of the medicinal uses of the plant largely matched the descriptions given in the book, which she could not read. Despite the visionary sources of her knowledge, her use of plant medicines was generally consistent with popular plant medicine as practiced throughout the mestizo community.

In keeping with her self-perception as openhanded with her knowledge, doña María was a vociferous proselytizer for the traditional uses of medicinal plants. In July 1997, for example, María was invited to speak at a forum on the sexual and reproductive rights of women under the auspices of the Red Nacional de Promoción de la Mujer, the National Network for the Advancement of Women, held at the Universidad Nacional Amazonía Peruana in Iquitos, to address the birthing and care of children. She was one of six women invited to speak to an audience consisting mostly of young mothers.

María had worked not only as a healer but also as a *comadrona*, midwife, and she demonstrated basic natal care, including how to bathe a baby properly, and, of course, the use of plant medicines—in particular, *cordoncillo*, shoestring pepper, traditionally used as a tea and as a vaginal wash after birth, in order to flush out excess blood.

In November 1991, having heard about it from a friend, doña María signed up for a course offered by the Associación de Médicos de Naturismo Práctico Tradicional de Loreto, intended to be a *curso de actualización y nivelación de médicina tradicional*, a refresher and overview of traditional medicine. María took the course in order to gain credentials for her healing and in the hope that she would learn new things helpful to her work. "This is what I do," she said, "and I wanted to learn more." The course was free, met twice a week for two hours in the evening, and lasted for two years, until October 1993.

The course, it turned out, was significantly below María's level of knowledge. Other students, she said, would sit quietly and listen; but she—and this is eminently in line with her personality—would actively tell what she knew about plant use and preparation, staying on in the course in order to help the other students. The teachers actively encouraged her participation, she said, telling her that she should be teaching the course because of her knowledge of traditional medicine.

The key to healing with plants, according to doña María, is not only to know which plant can heal which conditions but also to understand the proper way to prepare the plants for use. After a month of trying to teach me plant identification, giving me the names and uses of more plants than I could possibly remember, she said to me, "We have all these plants here, cures for all sorts of diseases; now that you have learned about them, you must learn how to prepare them." And what I needed to learn I would learn, over time, from the plants themselves.

DIAGNOSIS

Mestizo shamans deploy a number of diagnostic tools to detect the presence and location of darts and other pathogenic objects in the bodies of their patients. One method of diagnosis is by touch. The place where the sickness is lodged may be warm or cold to the touch; rheumatism feels cold, for example, and an inflammation feels hot. The place may also be indicated by its *pulsario* or pálpito, a pulsation or throbbing, which indicates to the touch the presence of a magical dart. Pablo Amaringo says that shamans invoke the electric eel because its electromagnetic waves sensitize them to perceive pulsations in their patients.[3] Don Sergio Freitas says that he is able to identify a sickness by the smell of the patient.[4] Piedras encantadas, magic stones, are believed to stick to the place on the body where the dart is lodged for several hours, suck out the sickness, and then drop off.

In addition, doctor ayahuasca reveals where the sickness is located. Don Agustin Rivas says that the shaman who has drunk ayahuasca can see into the skeleton, brain, organs, or intestines of the patient; sometimes the shaman may see something white in the bones and knows that something is wrong.[5] For example, "I looked into Benjamin's head, and saw his brain like a light, very clearly. Sitting in his brain was a little green leaf. The borders of the leaf were serrated and looked like they had been cut."[6] When shamans touch a patient, Pablo Amaringo says, their brains immediately give a picture of what might be wrong.[7]

The Shuar, the Achuar, and the Aguaruna all say that the shaman can visually penetrate the body of the patient—that ayahuasca makes the body transparent, so that the shaman can see the darts shot into it as glowing dots of varying color and luminosity.[8] Piro shamans drink ayahuasca in order to see the sorcery objects glowing within "the ordinary opacity of the human body."[9] A Shapra shaman once told me that ayahuasca was a spiritual x-ray machine with which he could see the location of the magic darts inside a patient. Canelos Quichua shamans see the intrusive object—a spider, darts, a cutting or stinging creature—encased in blue mucus within the body.[10] Some shamans maintain that they can distinguish different types of sorcery by observing the aura around the patient; zigzagging lights indicate an attack by a chontero; small waves crossed by dark lines indicate that the patient has been hit by a *huaní*, a crystal arrow shot from a steel bow.[11] A Tukano shaman describes what he sees: "We, too, can see the splinters and stones. . . . These splinters have different colors: white, red, and whitish. . . . The splinters make us feel sharp pains. There are other, similar splinters. On another splinter there is a bushel of hair, like a sprout. On the other side it is yellow and yellowish. This splinter, too, causes fever and vomiting." And he adds: "White people do not know anything about all this."[12]

In addition, the location and nature of the sickness may be pointed out by the attending spirits, the maestros de la medicina, the doctores, the extraterrestrial doctors from distant planets or galaxies, the plant spirits, the souls of ancient and powerful shamans, doctors from England or Japan, who communicate mentally or speak clearly into the ear of the shaman. They appear to don Rómulo Magin as Peruvian military officers; they appear to don Roberto as dark-skinned, almost naked, wearing only short skirts; they appear to painter Elvis Luna as brilliant celestial beings like angels.

These spirits speak in many languages. Sometimes they speak in castellano, Spanish, sometimes in idioma, tribal languages. Thus, doña María's spirits speak to her in a language she calls Inca—that is, Quechua—which is perfectly comprehensible to her, although she herself speaks no Quechua. Don Roberto is attended by outer space spirits who speak in computer language.

The spirits may communicate mentally, or they may use clearly audible speech to diagnose and prescribe: they speak directly into the shaman's ear, telling what is wrong, what icaros to sing, where to suck out the sickness or malignant darts, whether to use a sweat bath, what plants to prepare. Don Roberto hears this as a voice speaking clearly and distinctly in his ear. "Suck in this place," he told me the voice tells him. "Blow mapacho smoke in that place. Use this icaro." He spoke this directly into my ear, with startling clarity.

Finally, a shaman has many independent sources of information—questioning the patient, talking to the family of the patient, overhearing the conversations of patients and families as they wait for the healing session to begin. The shaman, too, may be a member of the community to which the patient belongs, and may well have access to current news, rumors, and gossip about the patient and about the patient's family, affairs, business, and enemies.

We can distinguish between general and specific diagnoses. A shaman may be able to diagnose a magical attack by a sorcerer; it is, as a general rule, up to the patient—perhaps with some prompting—to discover *why* the attack was made. This can require a patient to make a searching inventory of moral failure, breaches of trust, lack of generosity, or failures of reciprocity, and may require that the patient allow the ayahuasca to reveal, in a vision, the face of the sorcerer, the business rival, or the seducer of a beloved. Sometimes the shaman will have a vision or a dream of the evildoer; but, of course, as don Roberto once reminded me, such a vision is useless if the shaman does not know the identity of the person seen, which then has to be supplied by the patient in any case. Sometimes the shaman asks the spirit of ayahuasca to convey to the patient a specific vision of who caused the illness; in such cases, the patient is convinced of the diagnosis not only by what the shaman says but also because the patient has personally seen the face of the one who cast the spell.[13]

ORDINARY HEALING

A significant percentage of a mestizo shaman's practice is not in ayahuasca ceremonies, and does not involve either the shaman or patient drinking ayahuasca at all. Much of what the shaman does I have come to think of as *ten-minute healings*, in which the shaman sucks the sickness from the patient's body, seals and protects the body with shacapa and tobacco smoke, and then prescribes plant medicine for recovery from the continuing effects of the physical intrusion. This is the bread-and-butter work of the shaman, just as in the clinic of any general practitioner.

The Shaman's Tools

In the Upper Amazon, there are a number of medical specialists who are not shamans—for example, *parteras*, midwives; *hueseros*, bonesetters; oracionistas, prayer healers; *espiritistas*, spiritists; and *vaporadoras*, givers of steam baths. They differ from shamans in that they have not been taught by ayahuasca. Unlike shamans, they have not undergone la dieta; they have not established relationships of intimacy with the healing and protective spirits of plants and animals. They have not nurtured their protective phlegm; they do not possess magical darts. Moreover, their healing does not use three distinctively shamanic healing tools—shacapar, rattling with the leaf-bundle rattle; chupar, sucking out pathogenic objects; and soplar, blowing tobacco smoke.

Doña María began her healing career as an oracionista, a prayer healer, strongly influenced by the folk Catholicism and traditional Hispanic medicine of Amazonian Peru, as well as by her own idiosyncratic dreams and visions. She was also influenced by mestizo shamanism. Even as a child, she used the term *icaro* to refer to the oraciones, the prayer songs, she made up and sang while walking to and from school, and later sang for her patients.

She healed by singing these prayers and laying her hands on the heads of her patients. She protected herself with strong sweet smells, drinking the commercial cologne agua de florida, the commercial mouthwash Timolina, and camphor dissolved in aguardiente, sometimes adding camalonga, the seeds of the yellow oleander. These increased the fuerza, power, of her healing, she said, and made her prayers *muy poderosa*, full of divine power.

She used tobacco—her father had been a tabaquero—to induce and augment her visions. She swallowed the smoke of finos, commercial cigarettes, deep into her stomach; she drank a cold-water infusion of tobacco, letting it steep, squeezing out the water through a cloth, and drinking it, with the appropriate prayer. In fact, to prepare herself for her first drink of ayahuasca with don Roberto, she first drank a mixture of tobacco, camphor, camalonga seeds, and agua de florida cologne.

Once she had become his apprentice, don Roberto taught doña María to drink ayahuasca, and how to undertake the restricted diet in the monte, the jungle wilderness. Where she had previously worked with *plantas*, plants, of which the leaves are primarily used in medicine, he taught her *palos* as well, hardwood trees, of which primarily the roots, bark, or resin is used. And don Roberto taught her about transcorporación, and she learned how to call into her body the spirit of Oscar Rosindo Pisarro, a deceased Rosicrucian, to come help her in her healing and work through her.

Probably most important, in addition to drinking ayahuasca, doña María acquired during her training with don Roberto the foundational triad of mestizo shamanism—shacapar, using the leaf-bundle rattle; soplar, blowing tobacco smoke over and into the patient's body; and chupar, sucking. Although she had smoked finos, commercial cigarettes, this had been to induce visions, not to blow over patients. Don Roberto had introduced her to mapacho; and, as doña María told me, "Without mapacho, there is no soplando." And she learned to rattle, rather than lay her hands on top of her patient's head, as she had before in her prayer work. María loved using the shacapa. "The shacapa," she used to say, "is my pistol."

And she learned to suck. While María's prayer healing practice had not included chupando, sucking, it was later analogized to the cognate practice of jalando, pulling or drawing with her mouth from a distance, just as her laying on of hands was analogized to the use of the shacapa. Indeed, María never took up chupando, the sort of full-contact vigorous, noisy, dramatic sucking used by don Roberto, but, rather, used the more sedate and ladylike jalando throughout her later career.

Ten-Minute Healings

The key features of the ten-minute healing are the shaman's tools—shacapar, rattling with the shacapa leaf-bundle rattle; soplar, blowing tobacco smoke; and chupar, sucking out the sickness—along with the singing of the appropriate icaro. Don Agustin Rivas says about this ten-minute healing: "I was grateful that I had learned how to heal with tobacco, instead of healing like the brujos who have to do such a long ritual for healing that a patient can die before they're finished."[14] Sometimes a brief healing will end with a recommendation that the patient come to don Roberto's house on a Tuesday or Friday night to drink ayahuasca.

Here is an example of a ten-minute healing, from a patient's perspective. Once, I asked don Roberto to work on my left knee, where I had a replacement anterior cruciate ligament, and which sometimes ached in the jungle humidity. I sat in a chair, and don Roberto, with doña María present, blew tobacco smoke from a mapacho cigarette all over my body and into the top of my head, with that untranscribable whispery sound, *pshooo*. He began to rattle his shacapa, along with a soft tuneless whistle, which gradually grew into a whispered song and then an icaro, all the while rhythmically shaking the shacapa over my body; he burped and belched, drawing up his mariri. Then he knelt next to me and began to suck the side of my knee—and I mean *really* suck, with the skin drawn into his mouth, with great suction, bordering on the painful. Clearly, whatever pathogen was in my knee was not repulsive; there was no dramatic gagging and spitting, as in his ayahuasca ceremonies. He would release his mouth, take a breath, blow more smoke, and suck again. This went on for several minutes. Finally, he blew tobacco smoke one last time on my knee, blew smoke all over my body and into the top of my head, and shook the shacapa all over my body, singing his icaro. Then we were done.

Doña María then applied her own mixture of grasa de búfalo to my knee.

I asked her what plant spirits had attended the healing and what they had looked like. She appeared genuinely surprised: "Didn't you see them?"

This is why, by the way, neither don Roberto nor doña María can predict how they would treat a particular sickness in the future, or provide correlations between diagnoses and treatments. They do not know what the plant spirits will direct in any particular case in the future; but they can discuss which plants can be generally used for particular conditions, and they can say what they have been led to do for particular conditions in the past.

CLEANSING

Doña María's healing practice incorporated both inner and outer cleansing. Inner cleansing, of course, is la purga, vomiting and purgation. Outer cleansing included her baño de flores, flower bath, which she often called simply limpia, cleansing; the *sahumerio*, sweat bath; and, less frequently, what she called *sahumerio boliviano*, the Bolivian sweat bath, smudging a patient with dried herbs or aromatic woods such as *palosanto*. *Cuerpo limpio, espiritu tranquillo*, she would tell me: *Clean body, peaceful spirit.*

Flower Bath

The limpia, cleansing bath, or baño de flores, flower bath, has many functions among Amazonian mestizos. Sick or feverish children are frequently bathed with water containing flowers or herbs. A persistent run of bad luck and misfortune—called *saladera*—is invariably caused by sorcery, which is believed to manifest as salt on the skin;[15] sorcery is sometimes just called *sal*, salt.[16] Saladera is treated with a cleansing flower bath, which washes away the sorcery, rather than by sucking out a pathogenic object. A flower bath, using strongly scented herbs, flowers, and commercially prepared perfumes, imparts the sort of strong sweet smell that can help protect against sorcery. And flower baths may be used to bring good luck in love, when given in conjunction with a huarmi icaro, woman icaro.[17]

Doña María's cleansing practices were interconnected; when a patient could not purge enough to satisfy her by drinking ayahuasca, she would "unblock" the patient with a flower bath. She would first give the patient the leaves and fruits of the achiote, annatto, itself popularly used as an emetic, grating the leaves and fruits together, filtering out the seeds and pulp by squeezing through a cloth, and mixing with water, which the patient would drink. The bath was then her regular cleansing baño de flores, but with a special icaro. In fact, doña María's limpia was most often the same, although additional plants might occasionally be added; what varied was the icaro that she sang while pouring the water. Some of her most beautiful songs were sung over her flower baths.

Sweat Bath

The sahumerio, steam bath, is also used for removing sorcery from the skin and, by its penetrating qualities, may drive out invasive pathogenic objects as well. The steam bath is applied by having the patient sit in a chair, naked,

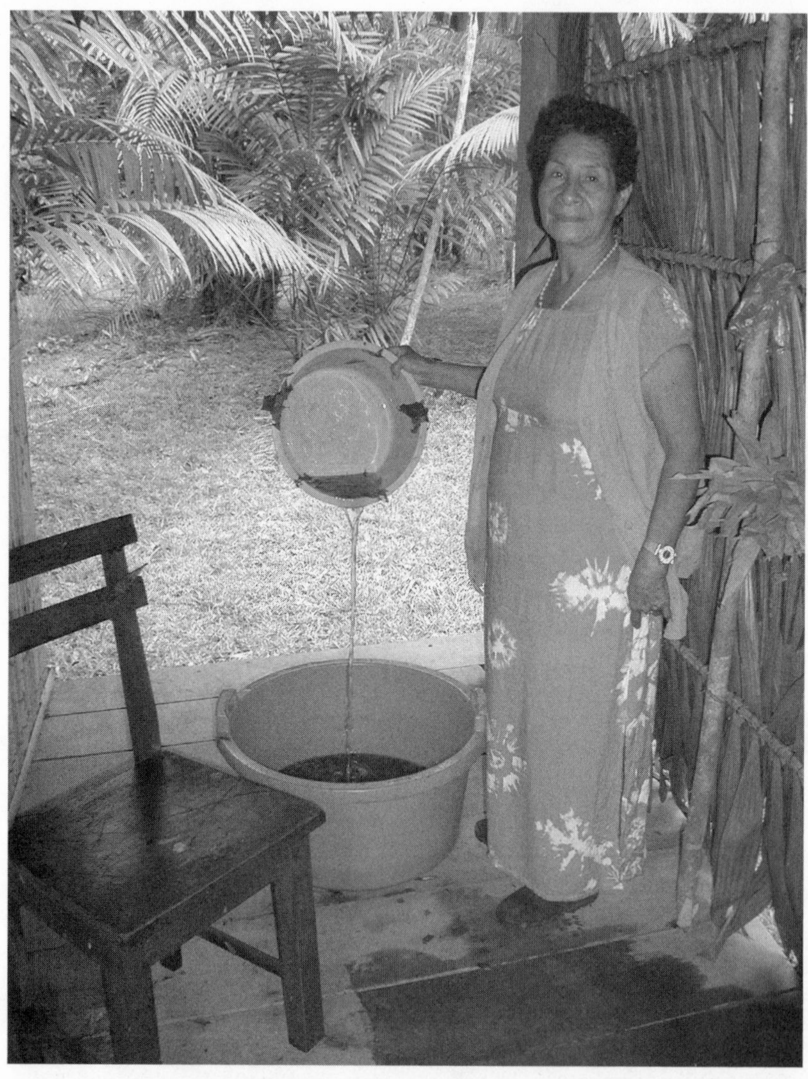

FIGURE 7. Doña María with her healing and cleansing bath.

wrapped in a blanket or poncho. Water with plants in it is heated almost to a boil, the bucket of steaming hot water is placed beneath the chair and inside the hanging blanket or poncho, and the steam is allowed to rise. Steam can also be applied to the face and head the same way, with a towel or cloth draped around the head, while the patient bends over a basin of steaming water.

Among indigenous peoples of the Upper Amazon—Shipibo, Anáshinka, Machiguenga—a practitioner called a vaporadora, almost always a woman, makes use of a similar sort of herbal steam bath.[18] Vaporadoras are not shamans but are rather like parteras, midwives, or hueseros, bonesetters—medical specialists who do not use sucking and blowing tobacco smoke in their practice.

This steam therapy is practiced by putting red-hot rocks or axe heads into a pot with water and herbs and then having the patient squat over the pot wearing a cushma, which keeps the steam inside, like a tent. Afterward, the vaporadora throws away the water, examines the herbs remaining in the pot, and often finds some pathogenic object—a nail, a thorn, a piece of bone or charcoal—that was expelled from the patient.[19] "With my medicine I soothe the patients," says Susana Avenchani Faman, a vaporadora. "Through the spirit of the leaves that are boiled for steam, the patient will be calmed."[20]

Doña María was something of a specialist in steam baths. The plants she used were almost always *plantas brujas*, sorcerer plants, dark in color. Doña María frequently called these plants morado, literally "purple" but generally meaning dark—dark-skinned people in the Amazon are morado—although some of these plants are, in fact, purplish in color. These sorcerer plants she frequently paired with another plant she called *verde*, literally "green" but here meaning generally lighter in color—for example, the plant called, variously, *piñon negro*, *piñon rojo*, and piñon colorado, dark piñon, as opposed to *piñon blanco*, light piñon, which she called *piñon morado* and *piñon verde*, respectively. Similarly, patiquina plants have a wide variety of leaf colors and patterns—which makes them popular houseplants in North America—and these too doña María generally grouped into *morada* and verde varieties. The dark plants are among those used by sorcerers to inflict harm and are, therefore, most powerful for healing and protection.

Doña María's antisorcery sweat bath contained the sorcery plants and catahua. Don Artidoro Aro Cardenas, a perfumero, a specialist in strong sweet odors, says that, during a sweat bath with piñon colorado, "you can actually see the phlegm, which is the bad magic, appear on the patient's skin as it comes out of the body."[21] It is also possible to buy prepackaged *sahumeria* bundles at the herb market in Belén in Iquitos.

Sometimes the expulsion of a pathogenic object during a sweat bath can be quite dramatic. Doña María told me how, after she had studied with don Roberto for about six months, she had treated a very sick woman, very thin and pale, very debilitated. When doña María looked at the woman, she heard a voice speak clearly in her ear: "This woman has an animal in her womb, because of sorcery."

Now, a woman having an animal in her womb is not that unusual a diagnosis among mestizos. Pablo Amaringo tells of a woman who had the larva of a boa implanted in her womb.[22] Anthropologist Jean-Pierre Chaumeil kept a calendar of the healing activity of Yagua shaman José Murayari for two months, during which time the shaman healed two cases of animals in the womb, both involving mestizo women.[23] Doña María asked the woman how long she had been sick; three months, the woman replied. "We have to take this animal out of your womb as soon as possible," María told her, "because it comes from sorcery."

What the plant spirits reveal is not only a diagnosis but, perhaps even more important, an *etiology*. In this case, the woman's husband had been having an affair with another woman, had left his wife for his mistress, and wanted nothing more to do with his wife or their children—not an uncommon story, even outside the Amazon. Still, in this case the mistress was using sorcery to get rid of her rival. What the woman needed, the spirits told María, speaking clearly in her ear, was an arcana, protection, from the sorcery of her husband's mistress, and they told her what plants she should use to heal the woman and what icaros she should sing. So María prepared a sahumeria, sweat bath, for the woman, containing green and purple patiquina to fight the sorcery, and other powerful plants to drive out the animal—catahua, a laxative; *guaba*, a diuretic; *ají*, hot chili pepper; and the commercial disinfectant Creolina.

While the plants and water came to a boil, doña María prayed, and she blew tobacco smoke into the woman, for protection, through the crown of her head. She had the woman strip, except for a skirt around her waist, and squat over the steam, with her legs open as if having a baby, just for a few minutes, because the woman was so weak. Doña María began to sing an icaro, and the sorcery left the woman's womb through her vagina, like a *cohete*, a rocket—*whoosh! pung!* said doña María, illustrating. The sorcery looked like a white rabbit—a flash of something like cotton and then a gush of blood. "What? What?" the woman cried out, and then they began to pray together, thanking God for the healing, while blood rushed from the woman's vagina.

Doña María blew more tobacco smoke into the woman's body, sealed her hands and forehead with drops of camalonga, and made the woman a hot drink of oregano and arnica, to seal her womb. Six days later the woman returned; although the woman had no money, doña María continued to treat her. "Don't think bad thoughts about your husband and his girlfriend," María told the woman. "They will get paid back for what they did." And María allowed the woman to pay her with her prayers. A year and a half later, the woman came to María with some money, but María refused to accept it, telling the woman to use the money to take care of her children.

POULTICES

Among doña María's plant healing practices was the application of poultices; the word she used was *patarashca*, which is also the word used for a serving of fish that has been wrapped in one of the large leaves of the *bijao* palm and barbecued on a grill.[24] Doña María's patarashca generally consisted of the chopped up leaves or stems of plantas brujas, sorcerer plants, wrapped in a leaf; the patient puts the poultice on the place where the pathogenic object is located, leaves it on overnight, and then burns it in a fire the next day. This weakens the sorcery. The used poultice is not to be thrown away; it has pulled out the sorcery and is now dangerous to handle. Among the plants doña María uses in her poultices are mapacho, patiquina, toé, catahua, and ají.

Poultices are also used for the healing of snakebite. Mestizos and indigenous peoples in the Upper Amazon use a wide variety of plants for this purpose: ethnobotanists James Duke and Rodolfo Vasquez list twelve genera used to treat snakebite; Richard Evans Schultes and Robert Raffauf list twenty-nine. Shamans all have their own songs to drive out venom and heal snakebite, usually called, generically, *icaro de víbora*, pit viper song. Don Roberto has his own snakebite icaros; he applies a patarashca made of a banana leaf, wrapped around the site of envenomation, and filled with the finely chopped tuber of jergón sacha, changed every few hours. He also uses *ishanga blanca*, white nettle, and *cocona*, as well as chewed leaves of mapacho applied directly to the wound. The patient may be given a cold-water infusion of jergón sacha to drink or cocona fruit boiled with sugar.

DOÑA MARÍA'S LOVE MEDICINE

Doña María was known particularly for her pusanguería, love medicine, her ability to make pusangas, love spells and potions. Pusanguería is widely distributed in the Upper Amazon. A love potion is called *puságki* among the Aguaruna, *pusanga* among the Campa, and *posanga* among the Machiguenga;[25]

Snakebite

There are two families of venomous snakes in the Upper Amazon—the Crotalidae or pit vipers and the Elapidae or coral snakes. The Crotalidae are called pit vipers because they have a pit or depression between the eye and the nostril on each side of the head, which functions as an extremely sensitive infrared heat-detecting organ. In the United States, there are three genera of the Crotalidae family—the copperhead, the cottonmouth or water moccasin, and fifteen species of rattlesnake.[1]

In the Amazon, the medically important coral snakes consist of fifty-three species in the genus *Micruris*. Like the northern species, they have various combinations of black and brightly colored rings. They are secretive and rarely encountered; envenomation by these snakes appears to be rare.[2] In the whole of Brazil, only 0.65 percent of all snakebites reported from 2001 to 2004 were attributed to coral snakes, and, in those 486 cases, there were no fatalities.[3]

The snakes of most medical concern are therefore the thirty-one species of pit viper somewhat indiscriminately referred to by the name *fer-de-lance* or *lance head*, all in the genus *Bothrops* and all very similar looking, with long bodies and large triangular heads. The lance heads live in the lowland jungle and average four to six feet in length, although they may grow as long as eight feet. They are generally tan with dark brown diamond-like markings along their sides and are very well camouflaged. Amazonian pit vipers—as opposed to the colorful coral snakes—have clearly chosen crypsis over warning; it is easy to pass very close to a fer-de-lance without noticing it.[4] Species of *Bothrops* account for 90 percent of the snakebites in South America.[5]

Mestizos in the Upper Amazon generally refer to the various *Bothrops* species as *víbora*, the usual Spanish term for a pit viper, or as *jergón*. The Spanish term *cascabel*, rattler, usually refers to the genus *Crotalus*, which is not found in neotropical environments but, rather, in dry habitats such as the savannas in Guyana.[6] In the Upper Amazon, the term *cascabel* refers instead to juveniles of the genus *Bothrops*, probably because the young have yellow tails.[7]

The Amazonian bushmaster or *Lachesis muta*—the Latin name means *silent fate*—is the largest pit viper in the world, reaching lengths up to twelve feet. Usually called by the Quechua term *shushupi*, the bushmaster is found in the lowland rain forest throughout the Amazon. It is generally a coppery tan with dark brown diamond-shaped marks on its back, rather than on its side. It is active at twilight and night and coils up in the buttresses of large trees or under roots and logs. After having fed, a bushmaster will remain in place until it has digested its prey, a period of two to four weeks.

Because of its length, a bushmaster can strike over a long distance; because of its large fangs, it can deliver a large dose of venom—probably the largest venom dose of any pit viper. However, bushmasters are very reclusive and therefore rarely encountered; many experienced tropical herpetologists have yet to see their first wild specimen. As a result, few envenomations actually occur, although the fatality rate is reportedly high.[8] I have been unable to find information about the age, physical condition, or treatment of reported fatalities.

Pit viper venom is a complex mixture of enzymes, which varies from species to species and which is designed to immobilize, kill, and digest the snake's prey.[9] The venom works by destroying tissue, and is capable of causing significant, sometimes disfiguring local tissue damage; but deaths—at least in the United States, where records are available—are very rare and limited almost entirely to children and the elderly.

Indeed, many pit viper strikes are dry and inject no venom, even when there are fang marks; and the amount of venom discharged can vary from little or none to almost the entire contents of the glands. Additionally, Crotalids can differ significantly in the toxicity of their venom, even within a single litter. With that said, pit viper envenomation can be excruciatingly painful—one expert has said that on a pain scale of 1 to 10, rattlesnake bites are an 11—and the discomfort can last for several days. The envenomated extremity can also become frighteningly ugly, leading to panic in both the patient and the caregiver. Greater or smaller areas of the extremity can turn blue or black, swell alarmingly, and develop large blood blisters. It is altogether an unpleasant experience.

However, most cases result in several days of serious misery and then recovery. More rarely, skin grafts may be necessary.[10] The fatality rate even for untreated pit viper bites is low, and the reported rate of permanent local injury is less than 10 percent.[11] In most cases, swelling and reduced function, even without antivenin, last for two or three weeks.[12]

It is hard to judge the effectiveness of any of the remedies used for snakebite in the Upper Amazon. There are few records; there is little long-term follow-up; Crotalid envenomation is frequently self-limiting. Moreover, a pit viper strike can create both a puncture wound and severely compromised tissue; therefore, in the jungle environment, sepsis must be a frequent complication. There is evidence that a number of plants traditionally used to treat snakebite—especially those in the family Urticaceae, such as ishanga blanca—have anti-inflammatory, immunomodulatory, and therefore potentially antivenom activity, which remains to be investigated.[13]

NOTES

1. Sullivan, Wingert, & Norris, 1995, pp. 681–683, 704–705.
2. Fan & Cardoso, 1995, p. 668; Minton & Norris, 1995, p. 713.
3. Manock, Suarez, Graham, Avila-Aguero, & Warrell, 2008, p. 1128.
4. Kricher, 1997, pp. 315–316; Minton & Norris, 1995, pp. 714–715.
5. Fan & Cardoso, 1995, p. 668.
6. Iwokrama International Centre for Rain Forest Conservation and Development, n.d.
7. Armed Forces Pest Management Board, 2008; Russell, n.d.
8. Fan & Cardoso, 1995, p. 679; Kricher, 1997, p. 317; Minton & Norris, 1995, p. 715.
9. Sullivan et al., 1995, p. 685.
10. Dart & Gold, 2004; Fan & Cardoso, 1995, pp. 673–674; Minton & Norris, 1995, pp. 718–719.
11. Gomez & Dart, 1995, p. 642; Sullivan et al., 1995, p. 702.
12. Dart & Gold, 2004, p. 1562.
13. Badilla, Chaves, Mora, & Poveda, 2006.

a Machiguenga song says, in part, "My brother is going to smear her with a posanga, and she is going to cry, my sister-in-law."[26] In Guyana and the Venezuelan Amazon, plant remedies called *pusanas* are used to gain sympathy or love or to gain success in hunting or fishing.[27] The Baniwa of Brazil use the term *pusanga* to refer to a charm made from a thin, crawling vine called *munutchi* that produces a powerful perfume. Girls use the leaf of this vine to cause boys to have terrible headaches.[28]

Just as there is folk medicine and folk sorcery, there are traditional pusangas, and doña María knew a tremendous number of these. Some are relatively straightforward. If you take a woman's vaginal secretions from her clitoris, she said, and rub it on your upper arm, you will become attractive to women. Similarly, if you take the vulva of a *bufeo colorado*, pink dolphin—creatures who transform themselves into irresistibly seductive human figures—and tie it around your upper arm, you will be attractive to women, especially if you can manage to have the charm touch the woman.

Another pusanga trick uses the leg bone of the *tanrrilla* bird, the sunbittern; these wading birds have long thin hollow leg bones, which are used, also, as the stem of the wooden *cachimbo*, pipe, in which one smokes mapacho or other psychoactive plants, such as the leaves of the toé plant or the bark of the ayahuasca vine. Apparently the use of the sunbittern in love magic is related to the fact that the bird achieves a spectacular erection.[29] If, when you shoot the bird, it falls on its back, the leg bone is no good; but the leg bone may be used if the bird falls on its chest. Remove the left leg bone, doña María instructed me, and bury the bird in the sand, mouth up. Then take the hollow leg bone and look through it *three times* at the person whose attentions you wish to attract—like looking through a telescope. For example, she said, if a woman you want is walking while you are looking at her, she will start to look around for you; by the time you have looked at her three times, she will be in love with you. But if you change your mind later, doña María warned, and no longer want her, that is too bad; she will continue to pursue you.

However, the most potent form of love magic, predictably, involves the use of plants. For example, plants that cling, such as lianas and vines, are often used for love medicine, especially the *renaco*, strangler fig, which clings to its support tree like a devoted lover. *Amor seco* has small prickly leaves that cling to the clothing or skin of passersby, and is similarly considered useful in love medicine. The plant called *sacha corazón* has heart-shaped leaves and clings to the trunks of trees; it is thus used not only in love medicine but also in the treatment of diseases related to the heart and blood.

The *buceta* plant, as do many plants in the Amazon, comes in two forms—

hembra, female, and *macho*, male. The female plant has two leaves on each stalk, the smaller of which clings to the underside of the larger and looks very much like a vagina—clearly a pusanga signature; in fact, the word *buceta* means vagina in slang Brazilian Portuguese.[30] Doña María made a buceta potion, which is to be applied to the inside of the vagina; the potion causes such intense pleasure for the male partner, she told me, that he will never leave his lover. She noted that her buceta potion was popular among prostitutes.

The use of such pusangas is very widespread; both men and women may be *pusangueado*, ensorcelled by love magic.[31] Peruvian newspapers carry classified advertisements for ready-made pusangas "to conquer, control, and attract your impossible or resisting lover." It is now, of course, possible to buy pusangas for all purposes on the Internet. In a plot worthy of O. Henry, anthropologist Marie Perruchon tells how she and her Shuar husband once turned out to have placed love spells on each other.[32]

It is important to note that pusangería includes not only sexual magic but the enhancement of personal attractiveness for the purposes of business as well. The *shimipampana*, arrowroot plant, has a root that is considered to look like a fist and therefore is used as a pusanga to tame a *mujer mala* or *mujer celosa*, an ill-tempered or jealous woman. The root is crushed, doña María told me, and put into the woman's *café con leche*. In addition, the root can be rubbed between the hands, and the resulting liquid is mixed into a lotion that, when applied to the face, will guarantee success in business negotiations or bring justice in court. Perfumero Javier Arévalo similarly recommends a pusanga of *alacransillo*, heliotrope, for good fortune in legal affairs:[33] the plant's small lavender flowers are curved in a way that resembles the stinging tail of the *alacrán*, scorpion.

Most important, doña María made a mixture of dried and powdered plants she called *diez podéres*, ten powers, because it contained ten plants, some of which have been difficult to identify, although doña María gave me a sufficient supply of the finished product to meet my personal needs for the foreseeable future. In fact, over several conversations, doña María named more than ten plants as ingredients of her pusanga. This may be because from time to time she conflated several different recipes, or because some of the plant names she used were in fact synonymous. The pusanga powder is used by dissolving it in cologne or aguardiente, distilled cane liquor, and applying it like perfume. Most commonly used among the colognes, of course, is agua de florida; but, when making a romantic pusanga powder for a woman, perfumero Javier Arévalo suggests instead the use of the fragrance Tabu.[34]

One who wears this pusanga becomes irresistible in matters of both love and business. The ingredients include renaco, strangler fig: cariñito, little love; *mashushingo*; shimipampana, arrowroot; *motelillo*; amor seco, dry love; *pinshacallo*, toucan's tongue; *lengua de perro*, dog's tongue; and *sangapilla*. There are a number of variations of this recipe; but the key ingredients are the renaco, strangler fig; lengua de perro, dog's tongue; and cariñito, little love plant.

When making this pusanga, doña María would stay in the monte, the highland jungle, for four days, smoking mapacho, singing the icaros of the plants to be used, and observing la dieta, the diet, especially avoiding salt and sugar. On the first day, she would rise early, go into the jungle, and spend the day gathering the necessary plants. She would spend the remaining days preparing the pusanga—cutting up and drying the plants, grinding them, and finally sifting them through a new clean cloth to make a fine powder. All this time she would sing the icaros of the plants, and especially the song of a spirit named Mayita, who is the genio, spirit, of the pusanga.

Mayita is an elegant beautiful woman, a *perfumera* and *hechicera* and *pusanguera*—a caster of spells who creates love potions through the use of perfumes. When doña María sings her icaro, Mayita comes and dances before her, wearing necklaces of plants, accompanied by many other women. Doña María especially can smell Mayita's very fragrant perfume; it is this perfume that enters into the pusanga and gives it power. Other spirits may come as well—the yacurunas, the water people, and the sirenas, mermaids, the sexually seductive dwellers beneath the water.

Sometimes the pusanga is, in effect, a special-purpose commission: a man or woman has come to her with a specific love object in mind. In such a case, while doña María sings, she calls the names of the man and woman for whom the pusanga is intended, bringing together their spirits under a yarina, ivory palm, whose leaves are used to thatch houses and which therefore symbolizes marriage. "Under the renaco tree," she sings, "I will put you with this spell," so that nothing will ever separate them. Their spirits are como un viento, like a wind; they leave and enter through their coronas, the crown of their heads; when the soul has left the body, she says, it is haire, air. She brings the souls of the man and woman together; where a man has left his wife for another, for example, he will begin to dream of his wife and feel sad for having left her. Such a pusanga can take as long as fifteen days to create, or even longer, singing the icaro of Mayita every Tuesday and Friday, during the regular ayahuasca healing ceremony, for three months, whereupon the straying husband will have returned.

Don Emilio Andrade similarly whistles the *icaro de la piedra*, song of the stone, which calls the souls of the man and woman along with a spinning black stone. He attaches the souls to the rotating stone; the woman feels dizzy and afraid, and she clings to the man at her side, loving him forever. Or he uses the *icaro de la arañita*, song of the little spider, calling a spider to weave a web around the souls of a man and woman. The sleeping woman dreams of the man and, upon waking, thinks of him and tries to contact him.[35] Don José Curitima Sangama, a Cocama shaman, not only calls the soul of the beloved with song but also places a doll on the altar and perfumes it with sweet plants, the fragrant palm sangapilla, the orchid named *huacanqui*, which in Quechua means *You will cry*. "And if the girl doesn't love you," he says, "the black boa lends us its colors, and we adorn the face of the doll with the colors of the black boa. We also lend the doll its tongue. These are the secrets of love magic."[36]

Doña María sees her use of pusanguería as consistent with her practice of pura blancura, the pure white path. She will not, she says, supply a pusanga to a married person in order to have an extramarital affair; that is, she says, against the laws of God. Perfumero don Artiduro Aro Cardenas takes a similar position regarding his use of pusangas. "Supposing the man has gone off and left his family," he says. "I pull him back so he returns to his home so the family can consolidate again. In a short time he will be thinking of his children and his wife, and he comes back. . . . I call his spirit back to his family home. I blow smoke to reunite them."[37]

Doña María has rebuked her colleagues who use their pusanguería to get sex, especially from *turistas gringas*. One such shaman was a young man, whom I knew, who had a thriving urban practice in Iquitos, worked with several promoters of ayahuasca tours, and had a number of highly emotion-charged affairs with American and European tourists—including, purportedly, an Italian countess—with claims and counterclaims of financial and sexual exploitation. Doña María saw in a vision that he kept his pusangas under his bed, and she told him, in no uncertain terms, to throw them out. But he did not—perhaps predictably—listen to her. The young shaman for a time promoted his ayahuasca tours on his own Web site.

Don Roberto also does pusangería when he is asked, but he defers to doña María's expertise in this area. He also collects plants, which he dries and powders; but the pusanga must be curado, cured—don Roberto says that you must *darle fuerza*, give it power—by the icaro, of which the most common is simply called the huarmi icaro, woman icaro. Most healers have their own huarmi icaro, learned from the appropriate plants; as with other generically named icaros, such as the icaro de ayahuasca, each one is different. The imanes, spirits, of the plants in the pusanga, he says, look like little boys and young girls; but it is their smell that gives the potion its fuerza, power.

There are limitations to the power of a pusanga. If love is imposed on an unwilling victim, the effect will last only around three months and then will fade—or turn to hatred. Realizing that one has been manipulated in this way is thought to cause rage and conflict.[38] In one case with which I am familiar, a man seduced a fifteen-year-old girl with a pusanga prepared, I am told, by don Roberto; he married her and had several children with her. But they began to fight and argue, the love generated by the pusanga faded away, and she went to don Roberto for a counter-pusanga, so that she could be free of her husband; don Roberto refused, because they were now married and had children. So she took a lover instead.

MALE POTENCY ENHANCERS

Very popular forms of Amazonian plant medicine are male sexual enhancers, sold in stalls and shops all over the Upper Amazon. These drinks are probably as well known for their names as for their ingredients: Rompecalzón, Rip-Your-Shorts; Levántate Lázaro, Arise Lazarus!; Para Para, Stand Up! Stand Up!; Tumba Hembra, Knock Her Over; Siete Veces Sin Sacar, Seven Times without Pulling Out; Levántate Pájaro Muerto, Arise Dead Bird!—the word *pájaro*, bird, being Peruvian Amazon slang for penis.

These aphrodisiacs are made from both plants and animal parts, the latter primarily the *ullo*, penis, of various animals—the *achuni*, coatimundi, a relative of the raccoon, which is believed to have a penis that is always erect; the *machín*, capuchin monkey; and the *lagarto negro*, black caiman.[39] It is popularly said that ingesting achuni ullo induces a priapism so profound as to survive death, requiring that a hole be cut in the coffin to accommodate it.[40]

Two plants in particular are thought to have male potency enhancement effects—chuchuhuasi and *clavohuasca*, clove vine. Clavohuasca is reputed to work as a libido enhancer for women as well. Interestingly, both of these—along with a number of the plants with which they are mixed—are considered hot plants, used to treat cold conditions, such as arthritis and rheumatism; in addition, the bark with which they are mixed comes from trees that produce strong durable hardwood used in construction for posts, supports, and uprights—a good example of the doctrine of signatures. The most frequently used hardwoods for this purpose are *cocobolo*, *cumaseba*, huacapú, icoja, and tahuari.

Some recipes are relatively straightforward: the chuchuhuasi drink is a maceration in aguardiente of chuchuhuasi bark; *abejachado* is the chuchuhuasi drink with honey added; achuni ullo, coatimundi penis, is a maceration in aguardiente of scrapings from the dried penis of a coatimundi. More complex recipes can add to chuchuhuasi both hot plants, such as *abuta* and *ipururo*, and the bark of such hardwood construction trees as huacapú and cumaseba, mixed with honey. The various Rompecalzón recipes use, in similar fashion, clavohuasca bark instead of chuchuhausi. Empirical studies of efficacy, I am sad to say, are lacking.

General tonics such as Siete Raíces, Seven Roots, and Veintiún Raíces, Twenty-one Roots, often contain chuchuhuasi or clavohuasca or both, and thus claim potency enhancement along with their numerous other benefits. The term *raíces* is metaphorical, since most of the ingredients are tree bark rather than roots. The ingredients can vary from place to place; here are four different recipes for Siete Raíces:

- chuchuhuasi, *mururé*, *huacapurana*, cumaseba, tahuari, icoja, huacapú
- chuchuhuasi, clavohuasca, mururé, huacapurana, cumaseba, cocobolo, ipururo
- chuchuhuasi, clavohuasca, *sanango*, *renaquilla*, *cascarilla*, cocobolo, ipururo
- chuchuhuasi, clavohuasca, chiricsanango, cascarilla, *huanarpo*, *maca*, ipururo

The capinurí palm is also worth mentioning. The ends of its fallen branches look remarkably like erect penises, and wearing a two- or three-inch piece of the branch end on a string around the neck is considered to increase virility—another example of the doctrine of signatures. The phallic ends of the branches are also the subject of a great deal of ribald humor.

CHAPTER 19

TYPES OF SHAMAN

There have been relatively few investigators who have studied the healing practices of the mestizos in the Peruvian Amazon. All of them—anthropologist Luis Eduardo Luna, medical anthropologist Marlene Dobkin de Ríos, and Jacques Chevalier, an expert in social anthropology and political economy—have characterized the healers they worked with as *shamans*.[1] And, indeed, both don Roberto and doña María have been perfectly comfortable being called—and calling themselves—*chamánes*.

Of course, in all likelihood, the term *chamán*, shaman, has only recently been introduced into mestizo professional classifications. Mestizo healers generally call themselves not shamans but vegetalistas, curanderos, médicos, *curiosos*, and *empíricos*.[2] The term *brujo*, sorcerer, is today often used pejoratively, to refer to a person who uses shamanic power to harm others—for money, for revenge, or just out of spite. But don Agustin Rivas Vasquez, a mestizo shaman from Tamshiyacu, says, "Back then the word shaman wasn't known, only now we know the word. Earlier we were all brujos, some doing good and some doing evil."[3] To the extent that the term *brujo* connotes power, shamans may embrace it; one shaman advertises himself in the newspaper, proudly, as *el unico brujo que tiene pacto con el diablo*, the only brujo who has made a pact with the devil.

Many mestizo shamans refer to themselves as vegetalistas—that is, those who have received their power from the *vegetales*, plants.[4] The boundaries of this term are uncertain. According to Luna, this term distinguishes vegetalistas from such other healers as oracionistas, prayer healers, and espiritistas, spiritist healers.[5] Chevalier opposes vegetalismo to brujería, sorcery.[6] Followers of the Brazilian new religious movements use the term *vegetalismo* to refer to both mestizo and indigenous ayahuasca shamanism in the Upper Amazon, in contrast to their own practices.[7] Among mestizos in the Peruvian Amazon, the term *vegetalismo* is often used to distinguish mestizo shamanism from that of indigenous peoples.

Other of these terms are used as well. Cesar Zevallos Chinchuya, a Campa healer, calls himself a médico.[8] Doña María and don Roberto describe themselves as curanderos, healers, which they oppose to brujos, sorcerers.[9] Don Francisco Montes Shuña, on the other hand, uses the term *curandero* not as opposed to *brujo* but to indicate a mestizo healer as opposed to an indigenous one.[10]

SPECIALIZATIONS

Perhaps most often used are terms referring to a practitioner's specialty or subspecialty, just as we might more readily describe a biomedical practitioner as, say, a *pediatrician* rather than more generically as a *doctor*. Such terms indicate the teacher plants with which the shaman has undertaken la dieta and with which the shaman has formed a special relationship.

Throughout the Upper Amazon, the three most important psychoactive plants are the three hallucinogens mapacho, toé, and ayahuasca, which embody the primary functions of protection, power, and teaching. Thus, there are three primary shamanic specialties, based on which of these plants the shaman uses to diagnose sickness and to contact the healing and protective spirits—tabaquero, toero, and ayahuasquero.

Then there are what we can call *subspecialties:*[11]

- *paleros* use the bark and resin of palos, large hardwood trees, such as ayahuma, *hacapú*, chullachaqui caspi, remocaspi, cumaseba, *huayracaspi*, icoja, and tahuari; the distinction is between plantas, plants, of which the leaves and stems are primarily used, and palos, trees, of which primarily the roots, bark, or resin is used
- *sananqueros* are expert in the use of a heterogeneous group of plants called sanango, especially chiricsanango
- *camalongueros* use the seeds of the camalonga, yellow oleander, usually dissolved in aguardiente along with camphor and white onion
- *catahueros* use of the resin of the catahua tree
- *perfumeros* are experts in the use of fragrant plants as well as commercially prepared colognes, such as agua de florida
- *ajosacheros* use drinks made from ajo sacha

- *tragueros* use *trago* or aguardiente, distilled fermented sugarcane juice
- *encanteros* use magic stones

These subspecialties frequently combine with primary specialties: a shaman can be a palero ayahuasquero, perfumero ayahuasquero, or, like don Roberto, a sananguero ayahuasquero. None of this is exclusive; ayahuasqueros smoke

Sanangos

Don Roberto is well known as a sananguero—that is, an expert in the use of a group of plants collectively known as sanangos. The best known of these plants is chiricsanango. But there are, in fact, two *Brunfelsia* species called chiricsanango—*B. grandifloria* and *B. chiricaspi*, the first also called *chuchuhuasha* and the second also called *chiricaspi*. Note that the Quechua term *chiric*, cold, chills, appears in the names of both plants. Note too that chuchuhuasha is a different plant from chuchuhuasi, although understandably their names are sometimes confused. To add to the confusion, the poet César Calvo distinguishes—on what basis I do not know—between red and white chuchuhuasha.[1]

Moreover, the sanangos include not only chiricsanango but also *motelosanango*; a variety of species in the genus *Tabernaemontana*, called, without much consistency, lobosanango, *uchusanango*, or *yacusanango*; a variety of species in the genus *Bonafousia*, called *cocasanango* or *sanango macho*; and a variety of species in the genus *Faramea*, called *caballosanango* or yacusanango. Just about any of these species may be called, simply, sanango.[2]

It is not clear to me what these plants have in common. Chiricsanango causes chills and tingling when ingested, and is therefore considered a cold plant, used to treat hot conditions—fever, diarrhea, wounds, and inflammations. But motelosanango is a hot plant, which has, as mestizo shaman Manuel Córdova says, "the effect of warming the blood," and is used to treat cold conditions, such as arthritis, rheumatism, and erectile dysfunction.[3]

Nor can I detect any overriding physical resemblance among the sanangos; for example, as far as I can tell, the cordate leaves of motelosanango look nothing like the elliptic leaves of chiricsanango. Interestingly, several *Tabernaemontana* species contain ibogaine;[4] ethnobotanist Norman Bisset reports that *Tabernaemontana sananho* is used as an arrow poison.[5] Famed ethnobotanists Richard Evans Schultes and Robert Raffauf in effect throw up their hands. "The Peruvian name *sanango*," they write, "indicates that this shrub has a medicinal use."[6]

NOTES

1. Calvo, 1981/1995b, p. 211.
2. For example, Gentry, 1993, p. 242; Schultes & Raffauf, 1990, p. 383.
3. Lamb, 1985, pp. 174–175.
4. Van Beek, Verpoorte, Svendsen, Leeuwenberg, & Bisset, 1984.
5. See Bisset, 1992; Duke & Vasquez, 1994, p. 164.
6. Schultes & Raffauf, 1990, p. 383.

mapacho, ingest toé, and drink camalonga. On the other hand, don César Zevallos Chinchuya, a Campa toero, sees the specialties as rivals. Ayahuasqueros are his mortal enemies, he says: ayahuasca is a creeping bush, and toé is a small tree; they cannot mingle.[12] A similar belief—that toé is antagonistic to the ayahuasca spirit—is also found among the related Ashéninka.[13] Zevalos also considers the catahuero to be his dangerous enemy, since catahua is used to kill rather than heal.[14]

Other commonly used terms with the *-ero* suffix indicate what we can call shamanic practice areas—for example, *pusanguero*, a maker of love potions; *curandero*, a healer of sickness; *shitanero*, a practitioner of shitana, sorcery; *hechicero*, a caster of evil spells; *chontero*, a sorcerer who inflicts harm with magic darts. These practice areas are independent of plant specializations: a chontero might be an ayahuasquero or a tabaquero; a tabaquero might be both a curandero and a pusanguero. Still, some subspecialties and practice areas tend to go together: a perfumero, for example, is likely to be a pusanguero.

PRESTIGE AND HIERARCHY

Sources of Prestige

There is an often unspoken hierarchy among mestizo shamans. There is, first, a relatively informal ranking based on length of practice, the number and length of dietas, the number and types of plants that have been mastered, and the number and quality of icaros in their repertoire.[15] Icaros become increasingly prestigious as they incorporate words from indigenous languages, unknown archaic tongues, and the languages of animals and birds; the more obscure the language, the more power it contains—and the more difficult it is to copy.

Additionally, prestige is acquired by association with indigenous traditions, on the one hand, and with Western biomedicine, on the other. The former is based on the mestizo assumption that jungle Indians are the ultimate source of shamanic knowledge and that any powers acquired directly from them are of particular value.[16] The latter is based on the social status of urban biomedicine and is manifested in the use of imagery involving hospitals, surgical scrubs and masks, medical procedures, and spirits dressed as doctors and nurses.[17] Reference to these two sources of prestige may be found in the way don Roberto and doña María dress for their ayahuasca ceremonies. Don Roberto wears a crown of feathers and a shirt inscribed with Shipibo Indian designs; doña María would often wear a long white coat, like that of a doctor.

The Banco

A mestizo healer of the greatest power and repute is often called a *banco*, bench, seat. Bancos are credited with remarkable abilities, such as being in two places at once.[18] A banco has the power to fly with speed and skill, has acquired powers of healing, and can transform into all sorts of animals—alligators, boas, dolphins, and birds;[19] a *banco puma* is able to change into a jaguar.[20]

To become a banco, one must diet for more than forty years; that is why most bancos are old, and most never leave their place in the jungle.[21] The term can be combined with terms for specialties: a shaman can be a banco ayahuasquero, banco tabaquero, or banco sananguero.

The term *banco* appears to be a loan of the word *banku* used among the indigenous Canelos Quichua, Lamista, and Shuar for particularly powerful shamans.[22] Among the Napo Runa, the bancu is said to be the most powerful kind of yachac. The supai, spirits, reside within him: it is from these spirits that the shaman derives his power; he is their seat.[23] Among the Canelos Quichua, a banco is a "living seat" for the souls of ancient shamans; among the Lamista, a banku is a powerful shaman who keeps the souls of powerful shaman ancestors in his yachay, magical phlegm.[24] The Shuar believe that bankus—who, they say, do not exist anymore—were those shamans who could be possessed by the spirit of a dead person and let it speak through their mouths.[25] The Achuar panku is likewise the highest form of shaman, through whose mouth speak the spirits of the dead—able to diagnose a sickness, reveal the responsible sorcerer, and give an infallible prognosis.[26]

Among mestizos, it is said that when bancos go into trance they need three apprentices to take care of them, to blow tobacco smoke on their feet, back, and crown of their head. It is during this trance that the banco can summon the spirits of the dead, who speak with the shaman, who is lying facedown within a mosquito net. The dead then tell the shaman how they died, and the shaman can convey this information to the bereaved family.[27]

The *Muraya*

Another status term found among mestizo healers is *muraya*. There is little consistency in the use of this term. Don Agustin Rivas gives a status hierarchy beginning with *muraillo*, then muraya, then *alto muraya*, then *altomando muraya*, and finally banco, the highest level of knowledge, which requires a diet of a full year, living alone in the jungle with no sex and eating only rice, plantains, and occasionally monkeys from the jungle. Don Agustin "graduated" to alto muraya in a dream about his teacher don Ramon, and to altomando muraya in a special ceremony.[28] The term *muraillo* appears to be an *-illo* diminutive of *muraya*; the sequence thus is little muraya, high muraya, high command muraya, and banco.

Just as the term *banco* appears to have been borrowed from the Shuar, Lamista, and other indigenous peoples, the term *muraya* appears to have been borrowed from the Shipibo-Conibo word *muraya* or *meraya*. Some consider the term *muraya* to be the ordinary Shipibo-Conibo term for shaman or sorcerer;[29] more likely, the term *muraya* or *meraya* refers to a special class of shaman distinguished from—and held in higher esteem than—the ordinary ayahuasca healer, called onanya.[30]

Literally, the term *onanya* means *one who knows*, and *meraya* means *one who meets*. One Shipibo shaman, when asked whether he was an onanya or meraya, replied that, when he was young, he could disappear from within his mosquito net, change into a jaguar, or have a double who could travel great distances, and thus was a meraya; but now that he had lost these powers through age, he was an onanya.[31] Indeed, there are currently very few meraya left among the Shipibo.[32]

The term *meraya* thus seems to indicate a set of powers very similar to those of the banco. Strikingly, one Shipibo woman, not herself a shaman, says that the meraya have now all disappeared, but that they could be possessed by the souls of dead people, who would speak through the meraya's mouth several months after their death to name the sorcerers who had killed them. There is thus reason to believe that the meraya—like the banco—was distinguished from other shamans by giving voice to the dead and by providing a home for the souls of powerful dead shamans.[33]

The *Sumi*

The term *sumi* or *sume* is used primarily to refer to a master shaman who has the ability to go at will into the underwater realms. Pablo Amaringo says that sumis are those able to go under the water; a *sumiruna* is "capable of entering the water as if it were the easiest thing in the world."[34] Luis Eduardo Luna annotates Amaringo's expression *witch sumiruna* as "a witch that can go under the waters."[35]

This is an important skill. The other-than-human persons who live under the water are often viewed as having great knowledge of healing and magic songs, which they may be willing to share with an intrepid shaman. In addition, these beings are sexually voracious and may kidnap humans for sexual purposes; a shaman must be able to compel them to give up their captives, often using icaros learned from the underwater beings themselves. It is not clear to me where the term *sumi* comes from. The term *sumiruna*—that is, sumi person—is often used synonymously.

Don José Celso tells a story of how he almost became a sumi. While he was drinking ayahuasca, a gigantic boa came to devour him, but he hesitated to enter the creature's mouth. If he had, he says, the boa would have vomited him into the underwater world.[36] The artist Elvis Luna, commenting on a painting he made of mermaids, says that the mermaids are celebrating because soon a newly kidnapped man will be brought to their world: "They enchant the man with their sublime singing and their beauty. The moment the man is taken underwater the mermaids encircle him as part of his welcome to their world." But the man they have abducted is in fact an apprentice shaman; he has just two days to establish a relationship with the mermaids in order to get their blessings, their spiritual knowledge. During these two days he must be rescued by a sumi, a specialized shaman of the water who is monitoring the apprentice. "If two days have passed and he is not rescued," the artist writes, "the man will experience an eternity in every day that he is underwater."[37]

There are stories of great shamans who travel underwater, to see the great cities of the mermaids and water people and to learn their songs and medicine. It is not clear whether these journeys are visionary, like visits to other planets, or are intended to be physical. Don Emilio Andrade claims that juice from the shoots of the raya balsa, water chestnut, along with the appropriate diet, allows one to travel underwater; don José Coral says the same of renaco, strangler fig.[38] Don Alejandro Vasquez Zarate does not believe that it is possible to travel bodily under the water;[39] but many shamans report visions of the great cities of the water people.

Don Francisco Montes Shuña speaks of his uncle, don Manuel Shuña, a banco sumi, who could live and work in the water realm with the mermaids, and who had a sexual relationship with a mermaid who taught him many things; and of his grandmother, Trinidad Vilces Peso, a sumiruna who had control over the spirits of the water, could enter the aquatic realms and transform into a fish, and died at the age of 108 to become a doctora for the dolphins.[40]

There is little consistency among shamans about the relationship of the terms *banco*, *muraya*, and *sumi*. The term *banco* appears to be the most general; one can be a banco muraya or a banco sumi, meaning a muraya or sumi of the highest level;[41] on the other hand, one can apparently be a sumi muraya as well.[42] Sometimes these terms are related to mastery of the three realms of earth, water, and air. According to Asháninka shaman don Juan Flores Salazar, the banco muraya is master of plants and animals on the land, and the banco sumi is master of the underwater realms.[43] Anthropologist Françoise Barbira Freedman reports that among the Lamista it is, rather, the banco muraya "who has gained access to the underwater connections in the cosmos,"[44] and Pablo Amaringo in his paintings frequently depicts murayas descending into the waters and interacting with the beings who dwell there.[45] Pablo Amaringo says that the banco is master of earth and sky, the muraya is master of water and earth, and the sumiruna is master of all three realms;[46] elsewhere he says that it is the banco who is the master of the three realms.[47] Clearly we are not dealing with a system here.

PART II

AYAHUASCA

CHAPTER 20

AN INTRODUCTION TO AYAHUASCA

Ayahuasca is a hallucinogenic drink made from the stem of the ayahuasca vine. The ayahuasca drink is sometimes, but rarely, made from the ayahuasca vine alone; almost invariably other plants are added. These additional ingredients are most often the leaves of any of three *compañeros*, companion plants—the shrub *chacruna*, the closely related shrub *sameruca*, or a vine variously called *ocoyagé*, *chalipanga*, *chagraponga*, and *huambisa*.

Additional plants may be added to this basic two- or three-plant mixture. One report lists fifty-five different plant species that have apparently been used as ayahuasca "admixture plants,"[1] and another lists more than 120.[2] Whatever plants the drink may have in addition to ayahuasca, the drink is still called ayahuasca.

So, already there is confusion. The term *ayahuasca* refers both to the vine and to the hallucinogenic drink made from the vine, almost always with one or several additional ingredients. This usage is an example of what we can call *Amazonian synecdoche*—naming something after just one of its components. For example, the term *camalonga* refers both to the yellow oleander and to a shamanic drink made not only of yellow oleander seeds but also of garlic or white onion, camphor, and aguardiente, distilled fermented cane juice. Similarly, the term *grasa de búfalo*, buffalo fat, refers both to buffalo fat specifically and to an ointment used for the relief of joint pain, of which buffalo fat is one of many ingredients.

The term *ayahuasca* is in the Quechua language. The word *huasca* is the usual Quechua term for any species of vine. The word *aya* refers to something like a separable soul and thus, also, to the spirit of a dead person—hence the two common English translations, "vine of the soul" and "vine of the dead." The

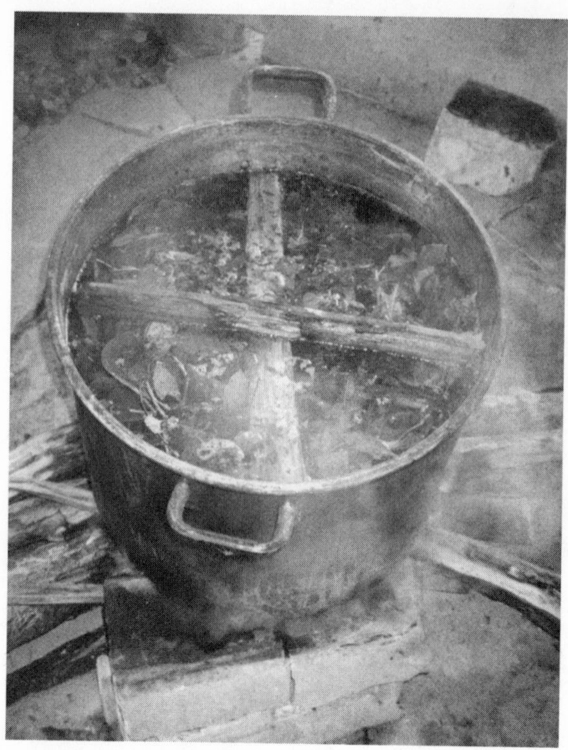

FIGURE 8. Cooking the ingredients for the ayahuasca drink.

word *ayahuasca* can apparently have either connotation, depending largely on cultural context. Quechua speakers in Canelos or on the Napo, as well as the mestizo shamans with whom I have worked, translate the word into Spanish as *soga del alma*, vine of the soul;[3] people on the Bajo Urubamba often translate the word as *soga de muerto*, vine of the dead, based on a local association of the jungle generally, and ayahuasca in particular, with a malicious ghost called a bone demon, which seeks to eat people or kill them through violent sexual intercourse.[4]

The ritual use of ayahuasca is a common thread linking the religion and spirituality of almost all the indigenous peoples of the Upper Amazon, including the mestizo population; it seems probable that the shamanic practices of most of western Amazonia—Brazil, Venezuela, Colombia, Ecuador, Peru, Bolivia—form a single religious culture area. Ayahuasca use is found as far west as the Pacific coastal areas of Panama, Colombia, and Ecuador; southward into the Peruvian and Bolivian Amazon; among the Indians of Colombia; among the Quichua, Waoroni, Shuar, and other peoples of Ecuador; and in Amazonian Brazil.[5] Luis Eduardo Luna has compiled a bibliography of more than three hundred items and has enumerated seventy-two indigenous groups reported to have used ayahuasca.[6]

The ayahuasca drink has several primary actions: it is a hallucinogen, emetic, purgative, and vermifuge. In fact, there is reason to think that the ayahuasca vine was first used for its emetic, purgative, and vermifuge activities.[7] Even today, the ayahuasca drink is often called, simply, la purga, and is used to induce violent vomiting, with hallucinations considered side effects;[8] indeed, ayahuasqueros are sometimes called *purgueros*.[9] But the emetic effect of the ayahuasca drink has spiritual resonance as well; vomiting shows that the drinker is being cleansed. *La purga misma te enseña*, they say; vomiting itself teaches you.[10]

Interestingly, given the emetic effect of the ayahuasca vine, the term used by mestizo shamans to describe the hallucinatory mental state induced by ayahuasca is *mareación*, from the verb *marearse*, to feel sick, dizzy, nauseous, drunk, seasick. When the ayahuasca has taken hold and one is hallucinating, one is said to be mareado; it is a good thing to be buen mareado after drinking ayahuasca. The term has been extended to include the effects of psychoactive plants such as toé that have no emetic effect.

It is harmaline, one of the β-carboline components of the ayahuasca vine, that makes the ayahuasca drink such a potent emetic and purgative. These gastrointestinal effects appear to be related to the ability of harmaline to inhibit peripheral monoamine oxidase-A (MAO-A); overdosing on an MAO inhibitor—they are sometimes used as antidepressants—is known to cause nausea and vomiting.[11] Harmaline is also found in Syrian rue, *Peganum harmala*, from which it was first isolated and after which it was named;[12] like the ayahuasca vine, Syrian rue has been used as an emetic and vermifuge. Doses of harmaline as small as 200 mg orally produce nausea, vomiting, and diarrhea in human volunteers. Five grams of Syrian rue seeds produce mild nausea and vomiting; higher doses produce both vomiting and diarrhea, in some cases serious enough to be incapacitating.[13] It also appears that there is habituation to the emetic and purgative activity of harmaline: shamans, who have drunk ayahuasca hundreds or thousands of times, seldom exhibit its emetic or purgative effects.

Rather, for the shaman, ayahuasca is a teaching plant; it is through the hallucinogenic power of the ayahuasca drink that the hundreds of healing plants, including the plants used for magical attack and defense, reveal their appearance and teach their songs. It is the ayahuasca drink that nurtures the shaman's phlegm, the physical manifestation of shamanic power within the body, used both as defense against magical attack and as a container for the magic darts that are the shaman's principal weapon.

On Terminology

The Quechua term *ayahuasca* is used primarily in present-day Peru and Ecuador; in Colombia the common term for both the vine and the drink is *yagé* or *yajé*, from the Tukano language. The Shuar of the Upano Valley in southeastern Ecuador call the vine *natém*, the companion plant *yaji*, and the drink *natém*, after the vine;[1] the closely related Aguaruna call the vine *datém*, the companion plant *yáhi*, and the drink *yáhi*, after the companion plant.[2] In both cases, the term *yaji* or *yáhi* probably refers to *Diplopterys cabrerana*. Luis Eduardo Luna has listed forty-two indigenous names for ayahuasca.[3]

Diplopterys cabrerana was previously classified as *Banisteriopsis rusbyana*, and the change in nomenclature has led to some confusion. The term *chagraponga* is apparently used in Colombia, and *ocoyagé* and *huambisa* are used in Peru, but there is considerable inconsistency. *Chalipanga*, a variant of the Colombian term, is used in Peru; *yagé oco*, an inversion of the Peruvian term, is used in Colombia.[4] The word *oko* means "water" in all the Tukanoan languages.[5] Some mestizo shamans around Iquitos refer to ocoyagé simply as yagé, the Colombian term for ayahuasca, confusing things still more. Jimmy Weiskopf claims that ayahuasca drinks made with chacruna are characteristically found in the Iquitos area, and those made with chagraponga in the Putumayo;[6] Marie Perruchon indicates that the Shuar combine the ayahuasca vine exclusively with chagraponga to make their hallucinogenic natém,[7] but the identification is no clearer here than it is in Michael Harner's work.[8] My experience has been that there is too much individual variation in the drinks prepared by different shamans to support much generalization; for example, for a period of time, don Roberto made his ayahuasca drink with leaves of both chacruna and ocoyagé; don Rómulo Magin, also near Iquitos, used chacruna and his own cultivar of sameruca.

The term *sameruca* appears to derive from the Shuar word *samiruk*.[9] Some mestizo shamans, such as don Rómulo Magin, consider *Psychotria carthaginensis* and *P. viridis* to be simply different types of chacruna, which can be used interchangeably; others, such as don Roberto, distinguish *P. viridis* by the term *chacruna legítima*, genuine chacruna.

NOTES

1. Perruchon, 2003, p. 216.
2. Brown, 1978, pp. 121, 123.
3. Luna, 1986c, pp. 171–173.
4. Weiskopf, 2005, pp. 148–151.
5. Schultes & Raffauf, 1990, p. 282.
6. Weiskopf, 2005, pp. 151–152.
7. Perruchon, 2003, p. 216.
8. Harner, 1971, p. 153.
9. The term is used by Shuar shaman Alejandro Tsakimp in Rubenstein, 2002, p. 141.

Combining the Plants

How in the world did indigenous peoples in the Upper Amazon come up with the idea of combining DMT with an MAO inhibitor? Many mestizo shamans will claim, of course, that the plants themselves taught humans how to do this. Other commentators point to some mysterious ecological wisdom found only in indigenous peoples. I think the answer is simpler. I think people were looking for a better way to vomit.

Excessive levels of serotonin in the brain may cause nausea and vomiting as a result of the vagus nerve being overstimulated. Diarrhea may also occur, as peripheral serotonin in the digestive tract stimulates intestinal motility.[1] It is not clear what role, if any, DMT plays in modulating the emetic response to harmaline.

I have found no direct evidence that either of the usual companion plants, chacruna or ocoyagé, has emetic or purgative properties. However, it is noteworthy that two *Psychotria* species, *P. ipecacuanha* and *P. emetica*, are widely used emetics, the former in Brazil and the latter in Peru.[2] *P. ipecacuanha* is the source of the widely used emetic syrup of ipecac. In the Colombian Vaupés, a shrub whose leaves are added to the ayahuasca drink, and which Schultes and Hofmann have identified as ocoyagé, is called by the Tukano "the ayahuasca that makes you vomit."[3]

If the companion plants have any emetic properties of their own, it is plausible to hypothesize that the ayahuasca vine and its companion plants were first combined in order to synergize or modulate their emetic and purgative effects, with the serendipitous result of creating an effective delivery form for DMT.

NOTES

1. Callaway, 1999, p. 255.
2. See generally Grieve, 1931/1971, pp. 432–434.
3. Schultes & Hofmann, 1992, p. 121.

It is in fact the companion plant—chacruna or ocoyagé or sameruca—that contains the potent hallucinogen dimethyltryptamine (DMT). But while DMT is effective when administered parenterally, it is, when taken orally, inactivated by peripheral MAO-A, an enzyme found in the lining of the stomach, whose function is precisely to oxidize molecules containing an $-NH_2$ amine group, like DMT.[14]

There are thus two ways to ingest DMT or plants containing DMT. The first is by *parenteral* ingestion—using a route other than the digestive tract, such as smoking, injection, or inhalation—which bypasses the MAO in the stomach lining.[15] A number of indigenous peoples around the Orinoco Basin in Venezuela inhale a snuff called *epená*, made from the sap of several trees in the genus *Virola* that contain large amounts of DMT;[16] and the Guahibo Indians of the Orinoco Basin use a snuff called *yopo*, also called *cohoba*, *vilca*, and *huilca*, made from the DMT-rich plant *Anadenanthera peregrina*.[17] Ethnographer

Patrick Deshayes has described how the Cashinahua and other peoples along the Río Purus produce a finely ground crystalline form of chacruna mixed with ground tobacco, which shamans inhale using a snuff tube while drinking ayahuasca, in order to speed their visions.[18]

It is also possible to mix the DMT with an MAO *inhibitor* that prevents the breakdown of DMT in the digestive tract. That is just what the ayahuasca vine contains—the β-carbolines harmine, harmaline, and tetrahydroharmine, which are potent inhibitors of MAO-A. Combining the ingredients of the ayahuasca drink allows the DMT to produce its hallucinogenic effect when orally ingested—a unique solution that apparently developed only in the Upper Amazon.[19]

It is probably worth noting that the ayahuasca drink tastes *awful*. It has an oily, bitter taste and viscous consistency that clings to your mouth, with just enough hint of sweetness to make you gag. The taste has been described as being bitter and fetid, like forest rot and bile, like dirty socks and raw sewage, and like a toad in a blender.[20] There are also significant differences between parenterally administered DMT and the ayahuasca drink. The effects of parenterally administered DMT appear with startling rapidity; as one user colorfully put it, "The kaleidoscopic alien express came barreling down the aetheric superhighway and slammed into my pineal."[21] In addition, these effects are short-lived—not much longer than thirty minutes—which at one time earned DMT the street appellation *businessman's lunch*.[22] On the contrary, the effects of the ayahuasca drink appear slowly, even slyly, in thirty to forty minutes, and then last approximately four hours, depending on the strength and constituents of the particular mixture.

Remarkably, while tolerance to the emetic and purgative effects of harmaline develops over time, consistent users of DMT, such as shamans, do not develop tolerance for its hallucinogenic effects.[23]

CHAPTER 21

VOMITING

There is no doubt that ayahuasca makes you vomit. There is some consolation in the fact that the vomiting will ease with continued experience; shamans seldom vomit. There is more consolation in the fact that the vomiting is considered to be cleansing and healing. But the vomiting is certainly distressing to a gringo, who has been taught that vomiting is wretched and humiliating.

Ayahuasca vomiting has become something of a literary trope. Poet Allen Ginsberg has described the physical part of his ayahuasca experiences. "Stomach vomiting out the soul-vine," he writes, "cadaver on the floor of a bamboo hut, body-meat crawling toward its fate."[1] William S. Burroughs writes: "I must have vomited six times. I was on all fours convulsed with spasms of nausea. I could hear retching and groaning as if I was some one else."[2] Novelist Alice Walker speaks of the effect of ayahuasca on her protagonist—horrible-tasting medicine, gut-wrenching nausea and diarrhea, "waves of nausea . . . like real waves, bending her double by their force."[3] Chilean American novelist Isabel Allende describes how she was doubled over with nausea, vomiting bile, "vomiting a foam that was whiter with each retching."[4]

Anthropologist Michael Taussig, investigating the shamanism of the Colombian Putumayo, felt compelled to drink ayahuasca—he uses the Colombian term *yagé*—as part of his research. "Somewhere," he writes, "you have to take the bit between your teeth and depict yagé nights in terms of your own experience." And one gets the ineluctable impression that Taussig *hated* the experience of drinking ayahuasca, hated the corporeality of its effects, hated vomiting. He writes, "But perhaps more important is the stark fact that taking yagé is awful: the shaking, the vomiting, the nausea, the shitting, the tension." It is, he says, "awful and unstoppable." His description of the experience is filled with metaphors of slime and nausea. The sounds he heard "were like those of the forest at night: rasping, croaking frogs in their millions by gurgling streams and slimy, swampy ground," "the sound of grinning stoic frogs squatting in moonlit mud." He writes that the "collective empathizing of nausea" at the healing session "feels like ants biting one's skin and one's head, now spinning in wave after trembling wave." He refers again and again to "the stream of vomit," "the streaming nasal mucus," "the whirling confusion of the prolonged nausea."[5]

But this is the reaction of a gringo. It is important to note that emetics and purgatives are widely used among the people of the Upper Amazon, who periodically induce vomiting in their children to rid them of the parasitic illnesses that are endemic in the region.[6] Vomiting is often induced in children and adults using the latex of ojé, also called *doctor ojé*, which is widely ingested throughout the Upper Amazon as a vermifuge; some shamans, such as don Agustin Rivas, use an ojé purge to begin la dieta.[7] Vomiting may be induced in children by giving them *piñisma*, hen excrement, mixed with verbena or *ñucñopichana*, sweet broom, along with other horrifying components, including pounded cockroaches and urine.[8] I have no doubt that this is an effective emetic.

The Piro believe that eating game leaves residues in the body, which accumulate with time, causing fatigue and depression; vomiting—especially by drinking ayahuasca—expels these residues from the body.[9] Communal vomiting is also found among indigenous Amazonian peoples. The Achuar Indians drink a hot infusion of *guayusa* as a morning stimulant, much as we drink coffee, after which all of them, including the children, vomit together.[10] Apparently the vomiting is not due to any emetic effect of the drink but, rather, is learned behavior.[11] Here in the jungle, vomiting is easy, natural, expected; the strangled retching of a gringo like me comes from shame.

Perhaps that is the first lesson I received from el doctor—to open myself up, let go of shame, give up control, hand myself over to the plant.

CHAPTER 22

QUESTIONS IN THE STUDY OF AYAHUASCA

THE ROLE OF THE β-CARBOLINES

There has been a continuing question about the role of the ayahuasca vine in the ayahuasca drink. As we have discussed, the ayahuasca vine contains three primary harmala alkaloids—the β-carboline derivatives harmine, tetrahydroharmine (THH), and harmaline.[1] Harmine is usually the primary constituent, followed first by THH and then by harmaline. There is no question that harmine, harmaline, and other β-carbolines are powerful reversible inhibitors of MAO.[2] And the MAO-inhibiting β-carbolines in the ayahuasca vine may also potentiate the actions of psychoactive alkaloids other than DMT—for example, nicotine from mapacho or the primary tropane alkaloids from toé.[3]

The question is: Apart from these actions, do these β-carbolines contribute to the nature or quality of the ayahuasca visionary experience? The accepted wisdom answers no.[4] A study of the ayahuasca drink used by the syncretic religious movement União do Vegetal in Brazil, for example, concluded that the harmala alkaloids "are essentially devoid of psychedelic activity" at doses found in the drink.[5]

A number of experiments with harmine—the primary β-carboline in the ayahuasca vine—would seem to bear out this assessment. Chemist Alexander Shulgin has reviewed the self-experimentation literature and concludes that harmine has inconsistent effects, which have in common that not much either pleasant or interesting happens—pleasant relaxation and withdrawal in one case; dizziness, nausea, and ataxia in another.[6] Researchers who have self-administered harmine have reported an increase in belligerence, fleeting sensations of lightness, transient subjective effects, mild sedation at low doses and unpleasant neurological effects at higher doses, and no "notable psychoactive or somatic effect."[7] Some researchers have expressed doubts that harmine is psychoactive at all.[8]

Jonathan Ott gives several accounts of his own experiences with ingesting infusions of the ayahuasca vine or other β-carboline-rich plants without DMT companion plants. During one shamanic ceremony, he drank an infusion of the ayahuasca vine mixed only with a small number of guayusa leaves, which contain caffeine but no tryptamines, which he intended to counteract what he believed would be the soporific effects of the drink. According to Ott, the caffeine content was insufficient for that purpose; he had to fight off sleep. He could see, he writes, why β-carboline-enriched infusions had been used traditionally as sedatives.[9]

There are two reasons, however, to question the common wisdom. The first is the work of Claudio Naranjo, who administered harmaline—not harmine—to thirty-five volunteers, by mouth and intravenously, under laboratory conditions.[10] Harmaline, he reports, was "more of a pure hallucinogen" than other psychoactive substances, such as mescaline, because of the number of images reported and their realistic quality—what Naranjo calls their "remarkable vividness."[11] "In fact," he writes, "some subjects felt that certain scenes they saw had really happened, and that they had been disembodied witnesses of them in a different time and place."[12] The volunteers often described landscapes and cities, masks, eyes, and what we elsewhere call *elves*—vividly realized animal and human figures, angels, demons, giants, and dwarfs.[13] If this study is credible, there are grounds to believe that, among the β-carbolines, at least harmaline, at sufficient doses, has independent hallucinogenic properties, phenomenologically very similar to those of DMT.

Shulgin's review of the self-experimental literature with regard to harmaline provides some confirmation of the reports of Naranjo's volunteers. A 500-mg oral dose produced nausea and a complete collapse of motor coordination—"I could barely stagger to the bathroom," one person reported—along with eyes-closed eidetic imagery and "tracers and weird visual ripplings" with open eyes.[14]

It is even more interesting to look at the effects of Syrian rue, which contains pretty much equal quantities of harmine and harmaline, as opposed to the proportionally much smaller amount of harmaline usually found in the ayahuasca vine. Oral ingestion of ground Syrian rue seeds caused intense eyes-closed hallucinations of "a wide variety of geometrical patterns in dark colors," which evolved into more concrete images—"people's faces, movies of all sorts playing at high speeds, and animal presences such as snakes." Oral ingestion of a fivefold greater dose, as extract, caused "zebra-like stripes of light and dark"—visual effects that had "a physicality unlike those of any other entheogen I'd experienced." In a second trial at the same dose, the participant saw "strange winged creatures" and traveled to "jungle-like places, full of imagery of vines, fountains, and animals."[15] In the same way, case reports of overdoses of Syrian rue describe its effects as including both visual and auditory hallucinations.[16]

Now the amount of harmaline in any sample of ayahuasca vine or drink is, as we shall see, extremely variable; it is a matter of controversy whether *any* infusion of the ayahuasca vine contains enough harmaline to cause the effects reported above. Jonathon Ott, whose views deserve respectful attention, says that the amount of harmaline in a single 200-ml drink of ayahuasca would be insufficient to produce the effects reported by Naranjo.[17]

Yet the accepted wisdom is challenged by ethnography as well. Among mestizo shamans, an ayahuasca drink made solely from the ayahuasca vine is sometimes ingested orally for hallucinogenic effects of a particular "dark" nature. In addition, ayahuasqueros, virtually universally, say that it is the ayahuasca vine that provides the fuerza, power, and DMT-rich plants such as chacruna that provide the luz, light, in the ayahuasca experience. In Colombia, the shamans say that the companion plant *brilla la pinta* makes the visions brighter;[18] among the Shuar, the companion plant is not considered to have any hallucinogenic effects but, rather, to make the visions clearer, and is in fact occasionally omitted.[19] Don Manuel Córdova Ríos agrees: Chacruna leaves, he says, "serve only . . . to make the visions clearer."[20] The great ethnobotanist Richard Evans Schultes reports that certain Colombian Indians smoke leaves of the ayahuasca vine;[21] under certain circumstances, don Roberto recommends smoking the bark.

Schultes himself, at Puerto Limón, drank an infusion derived solely from ayahuasca bark, and he experienced "subtle visions, blues and purples, slow undulating waves of color."[22] Then, a few days later, he tried the mixture with chagraponga. The effect was considerably brightened—"reds and golds dazzling in diamonds that turned like dancers on the tips of distant highways."[23] Author Daniel Pinchbeck—I do not know where he got this information—says that β-carbolines taken alone "create subtle, monochromatic hallucinations that are soft, warm, and humanized."[24] As one curandero told me, visions with the ayahuasca vine alone are dark and dim; the chacruna makes the vision come on like this: *whoosh!* he said, moving his closed hand rapidly toward my face, the fingers opening up as it approached. Luis Eduardo Luna, one of the leading investigators of Amazonian mestizo shamanism, reports that often a larger amount of the ayahuasca vine is added to the ayahuasca drink than is needed for MAO inhibition, precisely because of its ability to produce strong visual hallucinations.[25]

Interestingly, some users of parenterally administered DMT, and even of hallucinogens other than DMT, potentiate the effect by acute pretreatment with an MAO inhibitor. These hallucinogens are active by themselves, and it is difficult to see what benefit would be derived from inhibition of peripheral MAO. This too suggests that harmaline has actions on its own that would contribute to the hallucinogenic response.[26] For example, among the Piaroa of the Venezuelan Amazon, shamans inhale a snuff, generally called yopo, made from the pulverized seeds of the DMT-rich plant *Anadenanthera peregrina*, but also orally ingest a drink made from the ayahuasca vine prior to inhaling yopo, and add the vine to the ground seeds. The two plants work together, they say; drinking the vine is especially important when particularly strong visions are required.[27]

There is also some reason to believe that THH may be in part responsible for the hallucinogenic effects of the ayahuasca vine, either by itself or acting synergistically with other β-carboline compounds. In 1957 Hochstein and Paradies had already conjectured—"astutely," in the words of Jonathon Ott—that harmaline and THH might have "substantial psychotomimetic activity in their own right."[28] Strikingly, among members of the ayahuasca-using União do Vegetal church in Brazil, experienced users seem to prefer ayahuasca drinks where THH concentrations are high relative to harmine and harmaline. They explain that such drinks deliver more "force" to the experience.[29] It is therefore surprising that so little research has been done on THH. Alexander Shulgin, in his search of the self-experimentation literature, found only a single and entirely unhelpful report. "More studies on tetrahydroharmine," he says, "are absolutely imperative."[30]

Similarly, additive and—especially—synergistic studies of harmala alkaloids have not been performed. The ethnographic evidence strongly suggests that interactive effects are important and are yet to be investigated.

VARIABILITY AND DOSAGE

Variability in Component Plants

Another issue in understanding the ayahuasca drink is that plants of the same species, and different batches of the ayahuasca drink made from plants of the same species, may differ markedly in their chemical composition. Four different analyses of the DMT content of ocoyagé leaves, from different areas of the

Upper Amazon, report the mean DMT content ranging from 0.17 to 1.46 percent, a greater than eightfold difference.[31] Five analyses of the DMT content of chacruna leaves, similarly from a variety of sources, report the amount of DMT as ranging from undetectable to 1.77 percent, with mean DMT content differing from one study to another by an order of magnitude, from 0.10 to 1.00 percent.[32] Note the finding that some chacruna leaves apparently contained *no* detectable level of DMT; an ayahuasca drink made from such leaves should, according to the common wisdom, have no psychoactive effect at all, or any effect would be due entirely to other psychoactive substances. In the same way, six analyses of the β-carboline content of dried stems of the ayahuasca vine report amounts ranging from 0.05 to 1.44 percent, a twenty-eight-fold difference. Mean values reportedly vary from 0.21 to 1.01 percent, a fivefold difference.[33]

Why should this be so? The chemical constituents of plants, especially in the rain forest, can differ significantly depending upon microclimatic conditions. Adjacent plants, gaps in the canopy, the presence of clearings for swidden agriculture, the nature of the soil, and consequent variations in temperature, water, and sunlight—all these can affect the type and quantity of plant chemicals.[34] The ayahuasca vine may also differ in its chemical composition depending on its age and even the height of the section that is cut for use.[35] Anthropologist Gerardo Reichel-Dolmatoff makes the same point—that the chemical composition of the local soil is likely to influence the potency of the plant, and that Tukano men, fully aware of these differences, will go to great pains to collect the ayahuasca vine at some remote part of the jungle.[36] Chemist Jace Callaway reports that DMT levels in the leaves of a single chacruna plant varied according to the time of day they were collected, with the highest levels of DMT found in leaves collected at dawn or before dusk and the lowest levels found in leaves collected at midnight and midmorning, with values remaining low through the hotter part of the day.[37]

Further, a number of Amazonian shamans have developed their own plant cultivars, which they grow in their own gardens, and which may differ significantly in chemical constitution from other cultivars or the same species growing wild. Don Rómulo Magin, for example, had a large bush of sameruca growing in his front yard, which he would use to prepare his ayahuasca drink, and which probably differed in significant ways from wild sameruca, as well as from both wild and cultivated chacruna. Almost all the shamans in Colombia use ayahuasca vines that are deliberately planted for use in preparing the ayahuasca drink;[38] among these Colombian shamans, the culminating stage in the shamanic apprenticeship is when the master gives the apprentice vines to plant in his own garden.[39] In Peru, on the other hand, many mestizo shamans consider wild ayahuasca to be more potent, and they will seek out an *abuelo*, a grandfather plant, old and powerful, deep in the jungle, whose location they keep secret.[40] Cocama shaman don José Curitima Sangama has planted his own ayahuasca in the monte, the highland jungle, where it will grow undisturbed; he has been told that, in the new global economy, ayahuasca is a cash crop.[41]

Frequently, too, mestizo shamans will make distinctions among plants considered by Europeans to be the same species. For example, they will distinguish different types of ayahuasca vine—red ayahuasca, white ayahuasca, yellow ayahuasca, black ayahuasca; *cielo* ayahuasca, sky ayahuasca; *lucero* ayahuasca, bright star ayahuasca; *trueno* ayahuasca, thunder ayahuasca; and ayahuasca cascabel, rattle ayahuasca, which is the best ayahuasca of all. These distinctions are often based on the types of visions produced, rather than on the morphology of the plant.[42] Attempts are made to coordinate these various classifications: yellow ayahuasca is said to be the same as sky ayahuasca, and black ayahuasca is the same as thunder ayahuasca.

Similarly, the Ingano Indians recognize seven kinds of ayahuasca, the Siona recognize eighteen, and the Harakmbet recognize twenty-two, distinguished on the basis of the strength and color of the visions, the trading history of the plant, and the authority and lineage of the shaman who owns the plant. All of these variations are a single botanical species, yet shamans can distinguish these varieties on sight, and shamans from different tribes identify these same varieties with remarkable consistency.[43] Indigenous ayahuasqueros look at the shape of the vine, the color and texture of the bark, the shape and softness of the leaves, and the overall nature of the cylindrical shape of the vine, not to mention its smell and taste.

In Brazil, members of the ayahuasca-using União de Vegetal church distinguish two varieties of *Banisteriopsis caapi*, which they call *tucanaca* and *caupurí*. The tucanaca variety is a smooth vine that grows in the cooler climate of southern Brazil and is known to have a mild purgative effect; the caupurí variety is a knobby-looking vine with large internodes, which grows in the hotter jungles of northern Brazil and is known as a powerful purgative. A comparison of the mean content of the three β-carbolines in the dried bark of these two varieties of ayahuasca vine shows striking differences: caupurí has more than twenty-six times as much THH as tucanaca and more than six times as much harmaline.[44] These results indicate, once again, both significant differences in chemical composition among ayahuasca vines and indigenous ability to recognize variants of the same species and correlate these differences with differing physiological effects.

Variability in the Ayahuasca Drink

Six analyses have also measured the mean amount of DMT and β-carbolines found in samples of the ayahuasca drink, all made with chacruna, from the Upper Amazon and from Brazil.[45] The mean amount of DMT in the different studies ranged from 12.5 to 60 mg/100 ml, and the mean amount of total β-carbolines ranged from 20 to 668.33 mg/ml, more than an eighty-fold difference. In two samples analyzed by Callaway, one from the União do Vegetal and one from the Shuar, no DMT was detected at all.[46] Equally striking is the variability in the amount that each researcher took to be a *dose* of the ayahuasca drink—an amount that varied from 50 to 240 ml, almost a fivefold difference.

Similarly, where we have information about individual β-carbolines in ayahuasca drinks, the variability is just as striking. Four analyses of the individual β-carboline content of ayahuasca drinks report that mean harmine levels differ thirty-fold, and THH differs forty-fold, among the three analyses.[47] In four samples, the investigator reports that harmaline was so low as to be below the level of detection;[48] in another, the level of harmaline was actually higher than that of harmine.[49]

Again, why should this be so? The drinks will vary, of course, depending on the alkaloid content of their ingredients. Additional factors affect the finished drinks, particularly the method of preparation. Among some Amazonian people, the ayahuasca drink is prepared simply as a cold infusion of macerated vine, without cooking the plant.[50] In my experience, the drink is always prepared by cooking, sometimes in two stages—first with the plant materials boiled in water, and second, after decanting the plant material, to produce a reduction of the liquid alone. The part of the ayahuasca vine used in the preparation of the drink apparently varies from place to place as well, with some shamans scraping off the outer layer, some leaving it on, and some using the bark alone.[51] Again, in my experience, the entire vine has been used, pounded with a hammer and rendered into long stringy fibers that are then boiled in the water along with leaves of the companion and modulator plants. Cooking time in particular is a race between extracting all the relevant constituents from the plants, on the one hand, and boiling away the more volatile constituents on the other. The mixture may be boiled once or several times and for differing amounts of time; additional plant materials may or may not

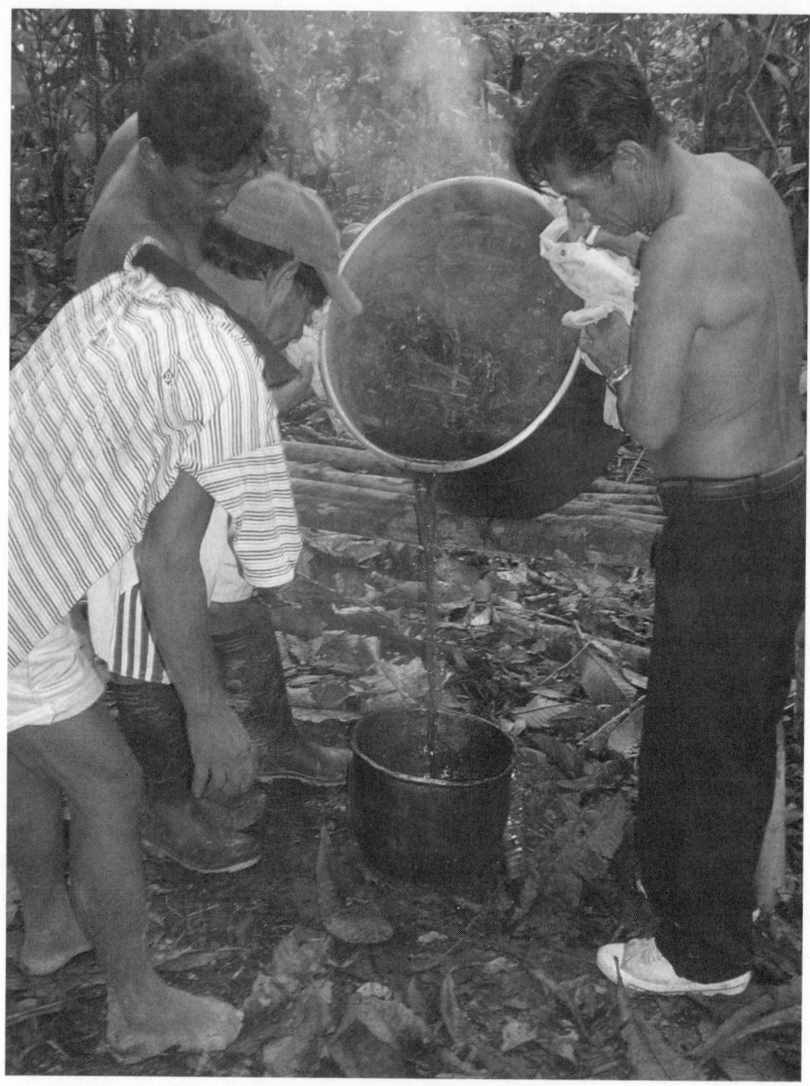

FIGURE 9. Pouring off the ayahuasca.

be added during the cooking process. Storage, too, can affect the quality of the ayahuasca drink, with the quality of the psychoactive effect often claimed to change as the drink ages.

Moreover, the ayahuasquero decides just how much ayahuasca drink will be given to any participant; in effect, the ayahuasquero titrates dosage to effect. The ayahuasquero fills the cup with the amount considered appropriate for the person drinking it. I have been given—after some discussion—a smaller amount of ayahuasca to drink at the next session after a particularly spectacular purge. Alternatively, I have been called back up to the ayahuasquero and given—to my dismay—a second and even a third drink of ayahuasca at a single session. In addition, a specific psychoactive effect may be orchestrated not only by dose but also by additional plants, either mixed into the ayahuasca drink or ingested separately—for example, by smoking the leaves of the toé plant after drinking the ayahuasca, or by smoking the bark of the ayahuasca vine in addition to drinking the ayahuasca drink.

The idea of deliberate titration to end point by adjusting dosage may be illustrated by looking at the mean DMT content of ayahuasca drinks not as mean mg/100 ml, as we did above, but, rather, as mean mg/*dose*. When we do that, the total β-carbolines in the ayahuasca drinks vary as widely as we have come to expect, ranging from 20 to 416 mg/dose. But the amount of DMT becomes remarkably constant, with a range of just 25 to 36 mg/dose and a mean of 30 mg/dose. It certainly seems that 30 ± 5 mg of DMT is considered, from the Upper Amazon to Brazil, an optimal dose, and that the leaders of ceremonies are able to judge just what amount of the drink they had made contains just that much DMT.

THE SINGLE ACTIVE MOLECULE

An even deeper issue in understanding ayahuasca lies in the attempt to relate its psychoactive effects to specific active molecules. There are several reasons why people try to do this. Many North Americans seek ways to evade the emetic and purgative effects, the ferocious physicality of the ayahuasca experience. That is why they seek parenteral ingestion of DMT, primarily through smoking—to eliminate the need for the vomit-inducing harmala alkaloids. That is why psychonautic tourist Daniel Pinchbeck says that the smokable or injectable form of synthetic DMT is "modern science's greatest contribution to archaic Amazonian spirituality."[52]

We tend to think this way because modern science has in fact *defined* medicines as having only one compound that is bioactive. This approach solved some practical problems, such as the need to patent and standardize medicines.[53] The idea has been that the medicinal or psychoactive effects of a plant are accounted for by specific chemicals, and that the best medicine consists of standardized, predictable dosages. Science journalist Joel Swerdlow suggests: "The study of whole plants and combinations is rare—largely because single active compounds, particularly those that have been modified, are easiest to patent and because FDA regulations encourage this approach."[54]

There are several problems with the assumption that the ayahuasca experience is due to its single active molecule. First, there is a significant *experiential* difference between drinking ayahuasca and an intravenous injection of dimethyltryptamine. Differences in the rapidity of onset and duration of the experience mean differences in the amount of time available for contemplation and exploration; the presence or absence of purging means differences in the experience of corporeality and catharsis; the harmala alkaloids—and even MAO inhibition itself—may make independent contributions to the quality or contents of the experience.

Further, emphasis on a single active molecule has prejudiced consideration of whole plants, which can contain dozens of bioactive substances.[55] There is little doubt that every plant contains a unique mix of multiply-interacting substances in complex additive, synergistic, and antagonistic relationships, presumably in a variety of feedback loops. The fact that it is *difficult* to describe these relationships is no reason to decide that they are unimportant. Yet, once it has been determined that the companion plant—chacruna, sameruca, chagraponga—contains DMT, the inquiry stops. Still, mestizo shamans select particular companion plants—and combinations of companion plants—for their specific effects. If their only function is to provide the single active molecule dimethyltryptamine, what is there to choose among them?

Similarly, if the purpose of the ayahuasca vine is to contribute a single active molecule, or even just a few active molecules, whose function is to inhibit peripheral MAO, then it should not matter if another plant is substituted, as long as it contains the same molecules. But substituting, say, Syrian rue for the ayahuasca vine, even though the rue contains the same harmala alkaloids, does apparently make an experiential difference. The experience with rue has been described as crystalline, cold, overwhelming, erratic, and uncaring, compared with that of the ayahuasca vine, which has been described as warm, organic, friendly, and purposeful.[56] This may be because the harmala alkaloids are in different proportions in the two plants: levels of THH are higher in the ayahuasca vine, and harmaline is higher in rue.[57] Experiential differences might also be due to the fact that rue contains tannins and quinazoline alkaloids not found in the ayahuasca vine.[58] Thus, too, self-experimenters tend to use only the minimum amount of rue necessary to inhibit MAO; using more apparently serves no purpose other than increasing the emetic effect. But the amount of ayahuasca vine can be increased beyond the minimum necessary, and increasing the amount is claimed to add a special dimension to the experience.[59]

Finally, the focus on single active molecules ignores *context*. The terms *pharmacologicalism* and *pharmacological determinism* have been coined to capture the

Ayahuasca Analogues

Substituting other plants for the ayahuasca vine and the companion plants—chacruna, sameruca, chagraponga—is part of a quest for what are called *ayahuasca analogues*—duplications of the ayahuasca drink "compounded with the correct percentages of DMT and beta-carbolines" but using materials more readily available in North America.[1] One of the most commonly used alternative sources of β-carbolines is the plant *Peganum harmala*, also called Syrian rue, which grows wild in the western states, and is available in South Asian and Middle Eastern groceries under the name *esfand* or *harmal*.[2] Potential North American sources of DMT include a variety of plants in the genera *Acacia*, *Desmanthus*, *Phalaris*, and *Mimosa*.[3] There are a number of neologisms for these analogues both generally, such as *pharmahuasca*, *anahuasca*, and *gaiahuasca*, and for specific combinations, such as *mimosahuasca* and *acaciahuasca*.[4]

NOTES

1. McKenna, 1989, p. 202. See DeKorne, 1994, pp. 91–101; Ott, 1994, pp. 51–70.
2. Ott, 1994, pp. 80–85; Shulgin & Shulgin, 1997, pp. 294–295.
3. Callaway & McKenna, 1998, p. 491; Ott, 1994, pp. 81–84, 86; Shulgin & Shulgin, 1997, pp. 418, 537.
4. See Shulgin & Shulgin, 1997, pp. 294–295. For a literary account of ingesting a mixture of the bark of *Minosa hostilis* and a powdered extract of Syrian rue, see Pinchbeck, 2002, pp. 141–143.

often unstated premise that the effects of a substance are entirely determined by its chemical structure, thus ignoring the effects, among other things, of traditional ceremonial settings, the authoritative presence of a healer, social pressures both within and outside the ceremony, and expectations of particular outcomes.[60] It ignores as well the presumably complex interactions *among* plants deliberately used for modulatory effects during the ceremony, including not only nicotine and other tobacco alkaloids but also any of the scores of additional plants that may be added to the ayahuasca drink.

THE TELEPATHY MEME

When harmine was first isolated from the ayahuasca vine, and before it was identified as the same compound found in Syrian rue, *Peganum harmala*, it was called, variously, banisterine, yagéine, and, interestingly, telepathine. Apparently it was a traveler named Rafael Zerda Bayón who first claimed, in 1915, that ayahuasca visions were telepathic—an idea reiterated by pharmacologist Alexandre Rouhier in 1924—and suggested the corresponding name telepathine for its active constituent. The name was then used by Colombian physician Guillermo Fischer Cárdenas when he actually isolated the compound in 1923. In 1932, a brief article appeared in *Science News*—and then apparently summarized in *Modern Mechanics*—describing how a drink made from the plant yage induces "magnificent and terrifying visions in motion picture form," and is said to grant the power to see things at a distance—"like mediums in a trance."[61] In 1939, it was determined that banisterine, yagéine, and telepathine were all the same as harmine, and that is the name that has been used ever since.[62]

And that probably would have been the end of that, except that American novelist William S. Burroughs ended his first book—originally published in 1953 as *Junky*, under the pseudonym William Lee—with a brief meditation on yagé. "I read about a drug called yage, used by Indians in the headwaters of the Amazon," he wrote. "I decided to go down to Colombia and score for yage. . . . I am ready to move on south and look for the uncut kick that opens out instead of narrowing down like junk." The last sentence in the book says, "Yage may be the final fix." Burroughs picked up on the name telepathine—which was, in fact, no longer being used—and noted that ayahuasca "is supposed to increase telepathic sensitivity."[63]

Hernando García Barriga, writing in 1958, added to the telepathy narrative. "Savage Indians," he wrote, "who have never left their forests and who, of course, can have no idea of civilized life, describe, in their particular language, and with more or less precision, the details of houses, castles, and cities peopled by multitudes."[64] What—other than ayahuasca-induced telepathy—could possibly be the source of such knowledge? Psychiatrist Claudio Naranjo had similar thoughts in 1967, but in the opposite direction. When he gave city dwellers harmaline—note that this is not the same as harmine, although related to it, and also a constituent of the ayahuasca vine—they reported that they saw tigers and jungle imagery.[65] Clearly the synthetic chemical had somehow connected Naranjo's subjects mentally to the jungle.

Of course, none of this took into account other possible reasons for these results. As anthropologist Gerardo Reichel-Dolmatoff has pointed out, even isolated Indians in 1958 knew a lot about cities, having been told about them by missionaries, soldiers, rubber tappers, traders, and travelers, and having seen pictures in calendars and magazines.[66] And we have no idea what expectations Naranjo's volunteers brought to their experience, although I think we can make a pretty good guess. But so embedded had this meme become that, in 1967, a Haight-Ashbury resident told physician Andrew Weil that Eskimos given ayahuasca saw visions of huge cats.[67]

Then, in 1971, Charles Lamb published *Wizard of the Upper Amazon*, which purported to be a transcription of the true story of Manuel Córdova Ríos, an Iquitos ayahuasquero who claimed that, when he had been kidnapped by

Indians in his youth, he had learned their language during group telepathic ayahuasca sessions, been made their chief, and finally returned to become a healer for his urban clientele.[68]

The reliability of this account has been seriously challenged.[69] But the telepathy meme it contained was passed along by best-selling writer Andrew Weil in his first book, *The Natural Mind*, published in 1972. Weil was particularly fascinated by the alleged "group vision sessions in which all participants see the same visions"—that is, visions of jungle cats, other animals, enemy tribes, and village scenes—which he took as evidence for the "reality of shared consciousness."[70] Weil was so enthusiastic about Córdova Ríos's alleged telepathic experiences that he wrote a glowing introduction when the book was, at his suggestion, reprinted as a paperback in 1974. Ayahuasca, he wrote, "has long been credited with the ability to transport human beings to realms of experience where telepathy and clairvoyance are commonplace. When German scientists first isolated harmaline, an active principle of ayahuasca, they named it 'telepathine' because of this association."[71] I suppose only a pedant would point out that it was harmine, not harmaline, that was named telepathine; or that Fischer Cárdenas did not name the compound he isolated after his own experience; or that he was Colombian, not German.

In this introduction, Weil referred to what was apparently his only experience with ayahuasca, which must therefore have taken place before 1974, while he was traveling in Colombia, and which was evidently quite miserable, leaving him violently sick and spending most of the night lying in a mud puddle.[72] In his next book, Weil gives a much more detailed account of this experience. But, by this time, he seems to have lost much of his initial enthusiasm for the alleged telepathic qualities of ayahuasca; he specifically points out that there were no jungles or jaguars in his visions, and no "telepathic news bulletins of distant events."[73]

Meanwhile, Kenneth Kensinger, a missionary and anthropologist who had worked for many years with the Cashinahua, echoed the narrative of Hernando García Barriga. Several Cashinahua, he wrote in 1973, "who have never been to or seen pictures of Pucallpa, the large town at the Ucayali River terminus of the Central Highway, have described their visits under the influence of ayahuasca to the town with sufficient detail for me to recognize specific sights and shops."[74] And he echoes Manuel Córdova Ríos as well. According to Bruce Lamb, during a particularly intense ayahuasca session, Córdova Ríos saw his mother dying; when he returned to the home of his youth, he learned that she had died just as he had seen.[75] Kensinger similarly reports that, after one ayahuasca session, six of the nine participants told him that they had seen the death of his mother's father, two days before Kensinger himself was informed of the death by radio.[76]

And then, in 1981, Peruvian poet César Calvo Soriano wrote a novel of acknowledged genius entitled *Las tres mitades de Ino Moxo y otros brujos de la Amazonía*, which he based on the story of Manuel Córdova Ríos. He described how the shaman Ximu telepathically controlled the visions of his young apprentice, "calibrating the hallucinogenic apparitions in the mind of the young man. . . . The slightest gesture of the old man developed in his consciousness the caresses of an order. Whatever Ximu thought was seen and heard by the boy. They understood each other through flashes of lightning and through shadows, amid slow visions and colors, and Ximu began to confide his patience and his strength."[77]

So the meme continues, with frequent invocations of the old name telepathine. David Luke, for example, is a parapsychology researcher at the Centre for the Study of Anomalous Psychological Processes at the University of Northampton in England. Interviewed by James Kent, the former editor of *Entheogen Review* and *Trip* magazine, Luke spoke about telepathy with ayahuasca, "because ayahuasca is reputedly quite potent in inducing telepathic and clairvoyant experiences. One of the active principles, harmaline, was even called 'telepathine' when it was first isolated from this decoction in the 1920s."[78] Countercultural writer Paul Krassner, in his book *Magic Mushrooms and Other Highs: From Toad Slime to Ecstasy*, says that "shamans say that ayahuasca is 'very telepathic,' and years ago, after also experiencing a ceremony, the first scientist to isolate the psychoactive alkaloid in ayahuasca named the chemical 'telepathine.'"[79]

What is interesting about this persistent meme is not that it is wrong but, rather, that it is correct, although translated into ill-fitting Western clothes. As we have seen, Upper Amazonian shamans maintain that drinking ayahuasca gives them visual and auditory information about events that are remote in both time and space. In the Upper Amazon, too, one of the key features of icaros, a shaman's magic songs, is that they have the ability to modulate the visionary effects of ayahuasca and other psychoactive plants, both for the shaman who is singing the icaro and for a patient or apprentice to whom the shaman has given the medicine. Most important, songs can also modulate the *contents* of the visions of a patient or apprentice. This is, I think, just what César Calvo was referring to in the passage quoted above; similarly, when doña María tired of my incessant questions, she would tell me, "I will show you," which meant that I should expect my next ayahuasca visions to give me the answers I was looking for.

CHAPTER 23

PHENOMENOLOGY OF THE AYAHUASCA EXPERIENCE

THE STAGES OF THE AYAHUASCA EXPERIENCE

Based on my own experience, discussions with others, and review of the ethnographic literature, the ayahuasca experience appears to unfold in three phases.[1] In the first phase, there are geometric figures, sometimes spinning or whirling, fireflies, rippling water, raindrops, van Gogh deep space stars and galaxies, and eyes; in fact, disembodied eyes and eyelike shapes are frequently found in Amazonian visionary art.[2] Of interest are the apparently frequent Greek key designs reflected in indigenous ayahuasca art—for example, in Tukano basketry and Shipibo pottery and embroidery; these patterns were consistently a part of the first phase of my experiences. Poet César Calvo gives a description of this stage: "When I closed my eyelids, something like arabesques appeared, complicated decorations of iridescent light and shadows. . . . They seemed to be animated, moving against a backdrop of geometric figures, pointed planets, great rocks carved with outlines of ancient animals, an unending diversity of forms."[3] Anthropologist Gerardo Reichel-Dolmatoff reports a similar experience—geometric shapes, fireworks, jets of water, semicircles, lights, multiplying circles, hexagons, eyes, colors, and stylized palm trees, lasting about twenty minutes.[4]

The second phase consists of what we may as well call contact with the spirit world, often through interaction with other-than-human plant and animal spirits, sometimes through *visionary information*—distant scenes, the whereabouts of missing relatives, the location of lost objects, the identity of the sorcerer or sorcery responsible for a sickness. These visionary landscapes often incorporate the geometric designs of the first phase: rooms may be lined with complex tessellations, faces may appear covered with patterns, a grassy area may be revealed as an oriental carpet covered with complex designs.

The third phase begins as the visions begin to fade, the nausea lessens, and one slips into a state of physical weakness and lassitude, sometimes with short, quiet, pleasant visions.

Indigenous cultures in the Amazon are similar. Among the Cashinahua, visions seen during the collective ritual drinking of ayahuasca—geometric designs, transformations of figures such as snakes, reptiles, and vines—are called *dami*. Rapidly changing dami are the only images perceived by beginners or at the initial stage of the effect of the ayahuasca; they are said to be *nixi pae besti*, "only vine things." To go beyond the dami images requires the good will and generosity of the owner or parent of the vine, called *yube*, spirit of the boa. If the spirit of the boa is stingy with the drinker, he will not see anything or at most "only vine things." The real images to be seen are yuxin—beings with the appearance and agency of human beings.[5]

The Sharanahua, too, distinguish between an initial stage, characterized by visions of shifting shapes and colors, colored beads and scrolls, growing larger, becoming like ropes or snakes; and a subsequent stage, characterized by visions of the spirits—beautiful women, dancing, with painted decorations and feathered headdresses. The beads and scrolls, vines and snakes, of the first phase indicate only that the visionary state is about to begin. They are not the spirits and are not, the Sharanahua say, of any importance. The spirits come only by singing, and therefore appear only to one who knows the songs that call them; young men see only the snakes, which terrify them.[6]

Among the Piro, the ayahuasca experience begins with the sound of wind rushing through the jungle, followed by what they call the *little lights* glittering in the dark. It is only after this that the spirits arrive, singing; these spirits, they say, are the *kayigawlu*, the real vision. Artemio Fasabi Gordon, son of a well-known Piro shaman, don Mauricio Roberto Fasabi, told anthropologist Peter Gow how he had drunk ayahuasca often in his youth but had not seen anything—only "those little glittering lights that the night makes."[7] One Cubeo described this first phase as "a room spinning with red feathers."[8]

Similarly, among the Tukano there are three stages of ayahuasca experience. Shortly after drinking, after an initial tremor and the sensation of rushing winds, there is a state of drowsiness in which the person concentrates with half-closed eyes upon the luminous flashes and streaks that appear—flickering and floating star and flower shapes, symmetrical kaleidoscopic patterns, eye-shaped motifs, concentric circles, chains of brilliant dots. It is in the second stage that pictorial images take shape, and the drinker can see people and animals, unknown creatures, spirit beings—the River of Milk, the Snake Canoe, the boa, the anaconda, the Master of the Animals of the jungle and waters, gigantic prototypes of the game animals. In the third stage, the images disappear, leaving soft music, wandering clouds, and a state of blissful serenity.[9]

Another important point is that first-time drinkers of ayahuasca, especially gringos with great expectations, often have disappointing experiences—no visions, no ecstasies, just profound nausea, explosive vomiting and retching, distressing diarrhea, and rubbery legs. Doña María and don Roberto explain this by saying that there must first be la purga, purgation and cleansing, before the ayahuasca can begin to teach. Don Agustin Rivas says the same: "After the body is rid of toxins," he says, "then one begins to see the real spirits."[10] Don Julio Jerena expresses the same thought. "I was going to paint him with the colors of ayahuasca," he says of a gringo patient who, eager for visions, had done nothing but vomit. "But when I looked inside him I realized that he was like a living room that was full of broken furniture, garbage on the ground, peeling walls. Who would paint a room like that? No one. So I had to spend the night cleaning it all out to get it ready for painting."[11] Don Pacho Piaguaje, a Siona shaman, puts it this way: "Ayahuasca is like a wild animal that must be approached with great caution. It will not allow you to make full contact until it knows you very well."[12]

Under such circumstances, issues of set and setting become very important. First-time drinkers of ayahuasca are often *eager* for visions, have read about the visions of others, and expect miraculous exploding cosmic pinwheels. "The ayahuasca must be weak," they say; but in fact it can take several sessions—and numerous wrenching purges—before the drinker is able to see what the teacher plant is ready to show. Novelist William S. Burroughs and poet Allen Ginsberg both confessed serious disappointment with their first experience of ayahuasca.[13]

This is true even of those who become shamans. Doña María had no visions until the third time she drank ayahuasca. Don Emilio Andrade Gómez, a mestizo shaman, says: "The first three times I took ayahuasca I did not see anything, but I continued being on a diet. The fourth time I saw something. That made me believe that it was indeed true what they said. The fifth time I took the brew I really had a vision."[14] Shipibo shaman don Leoncio Garcia Sampaya drank ayahuasca for three months before he had a vision—and then it was tremendous, overwhelming. "Probably I was learning from the spirits during the diet," he says, "but I didn't understand."[15]

Thus, too, the *accounts* of first- or second-time use must be read with awareness that such reports frequently recount the effects of expectation rather than the effects of the drink, or at least attempt to put the best interpretation on the experience. Finally, some shamans may mix some toé—rich in scopolamine—into the ayahuasca drink, at least the first time or two they give it to a gringo who has not drunk it before, so that the client is not disappointed at the lack of any dramatic effect. This may account for some unusually vivid and frightening first experiences. Don Roberto may, under such circumstances, have the person smoke toé leaves in a cachimbo, a wooden pipe.

It can sometimes take several experiences to get beyond the geometric shapes, kaleidoscopic patterns, eyelike figures, and even cartoon characters that seem to characterize the first stage of the ayahuasca experience. Why is this? Since ayahuasca visions either are embedded in the hallucinator's ordinary perceptual space or constitute the entire perceptual field, they clearly require considerable processing. Perspective must be retained and, as the observer or object moves, continuously updated; spatial relations among objects must be constantly readjusted. And to the extent that lifelike three-dimensional interactive figures are *constructed* by the mind, it may be that the process takes some practice. That may be why, too, gringos report early experiences of stick figures and relatively simple cartoon faces and persons.

FEATURES OF THE AYAHUASCA EXPERIENCE

Lucidity

Significantly, ayahuasca does not affect lucidity or clarity of thought. There is no sense of being narcotized, no decrease in alertness, no inability to process linearly. I have certainly been *puzzled* from time to time by what was going on, but I have never felt impaired in my ability to *reason* about it. I could walk in a crooked line in order to avoid banging my shins on cast-iron lawn furniture while, simultaneously, understanding that the furniture was a hallucination. Similar results have been found in DMT experiments; reasoning and thinking were, for most participants, reportedly unaffected.[16] Indigenous reports of ayahuasca experiences indicate that visions appear with "complete awareness of what is going on."[17] Similarly, there appears to be little *distancing* in ayahuasca visions, which appear from a first-person point of view. Finally, visions are sometimes more vivid with eyes closed, but not necessarily; many visions are perfectly clear with the eyes open, embedded into ordinary perceptual space.

> *Example* 1. I am drinking ayahuasca with don Rómulo in his jungle hut. The moonlit clearing is filled with black cast-iron lawn furniture, chairs and low tables, intricately filigreed, clearly visible in the

> moonlight. The pieces of lawn furniture are fully integrated into my perceptual space, blocking the visible area behind them, changing their spatial relationship and perspective as I walk among them, solid and heavy. When I walk across the clearing, held up on my rubbery legs by don Rómulo's son, we walk in a zigzag line, to avoid banging my shins against the tables. I do this even though I *know*, in my fully functional rational mind, that there is no lawn furniture in the jungle.

This effect was reported by Strassman's DMT participants as well. Usually there was little difference between what participants saw with their eyes opened or their eyes closed, although opening the eyes often caused the visions to overlay what was in the room.[18]

Time Dilation

Ayahuasca frequently induces a sense of *time dilation*: things seem to take a long time. The ayahuasca session seems to last much longer than the clock would indicate; each icaro seems to last as long as a Wagner opera, when, by my watch, it has been only fifteen or twenty minutes. Psychologist Benny Shanon reports similar experiences. "Feeling so much had happened," he writes, "I reopened my eyes only to discover—by looking at my watch—that barely two minutes had elapsed. The contrast between perceived time and real time was striking."[19]

Synesthesia

Synesthesia—what Shanon, in his extensive phenomenology, calls *intermodal effects*—is a prominent effect of ayahuasca.[20] There can be a sensory convergence of vision, sound, and smell; icaros create visions, smells produce sounds. Among mestizo shamans, the icaros modulate the visions not only of the shaman but of those who hear the icaro as well. The icaros speak of a medicine as "my painted song," "my words with those designs," or "my ringing pattern." Two writers have tried to capture this aspect of the ayahuasca experience. Poet César Calvo writes, "I see him reach over the neck of his cushma and extract a bottle of Florida water. Later he comes close and sprinkles me with the music that pours from the open bottle."[21] Or again: "The fresh air was something I could see, and sometimes a sound was like a texture of feathers that I could touch. All of my senses were one, communicated between themselves: I could listen with my fingers, touch with my eyes, sense those visions with my voice."[22] And novelist Peter Matthiessen describes part of a solitary ayahuasca session: "Somewhere, somewhere there was singing. . . .

The chords were multicolored, vaulting like rockets across his consciousness; he could break off pieces of the music, like pieces of meringue."[23] In the paintings of Pablo Amaringo, many elements that appear purely decorative—multicolored spirals and waves—are in fact visual expressions of music.[24]

Among the Shipibo, the designs painted on their bodies, homes, boats, tools, household goods, and clothing represent sacred patterns derived from a cosmic anaconda whose skin embodies all possible designs. The Shipibo shaman, after drinking ayahuasca, sees such a luminous design in the air; when this design floats down and touches the shaman's lips, it becomes transformed into a song the shaman sings. Different elements of the song relate to different elements of the design; for example, the end of each verse is associated with the end curl of a design motif. The shaman sings, "I see brilliant bands of designs, curved and fragrant"—a synesthesia of sound, vision, and smell.[25] Shipibo shamans employ these patterns to reorder the bodies of persons who are ill. Certain diseases are thought to be caused by harmful designs that the shaman must magically unravel and replace with orderly designs.[26] The shaman's song penetrates and reorders the patient's body in the form of harmonious geometric designs: "At first, the sick body appears like a very messy design. After a few treatments, the design appears gradually. When the patient is cured, the design is clear, neat, and complete."[27]

Among the Shipibo, visionary designs become songs; among the Cashinahua, songs become visionary designs. When Cashinahua drink ayahuasca, their songs describe their journeys in the spirit world; at the same time, designs that are drawn by the songs they sing help them orient themselves in the spirit world. The designs function as paths to be followed away from and back to normal space and perception. "One should always stay inside the design," the Cashinahua say, "in order to not get lost."[28] Like the Shipibo, the Cashinahua paint these maps their songs create: different worlds are represented as houses with doors to be entered and paths linking the different contained spaces—houses, worlds, bodies; spots represent stars.[29]

Similarly, in a Tukano creation story, the sounds made by the firstborn mythic child are the tastes and visions of ayahuasca, "for as soon as the little child cried aloud, all the people who were in Diawi became intoxicated and saw all kinds of colors."[30] Indigenous myths from southern Colombia speak of yagé-created Solar Men playing melodies on flute or drum, with each melody transforming into a different color: "When the world was illuminated, all this symphony of colors and the music brought forth understanding to humankind, creating intelligence and language."[31]

Gap Filling

A significant effect of ayahuasca—and one that will be important when we consider Charles Bonnet syndrome in the next chapter—is that ayahuasca serves as a *gap filler* in ambiguous visual stimuli and probably auditory stimuli as well. In other words, ayahuasca constructs visual *meaning* out of bits and pieces of perception, a sort of perceptual *bricoleur*.

> *Example 2.* I have drunk ayahuasca, and I am now off by myself in the jungle, suffering simultaneously from vomiting and diarrhea. I will discover, the next day, to my immense regret, that I am in fact squatting over an anthill, but at the time I am so focused on my intestinal disquietude that I do not notice the angry ants. I see, on the ground to my left, a small Confederate flag, perhaps eight inches long, on a slender stick—the sort of flag bystanders wave at a parade. It is perfectly formed, three-dimensional, *present*. My mind tells me it is a hallucination; my senses tell me it is real. I reach over and touch it, and immediately the flag *decomposes* into its component parts—twigs, leaves, jungle detritus. I remove my hand, and the flag reconstitutes itself. There it is again, real, actual, indisputable.

Here the ayahuasca drink has taken ambiguous visual stimuli—a jumble of uninterpretable sticks, twigs, leaves, shadows, and moonlight on the jungle floor in the nighttime darkness—and done me the favor of turning them into something coherent and meaningful. I do not have the slightest idea why this should turn out to be a Confederate flag. I do not believe that the Confederate flag has any particular psychological significance for me; it is as if the ayahuasca has searched my visual memory banks and come up with something that would fill in the perceptual gaps and make the stimuli meaningful.

> *Example 3.* I am living at don Rómulo's tambo, his jungle hut, where we have ayahuasca ceremonies in a small cleared area in front of his hut. I know that the ayahuasca is taking effect when the grass in that clearing becomes, in the moonlit dark, a highly detailed Persian carpet. The complex and detailed pattern of the carpet remains consistent even when I examine it closely; but when I *touch* the carpet, it feels like grass—and just in the spot I touched it, the carpet disappears, and I see a small patch of grass, seemingly growing in the middle of the carpet.

This gap-filling effect of ayahuasca explains many visions reported by others as well. William S. Burroughs saw, instead of a Confederate flag, Easter Island masks: "The hut took on an archaic far-Pacific look with Easter Island heads carved in the support posts."[32] Wade Davis saw plants in his friends' hair and snakes on the ground of the hut: "There were rainbows trapped inside their feathers. In their hair were weeping flowers and trees attempting to soar into the clouds. Leaves fell from the branches with great howling sounds. . . . Then the ground opened. Snakes encircled the posts of the maloca and slipped away into the earth."[33] César Calvo writes of an ayahuasca experience: "I took the little box of matches and began to laugh inwardly, because the matchbox was the skull of a deer . . . knowing that it really was a matchbox. The same with the top of that small tree next to the wall: it was a canoe that was beached there. But at the same time, in the same way, it was just the top of the small tree!"[34]

Auditory Hallucinations

The same gap-filling phenomenon may apply to auditory hallucinations as well. Ayahuasca drinkers often hear what they describe as the sound of flowing water, loud rushing sounds, the sound of wind rushing, the sound of rushing water, and the roar of rain or waterfall.[35] These ambiguous and amorphous sounds may then be constructed as *meaningful*—as sorrowful songs, unknown languages, people singing, the voice of a recently deceased friend, a brass band.[36] People ingesting DMT report similar experiences of hearing sounds described as high-pitched, whining, chattering, crinkling, or crunching.[37] One ayahuasca drinker reports hearing high-pitched chirps, like the sounds made by dolphins;[38] William S. Burroughs, drinking "oily and phosphorescent" ayahuasca in Colombia, describes how "larval beings passed before my eyes in a blue haze, each one giving an obscene, mocking squawk."[39] These sounds, too, are constructed as mysteriously meaningful. Users of DMT report hearing "alien music" and "alien languages," which may or may not be comprehensible.[40] Terence McKenna reports that he heard "a language of alien meaning that is conveying alien information."[41]

Example 4. I have drunk ayahuasca with don Antonio Barrera. I am sitting quietly, waiting for something to happen. Between my feet is a basin half-filled with water for me to vomit into. I have used the basin several times. I am absolutely convinced that a puppy dog has found its way into the thatched hut and is lapping up the water from the basin. I

> can hear the puppy clearly, hear the slight splash of water. I look down; there is no puppy; there are no ripples on the surface of the water. I look away, and I hear the lapping sounds again. This happens several times. The sounds are overwhelmingly realistic. It is the absence of the corresponding puppy that is puzzling.

Here again, I believe that ayahuasca, as perceptual bricoleur, has taken ambiguous auditory stimuli—the sounds of calling frogs in the jungle, the rustling of don Antonio's shacapa, the shifting and breathing of other people in the hut, the inchoate rushing sounds of ayahuasca itself—and given me a gap-filling *closest match*. I do not know why it turns out to be a puppy dog who has wandered into the hut; probably it does not matter. Rather, it is as if ayahuasca wants me to see things and hear things, *wants* me to find new meaning in my visual stimuli, *wants* me to see the world as strange and wonderful and unpredictable.

Sometimes visual and auditory hallucinations are neatly coordinated:

> *Example* 5. I am sitting in the dark jungle alongside the cleared area in front of don Rómulo's tambo. The cleared ground has become a Persian carpet, on which is scattered cast-iron lawn furniture, chairs and low tables, which I see in great detail and solidity, which I must be careful not to trip over. On the other side of the clearing is a large building with a terrace and a stone balustrade overlooking the lawn; dimly sensed people in evening clothes stroll on the terrace holding murmured conversations. The palm trees in the jungle are now in large pots on a terraced lawn. Clearly I have crashed a sophisticated party, and I am embarrassed to be making such a mess, vomiting into the potted palms.

Auditory perceptions of spirit speech are a central part of mestizo shamanic experience. Doña María and don Roberto are given patient diagnoses and prescriptions during healing ceremonies by plant spirits who speak clearly and distinctly, in Spanish, in their ears. Spirits use other languages as well. Doña María's spirits spoke to her in Inca—that is, Quechua—which she understood, although she did not speak Quechua. Both doña María and don Roberto, at the start of each healing ceremony, are attended by outer space spirits who speak in computer language. Doña María says they speak like this: *beep boop beep beep boop beep beep*; don Roberto says they sound like *ping ping dan dan*. Amazonian mestizo shamans also know the languages of birds and animals.

Don Rómulo Magin, for example, is fluent in the language of búhos, owls; their language, I am told, sounds like this: *oootutututu kakakaka hahahahaha.*

Explorable Space

What is most striking about ayahuasca visions is the sense of personal *presence*—first, that one is interacting with *persons* and second, that the persons are external, solid, three-dimensional, *real*.

I think that there may be two different sorts of experience that are frequently conflated under a single description. Many who drink ayahuasca report the visions as being like television or the movies—like "cinematographic films of a phantasmagoric nature."[42] Young Shuar today, for example, have a very relaxed attitude toward taking ayahuasca; they say that they "like it a lot because it's like watching a movie."[43] Anthropologist Luis Eduardo Luna speaks of people at ayahuasca ceremonies exclaiming, "How beautiful. This is like a movie!"[44] César Calvo has a character in his novel say that his ayahuasca vision was "as if I had watched a film while being drunk."[45] Such visions have a two-dimensional feel to them, like watching events unfold on a screen.

Other visions more immediately communicate *presence*, providing not only interaction with three-dimensional persons but also a sense of being embedded within a three-dimensional landscape capable of exploration. I think this distinction may be what doña María was trying to communicate to me when describing the difference between her tobacco and ayahuasca visions—that tobacco visions, unlike ayahuasca visions, are not very clear, but still reveal things; tobacco visions, she said, are like a movie. Pablo Amaringo explains this even more clearly: "It is only when the person begins to hear and see as if he were *inside the scene*, not as something presented to him, that he is able to discover many things."[46] I think this must be what the Cashinahua intend when they describe drinking ayahuasca as being a *bai*—that is, a sightseeing excursion with visits to the houses of friends and relatives along the way.[47]

Biophysicist and computer genius Clifford Pickover speaks of DMT allowing the user to enter a completely different environment "that some have likened to an alien or parallel universe," in which alien-like or elflike beings appear to live and interact with the user. "The DMT experience," Pickover writes, "has the feel of reality in terms of detail and potential for exploration."[48] This DMT space appears to be "an independent and consistent reality," he says;[49] this space is also often called "DMT hyperspace."[50]

Ayahuasca is thus often described as like "a portal to other worlds which exist alongside our own."[51] This sense of being in an explorable space not infrequently prompts comparisons to *tourism*; as Pablo Amaringo says, "I was like a tourist, always asking the spirits what is this and that, asking them to take me from one place to another, demanding explanations for everything."[52]

This sense of the reality of the ayahuasca experience is even encoded linguistically. In the Shipibo language, every declarative sentence has a mandatory marker for *evidentiality*. The direct evidential marker *-ra* indicates that the speaker makes the assertion from personal knowledge, and the reportative marker *-ronki* indicates that the speaker makes the assertion on the basis of information received from another. Accounts of dreams are regularly marked with *-ronki*; but, strikingly, accounts by shamans of what they have seen in an ayahuasca vision are regularly marked with *-ra*.[53] As linguist Pilar Valenzuela writes, "While ayahuasca visions are part of reality, dreams are not, and this distinction is encoded in the system."[54]

Elves and Spirits

Many reports of DMT use have in common what psychopharmacologist Daniel Perrine calls "a fairly bizarre claim" to be communicating with discarnate entities, usually referred to as *elves*, a term apparently first popularized by the prolific psychonaut Terence McKenna—specifically, "self-transforming machine elves," "tryptamine Munchkins," "hyperdimensional machine-elf entities."[55] In contrast to other psychedelics, McKenna says, DMT uniquely opened "an unanticipated dimension that involved contact with an alien intelligence. . . . Organized entelechies presented themselves in the psychedelic experience with information that seemed not to be drawn from the personal history of the individual or even from the collective human experience."[56] And he writes: "But in the Amazon and other places where plant hallucinogens are understood and used, you are conveyed into worlds that are appallingly different from ordinary reality. Their vividness cannot be stressed enough. They are more real than real . . . and you realize that you are not looking in on the Other; the Other is looking in on you."[57] Note again the sense of being in a foreign land described by Pablo Amaringo. Poet Dale Pendell writes that, for McKenna, "DMT opened the door to an entirely new dimension of reality, a dimension wholly *Other*. . . . The entities Terence encountered were alien. Like any good explorer, he tried to interact with them, to listen to what they had to say and to come back with a report."[58]

Sometimes this sense of presence is diffuse—dark-robed and faceless beings gathered to support me in my nausea; tall thin dark-skinned men in white shirts and white pants with black suspenders flitted on unknown errands among the participants at a ceremony. Poet Allen Ginsberg, drinking yagé in Pucallpa, writes of the whole hut seeming "rayed with spectral presences."[59] Writing of ayahuasca use on the Bajo Urubamba, anthropologist Peter Gow speaks of shamans seeing "a forest tree as a house full of people."[60] Piro shaman don Mauricio Roberto Fasabi calls these *ayahuasca people*. "They come when you drink ayahuasca," he says. "They join in, their songs are very beautiful!"[61] And sometimes the sense of presence is specific. Shuar shaman Alejandro Tsakimp reports that, when drinking ayahuasca, a "precious little woman, just lovely, kept appearing before me. Even now the woman is in the habit of appearing to me—very lovely and wearing different robes."[62]

Spirit Experiences

The presence of organized intelligent entelechies—what Peter Meyer calls *discarnate entities*—is a significant feature of ayahuasca experiences and perhaps the feature most important for understanding how ayahuasca brings about contact with plant and animal spirits.[63] Here are some examples:

> *Example 6.* I am drinking ayahuasca with don Winister Magin, a young shaman who is the son of don Rómulo Magin. His ayahuasca is made with sameruca; I find the visions dark, obscure. I walk to the edge of the clearing in front of his tambo in order to vomit. There at the edge of the jungle is a group of tall, dark figures, shapeless, faces hidden, as if dressed in the hooded robes of monks. But I know somehow that they are *persons*—other-than-human persons, surely—and that they are benevolent, gathered to help me.
>
> *Example 7.* I am drinking ayahuasca with don Antonio Barrera in a crowded tambo, filled with people who have come to be healed. It is almost pitch black, and people are sitting quietly, while don Antonio calls them up for healing, one by one, singing his icaros in the dark. I am bored; nothing seems to be happening except my being sick. Then I realize that, around the edges of the tambo, there are a number of tall young men, thin, with dark hair and skin, wearing white shirts and white pants with black suspenders. They move quickly, gracefully, and quietly around the crowd. They seem busy, helpful.
>
> *Example 8.* I am sitting with my head down, my elbows on my knees, unhappy because nothing much is happening, apart from vomiting. I am drinking ayahuasca with don Antonio, and he has decided that my visions are being blocked by an envious brujo, who does not want gringos learning any secrets. He decides, too, that I need to drink more ayahuasca, a prospect I find disheartening, but I manage to get down

another cupful without vomiting it back up right away. So I am just generally miserable, when I feel someone rubbing my head. I look up, and standing in front of me is a beautiful dark young Amazonian girl, wearing shorts and a white T-shirt, with long dark straight hair hanging down her back, and looking down at me with an absolutely radiant smile. My eyes are open; there is not a doubt in my mind that she is real. She is solid, three-dimensional, *present*. I can even sense the slight increase in air pressure one feels when close to a solid object. She is bathed in a brilliant light; I can see every detail of her features. She has one of the most joyous smiles I have ever seen. I stare at her for a while, basking in that smile; then I blink my eyes and she is gone.

Example 9. I am drinking ayahuasca with doña María and don Roberto. Then I am walking down a street in an urban setting, with no one around, near a vacant lot. I come upon a vendor with a wooden cart—two large wheels behind, two small wheels in front, a handle to push it with—who has necklaces for sale, hanging from wooden pegs, of the inexpensive sort that are tossed to the crowd at Mardi Gras in New Orleans. I buy one and see a small girl, maybe five or six years old, standing on the sidewalk. She is blond, muy gringa, dressed in a pale blue satin party dress, as if she is on her way to a birthday party. In fact, she is wearing a crown on her head, which looks like a cardboard crown covered with gold foil, which I take to be a sort of party costume. I hand her the necklace as a gift, and she stands there very still, like a statue, holding the rosary—that is how I think of it now—raised in her right hand, the golden crown on her head, covered in light on the broken sidewalk.

Example 10. I am drinking ayahuasca with don Rómulo and his son, don Winister. They are both singing icaros at the same time, but different ones, producing a decidedly eerie effect. Suddenly in front of me I see a beautiful green woman, lying back on a couch or bed; her arms and fingers are long; her body is covered in some kind of gauzy material. The moment is intense, erotically charged; I lean forward and kiss her. Whoa! says my rational mind. Is this all right? Are you allowed to have sex with plant spirits? The embrace is arousing; I wonder what my wife would say. The woman fades away, leaving me with a feeling of relief and disappointment.

Example 11. I am drinking ayahuasca with doña María and don Roberto. I see don Roberto dressed in his work clothes—white undershirt, dark pants, rubber boots. For some reason, his name in this vision is don Rosario. He is in front of a small tiled fountain that looks like a shrine; water comes out of the top and gathers in a pool at the bottom. He is kneeling on one knee before the fountain, reaching down into the pool, picking up drops of water with his thumb and two fingers, putting the water into his mouth.

Example 12. I am drinking ayahuasca with doña María and don Roberto. I find myself standing in the entry hallway of a large house in the suburbs. I open the front door and look out at a typical suburban street—cars parked at the curb, traffic going by, a front lawn, trees along the curb. Standing at the door is a dark woman, perhaps in her forties, her raven hair piled on her head, thin and elegant, beautiful, dressed in a red shift with a black diamond pattern. She silently holds out her right hand to me. On her hand is a white cylinder, about three inches long, which she is offering to me. I do not know what the white substance is.

I discussed both the young blond girl and the dark native woman with doña María and don Roberto. They immediately and unhesitatingly identified the first as ayahuasca and the second as maricahua, whom they call toé negro, the black datura. Maricahua is ingested by splitting the stem and eating a piece of the white inner pith about three inches long; they told me that the figure in the vision was handing me just such a piece of maricahua stem. As for my vision of don Roberto, doña María just nodded and said, "He is your maestro ayahuasquero, your ayahuasca teacher."

The Peter Meyer Reports

Peter Meyer calls such experiences "contact with discarnate entities" and has collected accounts from users of DMT. Here are some examples:

"I continued to fly on, over a ravine, leading up to a mountainside, and eventually saw a campfire. As I approached this, cautiously, I saw that on the other side of the fire was a human figure wearing a sombrero, whom I intuitively knew to be don Juan. He invited me to come closer, and spoke to me."[64]

"I found myself once again in the company of the 'elves,' as the focus of their attention and ministrations, but they appeared much less colorful and altogether preoccupied with the task at hand."[65]

"It was as if there were alien beings there waiting for me, and I recall that they spoke to me as if they had been awaiting my arrival, but I cannot remember exactly what was said."[66]

"I seemed to be aware of the presence of other beings in the same space, but had only fleeting glimpses of them, as if they were shy about appearing to me."[67]

"I seemed to be falling away, spiraling into some large, black void, after which I seemed to be in a bright, open space in the presence of two other beings. Their forms were not very clear, but they seemed to be like children, as if we were together in a playground."[68]

"The elves were telling me (or I was understanding them to say) that I had seen them before, in early childhood."[69]

"[The elves] peer toward me, watching, eyes bright and watching in small faces, then small hands to pull themselves, slowly, from behind and into view; they are small white-blond imp-kids, very old in bright, mostly red, togs and caps; candy-store, shiny, teasing and inquisitive, very solemn and somewhat pleased."[70]

The Rick Strassman Reports

In 1990, for the first time in almost twenty years, the FDA cautiously allowed researchers to study the effects of psychotropic substances on human beings.[71] Psychopharmacologist Rick Strassman at the University of New Mexico received funding from the National Institute on Drug Abuse for research on DMT with human volunteers, of whom there were eventually eleven, all experienced hallucinogen users. Strassman administered DMT intravenously in doses ranging from 3.5 to 28 mg—approximately 0.05 to 0.4 mg/kg. Intravenous instead of intramuscular administration was used after one participant in the preliminary testing, who was familiar with smoked DMT, complained that intramuscular injection did not match the rush of smoked street drug.[72]

Especially notable for our purposes were the reports of specific visual images—"a fantastic bird," "a tree of life and knowledge," "a ballroom with crystal chandeliers." There were "tunnels," "stairways," "ducts," and "a spinning golden disc." Participants became aware of and interacted with both human and nonhuman entities, including spiders, mantises, and reptiles, as well as elves, alien beings, and "a little round creature with one big eye and one small eye."[73] Usually there was little difference between what participants saw with their eyes opened or closed, though opening the eyes often caused the visions to overlay objects in the room.[74] For most participants reasoning and thinking were unaffected.[75]

Strassman points to the "impressive" number of volunteers—at least half—who perceived human and alien figures who in turn seemed to be aware of and interacted with the volunteers.[76] "When reviewing my bedside notes," he writes, "I continually feel surprise in seeing how many of our volunteers 'made contact' with 'them,' or other beings."[77] Research subjects used expressions like *entities*, *beings*, *aliens*, *guides*, and *helpers* to describe them; they appeared as clowns, reptiles, mantises, bees, spiders, cacti—and elves.[78] One volunteer reported: "That was real strange. There were lots of elves. They were prankish, ornery, maybe four of them appeared at the side of a stretch of interstate highway I travel regularly. . . . They were about my height. They held up placards, showing me these incredibly beautiful, complex, swirling geometric scenes in them."[79] There were many references to communication with these beings, some successful and some not. One volunteer reported: "There was an initial sense of panic. Then the most beautiful colors coalesced into beings. There were lots of beings. They were talking to me but they weren't making a sound. It was more as if they were blessing me, the spirits of life were blessing me. They were saying that life was good."[80] And again: "They were reptilian and humanoid, trying to make me understand, not with words, but with gestures";[81] "They were communicating in words";[82] "It was nonverbal communication";[83] "It was about to say something to me or me to it, but we couldn't quite connect."[84]

Artist Roger Essig has painted a picture of such a DMT being. He writes of his experience: "This image was inspired from my first unnatural encounter with the spirit molecule. An Entity that seemed extremely real and intelligent appeared before me with terrific precision and speed. It dissipated as soon as I imposed my will upon it. Many people have told me they have seen and felt Entities similar to this representation, it seems to be archetypally inherent within our inner domains."[85]

THE PHENOMENOLOGICAL UNIQUENESS OF AYAHUASCA

Ayahuasca, DMT, and the Classical Psychotropics

It is important to point out that these ayahuasca and DMT experiences are phenomenologically distinct from those of the classical insight- or depth-producing psychotropics—LSD, mescaline, and psilocybin. In many studies of these classical psychotropics, "bona fide hallucinations, to which the subjects reacted as real, were a minor consequence of the drug" and were rarely reported.[86] Drug researchers Peyton Jacob and Alexander Shulgin go so far as to say that, for these substances, the term *hallucinogen* is today "allowed as a euphemism, although that term is also inaccurate because hallucinations are not part of the usual syndrome."[87] Another drug researcher, David Nichols, agrees: "Hallucinogen is now, however, the most common designation in the

The Pharmacological Distinctiveness of DMT

There are reasons to believe that DMT is distinct from the classical entheogens not only phenomenologically but pharmacologically as well. A very rapid tolerance, known as tachyphylaxis, is produced on repeated administration of LSD, mescaline, and psilocin, the psychoactive metabolite of psilocybin;[1] daily administration of LSD, for example, results in almost complete loss of sensitivity to its effects by the fourth day.[2] Such tachyphylaxis is striking. When the CIA was doing secret human testing of hallucinogens in the 1950s, one report called the LSD results "the most amazing demonstration of drug tolerance I have ever seen."[3] Yet no such tolerance develops for the hallucinogenic effects of DMT;[4] for example, four sequential doses of DMT fumarate administered to volunteers at half-hour intervals gave no evidence of tolerance.[5]

Furthermore, in humans, cross-tolerance occurs among mescaline, LSD, and psilocybin but not between any of these and DMT.[6] Humans who are completely tolerant to LSD show no cross-tolerance to hallucinogenic doses of DMT.[7] The classical psychotropics function as agonists at the 5-HT_{2A} receptor site; DMT is an agonist at the 5-HT_{2C} and 5-HT_{1A} receptors as well.[8] Daily administration of LSD and the amphetamine hallucinogens selectively decreases cortical 5-HT_{2A} receptor density, which is, presumably, the mechanism by which tolerance develops;[9] but this does not occur with DMT.

NOTES

1. Nichols, 2004, pp. 141, 165.
2. Cholden, Kurland, & Savage, 1955; Isbell, Belleville, Fraser, Wikler, & Logan, 1956.
3. Quoted in Streatfeild, 2007, p. 67.
4. Goldberg, 2006, p. 269.
5. Strassman, Qualls, & Berg, 1996.
6. Balestrieri & Fontanari, 1959; Fenton, 2001, p. 478; Isbell, Wolbach, Wikler, & Miner, 1961; Tacker & Ferm, 2002, p. 1049; Geyer & Moghaddam, 2002, p. 694; Gillin, Kaplan, Stillman, & Wyatt, 1976; Morrison, 1998, p. 229.
7. Rosenberg, Isbell, Miner, & Logan, 1964.
8. Glennon, 1990; Spinella, 2001, p. 452.
9. Buckholtz, Freedman, & Middaugh, 1985; Buckholtz, Zhou, & Freedman, 1988; Buckholtz, Zhou, Freedman, & Potter, 1990; Leysen, Janssen, & Niemegeers, 1989; McKenna, Nazarali, Himeno, & Saavedra, 1989; Nichols, 2004, p. 141; Smith, Barrett, & Sanders-Bush, 1999.

scientific literature, although it is an inaccurate descriptor of the actual effects of these drugs."[88] Jonathon Ott, defending the term *entheogen*, states explicitly that the "shamanic inebriants did not provoke hallucinations," and that the term *hallucinogen* prejudiced the "transcendent and beatific states of communion with deity" he claims were characteristic of traditional use of visionary drugs.[89]

The vivid, mostly geometric visual illusions that are one of the hallmarks of such classical hallucinogens as LSD, mescaline, and psilocybin "are seldom perceived as having real outside existence."[90] While such patterns appear when drinking ayahuasca, they are usually preliminary to additional and different visions, and they are frequently perceived as external or as projected onto external surfaces—for example, the intricately patterned Persian carpet I would see on the cleared area in front of don Rómulo's jungle hut, or the patterned designs seen on the patient's body by the Shipibo shaman.[91]

To the contrary, Aldous Huxley speaks of mescaline as having cleansed his eyes—the doors of perception—and having allowed him to see the world as new in all respects, "as Adam may have seen it on the day of creation."[92] "For the artist as for the mescaline taker," he writes, using tropes that would become normative for psychotropic experiences in the future, "draperies are living hieroglyphs that stand in some peculiarly expressive way for the unfathomable mystery of pure being." The folds of his gray flannel trousers—an ironic fabric, under the circumstances—"were charged with 'is-ness.'"[93]

Reflections of Huxley can be found in many subsequent accounts. Albert Hofmann, discoverer of the psychotropic effects of LSD, speaks of "blissful moments when the world appeared suddenly in a new brilliant light and I had the feeling of being included in its wonder and indescribable beauty."[94] Andrew Weil speaks of mescaline creating "a sense of wonder, of just wonder and awe at the universe, at life, at consciousness."[95] Charles Tart says of his first mescaline experience, "This initial experience was profound. My worldview wasn't fundamentally changed, but it became alive. I never realized, for instance, that I had used the word 'beauty' all my life, yet I had never before known what 'beauty' meant."[96] None of them saw elves.

These experiences are frequently characterized by the psychoanalytic term *oceanic feeling*—as a dissolution of ego boundaries, a peak experience, a mystical experience, oceanic boundlessness, a temporal and spatial expansion of consciousness beyond the usual ego boundaries.[97] Such descriptions have been profoundly influential in the field of transpersonal psychology, in which such expanded self-concepts can "be considered to represent the degree of self-realization, or alternatively, spiritual development, transpersonal actualization, or other concepts central to much of transpersonal theorizing."[98] Freedman, in an influential essay, speaks of the experience in terms of *portentousness*—"the capacity of the mind to see more than it can tell, to experience more than it can explicate, to believe in and be impressed with more than it can rationally justify, to experience boundlessness and 'boundaryless' events, from the banal to the profound."[99]

Such descriptions are clearly different from those given for ayahuasca or DMT. It may be worth adding that the famed Amazonian ethnobotanist Richard Evans Schultes drank ayahuasca scores of times, but claims never to have had a "mystical experience."[100] Rather than any earthshaking experience, he once told William S. Burroughs, "all I saw was colors," and once told Claudio Naranjo, who asked him if he had seen jaguars, "Sorry, only wiggly lines."[101] The following two examples of my own experience may serve to illustrate this distinction. The first is an experience with ayahuasca, and the second is with huachuma, the San Pedro cactus, *Trichocereus pachanaoi*, rich in mescaline, close kin to the peyote cactus, a brother teacher plant.[102]

Example 13. I am sitting in a small jungle hut after having drunk ayahuasca. After a while, I notice that the walls are covered in a beautiful, perfectly regular tile pattern—white tiles bearing blue filigree designs. To my right, there is now a rectangular opening in the wall near the floor; through the opening, I can look down onto a lower level, which contains a rectangular swimming pool about ten feet square filled with rippling blue water. To the left of the pool is a stairway, on which young girls go up and down, wearing blue Peruvian school uniforms over white blouses. These things are absolutely clear, three-dimensional, *present*; I can hear the rippling of the water in the pool. What I see are things I cannot see without ayahuasca, as if they were in the same room

Ayahuasca Visions

The fact that ayahuasca or DMT experiences are *different* from those of the depth- or insight-producing psychotropics does not mean that they cannot be profound. Ayahuasca visions can be movingly beautiful—distant landscapes, other planets, brightly lit cities, crystal fountains in the midst of distant oceans, bright green leaves and raindrops on flowing water. Ayahuasca visions can tell us the sources of sickness—the failed relationships, the broken promises, the envy and arrogance of oneself and others—and point the way toward healing. Ayahuasca visions can be like myths—"profound, imaginative, other-worldly, universal or larger-than-life"—or like deeply salient dreams, "dreams of particular vividness or narrative coherence or notable personal significance; . . . dreams that appear to hold special significance for the dreamer's community."[1] I think that poet César Calvo captures this distinction when he writes that ayahuasca allows us "to live at the same time in this and in other realities, to traverse the endless, unmeasurable provinces of the night. . . . Instead of uncovering mysteries, it respects them. It makes them more and more mysterious, more fertile and prodigal." That is why the light of ayahuasca is black, he says; ayahuasca "irrigates the unknown territory: that is its way of shedding light."[2]

NOTES

1. Kirk, 1974, p. 25; Larsen, 1996, p. xix; Shafton, 1995, pp. 81–82.
2. Calvo, 1981/1995b, p. 177.

but in another, parallel dimension; what I do *not* see is some hidden beauty in the room itself, some depth of meaning in the untiled walls, anything *portentous*, except that I have opened a door to an alternative world, or am now able to see people and things in this world that I had not been able to see before.

Example 14. I am on a boat traveling at dusk along jungle rivers. A few hours earlier I had drunk huachuma. I am overwhelmed by the odors of the jungle, as if huge trumpet-shaped flowers are blooming just beyond my vision, as if I have tapped into the eternal cycles of blossom and decay. The jungle trees along the shore are primeval, approaching from vast distances, passing by me with stately grace and animal power. I see no *thing* that is new; what is different is the *way* I see what I have always seen, now rich with association, awe inspiring, wondrously beautiful.

Anthropologist Marie Perruchon, who is married to a Shuar and is herself an initiated uwíshin, shaman, puts it this way: ayahuasca "is a plant which has the effect that when you drink it, it allows you to see what otherwise is invisible, and it attracts the spirits. It is not that the ayahuasca takes one to another world, otherwise unreachable; it just opens one's eyes to what is normally hidden. There is only one world, which is shared by all beings, humans, spirits, and animals."[103]

Encultured Expectations in Human DMT Research

Rick Strassman's DMT research project ended prematurely, for a number of reasons. Strassman was himself a practicing Zen Buddhist, and he had hoped that his research would shed light on the relationship between hallucinogenic experience and spirituality. But Strassman came to believe that any benefits of the DMT experience were transient, even for volunteers who had incredibly intense and remarkable experiences during high-dose DMT sessions. Follow-up interviews with the first group of volunteers, one to two years after their DMT experiences, found little of what Strassman considered to be positive carryover into their daily lives. Even those who believed they had benefited inwardly from their high-dose DMT experience showed little outward evidence of making significant changes in their lives—for example, taking up a spiritual or psychotherapeutic practice, changing jobs, or increasing community service.

Strassman had apparently expected at least some of his volunteers to undergo life-changing experiences of depth or insight. "To my surprise and sadness," Strassman said in a later interview, "people's initial high-dose breakthrough sessions were beginning to sound a little hollow. I think this was because, by following our early volunteers, I saw that the drug experience itself had little substantial impact on most people's lives."[104] The relocations, marriages, or divorces that did occur in volunteers were all under way before their involvement in the studies. Instead of personal growth, the volunteers reported a disconcerting number of contacts with other-dimensional beings.

Strassman came to believe that this lack of long-term positive effect was the result of the experimental setting itself. The biomedical model, he concluded, was intrusive and dehumanizing, as was a neutral and nondirective supervising style. There needed to be more emphasis on *treatment*, he thought, and less on descriptive mechanistic brain-chemistry studies. DMT by itself had no beneficial effect, Strassman concluded; in fact, he became concerned that he was harming rather than helping his volunteers.

Other factors as well led to the cessation of the New Mexico research. Strassman had hoped to begin therapeutic work—as opposed to mechanistic studies in the hospital—with the longer-acting psilocybin, but the ethics committee refused to allow him to take his research out of the hospital setting. Off-site therapeutic work became even less likely when a volunteer on psilocybin had a paranoid reaction and fled the hospital. A graduate student began taking drugs with volunteers after hours, and undermined Strassman when he told the student to stop. Hoped-for colleagues did not arrive, and in fact began setting up their own foundations competing for scarce resources and colleagues. Long-term benefits were meager, and adverse effects were adding up. The frequency with which volunteers reported contact with other-dimensional beings was unexpected and personally disorienting to Strassman. His wife developed a serious illness, and they moved to Canada so she could be closer to family.

In addition, Strassman had begun a relationship with an American Zen Buddhist monastery in the early 1970s, which provided ongoing spiritual training and support. Many monks shared with him the importance of their earlier psychedelic experiences in choosing a spiritual lifestyle, which supported his emerging theories regarding psychedelics and mysticism. Buddhism also stimulated many of the ideas guiding the studies, providing the model for developing a new rating scale for DMT effects and informing Strassman's method of supervising drug sessions.

A disastrous conversation with a monk who knew little about psychotropics coincided with the terminal illness of the monastery's leader and the consequent lobbying for succession. The monk condemned Strassman's work, which caused formerly supportive monks to either turn silent or reverse long-standing support. The issue came to a head when Strassman published an

Strassman Redux

Strassman, after a hiatus, has now returned to hallucinogen research, joining with toxicologist and neurochemist Steven A. Barker to found the Cottonwood Research Foundation, whose projects include developing an ultrasensitive assay to detect naturally occurring tryptamine hallucinogens in humans, in both normal and nonnormal states, and an assessment of the effects of ayahuasca in a group of normal volunteers, with the goal of developing treatment protocols in collaboration with drug abuse treatment facilities.[1]

Strassman is still struggling with his earlier findings, which he describes as truly paradigm challenging and which, he says, he could not adequately integrate into his scientific worldview.[2] He has now collaborated with anthropologist Luis Eduardo Luna, a pioneer in the study of mestizo shamanism, and Ede Frecska, a psychopharmacologist who has worked with ayahuasca, to produce a volume of essays focusing on the use of psychedelics to journey to alien worlds. Here he focuses on reports of what he calls *invisible worlds* experienced by his earlier DMT volunteers, including their reported contacts with alien beings. These reports, he says, went far beyond any scientific training he had brought to the research. But he has had to accept, he now says, that the reports were descriptions of things that were *real*—that they occurred in reality, "although not in a reality we usually inhabit." He now hypothesizes that DMT, like a telescope or microscope, allows us access to a world previously unknown to our everyday perceptual apparatus.[3] He is, he says, teetering dangerously on the edge between respectable science and pseudoscience.[4]

NOTES

1. Strassman, 2007b.
2. Strassman, 2007a.
3. Strassman, 2008, p. 76.
4. Strassman, 2007a.

article linking psychedelics and Buddhism in *Tricycle: The Buddhist Review*. In this article, he said, among other things, that "dedicated Buddhist practitioners with little success in their meditation, but well along in moral and intellectual development, might benefit from a carefully timed, prepared, supervised, and followed-up psychedelic session to accelerate their practice."[105] The head temple called on Strassman to stop his work, which further wore down his remaining desire to continue the research. Several months after moving to Canada, he ended his work and returned all drugs and the last year of grant support to the federal government.[106]

This is an intriguing story, on many levels. For Strassman, it was important to note the effect of the experimental set and setting on the outcome of the DMT experiences. To the extent that the scientific protocol—and, importantly, its funding—depended on a hospital environment and biomedical approach, the setting may in fact have been subversive of long-term personal change.

But is long-term personal change what DMT is even about? With his own preexisting biases, both Buddhist and countercultural, Strassman thought that spiritual transformation was the end point of the hallucinogenic experience; he was unsettled by the frequently reported contacts with other-dimensional beings. Perhaps the hospital setting was less important than Strassman's own unmet expectations. Perhaps DMT—like ayahuasca itself—is not a psychotherapist but a teacher, leading where it intends—not to some sort of enlightenment, not to self-improvement, not to community volunteer work but, rather, into the dark and luminous realm of the spirits.

CHAPTER 24
MECHANISMS OF AYAHUASCA HALLUCINATIONS

DEFINITION OF HALLUCINATION

The term *hallucination* was apparently first used in its current sense in 1832 by French psychiatrist Jean Etienne Dominique Esquirol, who wrote that a hallucinating person has "the complete conviction of a sensation currently perceived, where there is no corresponding external object within the range of the senses to excite that sensation."[1] This classical definition has been generally repeated. A hallucination is "perception without an object";[2] "an internal image that seems as real, vivid, and external as the perception of an object";[3] "a sensory perception that has the compelling sense of reality of a true perception but that occurs without external stimulation of the relevant sensory organ."[4] Such definitions, we may briefly note, are naively metaphysical; the nonexistence of a perceptual object is taken to be unproblematic.

The definition has been further refined. A hallucination has been defined not only as occurring in the absence of an appropriate stimulus, and as having the full force or impact of a true perception, but also as being "not amenable to direct and voluntary control by the experiencer."[5] A phenomenological account of hallucinatory experiences, in contrast to both imagination and memory, lists five significant features: a hallucination is *involuntary*, arising without express volition; *believable*, appearing with the force of a present perception of empirical reality; *vivid*, rich enough in sensory qualities to claim committed awareness; *projected*, experienced as "out there," externally to the perceiving self; and *paranormal*, "tinged with the pathological," competing with ordinary perception.[6]

Entheogens

For the classical psychotropics—LSD, mescaline, psilocybin—Jonathan Ott, R. Gordon Wasson, and others coined the term *entheogen*, intended to mean something like "realizing the divine within" and referring to the primarily cognitive depth- or insight-producing nature of the LSD experience.[1] The term was supposed to apply equally to all the "shamanic inebriants," but, while it may describe at least some of the effects attributed to psychotropic mushrooms and cacti, the substances of most interest to those who coined the term, it seems to me to fit uneasily with the vivid lifelike hallucinations of ayahuasca.

NOTE

1. Ott, 1994, pp. 91–92 n. 1, 1996, pp. 103–105 n. 1; Ruck, Bigwood, Staples, Ott, & Wasson, 1979. See also Perrine, 1996, pp. 255–256; Stevens, 1987, p. 361.

AYAHUASCA AS A HALLUCINOGEN

There is no doubt that ayahuasca can produce hallucinations under any of these definitions—visual experiences that are solid, detailed, three-dimensional, animated, interactive, and embedded in ordinary perceptual space; auditory experiences that are immediate, external, directional, locatable in space, and often coordinated with visual experiences. Ayahuasca, then, can reasonably be said to be a *hallucinogen*, a term I will use without apology, despite the fact that the term has been deprecated and the term *entheogen* has been proposed in its place.

SPIRITS AS MISATTRIBUTION

In recent years, a widespread consensus has been reached about the nature of auditory hallucinations.[7] According to this consensus view, auditory hallucinations occur when the individual misattributes inner speech to a source that is external or alien to the self.[8] Hearing voices is thus really ego-alienated inner speech.[9] "The Voices were coming louder and faster," reports one person with schizophrenia, "startling me with their surprise visits to my brain. Only I didn't know they were in my brain. I heard them coming at me from the outside, as real as the sound of the telephone ringing."[10]

Most people take for granted the process of discrimination between our thoughts and images and the things we hear or see. However, there are grounds for supposing that we do not have a priori knowledge about whether perceived events are internal to ourselves and generated in our minds or are external to ourselves and generated by agencies other than the self.

The process of discrimination between these two kinds of events is known as *source monitoring* and has been studied by psychologist Marcia Johnson and her colleagues in a series of experiments with ordinary people.[11] This work has focused on judgments about the sources of memories, showing that human beings use a variety of cues when discriminating between memories of self-generated thoughts and memories of real events—such cues as contextual information, amount of cognitive effort required, and consistency with what is known about the normal behavior of people and the world. The observations suggest that discriminating between internal imaginary events and external real events is best thought of as a skill and, like all skills, can be learned, can be improved, and can fail. For our purposes, this means that source monitoring can also be *culturally mediated*. Johnson's suggestion that source-monitoring judgments are influenced by the inherent plausibility of perceived events helps to explain how culture can shift the boundary between hallucinatory and real experiences.[12]

A number of researchers have attempted to assess source-monitoring judgments in hallucinating people and nonhallucinating people. These studies generally report that hallucinating people perform differently as source monitors than do controls who are not hallucinating. People with schizophrenia who hallucinate, for example, have a more difficult time than either people with schizophrenia who do not hallucinate or people without schizophrenia in recalling whether they had thought up certain words by themselves or had been read those words by others.[13] These results may at least partially reflect the impact of beliefs and experiences on source-monitoring judgments, rather than any gross deficit in source-monitoring skills. Remember that Socrates let himself be guided by a voice that only he could hear and to which he occasionally referred as his *daemon*. Allowing his conduct to be guided by a hallucinatory voice was not a pathology but, rather, a crime; the daemon was not a god recognized in Athens. In fact, the daemon probably cost Socrates his life; it was the daemon who stopped him from defending himself at his trial and from escaping once he was sentenced to death.[14]

Thus, a person with schizophrenia has lost the usual distinction between what has been experienced and what has been imagined, between external stimuli and internally generated thoughts and memories.[15] Here, for example, is psychiatrist Harold Searles: "The deeply schizophrenic individual has, subjectively, no imagination. The moment that something which we would call a new concoction of fantasy, a new product of his imagination, enters his awareness, *he* perceives this as being an actual and undisguised attribute of the world around him."[16] To say that the schizophrenic has *no* imagination is basically the same as saying the person has no *normally functioning* imagination—that the schizophrenic takes the imagined to be real.

The symptoms of schizophrenia are thus predictable on the assumption that the disease involves misidentification of imaginings.[17] Indeed, the weakening of these ontological boundaries transcends pathology. The various modes of perceptual *imaginings*, such as visual and auditory imagery, share important features with the corresponding kinds of *perception*. We normally use the same descriptive terms for both internal imaginary perceptions and external real perceptions—sounds are *loud* or *distracting*; images are *dim* or *incomplete*. It is not difficult to confuse the two. I have had dreams so realistic and persuasive that it required serious thought to rule out that the events had actually occurred. I am not alone; people can find it difficult to remember whether they have actually seen something or simply formed a visual image of it.[18] Conversely, in a classic experiment, people were asked to visualize a banana, without knowing that there was in fact a just barely visible image of a banana on the screen in front of them. It was clear from their descriptions that what they took to be their internal images were really perceptions of the external picture.[19]

It is tempting to hypothesize that source-monitoring judgments—note that I said *judgments*, not *mistakes*—are a key element in ayahuasca hallucinations. It is important to bear in mind, too, that source monitoring can be affected by learning and, presumably, by culture; an experienced shaman may see spirits, even if vaguely, *all the time*, because a combination of ayahuasca, other psychoactive plants, learning, and social expectation may have systematically affected the source-monitoring process.

SPIRITS AS CONSTRUCTIONS

Here is the content of a series of visions—golden sparks, melting purple blobs, a dancing brown spot, snowflakes, saffron and light blue waves, a corona of light "like a chrysanthemum composed of thousands of radiating petals." Then, as the visions solidified, there appeared a Cuban flag flying over a bank building, an old lady with a gray umbrella walking through the side of a truck, a cat rolling across the street in a small striped barrel.

These are not ayahuasca visions. They are what writer James Thurber reported seeing after he became completely blind.[20] Neuroscientist Vilayanur Ramachandran believes that Thurber suffered from a neurological condition called Charles Bonnet syndrome.[21] One of Thurber's famous cartoons depicts a startled-looking woman sitting in a doctor's office looking at the giant rabbit in a suit and bow tie sitting behind the desk. *You said a moment ago that everybody you look at seems to be a rabbit*, the doctor says. *Now just what do you mean by that, Mrs. Sprague?* The cartoon in many ways depicts a typical Charles Bonnet hallucination—three-dimensional, integrated into perceptual space, persistent, coherent, interactive, *present*.

Thurber had been blinded in his right eye, accidentally, when he was six years old; as he grew older, the vision in his left eye began to fade as well, until, by the age of thirty-five, he was completely blind.[22] In his 1937 piece *The Admiral on the Wheel*, Thurber wrote of the spectacular things he saw despite the serious and growing deterioration of his vision—bridges rising lazily into the air like balloons; a "noble, silent dog" lying on a ledge above a brownstone house on lower Fifth Avenue; a "little old admiral in full dress uniform," his beard blowing in the wind and his hat set at a rakish angle.[23]

Charles Bonnet Hallucinations

One study of people with Charles Bonnet syndrome reports that hallucinatory episodes could last from a few seconds to several hours.[24] The patients described the content of their hallucinations as people, animals, plants, a large variety of inanimate objects, and sometimes complete scenes. The content of hallucinations was often mundane—for example, an unfamiliar person, a bottle, a hat. The hallucinations could also be funny; one woman saw two miniature policemen guiding a tiny villain to a tiny prison van. Some people saw translucent figures floating in the hallway, a dragon, people wearing one big flower on their heads, a beautiful shining angel, wonderful bunches of flowers, little circus animals, clowns, and—interestingly—elves. Indeed, many patients see people—a Canadian Mountie in full military dress; a group of Elizabethan figures; little girls playing in the yard, wearing white dresses with pink sashes and pink bows in their hair.[25]

Most patients described a large variety of hallucinations, differing in each hallucinatory episode; sometimes the sensation of specific objects returned, but stereotyped hallucinations, identical in every respect, were uncommon. Hallucinations contained both familiar and unfamiliar images, and they occurred both in black and white and in color. They could be clearer, equally clear, or less clear in comparison to reality. Most patients hallucinated only with their eyes open. Some perceived hallucinated objects as floating in the air or projected on a wall or ceiling; others reported that the objects fitted well into the surroundings—for example, an unreal person sitting in a real chair. Patients hallucinating while their eyes were closed perceived hallucinations in the dark subjective space in front of the eyes.

One patient described the experience this way: "The world was filled with hallucinations, both visual and auditory. I couldn't distinguish what was real from what was fake. Doctors and nurses standing next to my bed were surrounded by football players and Hawaiian dancers."[26] This same patient, during a discussion with Ramachandran, reported seeing a monkey—"extremely vivid and real"—sitting in the doctor's lap.[27] Visual and auditory hallucinations can be coordinated; one woman patient not only saw children in her left visual field but could also hear their laughter.[28]

A study using multiple-correspondence analysis and hierarchical cluster analysis reports a set of features characteristic of Charles Bonnet hallucinations.[29] The hallucinations occur when the patient is alert and with eyelids open; a sharply focused image suddenly appears, without any apparent trigger or voluntary control; the hallucinations are always outside the body and can last from a few seconds to most of the day.[30] The same study reports such hallucinations in conjunction with grief reactions. In fact, such auditory and visual hallucinations are a commonly documented part of the grief reaction, with as many as 70 percent of recently bereaved people experiencing either illusions or hallucinations of the deceased.[31] Ramachandran reports the case of a woman with Charles Bonnet syndrome who saw her recently deceased husband three times a week.[32]

In another study, factor analysis of structured interviews and questionnaires partitioned visual experiences into three clusters—visual perseveration and delayed palinopsia or recurring visual hallucinations; hallucinations of grotesque, disembodied, and distorted faces with prominent eyes and teeth; and hallucinations of extended landscape scenes and small figures in costumes with hats.[33] Another study reports a hallucination of an "elf in the woodshed."[34]

Gap Filling

Gap filling is the brain's way of dealing with gaps in the visual image. Migraine sufferers experience blind spots in the visual field, called scotomas, when a blood vessel goes into a spasm. Such a scotoma will blank out corresponding perceptual areas—a clock on the wall, for example. But the person does not see a blank or void where the clock used to be but, instead, a normal wall, with the region corresponding to the missing clock covered with the same color of paint or pattern of wallpaper as the rest of the wall.[35] More recent work has shown that such gap filling occurs even across large central scotomas caused by physical retinal damage;[36] it appears that gap-filled figures even generate afterimages.[37]

In a series of extraordinarily clever experiments, Ramachandran has explored the capacity of the visual process to fill in such perceptual gaps.[38] It is clear that such gap filling is capable of generating even complex perceptions. In one striking case, Ramachandran put up the numerals 1, 2, and 3 above a patient's scotoma and 7, 8, and 9 below. The patient saw a continuous column of numbers, with no gap in the middle. When asked to read the numbers aloud, the patient said, "Um, one, two, three, um, seven, eight, nine. Hey, that's very strange. I can see the numbers in the middle, but I can't read them. They look like numbers, but I don't know what they are." When asked if the numbers looked blurred, he replied, "No, they don't look blurred. They kind of look strange. I can't tell what they are—like hieroglyphics or something."[39]

It is probably worth noting that this report is consistent with the reports of lucid dreamers who attempt to read while dreaming. Such attempts are consistently difficult and usually unsuccessful; one test for determining whether one is dreaming is to try to read something. One dreamer reports, "When I have read several words in this way, partly forwards and partly backwards, something remarkable happens. Some of them have changed their shape; they no longer consist of the usual letters, but form figures which bear a distinct resemblance to hieroglyphics. And now I can see nothing but these symbols, each of which signifies a word or syllable, the ordinary letters having completely disappeared."[40] Similar experiences are found in hypnogogic imagery—for example, images of a printed book, in which, at most, a half a line can be read, usually nonsense.[41] It is plausible to hypothesize that these letters and hieroglyphics are being generated by processes similar to those used to fill in the column of numbers over the blind spot caused by the scotoma.

Such gap filling is in fact part of our everyday perceptions. Our retinal images are distorted, tiny, and upside down; most of the retina is nearly color blind and has severely limited powers of discrimination; the eye is in nearly constant motion;[42] yet we see a world that is relatively stable, detailed, and consistent. We are constantly filling in perceptual gaps—in a dog behind a wire fence, say, or one object partially obscured by another. It is clear, says Ramachandran, that the mind "abhors a vacuum and will apparently supply whatever information is required to complete the scene."[43] Philosopher Alva Noë puts it this way: "We experience the presence of that which we perceive to be out of view."[44]

Gap Filling and Ayahuasca

According to Ramachandran, the hallucinations of Charles Bonnet syndrome are an exaggerated version of such common imaginative and perceptual processes—precisely the same processes that account for gap filling in patients with scotomas.[45] Perception, under this theory, is the end result of interplay between current percepts and previously constructed and stored visual images from the past. This is a dynamic process. The higher visual centers receive a set of percepts, come up with best-match stored images, and project these back to the visual cortex, which uses them as perceptual gap fillers. In this way, the initial impoverished image is progressively refined; the resulting perception—a cat, a person, a Confederate flag—is the result of successive iterations of the matching and gap-filling process. As Ramachandran suggests, perhaps we are hallucinating all the time.[46]

There are several points of interest in this theorizing. First, it meshes closely with my own experiences of ayahuasca's gap-filling ability, described in the previous chapter. In addition, no one has attributed any psychopathology to any person with Charles Bonnet syndrome; the hallucinations apparently occur through normally operating visual mechanisms. Certainly there has been no discussion of any defect in source monitoring; apparently the hallucinations, acting through ordinary visual processes, are so compelling that they override culturally mediated source-monitoring judgments.

How does this happen? Normally, when we imagine, say, a rose, we do not *hallucinate* a rose. Ramachandran suggests that this is because we normally have real input coming in from the retina and optic nerve, even when the eyes are closed; there is always spontaneous activity in the retina. But where there is macular degeneration, or a scotoma, this visual input is completely missing, and internally generated images can assume vividness and clarity and have the irrevocable quality of real stimulus-evoked sensory experience. In other words, imagination produces weak images because there is competing real visual input; but when that competing input is absent, then, as Ramachandran says, we start confusing internal images with external reality.[47] In other words, partial blindness can affect source monitoring.

If that is the case, there is a continuum from the hallucinations of Charles Bonnet syndrome to ordinary, everyday perceptions—from the monkey on the neurologist's lap to the monkey in the enclosure at the zoo. What differentiates one from the other is, precisely, *source monitoring*—learned, fallible, alterable, culturally determined.

Imaginal Beings

In December 1913, Carl Jung first experienced what he was later to call *active imagination*. However, he did not talk about these experiences until twelve years later, when, in May and June 1925, he spoke for the first time of his inner development at two sessions of a series of weekly seminars he was giving in Zurich.[48] The contents of these lectures were not published until 1989;[49] but a partial account was given in 1962 by Aniela Jaffé in *Memories, Dreams, Reflections*, a purported autobiography of Jung that she largely wrote.[50]

In 1913, according to this account, Jung, profoundly distressed by his break with Freud, began to experiment with different ways to enter into his own imaginings. As James Hillman describes it, "When there was nothing else to hold to, Jung turned to the personified images of interior vision. He entered into an interior drama, took himself into an imaginative fiction and then, perhaps, began his healing—even if it has been called his breakdown."[51]

In this imaginal world, Jung began to confront and question the figures who appeared to him; and, to Jung's surprise, those imaginal persons replied to him in turn. "Near the steep slope of a rock," Jung says, "I caught sight of two figures, an old man with a white beard and a beautiful young girl. I summoned up my courage and approached them as though they were real people, and listened attentively to what they told me." And again: "I held conversations with him, and he said things which I had not consciously thought. For I observed clearly that it was he who spoke, not I."[52]

One of these imaginal people, a wise pagan whom Jung named Philemon, "seemed to me quite real, as if he were a living personality." Philemon spoke to Jung as follows: "He said I treated thoughts as if I generated them myself, but in his view thoughts were like animals in the forest, or people in a room, or birds in the air." It was this imaginal Philemon who taught Jung the reality of the psyche—"that there is something in me which can say things that I do not know and do not intend."[53]

Visionary Experiences

Active imagination shares important characteristics with a number of other experiences, often considered to be *anomalous*. Hallucinations, lucid dreams, DMT journeys, out-of-body experiences, false awakenings, waking dreams, apparitions, eidetic visualization, and active imagination are all characterized by a greater or lesser degree of presentness, detail, externality, and three-dimensional explorable spacefulness. We may call these, collectively, *visionary experiences*. Specifically, visionary experiences

- occur with the force of a present perception of external reality;
- have what appears to be the same quantity and quality of sensory detail as ordinary experiences;
- are experienced as external to the experiencer;
- occur in what seems to the experiencer to be an extended, three-dimensional, explorable perceptual space; and
- frequently involve interactions with apparently autonomous others.

We can, further, distinguish *overlapping* visionary experiences from *total* ones. An overlapping vision appears to occur within the otherwise normal perception of the environment—the monkey on the neurologist's lap, an apparition in the hallway, cast-iron lawn furniture in front of a jungle hut. A total vision substitutes an entirely different perceptual space for the ordinary

Visionary Experiences

Sometimes these sorts of visionary experience are called *anomalous experiences*, and have generally been ignored or pathologized by mainstream psychology. Recently, however, largely through the influence of Stanley Krippner, researchers have begun to pay more attention to these states, and the American Psychological Association has published a text entitled *Varieties of Anomalous Experience: Examining the Scientific Evidence*, which contains chapters on hallucinatory experiences, lucid dreaming, and out-of-body experiences, among other things.[1]

Eidetic visualization—the deliberate mental creation of minutely detailed three-dimensional landscapes, deities, and other beings—has been little investigated and has generally not been included among such anomalous experiences. Yet the practice is widespread, and lies at the heart of Tibetan Buddhist ritual meditation.[2] Interestingly, Jung disliked eidetic visualization, which he called "voluntary imagination," considering it, in contrast to active imagination, to be superficial and trivial.[3]

Psychologists Celia Green and Charles McCreery have characterized *all* such experiences, both overlapping and total, as *metachoric*, in the sense that, even where portions of the experience *appear* to occur in ordinary perceptual space, in fact the entire perceptual field has been replaced with a visionary one.[4]

NOTES

1. Cardeña, Lynn, & Krippner, 2000.
2. Beyer, 1973, pp. 68–81.
3. Casey, 2000, p. 213; Jung, 1921/1953–1977, p. 428.
4. Green, 1990; Green & McCreery, 1994, pp. 55–62; McCreery, 2006, p. 7.

environment—a lucid dreamer floating down a staircase; a runner hovering, looking down at her own body during a marathon; a vision of a golden child standing by a garbage-strewn empty lot. Either type of visionary experience may be multisensorial, incorporating vision, sound, and kinesthesia. Of course, there can be ambiguity. I may seem to awaken in my darkened room to see a figure standing in front of the dresser by the bed. If I have in fact awakened, then the figure appears to occur in my normal perceptual space; if this is, instead, a *false awakening*, and I am in fact dreaming, then clearly the vision has constructed not only the figure but my room as well.

Total visionary experiences convey the sense of being in an explorable environment, often in the presence of autonomous other-than-human persons. This sense has been discussed, in particular, by analysts describing active imagination—a world they call *imaginal*, and which I have here called visionary. For example, transpersonal psychologist John Rowan says, "It is crucial to understand that the imaginal world has a reality of its own, within the four walls of its own realm."[54] Here, Hillman says, "we have to engage with persons whose autonomy may radically alter, even dominate our thoughts and feelings."[55] Psychologist Mary Watkins says that one creates for oneself a *home in the imaginal*.[56] "The imaginal world," says Rowan, "is a world where real things happen."[57] Henry Corbin, a scholar of Sufism and Persian Islam, calls this visionary world the *mundus imaginalis*, "a very precise order of reality, which corresponds to a precise mode of perception."[58]

The same descriptions would fit a wide variety of total visionary experiences. People move through explorable landscapes—along a country road, through unfamiliar streets, high enough in the air to see the tops of the trees and small hills.[59] They interact with objects and people—push open a door, carry on a conversation, confront an angry father.[60] They turn corners and see unexpected things—a small chapel, a war memorial, a sunlit glade.[61] Unexpected events occur—a sparrow alights on one's hand, something with pointed ears scurries away, the hands of a clock suddenly move.[62] These descriptions come from active imagination, lucid dreams, out-of-body experiences, and false awakenings, but they have a striking phenomenological consistency.

These visionary experiences can also be characterized along two dimensions—first, according to the degree to which the experience is entered into intentionally; and, second, by the amount of control the experiencer exercises over the content of the experience. Active imagination would be high in intentionality and low on control; eidetic visualization would be high on both; and a Charles Bonnet hallucination would typically be low on both.

The same type of experience may occur at different points along these dimensions on different occasions. Hallucinations of the deceased are a commonly documented part of the grief reaction.[63] Such experiences are typically low on intention but may vary on control, to the extent that the bereaved attempts, for example, to engage the deceased in conversation or perhaps even attempts to call the deceased for purposes of communication. A lucid dreamer may—or may not—be able to control the actions of dream objects and persons, or be able to do so to varying degrees.

Several things follow from this discussion. First, it seems that ayahuasca experiences specifically, and shamanic experiences generally, fall within the class of visionary experiences. Shamanism seems to rank high on intentionality and relatively low on control, like active imagination. While the shaman can control his or her own actions while interacting with the spirits, the shaman has no direct control over the actions of the spirits; the shaman can ask a question, ask for help, even demand compliance, but most commonly cannot compel a particular response.

Tying shamanism to such experiences as lucid dreaming, active imagination, and eidetic visualization raises a number of interesting questions. Apart from their phenomenology, what do they have in common? To the extent that, at the time of experiencing them, they are *convincing*, detailed, explorable, then the line between the visionary and the everyday worlds is fluid, as source-monitoring experiments seem to show, and the line is shifted by culture, training, experience, and ayahuasca. El doctor, the teacher, teaches us to de-reify the world, to personify, to mythologize—to obliterate the boundaries, construct a visionary world from the detritus of the everyday, let us *see through*, turn the world into metaphor, into magic.

AYAHUASCA AND THE SPIRITS

These discussions of misattribution, construction, and the visionary provide a framework within which we can *begin* to think about the spirits shown to us by ayahuasca. First, the gap-filling qualities of ayahuasca are similar to—indeed, perhaps the same as—the gap-filling processes that are arguably the basis of *every* perception. What ayahuasca adds, then, is a reduction in the intensity of our source monitoring—precisely what Hillman calls *soul-making*, the relaxing of our stream of ontological judgments. The intensity of source monitoring is *learned behavior*, culturally determined; and what we see, in this luminous fused space, are precisely the spirits—and even our departed loved ones—to teach us what we do not know.

Here, then, is a model for understanding ayahuasca, for steering between

Endogenous DMT

DMT is widely distributed in the natural world. It is found, in the Amazon Basin, in the ayahuasca companion plants chacruna, sameruca, and ocoyagé; in several trees in the genus *Virola*, from whose sap the hallucinogenic snuff epená is made; and in the tree *Anadenanthera peregrina*, source of the hallucinogenic snuff yopo.[1] In North America, it is found in such trees and shrubs as *Mimosa hostilis*, *Acacia* spp., and *Desmanthus illinoensis* and in such grasses as *Arundo donax* and *Phalaris tuberosa*. It is also found, endogenously, in mice, rats, and human beings.[2]

No one seems quite sure what to make of this last fact. DMT has been identified in human blood, urine, brain tissue, and cerebrospinal fluid;[3] it apparently passes easily into the brain through the blood–brain barrier.[4] At first glance, the presence of DMT in the human body seems surprising—almost as surprising as the fact that bufotenine, the psychoactive toad venom, is found in human urine as well.[5]

But, in fact, the human body is full of tryptamines, including melatonin and the ubiquitous serotonin, all chemically related to the dietary amino acid tryptophan. Bufotenine and DMT are both formed from serotonin and tryptamine by the enzyme indolethylamine N-methyltransferase, which is ubiquitously present in human nonneural tissues.[6] Trace levels of endogenous psychoactive tryptamines thus appear to be the result of normal metabolic processes. The question is: Do they *do* anything?

The answer is: No one knows. In 1988, psychopharmacologist Jace Callaway—now well known as a member of the Hoasca Project studying the use of ayahuasca by the União do Vegetal in Brazil—proposed that, at night, serotonin becomes converted into DMT by the pineal gland and plays a central role in activating dreams.[7]

Psychopharmacologist Rick Strassman also thinks that the source of endogenous DMT is the pineal gland—coincidentally, the organ Rene Descartes considered the seat of the soul and the place where all our thoughts are formed. The pineal produces serotonin, melatonin, and β-carbolines, all with the same tryptamine core as DMT. So why not DMT as well?

Strassman claims that this pineal DMT has a variety of important effects. Given the avidity with which the brain draws DMT across the blood-brain barrier, he believes that endogenous DMT must be necessary for normal brain functioning.[8] He has proposed that a wide variety of anomalous experiences—psychotic hallucinations, mystical visions, alien-abduction experiences, and near-death experiences—are the result of abnormally high DMT levels in the brain.[9] In addition, high levels of DMT "may help mediate some of the more profound mental experiences people undergo"—that is, "mystical or spiritual experiences" such as those during birth, just before death, and in deep meditation.[10] Even more, he hypothesized that the "individual life force" enters the human fetus through its pineal gland and departs the body at death by the same route, each time triggering the release of a flood of DMT.[11]

As far as I know, these ideas remain speculative and unsupported by empirical research. For example, comparison of urine in people with schizophrenia and controls without schizophrenia has failed to show any systematic differences in DMT levels.[12] I know of no research comparing, say, blood DMT levels in normal controls and subjects immediately postpartum or postmortem, or in normal controls and persons in deep meditative states, or in dreaming and nondreaming sleepers, all of which ought to be relatively simple to do. There is also the question of whether endogenous DMT is supposed to have similar psychoactive functions in mice and rats.

Such speculations, too, have been dismissed on the grounds that the trace levels of DMT and other endogenous psychoactive tryptamines in the human body are insignificant metabolic by-products that are simply too small to have much effect; and this contention in turn has been rebutted by referring to trace amine receptors, where even tiny amounts of amines can elicit a surprisingly strong response.[13] But much of this speculation may have been superceded by a recent study demonstrating that the receptor to which endogenous DMT binds is in fact the sigma-1 receptor.

The sigma-1 receptor is widely distributed throughout the body, including the central and peripheral nervous system. Its function has remained unclear, and it was long considered an orphan receptor, without a known endogenous neurotransmitter of its own. Exogenous substances with a high affinity for the sigma-1 receptor include cocaine, heroin, dextromethorphan, haloperidol, methamphetamine, and PCP. For that reason, researchers took to calling the unknown sigma-1 neurotransmitter *endopsychosin* or sometimes, *angeldustin*.

This new research thus solves two puzzles at once. The mysterious endogenous ligand of the sigma-1 receptor is DMT. In addition, the study indicates that DMT may act at this receptor to regulate sodium ion channels in cells, and thus affect cell signaling processes. "The finding that DMT and sigma-1 receptors act as a ligand receptor pair," the authors conclude, "provides a long-awaited connection that will enable researchers to elucidate the biological functions of both these molecules."[14]

NOTES

1. Schultes, 1954; Seit, 1967; De Budowski, Marini-Bettòlo, Delle Monache, & Ferrari, 1974; McKenna, Callaway, & Grob, 1998; McKenna & Towers, 1985; Ott, 1996, p. 164.
2. Callaway & McKenna, 1998, p. 491; Ott, 1994, pp. 81–84; Shulgin & Shulgin, 1997, pp. 418, 537; Strassman, 2001, p. 48.
3. Strassman, 2001, p. 48.
4. Strassman, 2001, p. 53.
5. Forsström, Tuominen, & Karkkäinen, 2001; Kärkkäinen & Räisänen, 1992; Kärkkäinen et al., 2005; Ott, 2001; Räisänen, 1984.
6. Kärkkäinen et al., 2005.
7. Callaway, 1988.
8. Strassman, 2001, p. 55; Brown, 2007.
9. Horgan, 2006; Strassman, 2001, p. 53.
10. Brown, 2007; Strassman, 2001, pp. 55, 69, 73, 75.
11. Strassman, 2001, pp. 68–69.
12. Birchwood, Preston, & Hallet, 1992, p. 62; Gillin, Kaplan, Stillman, & Wyatt, 1976; Jacob & Presti, 2005, p. 931; McKenna et al., 1998, p. 68.
13. Jacob & Presti, 2005; Wallach, 2009.
14. Fontanilla et al., 2009.

ontological categories. If we are peopled by the gods just as we are peopled by voices, ayahuasca uses the raw material of the visual world to construct the outward manifestation of our inward reality. With ayahuasca, Socrates' daemon not only speaks but appears, to teach or terrify, constructed out of the ambiguous forms, the visual detritus of our own jungles. Is this what ayahuasca teaches, that the world is magical?

And there, it seems to me, lies the heart of the matter. It is a question of how we valorize our encounters. Whether ayahuasca lends solidity to imagination, or opens the door to the spirit realms, or transports the user to distant dimensions, it is still the quality of our meeting that matters, what we are willing to learn, whether we are willing to be taught by what we encounter, whether we will take our chances in the epistemic murk of a transformed world. Hillman, in his soul-making, makes all meetings magical, because he mythologizes the everyday; soul-making makes *everyone* a spirit. I like to recall what Joan of Arc says in George Bernard Shaw's *Saint Joan*:

> JOAN: I hear voices telling me what to do. They come from God.
> ROBERT: They come from your imagination.
> JOAN: Of course. That is how the messages of God come to us.[64]

And in an interview with the Dauphin:

> CHARLES: Oh, your voices, your voices. Why don't the voices come to me? I am king, not you.
> JOAN: They do come to you; but you do not hear them.[65]

CHAPTER 25

OTHER PSYCHOACTIVE PLANTS

Much attention has been focused, understandably, on the basic ayahuasca drink, made from the ayahuasca vine and any of several plant sources of dimethyltryptamine—chacruna, chagraponga, and sameruca. But mestizo shamans are both eclectic and experimental. They frequently mix additional plant materials into the ayahuasca drink; and in addition to the drink itself, they make use of a remarkable variety of potentially psychoactive substances—natural, commercial, and industrial, both individually and in combination.

THE BIG THREE

The Amazon bioregion supports a remarkable variety of plants that are psychoactive to one degree or another, and mestizo shamans have tended to utilize them all. Still, throughout the Upper Amazon, the three most important psychoactive plants are three hallucinogens—mapacho, toé, and ayahuasca, either singly or in various combinations. This psychoactive triad may be conceptualized as embodying, respectively, the primary functions of *protection*, *power*, and *teaching*. Among some indigenous peoples—Asháninka, Ashéninka, Piro, Shipibo—the Big Three have specific associations: ayahuasca is associated with knowledge of the forest and the spirits of the teaching plants; toé is associated with the beings of the water; tobacco is associated with the spirits of animals and birds, especially the hummingbird.[1]

The Role of Tobacco

Mapacho, tobacco, is the most important and almost universal shamanic plant in the Upper Amazon.[2] In many ways tobacco is more sacred than ayahuasca. Tobacco smoke invites and feeds the spirits; tobacco smoke purifies and protects the body; tobacco nurtures the magical phlegm; infusions of tobacco bring contact with the spirits. As don Emilio Andrade Gómez says: Without tobacco, you cannot use any plant.[3]

The same is true among indigenous peoples. Tobacco establishes communication with the spirits; it is the food of the spirits; it opens the mind to an understanding of the spirit world.[4] Swallowing or blowing tobacco smoke assures success in hunting; blowing tobacco smoke on an object reveals its true nature;[5] the scent of tobacco attracts the spirits.[6] Among the Shuar, for example, a sorcerer drinks green tobacco juice—a cold infusion of uncured tobacco leaves—to release a magic dart to be hurled at a victim. A shaman must constantly drink tobacco water to keep the darts fed so that they do not leave; a shaman cannot even go for a walk without taking along green tobacco leaves.[7]

Mapacho is a species of tobacco containing very high levels of nicotine and other psychoactive pyridine alkaloids—the highest nicotine levels of any tobacco species; leaves from this species contain more than 8 percent nicotine, as much as twenty-six times the amount found in the common cigarette tobacco in North America.[8] There is also reason to believe that psychoactive alkaloids other than nicotine are present in noncommercial varieties of tobacco.[9]

There is little doubt that tobacco by itself has psychoactive effects, including the ability to induce hallucinations.[10] The nicotine alkaloid in tobacco displays high acute toxicity,[11] and acute nicotine intoxication can have significant visual and auditory effects, including what anthropologist Johannes Wilbert, an expert on tobacco use in South American shamanism, calls "hallucinatory eschatological scenarios on a cosmic scale."[12]

It is difficult for North Americans to think of tobacco as a hallucinogen, in large part because the tobacco species used in commercial North American cigarettes have such a relatively low nicotine content, and because North American smokers ingest relatively small quantities, generally stopping when the desired mood alteration has been achieved. Interestingly, there have been scattered reports of hallucinations associated with smoking while wearing a transdermal nicotine patch.[13]

In addition, nicotine may be used by the shaman to modulate the effects of other psychoactive substances. The ingestion of tobacco may influence the effects of both ayahuasca and toé. For example, tobacco smoke may itself contain MAO inhibitors: smokers have 30 to 40 percent lower MAO-B and 20 to 30 percent lower MAO-A activity than nonsmokers.[14] In addition, nicotine may

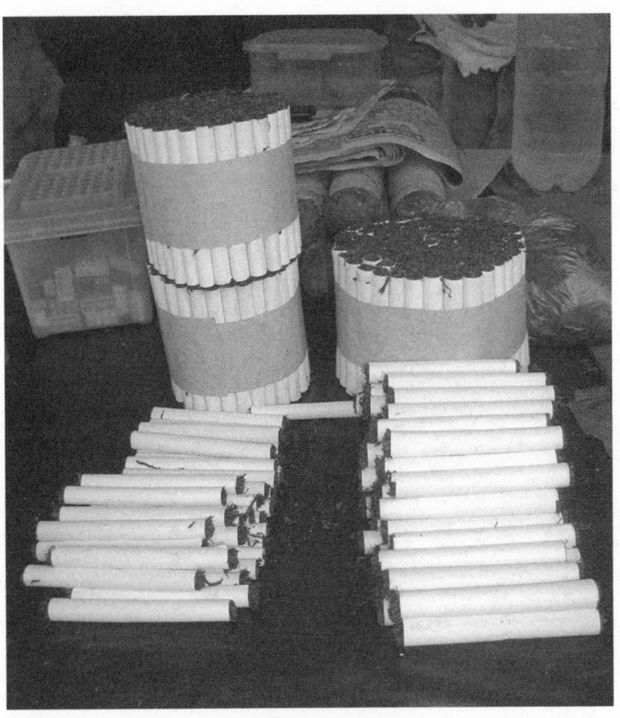

FIGURE 10. Mapacho in the Belén market.

modulate some of the cognitive effects of scopolamine, which is the primary psychoactive constituent of toé. In several studies, nicotine specifically helped to counteract the depression of performance produced by scopolamine on both rapid information and complex processing tasks.[15] This means that mapacho may ameliorate the cognitive deficits induced by toé while having no effect on its hallucinogenic properties.

Similarly, nicotine ingestion significantly improves the negative symptoms of schizophrenia—difficulty in abstract thinking, stereotyped thinking, social withdrawal, and blunted emotions—while having no effect on hallucinations. Nicotine ingestion also improves general psychopathology symptoms—poor attention, disorientation, unusual thought content, and poor impulse control. This may be one reason why people with schizophrenia tend to be such heavy smokers: they are medicating themselves. So smoking mapacho while drinking ayahuasca may well be a way to maintain cognitive lucidity and positive emotionality while not interfering with the hallucinatory experience.[16]

Indigenous Amazonian peoples ingest tobacco in every conceivable way—smoked, as a snuff, chewed, licked, as a syrup applied to the gums, and in the form of an enema.[17] Mestizo shamans consume tobacco as a cold-water infusion, in cigarettes, or in specially carved pipes; tobacco may also be added to the ayahuasca drink. Tobacco is smoked as cigarettes, hand-rolled in white paper, called mapacho in distinction from finos, commercial cigarettes; or else in pipes, called *shimitapon* or cachimbo.[18] The word *cachimbo* is Portuguese—hence the alternative pronunciation and spelling *cashimbo*—which in turn was probably derived from a West African language.[19]

Among the mestizos, the bowl of the pipe is often made from the dense reddish or purplish brown heartwood of the cachimbo tree, often carved with figures of snakes, birds, jaguars, or mermaids. Additional woods used for pipe bowls include *palisangre* and *quinilla*, which the Yagua often incise with symbols of the pipe spirit.[20]

Among mestizos the pipe stem is preferably made from the thin hollow leg bone of the tanrrilla, sunbittern, a wading bird with significant magical properties. I also own a pipe in the indigenous style whose stem is made from a monkey bone.[21] The Yagua make their pipe stems from the bone of a *panguana*, the tinamou bird.

Among mestizo shamans, such pipes are used to smoke not only tobacco but toé leaves and the bark of the ayahuasca vine as well. Some indigenous groups, such as the Yagua and the Ka'apor, also use pipes; there is reason to believe that, in some cases, such pipes have only recently come to replace rolled tobacco.[22]

The Role of Toé

Toé is the name given in the Upper Amazon to various species in the genus *Brugmansia*, including a wide variety of cultivars. César Calvo speaks of toé as "that other powerful and disconcerting hallucinogen."[23] It hardens the body; it makes one immune from sorcery; it builds up and maintains shamanic power.[24] Toé contains the primary tropane alkaloids hyoscyamine, atropine, and scopolamine;[25] it may be mixed into the ayahuasca drink, ingested in the form of raw plant materials or as a water infusion, or smoked in a cachimbo. Smoking the leaves produces a less intense experience than ingesting an infusion or raw plant materials. It is possible to buy *puros*, cigars, in the Belén market in Iquitos that are made of toé mixed with mapacho.[26]

Toé is considered one of the most powerful plants, a strong but dangerous ally. The intoxication induced by scopolamine and the other tropane alkaloids can last as long as four days, with often terrifying paranoid visions, followed by a calmer state and then retrograde amnesia, total or partial. Clinical signs and symptoms are those of the typical peripheral anticholinergic syndrome seen in any atropine poisoning—dilated pupils, dry mucous membranes, rapidly beating heart, fever, flushed dry skin, urinary retention, confusion, disorientation, and hallucinations. Rarely, seizures occur, and sometimes there are tactile hallucinations, such as crawling insects. Medical students have a mnemonic for this syndrome: blind as a bat, hot as a hare, dry as a bone, red as a beet, and mad as a hatter. Patients are often amnesiac for events between ingestion and recovery. Fatalities are rare but have been reported in children. Sometimes urinary retention is so severe as to require catheterization.[27]

Scopolamine overdose is recognized as a cause of acute paranoid hallucinatory psychoses, of a state of delirium like that associated with a very high fever, and of acute toxic psychosis, including confusion, agitation, rambling speech, hallucinations, paranoid behaviors, and delusions.[28] The hallucinations induced by scopolamine "are not of an agreeable, but on the contrary, of a terrifying and distressful kind."[29]

Here are two examples, both from the same emergency room.[30] A young man who had ingested *Datura straemonium*, rich in scopolamine, was admitted with agitation, delirium with persecutory ideation, and frightening hallucinations of being assaulted by animals. Similarly, a young woman who had ingested the same plant was agitated, with delirium, anxiety, auditory hallucinations, and frightening visual and tactile hallucination of green turtles walking on her. In both cases, the patients were restrained and treated with the antipsychotic drug cyamemazine, and both returned to normal after thirty-six and forty hours, respectively.

Similarly, the Centers for Disease Control have described an outbreak of heroin laced with scopolamine in several cities and the resulting "paranoia, hallucinations, and agitation" seen in emergency room patients.[31] It has been described as "a wild, crazed state, total disorientation, delirium, foaming at the mouth, a wicked thirst, terrifying visions that fuse into a dreamless sleep, followed by complete amnesia"; oscillating between extreme agitation and unconsciousness; "a loss of senses, visual disturbances, drying of the throat and mouth, visions (sometimes of a frightening character) and occasionally violent reactions requiring restraint."[32]

Don Agustin Rivas describes his first experience with toé as follows: "Five minutes after I drank toé, my body started to jerk all over, with my arms twitching and jerking. . . . My head ached, and I began to see demons, colors, strange men, animals, and aggressive snakes that wanted to bite me. I tried to remain still but it was impossible."[33] The Canelos Quichua say that *wanduj* makes one see distant things as if they were near and near things as if they were distant; the drinker sees the world of spirits, the dead, the future, souls; he stumbles and falls and crashes, frightening people, laughing when he should say *aiyaów!*[34]

One highland shaman told anthropologist Michael Taussig that when one drinks toé, one races around screaming, ripping off clothes, urinating all over the place, robbing things, without realizing what one is doing, like in a dream. "It's really awful," the shaman said, "not like yagé. It's as if your clothes come off. Your throat becomes dry, dry . . . and then this passes and you forget." The flower, he said, is "sweet like honey, but *strong*! Thus! *Boom*! Crash to the floor. Remember nothing. Nothing."[35]

The Shuar consider *maikua*, the raw juice of the green bark of the stem, to be the most dangerous and powerful hallucinogen. The effects begin within three or four minutes; the drinker is accompanied by an adult to hold him down if necessary when the drinker becomes delirious and tends to run off into the jungle. The vision can consist of two gigantic animals—often jaguars or boas—fighting each other, or a disembodied human head, or a ball of fire. When the vision gets near, the drinker must be brave enough to run forward and touch it, whereupon it instantly explodes and disappears.[36]

The visions given by toé are dark and frightening. Animals and humans that might in an ayahuasca vision appear to be potential allies appear in a toé vision to be menacing or terrifying. That is why toé is so powerful: it demands great courage; if you can survive the toé vision, the spirit world can hold few terrors. Thus toé hardens the body, makes it a cuerpo cerrado or cuerpo sellado, a body that is closed or sealed, makes one resistant to attack by sorcerers.[37]

THE QUESTION OF PSYCHOACTIVITY

A mestizo shaman has dieted with scores—perhaps hundreds—of plants, each of which has its own range of effects. Each plant becomes an ally in its own particular way. Some plants are powerful, grab you and shake you; some insinuate themselves gently into your dreams and thoughts. We often have very little information about the constituents of these plants; often there is uncertainty, as with camalonga, even about their identity in a given area of the Upper Amazon. And it must be confessed that there is similar uncertainty about the term *psychoactive*, especially as the plants are used by shamans during la dieta, because it is difficult to disentangle complex plant actions and to distinguish physical from psychological effects.

Chiricsanango

Here is an example. Chiricsanango causes chills and tingling and is therefore considered a cold plant, used to treat hot conditions—fever, diarrhea, wounds, and inflammations.[38] The medicine is made as a decoction of the leaves or bark or as an infusion of the roots.[39] The plant contains an alkaloid named scopoletin, but the effects of scopoletin are very different from those of the scopolamine in toé. The effect of ingesting chiricsanango can be dramatic—a tingling and vibrating sensation in the extremities, moving inward toward the head with ever increasing intensity, periodic waves of cold, tremors, electric vibrations penetrating the chest and back, stomach cramps, nausea, dizziness, vertigo, loss of coordination.[40] It is not at all clear to me whether chiricsanango has an independent psychoactive effect or whether altered consciousness is a result of its powerful physical effects; scopoletin is not itself known to be psychoactive.[41] But there is no question that chiricsanango is a very powerful ally, a healer, a strong protector, once it has shaken your bones.

FIGURE 11. Don Roberto with chiricsanango.

Catahua

In the same way, catahua is a very strong—even dangerous—teacher. Poet César Calvo says that catahua "is the worst of all: it makes your body rot, it burns you from the inside."[42] This is not an exaggeration. The latex contains toxic diterpene esters that can cause immediate skin inflammation, with edematous swellings and blisters; eye exposure can lead to temporary blindness; internally, the latex can cause debilitating intestinal cramps, vomiting, intestinal bloating, and diarrhea, followed by rapid heartbeat and impaired vision.[43] Where chiricsanango sends shivers to your bones, catahua puts knots in your intestines.

Catahua latex is traditionally used as a laxative and purgative—and as a fish poison.[44] Don Emilio Andrade Gómez whistles the *icaro de la catahua* before entering a dangerous lake; he throws a mixture of catahua, the toxic patiquina, and the pucunucho pepper into the water to drive away the yacuruna, the water people.[45] The medicine is learned by drinking a little bit of its latex after heating it in a water bath, or bringing it carefully to a boil, while the maestro ayahuasquero sings appropriate songs over it; a strict diet of several months is required.[46] Like other powerful plants with strong effects, catahua is considered a protector. "Catahua is always protecting me," says don Agustin Rivas, "and no malicious intent can affect me."[47] The physical effect is immediate; but the sense of protection—the opening of the mind and intuition—comes gradually.[48]

Ajo Sacha

On the other hand, ajo sacha, wild garlic, works slowly and gently. It is a warm plant, used to treat cold conditions such as arthritis and rheumatism; for this purpose, scrapings of the bark are mixed in water or aguardiente and drunk. Most often, ajo sacha is added to a limpia, bath, as a treatment for sore muscles, cramps, fatigue, aches, or flu and especially for saladera, bad luck caused by sorcery.[49] Ajo sacha contains several of the same sulfur compounds—primarily alliin and various allyl sulfides—as are found in garlic, none of which is considered psychoactive.[50] When dieting, it is ingested by drinking a macerate of the fresh scraped root. It tastes very much like garlic water, which some find to be unpleasant. Hunters drink ajo sacha to disguise their human scent; fishermen purify their bodies, tools, and canoes with ajo sacha to assure a good catch.[51]

Ajo sacha is considered a subtle ally, who influences the nature of dreams on following nights, making them peculiarly auditory; it is thus a source of

Camalonga

The plant called camalonga provides an example of ongoing uncertainty about the identity and effects of a shamanic plant. The name *camalonga* or *cabalonga* is shared by two different plants, the first term being more common in Peru and the second, in Colombia. The first of these two plants, sometimes distinguished as *camalonga negra*, may be any of several species in the genus *Strychnos*, including some that are used in the manufacture of the arrow poison *curaré*. The second, sometimes distinguished as *camalonga blanca*, is pretty clearly *Thevetia peruviana*, the yellow oleander, which is the plant used by don Roberto in making his camalonga drink—two yellow oleander seeds, one male and one female, white onion or garlic, and camphor mixed into aguardiente, distilled fermented sugarcane juice.

In Spanish generally, the word *cabalonga* refers to the almond-like seeds of the tree *Strychnos ignatii*, native to the Philippine Islands and China, which are popularly called *haba de San Ignacio*, St. Ignatius beans. In some parts of Peru, these imported seeds are worn as amulets, as they are in the Philippines, and are distinguished from the indigenous Amazonian *cabalonga de la selva*, jungle cabalonga.[1] Imported cabalonga is apparently highly valued. The dried pear-shaped fruits containing these seeds are rare and, according to ethnobotanist Christian Rätsch, are sold under the table at herb markets for exorbitant prices, with counterfeits sometimes substituted for the unwary.[2]

Apparently, Colombian shamans prefer to use seeds of plants of the *Strychnos* genus, while Peruvian shamans prefer to use the seeds of *Thevetia peruviana*. Although it is sometimes said that camalonga seeds may be added to the ayahuasca mixture, I have not found evidence that this is the case. In Peru, camalongueros are shamanic practitioners who specialize in the use of this camalonga drink.

I do not understand why the two camalongas are given the same name. The plants do not look even remotely similar, and the seeds—the part most often used by shamans—look as dissimilar as the plants. Moreover, the plants contain very different alkaloids, with very different physiological effects.

The yellow oleander, *Thevetia peruviana*, contains the powerful cardiac glycosides thevetin, thevetoxin, peruvoside, ruvoside, and nerifolin, which are found throughout the plant but are concentrated in the seeds. Ingesting yellow oleander seeds can cause abdominal pain; vomiting and diarrhea; dilated pupils; increased blood pressure, dizziness; stimulation of the smooth muscles of the intestine, bladder, uterus, and blood vessels; and a variety of arrhythmias, which can be fatal. Chewing the seed causes a drying, numbing, or burning sensation in the mouth and throat. The sap of the plant can cause skin irritation, sometimes blistering, and the plant has been used as a fish poison.[3]

On the other hand, the primary effects of plants of the *Strychnos* genus are muscular and neurological. The active constituent of these plants is strychnine, which increases the reflex irritability of the spinal cord, resulting in a loss of normal inhibition of the body's motor cells, in turn causing severe contractions of the muscles. Signs and symptoms of strychnine overdose include agitation, apprehension, fear, heightened startle reflex, restlessness, dark urine, muscle pain and soreness, and difficulty breathing, which can progress to rigid arms and legs, jaw tightness, painful muscle spasms, and finally uncontrollable arching of the neck and back, respiratory failure, and brain death. Death is usually due to asphyxiation resulting from continuous spasms of the respiratory muscles.[4] At very low doses, strychnine may give a sense of alertness, sensory acuity, and wakefulness; at one time it was widely prescribed in England as a tonic.[5]

I have seen only scant anecdotal evidence that strychnine ingestion causes prodromal dizziness or light-headedness. I am not sure what to make of the claim that true cabalonga can be identified by putting a tiny piece under your tongue and experiencing sensations of dizziness within a few moments.[6]

None of the constituents of either type of camalonga has been reported to be psychoactive. Neither appears to be widely used medicinally. *Strychnos guianensis* is used primarily as an ingredient in arrow poisons.[7] At Takiwasi, a center in Tarapoto devoted to the treatment of addictions using traditional Amazonian medicine, camalonga—specifically identified as the seed of a plant in the *Strychnos* genus—is reportedly administered to newly admitted patients for ten days, combined with a sugar-free diet, in a program to detoxify certain unspecified "energy disorders."[8]

Yellow oleander is used—as you would expect—as a purgative, and the leaves are used to treat toothache, presumably because of their numbing effect in the mouth. It is also considered an abortifacient, which is probably correct, given its stimulatory effect on the muscles of the uterus.[9]

NOTES

1. Giese, 1989, p. 258.
2. Rätsch, 2007, p. 606. Interestingly, according to Rätsch (2007, p. 606), in Mexico, just as in the Upper Amazon, the word *cabalonga* is used to refer both to *Thevetia peruviana* and to a *Strychnos* species, *Strychnos panamensis*.
3. Bose et al., 1999; Caravati, McCowan, & Marshall, 2004, pp. 1699–1700; Frohne & Pfänder, 2005, pp. 56–57; Maringhini et al., 2002; Nellis, 1997, pp. 145–147.
4. Flomenbaum, 2002, pp. 1383–1384; Harris, 2007; Henry, Little, Jagoda, & Pellegrino, 2003, pp. 152–153; Lewis, 1998, p. 985; Williams, 2004.
5. Shneerson, 2005, p. 80.
6. Faust & Bianchi, 1998, p. 249.
7. Castner, Timme, & Duke, 1998, p. 121; Dewick, 2001, pp. 324–327; Duke & Vasquez, 1994, p. 162; Plotkin, 1993, p. 309.
8. Mabit, 1996.
9. Castner et al., 1998, p. 124; Duke & Vasquez, 1994, p. 170.

icaros, magical songs, for all sorts of purposes.[52] Don Francisco Shuña dieted with ajo sacha while still a young boy; the first night after drinking it, he dreamed of a queen with a golden crown, her hands made of tree branches, telling him not to be afraid as a song entered into him like a spiral through the crown of his head. On a subsequent night the queen whistled the melody of an icaro so the boy could learn it.[53] Ajo sacha also enhances auditory perception in general; slowly and subtly, the jungle sounds become clearer, more meaningful; and in dreams the plants begin to sing.

AYAHUASCA RECIPES

Mestizo shamans often mix additional ingredients into the basic ayahuasca drink. In addition to the ayahuasca vine and its companion chacruna, chagraponga, or sameruca, some shamans may, at different times, add plants that are believed to modulate in some way the experience of the drink, such as ajo sacha, ayahuma, *bobinsana*, *capirona*, catahua, chiricsanango, lobosanango, mapacho, maricahua, mucura, pucalupuna, toé, or other plants, any of which may be psychoactive to one degree or another.[54]

Some shamans add several different plants to the ayahuasca drink. Don Roberto, for example, adds chiricsanango, toé, and maricahua. Other combinations of additional ingredients include bobinsana and lobosanango; toé and camphor; mapacho, toé, and bobinsana; ajo sacha, mucura, and guayusa; and toé, ajo sacha, and chiricsanango.[55] This practice may be disputed. "It is not always good to mix in so many things," says Pablo Amaringo. "It's better to make it each time with the chacruna and, if he so wishes, he may add another plant, always one at a time."[56]

Shamans may add plants to the basic drink for reasons other than to modify its psychoactive properties. For example, ayahuasca is a vine that requires strong trees for support; by analogy, some shamans add the bark of large strong trees to the drink—for example, huayracaspi, icoja, tahuari, and chullachaqui caspi—in order to provide similar support to those who drink it;[57] the harder the wood, the more power it can deliver.[58] Some add strong sweet smells, such as agua de florida, for the protection such smells give; some add tobacco for the same purpose. Some add plants to modulate the emetic effects of ayahuasca—ojé, an emetic, or *piripiri*, an antiemetic.[59] During la dieta, plants and other substances may be added for purely experimental reasons—to let the ayahuasca transmit the teachings of the added plant, its spirit, its uses, and its song.

COMBINATIONS

All of these potentially psychoactive materials may be consumed as part of la dieta, during the ayahuasca healing ceremony, or on other occasions. During a ceremony, the ayahuasca drink is seldom ingested in isolation; a shaman may ingest in addition significant amounts of mapacho, toé, camalonga, piripiri, camphor, agua de florida, aguardiente, and other substances. Sometimes a caffeine-rich infusion of guayusa is drunk—or its leaves are mixed into the ayahuasca drink—in order to kill the bitter taste of ayahuasca and, it is said, prevent a hangover the next morning.[60]

Over a career, a shaman has consumed an incredible variety of substances—not only hundreds of different plants but also any number of commercial products, including agua de florida, Timolina, Creolina, and camphor, often in combination. Don Roberto, for example, regularly drinks a mixture of camphor, camalonga, and aguardiente; doña María regularly drank a mixture of mapacho, camphor, camalonga, and agua de florida. Since these commercial products have genios, spirits, shamans may diet with them: Artidoro Aro Cardenas, a perfumero, has dieted with agua de florida, Timolina, and camalonga;[61] don Emilio Andrade Gómez has dieted with, among other things, agua de florida, camphor, and Creolina.[62] Clearly, the potential for complex synergistic and antagonistic interactions is immense.

PART III

CONTEXT AND SOURCES

CHAPTER 26
THE UPPER AMAZON CULTURE AREA

SOURCES OF MESTIZO SHAMANISM

Mestizo shamans derive their practices from numerous sources—the indigenous shamanism of the Upper Amazon, folk Catholicism, popular plant lore, traditional Hispanic medical theories and diagnoses, and the images and symbols of European biomedicine. I think of don Roberto, dressed in a crown of feathers and a shirt painted with Shipibo designs, welcoming spirits who descend from the sky in the form of extraterrestrial doctors speaking computer language; or doña María, dressed in a white coat like a biomedical doctor, singing the Ave Maria as a spell of protection before drinking ayahuasca. Guillermo Arévalo, a Shipibo shaman, says, "Right now in the Amazon, we can't say that there's any pure tradition. It's mixed. Even the indigenous are fusing together different cultural beliefs. This is not a bad thing, it's natural. When it comes out of positive intention, it's good."[1]

THE UPPER AMAZON AS A CULTURE AREA

Mestizo shamans are recognizably part of a larger Upper Amazonian religious culture area, characterized by a number of common features—the use of psychoactive plants; the presence of magical substances kept within the shaman's body; notions of sickness as caused by the intrusion of pathogenic objects; the ambiguity of shamanic ability to do both good and evil; the central sacrality of tobacco; the acquisition of songs from the spirits; the use of songs for the creation of both medicines and poisons; a focus on healing with the mouth through blowing and sucking; and the importance of singing, whistling, blowing, and rattling in both healing and sorcery.

FIGURE 12. Doña María with chacruna.

Travel and exchange have occurred throughout the western Amazon since long before the arrival of Europeans. What seems to the unfamiliar eye to be a vast undifferentiated landscape is in fact threaded with riverine highways navigable over long distances in dugout canoes. In addition to efficient canoe transport, indigenous people in the Amazon have always been able to cover long distances on foot, even carrying heavy loads, with remarkable speed. Anthropologists Blanca Muratorio and Michael Taussig have both provided nineteenth-century paintings and engravings that show indigenous porters carrying heavy burdens through the jungle highlands, including white men wearing frock coats and Panama hats, sitting on chairs strapped to the porter's back.[2]

Cultural exchange has been facilitated by trade throughout this area, dating back to pre-Columbian times, in such products as *pita* fiber, gold, salt, cotton, cinnamon, tropical fruits, and feathers; by rules of exogamy that require taking a bride from a village that speaks a different language; and by herbalists, traveling far distances, collecting medicinal plants from the Pacific coast to the lowland jungle, setting their blankets in the small markets, covered with their roots and stems, bark and leaves.[3] Arrow poisons have been widely used in this area, and the similarity of names—*curaré*, *wourali*, *ourari*, *urali*—indicate the frequent exchange of ideas and ingredients.[4]

The process of cultural exchange was accelerated by European colonization, when missionaries forced indigenous people to live together in *reducciones*, regardless of their tribal distinctions, so they could more easily be converted and controlled; and in particular by the rubber boom, where indigenous and mestizo people from the entire area, bound together by slavery and debt peonage, were transported long distances and put to work together as rubber tappers.[5] This process of interchange continues today in the urban slums of Iquitos and Pucallpa, in smaller Amazonian towns, and in the Peruvian army, in which local healers, thrown together with distant practitioners, have traditionally been able to exchange ideas.[6] Protestant missionaries use their light planes to fly indigenous people to large evangelical prayer meetings, where their guests use the opportunity to arrange marriages, negotiate political alliances, exchange news, and consult famous shamans—and where shamans can consult with each other.[7]

The shaman has always been a node in this interethnic network of social relations. Shamans seek to gain power from a variety of sources, including other ethnic groups. There is a belief, for example, that the magic darts of different groups are different from each other and can be extracted only by one who possesses darts of that particular type; thus a Quichua shaman will visit an Achuar shaman in order to exchange darts, or a Shuar will travel to a Canelos Quichua shaman to buy them.[8] In the same way, darts are considered more powerful if they have come from a great distance, so shamans in the jungle are reputed to travel as far as the northern Andes to acquire them.[9] Anthropologist Philippe Descola, as an exotic pale-haired stranger, reports being frequently importuned by Achuar shamans to share his darts with them.[10]

Shamans from some ethnic groups have reputations as being particularly powerful or particularly skilled in certain areas of specialization, such as love magic or sorcery. In the Amazon, most groups view others as being more powerful shamans than themselves, and therefore worth learning from. The Shuar say that the Canelos Quichua are powerful shamans;[11] the Cashinahua say the same of the Culina.[12] As one Amazonian Indian has put it, jokingly: Wherever you go, the great brujos are elsewhere.[13]

While all shamans are competitors, who may at any moment find themselves locked in mortal combat, they are also pan-Amazonian in outlook. A shaman faced with a difficult case may travel to drink ayahuasca with a powerful colleague, preferably far away, with a different culture and ethnic identity.[14] Shamans from different ethnic groups may care for each other's patients,

Arrow Poisons

Very few indigenous peoples of the Upper Amazon still hunt with blowguns. But using a blowgun and curaré-tipped darts was an efficient way to put food on the table; skilled hunters could even bring down small birds. The key, of course, was curaré, arrow poison, just as the key to fishing remains *barbasco*, fish poison. Sticking a dart in a wild pig gives you an angry pig; sticking a curaré-tipped dart in a wild pig gives you pig soup.

Historically, there have been two primary types of curaré used in the Amazon, which Europeans named not after their ingredients, which were a mystery, but after the three types of containers in which they were stored. Tube curaré, stored in hollow bamboo tubes, was used primarily in Peru, Ecuador, and western Brazil and was made from the vine *Chondrodendron tomentosum*. Calabash curaré, stored in small gourds, and pot curaré, stored in small clay pots, were used primarily in Colombia, Venezuela, and Guyana and were made from *Strychnos guianensis*.

These arrow poisons were usually complex mixtures, incorporating not only the primary active ingredient but also other plants, as well as snake venom, frog venom, or venomous ants—as many as thirty ingredients, which varied from group to group. The recipe was often kept as a commercial secret, in order to maintain regional monopolies. The mixture of bark and stems was pounded, boiled in water for about two days, and then strained and evaporated to become a dark, heavy, viscid paste with a very bitter taste. Additional plant material might be mixed in to make the preparation more glutinous, to stick more readily to blowgun darts or arrows.[1]

Plants of the *Strychnos* genus contain strychnine, a convulsant poison, which causes death by asphyxia because the respiratory muscles convulsively contract.[2] *Chondrodendron tomentosum*, on the other hand, contains the primary active alkaloids curarine and tubocurarine—the *tubo-* prefix is from storing the curaré in bamboo tubes—which interfere with the activity of the neurotransmitter acetylcholine, blocking nerve impulses at the neuromuscular junction. The result is the opposite of strychnine; rather than muscle contraction, tubocurarine produces limp relaxation of voluntary muscles. Death is caused by asphyxia because the respiratory muscles are too flaccid to function.[3]

A person hit by a poison dart of this sort is awake, aware, susceptible to pain, but unable to move. If breathing is supported by artificial respiration, recovery is complete in about thirty minutes, when the alkaloid has been metabolized.

These curaré alkaloids have two significant advantages for hunters. Since they result in muscle relaxation, animals hit by the darts fall out of trees onto the ground. Moreover, because these curaré alkaloids are absorbed very slowly from the intestine, animals killed by the poison darts can be eaten with impunity. The muscle-relaxing effect begins almost immediately upon hitting the bloodstream, but death from respiratory arrest can take a few minutes for birds and small prey and up to twenty minutes for larger mammals, such as tapirs. When I was staying among the formerly head-hunting Shapra in the borderlands between Peru and Ecuador, I was told that it can take fifteen or twenty darts to bring down a human being.

The strength of a batch of curaré can be tested in a number of ways—for example, by counting the number of times a frog can jump after being pricked or how many trees a monkey can leap after being hit. One-tree curaré is very potent; three-tree curaré can be used to take down live animals to be kept in captivity.[4]

Biomedicine has been profoundly interested in the neuromuscular properties of the curaré alkaloids. Tubocurarine has been studied for its use as a muscle relaxant in surgery, reducing the need for deep anesthesia, and as an aid to intubation or ventilation. A number of synthetic analogues have been developed, including succinylcholine and pancuronium, both of which have been used in executions by lethal injection.[5]

NOTES

1. See generally Davis, 1996, pp. 209–215; Dewick, 2001, pp. 324–327; Jones, 2007, pp. 29–30; Neuwinger, 1998, pp. 71–76; Prance, 2005, pp. 141–144; Schultes, 1989, pp. 34–35.
2. Flomenbaum, 2002, pp. 1383–1384; Harris, 2007; Henry, Little, Jagoda, & Pellegrino, 2003, pp. 152–153; Lewis, 1998, p. 985; Williams, 2004.
3. Dewick, 2001, pp. 325–326; Lattin & Fifer, 2002; Neuwinger, 1998, pp. 75–76.
4. Dewick, 2001, p. 324.
5. Denno, 2007; Dewick, 2001, pp. 325–326; Lattin & Fifer, 2002, pp. 286–289.

train each other's apprentices, and exchange visions, songs, knowledge, and power objects, such as stones or feather crowns. An Achuar shaman, for example, traditionally had to undergo apprenticeship with established shamans in different locations.[15] A Tukano apprentice was expected to live with a shaman of renown in a different region, for several months, even for a year or more, while receiving instruction.[16] Such communication among shamans has been maintained for centuries.[17]

Even though mestizo shamans are very individualistic, there is also a network of relationships among them, which may include transmitting new information or knowledge. Anthropologist Luis Eduardo Luna notes that such shamans often know others who live many kilometers away, and that shamans who live in the city have a communication network with those living in remote areas of the forest. One reason for these networks is that shamans are subject to magical attack by more powerful shamans, and a shaman who has been attacked may turn for protection to a shaman more powerful still.[18] Another reason is the satisfaction of knowing that their untimely death will be an affront to their friends and will be avenged.[19]

THE UNIQUENESS OF THE UPPER AMAZON

A remarkable feature of the Upper Amazon culture area is that it is a center from which radiates a larger culture area characterized by the use of psychoactive plants and fungi in shamanic work. These extensions spread westward across the Andes, eastward into Brazil, northward to the Mazatec and Huichol cultures of Mexico, and farther north into the Native American Church, which is in many ways a northerly extension of Huichol peyote use.

R. Gordon Wasson's well-publicized discovery—it was a front-page story in *Life* magazine—that Mazatec shaman María Sabina still used the ancient psychoactive mushroom teonanácatl in her healing rituals, coupled with the remarkable popularity of the early works of Carlos Castaneda, unleashed an abiding fascination with the use of psychoactive substances in religion generally and shamanism in particular.[20] But I think there is reason to believe that the extended Upper Amazon culture area may be *uniquely* characterized by the use of psychoactive plants and fungi in shamanic work, and that attempts to establish such use elsewhere—primarily in Siberia and North America—have failed to be persuasive.

Now, there is no question that psychoactive plants and fungi are widely used in indigenous cultures around the world. The question we are asking here, however, is not whether they are used, but whether they are used *by shamans for shamanizing*. And that raises a number of considerations.

Sometimes, of course, psychoactive plants or fungi are used outside any ceremonial context at all—for recreation, say, or to alleviate fatigue. For example, the hallucinogenic fungus *Amanita muscaria*, often called fly agaric, appears to have been most frequently used in Siberia *outside* of shamanism—to get a glimpse of what the shamans see, to prepare for all-night bardic performances, to alleviate the fatigue of heavy labor, or for recreational inebriation at weddings and feasts.[21]

Sometimes, too, psychoactive plants are used in a ceremonial context that does not involve shamanizing, such as in an ordeal or initiation. For example, the *iboga* plant, *Tabernanthe iboga*, is a central feature of the Bwiti religion, a revitalization movement in west-central Africa.[22] At low doses, iboga acts as a stimulant.[23] Its ability to suppress fatigue is of value at Bwiti ceremonies other than initiation, where participants must dance all night; low doses of iboga lighten the body, they say, so that it can float through the ritual dances.[24] But in initiatory rituals, very large hallucinogenic doses of iboga are ingested, in order for the initiates to contact the spirits of dead ancestors, to experience passing over to the land of the dead, to see the *bwiti*—that is, at once, the superior deity, the ancestors in the realm of the dead, and the great divine beings of the Christian pantheon.[25] It is only for purposes of initiation that sufficiently massive doses are ingested—fifteen to fifty times the normal threshold dose—to cause hallucinations, with the intention to "break open the head" of the initiate.[26] This does not appear to be a shamanic use.

We also find, surprisingly often, that psychoactive plants are used not by shamans but, rather, by nonshamans attempting to *emulate* shamans, by using psychoactive plants or mushrooms that shamans themselves do not use. Among the Siberian Koryaks, for example, ordinary people at one time would ingest fly agaric in order to attain visions like those of shamans, who apparently did not need it.[27] Among the Chumash and other indigenous peoples in south-central California, it can be important to acquire a *dream helper*, not just for shamans but for ordinary people as well: Falcon helps gamblers, Bobcat can help hunters, Otter can make one a good swimmer, Roadrunner helps midwives. Sometimes a dream helper appears in an ordinary dream; this is especially true for shamans, whose powers first appear in dreams during childhood. Conversely, to obtain a dream helper, common people rely heavily on *Datura*, which plays only a marginal role in the acquisition of shamanic power.[28]

And outside of the Upper Amazon culture area, shamans often claim that they do not *need* to ingest psychoactive substances in order to shamanize. Tatiana Urkachan, an eighty-two-year-old shaman in Kamchatka, told visitors that she never ingested the fly agaric mushroom herself, for she was too powerful a shaman to need it.[29] The Siberian Chukchi too believe that fly agaric is for weak shamans.[30]

We also have to look carefully at the relevant physical effects of the psychoactive plant or fungus claimed to be used by shamans, to see whether those effects are consistent with the demands of the shamanic performance. For example, small doses of fly agaric mushroom produce mild euphoria, suppression of fear, and feelings of increased strength or stamina; after ingesting the mushroom, for example, novelist Tom Robbins says he felt "invincibly strong," filled with "euphoric energy."[31] However, doses large enough to cause hallucinations—which appear to occur only rarely and sporadically—are physically incapacitating, with effects including drowsiness, confusion, muscle twitches, loss of muscular coordination, and stupor. It is difficult to see how a shaman could put on a physically demanding shamanic performance under such circumstances.[32]

In the same way, iboga, at sufficient dosages, acts as a hallucinogen; but the massive dose required to cause hallucinations is physically debilitating. Anthropologist James Fernandez notes that "initiates display a gross reduction in their ability to moderate or program motor activity." They eventually fall over and have to be carried to a special area where the visions are experienced.[33] Their bodies are described as *inert*—a condition incompatible with a shamanic performance.[34]

There are two separate questions here that are often conflated. One question is whether any particular shamanic culture, other than the one I have defined, *currently* uses psychoactive plants or fungi for shamanizing, or is reported to have used them for that purpose during the period for which we have historical records. A different question is whether, based on the answer to the first question, we can make legitimate inferences about the role of psychoactive plants or fungi in the *origins* of shamanism, or in its practice during prehistoric times.

Let us deal briefly with the second question. In order to make an inference from current practices, or the written record, to the practices of prehistoric shamans requires us to adopt the odd affectation of European colonialism that indigenous people are *without history*—that, unlike Europeans, they are unchanging in their isolation and innocence. But the assumption that indigenous practices are unchanging is demonstrably false—indeed, demonstrably false during the five hundred years within which indigenous practices have been recorded. We know, for example, that by the time the first European travelers brought home descriptions of Siberian shamanism, it had already been influenced by centuries of contact with Buddhism, Islam, and Russian Orthodox Christianity.[35] During the seventeenth and eighteenth centuries, Chukchi people from Siberia had contact with Inuit people from Alaska, through Russian trading posts within traveling distance of the Bering Strait.[36] We have no direct evidence of what Siberian shamanism—or, for that matter, *any* indigenous shamanism—might have been like before that time.

NEW RELIGIOUS MOVEMENTS IN BRAZIL

Discussion of the Upper Amazon culture area would be incomplete without some reference to its most recent eastward extension—the several new syncretic religious movements of Brazil in which ayahuasca plays a central sacramental role.[37] The Upper Amazonian contribution to these movements was the use of the basic ayahuasca drink, made from the ayahuasca vine and—exclusively—chacruna; no other companion plants, and no additional plants, are used in the drink. Other aspects of the Upper Amazon culture area, including its shamanism, were not imported; anthropologist Edward MacRae has specifically pointed out that Santo Daime has not incorporated such features of Amazonian shamanism as virotes, arcanas, phlegm, or Amazonian ideas of the moral ambiguity of the shaman.[38] Rather, ayahuasca was incorporated as a sacrament into a folk Catholicism that had already been profoundly influenced by spiritism and Afro-Brazilian culture.

These religions began in the 1930s, when many Brazilian immigrants moved southwest to the Amazon seeking work tapping rubber trees. Most of these impoverished Brazilian immigrants became sedentary *seringueros*, but came in contact not only with indigenous Amazonians but also with itinerant mestizo *caucheros* from the Upper Amazon. Three of these Brazilian immigrants—Raimundo Irineu Serra (1892–1971), Daniel Pereira de Mattos (1904–1958), and José Gabriel da Costa (1922–1971)—founded new religions, mixing African Brazilian, spiritist, and Christian elements with mestizo and indigenous use of ayahuasca.[39]

Santo Daime

The first Christian church to use ayahuasca as its sacrament was founded by Irineu Serra, a seven-foot-tall illiterate African Brazilian rubber tapper, the descendant of slaves. When he first drank ayahuasca, probably in the borderlands between Brazil and Bolivia, a woman appeared to him, calling herself the Queen of the Forest, whom Irineu identified with the Virgin Mary. She told him that ayahuasca was the sacred blood of Jesus Christ, giving light, love, and strength to all who would use it. Ayahuasca was henceforth to be called *daime*, "give me," as in "give me love, give me light, give me strength."

Toward the end of the 1920s, Irineu started to organize sessions in the town of Rio Branco, in the Brazilian state of Acre. Although he could not read, write, or transcribe music, his *hinos*, hymns, were soon put into written form by his followers. He became known as Maestre Irineu, the first great leader of the Santo Daime movement.[40] So important is his person that the double-armed cross of Caravaca, under the name *cruzeiro*, has been imported into the Santo Daime tradition, where it is present at all Daime works, and the second arm of the cross is held to refer to the second coming of Christ in the person of Maestre Irineu.[41]

As the number of his followers increased, Irineu organized his church and established its Christian-spiritist doctrine, which included belief in reincarnation and the law of karma. Christian elements included unconditional love for one's neighbors, veneration of Catholic saints, a belief in Jesus Christ as the Savior, and an understanding of Santo Daime as the doctrine of the Virgin and of Jesus Christ and of daime as the Blood of Christ.[42] In fact, the doctrine of Jesus Christ secreted itself within the sacred vine and leaf as Christ Consciousness—a seed that was destined to be replanted in humanity by Master Irineu.[43]

Irineu also instituted a specific ritual for the drinking of daime, with men and women separated in concentric circles, singing a set program of hymns. Santo Daime services center on healing. The structure is hierarchical and paternalistic; the main emphasis is on the doctrine as codified in hymns and ritual. The central focus for these Santo Daime ceremonies is the singing of hymns, which Serra claimed to have received while within the "force" of the daime.[44] Members of Santo Daime typically dance in an intricate two-step with men and women separated.[45]

Irineu died in 1971, but his center remained active. In 1972, one of his followers, Sebastião Mota de Melo (1920–1990), created a new center called the Centro Eclético de Fluente Luz Universal Raimundo Irineu Serra, the Raimundo Irineu Serra Eclectic Center of Fluid Universal Light (CEFLURIS). Other Santo Daime groups tracing their lineage to Irineu compete for the title *Alto Santo*, Holy Heights, after the location of the original Santo Daime church and community; none numbers more than a few hundred members.[46] Among other reasons, the split was sparked by differences about the legitimate successor to Irineu. The new center also adopted additional esoteric spiritist teachings, especially those of the Circulo Esotérico de Comunhão do Pensamento, a group based in São Paulo.[47] In addition, CEFLURIS, as opposed to Alto Santo, incorporated marijuana into its ayahuasca rituals, calling it *Santa María*, the plant of the Virgin Mary—a feminine spiritual force counterbalancing the masculine daime, which is God the Father.[48]

Under the charismatic leadership of Padrinho Sebastião, CEFLURIS began to operate in urban areas of many Brazilian states and later expanded into other European countries, the Americas, and Japan.[49]

Barquinha

Daniel Pereira de Mattos—called Frei Daniel by his followers—had been a friend of Irineu and a member of Santo Daime. In 1945, he developed his own religious movement, now known as Barquinha, Little Boat, based on the idea that adherents are sailors on the holy sea aboard the little boat of the Holy Cross.[50] Along with Santo Daime and the rural folk Catholicism of Brazil, Barquinha incorporated spiritism and West African spirit possession, especially from the Brazilian syncretic religion Umbanda. Among the spirits of Barquinha are *pretos velhos*, spirits of black slaves who had lived in Brazil, and *encantados*, beings such as mermaids and dolphins, borrowed from the Upper Amazon, as well as wood spirits and dragons.

In Barquinha services, participants drink daime while the leader sings the long Barquinha psalms, invoking the Catholic saints and the Barquinha spirits.[51] Men and women dance together, in a long snaking line. Barquinha rituals are directed primarily toward healing sickness, including serious physical disease, removing evil spirits, and countering witchcraft.[52] When spirit possession occurs, the spirit only partially occupies the body of the possessed, a process called *irradiação*, irradiation, for otherwise the possessed would be unable to withstand the experience.[53]

União do Vegetal

José Gabriel da Costa, known as Mestre Gabriel, created the União do Vegetal in 1961, after drinking ayahuasca near the Bolivian border. At the end of 1965, he went to Porto Velho, where he had earlier worked in a hospital, in order to develop his new religion, initially distributing ayahuasca to his followers in a small brick factory that he owned, and eventually building the first União do Vegetal (UDV) temple there, now called the Núcleo Mestre Gabriel. Shortly after his death in 1971, the movement took on its official name, Centro Espírita Beneficente União do Vegetal, and, in 1982, moved its general administration to Brasília.

The UDV has a highly hierarchic and initiatic structure, with the doctrine transmitted orally to selected candidates, who progress through the ranks by memorizing the exact words of the teachings and complying with strict rules of appropriate behavior. The church rejects any kind of spirit possession, as well as any emphasis on healing; the goal, instead, is, as the church puts it, an amplified degree of perception that permits the comprehension of reality with greater clarity and transcendence. UDV followers use the term *burracheira*—as opposed to the mestizo term *mareación*—to describe the effects of the drink; burracheira is described as a strange and unknown force, the combination of the force and the light of the ayahuasca—called *hoasca* or *vegetal*—in consciousness.[54]

The church combines a belief in reincarnation with the assertion that Jesus Christ is part of the divine totality and his word reveals the true path to salvation for humanity. At its services, the *mestre* distributes hoasca while participants remain seated, almost as if in a Quaker meeting, with long periods of silence, during which participants seek self-knowledge through balanced mental concentration, aided by the vegetal, alternating with sermons, teaching, and question-and-answer sessions with the leader. The UDV emphasizes the oral tradition in its doctrine, and during the rituals, the teachings of Mestre Gabriel are given in ways intended to foster individual transformation; hymns are sung, and *chamadas*, calls, similar to mantras, are chanted.[55]

The UDV has been particularly successful; it now has more than eight thousand members among all socioeconomic classes in more than forty urban centers throughout Brazil and has achieved a modest expansion outside the country as well.[56]

The Ayahuasca Drink

Under the auspices of Santo Daime and União do Vegetal, the use of ayahuasca has spread both to Europe, especially the Netherlands, and to the United States, especially San Francisco and Hawaii.[57] Approximately ten thousand regular participants take part in these new religions, typically twice a month and sometimes once a week.[58] This does not count the number of European and North American people who drink ayahuasca in ceremonies patterned, closely or loosely, on those practiced by Amazonian mestizo or indigenous ayahuasqueros.[59]

Followers of Santo Daime and Barquinha call their sacred drink *santo daime* or simply daime. The ayahuasca vine, which they call *cipo*, vine, or *jagube*, is the masculine, solar aspect of the drink; the added leaf is called *chacrona*, or *rainha*, queen, or simply *folha*, leaf, and is its feminine, lunar aspect. Followers of UDV call the drink hoasca or vegetal. The vine is called *mariri*, representing the masculine *força*, power, and the leaf is called *chacruna*, representing the feminine luz, light, in the combined drink. The UDV use of the word *mariri* in this context—the word is used by mestizo shamans to refer to both rarefied phlegm and magic songs—is striking.

CHAPTER 27
BEING MESTIZO

IQUITOS

Doña María lived in the city of Iquitos, in the middle of the bustling Mercado Modelo. Don Roberto lives much of the time in the port town of Masusa, at the mouth of the Rio Itayo, in the Mainas district, not far from Iquitos. They are both tied to Iquitos, although it is fair to say that doña María was far more urbanized than don Roberto, who maintains a close relationship with his jungle village and garden.

Iquitos is very noisy, because it is filled with three-wheeled motorcycle taxis, most of them with defective mufflers. There are few automobiles. Cars, like most consumer goods, must come to Iquitos up the Amazon from Brazil, and are thus very expensive. Iquitos can only be reached by air or river; until recently there were no roads; all the traffic to and from the surrounding jungle areas was by boat. Now there is a single sixty-mile road from Iquitos to the port of Nauta, which becomes impassable in the rain. In the Peruvian movie *Pantaleon y las visitadoras*—directed by Francisco Lombardi, a well-known and well-awarded filmmaker, starring Colombian film goddess Angie Cepeda and adapting a novel by Mario Vargas Llosa—Iquitos is depicted, in the words of one commentator, as "a steamy, prostitute-infected, Amazon river town in Peru full of cell phones, satellite dishes, and IBM laptops."[1] This is not far off the mark.

This is the city as it lives in the mestizo imagination—noisy, crowded, full of movement, driven by money, without plants. Iquitos, if you recall Werner Herzog's movie *Fitzcarraldo*, is where crazed rubber baron Brian Sweeney Fitzgerald, played by Klaus Kinski, dreams of building an opera house. The contradictions remain. The people who inhabit the jungles surrounding Iquitos have no electricity or running water except the river. Yet they can watch the latest North American programs on blaring old televisions when they come to town, by dugout canoe, to pick up supplies or sell jungle produce.[2]

MESTIZAJE

Doña María and don Roberto, and the community they serve, are usually called, and call themselves, mestizos, mixed people. *Mestizaje*—being mestizo, *de sangre mezclado*, of mixed blood—is a complex identity, a form of hybridity, contradictory and ambivalent. On the one hand, to be mestizo is simply to have a particular tribal identity; one can be mestizo in the same way as one can be Shuar, or Yagua, or Asháninka, or Shipibo. This mestizo identity is defined by such features as speaking Spanish as one's mother tongue, but often bearing an Indian surname; living by hunting, fishing, and slash-and-burn agriculture; not sleeping in a *maloca*, or large communal house in the jungle, but, rather, in a smaller, open, thatched single-family house on stilts by the river's edge, often clustered in a caserío, riverine community, with an inevitable soccer field; cutting one's hair in a European style and wearing mostly European-style clothing. The boundaries of this identity are porous; these features could apply, more or less, to any other tribal group in a process of acculturation. On the other hand, the mestizos are haunted by their hybridity, and they often define themselves specifically in opposition to the *nativos*, in the process borrowing and applying the terms of European colonialism.

The concept of mestizaje emerged from a colonial discourse that privileged the idea of racial purity and justified discrimination by a complex quasi-scientific taxonomy of racial mixtures.[3] In 1825, W. B. Stevenson, in his *Narrative of Twenty Years' Residence in South America*, produced a chart with twenty-three entries, detailing "the mixture of the different castes, under their common or distinguishing names," including *creole*, *mestiso*, *mulatto*, *quarteron*, *quinteron*, and *chino*.[4] Here we learn, for example, that the child of an Indian father and a white mother is one-half white, but the child of a white father and Indian mother is three-quarters white—testimony to the potency of white fatherhood.

The geography texts used in Peruvian schools sometimes estimate that 10 to 15 percent of the country's inhabitants are "white"—lighter-complexioned members of the middle and upper classes.[5] Generally circulated population figures indicate that Peru's population is 45 percent Indian, 37 percent mestizo, 15 percent white, and 3 percent black and Asiatic.[6]

For Amazonian peoples, mestizos are the descendants of marriages between immigrant white men and local Indian women. This interaction is conceptualized as the taming—the verb used is *amansar*, tame, calm down—of the wild natives through the attraction of white manufactured goods, and the seduction of the whites through the potent pusanguería, love magic, of native women.[7] Unlike North American Indians, Amazonian Indians are not conceptualized by the dominant culture as having been conquered but, rather, as having been *seduced*. The terms of this mutual seduction are compelling—on the one hand, manufactured goods; on the other, sexual magic. It is at this intersection that the mestizo stands.

The idea of mestizaje quickly disintegrates into its social components. Mestizos and Indians can be visually indistinguishable; some Indians have European ancestors, and many mestizos do not. The criteria defining these two groups are cultural and, increasingly, socioeconomic. In general, mestizos are persons of varying degrees of Indian ancestry who are accepted as participants in the dominant Hispanic culture. Indians, in contrast, adhere—or are perceived to adhere—to a different way of life, by their language, their style of dress, and their outlook, and are assigned a subordinate position in society. Hispanic whites and Hispanicized mestizos publicly worry from time to time about the presence of a large mass of indigenous people who are not assimilated into the national life—most notoriously novelist Mario Vargas Llosa, who argued that eradication of Indian culture was the sad but necessary price to be paid for their living a free and decent life.[8]

Indeed, pervasive social discrimination in Peru is explained and justified not in terms of race but in terms of cultural differences. This social convention is at the heart of Peruvian racism. Peruvian intellectuals define race with allusions to culture, the soul, and the spirit, which are claimed to be more important than skin color in determining the behavior of groups of people. This discourse legitimizes discriminatory practices against indigenous people by claiming that the discrimination is based not on innate biological differences, such as skin color, but on cultural ones.[9]

At the lower levels of the class structure, transition from Indian to mestizo status is readily accomplished by speaking Spanish and dressing in Western clothing. In the colonial period, it was basically a matter of language and place of residence; now, the transition from one culture to another is facilitated by financial and professional success.[10] That such transitions are considered economic rather than racial is evidenced by a saying that is pervasive throughout South America: *El dinero emblanquece*. Money whitens.

Nor should we assume that travel across this porous boundary is only in one direction. While mestizos can be Indians, or the descendants of Indians, who have shed their ethnic identity to enter the mestizo class, or they can be of Hispanic descent but land-poor, non-Indians can often just as easily become Indians as the reverse.[11] In fact, with the advent of governmental and NGO assistance for Indian groups, ribereño communities with predominantly mestizo families have also had reason to present themselves as "native." One troubling example comes from the Pacaya-Samiria region, where, in the early 1930s, a group of mestizos attacked a native village, killing and driving away the indigenous inhabitants, and then established a new community on the same site, which persists to this day. In the early 1990s, they successfully applied, with external assistance, for formal status as a "Native Community" in order to secure tenure of the lands around their village.[12] Such dissimulation is not unknown, in the age of casinos, in North America.

RIBEREÑO CULTURE

There have been relatively few works dealing specifically with the shamanism of the mestizos in the Peruvian Amazon. The reasons for this lie in the nature of the ethnographic enterprise. Amazonian history has largely been written by anthropologists, who have shown little interest in people who are not, in some obvious sense, indigenous. To the extent that anthropologists like to construct their subjects as pristine, primitive, and ahistorical, mestizos are considered acculturated and therefore uninteresting.[13] There are other reasons as well. Unlike people who are categorized as indigenous, mestizos have lacked political and economic organizations to represent them in regional, national, and international forums.[14]

If the term *mestizo* is a social classification, the term *ribereño*—derived from the noun *ribera*, riverbank—is a cultural one. The term *ribereño*, meaning something like "riverbank dweller," is often used interchangeably with *mestizo*;[15] ribereño culture is the culture of the Peruvian mestizo. But ribereño culture has spread beyond the social class of mestizos, and includes as well the descendants of detribalized Amazonian Indians and the descendants of early immigrants from different areas of Brazil, Peru, and other Andean countries.[16] When indigenous people of the Upper Amazon acculturate, they become ribereños.

The term *ribereño* refers to a distinct rural culture of smallholder farmers, fishers, hunters, and forest managers.[17] They are characterized by Spanish language; monogamous marriages; lack of overt tribal identification; single-family thatched houses on stilts by the water's edge, either singly or in small village clusters; a subsistence economy of shotgun hunting, net fishing, foraging, swidden-fallow agriculture, small animal husbandry, and wage labor activities; local transportation primarily by dugout canoe; and a religious life made up of noninstitutional folk Catholicism, ayahuasca shamanism, and belief in a wide variety of other-than-human persons inhabiting the jungle and river.[18]

The majority—85 percent—of the rural population of the Peruvian Amazon are known locally as ribereños. Even official native communities have a mixture of ribereño and indigenous members, all of whom speak Spanish, wear European clothing, and engage in similar subsistence activities. In such villages, Spanish is quickly replacing indigenous languages.[19] In one such village, on the Lower Ucayali, the inhabitants all considered themselves ribereños, spoke Spanish, engaged in the same combination of agriculture and foraging, and were descended from families that had lived along Amazonian rivers for many generations; yet these ribereños traced their heritage to at least five different ethnic groups.[20] In another ribereño community, located two hours down the Amazon River from Iquitos, the population was descended from three indigenous groups—Cocama, Napo Quichua, and Lamista.[21]

Ribereños who live close enough to Iquitos, Pucallpa, or any of the larger villages carry jungle produce—fish, game, turtles, caimans, fruit, cassava, plantains, hardwood, *suri* grubs—by dugout canoe or motorized *peque-peque*

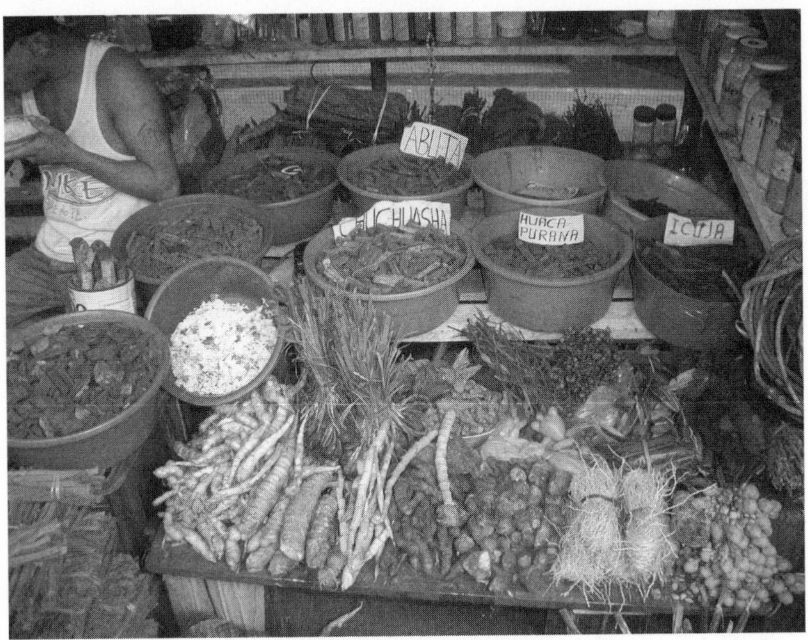

FIGURE 13. Medicinal plants in the Belén market.

to trade for money to buy manufactured goods, primarily clothing, shotgun shells, cigarette lighters, and batteries for radios and for the flashlights used for night hunting. A few hours in the vast and crowded Belén market in Iquitos makes clear the tremendous variety and quantity of food brought in from the jungle to the town.

Ribereños are fond of their own culture; displaced ribereños in Iquitos think of their jungle riverine environment with nostalgia. I was living with don Rómulo in his jungle hut, and his son had given us a ride in a peque-peque to the mestizo village of Indiana, where there was a rural tavern that sold distilled fermented sugarcane juice. I was sitting on a log on the bank of the Amazon River, nursing my glass of aguardiente, when one of the patrons came and sat beside me, somewhat the worse for wear. He put his arm around my shoulders and made a grand sweeping gesture, taking in the mighty river, the amazing sky, the wall of jungle. *Ese es paraíso*, he said, and liked it so much he said it again: *Ese es paraíso*. This is heaven.

The river is of central economic and symbolic significance to the ribereño. The river is the major source of food for local people and the main means of transport. All long journeys, and most short ones, are by dugout canoe; all settlements are on navigable waters. While there are paths that connect villages on the same side of the river, these tend not to be used for visiting between them; rather, they are an incidental product of hunting trails spreading out from the villages.

Peque-peque

The term *peque-peque* refers onomatopoetically to a dugout canoe with an old Briggs and Stratton outboard motor, which goes *pekepekepeke*. . . . The outboard motor has a long shaft, five or six feet; when the propeller gets fouled by weeds, it can be lifted out of the water and turned around into the boat to be cleaned.

The rivers of the Upper Amazon are filled with a great variety of watercraft, from dugout canoes to speedboats to *colectivos*, public water taxis. These colectivos can be quite large and, in addition to passengers, haul cargo and livestock up and down the major tributaries, stopping frequently at tiny ribereño villages, where prospective passengers wave at them from the riverbank. There are places onboard to hang your hammock, which is a necessity for journeys lasting several days, as going from Iquitos to Pucallpa. And there is every kind of boat in between—speedboats with 100-hp outboard engines, balsa-wood rafts, and passenger boats with outboard motors, a canopy of canvas or thatched palm leaves, and benches for twenty or thirty people.

Suri

Suri are the grubs of the palm beetles, *Rhynchophorus palmarum*, which grow in the stumps of chonta palms, primarily *Euterpe* and *Bactris* species, that have been felled to harvest their edible palm hearts. The grubs are fat, pale, curved, and large—up to five inches long. They are eaten by first using the thumb and forefinger to crush their mahogany brown head, which has a nasty pair of pincers; slicing the thin skin of the body with the thumbnail and opening it up lengthwise; plucking out the brown thread of the intestinal tract; and sucking out the white gelatinous contents. This is considered a great delicacy.

These internal contents are very greasy; I myself do not relish raw suri. But suri can be readily cooked in a pan, where they fry in their own fat, like bacon. Fried suri with ajo sacha, wild garlic, can be quite tasty. In markets throughout the Upper Amazon, vendors with small charcoal barbecues offer suri-on-a-stick. Famed ethnobotanist James A. Duke says, "Cooked, they are a great treat; better than fried oysters."[1]

Duke has proposed the development of renewable suriculture in the Amazon. Approximately 62 percent of the suri grub is protein. Insect fatty acids are highly unsaturated. Suri are rich in thiamin, zinc, riboflavin, copper, iron, and niacin.[2]

NOTES

1. Duke, 2006, p. 3.
2. See generally Duke & Vasquez, 1994, pp. 75–76; Hogue, 1993, p. 289; Walden, 1995, pp. 403–404.

Directions are generally expressed in terms of the river—other places are *abaja*, downriver; *arriba*, upriver; or *a la banda*, on the other side of the river. Special verbs are used for river travel. To go upriver is *surcar*, to plough, slice through; to go downriver is *bajar*, to go down; to cross the river is *chimbar*, a verb apparently not found outside the Peruvian Amazon.[22]

RUBBER

Mestizo shamanism is found in an arc from southern Colombia and Ecuador to northern Bolivia, through the present-day Peruvian *departamentos* of Loreto and Ucayali, westward along the Río Marañon, and spilling over eastward into western Brazil. This distribution is the result of historical factors, one of which was the great rubber boom—a period of about thirty-five years, approximately from 1880 to 1914, which transformed Amazonian culture in ways both profound and irremediable.

There are a number of rubber-producing trees in the Amazon, but two genera are of primary importance. *Hevea* species produce a latex called *siringa*, and

Castilloa species produce a latex called *caucho*.[23] To understand the formation of mestizo shamanism, we have to understand the biology of these two types of rubber trees.

The latex of *Hevea brasiliensis* was considered the finest in the Amazon. Moreover, this latex will flow from shallow incisions in the bark, and the tree can therefore be tapped for years without serious damage. But *Hevea* trees have two significant disadvantages. First, although they are capable of growing in the uplands, they are found primarily in low-lying periodically flooded areas, where they can be tapped only half the year, during the dry season.[24]

The ideal would therefore be to create upland plantations, where the trees could be readily tapped year-round. But here there is a second disadvantage. *Hevea* trees are susceptible to a fungal disease called *South American leaf blight*, caused by the fungus *Microcyclus ulei*, native to the Amazon. The fungus is transmitted from tree to tree, and effectively precludes growing the trees close together on plantations. The latex must be tapped from wild trees, which grow widely separated in the jungle—about two trees per hectare.[25]

A seringuero, a collector of siringa, lived in a hut, perhaps with a small garden, and regularly followed a path—called an *estrada*—that he cut through the jungle to two hundred or so *Hevea* trees, tapping half on one day and half on the next. Seringueros were essentially tenant farmers, held in peonage by constantly increasing debt, subject to disease, harsh weather, poor diet, and insect pests.[26] At some point, many gave up any hope of ever ending their bondage to the rubber trees.[27] At the same time, since seringueros were sedentary and steady sources of high-quality latex, rubber bosses and overseers had economic motives to limit violence and abuse of their tenants.[28]

Caucho, the latex of *Castilloa* trees, was considerably less desirable. Since the trees grew above flooded areas, they could be exploited year-round. But the trees could not be tapped, since incisions yield little latex. Rather, the latex had to be gathered all at once, with deep cuts in the trunk, branches, and roots, which produced a large amount of rubber but killed the tree.

A cauchero was therefore constantly looking for more caucho trees to drain. Caucheros frequently worked in teams, since it is almost impossible to bleed a large caucho tree alone. Always on the move, they were in constant danger of becoming lost in unfamiliar jungle; they could not grow gardens, as many seringueros did, and became increasingly indebted for supplies whose price was set arbitrarily by the rubber bosses to maintain indebtedness. If they became sick, no one would bother to look for them, because their location at any moment was unknown.[29]

The itinerant nature of caucho production required a permanently mobile labor force and constant territorial expansion.[30] Rubber bosses had no incentive to create long-term commercial ties with seminomadic and fungible caucheros.[31] The relative isolation of the rubber tappers allowed cauchero bosses to set up regimes of terror, using torture, mutilation, and murder to keep the collectors in line and producing as much caucho as possible.[32] This was most infamous among the Huitoto in the Colombian Putumayo, where anthropologist Michael Taussig has described a "culture of terror, space of death," and where egregious abuses of indigenous laborers shocked even those hardened to the excesses of extractive colonialism.[33]

Caucho collection was the predominant form of rubber production in the Upper Amazon.[34] And although caucho was considered less valuable than siringa, it could be gathered more quickly. A tapped *Hevea* tree yielded five to seven pounds of siringa annually; a seringuero might collect about 1,000 pounds of siringa in a year. In contrast, a mature *Castilloa* tree could yield 200 pounds of caucho in two days, and a pair of caucheros could collect 1,000 pounds of caucho in a month.[35]

Thus, as opposed to indigenous laborers, many of whom had been recruited to rubber tapping by *correrías*, slave raids, many mestizos became caucheros voluntarily, lured by the possibility of quick riches, only to find themselves *enganchado*, hooked, like a fish, by the system of *habilitación*, debt peonage.[36] Isolated, far from family, deep in the jungle, away from their beloved rivers, when mestizo rubber tappers became sick, they went to indigenous healers, including Yagua and Shipibo shamans.[37] In some cases, the caucheros became apprentices to those who had healed them, and upon their return home served their own communities with the skills they had learned.

The rubber boom in eastern Peru saw a massive migration of mestizos from west to east, a shift from agriculture to extraction, and a move from river to jungle.[38] Entire areas were depopulated by 50 percent or more all over the lowlands as rubber contractors removed populations for work.[39] In the town of Moyobamba the population dropped from fifteen thousand inhabitants to seven thousand between 1859 and 1904; the indigenous village of Jeberos saw a population decline from three thousand to three hundred in the same period.[40]

The rubber bust reversed these trends.[41] The price of rubber fell precipitously on the international market; the tapping of wild trees in the jungle could not compete with *Hevea* plantations in Asia, where there was no leaf blight. The mestizo rubber tappers migrated westward, back to their riverine homes, their communities, and their swidden gardens, bringing with them the healing they had learned from the indigenous people of the jungle.

MESTIZO AND INDIAN

There is a complex and often troubled relationship between mestizos and natives, encapsulated in the tale told by Manuel Córdova Ríos, an Iquitos ayahuasquero who claimed he had been kidnapped by Indians, taught their language, and made their chief, finally escaping with their shamanic secrets. The appeal of the tale is archetypal: a civilized person is stolen away by the savage hidden people of the wild places, learns their ways, becomes their chief, and brings their redemptive secrets back to the civilized world.

This tale feeds into the mestizo assumption that jungle Indians are the ultimate source of shamanic knowledge, and that any powers acquired directly from them are of particular value.[42] As anthropologist Jean-Pierre Chaumeil notes, there are few mestizo shamans who do not claim to have had at least one native teacher or who do not assert the indigenous origins of their knowledge.[43] At the same time, to the mestizo, natives are dangerous, unpredictable, treacherous, and sensual; Córdova Ríos, for example, began his life with

Manuel Córdova Ríos and César Calvo Soriano

The story of Manuel Córdova Ríos is recounted by Bruce Lamb as he purportedly heard it from the mouth of Córdova Ríos himself.[1] There is little doubt that Córdova Ríos was, in fact, a skilled and knowledgeable mestizo shaman; but the plausibility and veracity of the story he told have been challenged and defended.[2]

The story, as told by Lamb, has had two unexpected literary children—a lengthy poem about Córdova Ríos written by Pulitzer prize–winning poet and translator W. S. Merwin and a novel of acknowledged genius by César Calvo Soriano, an important Peruvian novelist and poet.[3] Calvo, a native of Iquitos, is perhaps best known in North America as the author of the poem *María landó*—a *landó* is an Afro-Peruvian song form—set to music by famed Peruvian singer Chabuca Granda and heartbreakingly rendered by Afro-Peruvian singer Susana Baca.[4] Calvo's novel, *Las tres mitades de Ino Moxo y otros brujos de la Amazonía,* The Three Halves of Ino Moxo, builds its mythic structure on the tale told to Lamb by Córdova Ríos. The multilayered novel takes place in the mind of its author, searching in the jungle for the healer under his Indian name Ino Moxo, during a single night, illumined by ayahuasca mixed with toé, "that other powerful and disconcerting hallucinogen."[5]

NOTES

1. Lamb, 1971/1974, 1985.
2. Carneiro, 1980; de Mille, 1990, pp. 452–453; Dobkin de Ríos, 1972a; Ott, 1996, pp. 234–237; Lamb, 1981a, 1981b; Luna & Amaringo, 1993, p. 19.
3. Merwin, 1994; Calvo, 1981/1995b.
4. Calvo, 1995a, Track 1; see Feldman, 2003, pp. 158–160, and generally, 2006.
5. Calvo, 1981/1995b, p. xii.

the Indians as an unwilling captive, just as humans can be kidnapped and held captive in the sensual worlds of underwater beings; the Indians are specialists, after all, in pusanguería, love magic.

Some of this tension is reflected in the concept of *cungatuya*, a potentially fatal sickness that slowly closes the throat of the patient, until the person is unable to speak, eat, or drink.[44] It is caused by a sorcerer sending a *mashu*, bat, to drop its phlegm or saliva into water that the victim then unknowingly drinks; the bat phlegm or saliva turns into worms that cause wounds in the victim's throat and which must removed by a healer sucking them out.[45] In San Martín, according to anthropologist Françoise Barbira-Freedman, the mestizos believe that this sickness is spread by Indians; and at feasts, weddings, and markets, mestizos warn each other about watching for phlegm in shared glassware.[46] As in other contexts with which we may be more familiar—drinking fountains and bus seats, for example—the Other is viewed as a source of dangerous contamination.

THE CHACRA

Of central importance in ribereño life is the chacra, the swidden or slash-and-burn garden. This is true also of many Amazonian peoples, for whom gardens—and garden magic—are a central feature of the domestic economy. A chacra is made by clearing an area of forest, burning the felled trees and other vegetation, clearing the movable remaining vegetation and reburning it, and then planting yuca, manioc, plátano, and other cultivated plants and trees such as beans, palms, pineapples, papaya, and mango. After several years, when the nutrients derived from the ash have been exhausted, the garden is abandoned to become new-growth jungle, and a new garden is created. Such gardens frequently demonstrate a sophisticated understanding of ecological interrelationships among domesticated and wild plant species.

Yuca is a staple crop for small swidden agriculture and a primary source of carbohydrate in the Amazon. Plátano, another staple source of carbohydrate, is eaten boiled or fried. Although sometimes called *banano*, these are plantains, not bananas. For reasons I do not understand, the people among whom I have lived in the Amazon call bananas *manzano*, apples, or *manzanito*, little apples.

Shamans frequently plant their own sacred and healing plants, primarily ayahuasca, chacruna, toé, and mapacho. Don Rómulo Magin, for example, had a large bush of sameruca growing in his front yard, which he would use to prepare his ayahuasca drink. Almost all the shamans in Colombia use

Yuca

All yuca roots contain a poisonous cyanogenic glycoside. The two kinds of yuca—*dulce*, sweet, and *brava*, bitter—differ in how this chemical is distributed. Sweet yuca can be eaten simply by peeling off the bark and boiling the root. In bitter yuca the poison is spread throughout the root and must be extracted before consumption; this is done by peeling and grating the root, and then squeezing out the poisonous juice in a long mesh sleeve that serves as a yuca press.[1]

The two varieties are not clearly different in shape or color, so they can be difficult for the unsophisticated to tell apart. Often it is simply a matter of knowing which type was planted; but, in addition, sweet yuca has two easily removable skins, a thinner outer one and a thicker inner one, while bitter yuca has a single skin that is difficult to remove.[2]

Among indigenous peoples of the Upper Amazon, cooked yuca is thoroughly chewed by the women and spit into a pot, where it ferments into *masato*, a virtually universal recreational drink, regularly offered in hospitality and not to be refused. Drinking masato—and it really is as awful as it sounds—is so common that a wife will make her husband his own masato bowl, which he carries with him when visiting friends or neighbors. When I was living with the Shapra, I knew I had been accepted when I was given my own masato bowl to carry with me.

NOTES

1. A detailed description of this process is found in Guss, 1990, pp. 28–30; see also Schultes & Raffauf, 1990, p. 181; Walden, 1995, p. 404.
2. Lovera, 2005, p. 41.

ayahuasca vines that are deliberately planted for their use in healing ceremonies, as do many in Ecuador.[47]

Indeed, *all* the forms of toé in the Amazon are considered to be cultivars. Ethnobotanist Wade Davis points out that the grotesque forms of many of these cultivars, generally called *borrachero* in Colombia, "are caused by viral infections. The Indians note that the varieties breed true and that each has quite specific pharmacological properties that can be manipulated by the shaman."[48] These borrachero cultivars are given distinct names—*munchiro borrachero, culebra borrachero*.[49] In fact, culebra borrachero, a small tree containing high concentrations of scopolamine, classified botanically as *Methysticodendron amesianum*, may not be a distinct genus at all but, rather, a highly atrophied form of toé—the result of a viral infection or mutation recognized and cultivated for its psychoactive effects.[50]

A chacra is a cleared space, *limpia*, clean, just like the ubiquitous soccer field or the wide clear path leading into the village from the riverbank—plantless, the result of human action, nonjungle.[51] Conversely, the monte is despoblado, unpeopled, the place of least human cultural interference, the place of

Plátanos

It is surprisingly difficult to find bananas in villages in the Upper Amazon. Plantains are distressingly common, eaten at almost every meal. Roasted plantains are tasteless and dry, and I got really tired of them; fried plantains are generally more palatable, but may be forbidden during la dieta. It was a great treat when someone would bring a bunch of sweet bananas in from the jungle.

jungle spirits and wild Indians.[52] They are wild because they live away from the rivers and out of contact with riverine commerce, in the center of the jungle; they are naked, and they eat their food raw and without salt. In short, they live with a minimum of cultural mediation between the jungle and themselves.[53]

Jungle Indians may be referred to contemptuously as chunchos, devoid of civilization and thus with no culture—even, from the viewpoint of official Peru, without legal existence, uninscribed in civil registers and therefore not citizens; uncivilized, unbaptized, naked, hunting with bows and arrows, without salt.[54] The savagery of the indigenous is exemplified by their saltlessness. Outsiders being given food by indigenous hosts can insult them by asking for salt. Anthropologists Norman and Dorothea Whitten describe a Catholic priest and his entourage at a Canelos Quichua celebration, telling each other how the *indios* use no salt. "They even eat raw meat," says one. "And they grow no crops," says another.[55]

Chacras that have been left fallow are called *purmas*.[56] The term includes a wide range of fields, from recently overgrown chacras to thirty-year-old successional forest.[57] Purmas continue to be utilized for building materials, including hardwood poles and palm leaves, and a variety of fruits.[58] Purmas also provide food and low dense brush for cover and nesting for a number of game animals—armadillos, agouti, paca, opossum, spiny rats—which are called, collectively, *purmeros*.[59]

Purmas are not simply abandoned chacras; they are the result of active forest management. When chacras are cleared, the seedlings of useful trees are often spared and protected, to be utilized when the chacra is left fallow.[60] These plants include fruit trees intended to attract game animals, which are primarily frugivores;[61] white-lipped peccaries, for example, consume a diet composed of 66 percent fruit, primarily palm fruits.[62]

MESTIZO CULTURAL GEOGRAPHY

Among the mestizos, social relationships are often expressed geographically, as horizontal spatial relationships. A feature of ribereño culture is a persistent

Soccer

Soccer—which is, of course, *fútbol*—is played and followed with almost religious intensity throughout Peru. According to sociologist Julio Cotler, soccer played a major role in forging a Peruvian national identity when, in 1970, the Peruvian national team surprisingly eliminated top-ranked Argentina to qualify for the Mexico Cup. For the first time, the games were broadcast nationwide, and soccer became a national passion.[1] Indeed, when, in 1996, Movimiento Revolucionario Túpac Amaru (MRTA) guerillas captured the Japanese embassy in Lima and held seventy-two hostages for 126 days, the occupation was broken by a surprise raid when the guerillas had gathered for their daily afternoon soccer game.[2]

Iquitos has two professional soccer clubs—Colegio Nacional Iquitos and Hungaritos, the Hungarians—and several amateur leagues, as well as an endless stream of pickup street games, which can last for hours and are played right through the pouring rain.[3] Ribereño villages throughout the Upper Amazon have soccer fields, and often a game is played every day in the evening.

Because some of these ribereño villages are small, they often play a downsized version of soccer called *fulbito*, with five or six players on a side. Famed writer Mario Vargas Llosa, in his novel *The City and the Dogs*, describes a fulbito game: "They wore sneakers, . . . and they made sure the ball was not fully inflated, to keep it from bouncing. Generally they kept the ball on the ground, making very short passes, and trying for goals from very close, without kicking hard."[4] Fulbito is thus a close sport, sometimes even played indoors; the MRTA guerillas were playing fulbito in the embassy grand dining room when the raid occurred. Some commentators have claimed that playing fulbito rather than soccer from childhood has kept Peruvian soccer players from developing kicking power, so that they are considered skilled rather than strong opponents.[5]

Games played against neighboring villages are a major social event and may involve three or four communities, with wagering, feasts, beer, dancing, and battery-operated CD players blaring cumbias. These games can be very exciting, especially in the rainy season, because the fields become quite muddy and slippery, with spectacular wipeouts, and everyone winds up covered in mud.[6]

The enculturation of indigenous groups to the ribereño lifestyle almost inevitably includes the adoption of soccer.[7]

NOTES

1. Smith, 2005.
2. Guevara, Loveman, & Davies, 1997, p. 302; Whyte, 2005, pp. 24–25.
3. Witzig, 2006, pp. 340, 342.
4. Vargas Llosa, 1963, p. 27.
5. Aranibar, 2006.
6. Chibnik, 1994, pp. 92–93; Witzig, 2006, p. 343.
7. See Johnson, 2003, pp. 37, 126–127; Witzig, 2006, pp. 344–346.

dualism of river and jungle, water and earth, *yacu* and *sacha*. Each realm has its own gigantic guardian serpent—*yacumama*, mother of the water, the great anaconda, and *sachamama*, mother of the jungle, the great boa. Each realm has its own supai, mysterious other-than-human inhabitants—yacuruna, the Water People, the owners of the rivers, and *sacharuna*, the Jungle People, the owners of the jungle, the chullachaquis. This dualism is reflected also in the distinction between the ribereño, who dwells on the river, and the Indian, who dwells in the jungle, and between the chacra, swidden garden, which is cleared and cultivated, and the monte, jungle, which is wild and unmanaged.

The mestizos also maintain a threefold model of the relationships among Amazonian peoples. The *ciudad*, city, such as Iquitos or Pucallpa or Puerto Moldanado, is the home of knowledgeable whites, the commercial and cultural center, and the source of manufactured goods such as shotgun shells and flashlight batteries. The monte, jungle, is the home of Indians, uncivilized but skilled in magic and jungle lore. Ciudad and monte are the extreme poles of human space. Mediating between the two are the mestizos, moving between city and jungle, carrying commodities out of the jungle and manufactured goods out of the city, acting as the pivot of knowledge.[63]

The spatial category that connects city and jungle is the river; once again, the river dweller, the ribereño, mediates between white and Indian. This geographical model is also expressed in terms of river *direction*. From the mestizo point of view, the city is always abaja, downriver, and *afuera*, outside; the jungle is arriba, upriver, and *en el centro*, toward the center. Movement downriver toward the city takes one away from the jungle, the center, from stillness to noise, from wildness to commerce. The same spatial model occurs on a smaller level *within* towns and villages, divided up into *barrios*, quarters, with the shops, bars, and houses of the mestizo population concentrated in the center of town, "by the river," while native people live away from this center, "towards the forest."[64]

GENDER AND COLOR

Among Amazonian mestizos, the world is often viewed in terms of male and female, macho and hembra. Not only animals but also plants—even inanimate objects—appear in both male and female forms; rain, for example, can be male or female, depending on the force with which it falls; if a plant species has two varieties, one with thorns, the one with thorns is considered male.[65] The plant mucura, for example, considered by botanists to be a single species, is held by mestizos to have a male form with round leaves and a female form with elongated leaves.[66] The red huayruro seed is considered to come from the female and the red and black huayruro seed from the male form of a single

The Jungle Cookbook

FOOD

Gerineldo Moises Chavez, my jungle survival instructor, taught me that it is impossible to go hungry in the jungle. The jungle is filled with game, fish, and wild plants, all ready to be gathered and eaten.

Small game is a staple in the diet of both mestizo and indigenous peoples. Frequently hunted mammals include large rodents—such as *añuje*, agouti; *majás*, paca; *pacarana*; and *ronsoco*, capybara—and small spiny rats, called generally *rata*, rats, *ratón*, mice, or *sacha cuy*, wild guinea pigs. In addition, small game mammals include *carachupa*, armadillo; *intuto*, opossum; huangana, white-lipped peccary, and sajino, collared peccary; sachavaca, common tapir; *venado*, gray and red brocket deer; and monkey, especially *coto*, howler monkey, and *maquisapa*, spider monkey.

There is also an amazing abundance and variety of fish in the Upper Amazon. For both mestizo and indigenous peoples, the lakes and rivers are an endless source of food, with more than two thousand species of freshwater fish.[1] Machiguenga greet strangers by asking, "Are there fish in the river where you live?"[2]

There are catfish of all sorts—*carachama*, *doncella*, *maparate*, *shirui*, and especially the delicious *dorado*, which can grow to a hundred pounds in deep river channels and oxbow lakes. Other commonly caught fish include *acarahuazú*, boquichico, *corvina*, *gamitana*, *lisa*, *palometa*, and *sábalo*, as well as *paña*—better known under the Portuguese name *piranha*—and paiche, the largest freshwater fish in the world, whose flaky and delicately flavored flesh has been featured in *Gourmet Magazine*.[3]

The rivers also yield turtles—*taricaya* and *charapa*, the latter routinely exceeding thirty inches in width—and their eggs, laid on the sandy beaches, as well as lagarto negro, black caimans, which as adults range from eight to ten feet long.[4] Everyone likes suri, the grubs of palm beetles.

In addition to the fruit that grows in their active gardens, ribereños forage fruit and edible plants from fallowed gardens and the jungle. Among the most important fruits are the palm fruits—huicungo, *ungurahui*, *aguaje*, and pijuayo—which are eaten fresh, made into drinks—*ungurahuina*, *aguajina*, or *pijuayina*—and even, in the cities, made into frozen desserts.[5] One survey of a ribereño village near Iquitos lists thirty-eight plant species collected from fallowed gardens and jungle, including palm fruits, bananas, pineapples, lemons, oranges, cashews, breadfruit, and sugarcane.[6]

HUNTING

The ribereño weapon of choice for small game hunting is a 16-gauge shotgun. In North America, we generally use 20-gauge shotguns for birds and 12-gauge for larger game; the 16-gauge is, in fact, an excellent all-around shotgun, useful for hunting medium-size jungle game—tapir, capybara, agouti, peccary, monkey.

Hunters tend to follow existing trails or canoe along local streams to established *campamentos*, campsites, or tambos, huts. From these locations, they cut trails to salt licks, watering holes, ravines, and fruiting trees—places where they know animals tend to congregate.[7] Hunters generally do not track game; rather, they have a detailed knowledge of animal behavior, and carry their shotguns to places where animals are likely to be found. They are also skilled at imitating animal cries and at locating any animals that respond.

When moving through the jungle, as when pursuing game, ribereño hunters are skilled at leaving sign. Trails are cleared with the ubiquitous machete; but, just as important, what appears to be almost casual cutting of trailside growth is a way of leaving sign for the return trip, as is the similarly casual turning over of leaves while moving through the jungle. The underside of many jungle plants is lighter in color than the top; when you look back, the turned-over leaves mark a path as clearly as highway signs, if you know how to see them.

Hunters also canoe upstream from camp during the day and then drift silently downstream after dark, shotguns ready, using a flashlight to target eye shine at beaches where animals come at night to drink. Shooting platforms may be erected in trees near colpas, where animals come to drink and eat salty clay; or feeding sites, such as the base of a fruiting tree; or along cleared trails, where hunters wait at night with a shotgun and flashlight.[8] Shotgun booby traps with trip wires may also be set near salt licks and colpas.[9]

Trampas, traps, including both snares and deadfalls, baited with manioc or pijuayo fruit, are also commonly used to catch small game, including agouti, monkeys, and spiny rats.[10] The cleverest snare I have ever seen was taught to me by a Shapra, out past Lago Rimachi.

FISHING

There are four places in the Upper Amazon where a fisherman looks for fish. First, large and medium-sized rivers in low areas often form numerous meanders that, when the river changes course, become *cochas*, moon-shaped oxbow lakes. These cochas often have sediment settled on the bottom, relatively clear water, high temperatures, and therefore rapid plant growth, which in turn supports quite large fish populations. Sometimes too you can see strips of clear and very slow water in a river. These are quiet places where plankton tends to grow, and fish can often be found downstream. You can also find fish under *camalones*, places where aquatic vegetation has formed a dense mat on the surface of the water. Finally, fish love to move into the waters covering seasonally flooded forests.[11]

It is possible to take fish just with your hands. It is not as hard as it sounds; I have caught beautiful trout with my bare hands in a stream in the Esacalante Wilderness. In the Amazon, people wade close to shore in muddy water, gently feeling for fish under rocks and in the mud. In particular, the carachama, the armored sailfin catfish, constructs burrows in the muddy banks of the cochas and rivers in which it lives, each a few feet deep and generally angled downward. You only need to feel around for a burrow, reach in, and very carefully—because carachama have very sharp spines on their dorsal fins—pull a carachama out of its hole and toss it up onto the bank. They are delicious.

People in the Amazon often fish with hook and line—an innovation dependent on the availability of steel hooks and high test monofilament fishing line. All you have to do is tie a hook to a length of line on the end of a stick, put a piece of grasshopper on the hook, and toss the hook into the water. Especially in an overpopulated cocha, in just a few minutes you have caught a fish. You can do this over and over again; in half an hour, you have caught enough fish for several days. You can be creative and tie a piece of wood to the string as a float.

If you have a family to feed, you can set out a trotline with baited hooks. Hook-and-line fishing can be done where other methods do not work—at night; during the rainy season, when the water is turbid; in the main current of the river. It is considered to be—heck, it is—fun.

Fishing nets can be cast from a canoe or by wading out into the water. Casting a fishnet requires skill clearly beyond my own, although, to my chagrin, I have seen numerous young boys do it quite successfully.

Ribereños also fish using fish spears or bows and arrows—usually with barbed metal two-tined heads—either from a canoe or from shore, sometimes on the river right in front of the village. Spear and bow-and-arrow fishing is largely limited to the dry season, when rivers tend to be clear rather than silty. A fisher can also put a *tabaje*, a fish trap, across a cocha outflow. Tabajes are woven from strips of caña brava, giant cane, or *bombonaje*. I have seen two mestizo fishermen work a running stream by anchoring a woven barricade with sticks downstream, driving fish into the trap from upstream, and then gathering them by hand. In a few hours they had caught enough fish, after being dried and salted, to last for a week.

Fish poison is also widely used in the Upper Amazon. The term *barbasco* can be used to refer to fish poison in general or more specifically to *Lonchocarpus urucu*, which is of sufficient importance that some indigenous peoples cultivate it in their gardens. The procedure is simple: the root is dug up, carried to the fishing place, and pounded with sticks so that the milky sap can be drained into the water. The primary active ingredients are rotenone and deguelin, which affect gill function in fish, inhibiting their ability to breathe.[12] Within fifteen minutes or so fish begin to float on the surface of the water, where they can be collected by hand or in baskets, hit on the head with a machete, speared, or shot with a bow and arrow.[13]

Fishing with barbasco in a cocha is simple; squeeze the milky sap into the still water, watch it spread, and then collect the fish. It only takes one or two people to fish a cocha in this way. On the other hand, in a flowing stream or river, you have to build a dam at the upper end of the fishing area to slow the flow, and another at the lower end—sometimes with a woven basketry net—to make it easier to capture the stunned fish. Such temporary dam construction may require additional people, which can, of course, turn into a party.[14]

COOKING

Small mammals are generally gutted but not skinned. Once I was helping Moises field dress an agouti. "In North America," I said, "we generally take off the head." He looked at me as if I was crazy. "Lots of good things in the head," he said.

Once gutted, the entire animal is thrown onto a fire. When the hair has been singed, any remaining hair is removed by scraping. Ribereños may then roast the game over hot coals. The large rodents—agouti, paca, and capybara—have particularly tender meat and can be quite tasty when prepared in this way.[15] Moises was able to conjure remarkable meals out of jungle game, adding *albaca*, wild basil; ajo sacha, wild garlic; grilled plantain, panguana eggs, and palm heart salad; and ripe huito fruit for desert.

In indigenous villages, on the other hand, the carcass is chopped indiscriminately into pieces, put into a pot of boiling water without seasonings, and boiled like crazy. This is not gourmet cooking. I tried to introduce the Shapra to the idea of a nicely trimmed monkey roast, but they were uninterested. They preferred just to boil the bejeezus out of their meat and make monkey soup.

There are, I think, two reasons why small mammals are not skinned. First, there is no use for the skin. Indigenous peoples of the Upper Amazon appear to lack material goods because they can make anything they need very quickly from resources that are ready at hand. I have seen Shapra make a basket out of leaves in just a few minutes, fill it with gathered fruit, carry it back to the village, and simply discard it. It is easier to make the basket than it is to keep it. Second, there is reason to believe that the subcutaneous fat of small game is one of the few sources of fat in the indigenous diet. This may also account for the preference for boiling into soup, which preserves the fat, as opposed to roasting, which does not.

Nonmammalian small game—birds, turtles, caimans—is treated pretty much the same way: inedible parts, such as feathers and shells, are removed; everything else is chopped up and boiled. Attractive feathers are kept for making crowns and jewelry; other inedible parts are thrown away. One exception I have seen has been the drying of peccary hides to be carried downriver to market. I remember spending two days in a speedboat filled with the smell of gasoline in 55-gallon drums and a pile of raw peccary hides decomposing in the heat. Vividly.

Fish may be boiled with plantains or roasted directly on the fire. Fish is often prepared as a patarashca, wrapped in one of the large leaves of the bijao palm and placed on the hot coals.[16] La Patarashca, a restaurant in Tarapoto, serves doncella stuffed with shrimp in a sauce of cocona fruit, and as a patarashca with tomato, onion, and sweet chili.

When hunting is good, extra meat and fish are smoked and salted. Meat to be smoked is placed over the fire on a grating made of green wood; the smoking process may take several days. People often snack on the meat as it is being smoked; I recall a memorable snack of smoked salted monkey cheeks. Fish that has been salted and dried in the sun makes excellent pack food for long trips; fish may be salted and smoked or salted and dried in the sun on the kitchen roof. Fish preserved in this way can last for several months.[17] *Fariña*—coarsely ground dried yuca root—is the jungle survival food of the ribereño. It is light in weight and easy to pack, and, believe me, a little bit goes a long way. It tastes like the worst breakfast cereal you ever had. Fariña can be mixed with water, lemon, and—if you are not on la dieta—sugar, to make a drink called *shibé*, which is a significant improvement.

NOTES

1. Kricher, 1997, p. 200.
2. Johnson, 2003, p. 63.
3. Maxim, 2007.
4. Hiraoka, 1995, p. 217.
5. Bodmer, 1994, p. 131.
6. Pinedo-Vasquez, Zarin, & Jipp, 1995, pp. 247–248, Tables 10.5–10.6.
7. Claggett, 1998, p. 11.
8. Chevalier, 1982, pp. 61–62.
9. Hiraoka, 1995, p. 210.

10. Hiraoka, 1995, pp. 210–211.
11. U.N. Environment Programme, 1987.
12. Gupta, 2007; Ling, 2003, pp. 6–9.
13. See generally Hillard & Kopischke, 1992, pp. 97–98.
14. Chibnik, 1994, pp. 127–129; Hiraoka, 1995, pp. 212–221; Johnson, 2003, pp. 63–67.
15. Brownrigg, 1996; Hiraoka, 1995, pp. 206–207; Ríos, Dourojeanni, & Tovar, 1975.
16. Castonguay, 1990, p. 109.
17. Hiraoka, 1995, p. 221; Johnson, 2003, pp. 68–69.

plant; botanists consider these two plants to be different species in the same genus.[67] What mestizos consider the male and female forms of the buceta plant are classified by botanists in different genera entirely.[68]

Doña María frequently distinguished between male and female forms of the same plant; the *spirits* of many plants, too, can appear in either male or female forms—sometimes both at once, as in doña María's first vision of the ayahuasca spirit, in which two genios appeared, one on either side of her. Doña María once showed me two cubes of commercially prepared camphor, wrapped in clear plastic, while describing how she used camphor in some of her preparations. "One of these is male, and one is female," she said. I asked how she could tell. She looked more closely. "Oh, these are both female," she said. "The male ones are a little larger."

Mestizos also use colors as a classificatory device, typically distinguishing between light colors, usually white and green, and dark colors, usually red, purple, or black. Shamans come in two colors—on the one hand, light, which includes doña María's healing practice of pura blancura, pure whiteness, and, on the other, dark, which includes the magia negra, black magic, or, even worse, magia roja, red magic, of wicked sorcerers. Similarly, jaguars fall into two categories—the otorongo, or tawny jaguar, and the yanapuma, the black jaguar, which are regarded as two distinct species, with different habits; Western zoologists consider both animals to be the same species, with the latter being a rare melanistic form of the former.[69]

A distinction is also made between light and dark forms of the same plant—for example, toé blanco and toé negro, white and black toé, considered by botanists to be in completely different genera, but conceptually linked through their uses and effects; or ishanga blanca and *ishanga roja*, white and red *ishanga*, in different genera but both with stinging hairs used to treat snakebite; or *verbena blanca* and *verbena negra*, in different genera, but both considered to be cold plants to treat hot conditions such as fever and diarrhea.

Often the dark form of a plant is the one used in sorcery. Doña María often called the darker variety morado, purple or dark, and the lighter variety verde, green or light. Mestizos consider the plant called, variously, piñon rojo, piñon colorado, or piñon negro and the plant called piñon blanco, which botanists consider two different species in the same genus, to be the dark and light forms of the same plant, with the dark form being a planta bruja; the same is true for lupuna colorada and lupuna blanca. A similar distinction is drawn between the plant—or, perhaps, plants—called *patiquina morada* or *patiquina negra* and the plant called *patiquina blanca* or, often, just patiquina, which seem to be a confusing variety of *Dieffenbachia* species, with a variety of leaf patterns and colors. Dona María called these groups of plants, respectively, patiquina morada and *patiquina verde.*

CHAPTER 28

BEINGS OF EARTH AND WATER

Mestizos in the Upper Amazon have a variety of beliefs about the other-than-human persons who inhabit the hidden realms deep in the jungle and under the water.[1] These beings are often conceived as inhabiting the three realms of air, earth, and water; all of them are dangerous. They are different from the madres or genios, the spirits of plants and animals with whom the shaman interacts, although shamans often seek to enter into right relationship with these beings as well. Ordinary people may, to their sorrow, unintentionally and unexpectedly encounter these more or less corporeal other-than-human persons.

Consistent with the mestizo conceptual dualism of jungle and river, there are parallels between the realms of earth and water: the sachamama, mother of the jungle, the giant boa constrictor, matches the yacumama, mother of the water, the giant anaconda; the chullachaqui are often called sacharuna, people of the jungle, in parallel with the yacuruna, people of the water. There is also overlap among these figures; both the water people and the jungle people may have bodily deformities, with parts of their bodies turned around backward; both yacuruna and sacharuna trick people into entering their realms, where they are abducted and sequestered, often for sexual purposes. Chullachaqui and dolphins, mermaids and water people, can appear disguised in human form. All the water beings are sexually seductive; mermaids and yacuruna are often interchangeable.[2]

But there are differences as well. Beings of the jungle are frightening—indeed, able to turn one mad with fright; beings of the water are sexually dangerous—able to seduce, abduct, and steal you away forever.

WANDERING SOULS

The air, especially at night, is full of souls—souls of the dead, souls of departed and powerful shamans, and what doña Mari used to call almas olvidadas, forgotten souls, the wandering souls of those who were neglected and abused while alive. The wandering and sorrowful soul of a dead person may appear as a being called a *tunchi*.[3] An evil spirit of the dead, driven by malignancy rather than sorrow, is called a maligno or an *alma mala*, an evil soul.[4]

The term *tunchi* is multivalent in the Upper Amazon: among the Aguaruna, the term refers to a shaman;[5] among the Shuar, the term refers to a special kind of tsentsak, magical dart, made from certain small spiders;[6] among the Achuar, the term refers to a sickness caused by sorcery, as opposed to a *sunkur* or ordinary sickness.[7] Among mestizos, the tunchi is a wandering bodiless spirit that cannot be seen but can be recognized at night by its mournful whistle. As César Calvo says, few have seen it; many have heard it; everyone fears it.[8] A tunchi is the departed soul of a deceased human being;[9] children are taught that a whistle at night is a spirit of the dead.[10] Tunchis may cause sickness, especially the sickness called mal aire, bad air;[11] and the souls of the murdered dead seek revenge.

Although frightening to encounter, mostly tunchis are pathetic creatures, often birdlike, who can be kept away by tobacco smoke.[12] But you must never mock a tunchi, for the infuriated soul will chase you, whistling, so that even the most courageous become panic-stricken, fleeing to madness or death.[13] People in Iquitos may present themselves as skeptical, but, when pressed, everyone has a story about meeting a tunchi—or something that might have been a tunchi.[14]

Sometimes tunchis are those who have suffered a particularly tragic death, especially by drowning; sometimes humanlike ghosts of the drowned can be seen in phantom canoes, moving upriver, back toward their former homes.[15] You can hear them drifting alone in the jungle night, whistling like birds, like sorcerers. This is closely related to a widespread belief in *almas que recogen sus pasos*, souls retracing their steps—the shadowy souls of the still living visiting, shortly before their death, the places where they have lived. "I saw him walking on the street," someone will report, "and he was in the hospital dying!"[16]

There is a striking relationship between these wandering souls and nocturnal jungle birds. Take, for example, the *ayaymama* or potoo. The name *ayaymama* reflects the belief that these birds are transformations of children abandoned in the jungle by their mothers, and their disconsolate cry asks,

Ay ay mama, why have you abandoned me? During the day, the birds perch motionlessly out in the open, on the ends of branches or broken-off stumps, virtually invisible in the jungle, with their mottled brown or gray coloration. At night they hunt flying insects in swooping flycatcher-like flights from their exposed perch.

At night, too, their eyes are highly reflective, and their brilliant eye shine can be seen even at great distances; their cry, heard especially on moonlit nights, is one of the most haunting sounds of the jungle—melancholy and lamenting, a series of loud wailing notes that gradually descend in pitch. The cry starts out loud enough to be startling if you are close; and as you turn toward this mournful sound, there in the moonlit darkness you see the shining and seemingly disembodied eyes.

THE CHULLACHAQUI

The chullachaqui is a demon of the jungle, known to almost everyone in the Amazon, frightening and pathetic.[17] He is characterized by having one or both feet deformed—either both turned backward or one shaped like that of an animal, such as a deer or jaguar;[18] the name is Quechua, meaning *uneven feet*. The deformed foot is emblematic of his nature: turned backward, it leaves false tracks; but it cannot be disguised, revealing his identity. He takes on the form of a friend or relative, or of an animal to draw in hunters, and lures people deep into the jungle, where they become hopelessly lost. People thus stolen away he then abandons, makes sick, enslaves, or drives mad.

The poet César Calvo pictures chullachaquis as zombielike creatures—creations of great shamans, sculpted out of the air, or formed from kidnapped children. If a kidnapped child is charged with evil powers, the right foot becomes deformed, self-contradictory—an animal foot when the chullachaqui is in human form, a human foot when in animal form. But there is also a second type of chullachaqui—benevolent, a person of the good, "a deceit in the service of the truth," with no deformity. In either case, the kidnapped one does not return.[19]

Chullachaquis are also known as *yashingo*, *curpira*, *shapingo*, and *shapshico*. Two generic terms are also applied to chullachaquis—supai, demons, and *sacharuna*, jungle people. The term *sacharuna*, jungle people, makes the chullachaqui the land equivalent of the yacuruna, water people.

Yet there is something sad about the chullachaqui. He dwells alone in the inundated forest, where the chullachaqui caspi tree grows, or under lupuna trees, with which he has an "indissoluble agreement of love."[20] He keeps a

Colpas

A colpa is a watering place where animals come to drink and bathe and where there may be salty clay to eat. Water from a colpa may be used in pusanguería, love magic, since animals at a colpa, even enemies, are said to behave in peace and harmony. Perfumero Artidoro Aro Cardenas uses *agua de colpas* in his healing and protecting flower baths.[1]

NOTE

1. Castonguay, 1990, p. 29; Chaumeil, 1983/2000, p. 179; Heaven & Charing, 2006, pp. 149, 176.

garden in which he cultivates only *sacha caimito*, and lives on its fruits.[21] Sometimes he appears, comically, as a small man wearing huge red shoes, red pants, and a hat; he may be challenged to a wrestling match, and one who defeats him will be given good hunting and happiness.[22]

The chullachaqui is also *madre del monte*, mother of the wilderness, the master of animals; by following the appropriate diet, one can propitiate the chullachaqui, who will grant success in hunting but punish those who take too many animals. In this, the chullachaqui is like other madres of the jungle—the mothers of the trees, the mothers of the colpas—who protect their domains from foresters and hunters.[23]

There has thus developed, in the last few decades, a new version of the chullachaqui, born out of an increasing awareness of commercial encroachment on the jungle—the chullachaqui as defender of the forest, enemy of lumber and oil companies; he heals wounded animals and punishes those who cut down the trees and hunt animals out of greed.[24] "The chullachaqui is a protective spirit of the jungle," says one description, "who can harm or help people, depending on whether they mistreat or respect nature in the jungle."[25] This new chullachaqui "is generous with those who make rational use of the resources of the forest, but is harmful toward people who invade his space without permission and destroy its plant and animal resources."[26]

Don Agustin Rivas tells of a jungle encounter with a small man who had an aged face, curved nose, small brilliant eyes, and very small mouth, and was missing one foot. Although the man was dressed normally, don Agustin recognized him immediately as a chullachaqui. Don Agustin expressed his delight in finally meeting a real chullachaqui, and they smoked a pipe together; don Agustin mentioned that he had been having bad luck in hunting lately, and the chullachaqui said, "Those are my animals. You need to ask my permission first, and you have never asked me before shooting an animal. But today you're going to kill an animal." Don Agustin suddenly felt dizzy and fell to the ground in a faint; when he awoke, the chullachaqui was gone. Almost immediately, he came across a very large deer and shot it—a perfect shot through the heart.[27]

THE SERPENT MOTHERS

Two great snakes inhabit the land and water—the sachamama, mother of the jungle, the boa; and the yacumama, mother of the water, the anaconda. But these are not ordinary snakes. They are huge, as large as trucks, as large as steamboats, their eyes shining in the dark like searchlights. The sachamama lies still, looking like a fallen tree, for hundreds of years, attracting its prey with its rainbow hypnotic powers. When it moves, it knocks down trees like a bulldozer. It can be used as an arcana for protection and as a weapon for attack, when called by the proper icaro. The yacumama is thirty to forty feet long; its bones are marble, and its multicolored skin flashes in the light. It may in fact appear as a steamboat filled with people, and is sometimes called *supaylancha*, spirit boat—a battleship or submarine carrying powerful shamans, great doctors. Almost everyone who has been out on the water at night will tell at least one tale of a terrifying encounter with a yacumama.[28]

BEINGS OF THE WATER

While the jungle is fearsome and uncanny, the water is alluring, sexually dangerous. The three primary types of other-than-human persons that live under the water—water people, mermaids, and dolphins—overlap considerably in their attributes, abodes, and erotic dangers; they are all seductive spirits who live in great underwater cities, take human form, and entice or kidnap humans for sexual purposes. When fishermen do not return, when husbands disappear, when young girls do not come home at night or become mysteriously pregnant, the answer is clear: they have been seduced and abducted by the erotic creatures of the uncanny depths.

Such abductions are—like the water beings themselves—*physical*. In this they differ clearly from various types of soul loss, such as in the sickness called susto or manchari, where the physical body remains but the shaman must summon the soul to return. These beings of the jungle and the river, sacharuna and yacuruna, steal the body, and the shaman must persuade them to give it back.

All the water spirits are believed to live in beautiful cities in their underwater world, to which they carry their abducted victims, and which great shamans can visit, to learn their songs and secrets. These cities may be shared by water people and mermaids; dolphins may live there too, as guardians and police. Don Agustin Rivas tells how, during an ayahuasca vision, the sirenas, mermaids, took him to visit their realm beneath the Amazon. "There were buildings and beautiful women dancing in front of me," he says, "wearing celestial dresses of clear pink, and dresses made of algae with diamonds, snails and precious stones. They were riding on the backs of large serpents and invited me to journey with them. Sitting on these women's tails, I was traveling within the water of my vision." They took him to a spaceship, which they launched into outer space; the yacuruna traveled into space with him, singing the most beautiful and marvelous songs.[29]

Yacuruna

The yacuruna, water people, look more or less like human beings, except that they live underwater in beautiful cities, often at the mouths of rivers. Sometimes these cities are described as upside-down mirror images of human cities—that is, like reflections on the surface of the water. Here the yacuruna live in palaces of crystal with multicolored walls of fish scales and pearl, reclining on hammocks of gazelle feathers, under a mosquito net of butterfly wings. These tropes can be extended: the hammocks of the yacuruna are boas, their seats are turtles, their canoes are alligators.[30] In different accounts, yacuruna may be hairy, or have their heads turned backward, or even have deformed feet, like the chullachaqui.[31]

People stolen away by the yacuruna come in time to resemble their captors: first their eyes and then their head and feet turn backward. When the transformation is complete, the stolen one has turned into a yacuruna and can never return.[32] Or the yacuruna may turn around the head of the one they have abducted immediately, so that the person cannot find the way home, but must continue onward into their city under the water.

The yacuruna are also great healers and can be summoned to help the shaman in his work. The yacuruna may teach an abducted person the healing arts and, when trust has been established, turn the person's head toward the front again and let the person return to the human world.[33] Similarly, the yacuruna may be the source of shamanic powers.

Don Juan Flores Salazar tells of how his little sister was pulled under the water while swimming and disappeared. Years later she appeared to him and said that she was still alive, married to a yacuruna, turned into a mermaid, and a healer of the waters. He continues to consult with her, for she knows many remedies. He thinks that this is perhaps their destiny, for her to be a healer in the waters and him to be a healer on the land, to transmit their knowledge to each other.[34]

Belief in powerful underwater beings is found elsewhere in the Amazon. Among the Achuar, the tsunki are male and female spirits who resemble humans and dwell in rivers and lakes, very much like the yacuruna among the mestizos. Tsunki social and material life mirrors that of the Achuar; they are a source of shamanic powers, and they engage in sexual relations with humans. Married Achuar men speak casually about their double life with their human family, on the one hand, and their adulterous underwater tsunki family on the other.[35]

Among the Shuar, the shamanic power of the water people is made explicit, and they attribute great shamanic power to the tsunki. Indeed, Tsunki is the primordial first shaman, the source of all shamanic power, the origin of knowledge about the use of tsentsak darts, who continues to live beneath the waters in a house made of anacondas, using a turtle as a stool. Tsunki can give to favored shamans a type of tsentsak made of crystal, which are particularly deadly; and he can kill shamans with whom he is angry.[36] It is possible to receive tsentsak directly from Tsunki in a dream or vision, instead of receiving them from a human shaman.[37] It is sometimes said that only those who have had a vision of Tsunki can become shamans.[38] A Shuar shaman sings, *I am like Tsunki. I am like Tsunki*. And again: *I am sitting with Tsunki*.[39]

Tsunki lives in the whirlpools of the remote waterfalls and appears in the form of a beautiful woman, a water snake, or other water being.[40] Thus there is ambiguity: the term *tsunki* can refer to the water people generally; to a particular water person, often a seductive female with long hair and large breasts, at least as reported by men; and to Tsunki, the primordial shaman.[41] An Achuar widow or unmarried woman may become a shaman and remain celibate, except for her sexual relationship with Tsunki.[42]

The Achuar tell a story of a woman carried off by Tsunki, who dwelled with him under the water, where there were great towns built of stone and people traveled in canoes as swift as airplanes. She returned to visit her grieving mother, who thought her daughter had been eaten by an anaconda; but the woman had become a great shaman while living with Tsunki, and the people of her village sought to kill her as a sorceress. So the woman said, "If that's the way it is, I shall go away forever, back to my husband Tsunki." And she disappeared into the lake, never to return.[43]

Similarly, among the Canelos Quichua, the master of the waters is Sungui or Tsungui, symbolized by the anaconda, and may be male or female or both. When male, he sits on the turtle seat of power in a house whose poles are anacondas; when angry and fierce, Sungui becomes the rainbow; Sungui is the first shaman of the water people. Don Rodrigo Andi chants that he has acquired the power of Sungui from the great lagoon, that he now has powerful medicine with which to heal; he fends off pathogenic projectiles with the shield of Sungui.[44]

Mermaids

Amazonian sirenas, mermaids, look just like the mermaids of the classical European imagination—beautiful blond women with the tail of a fish, sometimes with several fish tails, who have melodious voices and hypnotic eyes and live in caves beneath the waters.[45] They travel on boas. Sometimes they even turn into boas; if the woman sleeping next to you turns into a boa during the night, that is a good sign that you have been seduced by a mermaid.[46] Like dolphins, they can transform into human beings and seek sex with human men, just as dolphins seek sex with human women. Handsome young fishermen in their boats are at constant risk of abduction by mermaids.[47] That is why some men go out fishing and never return.

Sirenas will seduce men with their sweet sad songs and carry them off to their underwater world. A sirena sings her songs on a lonely beach or on a precipice by the water. A young man who hears her song will approach and yield to her, abandoning everything and going off with her forever. The family of the one who has disappeared think he has drowned, but the body is never found; if they ask a shaman, he tells them that the young man has been bewitched by a sirena and has gone to live with her in her kingdom in the depths.[48] Or the missing person may speak through the mouth of the shaman: "I am alive in an underwater city where there are mermaids and men with fish tails. There are great doctors, and life is beautiful and eternal."[49]

Both mermaids and yacuruna can become powerful allies of the shaman. Mermaids can appear in ayahuasca visions singing beautiful icaros, by which they exercise power over the underwater world and which they will sometimes teach to a fortunate shaman. Like dolphins and yacuruna, mermaids can be powerful shamans, often summoned to aid in pusanguería, love magic. Offspring of humans and mermaids can be powerful healers, who live underwater and can be called among the healing spirits at an ayahuasca ceremony.[50] The word *yara* is sometimes used to denote a sexually seductive mermaid, with blond hair and mother-of-pearl skin. Don Agustin Rivas tells how, while following la dieta, a beautiful strange female spirit named Yara would appear to him at dawn, lift his mosquito net, and lie down with him. He would awake just before having sex with her.[51]

Dolphins

The bufeo colorado, pink dolphin (*Inia geoffrensis*), is considered a powerful shaman, which casts spells when it surfaces, perhaps because its blowhole makes blowing and whistling sounds similar to those made by a shaman.[52] Much dolphin behavior supports belief in their intelligence. They are curious, and they will swim near boats and approach swimmers in the water.[53] They will chase a school of fish, allowing fishermen to go upstream and set their nets; the dolphins will then remain on the outside of the nets, easily capturing any fish that escape—a curiously symbiotic relation between humans and dolphins.[54]

Mestizos firmly believe that dolphins seek sexual intercourse with human beings. A menstruating women in a boat is in particular danger; a dolphin will ram her boat and overturn it, dragging her to the river bottom for sexual intercourse, where the woman may drown. Dolphins also turn into human form in order to seduce women and to make children that will later serve them. They appear primarily as fair handsome men dressed in dapper white linen suits and Italian fedoras, who attend parties, buying drinks for everyone and stealing or seducing women amid the noise, confusion, and dancing.[55] An infatuated woman may disappear, having thrown herself into the river out of her desire to stay forever with her dolphin lover.[56] If a young woman is impregnated and the father is unknown, the pregnancy is often blamed on a nocturnal liaison with a dolphin, who presumably lured the maiden into the water.[57]

But just as chullachaquis cannot hide their deformed foot, dolphins cannot disguise their blowhole, and always appear wearing a hat; and they will not drink, since being drunk may break the spell and reveal their true identity. Such an interloper may be frightened away by removing his hat and revealing that he is really a dolphin.

In line with the attributed sexuality of the dolphin is the belief that female dolphin genitals are the same as—indeed, more desirable than—those of human females. It is said that no woman can compare with a female dolphin in the passion or skills of sex, "more delicious in love than a woman, more tasty," says poet César Calvo.[58] Stories are told of men who began to copulate with female dolphins and found it so pleasurable that they could not stop, until first their semen and then their blood was completely drained.[59] Don Agustin Rivas tells how, when he was thirteen years old, he in fact had sex with a dolphin that had jumped into his boat—a dolphin, he says, "with small breasts and pubic hair just like a woman." He thought the dolphin had jumped into his boat in order to have sex with him; he had heard "that dolphins could be more sexually gratifying than women," so he took off his pants and had sex with it.[60]

Dolphins are hunted not for food but for body parts. If a man wears the ear of a dolphin on his wrist, he will enjoy large and lasting erections;[61] the vulva of a dolphin tied on the upper arm makes one irresistible to women; hanging a dolphin tooth around the neck of a child will cure diarrhea; a powder made from the pulverized eye, fat, teeth, or penis of the dolphin may be used to seduce women.[62] A sorcerer can attack a woman using the penis of a dolphin, calling the spirit of the dolphin to inflict on the woman a voracious sexual appetite, which she then alleviates with every available man.[63] Because of the slaughter of pink dolphins for these purposes, the species is now listed as *vulnerable* on the Red List published by the International Union for the Conservation of Nature—that is, facing a high risk of extinction in the wild in the medium-term future.[64]

CHAPTER 29

HISPANIC INFLUENCES

Four features of traditional Hispanic medicine have significantly affected mestizo shamanism—the emphasis on limpia, external purification of the body, including flower baths; the doctrine of signatures; Hispanic cultural syndromes, such as susto and pulsario; and humoral medicine.

EXTERNAL CLEANSING

While the mestizo practice of vomiting and inner purgation clearly derives from indigenous Amazonian culture, the use of limpias, cleansing baths, and *sahumerias*, sweat baths, reflect Hispanic influences. Sahumerias are used for healing among Mexican Americans on the Texas border.[1] Limpias are an important part of Mexican healing,[2] and among Mexican Americans, *baños especiales de fortuna*, special baths of good luck, are used to protect people from *sacalio*, bad luck, just as baños de flores, flower baths, are used by mestizo shamans in cases of saladera.[3]

THE DOCTRINE OF SIGNATURES

Don Roberto knows hundreds of plants, at least in the sense that he is *familiar* with that many, in the same way that a biomedical physician probably knows hundreds of medicines. I think that most shamans—like most biomedical physicians—regularly use a few dozen plant medicines in their everyday routine practice and go outside that number only in difficult cases, perhaps after consultation with a specialist. Even so, I have often wondered how a shaman remembers all those plants.

The doctrine of signatures is often attributed to Paracelsus and was pervasive in Europe by the sixteenth century. The doctrine asserted that the inner virtues of a plant are manifest in its *signature*, or outer appearance—that God had mercifully ordained that humans could read the healing powers of plants from their physical characteristics.[4] For example, according to a seventeenth-century herbal, we can know that Saint-John's-wort is good for cuts and wounds because the leaves have holes in them, and the flowers, when putrefied, look like blood, "which teacheth us, that this herb is good for wounds, to close them and fill them up."[5] In addition, the yellow color of saffron suggests its usefulness for jaundice; the brain-like surface of a walnut indicates its value for head ailments; the spotted leaves of lungwort, appearing like pulmonary disease, indicates its potential to cure chest complaints.[6]

The system in Europe was likely as much mnemonic as it was philosophical. It was easy to remember that the small celandine was good for hemorrhoids because its root had small nodules that looked like swellings. It also helped that the name of the plant was pilewort.[7]

Mestizo shamans apparently inherited the doctrine of signatures from Hispanic culture. I have found little evidence that there was any indigenous Amazonian equivalent of this way of viewing plants. Ethnobotanist William Balée, in his extensive study of Ka'apor plant use, devotes several pages to the doctrine of signatures, only to conclude that, by and large, the doctrine does not apply to Ka'apor medicinal plant use. And, certainly, the subsequent descriptions of medicinal plants bear this out; not one description relates plant use to plant *form*, although some plants used to ensure good hunting are said to *smell* like the game animal against which they work.[8]

For most mestizo shamans, the doctrine of signatures is an unstated premise of much of their plant medicine. This is most clear in pusanguería, love medicine. *Clinging* plants, especially lianas and vines, announce their utility for love medicine, especially the renaco, strangler fig, which clings to its support tree like a devoted lover. In the same way, *buceta hembra* has two leaves on each stalk, the smaller of which clings to the underside of the larger and looks very much like a vagina; amor seco, dry love, has tiny sticky leaves that cling to the clothing or skin of passersby; sacha corazon, jungle heart, has heart-shaped leaves and clings to the trunks of trees, and is thus used not only in love medicine but also in the treatment of diseases related to the heart and blood. Perfumero don Artidoro Aro Cardenas adds another signature: a plant that attracts bright birds will also attract beautiful women.[9]

In the Upper Amazon, the system is probably more mnemonic than metaphysical: signatures provide a way to remember the uses of a plant. Here are some additional examples:

- Caña brava, giant cane, can grow more than thirty feet tall, straight up from the ground, even pushing its way through other plants—*como hombre muy macho*, doña María glossed for me. It is thus used to treat erectile dysfunction, called *hombre caido*, perhaps best translated as *male droop*.
- Uña de gato, cat's-claw, is a vine whose stems have small hooklike appendages, so the plant is used to claw out tumors and inflammations.
- Shimipampana, arrowroot, has a root that is considered to look like a fist, and therefore is used as a pusanga to tame an ill-tempered or jealous spouse. The root is crushed, doña María told me, and put into some café con leche. In addition, the root can be rubbed between the hands, and the resulting liquid can be mixed into a lotion that, when applied to the face, will guarantee success in business and in litigation.
- Sangre de grado, dragon's blood, a tree whose red latex looks like blood, is thus used to treat wounds, ulcers, and skin infections. I have also often heard the sap referred to, because of its color, as *sacha iodo*, jungle iodine. This is a new signature; the sap is good for wounds because it resembles the iodine of biomedicine.
- Jergón sacha, jungle viper, is a shrub with a brown-green-gray mottled stem that resembles the skin of several South American pit vipers. A drink made from the root is used to treat snakebite; a poultice, or the root itself, may be heated and pressed directly on the wound. It can also, doña María told me, be used to treat cancer, which also bites, like a snake.

HISPANIC CULTURAL SYNDROMES

The idea of "culture-bound syndromes"—*amok* in Malaysia, *koro* in Indonesia, perhaps anorexia nervosa in North America—has been the occasion of considerable debate in medical anthropology.[10] Still, there is little doubt that the names and descriptions of certain sicknesses—*susto*, *empacho*, *mal aire*—are found throughout Hispanic communities in both North and South America, and do not correspond to sickness concepts found in other communities.

Much research has been done on these Hispanic sicknesses and on their complexity and variety.[11] Among the Hispanic sicknesses that don Roberto and doña María have told me about, and which they regularly encounter in their practice, are susto, fright; pulsario, bloating; mal de ojo, evil eye; mal aire, bad air; and saladera, bad luck.[12]

Susto

Soul loss in mestizo shamanism is almost certainly derived from the Hispanic concept of susto, soul loss due to fright; indigenous Amazonian shamanic traditions of soul loss appear to be too distant geographically and conceptually—for example, among the Wakuénai—to have significantly contributed to the idea.[13]

Among the Hispanic diagnostic categories, susto is probably the one most commonly invoked by both don Roberto and doña María, and also probably the Hispanic sickness most investigated by researchers.[14] Don Roberto and doña María frequently use the term *manchari* for the same condition, presumably from the Quechua *manchay*, to be afraid.[15] People afflicted with susto are said to be *asustado* or often *caido*, fallen, since the inducing fright in childhood susto is often considered to have been a fall. Such people are thought to have suffered a loss of their soul because of fright: they commonly lose their appetite and strength; they are listless, restless, depressed, withdrawn, and lacking in motivation. They must be cured by restoration of their soul.[16] Children with susto have symptoms of vomiting, diarrhea, constant crying, and insomnia.[17]

Many people suffering susto have experienced a sense of inadequacy and helplessness even before the symptoms begin; anthropologists have given the examples of a man who experienced an attack of susto after an embarrassing accident at work that evoked laughter from onlookers, and a woman who suffered an attack after she got into a fight with her unfaithful husband and he hit her with a rock.[18] An epidemiological study of susto has reported that asustados differed from controls without susto in both physical symptoms and role stress—that is, loss of appetite, loss of weight, fatigue, and lack of motivation, on the one hand, and, on the other, discrepancies between their expectations and their performance in their prescribed social roles.[19] Poet César Calvo writes that manchari "is a different fear, more difficult than the fear we all know, the one even animals can sense. The manchari enters like a soul into a body, and the person in that body becomes incapable."[20]

The concept of susto functions as an etiological category. When a person suffers from certain forms of social dysfunction—listlessness, depression, lack of motivation—family members or a healer search the past for a frightening event that may have caused the soul to leave the body.[21] When persons believe that they are performing their social roles less adequately, according to their own criteria, than others in the community, the illness category of susto provides a framework within which to conceptualize their experience and seek appropriate healing; perceived social and personal failures are attributed to a culturally defined sickness. The cure is for the shaman to call back the soul with the appropriate icaro and the help of the appropriate spirits. The soul comes back into the body through the corona, the crown of the head, doña María told me, como un viento, like a wind—except for the lost souls of children, who always appeared to doña María as angels.

Pulsario

Doña María and—to a somewhat lesser degree—don Roberto introduce a number of additional Hispanic syndromes into their sickness discourse. The term *pulsario* appears to refer to virtually the same disorder that is called empacho elsewhere in Hispanic culture.[22] Empacho is caused by a lump of poorly digested or uncooked food believed to be blocking the intestines, manifesting as a feeling of gas and fullness in the abdomen, lack of appetite, stomach ache, diarrhea, and vomiting.[23] Pulsario has many of the same symptoms—diarrhea, pain, loss of appetite—and manifests as a lump in the stomach just above the navel. "Doctors call it an ulcer," doña María explained to me. The condition is caused by not eating regularly; doña María considered the sickness to be the result of anger or shame.

Children's Sicknesses

Doña María, given the nature of her healing practice, frequently referred to certain traditional Hispanic sicknesses to which children are especially susceptible—mal de ojo, the evil eye, and mal aire, bad air. Evil eye beliefs are found in many cultures, and encode differences between acceptable and dangerous forms of eye contact.[24] The harm caused by the evil eye is intimately connected to envidia, envy; the Spanish *envidia* is etymologically related to the Latin *invidere*, to look askance, to look with enmity. In Amazonian mestizo culture, the infliction of the evil eye may be caused by looking upon another with such envy or even inadvertently, by admiring a baby, for example. Courtesy requires that great care be taken not to look too long or too hard at a child. It may also be considered rude to look at a child without touching it.

The belief in mal aire is widespread in South America; it occurs, doña María told me, when "something evil passes by"—almas malas, malignos, demonios, tunchis. The disease can be contagious. When adults, out at night, encounter one of these wandering souls, it can touch them as they pass by—a shock, a shiver, an apprehension—and then they can bring the sickness home to their children. When such invisible vaporous malignancies pass by a baby, the symptoms resemble those of susto—diarrhea, vomiting, unrest, fever—not an uncommon childhood syndrome, often diagnosed in North America as a result of the invisible vaporous malignancy called a *virus*.[25]

There are different types of mal aire. Illness produced by the spirit of a dead person may be called *mal aire de difunto*.[26] There can be *mal aire del monte*, evil air from the jungle, and *mal aire del agua*, evil air from the water.[27] The cure for this sickness is a *baño*, bath, pungent with flowers and spices—*rosasisa*, *cominos*, cumin, all cooked together. The child should be bathed in this rapidly, doña María taught me, and the baby's head, soles of the feet, and palms of the hands should all be sealed with crosses.

HUMORAL MEDICINE

Humoral medicine conceives the universe as made of basic opposing qualities—in the Greek system, hot and cold, wet and dry—and physiological functioning as a set of interactions among basic *humors*—blood, phlegm, yellow bile, and black bile.[28] According to this theory, health is a matter of balance among humors and their qualities.[29]

In Hispanic communities in both North and South America, the original fourfold intersecting classification of hot, cold, wet, and dry has been truncated to considerations only of warming and cooling. Varying degrees of hot and cold are assigned to foods, activities, emotions, sicknesses, and therapies,[30] and the goal of medical treatment is to overcome temperature imbalance. In Guatemala, for example, diarrhea is classified as a cold disease, and therefore penicillin, a cold medicine, is not appropriate for treatment. But dysentery is considered a hot disease because of the presence of blood, and then penicillin is acceptable because the hot disease and the cold medicine balance each other.[31]

This hot–cold distinction seems to have disappeared entirely in South Texas Hispanic communities,[32] and it has become vestigial in the Upper Amazon, overshadowed by the location and extraction of darts and other pathogenic objects. Still, mestizo shamans specify cold plants, such as chiricsanango and chiricaspi, to treat hot conditions, such as fever, diarrhea, wounds, and inflammations.[33] Warm plants, such as abuta, ajo sacha, chuchuhuasi, clavohuasca, and ipururo have, as mestizo shaman Manuel Córdova Ríos says, "the effect of warming the blood" and are used to treat cold conditions, such as arthritis, rheumatism, and male sexual inadequacy.[34] We should not be surprised to find some lack of consistency in these attributions.

CHAPTER 30
FOLK CATHOLICISM

CATHOLICISM AND SHAMANISM

If you look at the mesa of many mestizo shamans, you will see the usual ritual implements—ayahuasca, agua de florida, camalonga, a shacapa—and a book. The book is a collection of Catholic prayers and protections.

Most mestizo shamans will tell you they are Catholic, and they are probably about as Catholic as most mestizos living in the Amazon.[1] More than 80 percent of Peruvians say they are Roman Catholic;[2] according to the 1981 census, 93 percent of the rural residents of Maynas province—within which Iquitos is located—are Catholic.[3] The Peruvian constitution recognizes Roman Catholicism as deserving of government cooperation; public schools offer mandatory classes in Catholic religion, from which non-Catholic parents must request an exemption in writing from the school principal.

This is not to deny that evangelical Protestantism has made significant inroads into Catholic hegemony. There are now estimated to be around 1.5 million members of evangelical churches in Peru. Few self-identified Catholics attend mass regularly. Thus the number of active Protestant churchgoers is comparable to that of practicing Catholics.[4] In many rural villages, while the Catholic Church is left padlocked, the Jehovah's Witnesses or Mormons or Adventists or some other Protestant group have set up a prayer group and a meetinghouse.[5] "Catholicism has the cathedral," one commentator notes, "but the Evangelical preacher has the crowds."[6]

In fact, there is a long-standing scarcity of Catholic priests throughout South America.[7] In the small ribereño villages along the jungle waterways, masses are performed infrequently; a priest may appear once or twice a year and hastily perform marriage ceremonies for all the cohabiting couples, sometimes after a man and woman have lived together for decades.[8] And there are also some not-so-subtle anticlerical attitudes among the ribereños. A popular toy is a carving of a Franciscan monk in a robe; pulling on a string lifts up the robe, and a huge erect penis pops up, like a jack-in-the-box. People think this is hilarious.

Such humor taps into the widespread belief in the immorality of the clergy.[9] And such disdain is often reciprocal. Anthropologists Norman and Dorothea Whitten tell of a Catholic priest castigating a number of Canelos Quichua participants in a celebration. They are drunkards and dope takers, the priest says, spending their time with ayahuasca when they should be working for their wives; the celebration is slothful and savage.[10]

Still, Roman Catholicism remains a singularly powerful cultural force. For example, in Iquitos, people will organize a *velada*—a ritual celebration in honor of a saint—or will arrange for a *misa de honras*, a memorial mass, to ask for protection from tunchis or malignos, the evil spirits of the dead.[11]

Catholicism interacts with shamanism as well. Shipibo shaman don Javier Arévalo Shahuano says that Christianity and shamanism work together. "But it has nothing to do with going to church," he adds. "You learn all this in the wilderness. The spirits there are the angels of each plant to which you add your will to heal the client. This is the will of Christ."[12] In the same way, Cocama shaman don José Curitima Sangama says that he works with the help of God, who after all created all the plants; in his icaros he calls upon La Virgen de Dolores, the Virgin of Sorrows.[13]

It is clear that doña María's healing practice—and many of her theories about her healing practice—were influenced by a folk Catholicism found widely among Amazonian mestizos. In the Peruvian Amazon, institutional Catholicism is identified primarily with the cities, which are able to support ecclesiastical institutions such as cathedrals, priests, masses, and festivals. Outside the cities, there is folk Catholicism—as political scientist Anthony Gill puts it, "the Catholic faith in a noninstitutional setting . . . a popular form of religiosity, typically found in areas that receive only sporadic visits from Catholic priests."[14]

Folk Catholicism manifests itself in many ways. Good luck charms, for example, often containing images of saints, may be carried or placed on small altars in the home. There are two types—*collages*, consisting of small items glued to a cloth-covered piece of cardboard, and *vials*, discarded vaccine bottles filled with objects suspended in oil and sealed with aluminum and rubber caps. Most are accompanied by small slips of paper listing and explaining their contents, often with a picture of a saint and a brief prayer.

The items included with such charms may include tiny horseshoes for luck, pieces of pyrite to attract money, lodestones to attract both money and luck, huayruro seeds for luck, pieces of what is called *vuelve vuelve*—come back! come back!—vine for the return of a lost love; pieces of various kinds of tree bark dyed bright colors, and small figures of saints—St. Anthony, patron of lovers; St. Cyprian, magician and patron of healers; and St. Francis, patron of animals. Sometimes a collage will include a god's eye wound on two small sticks; small saint-card images of Jesus, St. Anthony, or the Virgin Mary; or a tiny red candle.[15]

Among mestizo shamans, folk Catholicism manifests itself primarily in two ways—first, in viewing Jesus Christ and the Virgin Mary as particularly powerful healing and protecting spirits; and second, in using prayer books and spell books to remove evil and to ensure safety. There is no doubt that doña María was deeply devoted to the Virgin Mary and considered her to be a powerful and trustworthy friend. This is different, perhaps, in intensity, but not in kind, from her relations with other spirits. Doña María's oraciones, prayer songs, to Jesucristo were almost identical to those to other healing spirits. She sang to Jesus:

Nazareno poderoso
yo te pido bendiciones
para todo mis hermanos
presentas y ausentes
nari nari na reina
[Powerful Nazarene
I ask you for blessings
for all my brothers and sisters
present and absent
nari nari na reina]

In the same way—and in virtually the same words—she sang to, say, *ayahuasca doctorcito poderoso*. She would begin every ayahuasca ritual with numerous repetitions of the avemaría, Hail Mary, as an arcana.

A popular spell book is *The Sacred Cross of Caravaca*, which provides a number of lengthy prayers to various saints as well as *oraciones curativas*, brief prayers and spells for healing. "Tests repeated a thousand times," says the anonymous author, "have given us the absolute conviction of their efficacy; thousands of impartial and careful testimonials agree with us in proclaiming their value in every case." For example, there is a prayer against burns: "Fire is not cold. Water is not thirsty. Air is not hot. Bread is not hungry. San Lorenzo, cure these burns, by the power God has given you." Against cataracts, one may pray: "Cataract, cataract, formed of blood and water; in honor and glory of the Holy Trinity, may it be quickly healed"; and again: "Mother of San Simeón, advocate against cataracts. Clear is the moon; clear is the sun; clear let the vision be of N., by your intercession." And there is a prayer against a sore throat: "In Belén are three young girls: one sews, another spins, and another heals sore throats. One spins, another sews, and another heals sore throats."[16]

MAGIC

This folk Catholicism easily shades over into *magia*, magic. The term has traditionally referred specifically to the magical power of white people, in distinction to the power of indigenous Amazonian shamans: It was their magic that allowed the whites to come and steal the land.[17] This magic is found in books, particularly in *grimorios*, such as the *Book of San Cipriano* or the *Great Grimoire of Pope Honorius*, and in Spanish translations of the texts of nineteenth-century European occultism. This means that books on magia can be purchased at the market and learned by oneself, without needing a maestro for protection and guidance and without undergoing the training and suffering of sexual abstinence and the restricted diet. All you need do is buy the book and find the right spell.

But there is a price to pay. Some people say that the magic of the whites requires a pact with the devil. The prayers and spells in the books of magia can conjure up evil spirits who then harm the conjurer.[18] Doña María warned me that magic makes people *cruzado*, confused, burdened, tormented, because they have no guidance from a maestro. Buying magia in a bookstore requires no self-control; it is like dieting only long enough to become a sorcerer. To receive initiation from a shaman, one must undergo severe dietary, sexual, and other restrictions; but to become a magician you just to have to read the books on magic and follow their instructions. Being a magician is considered to involve less suffering than being a shaman; nor does it demand a great deal of self-control to become a magician.[19]

Here is an example of a magic spell from one version—there are many—of the *Book of St. Cyprian*, telling how a woman can make a man fall in love with her. The woman should get from the chosen man a coin, medal, pin, or other object, or part of an object, made of silver, which he has had with him for a period of twenty-four hours. She should approach the man holding the object in her right hand and with the other hand offer him a cup of wine, in which she has dissolved a pill, the size of a grain of millet, with the following composition—the head of an eel, a thimbleful of hemp seeds, two drops of laudanum, and six drops of her own blood, taken from her menstruation in the same month. As soon as the individual has drunk the cup of wine with this mixture, he will helplessly love the woman who gave it to him.[20]

THEISTIC SYNCRETISM

When doña María spoke of her life and work, she frequently put her palms together in a gesture of prayer and exclaimed, *¡Gracias a Dios!* Thanks to God!—especially when describing her narrow escapes from sorcerers. Her monotheism emerged in many of her theoretical constructs. For example, doña María learned from don Roberto that there are three *fuentes de la medicina*, sources of medicine—*tierra*, earth; *agua*, water; and haire, air. This is a typically Amazonian threefold cosmology, lacking the element of *fire* found in the fourfold European cosmologies derived from Greek thought. But María added her own theistic interpretation. "Many shamans do not know this," she told me. "One poder, power, comes through three *fuentes*."

Her explicit threefold cosmology was subsumed under an implicit vertical duality—that between arriba, above, and tierra, earth, below. The use of the term *tierra* instead of the more correlative term *abajo*, below, may be another instance of Amazonian synecdoche: here below are the three sources of medicine, of which tierra is one. This duality pervaded doña María's discourse. Arriba was explicitly identified with cielo, heaven, and tierra with *infierno*, hell. Similar implicit oppositions recurred frequently: below are the genios, plant spirits, and above are the *santos*, saints; below are the icaros, plant spirit songs, and above are oraciones, prayers. Similarly, doña María used two different words for the general concept of *power*: on the one hand was *fuerza*, which is the power of the shaman, related to tierra, earth; on the other was *poder*, which is the power of God, related to arriba, heaven. It is this divine poder, rather than the shamanic fuerza, which, doña María said, is manifested through *las tres fuentes de la medicina*.

Similarly, doña María considered herself to have had three types of teacher in her life—her earthly teacher, her heavenly teacher, and her spirit teacher. Her only human teacher had been don Roberto, who is of tierra, the earth. Somewhere between earthly and heavenly teachers was her spirit teacher, her spirit ally—Oscar Rosindo Pisarro, the deceased Iquitos Rosicrucian who entered her body and worked through her when she underwent transcorporación. But her true teacher was arriba, heaven above—the Virgin Mary and Jesus Christ, the threefold Padre, Jesucristo, and Espíritu Santo.

PART IV

MEETING MODERNITY

CHAPTER 31

AYAHUASCA MEETS GLOBAL MODERNISM

GLOBAL MARKETING

Ayahuasca—both the ayahuasca drink and ayahuasca shamanism—has been subject to the forces of globalization and modernity that have affected every other aspect of Amazonian life. The results of this encounter have been mixed, on both sides—on the one hand, new forms of literature and art, new religious movements, experiments in religious organization; on the other hand, oppression, exploitation, and the piracy of valuable traditional knowledge.

Doña María and don Roberto now perform their work within global currents. They are embedded in a world culture in which expansive markets, mass media, technological change, and hegemonic ideologies are shaping—and in turn are shaped by—their own local culture.[1] Ayahuasca shamanism is up for sale on the global market, promulgated through literature, art, and, of course, the Internet. The visionary ayahuasca paintings of Pablo César Amaringo are available to a world market in a sumptuous coffee-table book;[2] international ayahuasca tourists exert a profound economic and cultural pull on previously isolated local practitioners; ayahuasca shamanism, once the terrain of anthropologists, is now promoted in the New Age marketplace. Ayahuasca shamans, previously local and largely individual practitioners, have themselves adopted the rationalizing devices of modernity, primarily those of collective organization and professionalization.

Ayahuasca has been endorsed by international celebrities—Sting, Tori Amos, Oliver Stone.[3] Noted novelists—Isabel Allende, Peter Matthiessen, Paul Theroux, Alice Walker—have written about the ayahuasca experience;[4] Paul Simon has written a song about it.[5] Ayahuasca itself is now enmeshed in two worldwide markets—one for medicinal plants and one for psychoactive

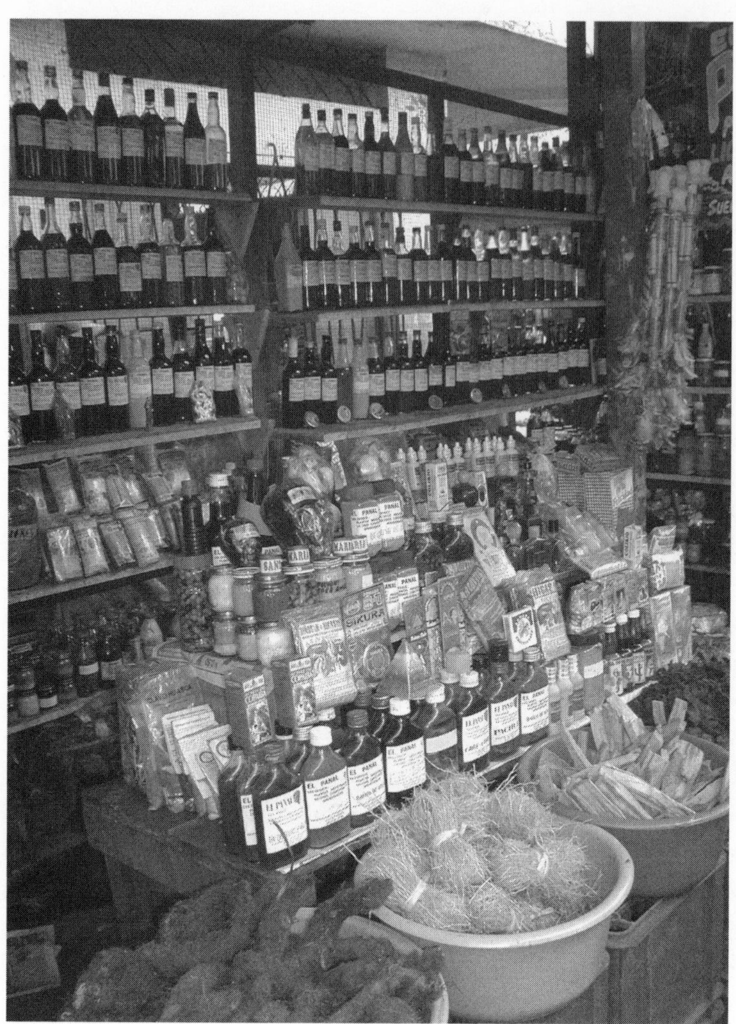

FIGURE 14. Medicine plants in the Belén market.

substances—and in the attempts of national governments and international agencies to control those markets, through mechanisms of patent law, international treaties, and criminal sanctions.

Don Roberto and doña María now live in what has been called a *community-world*.[6] In the presence of instantaneous communication, jet travel, migration, and the other hallmarks of global modernity, it is no longer realistic or possible to imagine that their culture or religious practice can be bounded or self-enclosed.[7] In the "mazelike condition" of global modernity, ayahuasca shamanism has become porous.[8]

CONTEMPORARY DISCOURSE

The degree to which don Roberto and doña María have incorporated biomedical and other contemporary imagery into their practice is striking. The spirits of many plants appear as doctors, often in surgical scrubs and masks. Doña María's coronación dream involved her initiation by doctors in pure white surgical scrubs performing operations in a great hospital; when don Roberto transcorporates, he journeys to huge hospitals, where he observes medical procedures and operations in progress. Both doña María and don Roberto are aided by doctores extraterrestreales, extraterrestrial doctors, or marcianos, Martians, who speak in computer language; don Rómulo Magin is helped in exactly the same way by jefes, chiefs, who descend from the sky dressed as Peruvian military officers.

The shamanism of the Upper Amazon is remarkably absorptive of such imagery. Amazonian shamans frequently have visions of great cities, often said to be located on other planets.[9] Sharanahua shamans sing of Peruvian spirits traveling up the Purús in a large boat filled with trade goods—metal pots, shotgun shells, guns, suitcases, whiskey.[10] One shaman living in Iquitos has a jet fighter plane he uses when attacked by strong sorcerers;[11] a shaman in Pucallpa receives magical keys in his visions, so that he can drive beautiful cars and airplanes.[12] One Shapra shaman, who lived in the jungle hundreds of miles from Iquitos, told me that he had a spiritual x-ray machine with which he diagnosed patients. When don Rodrigo Andi, a Canelos Quichua shaman, sings, the spirits bring him healing machines—an x-ray machine, blood pressure apparatus, stethoscope, and surgical light. He carries a shield of medicine he buys in a spirit drugstore on the Napo River. He is protected by noisy airplanes flying all around him—military planes, helicopters, cargo planes. "Here I am," he sings, "a shaman sitting in the center of aviation control."[13]

Such importations are not new; an earlier generation of Amazonian shamans frequently adopted the language of electricity, magnetism, and radio. Don Agustin Rivas, for example, has said that the yacuruna, water people, live beneath the waters so that "they cannot be disturbed with the energy of electrical technology" and that spirits are energies like radio waves.[14] Campa shaman César Zevallos Chinchuya says that the genio, plant spirit, places a powerful magnet in his mouth, which attracts the *atmósfera* or flemosidad of the patient's disease. His sucking works through this magnet; plants and mermaids bring him magnets with which to heal and harm; blowing tobacco smoke on the body magnetizes it.[15] Don Emilio Andrade also described his yachay, magical phlegm, as a sort of magnet, attracting the dart when he sucks at the place it is lodged.[16] Icaros especially are assimilated to magnetism. “Ximu sang icaros to them,” writes poet César Calvo, “magnetizing them and empowering with precise and sufficient powers.”[17] Zevallos says that icaros are “magnetic cures” and that protective icaros are “magnetic shielding.”[18]

Thirty years ago, too, don César Zevallos communicated with the spirits through radio waves, and was told where to find the proper cures in an invisible book. “Vomiting, diarrhea, fever. See book 72,001,” the spirits tell him. “Immediately ask the patient how long he has been taking the purgative. . . . Very good. Immediately look up page 42.”[19] At about the same time, a Sharanahua shaman sang this song of the radio: “Its Peruvian made it, the radio is talking. . . . Its white antenna, its fiery antenna up in the air. Its owner is talking, its fiery antenna, its fire talks.”[20]

More recently, Alberto Prohaño, a Yagua shaman in a remote village where a satellite telephone dish was recently installed, now talks with the spirits by telephone, using the pot in which the ayahuasca is cooked as what he calls a microreceiver. He blows tobacco smoke in the pot to clear the line, whistles, and puts his ear to the pot: “Hello! 1973, hello, 1-2-3-4-5. . . . Yes. . . . Over. . . . Operator? . . . Pepelucho needs help in business. We are going to help him. . . . Over. . . . Yes, for business, you know. . . . He is here, do you want to talk with him?” The shaman asks the spirits how much ayahuasca to use: “The amount, we need to know the amount, approximately how many centimeters? Two centimeters, okay.”[21]

Contemporary technology—lasers, spaceships, biomedicine—similarly pervades mestizo shamanism. The striking visionary paintings of Pablo Amaringo are filled with battleships protected by pyramid-shaped lasers; spaceships from the edge of the universe; spaceships from Venus, Mars, Jupiter, and Ganymede; beings from distant galaxies with skin as white as paper; electromagnetic boa constrictors; singing spaceships from the constellation Kima; magnetizing mirrors; poisonous space snakes from Mars; a spaceship of elves from Mars; and, of course, doctors and nurses performing spiritual medical procedures.[22]

Flashlights have become a tool of sorcery. Pablo Amaringo tells how a person’s eyes were harmed by a sorcerer shining a magic flashlight on them.[23] Among the Tukano, it is believed that during the dry season, at noon, a white foamy liquid exudes from small round holes in certain rock formations. This liquid, when touched, has the power to drive people insane. A shaman can protect himself from this liquid and, traditionally, would mix it with tobacco to be offered to an enemy, or sprinkle it on the enemy’s clothing or hammock.

Now the shaman need only smear the liquid on the back of a flashlight and shine its beam on the intended victim.[24]

Similarly remarkable is the degree to which Amazonian shamanism has continued—voraciously—to absorb and transform outside philosophical influences, just as it has done with Catholicism. Medical anthropologist Marlene Dobkin de Ríos discusses ayahuasquero don Hildebrando, who runs a clinic in Pucallpa and who combines indigenous shamanic practice both with folk Catholicism—the Virgin Mary appeared to him when he began his career as an ayahuasca healer—and with a new religious movement called Septrionism.[25] The spirits depicted in Pablo Amaringo's visionary paintings include Krishna, Vishnu, Shiva, and "the great gurus of India."[26] The Indic word *samadhi* turns up in the name of Queen Samhadi the Illuminated.[27]

Mestizo shamanism is now in a similar process of absorbing New Age terms and concepts. Typical of such syncretism is don Antonio Barrera Banda, a young mestizo shaman well known in Iquitos and the surrounding Tamshiyacu-Tahuayo area in the Upper Amazon. Don Antonio is literate in Spanish, and, when I first knew him, he was an insatiable and uncritical reader of everything he could find on spiritual practices outside of Peru. Given his relative isolation, the books he found were haphazard, and his knowledge was an idiosyncratic mix heavy with yoga and the martial arts. At the outset, his ceremonial practice was almost entirely traditional, although his explanations sometimes drew eclectically on his reading. Later, on his Web site, he promoted ayahuasca tours during which visitors could "honor their sacred being," "reach back in beyond ancestral common sharing," and "tap into the green soul of Pachamama itself."[28]

TAROT CARDS

A small but interesting bit of cultural syncretism is the use of Tarot cards by healers—to see whether a spouse is unfaithful and whether love magic is involved, to predict whether a proposed course of action will be fruitful, to find the identity of a thief. Marlene Dobkin de Ríos, who pioneered the study of mestizo shamanism, tells a fascinating story of how she became a curiosa, a Tarot card reader for dwellers in the slum community of Belén in Iquitos. She also provides an interesting statistic: given the number and meanings of the cards, and the way they are dealt, almost 90 percent of the readings predict misfortune, conflict, loss, or sickness. This is probably not inconsistent with mestizo expectations.[29] The practice has now spread from the mestizos to the

Shuar.[30] When some property of mine was stolen, one course of action to discover the thief was to consult a Tarot card expert.

AYAHUASCA VISIONS IN MODERN AMAZONIAN ART

Ayahuasca shamanism has also produced a distinct and highly influential style of contemporary art, primarily by mestizo artists, which was brought forcefully to the attention of European and American readers by the publication, in lavish reproductions and with detailed commentary, of the visionary art of former shaman Pablo Amaringo.[31] Entirely self-taught, Amaringo was encouraged by anthropologist Luis Eduardo Luna to expand his repertoire from portraits and landscapes to include recollections of his ayahuasca journeys. "When painting his visions," Luna writes, "he often sings or whistles some of the icaros he used during his time as a vegetalista. Then the visions come again, as clear as if he were having the experience again."[32]

One such vision directed don Pablo to use his artwork to speak of the spirit world and the difficult times faced by humanity. As a result, in 1988, he founded the Usko-Ayar Amazonian School of Painting in Pucallpa, dedicated to documenting the ways of life in the Amazon. The school's mission is the education of local youth in the care and preservation of the Amazon ecosystem. They are taught to visualize internally what they are going to paint—in other words, to regulate their attention in an attempt to evoke visions that can be shared with others.[33] The school has been made the subject of a short film directed by Luna.[34]

Important as well is Francisco Montes Shuña, another self-taught artist and a practicing shaman associated with the Sachamama Ethnobotanical Garden, which he founded in 1990, about 18 kilometers outside Iquitos. Unlike other art in this genre, his work employs natural pigments on bark, in the traditional indigenous manner. In 1999, his works appeared alongside those of Pablo Amaringo, Yando Ríos, and Elvis Luna at an exhibition at the October Gallery in London.[35]

In contrast with the abstract patterns in indigenous ayahuasca-inspired art, the work of these mostly mestizo artists is characterized by detailed and realistic depictions of the substantive content of their ayahuasca visions—the spirits, trees, and animals they have seen, as well as the shamans, patients, and audience of the healing ceremony. This art almost paradigmatically falls within what has now come to be called *outsider art*, sometimes *naive art*, and sometimes *visionary art*. It is "direct, intense, content-laden, eschatological, expressive, and formally inventive, and it offers glimpses of other modes of perception."[36] The colors are bright and nonnaturalistic; the perspective is nonscientific and two-dimensional.[37] The founding artists were almost entirely self-taught, drew on folk art traditions, used local and indigenous art materials, and produced works that were enormously detailed, personal, idiosyncratic, and visionary. The work of the Usko-Ayar school has been extremely influential, creating both a recognizable style and an international market for Amazonian shamanic art.

Traditional ayahuasca art and, especially, the new art of Pablo Amaringo, the Usko-Ayar school, and such independent practitioners as Elvis Luna and Francisco Montes Shuña have become accessible to a global audience through exhibits, both academic and commercial, and through the handsome publication of Pablo Amaringo's paintings.[38] The work of such painters is finding its way into the North American art market as well, at galleries and through the Internet. This accessibility has in turn created a strong interest in ayahuasca visions generally, stimulated ayahuasca tourism, and created local markets in Iquitos and Pucallpa for paintings in the Amaringo visionary style. As such depictions of ayahuasca experiences become normative, it may be that, rather than the experience prescribing the art, the art may begin to prescribe the experience.

ICAROS MODERNIZED

Icaros, the sacred songs of the Amazonian shamans, are traditionally sung either unaccompanied or with the rhythmic shaking of the shacapa, the leaf-bundle rattle. Recently, however, there has been some experimentation with additional instrumentation. Don Agustin Rivas Vasquez, for example, sings his icaros using a variety of drums, panpipes, maracas, a harmonica, and a stringed instrument of his own devising, as well as a variety of singing styles, some sounding very much like Peruvian popular music.[39] Flautist Tito La Rosa has backed the singing of Shipibo shamans Amelia Panduro, her son Milke Sinuiri, and José Campos with traditional Peruvian instruments—bone flutes, panpipes, conch shells, rattles, and whistling vessels—as well as contemporary percussion, violin, charango, and keyboard.[40] Similarly, musician Alonso Del Río served as an apprentice to don Benito Arévalo, a renowned Shipibo shaman, for three years, and now sings his own icaros accompanied by his guitar—and sometimes traditional Peruvian wind and string instruments—in a style close to folk music.[41]

North American musicians, too, have discovered icaros and have adapted them in a variety of ways. Dada World Data—consisting of Jim Sanders, Andre

Clement, and Dustin Leader—has put the icaros of Asháninka shaman don Juan Flores Salazar into jazz-inflected settings, using guitar, drums, bass, and keyboard, as part of a live multimedia performance project they call Maestro Ayahuasquero and as part of a series of films they are producing about don Juan, ayahuasca, and plant medicine.[42] Guitarist Bill Kopper has similarly backed, with guitar, sitar, bass, piano, and background vocals, the icaros of an Amazonian singer he identifies only as Cristina.[43]

Tulku is a group with constantly shifting membership gathered around musician and producer Jim Wilson. Wilson has worked with many of the most important figures in contemporary Native American music—Robbie Robertson, the Little Wolf Band, Walela, Joanne Shenandoah, and Primeaux and Mike. Much of Wilson's work has centered on cross-cultural musical collaborations—with Russian psychiatrist Olga Kharitidi on Siberian shamanism, with Consuelo Luz on ancient Sephardic prayers and traditional love songs in Ladino, with James Twyman on peace prayers from world religious traditions. Tulku has been part of this same collaborative process, mixing techno-beat, trance-ambient, and global musical traditions and voices; albums have included collaborations with Jai Uttal, Krishna Das, Primeaux and Mike, and Mamek Khadem. Now icaros have been added to the mix: the album *A Universe to Come* brought back original members Jai Uttal and Geoffrey Gordon, along with Consuelo Luz, Gina Sala, Sita Jamieson, and Shipibo shaman Benjamin Mahua.[44]

NEW SYNCRETISMS

As we have seen, mestizo shamanism is insatiably syncretistic. Potential sources of innovation in the future include contact with the Native American Church, the needs and presuppositions of gringo clients, and an expanding pharmacopeia of psychoactive plants.

Eagle and Condor

An interesting and unforeseen consequence of globalization is that there has been increasing contact among indigenous peoples of North and South America. These contacts have sometimes been grounded in a prophetic belief that, after five hundred years of oppression, the eagle and the condor—that is, North and South American indigenous peoples—will fly in the sky together.[45] In many ways, these contacts have followed established pan-Indian routes. For example, the Sun Dance has become a ritual symbol of Indian unity for many North American Indians. This symbolism goes back a long ways; in

1941, for example, Crow elders from Montana sought out Sun Dance leaders of the Wind River Shoshone in Wyoming for help in reconstructing their own Sun Dance, which they had abandoned in 1875 under pressure from missionaries and the federal government.[46]

Now the indigenous people of South America are also seeking access to this powerful symbolism. A group of Mexican Indians danced with Leonard Crow Dog in South Dakota in the 1980s, and they brought the Lakota-style dance back home. Crow Dog's father had a vision of tipis lined up from South Dakota to Mexico.[47] Indigenous people in Colombia and Chile too are seeking ways to bring Sun Dance traditions south to their own communities. As Sun Dancer Tomas Ramirez told me, "Nowadays it is a great and a huge motivation to see Mapuche people from Chile, Nasa from Colombia, and Mexicas dancing next to Lakota, Diné, or Ojibwe warriors."

In addition, there have been a number of contact points between shamanism in the Upper Amazon and the Native American Church (NAC). Some of these contacts have been personal: Valerio Cohaila, for example, an Aymara ayahuasquero from Tacna, Peru, is also a road chief in the NAC. Institutionally, there have been a number of conferences of NAC elders and South American indigenous healers, focusing on shared peyote and ayahuasca ceremonies, under such rubrics as Encuentro de Naciones Condor–Aguila. The Iglesia Nativa in Ecuador has done combined sacred pipe and ayahuasca ceremonies with Shuar shamans under the auspices of the Associación Tsunki, an association within the Federación Shuar.[48]

Not all such attempts at syncretism have gone well. Anthropologist Marie Perruchon, an initiated Shuar shaman, reports that NAC teachers at one such ceremony attempted to force uncongenial practices on the Shuar—imposing lower status on the women participants, excluding menstruating women from touching the sacred pipe, and interpreting the status of the condor in Shuar culture as like that of the eagle in indigenous North American cultures.[49] A recent Condor–Eagle Gathering of Nations held near Popayán, Colombia, was intended to bring together respected Colombian shamans and NAC elders; but it was so costly that indigenous Colombians could not attend and was instead filled with wealthier European tourists who, as one NAC participant put it, "were there just for the medicine."

New Psychoactives

Don Roberto and doña María have not had, as far as I know, any contact with Andean shamans, nor has there been, to my knowledge, any organized attempt to bring Andean and Amazonian shamans or healers together to discuss topics of mutual interest. Neither don Roberto nor doña María—nor, as far as I know, any other mestizo shamans in significant numbers—has shown any interest in joining any of the newly formed shaman organizations, perhaps due to the traditional individualism of these practitioners, and perhaps due to concerns about envidia, professional jealousy, and the stealing of professional secrets.

Interestingly, where interaction with Andean shamanism has occurred, it has been through the medium of huachuma—the San Pedro cactus, *Trichocereus pachanaoi*, rich in mescaline, close kin to the peyote cactus, and widely used by shamans in northern Peru.[50] This is consistent with the traditional Amazonian approach to learning: don Roberto and doña María are learning huachuma in the same way that they have learned the other healing plants—not from human teachers, but in dialogue with the plant itself.

Doña María had drunk huachuma twice when I first met her, and she drank it once more when I was with her. It was given to her by the owner of the lodge where she performed ayahuasca healing ceremonies for tourists. He in turn had learned huachuma from don Eduardo Calderón, a traditional Andean shaman who had developed a large North American clientele.[51]

"*Oh bonita!*" doña María said when I asked her about huachuma. "How wonderful!" The first time she drank it, she purged heavily, like a *paliza*, she said, like being beaten with a stick; it made her body shake and tremble and warmed her bones inside. The second time, the effect was not so drastic; it did not immobilize her. She said she had been afraid to drink huachuma, which I found remarkable from a person who had ingested such a tremendous variety of psychoactive substances; now she was eager to drink it again.

Huachuma, she told me, has much poder, power; note the use of the term *poder*, power of God, instead of *fuerza*, shamanic power. Doña María categorized huachuma as arriba, relating to heaven, in opposition to ayahuasca, which she categorized as tierra, relating to the earth. Huachuma visions are *mas espiritual*, more spiritual, she told me, than those of ayahuasca; it is *medicina de Dios*, medicine of God, a *bendición de Dios*, a blessing of God, like communion. Note here too how this opposes *el dios*, the masculine God, to la diosa, the goddess, the feminine ayahuasca. Huachuma, she told me, showed her primarily angelic spirits.

Don Roberto had drunk huachuma three times by the time I met him. He says that the vision of huachuma is very different from that of ayahuasca—it brings one less in contact with the spirits of the jungle, he says, and more in contact with santos, the saints; these santos he sees with huachuma are different from the genios, spirits, he meets with ayahuasca. With ayahuasca he meets persons; with huachuma he sees things differently. For example, one of the participants at the huachuma session turned into another person, glowing and luminous, with a long black beard. But don Roberto also understands the effect of setting on his experiences; his huachuma experience might be very different if he drank huachuma during an ayahuasca ceremony. It is, he says, an experiment to be tried.

When I drank huachuma with don Roberto and doña María, don Roberto's son Carlos, his shamanic apprentice, drank huachuma with us, for the first time; don Roberto wanted to show him what huachuma was like. Each time don Roberto drinks huachuma, he says, he learns more. The experience will have an effect on his work as a curandero; it is providing him with an additional source of fuerza, shamanic power, for his healing.

Both doña María and don Roberto are trying to incorporate this new experience into their own established cognitive sets. Doña María had a metaphysics well prepared to accommodate the experience of mescaline; it fit easily into her distinction between things that are arriba and things that are tierra. Don Roberto sees huachuma more as an additional source of his fuerza, whose diminution with age and eventual transmission to his son Carlos he is beginning to contemplate.

Gringo Tourists

The term *gringo* is not used pejoratively in Peru, as it is in, say, Mexico. The word means essentially a stranger or foreigner, not necessarily a norteamericano; to an Amazonian mestizo, someone from as exotic a place as Argentina—even someone from Lima—may be considered a gringo. Still, the term refers primarily to light-skinned foreigners of European appearance and thus, paradigmatically, to North Americans. Gringo tourists apply a great deal of pressure on mestizo shamans to produce ceremonies and interact with clients in ways consistent with their own expectations.

Both don Roberto and doña María have worked with gringo clients, most frequently ayahuasca tourists, whom they meet through Howard Lawler's El Tigre Journeys. Doña María told me gringos are pretty much the same as everyone else, except that many of them are cruzado, confused, burdened, tormented. She attributes this condition to the fact that many gringos have read about magic in books, especially while at university, yet had no maestros to give them guidance; this has left them open to *maldades*, evils, of all sorts. Thus ayahuasca tourists are conceptually assimilated to two groups—the colonizers who brought their powerful magia to the Amazon, and those mestizo and indigenous youths who are unwilling to undergo the deprivations of shamanic training and turn to books of magic instead.

Don Roberto believes that gringos tend to bring him mental problems for healing, while Peruvians bring physical problems; gringos, he says, are interested in spiritual matters, while Peruvians are seeking to heal illnesses or to gain information, such as who is sleeping with a spouse or who has cursed their business affairs. Don Roberto has treated Peruvians who are *deprimido*, depressed; but gringos come to him with *dolores inconcidos*, undiagnosed illnesses. Gringos, he says, seem primarily to have problems in their lives related to their childhood—deprivation, problems with their parents. He is astonished at the number of gringos who say that they were physically or sexually abused as children.

Other shamans who have worked with gringo clients have formed the same conception about gringos and their families. "Many of them suffer from depression," says Guillermo Arévalo, a Shipibo shaman from Puccalpa. "Many have been badly treated by their family . . . often from their fathers' behavior toward them. . . . There are other cases where women have suffered from rape trauma, caused by a father, brother, or friend." When asked how many of his clients have suffered rape trauma, he answered: "In my estimation, 80 percent among women. This causes me to think a lot about what goes on in developed countries."[52]

These are things for which the gringos have been unable to find cures at home, don Roberto says, so they come to him to receive the medicine of the plants. The plant spirits have told him to treat such illnesses as if they were susto, manchari, soul loss. Don Roberto's innovation in treating gringos is not that he creates new techniques but, rather, that he extends existing techniques to embrace new problems.

CHAPTER 32
AYAHUASCA TOURISM

CREATING THE RAIN FOREST

For five hundred years, the Amazon has been one of those "dark unruly spaces of the earth" that serve as a Rorschach test of the European imagination.[1] First, the *jungle* is "an emphatically nonparadisal space."[2] Novelist Barbara Kingsolver describes the jungle like this:

> The trees are columns of slick, brindled bark like muscular animals overgrown beyond all reason. Every space is filled with life: delicate, poisonous frogs war-painted like skeletons, clutched in copulation, secreting their precious eggs onto dripping leaves. Vines strangling their own kin in the everlasting wrestle for sunlight. The breathing of monkeys. A glide of snake belly on branch. A single-file army of ants biting a mammoth tree into uniform grains and hauling it down to the dark for their ravenous queen. And, in reply, a choir of seedlings arching their necks out of rotted tree stumps, sucking life out of death. The forest eats itself and lives forever.[3]

Every space is filled with life, she says—poisonous, ravenous, copulating, strangling, biting, sucking. Poet and naturalist Diane Ackerman speaks of the rain forest as a "world of cunning and savage trees," where she finds "a vibrant aqua-blue-and-yellow arrowhead frog" covered with poisonous mucus, "tiny but pungent with death."[4] German filmmaker Werner Herzog, who filmed both *Aguirre, the Wrath of God* and *Fitzcarraldo* in the rain forest west of Iquitos, says that the jungle is "fornication and asphyxiation and choking and fighting for survival and growing and just rotting away."[5] These are the tropes of the jungle in the European imagination: the jungle is disordered growth, unrestrained, sexual; the jungle is rank decay, cunning, savage, poisonous.

But, second, there is also another jungle in the European imagination—Edenic, virgin, a source of medicines. If the word *jungle*, with its connotations of dense impenetrability, is the key term for the savage wilderness, the word *rain forest* is the key term for the Edenic wilderness. Since the 1970s, the tropical rain forest has become the most powerful modern icon of unfallen, pristine, sacred land, acquiring ever stronger Edenic overtones, and has become increasingly synonymous with Amazonia;[6] so positive is its connotation that the adjective *rain forest* has become a marketing tool for cosmetics, theme restaurants, "ruggedly elegant outerwear," and gourmet ice cream. The rain forest is beautiful and radiant, a living cathedral enshrined in lavish coffee-table books.[7] But while the rain forest is beautiful, it is intensely vulnerable. Thus the jungle is savage and must be tamed; the rain forest is fragile and must be preserved. In either case, the land requires the intervention of European attitudes and technologies.

I do not understand any of this. My jungle survival teacher, Gerineldo Moises Chavez, taught me that the jungle is less dangerous than Lima. The jungle is filled with voracious, struggling, and triumphant life; you cannot go hungry in the jungle, Moises told me. And humans have always lived here, barefoot people happily raising babies where I had to be trained to survive.

In any current dialogue regarding tropical forests, the Amazon Basin is usually mentioned as a vital area to be left untouched and protected; yet archaeological, historical, and ecological evidence increasingly shows not only a high density of human populations in the past but also an intensively managed and constantly changing environment.[8] In much of Amazonia, it is difficult to find soils that are not studded with charcoal—clearly the result of human slash-and-burn agriculture.[9] During the early 1990s, McDonald's Corporation put out a brochure describing the company's rain forest policy, featuring a photograph of a shimmering grove, bright light slanting through tall trees, bare trunks soaring to the sky. The problem is that the photograph is not of a rain forest at all but, rather, another kind of woodland—"actually temperate conifers completely alien to the tropics."[10] A real rain forest, with parasitic lianas and epiphytes covering the trees, the canopy blocking the sky, was apparently insufficiently radiant for corporate advertising purposes.

SELLING THE NATIVE

Rain forest environmentalism sees the rain forest *native* as sharing the purity of the rain forest—closer to nature, less affected by the evils of the world, demonstrating the integrity of the unspoiled. The native of the rain forest is a monolithic figure, the keeper and companion of the plants and animals, an instrument to criticize our own civilization. That purity becomes associated with a wisdom we once had but have lost, and which we need to recover in order to rebuild what our technology has destroyed. Thus, the native is *our guide*—"our guide to nature, or our guide to the prehistoric past."[11] The wisdom of the rain forest stands ready to be reappropriated by the dominant culture.[12]

In 1982, the home furnishings department of Macy's in San Francisco had a show of primitive art from the Amazon. The display was set in a darkened area on the seventh floor, with jungle noises piped in through the sound system. Shoppers could read a brochure predicting how valuable the art would become and describing the perils faced by Macy's buyers in acquiring it. The brochure reiterates a number of themes that characterize popular attitudes toward Amazonian culture that persist today.[13]

First of all, as we might expect, the jungle is dangerous—or at least uncomfortable. It has "pesty to poisonous insects and snakes, piranha-infested waters dotted with colonies of crocodiles, unbearable heat and humidity and virtual isolation from the rest of the world. With these things in mind, the crew proceeded—carefully." Second, this dangerous jungle is filled with friendly, childlike natives. "There are twenty-three known Amazon cultures," the brochure says, incorrectly, "each one as diverse as the environment itself. But what was common to all was the warmth and excitement that greeted the crew when they arrived at the river banks. . . . The local chief would receive the travelers and then they would visit the houses to select the pottery, tools, baskets and other wares."

Moreover, these natives were innocent of commercial motives. "All of the pieces were made by traditional methods utilizing materials indigenous to the lush jungle environment. . . . Most importantly, these items were made for personal use, not commercial export, making them uniquely representative of tribal lifestyle and tradition." These pieces, the brochure repeats—the "pottery, baskets, weapons, tools, ceremonial masks and objects"—were not made for commercial purposes "but created by the Indians for their daily and ritual uses."[14]

Childlike, noncommercial—one wonders just what these Indians were *paid* for their crafts. Note the combination of tropes, designed to move merchandise: the savage wilderness braved; innocent natives eager for American consumers to possess their goods. This innocence has been projected on the Amazon Indian since the Spanish and Portuguese conquest; their indifference to commodities such as gold made them appear like children in the eyes of their conquerors.[15] As anthropologist Bernard McGrane expresses it, "The Other is inferior to the European because he is not, as the European is, capable of having a responsible relationship with the gold that surrounds him, and hence the European appropriation of it is justified. This formulation we may term the Other-as-Child."[16] The perception of the colonized culture as fundamentally childlike feeds into the fantasy of the colonial civilizing mission, which is quite self-consciously fashioned as a form of tutelage—"a disinterested project concerned with bringing the colonized to maturity."[17]

Presenting these indigenous household goods as items for American interior decoration creates what Margaret Dubin, an expert on Native American art, calls "a pervasive sense of disjuncture," a sense that these objects are out of place and unable to serve their original functions.[18] Once removed from their cultural context, Chippewa artist David Bradley says, such objects lose "their real value and their reason for existence. They are flat; they have become the possessions of collectors."[19] The stereotype of innocent natives obscures their modernity, ensures their disappearance as human subjects:[20] "Relegated to the silence of premodernity, living artists are transformed into objects, like mannequins in a museum diorama."[21]

Like the Edenic rain forest, Edenic childlike natives need our protection. It is not that our culture will corrupt theirs, as an adult might corrupt a child. Rather, they *have no culture*—they are in a *state of nature*—because their culture has been reduced to a contextless set of pan-Amazonian household goods.[22] They are the same as their environment; one is an idealized embodiment of the other; instead of a "multiplicity of worlds," complex groups and individuals with varying needs and desires, they become an endangered species.[23]

THE AYAHUASCA TOURIST

Ayahuasca tourism has brought new attention, new money, and new problems to traditional healers and their communities, and has created a market for the misrepresentation of traditional practices and the exploitation of eager and innocent tourists.[24] The marketing of ayahuasca shamanism is in many ways akin to the marketing of Amazonian household goods at Macy's—the dangerous yet pristine landscape; the spiritual natives eager for American consumers to possess their wisdom; the chance for the tourist, in imitation of the archetypal Córdova Ríos, to bring back the redemptive secrets of the Edenic rain forest, as decontextualized as an indigenous basket on a suburban wall.

A typical promotion for an ayahuasca trip to Peru promises "personal cleansing and transformation . . . a deep connection to Nature, and the opportunity for release on inner levels we may not have touched into before . . . a safe place where people can come for ceremony and healing . . . deep healing we can find in this jungle retreat."[25] Another ayahuasca tourist Web site speaks of "jungle shamanism, mysticism, and spiritual transformation through personal experience . . . transformation and personal growth . . . the mystery and transformational power of sacred traditional rituals."[26]

Key terms in such descriptions are *healing* and *transformation*. Cultural geographer Arun Saldanha has described the trance dance and drug culture he explored in Goa, India, in terms of a set of hedonistic practices—drugs, art, ritual, travel, the risky, the exotic, spiritualities borrowed from other populations—used by cultural outsiders for purposes of self-transformation. And this transformed self, he writes, is primarily a *state of mind*—consciousness, enlightenment, a liberation from modern bourgeois rationality, from the weights of home, work, school, church, aging, pain, and discipline.[27]

This description captures the rhetoric of many ayahuasca tourists: they speak of healing, spiritual growth, and transformation of all sorts—personal, planetary, psychological, and sacred transformation; ayahuasca ceremonies that are deeply, seriously, spiritually, or totally transformative.[28]

Ayahuasca tourists are primarily white, urban, relatively wealthy, well educated, and spiritually eclectic outsiders. In almost every case, the experience takes place outside the context of any long-term involvement with the struggles of the indigenous community from which the shaman comes—indeed, almost always without any involvement at all. And in almost every case, the goal is not an increased intellectual or scholarly understanding of the indigenous culture but, rather, personal spiritual growth, healing, and transformative experience. Anthropologist Michael Winkelman interviewed fifteen ayahuasca tourists in Manaus and found them to be seeking spiritual relations, personal spiritual development, personal self-awareness, emotional healing, and access to deeper levels of the self.[29]

Perhaps as important, they come to the shaman with their own set of etiological and nosological concepts, rooted primarily in popular psychology and the vocabulary of self-help. These clients come to the shamans to be transformed, to heal their inner wounds, to achieve some form of cathartic and redemptive insight. And they make related assumptions about the nature of shamans. "I thought I was going to be meeting spiritual, loving, wise shamans," lamented one such tourist in his journal, "but I haven't found any yet."[30] These concepts have two effects: they downplay the importance of the traditional shamanic interventions, such as sucking and blowing tobacco smoke; and they view ayahuasca as autonomously healing, as providing insight, cathartic realization, not unlike the empathy- or insight-producing psychotropics, the empathogens and entheogens the clients may be used to.

This concern for personal transformation over cultural understanding means that ayahuasca tourists may wind up paying for ceremonies that are far from traditional, incorporating, for example, mud baths, nude bathing, and acupuncture.[31] Anthropologist Marlene Dobkin de Ríos, one of the first investigators of ayahuasca shamanism among the mestizos in Iquitos, is particularly bitter about such transactions. She castigates both sides of what she calls an "evil and exploitative enterprise," both the "upscale, well-to-do, prominent" tourists on their never-ending search for self-actualization, and the unscrupulous practitioners who exploit them—middle-class men, she says, who "become instant traditional healers," fight among themselves, and make far too much money.[32]

On the other hand, anthropologist Luis Eduardo Luna, another early investigator of mestizo shamanism, has become a healer himself, a "neo-ayahuasquero," having founded the Wasiwaska Research Center for the Study of Psychointegrator Plants, Visionary Art, and Consciousness, located in southern Brazil. Here he provides "a secure and supportive environment for intense internal exploration," including ayahuasca sessions, holotropic breathwork, artistic expression workshops, lectures, and rain forest excursions. "I have had both mestizo and indigenous teachers," he says, "whom I now honor by doing my own work."[33]

In a wry and self-deprecating article, anthropologist Donald Joralemon discusses his reaction to the "commercialization" of traditional healer Eduardo Calderón by psychologist Alberto Villoldo, who conducts "spiritual tours" for outsiders to meet and practice with the shaman. Confronted with Calderón's embarrassing incorporation of New Age themes into his shamanic performance, Joralemon ironically writes, "I am a serious student of culture, not a two week tourist pilgrim. I know TRADITION when I see it. . . . My shaman informant never led any tour groups!"[34]

Joralemon finally takes a more nuanced view. Issues over "tradition" are *negotiable*. Calderón dealt with his local Peruvian clients in one context and with spiritual tourists in another, mediating between his own tradition and the expectations and understanding of outsiders, adapting to new social and cultural circumstances.

Still, the dilemma for traditional healers can be profound. Tourist dollars could allow shamans to support themselves while continuing to treat their community for little or nothing; but it could just as easily allow a privileged few to abandon their communities for a more affluent life in tourist towns or jungle lodges. A shaman can earn hundreds of dollars per month from shamanism students and $30 or more per person for onetime ceremonies, while others in the same area sell handicrafts for pennies. A shaman who has studied for years has to compete with tour guides who have learned to make ayahuasca, memorized enough icaros to get through a ceremony, and become, in the words of performance artist Guillermo Gómez-Peña, "a hyper-exoticized curio shop shaman for spiritual tourists."[35]

In response to accusations of selling out, one shaman said, "I am an innovator, adding to my ancestral knowledge." He says his people, the Shipibo, need to grow and change: "We can't just stay the same so that tourists can stare at the naked Indians in feathers and the anthropologists can treat us like a living museum."[36] Yet if shamans are too busy entertaining tourists to help their communities, the tradition will have become an empty commercial venture of the type condemned by Dobkin de Ríos.

One example of a successful integration of these concerns is Howard Lawler's El Tigre Journeys.[37] The organization seeks out traditional mestizo shamans and provides them with additional income for performing periodic healing ceremonies for foreign tourists. Groups are limited to twelve participants, and those who drink ayahuasca must observe traditional dietary restrictions. Participation includes trips to such ethnobotanical resources as the Alpahuayo-Mishana rain forest reserve and field station, operated by the well-respected Instituto de Investigaciones de la Amazonía Peruana. The shamans work part time and continue to serve their own communities. Ayahuasca healing sessions for tourists are also open, for free, to people who live in the local area. Especially important, ayahuasca tourism dollars are used to sponsor community development projects for nearby Bora, Yagua, and Huitoto villages —a building for a community medical clinic, a twelve-meter wooden-hulled boat and motor, a facility for a village-owned cooperative general store, and a community chicken farming project.

CHAPTER 33

AYAHUASCA AND THE LAW

THE CONTROLLED SUBSTANCES ACT

While it is apparently legal in the United States to possess the ayahuasca vine and its ß-carboline constituents, it is clearly illegal to possess DMT or any plants, such as chacruna, that contain DMT. Under Chapter 13 of the Controlled Substances Act, DMT is classified as a Schedule I drug, meaning that the Drug Enforcement Administration (DEA) has found that it has a high potential for abuse, has no currently accepted medical use in treatment in the United States, and lacks accepted safety for use under medical supervision.[1] A person who manufactures, distributes, or dispenses DMT, or possesses DMT with intent to manufacture, distribute, or dispense it, "shall be sentenced to a term of imprisonment of not more than 20 years."[2]

Both the plant chacruna and the ayahuasca drink that contains chacruna would seem to fall within the scope of this prohibition. Under the Controlled Substances Act, if DMT is a Schedule I hallucinogenic substance, then so is "any material, compound, mixture, or preparation which contains any quantity" of DMT.[3] Since chacruna and the ayahuasca drink are materials that contain some quantity of DMT, they are, by a plain reading of the statute, also Schedule I substances. Under this provision, it has generally been assumed that listing a major psychoactive component of a plant also lists the plant of which it is a part;[4] for example, the Drug Enforcement Administration notes that, in listing the active ingredient cathinone in Schedule I, any material that contains cathinone, including its source plant khat, is automatically listed along with it.[5]

CRIMINAL PROSECUTIONS IN THE UNITED STATES

The Peyote Precedents

On November 9, 1924, a Native American of the Crow Tribe named Big Sheep was charged with the crime of unlawfully having peyote in his possession.[6] The court refused to allow him to testify in his defense that he was a member in good standing of the Native American Church, or that members of that church used peyote "for sacramental purposes only in the worship of God according to their belief and interpretation of the Holy Bible, and according to the dictates of their conscience." The Supreme Court of Montana remanded the case for further proceedings at the trial level, noting that, while the Montana Constitution guaranteed the "free exercise and enjoyment of religious profession and worship," it also provided that the liberty of conscience thus secured did not "justify practices inconsistent with the good order, peace, or safety of the state, or opposed to the civil authority thereof."[7]

There was absolutely nothing remarkable about that observation. The religion clause of the First Amendment reads, "Congress shall make no law respecting an establishment of religion, or prohibiting the free exercise thereof." Yet legislatures make laws all the time that can, under some circumstances, burden the free exercise of religion—laws against murder, for example, that implicitly prohibit human sacrifice. At the time of *Big Sheep*, the leading precedent in this area was *Reynolds v. United States* (1878), in which the U.S. Supreme Court had ruled that the Mormon religious practice of polygamy was not protected by the free exercise clause of the First Amendment—indeed, that the First Amendment offered no protection to any religious act that contravened generally applicable legislation.[8] While Mormons were free to believe that polygamy was a religious duty, they just could not practice it—not because they were Mormons but because no one could practice it.

This line of reasoning continued to be the model for First Amendment free exercise jurisprudence. In *Prince v. Massachusetts* (1944), the Court held that a woman was subject to prosecution for violating the child labor laws when she brought her nine-year-old niece with her to sell religious literature on a street corner;[9] in *Braunfeld v. Brown* (1961), the Court upheld Sunday closing laws as applied to Orthodox Jewish businessmen who closed their shops on Saturday, rejecting the argument that forcing them to close their shops on a second day unduly burdened their religious practice.[10]

However, beginning in 1963, the Court signaled a new approach to First Amendment religious issues. In *Sherbert v. Verner* (1963), the Court held that a state could not simply deny unemployment compensation to a person whose unavailability for Saturday employment was religiously motivated. Rather, the state had to show a "compelling state interest" for its refusal to grant a religious exception to the regulation. The Court said that "no showing merely of a rational relationship to some colorable state interest would suffice." Only the gravest abuses, endangering "paramount interests," would allow the state substantially to infringe the free exercise of religion.[11] And the Court followed up this new approach in *Wisconsin v. Yoder* (1972), holding that the state interest in compulsory education was not sufficient to justify the state forcing Amish families, against their religious principles, to educate their children beyond the eighth grade.[12]

This new model of interpretation was first applied to peyote, by a state court, in *People v. Woody* (1964).[13] The California Supreme Court, following the 1963 decision of the U.S. Supreme Court, overturned the conviction of several Navajo members of the Native American Church for possession of peyote. The court found that the state had not met its burden of demonstrating a "compelling state interest" to justify refusing a religious exemption to its drug laws.

The effect of this case was predictable. Soon people were lined up at the courthouse doors seeking religious exemptions for drug use—the Neo-American Church, the Church of the Awakening, the Native American Church of New York, and a whole slew of criminal defendants claiming that the marijuana for which they had been arrested was for use in their religious practice.[14]

Not one of these claims for religious exemption for drug use was successful. Of all these claimants, only the Native American Church was able to establish a religious exemption to enforcement of generally applicable drug laws—and sometimes not even then. As late as 1975, an Oregon Appellate Court refused to find that the religious interests of the Native American Church outweighed legislative concern for "the health and safety of the people."[15]

Finally, in 1990, the U.S. Supreme Court slammed the door on the whole process. Alfred Smith and Galen Black had worked as counselors for a private drug rehabilitation organization. They were also both members of the Native American Church, and they were fired from their jobs because they had ingested peyote for sacramental purposes at a church ceremony. When they applied for unemployment compensation, they were determined to be ineligible for benefits because they had been discharged for work-related misconduct. Both the Oregon Court of Appeals and the Oregon Supreme Court, following then-existing U.S. Supreme Court precedent, concluded two things—first, that the religiously inspired use of peyote fell within the prohibition of the

Peyote Exemptions

After *Woody*, twenty-three states carved out exemptions for the Native American Church, both judicially and legislatively.[1] In addition, the National Conference of Commissioners on Uniform State Laws urged states adopting the Uniform Controlled Substances Act to include exemptions for the Native American Church similar to those of the federal government.[2]

Moreover, the Drug Enforcement Administration promulgated a regulation exempting "the nondrug use of peyote in bona fide religious ceremonies of the Native American Church" from the operation of the Controlled Substances Act.[3] In 1994, in light of the holding in *Employment Division v. Smith*, Congress amended the American Indian Religious Freedom Act to provide that "the use, possession, or transportation of peyote by an Indian for bona fide traditional ceremonial purposes in connection with the practice of a traditional Indian religion is lawful, and shall not be prohibited by the United States or any State."[4]

NOTES

1. For example, *State v. Whittingham*, 19 Ariz. App. 27, 504 P.2d 560 (1973), cert. denied, 417 U.S. 946 (1974); *Whitehorn v. State*, 561 P.2d 539 (Okla. Crim. App. 1977). For example, Ariz. Rev. Stat. Ann. 13-3402(B)(1)-(3)(1989); N.M. Stat. Ann. 30-31-6(D) (Supp.1989); Colo. Rev. Stat. 12-22-317(3) (1990); Mont. Rev. Codes Ann. §94-35-123 (1947); Kan. Stat. Ann. 65-4116(c)(8) (1985); Utah Code Ann. 58-37-3(3) (1986).
2. Uniform Controlled Substances Act (1994) §204, "Comment."
3. 21 CFR 1307.31 (1993).
4. 42 USC 1996a (1994).

Oregon statute, which "makes no exception for the sacramental use" of the drug; but, second, that such a prohibition was not valid under the Free Exercise Clause. Therefore, the state could not deny unemployment benefits to the respondents for having engaged in that practice.[16]

So far, so good. But the U.S. Supreme Court reversed the Oregon Supreme Court—and, although the Court struggled to deny it, itself—and held that there was simply no religious exemption from laws of general applicability: "To make an individual's obligation to obey such a law contingent upon the law's coincidence with his religious beliefs, except where the State's interest is 'compelling'—permitting him, by virtue of his beliefs, 'to become a law unto himself'—contradicts both constitutional tradition and common sense."[17]

Many commentators were surprised by what they perceived to be a sudden reversal of course by the Supreme Court.[18] There was a perception that the Court, in jettisoning the requirement that the state show a compelling interest before abridging a religious practice, had abandoned marginal and quirky religions to majoritarian tyranny, in contravention of the spirit of the First Amendment. In response, in 1993 Congress passed the Religious Freedom

Restoration Act (RFRA)—note the provocative title—which in effect enacted *Sherbert* into law.

RFRA (pronounced *refra*) prohibits government from imposing a substantial burden on a person's exercise of religion, even if the burden results from a rule of general applicability, *unless* the government can demonstrate that the burden is, first, in furtherance of a compelling governmental interest and, second, the least restrictive means of furthering that interest. RFRA's mandate applies to any branch of federal or state government, to all officials, and to anyone acting under color of law. The law is intended to apply to all federal and state law and the implementation of that law, whether statutory or otherwise and whether adopted before or after the date of RFRA's enactment.

The passage of RFRA was the legal equivalent of Congress poking a sharp stick into the Supreme Court's eye, and the Court responded accordingly. In *City of Boerne v. Flores* (1997), the Court held that RFRA was unconstitutional as applied to state and local governments.[19] The Court found that RFRA was a considerable congressional intrusion into traditional state and local prerogatives and general authority to regulate for the health and welfare of their citizens, and was not designed to identify and counteract state laws likely to be unconstitutional because of their treatment of religion. So, as of now, the protections of RFRA run against only the federal government, and do not temper the burdening of religious practices by the application of generally applicable state and local laws. If a Rastafarian is arrested for cultivating ganja in Topeka, Kansas, no matter how sincere his religious motivation may be, RFRA offers no protection.[20]

The União do Vegetal Case

The União do Vegetal (UDV) is a Brazilian new religious movement that utilizes the ayahuasca drink—which the UDV calls hoasca—in its church services. In 1999, federal agents raided the New Mexico home of a UDV church member who had three drums of ayahuasca. The officials seized the ayahuasca and threatened prosecution for possession of material prohibited by the federal Controlled Substances Act. In response, the church sued the U.S. attorney general and other federal law enforcement officials, contending that the application of the federal drug laws to the religious use of ayahuasca violated the Religious Freedom Restoration Act.

Although RFRA had been declared unconstitutional as applied to states and municipalities, it was still binding on the federal government. And the UDV was not being prosecuted under the drug laws of any state; rather, its ayahuasca had been seized by the United States, and the UDV argued that the federal government could not articulate a compelling state interest in preventing its religious use of ayahuasca. The UDV sought an injunction requiring the federal government to give the church its ayahuasca back.

The UDV had two important advantages. First, the UDV looks very much like a church of the sort with which an American court would be familiar—regularly scheduled ceremonies, a hierarchical structure, sober and orderly churchgoers, and a theology recognizably akin to that of Christianity.[21] Moreover, a formal psychiatric study introduced at trial showed significant differences between long-term members of the UDV who consumed ayahuasca at least two times a month in religious rituals and demographically matched controls who had never consumed ayahuasca—and not in the direction of dysfunction. Personality testing instruments showed UDV members to be more reflective, rigid, loyal, stoic, slow tempered, frugal, orderly, and persistent, with higher scores on measures of social desirability and emotional maturity than the controls. The ayahuasca-using participants also differed from the controls in being more confident, relaxed, optimistic, carefree, uninhibited, outgoing, and energetic, with higher scores on traits of hyperthymia, cheerfulness, stubbornness, and overconfidence. Significantly, on neuropsychological testing the UDV group demonstrated significantly *higher* scores on measures of concentration and short-term memory, despite the fact that many ayahuasca users reported significant psychiatric and substance abuse histories prior to their church membership.[22]

Now, there are certainly some problems with this study. UDV worship is a structured and stable environment. Participants remain seated, with long periods of silence during which they seek self-knowledge through mental concentration, aided by ayahuasca.[23] The ayahuasca-using participants had to have been members of UDV for at least ten years, with at least twice-monthly—that is, highly regular—attendance at these services. Thus, the ayahuasca users may have been preselected for personality traits of stability, persistence, and orderliness; self-reports of prior mental health problems by church converts may be viewed with some level of skepticism. Moreover, while subjects and controls were matched for age, ethnicity, marital status, and level of education, there was apparently no attempt made to control for regular churchgoing, a measure on which the ayahuasca users were preselected for perfect scores and which may well be correlated with personality traits for which they also scored high. Still, the study certainly gave no grounds to believe that long-term UDV church membership, along with concomitant twice-monthly drinking of ayahuasca, had caused any personality or cognitive detriment to its members.

Back in the Trial Court

So the parties are back before Judge James A. Parker in the U.S. District Court in New Mexico. The preliminary injunction issued by Judge Parker in 2002—having been first stayed by the Tenth Circuit and then upheld by the Tenth Circuit and the Supreme Court—is, for now, effectively the charter under which the União do Vegetal (UDV) may import and use the ayahuasca drink.[1] That preliminary injunction incorporated, at the request of the government, and after lengthy negotiations, thirty-six conditions intended to prevent the diversion of the ayahuasca drink to illegal nonreligious uses, and thus gave the government a significant role in regulating its importation; for example, while the government cannot limit the amount of ayahuasca imported, the Drug Enforcement Administration (DEA) can require the UDV to supply the social security numbers of anyone handling the ayahuasca drink outside of religious ceremonies.[2]

The government now argues that the Supreme Court decided just one thing—that the UDV has the legal right to import and distribute a Class I controlled substance, subject to all the pertinent DEA regulations and licensing requirements, unless and until the DEA grants a discretionary exemption. The UDV challenges any such government oversight, claiming that it unduly burdens its religious practices in violation of the Religious Freedom Restoration Act. The government says that the New Mexico court has no jurisdiction to hear that challenge because the UDV has failed to apply for an administrative waiver from those regulations under 21 C.F.R. §1307.3, the denial of which must be appealed to the D.C. Court of Appeals—and, indeed, is arguing against regulations that have not yet even been imposed.[3]

Presumably the district court wants to work out a reasonable and workable set of rules, involving record keeping, secure storage, and limitations on distribution, balancing government concerns over against the UDV's claim that its religious practice is unduly burdened by intrusive government supervision. Indeed, the Tenth Circuit has already noted two things. First, religious accommodations should avoid "burdensome and constant official supervision and management."[4] Second, in this case, "extensive judicial and administrative oversight" of the handling and use of the ayahuasca drink would likely be necessary to allow the UDV to practice its religion "while respecting the public interest in preventing the diversion of DMT and protecting the public health and safety."[5] The tension between these two statements remains unaddressed.

On March 8, 2009, U.S. District Judge Owen M. Panner followed the UDV precedent in finding that the Religious Freedom Restoration Act protects the use of ayahuasca as a sacrament by two Santo Daime churches in Oregon. Judge Panner entered a permanent injunction barring the government from penalizing the church for its ayahuasca use, and setting forth rules regarding importation, storage, and record keeping. The court specifically enjoined the government from requiring the churches "to conform their conduct to any regulations except as set forth" in the injunction itself. As of this writing, it is unknown whether the government will appeal.[6]

NOTES

1. *O Centro Espirita Beneficiente Uniao do Vegetal v. Ashcroft*, 314 F.3d 463 (10th Cir. 2002, emergency motion for stay pending appeal); *O Centro Espirita Beneficiente*

Uniao do Vegetal v. Ashcroft, 389 F.3d 973 (10th Cir. 2004, rehearing en banc), p. 976; *Gonzales v. O Centro Espirita Beneficente Uniao do Vegetal*, 546 U.S. 418 (2006).

2. *O Centro Espirita Beneficiente Uniao do Vegetal v. Ashcroft* (2002), p. 467.
3. *O Centro Espirita Beneficiente União do Vegetal v. Mukasey*, CIV. No. 00–1647 JP/RLP, Defendants' Motion to Dismiss (D. N. M. November 21, 2007), pp. 10–28; *O Centro Espirita Beneficiente União do Vegetal v. Mukasey*, CIV. No. 00–1647 JP/RLP, Plaintiffs' Response to Defendants' Motion to Dismiss (D. N. M. February 22, 2008); *O Centro Espirita Beneficiente União do Vegetal v. Mukasey*, CIV. No. 00–1647 JP/RLP, slip op. (D. N. M. June 19, 2008, order denying defendant's motion to dismiss Count 1), pp. 3–4.
4. Olsen v. DEA, 878 F.2d 1458 (D.C. Cir. 1989), pp. 1462–1463; *O Centro Espirita Beneficiente Uniao do Vegetal v. Ashcroft* (2002), p. 467.
5. *O Centro Espirita Beneficiente Uniao do Vegetal v. Ashcroft* (2002), p. 467.
6. *Church of the Holy Light of the Queen v. Mukasey*, No. CV 08-3095-PA, Slip op. (D. Or. March 9, 2009).

The second advantage was arguably even more important than the first. The president of the UDV in the United States was Jeffrey Bronfman, who is, unfortunately for the government, an heir to the Seagram's whiskey fortune and second cousin to the profoundly well-connected Edgar Bronfman Jr., chairman and CEO of Warner Music, among other things. Jeffrey Bronfman had the commitment and the resources to fight the seizure all the way to the U.S. Supreme Court.

And to the Supreme Court the case duly went, after both the trial court and the U.S. Court of Appeals for the Tenth Circuit handed victories to the UDV, first by issuing a preliminary injunction against the U.S. attorney general, the DEA, and other government agencies, requiring them to return the ayahuasca that had been seized from the group, and then by upholding the issuance of the injunction.[24] On February 21, 2006, in a unanimous ruling, Justice John G. Roberts Jr. affirmed the trial court's preliminary injunction preventing the federal government from enforcing a ban on the UDV's sacramental use of ayahuasca.[25] The Court held that the government had simply failed to demonstrate a compelling state interest in preventing the 130 or so American members of the UDV from practicing their religion: "Congress has determined that courts should strike sensible balances, pursuant to a compelling interest test that requires the Government to address the particular practice at issue. Applying that test, we conclude that the courts below did not err in determining that the Government failed to demonstrate, at the preliminary injunction stage, a compelling interest in barring the UDV's sacramental use of hoasca."[26]

Of course, the case is not over. All that has been litigated is the propriety of the initial preliminary injunction. There may yet be a trial, although the chances of an ultimate government victory over the UDV appear to be slim.

The Saga of Alan Shoemaker

On April 20, 2001, the Peruvian Air Force, working with the U.S. Drug Enforcement Administration, shot down a small missionary plane in the Peruvian Amazon, seriously injuring the pilot and killing the wife and newly adopted daughter of one of the missionaries, apparently because the plane was mistakenly believed to be carrying drugs. A report issued jointly by the United States and Peru, apparently as part of a CIA cover-up, put most of the blame on the plane's pilot, who allegedly had not filed a flight plan, a claim denied by the evangelical organization for which he worked.[27] The report also suggested that language problems—between the CIA-contract pilots of the surveillance plane that initially targeted the missionary plane as a drug courier and the Peruvians aboard the jet that did the actual shooting—contributed to the tragedy that left two Americans dead and the pilot seriously wounded. A highly skeptical analysis of the joint report, datelined October 24, 2001, appeared in the December 1, 2001, edition of the online activist newsletter *Narco News*, written by Peter Gorman, a former *High Times* editor-in-chief who had traveled in Peru for more than two decades as a journalist and consultant to the Museum of Natural History in New York. The report contained photographs of the bullet-riddled missionary plane, including close-ups of the smashed cockpit, taken by Alan Shoemaker.[28]

It is tempting to guess that the DEA and Shoemaker were not—and had not been for some time—strangers to each other. In October 1996, Shoemaker spent three days in the Gayabamba jail in Iquitos, pursuant to a formal government complaint that he was manufacturing and distributing ayahuasca contrary to the public health.[29] Such an action is astonishing, as there is nothing even remotely illegal about ayahuasca in Peru. But in Iquitos, it is not difficult to file a denuncio with the police, and the mere filing of such a complaint is enough to get the accused tossed in jail until he is able to extricate himself. It must be remembered that the DEA has a powerful presence in Iquitos, including a huge guarded complex outside the city, bristling with microwave towers. Clearly, someone—someone with connections—was sending Shoemaker a message.

Shoemaker had come to Iquitos in 1993, after studying huachuma and ayahuasca healing in Ecuador. In a 1996 magazine interview, he spoke of living a "magical life" and related how, in an ayahuasca vision, he had learned how to cure his mother of her liver cancer.[30] In Iquitos he met and married Mariella Noriega, a Peruvian national who, in 1998, started a company named Chinchilejo, Dragonfly, licensed to export plant materials from Peru. On January 29, 2001, Chinchilejo became the first and only Peruvian plant exporter to have a shipment seized by the DEA. The seizure was made after delivery was completed to Shoemaker's son by a previous marriage, who lived in Clarkston, Georgia, just outside of Atlanta, and who said that he was starting a wholesale plant business. The shipment, which had been exported with all the necessary Peruvian and international paperwork, consisted of 660 pounds of ayahuasca vine and 220 pounds of chacruna, seized on the grounds that the chacruna leaves contained DMT, a Schedule I controlled substance.[31]

Following this seizure, during the period approximately from May through July 2001, Shoemaker's wife undertook to charter a church in Iquitos, under the name Soga del Alma, Vine of the Soul, a Spanish translation of the word *ayahuasca*. Although Shoemaker has denied this, it is a good guess that one of the primary purposes of doing so was apparently to be able to invoke the legal protections of the Religious Freedom Restoration Act in the United States—the same act that the U.S. Supreme Court would later hold protected the UDV from seizure of its ayahuasca.

This development was greeted with great interest in the online Ayahuasca Forum, where Noriega solicited memberships and donations. Many of her statements seem calculated to give the church a sort of retrospective validity—that is, to demonstrate its existence, if not its name, prior to the date of the seizure. "Soga del Alma," she wrote, "is merely a formalization of the religion that has been in existence in the Amazon since the rubber tappers learned it from the indigenous, about 100 years ago. The ceremonies they have held since that time have remained the same. There has never been any formal name applied to these ceremonies which have always been very spiritual and healing. The act of registering it is something that should have been done years ago, but was not."[32]

Within a few days she was promising to provide application papers for forum members, whose names would then be entered in an official book in Peru and who would receive, in return, official certificates confirming membership in the church—perhaps, she said, even a smaller wallet-sized card as well.[33] And she repeats: Soga del Alma "is really only the formalization of the religion of the ayahuasqueros who have been holding sessions every Tuesday and Friday nights for the last 100 years."[34] Donations, however, were apparently slow in coming, and by the next year, Soga del Alma seems to have been a church without structure, governance, doctrine, congregations, ordinations, ministry, or membership—in brief, nothing that would make a U.S. judge or jury think Soga del Alma was a *religion*, rather than, say, a ragtag bunch of hippies seeking to evade the drug laws.

No arrests were made at the time of the seizure. Peter Gorman claims to have spoken to the DEA agent in charge of the airport where the confiscated plants were being stored. Gorman says that the agent in charge stated that the plants would be placed in a damp place in the airport where they would rot, and that Shoemaker would then have the option of fighting the seizure—which would have cost more than the plants were worth—or watching them putrefy. Gorman claims to have recorded this conversation.[35]

Then, on April 1, 2002, when Shoemaker flew from Iquitos to Miami to see his dying mother, he was picked up at Miami International Airport and told a sealed indictment had been handed down on January 22, 2002. Shoemaker was charged with intent to distribute a Schedule I controlled substance, along with a number of lesser charges. The primary charge carried a potential penalty of up to twenty years in federal prison. Shoemaker's lawyer at the time, Page Pate of Atlanta, said his client planned to use the ayahuasca drink made from the two plants—all 880 pounds of them—solely in religious ceremonies.[36]

Shoemaker was held in prison for fifty-nine days—one month in federal lockup in Miami before being transferred to hard-core lockdown in Atlanta for a month—then released on a $50,000 cash bond, with the stipulation that he wear an electronic ankle bracelet and remain at his late mother's home in Elizabethton, Tennessee, until the case was concluded. His wife and two children remained in Iquitos. Shoemaker's lawyer said, "This is an unwarranted extension of the so-called war on drugs to a substance that has no use as a recreational drug and doesn't pose any real threat or danger to American society. Government resources could be best used elsewhere." U.S. Attorney Bill Duffey stood by the charges. "This is a very dangerous hallucinogen," he said. "We will do whatever we can to keep it out of our district and prosecute anyone who tries to bring it in."[37] Meanwhile, on August 12, 2002, Judge James Parker of the U.S. District Court for the District of New Mexico ruled that the use of ayahuasca by the UDV was likely protected under RFRA and issued a preliminary injunction against the U.S. attorney general, the DEA, and other government agencies, requiring them to return ayahuasca that had been seized from the group in May 1999.[38] On September 4, 2003, a three-judge panel of the Tenth U.S. Circuit Court of Appeals in Denver upheld the issuance of the injunction.[39]

There are two important features of this case that make it different from the UDV case. First, Shoemaker—who had been described by one Peruvian journalist as "someone who seems to have been torn from the pages of a Henry Miller novel"—had few resources to finance his litigation;[40] and second, unlike UDV, he had no institutional structure to back up a claim to religious exemption under RFRA. Perhaps for that reason, Shoemaker, despite his wife's attempts to create a church identity, did not claim religious exemption from the drug laws, even though the defense was available.

Rather, he claimed that while DMT was a Schedule I controlled substance, the naturally occurring chacruna—as opposed to synthetic DMT—was not intended to be included under the Controlled Substances Act and was, therefore, legal. The same argument had already been rejected by Judge Parker in the União do Vegetal case in New Mexico.[41] On October 23, 2002, U.S. Magistrate Judge Alan Baverman declined to dismiss the indictment. The magistrate judge found that the Controlled Substances Act, while not specifying the vines or leaves as illegal substances, covers "any material" that contains DMT. The case was bound over for trial.

For reasons that are not clear, Shoemaker retained a different lawyer, Mark Sallee. On April 1, 2003, the magistrate judge granted Shoemaker's motion, unopposed by the government, to modify the special conditions of his bond, eliminating the electronic monitoring and the travel restrictions. Shoemaker claims that he had the full permission of the government to return to Peru—that, in the presence of Peter Gorman, he telephoned unspecified government officials on the day of his departure to confirm his understanding that he was free to leave the country.[42] And leave it he did, departing forthwith to rejoin his wife and children in Iquitos.

Then, on July 16, 2003, the magistrate judge scheduled a bond revocation hearing for the next week, at which Shoemaker would have to appear, explain why he had fled to Peru, and show cause why his bond should not be revoked; revocation of his bond would mean being remanded to jail to await trial. Shoemaker says that he was given just four days' notice and could find no way to return to the United States in time for the hearing. It is not at all clear to me why Shoemaker's attorney, Mark Sallee, was unable to obtain a one-week continuance of the hearing in order that his client might appear. To the suspicious mind, it might seem that these events were orchestrated for one purpose—to get Shoemaker out of the United States and then keep him out.

When Shoemaker failed to appear at the July 23 bond revocation hearing, the magistrate judge issued a bench warrant for his arrest. Shoemaker had now officially become a fugitive—a status he claims was the result of government action, not his own. "I did not declare myself a fugitive, they did," he says. "Do I want to be a fugitive? No. Did I ask to be a fugitive? No."[43] The offense with which Shoemaker is charged in the United States is not an extraditable offense in Peru. He is safe as long as he does not return to the United States.

Shoemaker is now quite publicly back in Iquitos with his wife and children. On July 9–15, 2005, he sponsored an international conference on ayahuasca in Iquitos, attended by such heavyweights as Dennis McKenna, Eduardo Luna, and Benny Shanon, as well as a number of indigenous curanderos. The event has continued, quite successfully, each year since. He has a lawyer looking into "certifying" Soga del Alma as a religion, with chapels all over the world—just like the União do Vegetal.[44] He has apparently learned this lesson: if you want an exemption under RFRA for the religious use of psychotropic plants, it is best to look as much as possible like an Episcopalian.

Why was Shoemaker prosecuted? There is no doubt that it was due in part to the size of the shipment; 880 pounds of plants—even 220 pounds of a plant containing a Schedule I controlled substance—may have been just too big to ignore. Interestingly, Shoemaker states, "The only thing that I have done was to take photos of the downed missionary plane."[45] Although the pictures were taken after the seizure, it is hard to believe that it was the first provocative act he had taken against the DEA. In fact, Shoemaker later wrote, "I am in my situation not because my wife shipped plants to my son in Atlanta. I am in this situation because Peter [Gorman] and I stood up for what we believe to be the real United States and put our face into those that were hired under misleading and false corporations to run amok on the Putamayo."[46]

CRIMINAL PROSECUTIONS IN OTHER COUNTRIES

Like the União do Vegetal in the United States, Brazilian new religious movements have achieved some legal success against criminalization in other countries. In 1985, Brazil's Federal Narcotics Council, Conselho Federal de Entorpecentes (CONFEN), and the Medicine Division of the Ministry of Health, Divisão de Medicamentos, apparently under pressure from the United States, made the ayahuasca drink illegal by placing it on the list of prohibited narcotics. The União do Vegetal brought a legal challenge against the new law, and CONFEN conducted two studies, in 1987 and 1988, investigating the use and effects of ayahuasca at the ceremonies in these churches, including drinking it themselves, and ultimately recommended that it be removed from the list of controlled substances. In June 1992, the Brazilian government declared that the use of ayahuasca for religious purposes had caused no social disruption and would not be prohibited.[47]

In early October 1999, police raids in several European countries resulted in the seizure of ayahuasca from members of the Santo Daime. In Amsterdam, the police raided a Santo Daime ceremony, confiscated the ayahuasca, and charged the group leader, Geerdina Fijneman, with conspiracy to distribute DMT, a Class I dangerous drug.[48] This raid on a church during a ceremony caused outrage and demonstrations in favor of legalization. The public prosecutor apparently offered to drop the charges, but Santo Daime's lawyer, Adele van der Plas, pushed for a trial, in order to obtain a clear judicial ruling on the legality of the church's ayahuasca use.

The case came to trial in May 2001. The church argued that the use of ayahuasca was fundamental to its religious practice, and that its right to religious freedom under Article 9 of the European Convention on Human Rights and Fundamental Liberties outweighed any potential threat to public health from the use of ayahuasca in the Santo Daime church. The court agreed. Prohibiting the defendant from receiving the most important sacrament of her religion, the court stated, "constitutes such a serious infrin\gement of her religious freedom that this infringement cannot be regarded as necessary in a democratic society." Based on the evidence presented that there are no appreciable health risks involved in the ritual use of ayahuasca, "greater weight should be attached to the protection of religious freedom." The court declared that the charges were not punishable, and acquitted the defendant.[49]

In Paris, the police similarly raided a Santo Daime church, jailed the leaders for three weeks, reportedly tapped the telephones of church members, and charged the association with embezzling as well as drug trafficking.[50] In Paris, few people heard of the Santo Daime arrests, and apparently few cared; there were no demonstrations. In January 2004, the six defendants were found guilty, variously, of illegally acquiring, possessing, and importing narcotics, and were given suspended sentences to terms in prison varying from four to ten months.[51]

In January 2005, these convictions were overturned by the court of appeals. The court noted that no regulation specifically listed ayahuasca as prohibited. The court further noted that the penal code and the health code prohibited "poisonous plants, substances, and preparations." The court took the term *substance* to mean a pure chemical substance, such as DMT, and the term *preparation* to refer to the pharmaceutical operation of mixing or dissolving such pure substances. Although the ayahuasca drink undoubtedly contained DMT, which is prohibited, the DMT did not get there by a process of *préparation*, as required by law, but, rather, by way of *décoction*, *infusion*, or *macération*. Such operations, the court said, cannot produce a *substance*, since the results are not homogeneous, and the components can still be isolated—for example, by chromatography—and extracted. Based on this reasoning, the court dismissed all charges against the defendants, and ordered the state to return the confiscated ayahuasca.[52]

But like many such technical victories based on statutory language, this one was Pyrrhic for the Santo Daime church. On May 3, 2005, just four months after the acquittal, the director general for health promulgated an order amending the list of substances classified as narcotics specifically to include not only *Banisteriopsis caapi*, *Psychotria viridis*, and *Diplopterys cabrerana* but also harmine, harmaline, and tetrahydroharmaline—in other words, just about every possible ingredient of the ayahuasca drink.[53]

THE UNITED NATIONS CONVENTION

In 1980, the United States ratified the U.N. Convention on Psychotropic Substances, in support of an international effort "to prevent and combat abuse of [psychotropic] substances and the illicit traffic to which it gives rise."[54] Very much like the Controlled Substances Act, the convention classifies substances according to their degree of safety and medical usefulness, with DMT in Schedule I, representing substances that are considered particularly unsafe and lacking any medical use.[55] Parties to the convention—more than 160 nations in all—must, under Article 7(a), prohibit "all use except for scientific and very limited medical purposes," with the following provision under Article 32(4): "A State on whose territory plants are growing wild which contain psychotropic substances from among those in Schedule I and which are traditionally used by certain small, clearly determined groups in magical or religious rites may, at the time of signature, ratification, or accession, make reservations concerning these plants, in respect of the provisions of article 7, except for provisions relating to international trade." Under this provision, the United States made a reservation for religious use of peyote by the Native American Church, and Peru made a reservation for the use of DMT "by certain Amazon ethnic groups in magical and religious rites and in rites of initiation into adulthood."[56] Neither the United States nor Brazil ever made a reservation for DMT.

Also like the Controlled Substances Act, the convention provides that "a preparation is subject to the same measures of control as the psychotropic substance which it contains" and defines *preparation* as "any solution or mixture, in whatever physical state, containing one or more psychotropic substances."[57]

Such international treaties are recognized by the Constitution as being the law of the land.[58] But treaties have no greater or lesser impact than other federal laws;[59] and where the provisions of a treaty, such as the convention, conflict with the provisions of a statute passed subsequent to the treaty, such as RFRA, the Supreme Court has held that the statute, to the extent of the conflict, supersedes the treaty.[60] Pursuant to the Psychotropic Substances Act of 1978, the United States implements its international drug-control treaty obligations, including the convention, through the Controlled Substances Act.[61]

In a drug prosecution in the United States, therefore, reference to the convention would appear to be superfluous. However, RFRA requires that courts strike a "sensible balance" between religious practices and compelling government interests.[62] In the União do Vegetal case, the government asserted three such compelling interests—health risks to members of the UDV, potential for diversion to nonreligious use, and adherence "to an important international treaty obligation" under Article 7(a).[63] It is on the basis of this last purported government interest that it becomes important to determine whether the ayahuasca drink, or the chacruna leaves from which it is made, falls within the scope of the convention.

That question has only partially been answered. The Supreme Court has unambiguously ruled that the ayahuasca drink is a solution or mixture of DMT under Article 1(f)(i) of the convention and therefore, under Article 3(1), is subject to the same measures of control as DMT itself.[64] But as the Court pointed out, the fact that the ayahuasca drink is covered by the convention does not automatically mean that the government has demonstrated a compelling interest in prohibiting the religious use of ayahuasca by a group such as the UDV.[65] In the União do Vegetal case, the government had failed to show at trial any compelling state interest in meeting its international obligations by complying with the convention—and, the Supreme Court said, had failed even to submit evidence concerning the international consequences of allowing the UDV to drink ayahuasca in its ceremonies.[66] So the question remains open as to whether, in some future case, the government can establish a sufficiently compelling interest in meeting its international obligations under the convention to overcome the demands of RFRA.

It is worth remembering that the convention itself seems to stake out room for claims of religious exemption. In Article 22(1)(a), it provides that each party shall treat any intentional offense as a punishable act "subject to its constitutional limitations" and, in Article 22(5), that such offences "shall be defined, prosecuted and punished in conformity with the domestic law" of the country involved. At first glance, this would certainly seem to include RFRA. The Supreme Court has so far declined to rule on this issue.[67]

The Court also asserted no opinion as to whether the *plants* from which the drink is made are covered by the convention—an issue to which we now turn.[68]

THE STATUS OF NATURAL HALLUCINOGENS IN THE UNITED STATES

Small quantities of chacruna, both live plants and dried leaves, in fifty-gram or two-ounce packets, are readily available on the Internet; and one occasionally hears claims that while possession or sale of DMT may be a felony, the Controlled Substances Act prohibits only synthetic DMT and not the DMT occurring naturally in plants, such as chacruna, or even in plant preparations, such as the ayahuasca drink—that it is in fact *legal* to possess plants containing DMT. The argument basically states that if Congress had wanted to ban such natural DMT, it would have done so, just as it explicitly banned both the plant peyote and the chemical mescaline.[69]

This claim has achieved the status of folklore but has not prevailed, as far as I have been able to ascertain, in any U.S. ayahuasca prosecution. Courts have had little difficulty in finding that the statutory regulation of "any material, compound, mixture, or preparation which contains any quantity" of DMT has a plain meaning that embraces both chacruna and the ayahuasca drink.[70] "When Congress speaks clearly," said Magistrate Judge Alan J. Baverman, rejecting the claim that the chacruna imported by Alan Shoemaker was not covered by the Controlled Substances Act, "the court must follow what Congress has stated."[71] Chief Judge James A. Parker, rejecting similar claims by the União do Vegetal, said that "the plain language of the CSA [Controlled Substances Act] clearly indicates that the statute's prohibition on DMT extends to" the ayahuasca drink, which is therefore "an illegal substance under the CSA."[72]

The claim that DMT-containing plants are not illegal is frequently buttressed by two documents. The first is a *Commentary on the Convention on Psychotropic Substances*, published by the United Nations and written by Adolf Lande, who served for many years as secretary of two international drug organizations, the Permanent Central Narcotics Board and the Drug Supervisory Body.[73] This commentary notes that the convention does not list any natural hallucinogenic materials, such as plants, in Schedule I, and comments that "plants as such are not, and it is submitted are also not likely to be, listed in Schedule I, but only some products obtained from plants."[74] This is because "the inclusion in Schedule I of the active principle of a substance does not mean that the substance itself is also included therein if it is a substance clearly distinct from the substance constituting its active principle."[75] Presumably plants are substances sufficiently distinct from their active principles to be excluded from regulation. This is, of course, precisely the opposite of the common reading of the Controlled Substances Act.[76]

More than that, the commentary seems to assume that simple preparations made from plants containing hallucinogenic substances are not regulated by the convention either. The commentary notes that "neither . . . the roots of the plant *Mimosa hostilis* nor *Psilocybe* mushrooms themselves are included in Schedule I, but only their respective active principles."[77] In two footnotes, the commentary then observes that "an infusion of roots" is used to consume *Mimosa hostilis* and that "beverages" are used to consume *Psilocybe* mushrooms.[78] One may infer that such infusions or beverages are as distinct from their active principles as were the roots or mushrooms from which they were made.[79]

The second document is a letter from Herbert Schaepe, secretary of the International Narcotics Control Board (INCB), the group responsible for enforcement of the convention, which was solicited by the prosecutor and submitted to the Dutch court in the Fijneman case. This document makes explicit what the commentary implies, stating, "No plants (natural materials) containing DMT are at present controlled under the 1971 Convention on Psychotropic Substances. Consequently, preparations (e.g., decoctions) made of these plants, including ayahuasca, are not under international control and, therefore, not subject to any of the articles of the 1971 Convention."[80]

Of course, the impact of these documents is doubly indirect. Neither is likely to persuade an American court to ignore the plain language of the Controlled Substances Act. And even if the two documents correctly state the intent of the convention, there is no reason why the United States may not regulate natural plant hallucinogens that the convention leaves unregulated. The question they raise, rather, is whether natural plant hallucinogens fall within the embrace of the convention such that the government can claim—in addition to other compelling interests—a compelling interest in enforcing their regulation under its treaty obligations.

Based on the reasoning of the commentary, Judge James A. Parker originally ruled in the União do Vegetal case that the ayahuasca drink does not fall within the embrace of the convention. The court reasoned that the ayahuasca drink, like the plants from which it is made, is sufficiently distinct from DMT to fall outside the treaty—a position then strongly rejected by both the Court of Appeals and the Supreme Court.[81]

Apart from this rejection by two appellate courts, there are questions about the legal force of both these documents in an American courtroom. First, they appear facially inconsistent with the language of the convention, which at least contemplates that natural substances may be regulated, by defining *psychotropic substance* as "any substance, natural or synthetic, or any *natural material* in Schedule I, II, III or IV."[82] Moreover, Article 32(4) allows states to make a reservation for the religious use of "plants growing wild which contain psychotropic substances from Schedule I." The fact that a specific reservation must be made to *exclude* such plants indicates that they are otherwise included.[83]

In addition, Judge Michael R. Murphy of the U.S. Court of Appeals for the Tenth Circuit has noted that the commentary was drafted by a single author, was published five years after the convention was negotiated, and is ambiguous on whether the ayahuasca drink—as opposed to the chacruna from which it is made—is prohibited by the convention.[84] Because the commentary was not written by the negotiators or signatories to the convention, it would not seem to be the sort of negotiating and drafting history, or postratification understanding of the parties, upon which courts traditionally rely in interpreting an agreement.[85]

Similar issues arise for the Schaepe letter. The secretary is not a voting member of the International Narcotics Control Board, and it is therefore not clear whether the letter expresses the opinion of the board or the personal opinion of its secretary. Indeed, it is apparently not up to the INCB, as an enforcement agency, to decide what substances are or are not controlled under the convention. On such grounds, Judge Murphy has pointed to "serious questions as to the relevance of the Secretary's opinion" regarding whether the ayahuasca drink is covered by the convention.[86] Even the Dutch court to which the letter was originally proffered refused to consider it, "because it is not implied by the Convention that the interpretation of the Convention by the United Nations International Narcotics Control Board must be regarded as official and binding."[87] While the interpretation of an international treaty by the agency charged with its negotiation and enforcement is usually given great deference by the courts, that agency in the United States is the State Department, not the INCB.[88]

Although the Supreme Court has clearly ruled that the ayahuasca drink is covered by the convention, the Court left unresolved the issue of *unmodified* natural plant hallucinogens, such as the chacruna leaves for which Alan Shoemaker was arrested. The commentary, the Court held, was irrelevant to the case before it, since what was at issue was the ayahuasca drink, not the chacruna leaves from which it was made. "To the extent the commentary suggests plants themselves are not covered by the Convention," the Court stated, "that is of no moment—the UDV seeks to import and use a tea brewed from plants, not the plants themselves, and the tea plainly qualifies as a 'preparation' under the Convention."[89] The question awaits resolution.

NATIONAL CULTURAL HERITAGE

Another recent development may have legal implications. On June 24, 2008, the Peruvian National Institute of Culture declared that indigenous ayahuasca rituals—"one of the fundamental pillars of the identity of Amazonian peoples"—are part of the national cultural heritage of Peru and are to be protected, in order to ensure their cultural continuity. The declaration was then published on July 12, 2008, in the *Boletin de Normas Legales*, Bulletin of Legal Regulations, the official government journal.[90] The National Institute of Culture is charged by statute with recording, publishing, and protecting the Peruvian national cultural heritage.

Ayahuasca, the institute says, is "a plant species with an extraordinary cultural history, by virtue of its psychotropic qualities and its use as a drink combined with the plant known as chacruna." This plant, the institute continues, "is known to the indigenous Amazonian world as a wise or teaching plant, which shows to initiates the very foundations of the world and its components. The effect of its consumption is to enter into the spiritual world and its secrets."[91]

But note that it was not the ayahuasca vine itself that was declared a national heritage but, rather, its *traditional knowledge and uses*. The declaration specifically distinguishes the effects of ayahuasca from those of other hallucinogens, due in part to "the ritual which accompanies its consumption, which leads to a variety of effects which are always within culturally defined limits, and with religious, therapeutic, and culturally affirmative intentions." Although the declaration vindicates the spiritual nature of the ayahuasca experience, it does so solely within the context of its role in traditional indigenous rituals. Strikingly, the resolution explicitly differentiates the traditional use and sacred character of indigenous ayahuasca rituals from "decontextualized, consumerist, and commercial western uses."[92]

CHAPTER 34
SHAMANS FIGHT BACK

SORCERY AS POLITICAL RESISTANCE

Napo Runa Indians who regularly go to work for the oil companies often have themselves cleansed with tobacco smoke by a shaman when they return to their villages. They are having themselves healed of wage labor; they are being cleansed of capitalism.[1] This is a small act of cultural resistance, affirming the validity of their traditional values over against those of their white employers.

Shamans are the knowledge-bearers of their cultures, repositories of myths, symbols, and values. The shaman thus embodies a cultural tradition, and may function as a catalyst for cultural resistance against oppression and assimilation.[2]

This should not be surprising. Shamanic power is involved in all community affairs; it is therefore inevitably involved in aggression, warfare, and the struggle for political and economic power.[3] Dark shamanism and assault sorcery especially have been viewed as acts of political resistance and thus as, essentially, acts of cultural healing. A dominant strand in the interpretation of South American shamanism has viewed it as resistance against the brutalities of colonialism, as an indigenous struggle for autonomy in the face of state control, and as a discourse about modernity—gun violence, slave trading, debt peonage, missionaries, epidemic disease, "the white man's materiality and spirituality."[4] Sorcery—like all shamanism—is political.

In this view, shamans play a role in resisting, ameliorating, and influencing the course of colonial contacts and history; they become the source and symbol of an indigenous culture capable of defending itself against colonial power and the national state.[5] As one Putumayo shaman reportedly told anthropologist Michael Taussig, "I have been teaching people revolution through my work with plants."[6] And the resistance can be more direct.

Sorcery, as a weapon of the weak, may be turned against the colonial oppressor just as it may be used to enforce internal norms of sharing and generosity.[7] It can function as a form of direct resistance—poisoning, killing, subverting the authority of colonial or oppressive powers. An example of such sorcery in the Guyanese Amazon is *canaima*;[8] in fact, it was the investigation of canaima by Neil Whitehead, a University of Wisconsin–Madison professor of anthropology, that initiated the current interest in what has been called dark shamanism and especially the view of assault sorcery as, in some sense, socially integrating and as a vehicle of resistance to political and colonial oppression.[9]

Among many indigenous peoples of the Guyanese Amazon, the term *canaima* refers both to a mode of ritual killing and to its practitioners, a form of dark shamanism involving the horrific mutilation and lingering death of its victim, who becomes, after death, the shaman's food. Whitehead places both the belief and the practice at the beginning of the nineteenth century, "as a defensive magico-military technique to ward off the new and overwhelming gun violence and slave trading"—a form of dialogue with and about colonizing modernity that continues to serve a variety of cultural purposes.[10] The *targets* of this dark shamanism are the wealthy and powerful generally, but also, in particular, avaricious whites and those who through contact with whites have acquired an unusual wealth of trade goods, by selling rubber or working in the mining areas.[11] A canaima practitioner can be recognized in part by his refusal to use Western-style clothing, matches, metal cooking pots, or guns.[12]

But such resistance may also involve multiple levels of *irony*. The colonizer, as cultural outsider, projects on the indigenous shaman the colonizing culture's own presuppositions concerning sorcery and indigenous savagery. In turn, to be effective, the colonized sorcerer must conform to the expectations and presuppositions of the colonizer—indeed, for purposes of resistance, may reinforce and enhance such projections by emphasizing just those features of indigenous sorcery the colonizer finds most gruesome, repugnant, and therefore terrifying. Thus the colony becomes a heart of darkness—a place, as anthropologist Neil Whitehead puts it, of "mystical terror and savage violence."[13] And this is so whether the indigenous attack sorcery is actually practiced or is simply a form of accusation.

This is the way Michael Taussig interprets shamanic healing in the Putumayo region of Colombia—as hidden political resistance to the terror and suffering experienced by the Indians during a brutal colonial history. Taussig originally came to Colombia as a dedicated Marxist physician, intending to minister to rural guerillas.[14] While doing this work, Taussig became fascinated by the historical violence in the area—he became, he says, a violence junkie—and intrigued by the fact that the Huitoto Indians, the most oppressed and marginalized people in Colombian society, were credited with possessing magical power, which they then made available to poor white colonists in the form of ayahuasca healing sessions.

This power was in fact, he says, a projection by the white colonizers onto the shamanic other; to the magic already possessed by indigenous shamans, "colonialism fused its own magic, the magic of primitivism."[15] The shaman then took this projected magical power, this image of shaman as *wild man*, to use in his own healing practice, which he made available to the civilized colonizer. And the shaman as *suffering healer*—suffering under the violence of the colonial state—comported with the official discourse of the colonial church.[16]

Thus the interaction of colonizer and shaman was not a one-way process where Indian culture was passively acted upon by external forces; nor was the result an organic synthesis or syncretism. Rather, the interaction was a "chamber of mirrors reflecting each stream's perception of the other," which "folds the underworld of the conquering society into the culture of the conquered, the peon, the slave."[17] In fact, these forces came full circle, with impoverished white colonists seeking redemption at the hands of the colonized natives. Taussig describes this encounter as one in which an indigenous shaman "heals the pain in the souls of the civilized."[18] So, through the sweep of colonial history, the colonizers provided the colonized with the image of the wild man—"a gift whose powers the colonizers would be blind to, were it not for the reciprocation of the colonized, bringing together in the dialogical imagination of colonization an image that wrests from civilization its demonic power."[19]

We need to be cautious, however, in applying such a grand narrative to the facts on the ground, and avoid—as anthropologist Marshall Sahlins expresses it—"translating the apparently trivial into the fatefully political."[20] Social anthropologist Caroline Humphrey, an expert on Mongolian shamanism, sees the shamanism Taussig describes as uniquely "reactive, absorptive, and frantically hyperaware of colonial powers and technology."[21] Anthropologist Michael Brown, who studied the shamanism of the Aguaruna of northeastern Peru, says that "society cannot be relegated to the conceptual status of a penal colony without . . . violating the complex and creative understandings of those for whom we presume to speak."[22]

Reducing shamanism to political resistance, Brown says, also undervalues the internal complexity of indigenous cultures, which have their own "internal fields of conflict and points of contention."[23] To the extent that resistance changes the distribution of power, status, and wealth, he says, it may challenge the internal status quo as much as it challenges the power of outsiders.[24] Anthropologist Sherry Ortner puts it this way: "Resistors are doing more than simply opposing domination. They have their *own* politics."[25] And indigenous resistance to acculturation may be supported by those nominally the oppressor, for their own reasons—for example, wanting the natives to return to their own environment, leaving them safe in their communal houses, rather than living in the city and appointed, say, secretary of education.[26]

Grand narratives of sociopolitical resistance, says medical anthropologist Arthur Kleinman, eventually undermine the genuine moral claims of indigenous suffering, and belittle "the personal pains and distress that sick persons bring to shamans, which shamans try to cure."[27] We must be careful that, in characterizing the shaman as heroic resistor, we are not—once again—mythologizing the shaman to suit our own projected needs. Far from resisting biomedicine, for example, the Amazonian shaman has adopted its symbols and power; rather than being a static reservoir of tradition, preserving culturally intact knowledge, shamanism has created—as it always has—"an actively produced hybrid medicine."[28]

AMAZONIAN SHAMANS' ORGANIZATIONS

There is, of course, no reason to believe that sorcery is not still used politically in the Amazon. But now there are additional tools, perhaps equally powerful, available to shamans—organizing and the law.

Shamans in the Amazon are not unaware of the problems brought about by their encounter with global modernity. On June 1 through 8, 1999, forty of the most prominent traditional healers from seven indigenous peoples convened in Yurayaco, Colombia, to hold an Encuentro de Taitas, a Meeting of Shamans, and to discuss the future of traditional medicine. One result of that meeting was the publication of two documents—a *Código de ética de la medicina indígena del piedemonte Amazónico Colombiano, Code of Ethics of Indigenous Medicine of the Foothills of the Colombian Amazon*, and the *Declaración del Encuentro de Taitas, Declaration of the Meeting of Shamans*, often called the *Yurayaco Declaration*.[29]

In addition, under a grant from the Amazon Conservation Team, an environmental group with headquarters in Washington, D.C., a very handsome commemorative volume was published, with beautiful color photographs of the participants and events.[30] Another result was the formation of an organization, the Unión de Médicos Indígenas Yageceros de la Amazonía Colombiana (UMIYAC), the Union of Indigenous Yagé Healers of the Colombian

Amazon, with the purpose, among other things, of establishing a certification procedure for shamans, apprentices, and disciples.[31]

The Yurayaco meeting recognized a number of problems with which the declaration and code of ethics were intended to deal. These included disunity among shamans; discrediting of indigenous medicine by *blancos*; disbelief in medicine and medicinal plants, and disrespect for shamans, among indigenous youth; belief by *gente blanca*, white people, that yagé is a harmful drug of no benefit; depletion of the rain forest, yagé, and medicinal plants; indigenous charlatans; misuse of yagé by nonindigenous people; trade in yagé and other medicinal plants; the problem of patents and ownership of plants; possible prohibition of yagé; and the relationship with the government health system.

The *Yurayaco Declaration* consists of fourteen points. For example, declaration number three states:

> Nonindigenous peoples are now acknowledging the importance of our wisdom and the value of our medicinal and sacred plants. Many of them desecrate our culture and our territories, traffic in yagé and other plants, dress like Indians, and act like charlatans. We note with concern that a new form of tourism is being promoted to deceive foreigners with purported services of *taitas* or shamans in several villages in the Amazon foothills. Even some of our own indigenous brothers do not respect the value of our traditional medicine and go around the villages and cities selling our symbols and misleading people.[32]

The declaration concludes with a request for support from nonindigenous peoples, an agreement to "work for the unity and defense of traditional medicine and offer our services for the health of indigenous peoples and humanity," and three concrete proposals—to initiate a certification process and code of ethics for practitioners of indigenous medicine, in order to facilitate recognition of the difference between shamans and charlatans; to travel throughout the Americas to bring the benefits of their medicine to indigenous peoples and to construct indigenous medical clinics for nonindigenous peoples as well; and to create UMIYAC, the Union of Indigenous Yagé Healers of the Colombian Amazon.[33]

Another organization, called the Associación de Shamanes Indígenas del Napo (ANISHIN), was founded in Ecuador in 1997, in response to decades-long legal attacks on traditional healers. Under the impetus, in part, of a Quechua ayahuasquero named don Léon Fidel Andy Grefa, who has been its president since 2006, ANISHIN has lobbied for legalizing the practice of *curanderismo* in Ecuador and has proposed that shamans be awarded academic credentials and employed in public hospitals.[34] These proposals were adopted by the Consejo Nacional de Salud, the National Board of Health, at its third Congreso por Salud y la Vida.[35]

A similar but apparently less politicized organization has also been established in Iquitos—Asociación de Médicos Vegetalistas de Iquitos, the Iquitos Association of Plant Healers, formed on June 17, 2001, under the sponsorship of the prestigious Instituto de Investigaciones de la Amazonía Peruana, a governmental research institute, and originally headed by famed ethnobotanist Elsa Rengifo.[36] The goal of the organization was primarily to promote the use of traditional plant healing practices, train new plant healers, and encourage the conservation of medicinal plant resources. As of 2003, two years after its founding, the organization had thirty-two member practitioners;[37] as of 2008, I am told, even the president and vice president of the organization were no longer actively involved.[38]

The effect of such attempts at organization and professionalization is not yet clear. To the extent that certification processes are established, they can be used politically against unpopular shamans and their apprentices, and they can constitute entry barriers that protect the interests of established shamans. Nor is it clear to what extent shamans in Peru or Ecuador or Colombia would be willing to sacrifice their autonomy and individuality, or to what extent noble intentions might be subverted by envidia and accusations of brujería—in other words, by shamanic business as usual.

THE AYAHUASCA PATENT CASE

Ayahuasca shamans encountered modernity as well when they discovered, to their considerable surprise, that an American had patented ayahuasca. In 1981, Loren Miller, director of the California-based International Plant Medicine Corporation, took a sample of ayahuasca back to the United States. Miller then patented it with the U.S. Patent and Trademark Office (PTO), claiming a new plant variety he called *Da Vine*, and in 1986 obtained exclusive rights to sell and breed the plant. It was not until ten years later that Amazonian indigenous people became aware that one of their sacred plants was now under U.S. patent law. By 1998, Miller had received, and ignored, repeated requests from indigenous groups to give up the patent.

Finally, the Coordinating Body for Indigenous Organizations of the Amazon Basin (COICA), a group based in Ecuador and representing over four hundred indigenous groups from eight countries, decided to take action. "Our goal is to have the ayahuasca patent annulled, and to teach all international biopirates a lesson," said Rodolfo Asar, communications director of COICA. The organization informed its members that Miller was an "enemy of indigenous peoples" and that "his entrance into all indigenous territory should be prohibited."

A war of words ensued. The organization posted a notice on its Web site stating that it would not be responsible for any physical harm to Miller if he ventured into indigenous territory. Miller said that he was given a sample of the plant by an indigenous community in Ecuador, but he refused to identify the community on the grounds that he wanted to protect residents from COICA, which he called a terrorist organization that had ruined the reputation of his business.

Charging that the patent was improperly issued, indigenous groups challenged the claim at the PTO, with the help of two Washington-based organizations, the Center for International Environmental Law and the Coalition for Amazonian Peoples and Their Environment. The Plant Patent Act of 1970 was intended to protect growers breeding new plant varieties, and requires the person requesting the patent to be the original breeder. Since ayahuasca is widely used throughout the Amazon and, botanical experts said, the patented plant was exactly the same as the natural variety, Miller could not claim to have been the "inventor" of the plant, and thus was not eligible for a patent. The shamans asked that the validity of the patent be reviewed on these grounds, and that request was approved.

Indigenous people of the Amazon have learned how to use photo opportunities. Querubin Queta Alvarado and Antonio Jacanamijoy Rosero, spiritual leaders of their people, appeared at the headquarters of the PTO wearing traditional garb—beads, feathers, and piranha teeth. Under their arms were official protest documents prepared by their attorneys.

In the fall of 1999, the PTO nullified the patent on the grounds that a specimen like Miller's had been on display at Chicago's Field Museum at least a year before he applied for a patent. "Our shamans and elders were greatly troubled by this patent," said Antonio Jacanamijoy Rosero. "Now they are celebrating."[39]

The celebration did not last.

While the PTO had accepted the arguments that the claimed plant variety was not distinctive or novel, it had not acknowledged the argument that its religious value warranted an exception from patenting. In apparent violation of its own procedures, the PTO allowed Miller to submit new evidence and arguments, centering on the differences between his ayahuasca plant and the museum reference plant. In January 2001, without having heard opposing views, the PTO reversed its rejection and, in April, issued a certificate allowing the patent to stand for the remaining two years of its term.

Ironically, after all his legal efforts, Miller was left with a patent that was essentially worthless. The patent he received protects only the specific genome of the patented plant and its asexually reproduced progeny—that is, exclusive rights over nothing more than his original plant and specimens grown from its cuttings. It does not give him rights over any other specimens of the ayahuasca vine, even specimens that may be identical in appearance.

Under the law, a patent applied for before 1995 expires seventeen years from the date it was originally issued. The ayahuasca patent expired on June 17, 2003. It cannot be renewed.[40]

CHAPTER 35

THE FUTURE

Mestizo shamanism in the Upper Amazon is expanding and declining at the same time: it is expanding at the expense of other indigenous shamanisms, and it is declining in the face of biomedicine, magic, and the reluctance of the young to undergo the sufferings required to become a shaman.

This does not mean that there is no *interest* in the shamanism of the Upper Amazon and particularly in the psychoactive effects of ayahuasca. That interest, in fact, is great. Every year since 2005, Alan Shoemaker has organized, on behalf of his organization Soga del Alma, a conference on ayahuasca shamanism in Iquitos, Peru. These gatherings have featured such heavyweights as Dennis McKenna, Luis Eduardo Luna, Pablo Amaringo, Jacques Mabit, and Benny Shanon, as well as a number of indigenous curanderos. There is no doubt that these gatherings achieve their aims. They bring together famous gringo scholars, psychonautic enthusiasts, serious seekers, and a variety of mestizo and indigenous shamans. Everyone gains an aura of legitimacy from this interaction, and the shamans pick up some much-needed cash. But then everyone goes home, and the shamans are left without what the tradition really needs—apprentices.

One reason shamanism is declining among Indians and mestizos is because young people do not want to keep the difficult diet;[1] young Shuar, for example, nowadays prefer to learn magic, by reading books and following their instructions, rather than undergo the restricted diet and sexual abstinence required to become a shaman.[2] Don Guillermo Arévalo, a well-respected Shipibo shaman from Puccalpa, says the same: "Many who are interested in shamanism don't want to submit themselves to diets with teaching plants. They prefer to have recourse to books of occult sciences."[3]

Don Mauricio Fasabi Apuela, a shaman from Lamas in San Martín, is willing to take on young people as apprentices in ayahuasca shamanism. He has had no takers. "I have no disciples here, just me," he says. "In the end they prefer the girls." Shaman Casimiro Izurieta Cevallos explains, "Youngsters today don't have the same curiosity." Don Mauricio agrees: "The youth of today don't want to learn."[4] Don Guillermo Arrévala concurs: "To function in this world of shamanism . . . demands a certain measure of discipline, to live within the rules. Young indigenous people in these times don't want to get involved in these studies. . . . They prefer not to submit themselves to that type of strenuous apprenticeship."[5] Young people do not even want to smoke mapacho, but only finos, says don José Curitima Sangama, a Cocama shaman. "They only smoke fine red store-bought packs of tobacco," he says, "and when they see us smoke black tobacco, they make fun of us, saying that that is for dirty witches."[6]

None of the four shamans with whom anthropologist Luis Eduardo Luna worked had a successor. They all told him that young people were not interested in or were unable to endure the diet and abstinence necessary for learning from the plant spirits. Their roles have been taken, they said, by charlatans who do not possess any knowledge of the plants.[7]

Don Roberto has had apprentices in the past, and he believes that other curanderos currently have apprentices, but, when pressed, he cannot name any who do. Although his son Carlos is now his apprentice, no one else in the local community is currently working with him or has asked to apprentice with him. The interest of gringos in his work will have no effect on this, he says; local people will either be interested or not regardless of what gringos do. The gringos, he shrugs, come for a single experience; few come to learn the ayahuasca path. But don Roberto is hopeful about the future of the type of healing he practices. "The medicine will continue," he says. He believes that more and more young people will take up the path once they understand the fuerza, power, that it gives them.

Many mestizo shamans continue to have patients, especially in poorer urban areas, such as in Iquitos or Pucallpa. But few mestizo shamans nowadays have apprentices. Without students, as one shaman put it, *no hay futuro*, there is no future.[8] And then a thing of great beauty and power will be gone.

APPENDIX A

PLANTS MENTIONED IN THE TEXT

Popular Name	Scientific Name	References	Other Names
abuta	*Abuta grandifolia*	BS 373–374; CTD 13; D 1–2; DV 13; GRO 151; LV 33; MR 12–13; PRC 37–40; R 155	*motelosanango, sanango*
achiote	*Bixa orellana*	BS 181–182; CTD 26–27; D 103–108; DV 31; G 282; GRO 151; MR 14–15; PRC 41–45; R 24, 59	
aguaje	*Mauritia flexuosa*	CTD 81; D 441–443; DV 114;G 182; HGB 69–70; see SR 354	
ají	*Capsicum* spp.	BS 493–494; D 157–162; G 797; LA 144–145; LV 42; MR 18–19; PRC 271; R 26, 61, 144, 146; SR 426	
ajo sacha	*Mansoa alliacea*	CTD 79; D 435–437; DV 112; G 281; GRO 153; LA 146–147; LV 56–57; MLT 356; MR 20–21; PRC 47–50; R 13, 16, 24, 155; SR 105; *Cordia alliodora*, BS 184; D 231–232	
ajosquiro	*Cordia alliodora*	BS 184; D 231–232; DV 55; *Gallesia* spp., G 680	
alacransillo	*Heliotropium indicum*	CTD 58; D 351–353; DV 86; *H. curassavicum*, B 187	
albahaca[a]	*Ocimum* spp.	BS 324–325; CTD 89; D 488–490; DV 124; GRO 153; LA 148–149; LV 59–60; MLT 356; MR 22–23; PRC 271; SR 221; see G 482	*pichana albaca*
amor seco	*Bidens* spp.	BS 127; CTD 25; D 98–101; DV 31; MR 28–29; R 55, 61, 145; *Desmodium* spp., D 260; DV 64; G 553; LA 154–155; PRC 272; see SR 237	
atadijo	*Trema micrantha*	DV 170; G 824[b]	

Popular Name	Scientific Name	References	Other Names
ayahuasca	*Banisteriopsis caapi*	BS 366; CTD 21; D 90–91; DV 28; G 578; GRO 151; LV 35–36; PRC 55–58; R 17, 25, 72, 155; SR 274–279	
ayahuma	*Couroupita guianensis*	D 237–238; DV 58; G 501; GRO 152; LV 45–46; MLT 357; MR 34–35; R 151	
ayasisa	*Tagetes erecta*	D 685–688; DV 165; MR 36–37; PRC 195–198; R 59	*rosasisa*
barbasco	*Lonchocarpus nicou*	D 257–258; DV 106; LA 158; PRC 272; R 155; SR 244; see G 535; *Tephrosia* spp., DV 167; LA 158; R 56; SR 258	
bellaquillo	*Thevetia peruviana*	D 709–712; DV 170; MR 42–43	*camalonga*
bijao	*Calathea lutea*	DV 36; G 148; R 62, 143, 151, 157; see SR 290–291; *C. allouia*, D 143–144	
bobinsana	*Calliandra angustifolia*	D 145–146; DV 38; G 523; LA 160–161; LV 40; MLT 357; PRC 273; R 63, 149	
bombanaje	*Carludovica palmate*	CTD 33; D 173–174; DV 44; G 116; see SR 155; *Irartea* spp., G 192	
buceta hembra	*Xanthosoma* spp.	R 63[c]	*cf. buceta macho*
buceta macho	*Anthurium* spp.	R 63	*cf. buceta hembra*
caballosanango	*Faramea* spp.	D 319; DV 77; see G 741	*yacusanango*
cachimbo	*Cariniana* spp.	DV 44; Feltwell, 2005, p. 26; Flores Sandoval, González Flores, & Trujillo Cuéllar, 2001; Miller, 1999, p. 17	
camalonga	*Thevetia peruviana*	BS 99–100; CTD 124; D 709–712; DV 170	*bellaquillo*
caña brava	*Gynerium sagittatum*	BS 434; DV 54, 137; MR 54–55; PRC 67–70; R 150	
capinurí	*Maquira coriacea*	CTD 80; DV 112; G 631; GRO 153; MR 56–57; R 151, 157	
capirona	*Calycophyllum* spp.	CTD 31; D 149–150; DV 38; G 727; LV 41; MLT 358; PRC 71–74; R 151, 157; SR 377	
cariñito	*Justicia pectoralis*	DV 99; G 209; GRO 152; R 147; SR 43–44; see D 394–396	*imancito*

Popular Name	Scientific Name	References	Other Names
carricillo	*Arthrostylidium* spp.	DV 24; *Olyra latifolia*, R 56	
cascarilla	*Ladenbergia magnifolia*	DV 102; R 18; *Cinchona officinalis*, BS 466–467, D 212–214	
catahua	*Hura crepitans*	D 360–362; DV 89; G 492; GRO 152; LA 168–169; LV 53–54; MLT 356; MR 60–61; PRC 274; R 24[d]	
chacruna	*Psychotria viridis*	CTD 107; DV 147; G 739; LV 65–66; SR 392–396	
chagraponga	*Diplopterys cabrerana*	LV 48; SR 281–282; see G 580	*chalipanga, huambisa, ocoyagé*
chalipanga	*Diplopterys cabrerana*	LV 48; SR 281–282; see G 580	*chagraponga, huambisa, ocoyagé*
chambira	*Astrocaryum chambira*	DV 25; G 187; HGB 204; MR 64–65; PRC 97–100; R 155, 158; see G 187; SR 348	
chiricaspi	*Brunfelsia chiricaspi*	DV 34; LV 38–39; SR 424; *B. grandifolia*, PRC 101–104; see D 127–128; G 791	
chiricsanango	*Brunfelsia grandiflora*	CTD 29; D 127–128; DV 34; GRO 151; LV 38–39; MR 68–69; SR 425; R 18, 26, 65, 150; *B. chiricaspi*, DV 34, LV 38–39; *B. chiricsanango*, MLT 358; see G 791	*chuchuhuasha, chiricaspi*
chuchuhuasha	*Brunfelsia grandiflora*	D 127–128; DV 34; LV 38–39; MR 68–69; see G 791	*chiricsanango*
chuchuhuasi	*Maytenus macrocarpa*	DV 114; G 327; GRO 153; LV 58; MLT 356; MR 70–71; PRC 105–108; R 24, 158; SR 126; *M. boaria*, D. 443–444; *Heisteria acuminata*, BS 394; LA 178	
chullachaquicaspi	*Remijia peruviana*	DV 149; SR 396–397; *Tovomita* spp., G 449, LV 72; MLT 357; R 24; see DV 170[e]	
clavohuasca	*Tynanthus panurensis*	CTD 125; D 725–726; DV 171; G 277; GRO 154; LV 73; MLT 356; MR 72–73; PRC 85–88; R 155, 157; *T. scabra*, BS 181	
cocasanango	*Bonafousia* spp.	DV 32; see G 242; *Tabernaemontana sananho*, D 684–685	*sanango macho*

Popular Name	Scientific Name	References	Other Names
cocona	*Solanum sessiliflorum*	CTD 120; D 647–648; DV 158; G 789; LA 180–181; MR 76–77; PRC 89–92; R 26, 144; SR 440–441	
copaiba	*Copaifera* spp.	D 228–230; DV 55; G 517–518: MR 80–81; PRC 93–96; see SR 236–237	
cordoncillo	*Piper aduncum*	CTD 101; D 548–552; DV 137–138; G 684; GRO 153; MR 82–83; PRC 275; R 25, 152, 158; SR 364–368; *Maclura tinctoria*, D 424–425	
cumaceba	*Swartzia polyphylla*	D 670; DV 162; G 529; GRO 154; MR 86–87; R 158	
fierrocaspi	*Minquartia guianensis*	D 456–457; DV 117; GRO 153; PRC 123	*huacapú*
floripondio	*Brugmansia suaveolens*	DV 33; LV 38; MR 194–195; SR 422; see G 791; *B. arborea*, BS 487–489; D 122–123; *Teliostachya lanceolata*, R 100	*maricahua, toé; cf. toé negro*
guaba	*Inga edulis*	BS 284; CTD 63; DV 93; G 519; see SR 242–244	*shimbillo*
guayusa	*Ilex guayusa*	BS 101–102; D 369; DV 92; G 249; LV 54; SR 80–81; *Piper callosum*, GRO 153; R 65, 143	
hierba luisa	*Cymbopogon citratus*	BS 431–432; CTD 48; DV 61; GRO 152; LA 190–191; PRC 276; SR 202–203; R 18, 25, 59, 65, 143; *Aloysia citriodora*, D 28–30	
huacanqui	*Masdevallia vetchiana*	Roque & León, 2006, p. 822	
huacapú	*Minquartia guianensis*	D 456–457; DV 117; G 669; MR 98–99; PRC 121–124; R 18, 25, 159; *Vouacapoua americana*, LV 75, MLT 357	*fierrocaspi*
huacapurana	*Campsiandra angustifolia*	D 150–151; DV 38; G 516; MR 100–101; LV 41; R 25; SR 234	
huachuma	*Trichocereus pachanaoi*	SR 154–157; see generally Glass-Coffin, 1998; Joralemon & Sharon, 1993; Sharon, 1972; *Echinopsis pachanaoi*, BS 200–201	
huacrapona	*Iriartea deltoidea*	CTD 66; DV 96; G 192; HGB 109	

Popular Name	Scientific Name	References	Other Names
huambisa	*Diplopterys cabrerana*	LV 48; SR 281–282; see G 580	*chagraponga, chalipanga, ocoyagé*
huasaí	*Euterpe* spp.	D 313–315; DV 75; G 198; HGB 124; R 16, 24, 156, 159[f]	
huayracaspi	*Cedrelinga cataneiformis*	DV 48; LV 43; MLT 357; *Sterculia apetala*, D 668	
huayruro	*Ormosia* spp.	BS 294; DV 125; G 541; MR 102–103; Smithsonian Tropical Research Institute, 2006a, 2006b; see SR 247–249[g]	
huicungo	*Astrocaryum murumuru*	DV 25; HGB 205; see G 187; SR 348; *A. huicungo*, DV 25; *A. macrocalyx*, DV 25; R 24, 159	
huiririma	*Astrocaryum jauarii*	DV 25; HGB 205; see G 187; SR 348	
huito	*Genipa americana*	CTD 55; D 324–327; DV 79; GRO 152; LA 194–195; MR 106–107; PRC 133–137; R 25, 55	
icoja	*Unonopsis* spp.	DV 172; G 236; GRO 154; MR 108–109; PRC 139–142; R 159; SR 60	
inayuga	*Maximiliana* spp.	DV 114; G 189; SR 356; *Attalea maripa*, D 79–80; HGB 115; but see SR 349	
inchaui	*Syagrus tessmannii*	DV 162; G 189; see HGB 140–149	
ipururo	*Alchornea castaneifolia*	DV 14; LV 33–34; MLT 356; MR 110–111	
irapay	*Lepidocaryum tessmannii*	CTD 72; DV 103; G 182; *L. tenue*, HGB 71	
ishanga blanca	*Laportea aestuans*	D 404–405; DV 103; PRC 277; R 26, 141; see G 827, 831	*cf. ishanga roja*
ishanga roja	*Urera* spp.	R 26; see D 730–731; DV 172	*cf. ishanga blanca*
ishpingo caspi	*Amburana cearensis*	DV 18; G 541–543	
jergón sacha	*Dracontium loretense*	CTD 49; D 275–277; DV 67; G 100; GRO 152; LA 200–201; MR 112–113; PRC 143–146; SR 86; R 16, 24, 66, 144, 152, 156, 159	
kapok	*Ceiba pentandra*	CTD 34; D 190–194; DV 48; G 288; LV 44	*lupuna; lupuna blanca*

Popular Name	Scientific Name	References	Other Names
lengua de perro	*Zamia ulei*	CTD 116–117; GRO 154; see DV 181; G 89; SR 153	
lobosanango	*Tabernaemontana* spp.	D 684–685; DV 164; LV 70; MR 178–179; SR 75–76; *Stenoselen eggersii*, DV 160; R 156, 159; *Faramea anisocalyx*, DV 77	*sanango, uchusanango, yacusanango*
lupuna	*Ceiba pentandra*	CTD 34; D 190–194; DV 48; G 288; LV 44; MLT 356; R 160	*lupuna blanca; kapok; cf. pucalupuna, lupuna bruja, lupuna colorada*
lupuna blanca	*Ceiba pentandra*	CTD 34; D 190–194; DV 48; G 288; LV 44	*lupuna; kapok*
lupuna bruja	*Cavanillesia umbellata*	DV 47; G 290; LV 43; MLT 356	*pucalupuna; lupuna colorada; cf. lupuna; lupuna blanca*
lupuna colorada	*Cavanillesia umbellata*	DV 47; G 290; LV 43; MLT 356	*pucalupuna; lupuna bruja; cf. lupuna; lupuna blanca*
machimango	*Eschweilera* spp.	DV 74; G 501–503; *Brosimum* spp., R 24; see SR 226–227	
mapacho	*Nicotiana rustica*	DV 123; G 797; LV 59; SR 432	
maricahua	*Brugmansia* spp.	D 126–127; DV 33; LV 37–38; SR 421; see G 791[h]	*floripondio, toé; cf. toé negro*
mashushingo	*Pavonia leucantha*	DV 132; see G 588	
mishquipanga	*Renealmia alpina*	CTD 108; DV 149; PRC 279; SR 472–473	
motelillo	*Fittonia verschaffeltii*	DV 78; R 143; see G 212; SR 41–42	
motelosanango	*Abuta grandifolia*	CTD 13; DD 1–2; V 13; LV 33; MR 12–13; PRC 37–40; R 17, 25	*abuta*
mucura	*Petivera alliacea*	BS 412–413; CTD 97; D 517–519; DV 133–134; LV 61; MLT 357; PRC 279; R 18, 25, 60, 120, 142, 152–153; SR 361	
mururé	*Brosimum acutifolium*	D 119–121; GRO 151; MR 132–133; PRC 215–218	*tamimuri*
ñucñopichana	*Scoparia dulcis*	CTD 112; D 614–617; DV 154; G 838; GRO 154; LA 222–223; LV 68; MLT 358; MR 136–137; PRC 155–158; R 18, 26, 143	

Popular Name	Scientific Name	References	Other Names
ocoyagé	*Diplopterys cabrerana*	LV 48; SR 281–282; see G 580	*chagraponga, chalipanga, huambisa*
ojé	*Ficus insipida*	CTD 54; D 320–322; DV 77–78; G 637; GRO 152; LA 224–225; LV 50; MLT 357; MR 138–139; PRC 159–162; R 17, 25, 153; SR 316	
palisangre	*Brosimum rubescens*	DV 33; GRO 151; R 160; see SR 312	
palosanto	*Bursera graveolens*	BS 198–199; D 132–133; DV 34; SR 116; see G 302; *Dalbergia ecastaphyllum*, D 253–254; *Sclerobium setiferum*, MLT 357	
patiquina	*Dieffenbachia* spp.	D 261–262; DV 66; G 102; LV 47; MR 156–157; PRC 280; R 56, 142, 146	*patiquina blanca; cf. patiquina negra*
patiquina blanca	*Dieffenbachia* spp.	GRO 152; see D 261–262	*patiquina; cf. patiquina negra*
patiquina negra	*Dieffenbachia* spp.	D 261–262; R 16, 24; *Xanthosoma violaceum*, GRO 154	*cf. patiquina, patiquina blanca*
pichana albaca	*Ocimum* spp.	CTD 89; D 488–489; DV 124; LV 59–60; MLT 356; see G 482	*albaca, albahaca*
pijuayo	*Bactris macana*	D 89; HGB 192; see G 187; SR 349; *B. gasipaes*, DV 28, GRO 151; R. 24[i]	
piñon blanco	*Jatropha curcas*	CTD 67; D 383–388; DV 98; GRO 152; LA 240–241; MR 160–161; PRC 183–186; R 24, 59, 69, 149; see BS 266–267; G 409; SR 180	*cf. piñon colorado, piñon negro, piñon rojo*
piñon colorado	*Jatropha gossypifolia*	D 388–391; LA 238–239; LV 55; R 56; see BS 266–267; G 409; SR 180	*piñon negro, piñon rojo; cf. piñon blanco*
piñon negro	*Jatropha gossypifolia*	CTD 68; D 388–391; DV 98; LV 55; PRC 187–190; R 69, 149; see BS 266–267; G 409; SR 180	*piñon colorado, piñon rojo; cf. piñon blanco*
piñon rojo	*Jatropha gossypifolia*	D 388–391; GRO 152; PRC 189; see BS 266–267; G 409; SR 180	*piñon colorado, piñon negro; cf. piñon blanco*
pinshacallo	*Xylopia benthamii*	DV 179; G 226–227; see SR 62	

Popular Name	Scientific Name	References	Other Names
piripiri	*Cyperus* spp.	D 249–251, 251; DV 61; G 120; LA 242–243; LV 46–47; MLT 356; PRC 281; R 17, 69, 142; SR 157–158	
plátano	*Musa paradisiaca*	BS 381–382; DV 120; CTD 85; LA 244–245; MR 162–163; R 25	
pona	*Socratea exorrhiza*	CTD 117; DV 157; G 192; *Wettinia drudei*, HGB 115[i]	
pucalupuna	*Cavanillesia umbellata*	DV 47; G 290; LV 43; MLT 356	*lupuna colorada; lupuna bruja*
pucunucho	*Capsicum annuum*	D 157–162; DV 40	
quinilla	*Manilkara bidentata*	DV 112; G 775; *Warszewiczia coccinea*, D 739–740	
raya balsa	*Montrichardia arborescens*	DV 118; G 102; LV 58–59; MLT 356	
remocaspi	*Aspidosperma excelsum*	D 77–78; DV 25; G 243; GRO 151; MR 166–167; R 23, 160; *Pithecellobium laetum*, MLT 357; *Swartzia polyphylla*, D 670	
renaco	*Ficus americana*	DV 77; see G 637; LV 51; MLT 357; SR 314–317; *F. insipida*, D 320–322	
renaquilla	*Clusia rosea*	CTD 39; DV 53; G 448; GRO 151; MR 168–169; R 17, 24, 146, 160	
rocoto	*Capsicum pubescens*	D 157–162; U.S. Department of Agriculture, National Resources Conservation Service, 2007; Wiersema & Léon, 1999, pp. 105, 609	
rosasisa	*Tagetes erecta*	D 685–688; GRO 154; MR 36–37; LA 248–249; PRC 195–198; R 59, 69; see G 359; SR 138–139	*ayasisa*
ruda	*Ruta graveolens*	BS 476–477; MR 172–173; see SR 405; *R. chalepensis*, DV 150; *Tagetes erecta*, D 685–688	
sacha caimito	*Chrysophillum caimito*	CTD 37: DV 51; G 775–776; SR 411; see D 210–211	
sacha corazon	*Caladium* spp.	DV 36; see G 104; SR 85; see D 142–143	
sameruca	*Psychotria carthaginensis*	DV 146; G 739; SR 392–393	

Popular Name	Scientific Name	References	Other Names
sanango	*Tabaerne-montana sananho*	D 684–685; DV 164; G 242; LV 70; MR 178–179; R 16, 23, 156; SR 74–76; Faramea spp., SR 383	*lobosanango, uchusanango, yacusanango*
sanango macho	*Bonafousia* spp.	DV 32; see D 684–685; G 242	*cocasanango*
sangapilla	*Chamaedorea fragrans*	HGB 95; *Costus spicatus*, D 235–236; *Cyclantus bipartitus*, R 147; see G 196	
sangre de grado	*Croton lechleri*	CTD 46; D 242–245; DV 58; G 411; GRO 152; LA 254–255; MR 180–181; PRC 207–210; R 17, 24, 74, 153; see SR 178	
shacapa	*Pariana* spp.	DV 128; Luna & Amaringo, 1993, pp. 32, 112, 140; see SR 192	
shimbillo	*Inga* spp.	CTD 63; DV 93; G 519; see SR 242–244	*guaba*
shimipampana	*Maranta arundinacea*	D 437–439; DV 112; GRO 153; MR 186–187; PRC 282; R 70–71, 87, 143; see G 150	
suelda con suelda	*Phthirusa* spp.	DV 136; GRO 153; LV 62; MLT 357; MR 188–189; R 17[k]	
tahuari	*Tabebuia* spp.	D 680–683; DV 164; G 268; GRO 154; LV 69–70; MLT 356; MR 192–193; PRC 211–214; R 154, 156, 161; SR 107–108; *Anthodiscus* spp., DV 22; G 323; LV 35; MLT 356	
tamimuri	*Brosimum acutifolium*	D 119–121; DV 32; G 632–633; MR 132–133	*mururé*
toé	*Brugmansia suaveolens*	CTD 28; D 123–125; DV 33; LV 37–38; MLT 358; MR 194–195; PRC 223–226; R 71, 149; SR 422; see G 791; *B. arborea*, D 122–123	*floripondio, maricahua; cf. toé negro*
toé negro	*Teliostachya lanceolata*	D 701; DV 167; LV 71; MLT 356; R 71, 142; SR 47–48; see G 209	*cf. floripondio, maricahua, toé*
uchusanango	*Tabernae-montana* spp.	DV 164; LV 70–71; MLT 356; R 23; SR 77–78	*lobosanango, sanango, yacusanango*
uña de gato	*Uncaria guianensis*	CTD 126–127; D 727–730; DV 172; G 721; LV 73; MR 202–203; PRC 237–242; R 18, 25; see SR 401; *U. tomentosa*, BS 467–468; *Macfadyena* spp., DV 108	*uña de gato blanco; cf. uña de gato roja*

Popular Name	Scientific Name	References	Other Names
uña de gato blanco	*Uncaria guianensis*	R 154, 161	*uña de gato; cf. uña de gato roja*
uña de gato roja	*Uncaria tomentosa*	R 154, 161	*cf. uña de gato, uña de gato blanco*
ungurahui	*Oenocarpus bataua*	G 198; GRO 153; HGB 130–131; PRC 233–236; R 161; *Euterpe* spp., D 313–315; *Jessenia bataua*, DV 99; see SR 353	
verbena	*Verbena littoralis*	BS 528–529; DV 174; PRC 243–246; R 26; SR 463–464	*verbena negra; cf. verbena blanca*
verbena blanca	*Stachytarpheta cayennensis*	R 71, 143	*cf. verbena, verbena negra*
verbena negra	*Verbena littoralis*	R 71, 143; *Stachytarpheta cayennensis*, D 663–664	*verbena; cf. verbena blanca*
yacusanango	*Tabaerne-montana sananho*	D 684–685; SR 75–76; *Faramea capillipes*, DV 77	*caballosanango, lobosanango, sanango, uchusanango*
yarina	*Phytelephas* spp.	CTD 99; DV 136; G 184; HGB 238; R 161	
yuca	*Manihot esculenta*	BS 267–268; D 431–433; DV 110; CTD 76–77; LA 284–285; MR 218–219; PRC 283; SR 181	

NOTE: BS = Bussmann & Sharon, 2007; CTD = Castner, Timme, & Duke, 1998; D = Duke, 2009; DV = Duke & Vasquez, 1994; G = Gentry, 1993; GRO = Galy, Rengifo, & Olivier Hay, 2000; HGB = Henderson, Galeano, & Bernal, 1995; LA = Lacaze & Alexiades, 1995, LV = López Vinatea, 2000; MLT = McKenna, Luna, & Towers, 1995; MR = Mejia & Rengifo, 2000; PRC = Pinedo, Rengifo, & Cerruti, 1997; R = Rengifo, 2001; SR = Schultes & Raffauf, 1990.

[a] Spelling variants include *albaca* and *alvaca*. The term *sharamasho* refers to wild basil species as well (PRC 282).

[b] D 242–245 identifies *atadijo* with *sangre de grado.*

[c] Castonguay (1990, p. 63) gives the word *labuceta* as the name of a *pusanga* plant.

[d] This tree is also called *catahua negra* (Luna & Amaringo, 1993, p. 106).

[e] *Chullachasi caspi* [*sic*] is identified as *Licania heteromorphia* (G 332); *Licania* spp. are elsewhere called *apacharama* (DV 105; G 332).

[f] Spelling variants include *asahí, asaí, huasahí,* and *huasi.*

[g] The seeds of the *huayruro* are considered to come in male and female forms: the solid red seed, *huayruro hembra*, considered female, is *Ormosia macrocalyx*; the red and black seed, *huayruro macho*, considered male, is *O. amazonica.* Photographs can be seen in Smithsonian Tropical Research, 2006a, 2006b.

[h] Doña María and don Roberto identify *maricahua* as the same plant as *toé negro, Teliostachya lanceolata.*

[i] *B. gasipaes* is probably the palm denoted by the Shuar term *uwí* (SR 351), rather than *Guilelma gasipaes* (Perruchon, 2003, p. 267 n. 9).

[j] This palm is probably not *Irartea exorhiza* (Luna & Amaringo, 1993, p. 88), since *Irartea* spp. have "non-spiny stilt roots" (G 192); Socratea is differentiated from *Irartea* by "stilt roots which are densely covered with spines" (CTD 117).

[k] A surprising number of genera are called *suelda con suelda* in Peru—*Adiantum latifolium* (D 21); *Ephedra americana* (BS 251–252), *Oryctanthus* spp. (D 492; DV 127; R 25), *Phoradendron* spp. (D 528–530; DV 135–136; G 568), *Psitticantus chanduyensis* (BS 355–356), and *Tristerix longibracteatus* (BS 355).

APPENDIX B

ANIMALS MENTIONED IN THE TEXT

BIRDS			
Popular Name	**English Name**	**Scientific Name**	**References**
ayaymama	potoo	*Nyctibius* spp.	CS 68–69; HB 234–235; PB 135–137; RG 223–226; SSLOP 198–199
camungo	horned screamer	*Anhima cornuta*	CS 19; HB 77; K 213; PB 111; RDT 79; RG 51–52; SSLOP 80–81
chajá	crested screamer	*Chauna torquata*	CS 19; see HB 77–78; SSLOP 80–81
cóndor	condor	*Vultur gryphus*	CS 23; HB 89; K 224; PB 121–122; RG 73; SSLOP 84–85
cushuri	cormorant	*Phalacrocorax* spp.	CS 14; HB 58; K 193; PB 104–106; RG 49–50; SSLOP 72–73
guacamayo	macaw	*Ara* spp.	CS 56; HB 198–202; K 267–268; PB 128–131; RDT 79; RG 183–186; SSLOP 166–167; see SaR 604
jabirú	jabiru	*Jabiru mycteria*	CS 18; HB 72; K 213–214; RG 72; SSLOP 38–39
manshaco	wood stork	*Mycteria americana*	CS 17; HB 70–71; K 213; RG 72; SSLOP 38–39
panguana	tinamou	*Crypturellas undulatus*	CS 2; HB 44; RDT 79; RG 33; SaR 605; SSLOP 32
pinsha	toucan	*Ramphastos cuvieri*[a]	CS 99; HB 330–331; RDT 79; RG 330–331; SaR 605; SSLOP 276
sharara	anhinga	*Anhinga anhinga*	CS 14; HB 59; PB 104–106; RG 50; SSLOP 72–73
tanrilla	sunbittern	*Eurypyga helias*	CS 39; HB 146; K 213; PB 110–113; RG 130; SSLOP 118–119

BIRDS, *continued*			
Popular Name	**English Name**	**Scientific Name**	**References**
trompetero	trumpeter	*Psophia* spp.	CS 35; HB 134–135; K 255–256; PB 119–121; RDT 80; RG 132; SaR 605; SSLOP 118–119

MAMMALS			
Popular Name	**English Name**	**Scientific Name**	**References**
achuni	coatimundi	*Nasua nasua*	B 204; E 153–154; ER 288–289; K 311; PB 206, 210; RDT 82; SaR 604
añuje	agouti	*Dasyprocta* spp.	B 193, 203; E 227–228; ER 463–466; K 303; PB 215, 217–218; RDT 81; SaR 604
bufeo colorado	pink dolphin	*Inia geoffrensis*	E 170–171; ER 319–321; K 205–206; PB 224–227
carachupa	armadillo	*Dasypus novencinctus*	B 193, 204; E 49–50; ER 104–105; K 309–310; PB 190–192; RDT 81; SaR 604
coto	red howler monkey	*Alouatta seniculus*	B 204; E 136–137; ER 265–266; K 152, 300–301; PB 202, 205; RDT 81; SaR 604
huangana	white-lipped peccary	*Tayassu pecari*	B 193, 203; E 176–177; ER 334–335; K 305–306; PB 210–214; SaR 604; T. albirostris, RDT 82, 91
intuto	opossum	*Didelphis marsupialis*	E 14–16; ER 54; K 314; PB 187–189; D. azarae, RDT 81
machín	capuchin monkey	*Cebus* spp.[b]	B 193, 204; E 127–130; ER 258–259; K 296–297; PB 201, 203; RDT 81, 92, 204
majás	paca	*Agouti paca*[c]	B 193, 203; E 224–225; ER 462–463 K 304; PB 215, 217–218
maquisapa	white-bellied spider monkey	*Ateles belzebuth*	B 204; E 143; ER 267–268; K 153, 298–299; PB 201–202, 205; RDT 81, 90; A. chamek, SaR 604
otorongo	tawny jaguar	*Panthera onca*[d]	E 168; ER 302–303; K 312; PB 207–210; RDT 82, 90, 92; SaR 604
pacarana	pacarana	*Dinomys branickii*	E 225–226; ER 454
rata	spiny rat	*Proechymis* spp.	E 232–233; ER 492–498; K 304

MAMMALS, *continued*			
Popular Name	**English Name**	**Scientific Name**	**References**
ronsoco	capybara	*Hydrochaeris hydrochaeris*	B 204; E 223–224; ER 460–461; K 207–208; PB 215–219; RDT 81; SaR 604
sachavaca	common tapir	*Tapirus terrestris*	B 193, 203; E 173–174; ER 329–330; K 306–307; PB 219–221; RDT 92; SaR 604
sajino	collared peccary	*Tayassu tajacu*	B 193, 203; E 175–176; ER 335–336; K 305; PB 210–214; RDT 82; SaR 604
venado	deer	*Mazama americana*	B 193, 203; E 178; ER 344–345; PB 211–212, 214; SaR 604; see RDT 82, 90, 92
yanapuma	black jaguar	*Panthera onca*[e]	E 168; ER 302–303; K 312; PB 207–210; RDT 82, 90, 92

REPTILES			
Popular Name	**English Name**	**Scientific Name**	**References**
boa amarilla	boa constrictor	*Boa constrictor*	BB 205–206; D 355; PB 82–86; K319K 208; RDT 78
boa negra	anaconda	*Eunectes murinus*	BB 211–212; D 357–358; PB 82–86; K 319; RDT 78
cascabel	rattler	*Bothrops* spp.[f]	
charapa	great river turtle	*Podocnemis expansa*	BB 146–147; K 210–211; RDT 78
jergón	fer-de-lance	*Bothrops* spp.	BB 268–269; D 390–391; K 315–316 ;PB 82–86; RDT 78
lagarto negro	black caiman	*Melanosuchus niger*	BB 135; D 328–329; K 209–210; RDT 78; SaR 604; *Caiman niger*, PB 77
shushupe	bushmaster	*Lachesis muta*	BB 272–273; D 391–392; K 317; PB 82–86; RDT 78
taricaya	yellow-spotted river turtle	*Podocnemis unifilis*	BB 148–149; PB 78, 80; RDT 78; SaR 604; see D 326–327
vibora	fer-de-lance	*Bothrops* spp.	BB 268–269; D 390–391; PB 82–86; K 315–316

FISH			
Popular Name	**English Name**	**Scientific Name**	**References**
acarahuazú[g]	oscar	*Astronotus ocellatus*	AA 267; FP 3612; OV 20; RDT 76, 92; SaR 606; *A. crassipinis*, OV 20
boquichico	black prochilodus	*Prochilodus nigricans*	AA 261–263; FP 11984; OV 11; RDT 76, 92; RKF 67; SaR 606; *P. vulginum*, C 128

FISH, *continued*			
Popular Name	**English Name**	**Scientific Name**	**References**
carachama	sailfin catfish	*Pterygoplichthys multiradiatus*	C 128; FP 4793; OV 18; RDT 76, 92; RKF 366; SaR 606
corvina	black curbinata	*Plagioscion auratus*	C 128; OV 20; RDT 76; *P. squamosissimus*, FP 4310; SaR 606
doncella	barred sorubim	*Pseudo-platystoma fasciatum*	AA 252; FP 6410; OV 15; RDT 76; SaR 606
dorado	gilded catfish	*Brachy-platystoma flavicans*	AA 249; *B. filamentosum*, OV 14; *B. rousseauxii*, RKF 435; *Ilisha deauratus*, C 128; RDT 77
gamitana	tambaqui	*Colossoma macropomum*	FP 263; OV 8; RKF 123; SaR 606; *C. bidens*, C 128; RDT 76, 92
lisa	banded leporinus	*Leporinus fasciatus*	C 128; FP 5352; OV 12; RDT 76, 92; RKF 75–77; SaR 606
maparate	highwaterman catfish	*Hypophthalmus edentatus*	OV 15; RKF 436; SaR 606; FP 4533; *H. marginatus*, OV 15, FP 25736; *Epapterus dispilurus*, FP 47660, OV 14, RDT 76, RKF 475
paiche	arapaima	*Arapaima gigas*	C 128; FP 2076; OV 6; RDT 76, 77, 92; RKF 31; SaR 606
palometa		*Mylossoma duriventris*	AA 257; C 128; FP 12977; OV 10; RDT 76; RKF 187; SaR 606; *Metynnis* spp., OV 8; RKF 184
paña	piranha	*Serrasalmus* spp.	C 128; FP 11964, 11970, 51194, 51196, 58140; OV 9; RDT 76–77; RKF 190–192; SaR 606
sábalo		*Brycon* spp.	AA 253; C 128; FP 14171, 25516, 51095; OV 7; RDT 76, 92; RKF 175–178; SaR 606; *Salminus* spp., OV 9
shirui	corydoras	*Corydoras* spp.	FP 12156, 12159, 12168, 12199, 13109, 46041, 46044, 46066, 46102; SaR 606; *Hoplosternum thoracatum*, OV 16; RDT 77

NOTE: AA = Araujo-Lima & Alvarez-León, 2003; B = Brownrigg, 1996; BB = Bartlett & Bartlett, 2003; C = Chibnik, 1994; CS = Clements & Shany, 2001; D = Duellman, 2005; E = Emmons, 1997; ER = Eisenberg & Redford, 1999; FP = Froese & Pauly, 2008; HB = Hilty & Boyd, 1986; K = Kricher, 1997; OV =

Ortega & Vari, 1986; PB = Pearson & Beletsky, 2008; RDT = Ríos, Dourojeanni, & Tovar, 1975; RG = Ridgely & Greenfield, 2001; RKF = Reis, Kullander, & Ferraris, 2003; SaR = Saldaña & Rojas, 2004; SS-LOP = Schulenberg, Stotz, Lane, O'Neill, & Parker, 2007.

Fish identifications should be viewed with some skepticism. Some species have many different common names; some common names are used to refer to many different species. *Colossoma bidens* is called both *tambaqui* and *gamitana*; *Brachyplatystoma flavicans* is called both *dorado* and *bagre*. Conversely, a fish called *bagre* could be any of twenty different species; the popular name *carachama* refers, in Peru alone, to fifteen different fish species. Citations to FP are to FishBase species identification number, and English names are those given by the American Fisheries Societies wherever possible.

[a] *Ramphastos cuvieri* of southern Colombia, Peru, Bolivia, and western Brazil is probably the same as *R. tucanus* of northeast Colombia to Guyana (HB 331).

[b] There are two *Cebus* species generally distinguished in the Peruvian Amazon—*machín blanco*, white capuchin, sometimes *mono blanco*, white monkey, *C. albifrons*; and *machín negro*, black capuchin, sometimes *mono negro*, black monkey, *C. apella* (B 193, 204; E 127–130; RDT 82; SaR 604; see Aquino & Encarnación, 1994; Soini, 1972).

[c] The genus name *Agouti* for the paca is confusing, because the paca is not an agouti; the various species of agouti, generally called *añuje* in the Peruvian Amazon, belong instead to the genus *Dasyprocta*. For that reason, the genus of the paca is sometimes given the name *Cuniculus*.

[d] The species is alternatively *Felis onca*. The jaguar is often called *tigre* in the Upper Amazon.

[e] Mestizos consider the *otorongo* and the *yanapuma* to be distinct species; Western zoologists consider both animals to be *Panthera onca*, with the yanapuma a melanistic form.

[f] In the Upper Amazon, where there are no rattlesnakes, the term *cascabel* is used to refer to juveniles of the genus *Bothrops*, probably because juvenile *B. atrox* have yellow tails (Armed Forces Pest Management Board, 2008; Russell, n.d.).

[g] Spelling variants include *acarahuasú* and *carahasú*.

NOTES

INTRODUCTION

1. Hood, 1996.

CHAPTER 1

1. Hankiss, 1981, p. 204.
2. Patai, 2001, p. 276.
3. Patai, 1988, p. 18; emphasis in original.

CHAPTER 2

1. It is possible that the term *mesa* was borrowed from the shamans of the northwestern Peruvian tradition, whose elaborate mesas are a central feature of their healing ceremonies. See, for example, the discussions in Joralemon & Sharon, 1993; Skillman, 1990.
2. Cebrián, 2005, p. 178.
3. Quoted in Tindall, 2008, p. 219.
4. See Luna, 1986c, p. 94.
5. Tindall, 2008, p. 191.

CHAPTER 3

1. Laderman & Roseman, 1996, p. 1; emphasis added.
2. Laderman & Roseman, 1996, p. 2.
3. Schechner, 1994, p. 183.
4. Hutton, 2001, p. 85.
5. Gómez-Peña, 2000, pp. 232–233.
6. Schechner, 1994, p. 184.
7. Schechner, 1988, pp. 50–51; see also Schechner, 1971.
8. Schechner, 1985, p. 5.
9. Schechner, 1985, p. 10.
10. Turner, 1969, p. 82; for discussion, see Duntley, 1993, p. 4.
11. Howe, 2000, p. 63.
12. Schechner, 1994, p. 185.
13. See, for example, Brown, 1988.
14. Sullivan, 1988, p. 459.
15. Schechner, 1994, p. 185.
16. Carlson & Shield, 1989; May, 1989, p. 108; Krippner, 1989, p. 112; Krieger, 1989, pp. 125–126; Kübler-Ross, 1989, p. 127; Johnson, 1989, p. 131.

17. Vizenor, 1997, p. 52; Brown, 1988, p. 103; Crocker, 1985, p. 237.
18. Hugh-Jones, 1994, p. 35.
19. Hutton, 2001, p. 90.
20. Laderman & Roseman, 1996, p. 6.
21. Strathern, 1995, p. 127.
22. Kendall, 1996, p. 50.
23. Katz, 1982, p. 107; for discussion see Turner, Blodgett, Kahona, & Benwa, 1992, p. 200.
24. Cited in Kalweit, 1992, p. 114.
25. Cited in Hutton, 2001, p. 94.
26. Cited in Hutton, 2001, p. 95.
27. La Barre, 1972, p. 319.
28. Singer, 1990, p. 444.
29. Singer, 1990, pp. 448–449.
30. Radin, 1926/1983, p. 103.
31. Radin, 1926/1983, pp. 110–111, 125.
32. Lévi-Strauss, 1958/1963, pp. 175–178.
33. See discussion in Glucklich, 1997, pp. 168–169.
34. Descriptions are given in Christopher, 1973, pp. 74–81; Cooper, 1944; Dunning, 1959, pp. 178–180; Feraca, 1998, pp. 3–44; Flannery, 1944; Hallowell, 1942; Holy Bull, 2000; Hultkrantz, 1992, pp. 37–39; Lewis, 1992, pp. 71–105; Powers, 1984.
35. Burger & Neale, 1995, p. 51; Hallowell, 1942, p. 74.
36. Dow, 1986, pp. 108, 110.
37. Drury, 1982, p. 1.
38. Harris, 1992, p. 412.
39. Harner, 1980, pp. 115–117.
40. Sullivan, 1988, p. 659.
41. Descola, 1993/1996, pp. 332–333.
42. Dow, 1986, p. 110; Bear, 2000, pp. 126–127; Gorman, 2006.
43. Perruchon, 2003, p. 218.
44. La Barre, 1972, p. 320.
45. Hallowell, 1942, p. 19.
46. Burger & Neale, 1995, p. 52.
47. Burger & Neale, 1995, p. 130.
48. Burger & Neale, 1995, pp. 6, 130.
49. Briggs, 1996, p. 187; Mattingly, 2000, p. 200.
50. Mattingly, 2000, p. 181.
51. See Mattingly, 2000, p. 199.

CHAPTER 4

1. Brown, 1989, p. 8.
2. Doore, 1988.
3. Harner, 1980, p. xii, 1988a, p. 182, 1989, p. 137.
4. Luna & Amaringo, 1993, p. 13.
5. Heinze, 1991, p. 7.

6. Perruchon, 2003, p. 214.
7. Buchillet, 2004, p. 118.
8. Buchillet, 2004, pp. 117–118.
9. Grof, 1994, p. 23; see also Kalweit, 1989.
10. Shoemaker, 1997b, p. 40.
11. Brown, 1986, pp. 60–61, 200 n. 3; Whitten, 1976, p. 146.
12. Adams, 1997, p. 113; Hillman, 1976/2000, p. 118, 1983a, p. 34; Moore, 1989, p. 112.
13. Moore, 1989, p. 112.
14. Moore, 1989, p. 113.
15. Moore, 1989, p. 112.
16. Hillman, 1988, p. 10.
17. Buber, 1947/1965, p. 14.
18. Lévinas & Kearney, 1986, p. 23.
19. See Welwood, 2000, pp. 11–14.
20. Kornfield, 1989, p. 150.
21. Harvey, 2003, p. 8.
22. Eliade, 1951/1964, pp. 264–265, 500. For critiques, see Balzer, 1997, p. xvi; Harvey, 2003, p. 16; Noel, 1997, p. 34.
23. Smith, 1987, pp. 2, 122 n. 2.
24. Eliade, 1951/1964, pp. 264–265, 269. See Noel, 1997, pp. 35–36; for a lengthy critique, see Smith, 1987.
25. Eliade, 1951/1964, p. 500.
26. Eliade, 1951/1964, p. 500.
27. Wasson, 1972b, pp. 197–200; Wasson & Wasson, 1957, p. 295.
28. Estrada, 1981, p. 55.
29. Estrada, 1981, p. 73.
30. Letcher, 2007, p. 104.
31. Estrada, 1981, p. 55.
32. Estrada, 1981, p. 25; Letcher, 2007, p. 104.
33. Letcher, 2007, p. 86.
34. Letcher, 2007, p. 100; Metzner, 1971, p. 104.
35. Znamenski, 2007, p. 128.
36. Estrada, 1981, p. 86.
37. Estrada, 1981, pp. 90–91.
38. Letcher, 2007, p. 102; Wasson, 1980, p. 28; Estrada, 1981, p. 55.
39. Vizenor, 1997, p. 52.
40. Crocker, 1985, p. 237.
41. Clastres, 1989, p. 144.
42. Perruchon, 2003, p. 266.
43. Cebrián, 2005, p. 27; my translation.
44. Brown, 1988, p. 114; Buchillet, 2004, p. 109.
45. Hugh-Jones, 1994, p. 35.
46. Douglas, 2005, p. 90.
47. Uzendoski, 2005, p. 58.
48. Métraux, 1949, p. 598.

49. Buchillet, 2004, p. 110; Chaumeil, 1983/2000, p. 65; Brown, 1989, p. 10.
50. Quoted in Charing, 2007a.
51. Rubenstein, 2002, p. 243.
52. Perruchon, 2003, p. 226.
53. Siskind, 1973a, p. 168.
54. Hugh-Jones, 1994, p. 36.
55. See also Freedman, 2000, p. 113.
56. Perruchon, 2003, p. 235.
57. Beckerman & Yost, 2007, p. 162.
58. Chacon, 2007, p. 539.
59. Whitehead, 2002, p. 205; Whitehead & Wright, 2004, p. 4.
60. Brown, 1989, p. 10.
61. Fausto, 2004, pp. 171–172.
62. Lagrou, 2004, p. 268 n. 2.
63. Chaumeil, 1983/2000, pp. 120–121.
64. Jackson, 1983, p. 198; Reichel-Dolmatoff, 1975, pp. 86, 241 n. 21.
65. Brown, 1988, pp. 103–104.
66. Freedman, 2000, p. 113.
67. Quoted in Rubenstein, 2002, p. 22.
68. Chaumeil, 1983/2000, pp. 62, 66, 219.
69. Lagrou, 2004, pp. 248–249.
70. Perruchon, 2003, p. 236.
71. Brown, 1988, p. 104, 1989, pp. 8, 10.
72. Dubé, 2003; Little, 2003.
73. Brown, 1988, p. 114.
74. Clastres, 1989, p. 144, 1994, p. 64.
75. Rubenstein, 2002, p. 244.
76. Buchillet, 2004, p. 124.
77. Wilbert, 2004, p. 28.
78. Lagrou, 2004, pp. 258, 262.
79. Goldman, 1979, p. 266.
80. Siskind, 1973a, p. 166.
81. Lagrou, 2004, p. 268 n. 2.
82. Descola, 1993/1996, p. 331.
83. See, for example, Hendricks, 1993, p. 290.
84. Brown, 1989, p. 10.
85. Freedman, 2000, p. 113.
86. Hugh-Jones, 1994, p. 71.
87. Chevalier, 1982, p. 402.
88. Perruchon, 2003, p. 225.
89. Taussig, 1987, p. 246.
90. Perruchon, 2003, pp. 236, 266.

CHAPTER 5

1. Dobkin de Ríos & Rumrrill, 2008, p. 45.

2. Bear, 2000, p. 133.
3. Castonguay, 1990, p. 90.
4. See Luna, 1986c, p. 50.
5. Luna & Amaringo, 1993, p. 60 n. 105.
6. Muratorio, 1991, p. 64.
7. Calvo, 1981/1995b, p. 111.
8. Quoted in Charing, 2007e.
9. See Dobkin de Ríos, 1973; Luna, 1984b, 1986c, pp. 51–55.
10. Calvo, 1981/1995b, p. 155.
11. Bear, 2000, pp. 131–132; Castonguay, 1990, p. 21.
12. Cebrián, 2005, p. 38.
13. Luna, 1986c, p. 45.
14. Chevalier, 1982, p. 346.
15. Luna & Amaringo, 1993, p. 56.
16. Quoted in Slawek, 2007.
17. Luna, 1986c, p. 52.
18. Sammarco & Palazzolo, 2002.
19. Quoted in Rubenstein, 2002, p. 153.
20. Silva, 2004, p. 195.
21. Silva, 2004, p. 196.
22. Schultes & Raffauf, 1992, p. 79.
23. Chaumeil, 1983/2000, pp. 9–10.
24. Muratorio, 1991, p. 181.
25. Quoted in Charing, 2007a.
26. See Luna, 1986c, p. 55.
27. Quoted in Cloudsley & Charing, 2007.
28. Luna, 1984b.
29. Quoted in Cloudsley & Charing, 2007.
30. Quoted in Rubenstein, 2002, p. 153.
31. Quoted in Slawek, 2007.
32. Quoted in Heaven & Charing, 2006, p. 52. The jealousy of the plants is reiterated in Chevalier, 1982, p. 348.
33. Quoted in Cloudsley & Charing, 2007.
34. Descola, 1993/1996, p. 339.
35. Quoted in Muratorio, 1991, p. 181.
36. Vargas Llosa, 1987/2001, p. 196.
37. Quoted in Muratorio, 1991, p. 215.
38. Quoted in Heaven & Charing, 2006, p. 52.
39. Luna, 1986c, p. 54.
40. Castonguay, 1990, p. 32.
41. Castonguay, 1990, p. 32.
42. Chevalier, 1982, p. 404 n. 19.
43. See Luna, 1986c, p. 54; Shoemaker, 1997a.
44. Quoted in Rubenstein, 2002, p. 153.
45. Payaguaje, 1990/2001, p. 231.

46. Freedman, 2000, p. 113; see Gow, 2001, p. 150.
47. Bear, 2000, pp. 132–133; Wilcox, 2003, p. 107.
48. Luna, 1984b.
49. Bear, 2000, p. 144.
50. Quoted in Hvalkof, 2004, p. 213.
51. Luna, 1986c, p. 66; Luna & Amaringo, 1993, p. 48 n. 80.
52. Luna, 1986c, p. 159.
53. Luna, 1986c, p. 63.
54. See Luna, 1986c, p. 71.
55. Heaven & Charing, 2006, p.140.
56. Luna, 1986c, p. 103, 1992, p. 238.

CHAPTER 6

1. Luna, 1992; Chávez, 2001, p. 143.
2. The most important reporting on icaros has been by Luis Eduardo Luna, in three largely overlapping publications (1984b, 1986c, 1992) based on his Iquitos fieldwork. In addition, there has been a very brief article by Rosa Alarco (1965/1985) and two articles analyzing the icaros sung during a single ayahuasca session (Katz & Dobkin de Ríos, 1971; Stocks, 1979). Alfonso Padilla (1984) wrote a musical analysis of seven icaros collected by Luna during his first period of fieldwork, published as an appendix to Luna, 1984b. Transcriptions of eight icaros are found in Luna, 1986c, pp. 174–180; and two others are transcribed in Luna & Amaringo, 1993, pp. 39–41, and Katz & Dobkin de Ríos, 1971. Icaros from a variety of mestizo ayahuasqueros are available on a number of CDs, videos, and audiocassettes. The line between commercially produced and homemade CDs is increasingly blurred with the increasing capabilities of relatively inexpensive computers; such small-scale CDs of icaros turn up from time to time on such outlets as eBay. Those interested in hearing a variety of mestizo icaros can try Campos, 2000; Garcia Sampaya, Montes Shuña, Gerena Pinedo, & Torres Devila, 2003; Gonzales Ramirez, 1998; Guerra Gonzales, 1987, 2001; Luna, 1984c, 1987; Montes Shuña, Laiche Celis, Coral, & Peña Shuña, 2001; Mossembite, 1983; Murayay, 2007; Panduro Vasquez, 2000; Rivas, 1988, 1998; Tangoa Paima, 2004.
3. Cebrián, 2005, p. 54; my translation.
4. Sammarco & Palazzolo, 2002.
5. See, for example, Hill, 1992, pp. 184–192; Illius, 1992, pp. 65–68, 71–73; Kracke, 1992, pp. 130–134; Pollock, 1992, pp. 32–34; Siskind, 1973c, pp. 31–37; Weiss, 1973, pp. 44–46.
6. Langdon, 1992b, p. 16.
7. Viveiros de Castro, 1994, p. 204.
8. Townsley, 2001, p. 267.
9. Snyder, 1969, p. 122, reprinted in 1973, p. 399, 1983, p. 93.
10. Snyder, 1975, p. 3, reprinted in 1977b, p. 12.
11. Rothenberg, 1968, p. 424, reprinted in 1981a, p. 186.
12. Rothenberg, 1976, p. 11, reprinted in 1981b, p. 134; Snyder, 1976, pp. 19–20, reprinted in 1977a, pp. 36–37, 1979/1980, p. 171.

13. Calvo, 1981/1995b, p. 70.
14. See Cebrián, 2005, p. 52.
15. Luna & Amaringo, 1993, p. 106 n. 155.
16. Gow, 2001, pp. 145–147.
17. For an example, see Bear, 2000, p. 118; Shoemaker, 1997a.
18. Slawek, 2007.
19. Demange, 2002.
20. Bear, 2000, pp. 133, 184.
21. Sammarco & Palazzolo, 2002.
22. Luna & Amaringo, 1993, p. 27.
23. Luna & Amaringo, 1993, p. 82.
24. Guerra Gonzales, 2001, track 10; Luna, 1986c, p. 107, 1992, p. 244; Luna & Amaringo, 1993, pp. 56, 60.
25. Luna & Amaringo, 1993, p. 64.
26. Luna & Amaringo, 1993, p. 62.
27. Luna & Amaringo, 1993, p. 98.
28. Luna & Amaringo, 1993, p. 58.
29. Panduro Vasquez, 2000, track 5.
30. Chávez, 2001, pp. 143–144.
31. Guerra Gonzales, 2001, track 3; Luna & Amaringo, 1993, p. 128.
32. Luna, 1984b.
33. Luna & Amaringo, 1993, pp. 54, 74.
34. Luna, 1992, p. 246.
35. Luna & Amaringo, 1993, p. 122.
36. Rivas, 1998, track 10.
37. Luna, 1992, p. 240.
38. Panduro Vasquez, 2000, track 12.
39. Luna & Amaringo, 1993, p. 56.
40. See Garcia Sampaya, Montes Shuña, Gerena Pinedo, & Torres Devila, 2003.
41. Panduro Vasquez, 2000, track 9.
42. Luna, 1986c, p. 103.
43. Guerra Gonzales, 2001, track 6; Panduro Vasquez, 2000, track 14.
44. Guerra Gonzales, 2001, track 5.
45. Luna, 1992, p. 246.
46. Luna & Amaringo, 1993, p. 64.
47. Luna & Amaringo, 1993, p. 112.
48. Chávez, 2001, pp. 143–144.
49. Luna & Amaringo, 1993, p. 142.
50. Luna, 1986c, p. 103.
51. Luna & Amaringo, 1993, p. 138.
52. Luna, 1986c, p. 103, 1992, pp. 238–239.
53. Quoted in Dobkin de Ríos & Rumrrill, 2008, p. 64.
54. Calvo, 1981/1995b, p. 155.
55. Sammarco & Palazzolo, 2002.
56. Luna, 1986c, p. 100.

57. Tindall, 2008, pp. 189, 191.
58. Calvo, 1981/1995b, p. 244.
59. Calvo, 1981/1995b, p. 140.
60. Lamb, 1985, p. 165.
61. Calvo, 1981/1995b, p. 69.
62. Luna & Amaringo, 1993, p. 118.
63. Luna & Amaringo, 1993, pp. 110–112.
64. Luna, 1992, p. 240.
65. Luna & Amaringo, 1993, p. 27.
66. Perruchon, 2003, p. 255.
67. Bear, 2000, pp. 118–119.
68. Luna & Amaringo, 1993, p. 93.
69. Luna, 1992; Luna & Amaringo, 1993, p. 38.
70. See Luna, 1986c, p. 107.
71. Luna, 1986c, p. 150.
72. Calvo, 1981/1995b, pp. 173–174.
73. Martin, 2005, p. 5.
74. Chaumeil, 1983/2000, pp. 127–128.
75. See Luna, 1992, p. 242.
76. Martin, 2005, p. 4. For recorded examples of Shipibo shamanic singing, see Martin, 2006.
77. Shoemaker, 1997a.
78. Dobkin de Ríos & Rumrrill, 2008, pp. 58, 60, 63–64, 153. Don Agustin Rivas makes a distinction—which I have not heard elsewhere—between icaros, which are tunes without words, and mariris, which are icaros with words (Bear, 2000, p. 110).
79. Calvo, 1981/1995b, p. 140.
80. Chaumeil, 1992, pp. 102–103.
81. Rothenberg, 1968, p. 386.
82. Cebrián, 2005, p. 53; Luna, 1986c, p. 122 n. 71.
83. Quoted in Charing, 2007b.
84. Siskind, 1973a, p. 135.
85. Slawek, 2007.
86. Cebrián, 2005, p. 265.
87. Townsley, 2001, pp. 267–268.
88. Taylor & Chau, 1983, pp. 96, 98.
89. Perruchon, 2003, pp. 229, 240–241, 245.
90. Vidal & Whitehead, 2004, pp. 56, 59.
91. Seeger, 2004, p. 33.
92. See Eliade, 1951/1964, pp. 168–180; Sullivan, 1988, pp. 426–427.
93. Sullivan, 1988, pp. 428, 656.
94. Métraux, 1949, p. 573.
95. Chaumeil, 1983/2000, p. 73.
96. Viveiros de Castro, 1994, p. 221.
97. Brown, 1986, p. 62; Perruchon, 2003, pp. 224, 267 n. 7; Whitten & Whitten, 2008,

p. 70; Descola, 1986/1994, p. 164, 1993/1996, p. 317; Chaumeil, 1983/2000, p. 73; Colson, 1977, p. 60; Sullivan, 1988, p. 435.

98. Muratorio, 1991, pp. 185, 263; Whitten & Whitten, 2008, p. 70.

99. Hugh-Jones, 1994, p. 49.

100. Cebrián, 2005, p. 59; Luna & Amaringo, 1993, p. 33 n. 42.

101. Grossman, 2006.

102. Luna & Amaringo, 1993, p. 33 n. 42; Weiskopf, 2005, p. 217.

103. De Civrieux, 1980, p. 23; Sullivan, 1988, p. 43.

104. Reichel-Dolmatoff, 1975, p. 94.

105. Reichel-Dolmatoff, 1968/1971, pp. 114, 129.

106. Gilbert & Pearson, 1999, pp. 39, 60.

107. Shepherd, 1992, p. 149.

108. Irigaray, 1985, pp. 25–26. See also Classen, 1990; Corbin, 1986; Howes, 1988; Jackson, 1989; Stoller, 1989, 1996.

109. Gilbert & Pearson, 1999, p. 87.

110. Shepherd, 1992, p. 148.

111. Gow, 1995, p. 43.

112. Gow, 1995, p. 43.

113. Gell, 1995, p. 236.

114. Gell, 1995, p. 235.

115. Jernigan, 2008.

116. Gell, 1995, pp. 237–238.

117. Gell, 1995, p. 240.

118. Goldman, 1979, pp. 210–211; Shanon, 2002, p. 59; Harner, 1973a, p. 15; Whitten & Whitten, 2008, p. 70.

119. Goldman, 1979, pp. 210–211; Lamb, 1985, p. 178; Shanon, 2000, p. 19; Flores & Lewis, 1978, p. 155; Harris, 2008, p. 61; Siskind, 1973a, p. 145.

120. Strassman, 1994, p. 112.

121. Gracie & Zarkov, 1985.

122. McKenna, 1991, p. 38.

CHAPTER 7

1. Strathern & Stewart, 2004, p. 315.

2. Métraux, 1949, p. 598; Sullivan, 1988, p. 419.

3. Luna, 1986c, p. 112.

4. Muratorio, 1991, p. 268; Whitten & Whitten, 2008, p. 61.5. See Métraux, 1967, pp. 91–92, 1944, p. 214.

6. Métraux, 1967, pp. 91–92; my translation.

7. Dobkin de Ríos & Rumrrill, 2008, pp. 58, 60, 63–64, 153.

8. Pollock, 1992, p. 27, 2004, pp. 202–206.

9. Langdon, 1992a, pp. 47–48.

10. Luna, 1986c, p. 112; for a full discussion, see Harner, 1973a, pp. 17–20.

11. Illius, 1992, p. 65.

12. Descola, 1993/1996, p. 336.

13. Brown, 1986, pp. 60–61, 200 n. 3.

14. Gentry, 1993, p. 187; Henderson, Galeano, & Bernal, 1995, pp. 188, 195; see Luna & Amaringo, 1993, p. 62. Duke & Vasquez, 1994, p. 75; see Luna & Amaringo, 1993, p. 70.
15. For example, Luna & Amaringo, 1993, pp. 70, 116.
16. Chevalier, 1982, p. 397 n. 13.
17. Perruchon, 2003, p. 267 n. 9; Iglesias, 1989, p. 82; Rodríguez, 1999, p. 291.
18. Perruchon, 2003, pp. 190, 237.
19. Calvo, 1981/1995b, p. 259.
20. Buchillet, 2004, p. 114; Fausto, 2004, p. 174 n. 8; Gow, 2001, p. 149; Jackson, 1983, p. 198; Lagrou, 2004, p. 266; Luna, 1986c, p. 31; Luna & Amaringo, 1993, pp. 70, 106; Reichel-Dolmatoff, 1975, p. 95; Whitten, 1976, p. 146.
21. Lagrou, 2004, p. 266.
22. Luna & Amaringo, 1993, p. 70.
23. Wilbert, 2004, pp. 28, 43.
24. Harner, 1971, pp. 158–159; Luna, 1986c, pp. 93–94.
25. Perruchon, 2003, pp. 237–238.
26. Chaumeil, 1983/2000, p. 119.
27. Brown, 1986, p. 60.
28. Whitten, 1976, p. 146; see also Whitten & Whitten, 2008, p. 78.
29. Sullivan, 1988, p. 407; Whitten, 1976, p. 146.
30. Descola, 1993/1996, p. 335.
31. Whitten & Whitten, 2008, p. 78.
32. Chaumeil, 1983/2000, p. 119.
33. Whitten & Whitten, 2008, p. 77.
34. Whitten & Whitten, 2008, pp. 60, 66, 71, 80.
35. Harner, 1973a, pp. 23–24.
36. Descola, 1993/1996, p. 332.
37. Sammarco & Palazzolo, 2002.
38. Luna, 1992, p. 236.
39. Luna, 1986c, p. 110.

CHAPTER 8

1. Perruchon, 2003, p. 225.
2. Quoted in Descola, 1993/1996, p. 337.
3. Perruchon, 2003, p. 225.
4. Brown, 1986, pp. 60–61, 200 n. 3; Whitten, 1976, p. 146.
5. Koch, 2000, p. 52.
6. Luna, 1984b, 1986c, pp. 37–39, 43–44.
7. Perruchon, 2003, p. 224.
8. Reichel-Dolmatoff, 1975, p. 107.
9. Harner, 1973a, p. 24.
10. Luna, 1986c, p. 110.
11. Langdon, 1992a, pp. 47–48.
12. Illius, 1992, p. 65.
13. Harner, 1973a, pp. 17–19; Perruchon, 2003, p. 224.

14. Quoted in Rubenstein, 2002, p. 159.
15. Métraux, 1967, p. 90.
16. Descola, 1993/1996, pp. 337–338.
17. Perruchon, 2003, pp. 244–245.
18. Perruchon, 2003, p. 231.
19. Reichel-Dolmatoff, 1975, pp. 80, 240 n. 6.
20. Perruchon, 2003, p. 228.
21. Descola, 1993/1996, p. 338.
22. Reichel-Dolmatoff, 1975, p. 82.
23. Freedman, 2000, p. 113; Gow, 2001, p. 150.
24. Perruchon, 2003, pp. 189, 340.
25. Perruchon, 2003, p. 235.
26. Buchillet, 2004, p. 125.
27. Harner, 1973a, pp. 17–19.
28. Sullivan, 1988, pp. 407, 763 n. 365; Whitten 1976, pp. 146–147.
29. Luna, 1986c, pp. 110, 116, 1992, p. 236.
30. Quoted in Charing, 2007a.
31. Perruchon, 2003, p. 230.
32. Perruchon, 2003, pp. 189, 230, 340.
33. Descola, 1993/1996, p. 345.
34. Luna & Amaringo, 1993, pp. 26–27.
35. Sammarco & Palazzolo, 2002.

CHAPTER 9

1. Buchillet, 2004, p. 111.
2. Viveiros de Castro, 1994, p. 223.
3. Chaumeil, 1983/2000, pp. 119–120; Reichel-Dolmatoff, 1975, p. 89.
4. Bear, 2000, p. 200.
5. For example, Baer, 1992, p. 86; Bartolomé, 1979, pp. 132–133; Brown, 1986, p. 62; Descola, 1993/1996, p. 331; Harner, 1973a, pp. 23–25; Hill, 1992, p. 198; Wright, 1992, pp. 164–165.
6. Baer, 1992, p. 86.
7. Reichel-Dolmatoff, 1975, p. 90.
8. Wright, 1992, p. 165.
9. Descola, 1993/1996, p. 331.
10. Brown, 1986, p. 62; Harner, 1973a, pp. 23–25.
11. Chaumeil, 1983/2000, pp. 119–120.
12. Quoted in Bartolomé, 1979, p. 133.
13. Ritzenthaler, 1963, pp. 321–322.
14. Maddox, 1923, pp. 80, 190–192.
15. Whiting, 1950, p. 214.
16. Bear, 2000, p. 17.
17. Bear, 2000, pp. 126–127.
18. Dow, 1986, p. 108.
19. Gorman, 2006.

20. Luna & Amaringo, 1993, p. 25.
21. Fock, 1963, pp. 105–108; Sullivan, 1988, p. 286, 854 n. 136.
22. Chaumeil, 1983/2000, p. 125.
23. Matteson, 1954, p. 84; Johnson, 2003, p. 214.
24. Whitten & Whitten, 2008, p. 62.
25. Hendricks, 1993, p. 164.
26. Varese, 1973/2002, p. 128.
27. Butt, 1956, pp. 50–54; Sullivan, 1988, p. 435.
28. Sullivan, 1988, p. 318; Viveiros de Castro, 1979, p. 43.
29. Fulop, 1954, p. 115; Sullivan, 1988, p. 390.
30. Johnson, 2003, p. 214.
31. Chaumeil, 1983/2000, p. 125.
32. Métraux, 1967, pp. 90–91.
33. Luna, 1986c, p. 91.
34. Cebrián, 2005, p. 154; Perruchon, 2003, p. 247.
35. Bear, 2000, p. 145.
36. Luna & Amaringo, 1993, pp. 25–26.
37. Clastres, 1972, p. 262; Sullivan, 1988, p. 292.
38. Harner, 1973a, pp. 17–19; Sullivan, 1988, pp. 407, 763 n. 365; Whitten 1976, pp. 146–147.
39. See generally Sullivan, 1988, p. 658, 1994.

CHAPTER 10

1. Harvey, 2003, p. 9.
2. Hallowell, 1975, 1992; for an extended discussion, see Harvey, 2006, pp. 33–49.
3. Blackburn, 1975, p. 66; for further discussion, see Morrison, 2000.
4. Abram, 1997, pp. 9–10; emphasis in original.
5. Bird-David, 1999, p. 67.
6. Salmón, 2000, p. 1327.
7. Abram, 1997, p. 13.
8. See generally Chichester, 2005; Harvey, 2005, 2006, pp. 5–9.
9. Harvey, 2005, p. 83.
10. Quoted in Viveiros de Castro, 2005, p. 40.
11. Viveiros de Castro, 2005, p. 40, see also 1998/2002, p. 309.
12. Langdon, 2004, p. 307.
13. Lenaerts, 2006.
14. Baer, 1994, p. 224, quoted in Viveiros de Castro, 1998/2002, p. 322 n. 9, 2005, p. 38.
15. Viveiros de Castro, 1998/2002, p. 308, 2005, p. 38.
16. Viveiros de Castro, 1998/2002, pp. 310–312, 2005, pp. 43–47.
17. Viveiros de Castro, 1998/2002, p. 308, 2005, p. 38; Uzendoski, 2005, p. 39.
18. Viveiros de Castro, 2005, p. 38.
19. Rivière, 1994, p. 256, quoted in Viveiros de Castro, 1998/2002, p. 308, 2005, p. 38.
20. Viveiros de Castro, 2005, p. 60.
21. Viveiros de Castro, 2005, p. 50.

22. Gow, 2001, p. 142.
23. Viveiros de Castro, 1996, p. 183.
24. Fausto, 2004, p. 171.
25. Goldman, 1979, p. 263.
26. McKenna, 1991, p. 27.
27. Jung, 1955/1997b, ¶706, p. 167, see also 1947/1997e, p. 164.
28. Jung, 1962/1997a, p. 28.
29. Cwik, 1995, p. 138; Jung, 1958/1997d, ¶186, p. 58.
30. See Hillman, 1983b, p. 55; Jung, 1962/1997a, p. 30.
31. Jung, 1935/1997c, ¶397, p. 145.
32. Hillman, 1983b, p. 62.
33. Ulanov & Ulanov, 1999, p. 41.
34. Hillman, 1975, p. 2.
35. Ramachandran, 1998, p. 107.
36. Winkelman, 2000, p. 50.
37. Turner, 1992, p. 28.
38. Goodman, 1990, p. 55.
39. Shweder, 1991, p. 347.
40. Blain, 2002, p. 153.
41. Hillman, 1983a, p. 36.
42. Hillman, 1975, p. xv.
43. Hillman, 1990, pp. 122–123; emphasis in original.
44. Hillman, 1975, p. xvi; emphasis altered.
45. Hillman, 1983a, p. 37.
46. Hillman, 1975, p. 136.
47. Adams, 1997, pp. 104–105.
48. Hillman, 1975, p. xvi.
49. Hillman, 1983a, p. 19.
50. Hillman, 1975, p. 12; emphasis removed.
51. Hillman, 1975, p. 13.
52. Calvo, 1981/1995b, p. 175.
53. Luna & Amaringo, 1993, pp. 34, 54–55, 106–107.
54. Chevalier, 1982, p. 371.
55. Quoted in Narby, 1999, p. 31.
56. Quoted in Gebhart-Sayer, 1986, p. 196.
57. Hamsa, 2007.
58. Gow, 2001, p. 148.
59. Quoted in Dobkin de Ríos & Rumrrill, 2008, p. 61.

CHAPTER 11

1. Luna, 1986c, p. 90.
2. Calvo, 1981/1995b, p. 155.
3. Luna & Amaringo, 1993, p. 21 n. 15.
4. Luna, 1984b.
5. See generally Luna, 1986c, pp. 90–94; Luna & Amaringo, 1993, p. 18 n. 12.

6. Luna, 1986c, p. 91.
7. Sammarco & Palazzolo, 2002.
8. Tindall, 2008, p. 165.
9. Luna & Amaringo, 1993, p. 88; the accompanying painting depicts curanderos swallowing virotes made from these four types of palms.
10. For the use of spirit birds in sorcery among the Shuar, see Harner, 1973a, p. 21.
11. The timelito is apparently a small shore bird, which I have been unable to identify.
12. Luna, 1984b, 1986c, pp. 90–92.
13. Bear, 2000, pp. 209–210.
14. Luna, 1986c, p. 92.
15. Luna, 1984b.
16. Panduro Vasquez, 2000, tracks 1–4.
17. Tindall, 2008, p. 218.
18. Luna, 1986c, p. 160; Luna & Amaringo, 1993, p. 18 n. 12; Taussig, 1987, p. 408.
19. Perruchon, 2003, p. 247.
20. For a photograph of Florida Water on a Vodou altar in Brooklyn, see Turner, 1999, p. 132.
21. See generally Yronwrode, 2003b, for a brief history of the commercial Florida Water and Kananga Water, as well as recipes for making your own.
22. Luna, 1986c, p. 146 n. 88.

CHAPTER 12

1. For example, Luna, 1986c, p. 88.
2. Shanon, 2002, pp. 61, 116–117.
3. Schultes & Raffauf, 1992, p. 24.
4. Bear, 2000, pp. 135, 142. The term yara is often applied generically to mermaids.
5. Lagrou, 2004, pp. 257, 269 n. 9; see Saladin d'Anglure & Morin, 1998, p. 60.
6. Muratorio, 1991, p. 182.
7. Muratorio, 1991, p. 257 n. 2.
8. Muratorio, 1991, pp. 184, 215.
9. Perruchon, 2003, p. 322.
10. Descola, 1993/1996, p. 325.
11. Silva, 2004, p. 195.

CHAPTER 13

1. This distinction was first drawn by Fabrega (1974) and Kleinman (1980).
2. Finkler, 1985/1994b, p. 5.
3. Good, 1994, p. 133.
4. Turner, 1984, p. 206.
5. Cassell, 1976, p. 48.
6. Garro & Mattingly, 2000, p. 9.
7. See Strathern & Stewart, 1999, p. 7.
8. For a comparison between biomedicine and "sacred healing," see Finkler, 1994a.
9. Strathern & Stewart, 1999, p. 192.
10. Good, 1994, p. 24; emphasis added.

11. Helman, 1985, p. 294.
12. Hahn, 1995, p. 14; or, again, sicknesses are "unwanted conditions of self, or substantial threats of unwanted conditions of self" (p. 22).
13. Dobkin de Ríos, 1972b, p. 78; Hvalkof, 2004, p. 57; Kamppinen, 1990, 1997; Perruchon, 2003, p. 233.
14. Perruchon, 2003, p. 233.
15. Bear, 2000, p. 212.
16. Luna, 1986c, p. 121; Perruchon, 2003, pp. 236–237.
17. Luna, 1986c, p. 121; Perruchon, 2003, pp. 236–237.
18. Descola, 1993/1996, p. 330; Dobkin de Ríos, 1972b, p. 78, 1992, p. 51; Kamppinen, 1989, 1997; Luna, 1986c, p. 121; Perruchon, 2003, pp. 237–238; Teixera-Pinto, 2004, p. 239.
19. Descola, 1993/1996, p. 330.
20. Perruchon, 2003, p. 233.
21. Perruchon, 2003, p. 239.
22. Descola, 1993/1996, pp. 330–331.
23. Quoted in Hvalkof, 2004, p. 210.
24. Bear, 2000, p. 212.
25. Young, 1983.
26. Foster & Anderson, 1978, pp. 53–70.
27. See generally the discussion in Helman, 1990, pp. 110–113.
28. See Whitehead, 2002, p. 69.
29. Carneiro, 1977, p. 222, quoted in Heckenberger, 2004, p. 187.
30. Chevalier, 1982, p. 377.
31. Buchillet, 2004, p. 112.
32. Reichel-Dolmatoff, 1975, p. 100.
33. Jackson, 1983, p. 198.
34. Goldman, 1979, p. 266.
35. Chaumeil, 1983/2000, pp. 251–252.
36. Mentore, 2004, pp. 142, 149.
37. Lagrou, 2004, p. 249.
38. Whitehead, 2002, p. 256 n. 20.
39. Langdon, 2004, p. 308.
40. Taussig, 1987, p. 394.
41. Buchillet, 2004, p. 117.
42. Buchillet, 2004, p. 117.
43. Saler, Horton, & Lothrop, 1970, p. 133.
44. Glass-Coffin, 2001, pp. 50–51; my translation.
45. Taussig, 1987, p. 393.
46. Taussig, 1987, p. 397.
47. Dobkin de Ríos, 1972b, p. 85.
48. Buchillet, 2004, p. 117; Charing, 2007c; Dobkin de Ríos, 1972b, p. 86.
49. Dobkin de Ríos, 1972b, p. 86.
50. Kamppinen, 1997, pp. 9–10.
51. Scott, 1990, pp. 143–144; see Joralemon & Sharon, 1993, p. 264.

52. Perruchon, 2003, p. 259.
53. Heaven & Charing, 2006, pp. 142, 146.
54. Chevalier, 1982, p. 383; Perruchon, 2003, p. 256.
55. Chevalier, 1982, p. 378.
56. Luna, 1986c, p. 121 n. 70.
57. Duke & Vasquez, 1994, p. 47.
58. Dobkin de Ríos, 1972b, p. 86; Luna & Amaringo, 1993, pp. 27, 108.
59. Charing, 2007c; Dobkin de Ríos, 1972b, p. 86.
60. Chaumeil, 1983/2000, p. 123.
61. Buchillet, 2004, p. 113; Jackson, 1983, p. 198.
62. Goldman, 1979, pp. 268–270.
63. Lagrou, 2004, p. 265.
64. Lagrou, 2004, p. 253.
65. Lagrou, 2004, p. 249.
66. Chevalier, 1982, p. 378.
67. Buchillet, 2004, pp. 115–116; Jackson, 1983, p. 198.
68. Scott, 1990, pp. 143–144.
69. Taussig, 1987, p. 394.
70. Buchillet, 2004, p. 116.
71. Taussig, 1987, pp. 393–394.
72. Lagrou, 2004, pp. 253–254, 266–267.
73. See Heckenberger, 2004, pp. 179–180.
74. Wright, 2004, p. 87.
75. Charing, 2007a.
76. Lagrou, 2004, p. 253.
77. Gow, 2001, p. 149; Teixeira-Pinto, 2004, p. 239.
78. Pollock, 2004, p. 207.
79. Gow, 2001, p. 149.
80. Siskind, 1973a, p. 167.
81. See, e.g., Fausto, 2004, pp. 158–159.
82. Reichel-Dolmatoff, 1975, p. 44.
83. Goldman, 1979, p. 263.
84. See Buchillet, 2004, p. 117.
85. Pollock, 2004, p. 205.
86. Heckenberger, 2004, p. 180.
87. Gray, 1997, pp. 30, 111.
88. Langdon, 2004, p. 307.
89. Descola, 1993/1996, p. 347.
90. Perruchon, 2003, pp. 199–200, 227.
91. Teixera-Pinto, 2004, pp. 239–240.
92. Stewart & Strathern, 2004, pp. 12, 27–28.
93. Pollock, 2004, p. 206.
94. Finkler, 1985/1994b, p. 52.
95. Bear, 2000, p. 32.
96. Bear, 2000, p. 111.

97. Luna & Amaringo, 1993, p. 25.
98. Buchillet, 2004, p. 119.
99. Teixera-Pinta, 2004, p. 239.
100. Gray, 1997, p. 111; Perruchon, 2003, pp. 199–200.
101. Perruchon, 2003, pp. 199–200.
102. Quoted in Rubenstein, 2002, p. 205.
103. See Whitehead, 2002, pp. 92–94.
104. García, 2002, pp. 39–40.
105. Muratorio, 1991, p. 224.
106. Goldman, 1979, p. 266.
107. Muratorio, 1991, p. 224.
108. García, 2002, p. 46.
109. García, 2002, p. 46; Muratorio, 1991, p. 224.
110. García, 2002, p. 46; Muratorio, 1991, p. 224.
111. Muratorio, 1991, p. 225.
112. García, 2002, p. 46.

CHAPTER 14

1. Muratorio, 1991, p. 222; see also Chibnik, 1994, pp. 91–92.
2. Taussig, 1987, p. 278.
3. Tanner, 2007.
4. Lewis, 1993, p. 194.
5. Desjarlais, 1996, pp. 151–152. An exception is Finkler (1985/1994b), who has studied the outcomes of treatment by spiritualist healers in Mexico.
6. Kleinman & Kleinman, 1995, p. 96; see generally Kleinman, 1992/1995.
7. Kleinman, 1992/1995, p. 275 n. 17.
8. Scott, 1985, p. 348.
9. Kleinman, 1992/1995, p. 123.
10. Kleinman, 1992/1995, pp. 126, 134, 140.
11. Lock & Scheper-Hughes, 1996, p. 67. On illness as resistance to unbearable life situations, see also Brodwin, 1992; on illness as an expressed reaction to a previous physical attack—including domestic assaults—by another person, in some cases years later, see Strathern & Stewart, 1999, pp. 97–98.
12. Kleinman, 1992/1995, pp. 144–146.
13. Elliott, 2000.
14. Hacking, 1995, 1998.
15. Rubel, O'Nell, & Collado-Ardon, 1984.
16. Helman, 1990, pp. 235–236.
17. Good, 1994, p. 128.
18. Good, 1994, p. 128.
19. Sarbin, 1986, pp. 8, 19.
20. Ricoeur, 1983, p. 177, 1983/1984, pp. 65, x, see also 1984/1985, p. 61.
21. Ricoeur, 1984/1985, p. 66.
22. Simms, 2003, p. 80.
23. Todorov, 1968/1981, pp. 43–45.

24. Kirmayer, 2000, p. 172.
25. Ricoeur, 1981, p. 278.
26. Good, 1994, p. 121.
27. Good, 1994, p. 144.
28. Ricoeur, 1981, p. 278.
29. Csordas, 2002, p. 166; Frank, 1961/1974.
30. Eisenberg, 1981, p. 245.
31. Moerman, 1997, p. 251.
32. Brody, 1987.
33. Whitehead, 2002, p. 256 n. 20.
34. See also Helman, 1981, 1990, pp. 90–91.
35. Joralemon & Sharon, 1993, pp. 211–213.
36. Calvo, 1981/1995b, p. 139.
37. See Lock, 1988; Lock & Scheper-Hughes, 1996.
38. Joralemon & Sharon, 1993, p. 258.
39. For example, Muratorio, 1991, p. 222.
40. Calvo, 1981/1995b, p. 140.
41. Taussig, 1987, p. 395.

CHAPTER 15

1. Eliade, 1951/1964, pp. 264–265, 269, 500. For critiques, see Balzer, 1997, p. xvi; Harvey, 2003, p. 16; Noel, 1997, pp. 34–36; Smith, 1987, pp. 2, 122 n. 2.
2. Lagrou, 2004, p. 261.
3. Gow, 2001, p. 139.
4. In Hendricks, 1993, p. 290.
5. Brown, 1986, p. 62.
6. Lamb, 1985, p. 127.
7. Slawek, 2007.
8. Muratorio, 1991, pp. 230–234.
9. Quoted in Dobkin de Ríos & Rumrrill, 2008, p. 62.
10. See Luna, 1986c, p. 94.
11. See, for example, Cebrián, 2005, p. 27.
12. Luna, 1984b.
13. Luna, 1986c, p. 94; Luna & Amaringo, 1993, p. 15.
14. Weiss, 1973, p. 44.
15. Reichel-Dolmatoff, 1975, p. 104.
16. Johnson, 2003, pp. 212, 215–216.
17. Whitten & Whitten, 2008, pp. 71, 78–79.
18. Chaumeil, 1983/2000, p. 69.
19. Perruchon, 2003, p. 196.
20. Déléage, n.d.; Valenzuela & Valera Rojas, 2005.
21. Descola, 1993/1996, pp. 344–345.
22. Muratoria, 1991, p. 184.
23. Muratorio, 1991, p. 213.
24. Muratorio, 1991, p. 185.

25. Muratorio, 1991, pp. 230–234.
26. Jakobsen, 1999, p. 4; Shirokogoroff, 1935/1982, p. 274.
27. Harvey, 2003, p. 9.
28. Bowie, 2000, pp. 199–200.
29. Perruchon, 2003, p. 230.
30. Perruchon, 2003, pp. 189, 340.
31. Perruchon, 2003, pp. 227–228.
32. Brown, 1986, pp. 62, 64.
33. Fausto, 2004, pp. 161, 174 n. 8.
34. Descola, 1993/1996, p. 345.
35. Luna, 1984b.
36. See Luna, 1986c, p. 133.
37. Luna, 1986c, p. 135.
38. Luna, 1986c, pp. 133–135.
39. Eliade, 1951/1964, p. 6; Humphrey & Onon, 1996, p. 31; Vitebsky, 1995, pp. 10–11, 2000, pp. 56–57.
40. Dodds, 1951, p. 88 n. 43.
41. Rouget, 1980/1985, pp. 18–19.
42. Harner, 1988b, p. 8; emphasis in original.
43. See, for example, Rouget, 1980/1985, p. 23.
44. Findeisen, 1957, p. 237; Reinhard, 1976; Siikala, 1992, pp. 11, 21; see also Eliade, 1961, p. 155.
45. Jakobsen, 1999, p. 7.
46. Oppitz, 1981.
47. For example, Hultkrantz, 1992, pp. 19, 158.
48. Hultkrantz, 1996, p. 16.
49. Siikala, 1992, pp. 11, 21.
50. Anisimov, 1958, pp. 100–105.
51. Hutton, 2001, pp. 87–90.

CHAPTER 16

1. Luna & Amaringo, 1993, p. 84 n. 133.
2. Slawek, 2007.
3. Luna & Amaringo, 1993, p. 84 n. 133.
4. Brown, 1985, p. 378.
5. Slawek, 2007.
6. Cebrián, 2005, p. 57.
7. Sammarco & Palazzolo, 2002.
8. Slawek, 2007.
9. Slawek, 2007.
10. Fock, 1963, pp. 123, 126; Sullivan, 1988, p. 403.
11. Fock, 1963, p. 127; Sullivan, 1988, p. 403.
12. Brown, 1985, 1986, p. 57.
13. Reichel-Dolmatoff, 1979/1997a.
14. Reichel-Dolmatoff, 1975, pp. 79, 90.

15. Chaumeil, 1983/2000, p. 123.
16. Baer & Snell, 1974, p. 69; Sullivan, 1988, p. 418.
17. Baer, 1992, pp. 86–87.
18. Luna & Amaringo, 1993, p. 84 n. 133; Whitten, 1985, p. 109; Whitten & Whitten, 2008, p. 66.
19. Whitten & Whitten, 2008, p. 60.

CHAPTER 17

1. Quoted in Pendell, 2005, p. 145.
2. Hvalkof, 2004, p. 59.
3. Lenaerts, 2006.
4. Perruchon, 2003, p. 195.
5. Harner, 1971, p. 155.
6. Brown, 1986, p. 61; Descola, 1993/1996, p. 330.
7. Lagrou, 2004, p. 244; see Kensinger, 1973, p. 13 n. 6.
8. Ministerio de Salud del Perú, 2002; Tournon, 1991.
9. Quoted in Luna & Amaringo, 1993, p. 18.
10. Vidal & Whitehead, 2004, p. 56.
11. Buchillet, 1992, 2004, p. 111.
12. Hvalkof, 2004, p. 59.
13. Reichel-Dolmatoff, 1975, p. 81.
14. Wright, 2004, pp. 86–87.
15. Chevalier, 1982, p. 364.
16. Lagrou, 2004, pp. 249, 258.
17. Perruchon, 2003, pp. 245, 255; on mestizo use of Tarot cards for medical diagnosis, see Dobkin de Ríos, 1969, 1972b, pp. 88–91, 2006.
18. Perruchon, 2003, p. 177.
19. Luna, 1986c, p. 108.
20. See Buhner, 1996, p. 26, 2002, pp. 26, 32–33, 35.
21. Swerdlow, 2000, pp. 6–7; a very similar story is in Tindall, 2008, p. 254.
22. Lamb, 1985, p. 165.
23. Luna & Amaringo, 1993, pp. 110–112.
24. Calvo, 1981/1995b, p. 191.
25. Cebrián, 2005, p. 126.
26. Calvo, 1981/1995b, p. 212.
27. Calvo, 1981/1995b, p. 211.
28. Chevalier, 1982, p. 344.

CHAPTER 18

1. For example, Lacaze & Alexiades, 1995, containing seventy-seven plant descriptions; Mejia & Rengifo, 2000, containing 105 plant descriptions; and Pinedo, Rengifo, & Cerruti, 1997, containing fifty-two plant descriptions.
2. Mejia & Rengifo, 2000.
3. Luna & Amaringo, 1993, p. 130.
4. Luna, 1986c, p. 123.

5. Bear, 2000, p. 212.
6. Bear, 2000, p. 126.
7. Luna & Amaringo, 1993, p. 128.
8. Brown, 1986, p. 62; Descola, 1993/1996, pp. 322, 329–330; Perruchon, 2003, p. 190.
9. Gow, 2001, pp. 135, 139.
10. Whitten & Whitten, 2008, pp. 66, 71, 80.
11. Luna & Amaringo, 1993, p. 70.
12. Quoted in Reichel-Dolmatoff, 1975, pp. 95–96.
13. Luna, 1986c, pp. 131, 147.
14. Bear, 2000, p.74.
15. See generally Dobkin de Ríos, 1981. See Duke & Vasquez, 1994, p. 133; Heaven & Charing, 2006, p. 177; Luna, 1986c, p. 137.
16. For example, Taussig, 1987, p. 252.
17. Luna, 1986c, p. 108.
18. Hvalkof, 2004, p. 59.
19. Hvalkof, 2004, p. 59; Lenaerts, 2006.
20. Quoted in Hvalkof, 2004, p. 222.
21. Quoted in Heaven & Charing, 2006, p. 177.
22. Luna & Amaringo, 1993, pp. 110–112.
23. Chaumeil, 1983/2000, p. 247.
24. Castonguay, 1990, p. 109.
25. Brown, 1986, pp. 153–160; Chevalier, 1982, pp. 384–389.
26. Rosengren, 2000, p. 232.
27. Vidal & Whitehead, 2004, p. 56.
28. Wright, 2004, pp. 95, 106 n. 17.
29. Luna & Amaringo, 1993, p. 118 n. 168.
30. Kulick, 1998, pp. 3, 84, 108.
31. See Castonguay, 1990, p. 114.
32. Perruchon, 2003, p. 255.
33. Heaven & Charing, 2006, p. 150.
34. Heaven & Charing, 2006, p. 150.
35. Luna, 1986c, p. 105, 1992, p. 241.
36. Quoted in Dobkin de Ríos & Rumrrill, 2008, p. 64.
37. Quoted in Charing, 2007d.
38. Perruchon, 2003, p. 255.
39. Castonguay, 1990, p. 11; Emmons, 1997, pp. 153–154.
40. Bear, 2000, pp. 158–159.

CHAPTER 19

1. Chevalier, 1982, p. 13; Dobkin de Ríos, 1992; Luna, 1984b, 1986c, p. 14; Luna & Amaringo, 1993, p. 12.
2. Cebrián, 2005, pp. 24–25; Chevalier, 1982, p. 340; Luna, 1986c, p. 32.
3. Bear, 2000, p. 18.
4. Luna, 1984b, 1986c; Luna & Amaringo, 1993, pp. 12–13.

5. Chaumeil, 1992, p. 104; Luna, 1984b. On spiritist healing, see Bragdon, 2004; Bronson, 1983; Koss-Chiono, 2005; Tsemberis & Stefancic, 2000. An excellent summary of spiritist doctrine in South America is Dobkin de Ríos & Rumrrill, 2008, p. 1923.
6. Chevalier, 1982, p. 381; Luna, 1986c, p. 32.
7. Marcelo Simão Mercante, personal communication, June 26, 2003.
8. Chevalier, 1982, p. 361.
9. They often make this same distinction in terms of colors. Don Roberto and doña María say that they are pura blancura, followers of the pure white path, as opposed to brujos, sorcerers, who practice magia negra, black magic, or the even worse magia roja, red magic.
10. Sammarco & Palazzolo, 2002.
11. See generally Luna, 1986c, p. 32; Luna & Amaringo, 1993, p. 13.
12. Chevalier, 1982, pp. 340 n. 4, 349.
13. Hvalkof, 2004, p. 59.
14. Chevalier, 1982, pp. 340 n. 4, 349.
15. Demange, 2002; Luna & Amaringo, 1993, p. 38. Again, this notion is widespread in the Amazon. Among the Araweté, a shaman is evaluated according to his singing style and the originality of his songs (Viveiros de Castro, 1994, p. 225).
16. Gow, 1996, p. 96.
17. For a painting of such a "spiritual heart operation," see Luna & Amaringo, 1993, p. 103.
18. Sammarco & Palazzolo, 2002.
19. Bear, 2000, pp. 18, 132.
20. Luna & Amaringo, 1993, p. 134 n. 180.
21. Sammarco & Palazzolo, 2002.
22. Luna & Amaringo, 1993, p. 32 n. 37. Harner (1971, p. 119) sees the loan going in the other direction—from Spanish *banco*, which indicates the part of the placer mining apparatus that retains the gold-bearing gravel. *Banku* thus refers to a shaman believed to be a similarly rich repository of shamanic power.
23. Uzendoski, 2005, p. 58; see also Muratorio, 1991, pp. 181, 184, 260.
24. Luna & Amaringo, 1993, p. 32 n. 37; Whitten, 1976, p. 149.
25. Perruchon, 2003, p. 196.
26. Descola, 1993/1996, p. 344.
27. Sammarco & Palazzolo, 2002. A painting of a banco under a mosquito net while celestial spirits descend on him is in Luna & Amaringo, 1993, p. 100.
28. Bear, 2000, pp. 18, 137, 191, 203–205.
29. Chevalier, 1982, p. 350; Gebhart-Sayer, 1984, p. 44.
30. Ministerio de Salud del Perú, 2002, pp. 107–108.
31. Tournon, 1991.
32. Silva, 2004, p. 195.
33. Déléage, n.d.; Valenzuela & Valera Rojas, 2005, p. 114.
34. Luna & Amaringo, 1993, pp. 74, 128.
35. Luna & Amaringo, 1993, p. 140.
36. Luna, 1984b.

37. Luna, 2005.
38. Luna, 1984b.
39. Luna, 1984b.
40. Sammarco & Palazzolo, 2002.
41. Calderwood, 2008, p. 20; Charing & Cloudsley, 2006, p. 18; Freedman, 2000, p. 118; Gow, 1996, p. 105; Sammarco & Palazzolo, 2002.
42. Tindall, 2008, p. 209.
43. Tindall, 2008, p. 209.
44. Freedman, 2000, p. 118.
45. Luna & Amaringo, 1993, pp. 82, 84, 86, 106, 124.
46. Luna & Amaringo, 1993, p. 32.
47. Luna & Amaringo, 1993, p. 128.

CHAPTER 20

1. McKenna, Luna, & Towers, 1995.
2. López Vinatea, 2000.
3. Mercier, 1979, p. 352; Whitten, 1976, p. 305.
4. Gow, 1991, pp. 187, 191, 1995, p. 54.
5. On the Pacific coastal areas, see Reichel-Dolmatoff, 1960. On the Peruvian and Bolivian Amazon, see Alexiades, 1999; Andritzky, 1989a, 1989b; Arevalo, 1986; Baer, 1969, 1979, 1992; Baer & Snell, 1974; Bear, 2000; Brown, 1978, 1986, 1988, 1989; Carneiro, 1964; Chaumeil, 1983/2000; Chaumeil & Chaumeil, 1979; Chevalier, 1982; Desmarchelier, Gurni, Ciccia, & Giulietti, 1996; Dobkin de Ríos, 1970a, 1970b, 1971, 1972b, 1973; Friedberg, 1965; Gebhart-Sayer, 1984, 1985, 1986; Illius, 1992; Johnson, 2003; Katz & Dobkin de Rios, 1971; Kensinger, 1973; Kusel, 1965; Langdon, 1979; Luna, 1984a, 1984b, 1986c, 1991a, 1992, 2003; Luna & Amaringo, 1993; Rusby, 1923; Shepard, 1998; Siskind, 1973a, 1973b, 1973c; Stocks, 1979; Weiss, 1973, 1975; White, 1922. On the peoples of Colombia, see Bristol, 1966; Brüzzi, 1962; de Calella, 1935, 1944a, 1944b; Goldman, 1979; Koch-Grünberg, 1909–1910, 1923; Morton, 1931; Reichel-Dolmatoff, 1944, 1968/1971, 1969, 1970, 1972, 1975; Taussig, 1987; Uscátagui, 1959. On the peoples of Ecuador, see Davis & Yost, 1983a, 1983b, 1983c; Descola, 1986/1994, 1993/1996; Harner, 1971, 1973a, 1973b, 1973c; Marles, Neill, & Farnsworth, 1988; Mercier, 1979; Naranjo, 1975, 1979, 1983; Perruchon, 2003; Whitten, 1976. On Amazonian Brazil, see Ducke, 1957; Lowie, 1946; Prance, 1970; Prance, Campbell, & Nelson, 1977; Prance & Prance, 1970.
6. Luna, 1986a, 1986b; Luna & Amaringo, 1993. For reviews of the literature, see Naranjo, 1983; Ott, 1994, 1996; Reichel-Dolmatoff, 1975; Schultes & Hofmann, 1980.
7. Among the Campa Indians, ayahuasca is known as *kamárampi*, vomitive, emetic—a valued effect, associated with cleansing (Chevalier, 1982, p. 406 n. 22; Johnson, 2003, p. 217; Weiss, 1973, pp. 43–44).
8. Etkin (1986, p. 18) argues that the diarrhea and vomiting induced by the ayahuasca vine were its primary action, intended as treatment for intestinal infections, with psychoactivity used solely as a dosage marker; see also Rodríguez & Cavin, 1982.
9. Luna, 1984b.

10. Demange, 2002.
11. Lewis, 1998, p. 714.
12. McKenna, 1999, p. 193; Ott, 1996, p. 204; Schultes & Hofmann, 1992, p. 53.
13. Shulgin & Shulgin, 1997, pp. 444–448.
14. Hanson, 2005, p. 211.
15. See Bigwood & Ott, 1997, pp. 57–58; McKenna, Callaway, & Grob, 1998; Ott, 1996, p. 164; Stafford, 1992, p. 322; Strassman, 1991.
16. Schultes, 1954; Seit, 1967.
17. De Budowski, Marini-Bettòlo, Delle Monache, & Ferrari, 1974; McKenna & Towers, 1985; McKenna et al., 1998; Ott, 1996, p. 164.
18. Deshayes, 2002, p. 71.
19. Davis, 1995; McKenna et al., 1995; McKenna et al., 1998; McKenna, Towers, & Abbott, 1984; Nichols, Oberlender, & McKenna, 1991; Shulgin, 1978; Schultes, 1972.
20. Allende, 2008, p. 210; Piccalo, 2008; Hancock, 2005.
21. Arkenberg, 2006, p. 205.
22. Perrine, 1996, p. 237.
23. Goldberg, 2006, p. 269.

CHAPTER 21

1. Ginsberg, 1961, p. 96.
2. Burroughs & Ginsberg, 1963/1975, p. 30.
3. Walker, 2004, p. 52.
4. Allende, 2008, pp. 211–212.
5. Taussig, 1987, pp. 406–407, 410, 412, 438.
6. Dobkin de Ríos, 1972b, p. 127. Numerous plants of the Upper Amazon used as emetics and purgatives are given in Schultes & Raffauf, 1990; of the fifty rain forest plants discussed by Taylor (1998), twelve are listed as vermifuges.
7. Bear, 2000, p. 133.
8. Bear, 2000, p. 21.
9. Gow, 2001, p. 139.
10. Duke & Vasquez, 1994, p. 92.
11. Lewis et al., 1991.

CHAPTER 22

1. Callaway et al., 1996; Der Marderosian, Pinkley, & Dobbins, 1968; Hashimoto & Kawanishi, 1975; Hochstein & Paradies, 1957; McKenna, Callaway, & Grob, 1998; McKenna, Towers, & Abbott, 1984; Poisson, 1965; Rivier & Lindgren, 1972; Schultes, Holmstedt, & Lindgren, 1969. Tetrahydroharmine is also called d-leptaflorine, since it was originally isolated from *Leptactinia densiflora*; harmaline is also called dihydroharmine.
2. Buckholtz & Boggan, 1977; Lindgren, 1995, p. 347; Udenfriend, Witkop, Redfield, & Weissbach, 1958.
3. Callaway et al., 1999; Ott, 1994; Pinkley, 1969; Schultes, 1957.
4. Callaway et al., 1999; McKenna et al., 1998.
5. Callaway, Airaksinen, McKenna, Brito, & Grob, 1994, p. 386.
6. Shulgin & Shulgin, 1997, pp. 455–457.

7. Halpern, 1930a, 1930b; Slotkin, DiStefano, & Au, 1970; Leuner & Schlichting, 1989; De Smet, 1985.
8. Turner, Merlis, & Carl, 1955.
9. Ott, 1994, p. 55.
10. Naranjo, 1967, 1973b. For a sharply worded critique, see Ott, 1996, p. 260 n. 3.
11. Naranjo, 1967, p. 390.
12. Naranjo, 1967, p. 390.
13. Naranjo, 1973b, pp. 178–190.
14. Shulgin & Shulgin, 1997, pp. 445–447.
15. Shulgin & Shulgin, 1997, p. 447.
16. Frison, Favretto, Zancanaro, Fazzin, & Ferrara, 2008.
17. Naranjo, 1973b; Ott, 1996, p. 260 n. 3.
18. Weil, 1980/1998, p. 128; Weiskopf, 2005, p. 122.
19. Perruchon, 2003, p. 216.
20. Lamb, 1985, p. 178.
21. Luna, 1986c, p. 59.
22. Davis, 1998, p. 163.
23. Davis, 1996, p. 216.
24. Pinchbeck, 2002, p. 140.
25. Luna, 1984b.
26. Bonson & Baggott, 2002, pp. 236–237. In this regard, too, it is interesting to note that animals trained to respond to the effects of harmaline identify 2,5-dimethoxy-4-methylamphetamine, or DOM, also called STP, a phenethylamine hallucinogen, as having effects similar to those of harmaline (Bonson & Baggott, 2002, p. 237).
27. Rodd, 2008.
28. Ott, 1994, p. 35; Hochstein & Paradies, 1957.
29. Callaway, 1999, p. 267.
30. Shulgin & Shulgin, 1997, p. 586.
31. Agurell, Holmstedt, & Lindgren, 1968; Der Marderosian et al., 1968; McKenna et al., 1984; Poisson, 1965; see Ott, 1994, Table II-B, p. 40.
32. Callaway, Brito, & Neves, 2005; Callaway et al., 1999; Der Marderosian, Kensinger, Chao, & Goldstein, 1970; McKenna et al., 1984; Rivier & Lindgren, 1972; see Ott, 1994, Table II-B, p. 40.
33. Callaway et al., 1999; Hochstein & Paradies, 1957; McKenna et al., 1984; Poisson, 1965; Rivier & Lindgren, 1972; Schultes et al., 1969; see Ott, 1994, Table II-A, p. 38.
34. See generally Chen & Saunders, 1999; Hunter & Aarssen, 1988; Stuller, 1995.
35. Reichel-Dolmatoff, 1975, p. 198; Weiskopf, 2005, pp. 128–129.
36. Reichel-Dolmatoff, 1975, pp. 198–199; Weiskopf, 2005, p. 127.
37. Callaway, 1999, p. 268; Callaway et al., 2005, pp. 146–149. Special care was taken to select leaves at equivalent stages of development.
38. Weiskopf, 2005, p. 114.
39. Weiskopf, 2005, p. 125.
40. Luna, 1986c, p. 144 n. 85.
41. Quoted in Dobkin de Ríos & Rumrrill, 2008, p. 61.

42. Luna, 1986c, p. 151.
43. Davis, 1996, p. 218; Junquera, 1989, pp. 52–53; Weiskopf, 2005, pp. 123–125.
44. Callaway, 1999, p. 267. These results appear not to have been replicated in Callaway et al., 2005, p. 146.
45. Callaway, 2005; Callaway et al., 1999; Der Marderosian et al., 1970; Liwszyc, Vuori, Rasanen, & Issakanen, 1992; McKenna et al., 1984; Rivier & Lindgren, 1972; see also Ott, 1994, Table II-C, p. 41.
46. Callaway, 2005, p. 153.
47. Callaway, 2005; Callaway et al., 1999; McKenna et al., 1984; Rivier & Lindgren, 1972.
48. Callaway, 2005; Rivier & Lindgren, 1972. For a general discussion, see McKenna et al., 1998, p. 66; Ott, 1994, pp. 33–50.
49. McKenna et al., 1984; Ott, 1994, p. 37.
50. Weiskopf, 2005, pp. 115–116.
51. Weiskopf, 2005, pp. 118–119.
52. Pinchbeck, 2002, p. 212.
53. Swerdlow, 2000, p. 244.
54. Swerdlow, 2000, pp. 117, 290.
55. Swerdlow, 2000, pp. 47, 232.
56. These descriptions are derived from a discussion on the Ayahuasca Forums Web site; see Druiddream, 2004; Ichinen, 2004; Napoleon Blownapart, 2004.
57. Shulgin & Shulgin, 1997, pp. 298, 585.
58. Laing, 2003, p. 110; Ott, 1996, p. 204; Shulgin & Shulgin, 1997, p. 454.
59. Gayle, 2007; Mirante, 2008a, 2008b; see also Luna, 1984b.
60. Tupper, 2006, p. 4; DeGrandpre, 2006, pp. 27, 239.
61. "Drug made from Indian plant," 1932; "Drug said to cause clairvoyance," 1932.
62. Ott, 1996, pp. 210, 233; Rouhier, 1924.
63. Burroughs, 1953/1977, pp. 151–152.
64. García Barriga, 1958, quoted in Reichel-Dolmatoff, 1975, p. 233 n. 43.
65. Naranjo, 1973a, pp. 125, 170, 1973b, pp. 183–185, 1987.
66. Reichel-Dolmatoff, 1975, p. 233 n. 43.
67. Weil, 1980/1998, pp. 101–102.
68. Lamb, 1971/1974.
69. Carneiro, 1980; de Mille, 1990, pp. 452–453; Dobkin de Ríos, 1972a; Ott, 1996, pp. 234–237. For defenses, see Lamb, 1981a, 1981b; Luna & Amaringo, 1993, p. 19.
70. Weil, 1972/1986, pp. 182–184.
71. Weil, 1974, p. vi.
72. Weil, 1974, p. xi.
73. Weil, 1980/1998, pp. 122–123.
74. Kensinger, 1973, p. 12 n. 4.
75. Lamb, 1971/1974, pp. 184, 198.
76. Kensinger, 1973, p. 12 n. 4.
77. Calvo, 1981/1995b, pp. 173–174.
78. Kent, 2007a.
79. Krassner, 2004, p. 122.

CHAPTER 23

1. There are numerous first-person accounts of ayahuasca experiences: Allende, 2008, pp. 210–213; Davis, 1996, pp. 487–490; Delacroix, 2000; Descola, 1993/1996, pp. 205–209; De Wys, 2009; Dobkin de Ríos, 1972b, pp. 125–128; Freedman, 2000; Harner, 1980, pp. 1–9; Krippner & Sulla, 2000; McKenna, 1989; Reichel-Dolmatoff, 1975, pp. 155–167; Salak, 2005; Shanon, 2002; Taussig, 1987, pp. 435–446; Tindall, 2008; Torres, 2000; Wilcox, 2003. Several self-reports are collected in Luna & White, 2000, pp. 81–126; Metzner, 1999. Fictional accounts are in Matthiessen, 1965, pp. 87–104; Theroux, 2005, pp. 77–101; Walker, 2004, pp. 51–53.
2. These initial visual experiences are sometimes (e.g., Reichel-Dolmatoff, 1978/1997b) taken to be *phosphenes*, geometric entoptic phenomena—the lines, curves, circles, and occasionally complex structures, such as oscillating pinwheels or fireworks-type patterns, caused by discharges of activity of the retina and the occipital cortex of the brain (Aiken, 1998, p. 158; Peters, 1994, p. 8; see also Hodgson, 2000). A particularly thorough and relevant account is Carr, 1995.
3. Calvo, 1981/1995b, p. 210.
4. Reichel-Dolmatoff, 1975, pp. 165–167.
5. Lagrou, 1999.
6. Siskind, 1973a, pp. 132–133, 135–137.
7. Gow, 2001, pp. 37, 138–139, 147.
8. Goldman, 1979, p. 210.
9. Reichel-Dolmatoff, 1968/1971, p. 107, 1972, pp. 103–104, 1975, pp. 171–173, 179–180, 1978/1997b, pp. 244, 248.
10. Bear, 2000, p. 214.
11. Quoted in Gorman, 2006.
12. Quoted in Weiskopf, 1995.
13. Burroughs & Ginsberg, 1963/1975, p. 21; Miles, 2000, p. 266.
14. Quoted in Luna, 1986c, p. 45.
15. Quoted in Charing, 2007e.
16. Strassman, 2001, p. 148.
17. Chacón, 2001, p. 167; my translation.
18. Strassman, 2001, p. 146; see also Shanon, 2002, pp. 68–85.
19. Shanon, 2002, p. 227, see also 2001.
20. Shanon, 2002, p. 189. On synesthesia generally, see Marks, 2000.
21. Calvo, 1981/1995b, p. 215.
22. Calvo, 1981/1995b, p. 210.
23. Matthiessen, 1965, pp. 90–91.
24. Luna & Amaringo, 1993, p. 38.
25. Gebhart-Sayer, 1985, p. 172.
26. Gebhart-Sayer, 1984, 1985, 1986.
27. Gebhart-Sayer, 1985, p. 164. See also Gow, 1999; Lathrap, 1976; Lathrap, Gebhart-Sayer, & Mester, 1984.
28. Lagrou, 1999.
29. Lagrou, 1999.

30. Fulop, 1954, pp. 125–128. See Sullivan, 1988, p. 287.
31. Ramírez de Jara & Pinzón Castaño, 1992, pp. 295–296.
32. Burroughs & Ginsberg, 1963/1975, p. 29.
33. Davis, 1996, p. 489.
34. Calvo, 1981/1995b, p. 216.
35. Goldman, 1979, pp. 210–211; Shanon, 2002, p. 59; Harner, 1973a, p. 15; Whitten & Whitten, 2008, p. 70.
36. Lamb, 1985, p. 178; Shanon, 2000, p. 19; Goldman, 1979, pp. 210–211; Flores & Lewis, 1978, p. 155; Siskind, 1973a, p. 145.
37. Strassman, 1994, p. 112.
38. Topping, 1999.
39. Burroughs & Ginsberg, 1963/1975, p. 30.
40. Gracie & Zarkov, 1985.
41. McKenna, 1991, p. 38.
42. Shanon, 2000, p. 18.
43. Perruchon, 2003, p. 222.
44. Luna, 1986c, p. 150.
45. Calvo, 1981/1995b, p. 216.
46. Luna & Amaringo, 1993, p. 27; emphasis added.
47. Kensinger, 1973, p. 11.
48. Pickover, 2005, p. 84.
49. Pickover, 2005, p. 84.
50. Meyer, 1994, p. 186; Tramacchi, 2006, p. 91.
51. Lyttle, 1993, p. 202. For a critique of the ideas of McKenna, Pickover, and other elf advocates, and access to the ongoing debate, see the e-mail correspondence of James Kent (2004), the former editor of *Entheogen Review* and *Trip* magazine.
52. Luna & Amaringo, 1993, p. 27.
53. Aikhenvald, 2004, pp. 346, 348–349; Valenzuela, 2003, pp. 51, 58.
54. Valenzuela, 2003, p. 58.
55. Perrine, 1996, p. 284; McKenna, 1991, p. 37.
56. McKenna, 1991, p. 27.
57. McKenna, 1991, p. 78.
58. Pendell, 2005, pp. 232, 236; emphasis in original.
59. Burroughs & Ginsberg, 1963/1975, p. 56.
60. Gow, 1995, p. 55.
61. Quoted in Gow, 2001, p. 141.
62. Quoted in Rubenstein, 2002, p. 159.
63. Meyer, 1994.
64. Meyer, 1994, p. 175.
65. Meyer, 1994, p. 174.
66. Meyer, 1994, p. 176.
67. Meyer, 1994, p. 178.
68. Meyer, 1994, p. 179.
69. Meyer, 1994, p. 174.
70. Meyer, 1994, p. 173.

71. Perrine, 1996, p. 284.
72. Strassman, 1992; Strassman & Qualls, 1994; Strassman, Qualls, Uhlenhuth, & Kellner, 1994. See generally Strassman, 2000; for a detailed account of the nature and procedures of the New Mexico DMT experiments, see Strassman, 1991, 1994.
73. Strassman, 1994, 2001, p. 147.
74. Strassman, 2001, p. 146.
75. Strassman, 2001, p. 148.
76. Strassman, 2001, pp. 185, 147.
77. Strassman, 2001, p. 185.
78. Strassman, 2001, p. 185. The prankishness and general high spirits of these elves are often reported, particularly by Terence McKenna, whose own prankishness apparently matched their own. For example, McKenna reports the following exchange: "And so then I said: 'Aha the creatures in the DMT flash are Traders. . . . They're Traders.' And that's what this weird feeling is—it's a business environment in there. [*laughter*] We're having a business meeting. They're saying . . . and then the objects! Then I remembered—the objects . . . they're trade goods! They're saying: 'How about thissss! How about This!'" (1990; ellipses in original). McKenna was an idiosyncratic and tremendously engaging speaker; a large collection of recordings, transcripts, and videos can be found at the Terence McKenna Land Web site, http://deoxy.org/mckenna.htm.
79. Strassman, 2001, p. 188. Similarly: "I saw strange creatures, they were dwarves or something, they were black and moved about" (p. 188); "I was living in a world of orange people" (p. 188); "There were at least two presences, one on either side of me, guiding me to a platform" (p. 189); "I felt a dragonlike presence" (p. 191); "There were these three guys or three things" (p. 192); "There was a human, as far as I could tell, standing at some type of console, taking readings or manipulating things" (p. 194); "These beings were friendly" (p. 197); "Then I felt like I was suddenly in the presence of an alien or of aliens, vaguely humanoid" (p. 204); "There were insectlike intelligences everywhere" (p. 209); "Suddenly, beings appeared. They were cloaked, like silhouettes. They were glad to see me" (p. 214).
80. Strassman, 2001, p. 190. Similarly: "There was something outlined in green. . . . She was showing me, it seemed like, how to use this thing. It resembled a computer terminal. I believe she wanted me to communicate with her through that device" (p. 209).
81. Strassman, 2001, p. 191.
82. Strassman, 2001, p. 192.
83. Strassman, 2001, p. 207.
84. Strassman, 2001, p. 197. Similarly: "They were pouring communication into me but it was just so intense" (p. 209); "A male presence tries to communicate with me, but I don't understand" (p. 212); "They told me there were many things they could share with us when we learn how to make more extended contact" (p. 215); "I realize the intense pulsating buzzing sound and vibration are an attempt by the DMT entities to communicate with me" (p. 208).
85. Essig, 2001.

86. Szára, 1994, p. 34. See Cohen, 1985; Fischman, 1983; Freedman, 1968; Hollister, 1962; Morrison, 1998, p. 231.
87. Jacob & Shulgin, 1994, p. 74.
88. Nichols, 2004, p. 132.
89. Ott, 1995.
90. Szára, 1994, p. 40. Morrison (1998, p. 231) suggests that these visual distortions are more appropriately termed *illusions*.
91. Gebhart-Sayer, 1985; Gow, 1999; Lathrap, 1976; Lathrap et al., 1984.
92. Huxley, 1954, p. 17.
93. Huxley, 1954, p. 33.
94. Hofmann, 2001, p. 123.
95. Weil, 2002, p. 124.
96. Tart, 2001, p. 48.
97. Szára, 1994, p. 41; Richards, Rhead, DiLeo, Yensen, & Kurland, 1977; Richards, 1978; Hermle et al., 1992; Grof, 1988, p. 38.
98. Friedman, 1983, p. 39.
99. Freedman, 1968, p. 331.
100. Forte, 2000a, p. 90 n. 5.
101. Quoted in Kandell, 2001; quoted in Shulgin & Shulgin, 1991, p. 67.
102. On chemical analysis of the San Pedro plant, see Crosby & McLaughlin, 1973; Helmlin & Brenneisen, 1992; Lundstrom, 1970; Poisson, 1960; Turner & Heyman, 1961. On huachuma shamanism in northern Peru, see Glass-Coffin, 1998; Joralemon & Sharon, 1993; Sharon, 1972.
103. Perruchon, 2003, p. 218.
104. Scotto & Kent, 2001.
105. Strassman, 1996.
106. Strassman, 2001, pp. 266–309.

CHAPTER 24

1. Esquirol, 1832, quoted in Green & McCreery, 1994, p. 170 n. 3; cited in Bentall, 2000, p. 86, and Horowitz, 1970, p. 8; my translation.
2. Casey, 1991, p. 82.
3. Horowitz, 1970, p. 8.
4. American Psychiatric Association, 1994, p. 767. For a review of the history of the concept of hallucination, see Leudar & Thomas, 2000, pp. 8–14.
5. Slade & Bentall, 1988, p. 23.
6. Casey, 1991, pp. 83–88.
7. Bentall, 2000, p. 99.
8. Bentall, 1990, 2000; Frith, 1992; Hoffman, 1986; Thomas, 1997.
9. Leudar, Thomas, & Johnston, 1992, 1994; Leudar, Thomas, McNally, & Glinski, 1997.
10. Schiller, 1994, p. 21. On the history of verbal hallucinations and a compelling attempt to depathologize them, see Leudar & Thomas, 2000; on attempts to distinguish pathological and nonpathological inner voices, see Heery, 1989; Liester, 1996.

11. Johnson, Hashtroudi, & Lindsay, 1993; Johnson & Magaro, 1987. Christopher Frith (1992, p. 73) calls this *self-monitoring*.
12. Bentall, 2000, p. 102.
13. Bentall, Baker, & Havers, 1991.
14. Leudar & Thomas, 2000, p. 7.
15. Currie, 2000, p. 173; Frith, 1992, p. 84.
16. Quoted in Sass, 1994, p. 19.
17. Currie, 2000, p. 178.
18. Kosslyn, 1994, p. 55; Reisberg & Leak, 1987.
19. Brown & Herrnstein, 1981; Currie, 2000, p. 179.
20. The first description is in a letter to his ophthalmologist, quoted in Ramachandran, 1998, p. 86; the second is in Thurber, 1937/1945, p. 107.
21. Ramachandran, 1998, p. 87.
22. Grauer, 1994, p. 66; Ramachandran, 1998, p. 85.
23. Thurber, 1937/1945, pp. 107–109.
24. Ramachandran, 1998; Teunisse, Cruysberg, Hoefnagels, Verbeek, & Zitman, 1996.
25. Mogk, Riddering, Dahl, Bruce, & Brafford, 2000, pp. 118–119.
26. Ramachandran, 1998, p. 106.
27. Ramachandran, 1998, p. 107.
28. Ramachandran, 1998, p. 105.
29. Schultz, Needham, Taylor, & Shindell, 1996.
30. Fernandez, Lichtshein, & Vieweg, 1997.
31. Bentall, 2000; Grimby, 1993; Reese, 1971.
32. Ramachandran, 1998, p. 106.
33. Santhouse, Howard, & ffytche, 2000.
34. Needham & Taylor, 2000.
35. Ramachandran, 1998, p. 89.
36. Zur & Ullman, 2003.
37. Shimojo, Kamitani, & Nishida, 2001.
38. Ramachandran, 1991, 1992, 1993, 1998, pp. 88–104.
39. Ramachandran, 1998, p. 101.
40. Quoted in Green & McCreery, 1994, p. 107.
41. Green & McCreery, 1994, p. 109.
42. Noë, 2002, p. 2.
43. Ramachandran, 1998, p. 89.
44. Noë, 2002, p. 10.
45. Ramachandran, 1998, pp. 111–112.
46. Ramachandran, 1998, p. 112.
47. Ramachandran & Hirstein, 1999, p. 95.
48. Jaffé, 1962/1963, p. vii.
49. Jung, 1989.
50. Jung, 1962/1963, pp. 170–199.
51. Hillman, 1983b, p. 54.
52. Jung, 1962/1997a, pp. 28, 30.
53. Jung, 1962/1997a, p. 30.

54. Rowan, 1993, p. 63.
55. Hillman, 1983b, p. 55.
56. Watkins, 1976, p. 124.
57. Rowan, 1993, p. 54.
58. Corbin, 1972/2000, p. 71.
59. Jung, 1935/1997c, ¶394, p. 144; quoted in Green & McCreery, 1994, pp. 1–2; Alvarado, 2000, p. 184.
60. Jung, 1935/1997c, ¶394, p. 144, 1962/1997a, pp. 28, 30; Laberge & Gackenbach, 2000, p. 169.
61. Jung, 1935/1997c, ¶394, p. 144; Green & McCreery, 1994, pp. 1–2, 11.
62. Green & McCreery, 1994, p. 11, 69; Jung, 1935/1997c, ¶394, p. 144.
63. Bentall, 2000; Grimby, 1993; Reese, 1971.
64. Shaw, 1924/1931, p. 967.
65. Shaw, 1924/1931, p. 987.

CHAPTER 25

1. Silva, 2004, p. 191.
2. Wilbert, 1987, p. 4.
3. Luna, 1986c, p. 159.
4. Schultes & Raffauf, 1992, p. 92.
5. Chaumeil, 1983/2000, p. 126; Harner, 1971, p. 60.
6. Gow, 2001, p. 138.
7. Harner, 1971, pp. 136, 157, 163–165.
8. SensIR Technologies, 2000; University of Iowa Hospitals and Clinics, n.d.
9. Goodman, 1994, p. 25; Janiger & Dobkin de Ríos, 1976.
10. Schultes & Raffauf, 1990, pp. 432–436; Wilbert, 1987, pp. 133–137; Goodman, 1994, p. 25.
11. Ott, 1997, p. 81.
12. Wilbert, 1991, p. 185. See generally Wilbert, 1987, pp. 162–171; Wright, 1992.
13. Fouldes & Toone, 1995; Scurlock & Lucas, 1996.
14. Berlin & Antheneli, 2001.
15. Everitt & Robbins, 1997; Wesnes & Revell, 1984; Wesnes & Warburton, 1984.
16. Patkar et al., 2002; see also Arehart-Treichel, 2002.
17. Schultes & Raffauf, 1992, p. 87.
18. Bear, 2000, p. 204.
19. Balée, 1994, p. 29.
20. Chaumeil, 1983/2000, p. 71.
21. See Castonguay, 1990, p. 25.
22. Balée, 1994, p. 29; Chaumeil, 1983/2000, p. 71.
23. Calvo, 1981/1995b, p. xii.
24. See Gow, 2001, p. 136.
25. Bristol, Evans, & Lampard, 1969; Duke & Vasquez, 1994, p. 33; Yasumoto, 1996, p. 242.
26. Grossman, 2008.

27. See generally Arouko et al., 2003; Birmes et al., 2002; Chan, 2002; Marc et al., 2007.
28. Ziegler & Tonjes, 1991; Perrine, 1996, p. 178; Novartis Consumer Health, Inc., 1998.
29. Lewin, 1931/1964, quoted in Schultes & Raffauf, 1992, p. 57.
30. Marc et al., 2007.
31. Centers for Disease Control, 1996.
32. Davis, 1996, p. 146; Whitten & Whitten, 2008, p. 72; Schultes & Raffauf, 1990, p. 421.
33. Bear, 2000, p. 143.
34. Whitten & Whitten, 2008, pp. 72–73.
35. Taussig, 1987, p. 456; ellipses in original.
36. Harner, 1971, p. 138.
37. See Taussig, 1987, p. 408.
38. Schultes & Raffauf, 1990, pp. 424–425.
39. Castner, Timme, & Duke, 1998, p. 29.
40. See Plowman, 1977.
41. Schultes & Raffauf, 1992, p. 36.
42. Calvo, 1981/1995b, p. 211.
43. Frohne & Pfänder, 2005, p. 183; Nellis, 1997, pp. 174–175.
44. Duke & Vasquez, 1994, p. 89; Mejia & Rengifo, 2000, pp. 60–61; Schultes & Raffauf, 1990, p. 180.
45. Luna, 1992, p. 237.
46. Luna, 1986c, p. 102; Luna & Amaringo, 1993, p. 108 n. 156; Schultes & Raffauf, 1990, p. 180.
47. Bear, 2000, p. 134.
48. Bear, 2000, pp. 144–145.
49. Castner et al., 1998, p. 79; Duke & Vasquez, 1994, p. 112; Mejia & Rengifo, 2000, pp. 20–21.
50. Taylor, 2006a.
51. Hiraoka, 1995, p. 213.
52. See Lumby, 2000.
53. Sammarco & Palazzolo, 2002.
54. For a collection of recipes for the ayahuasca drink as prepared by ten different mestizo shamans, see López Vinatea, 2000, pp. 23–24; on "additive plants" generally, see McKenna, Luna, & Towers, 1995.
55. Cebrián, 2005, p. 41 n. 34; Chaumeil, 1983/2000, p. 321; López Vinatea, 2000, p. 23; Duke & Vasquez, 1994, p. 7.
56. Luna & Amaringo, 1993, p. 48.
57. Cebrián, 2005, pp. 197–198; Luna, 1986c, p. 67.
58. Sammarco & Palazzolo, 2002.
59. Taylor, 2006b.
60. Duke & Vasquez, 1994, p. 92; Schultes & Raffauf, 1990, p. 80.
61. Heaven & Charing, 2006, p.140.
62. Luna, 1984b, p. 146.

CHAPTER 26

1. Quoted in Onnie-Hay, 2006.
2. Muratorio, 1991, cover illustration and Figure 4; Taussig, 1987, pp. 295–303. Typically, Taussig presents these *silleros*—the word comes from *silla*, chair—as debased and exploited by their employment, while Muratorio reports them as proud of their strength and skill and contemptuous of their cargoes.
3. Oberem, 1974; Lowie, 1948, p. 29; Taussig, 1987, pp. 284–285. See generally Ríos Zañartu, 1999, pp. 54–59.
4. Sheldon & Balick, 1995, p. 50.
5. For an excellent history of this era, see Stanfield, 1998.
6. Luna, 1986c, pp. 26, 28.
7. Descola, 1993/1996, p. 360.
8. Descola, 1993/1996, p. 335; Whitten & Whitten, 2008, p. 78.
9. Descola, 1993/1996, p. 342.
10. Descola, 1993/1996, p. 343.
11. Perruchon, 2003, p. 244.
12. Siskind, 1973a, p. 166.
13. Taussig, 1987, p. 179.
14. Whitten & Whitten, 2008, p. 75.
15. Kelekna, 1994, p. 235.
16. Reichel-Dolmatoff, 1975, p. 78.
17. Muratorio, 1991, pp. 219–222.
18. Luna & Amaringo, 1993, p. 114.
19. Descola, 1993/1996, p. 347.
20. Wasson, 1957, see generally 1972b; Castaneda, 1968, 1971, 1972, see also 1973. For critical reviews of Castaneda, see de Mille, 1976, 1990; Fikes, 1993; Harris, 1979, pp. 315–324; La Barre, 1989, pp. 271–275, 307–308; Letcher, 2007, pp. 214–216; Noel, 1976; Wasson, 1972a. For examples of this abiding fascination, see the articles collected in Forte, 2000b; Furst, 1972; Grob, 2002; Harner, 1973d; Roberts, 2001. Anthropologist Alice Kehoe (2000, pp. 64–65) renders *all* shamanism drug-free by refusing to call South American religious specialists shamans.
21. Dunn, 1973; Hutton, 2001; Letcher, 2007, p. 134; Saar, 1991.
22. See generally Schultes & Hofmann, 1992, pp. 112–115; Spinella, 2001, pp. 360–371.
23. Dobkin de Ríos, 1984/1990, p. 161; Ott, 1996, pp. 371–372.
24. Fernandez, 1972, pp. 243–244, 248, 250; Paicheler & Ravalec, 2004/2007, p. 7.
25. Dobkin de Ríos, 1984/1990, p. 164; Fernandez, 1972, p. 241.
26. Fernandez, 1972, p. 248; Ott, 1996, p. 372.
27. Jochelson, 1908, p. 120.
28. Applegate, 1978; Pendell, 2005, pp. 248–249.
29. Letcher, 2007, pp. 135–137; Salzman, Salzman, Salzman, & Lincoff, 1996.
30. Znamenski, 2007, p. 134.
31. Quoted in Znamenski, 2007, p. 132.
32. Arora, 1986, pp. 894–895; Stone, 2003, p. 104.
33. Fernandez, 1972, pp. 249–250.

34. Paicheler, 2004/2007, p. 67.
35. Letcher, 2007, p. 133.
36. Kehoe, 2000, p. 48.
37. The scholarly literature on these new religious movements is extensive: see Beynon, 1993; Brandão, 1993; Frenopoulo, 2004; Groisman & Sell, 1996; Henman, 1986; Krippner & Sulla, 2000; Labate & Araújo, 2002; Larsen, 2000; Liwszyc, Vuori, Rasanen, & Issakanen, 1992; Lowy, 1987; Luna, 2003; Luna & White, 2000; MacRae, 1992, 1999, 2000, 2004; Ott, 1996, pp. 242–244, 266–268 n. 9; Polari de Alverga, 1984/1999; Prance, 1970; Quinlan, 2001; Richman, 1990–1991; Schinzinger, 2001; Soibelman, 1996. An important collection of hymns in these religious movements, in English and Portuguese, translated by Steven White, is found in Luna & White, 2000, pp. 135–144. Of course, there is a lot of information on the Internet—in particular, the official União do Vegetal Web site, http://www.udv.org.br/, and the Centro Eclético de Fluente Luz Universal Raimundo Irineu Serra Web site, http://www.santodaime.org/indexy.htm.
38. MacRae, 1992, p. 129.
39. Luna, 2003; Luna & White, 2000, pp. 6–7. The best brief introduction is MacRae, 2004.
40. Krippner & Sulla, 2000; Luna, 2003.
41. Dawson, 2007, p. 72; Polari de Alverga, 1984/1999, p. 25; MacRae, 2000, p. 104.
42. MacRae, 2004.
43. Goldman, 1984/1999, p. xxiv.
44. Krippner & Sulla, 2000.
45. Callaway, 1999, p. 264.
46. MacRae, 2004.
47. Frenopoulo, 2004, p. 23.
48. MacRae, 1998, 2004; Weiskopf, 2006.
49. Luna, 2003; Luna & White, 2000, pp. 6–7.
50. MacRae, 2004.
51. MacRae, 2004.
52. MacRae, 2004.
53. Callaway, 1999, p. 264; Frenopoulo, 2004; Luna, 2003; Luna & White, 2000, pp. 6–7; MacRae, 2004.
54. MacRae, 2004.
55. Calloway, 1999, p. 264; Luna & White, 2000, pp. 6–7.
56. Luna & White, 2000, pp. 6–7; MacRae, 2004.
57. Luna, 2003; Luna & White, 2000, pp. 6–7.
58. Callaway, 1999.
59. See, for example, Piccalo, 2008.

CHAPTER 27

1. Fuguet, 2001, p. 66.
2. Valenti, 2000, p. 6; see generally Paerregaard, 1997.
3. Ashcroft, Griffiths, & Tiffen, 2000, p. 136.
4. Reproduced in Pratt, 1992, p. 152.

5. Werlich, 1978, p. 12.
6. Masterson, 1991, pp. 5–6. The same figures are given by sources as diverse as the Central Intelligence Agency (2006) and *The New York Times* (2004).
7. See Gow, 1996, p. 99.
8. Masterson, 1991, pp. 5–6; Werlich, 1978, p. 12; Vargas Llosa, 1990, p. 52, quoted in Sá, 2004, p. 251.
9. De la Cadena, 2000, pp. 1–3, 46.
10. Masterson, 1991, pp. 5–6.
11. Crandon-Malamud, 1991, p. 241 n. 2.
12. Coomes & Barham, 1997.
13. See Gow, 1991, pp. 1–2, 263–264, 293.
14. Hiraoka, 1992, p. 135.
15. The equivalent Portuguese terms are *ribeirinho* and *caboclo* (Slater, 2002, p. 229 n. 44; see Santos-Granero & Barclay, 2000, p. xiv).
16. Luna & Amaringo, 1993, p. 9.
17. Padoch & de Jong, 1987; Pinedo-Vasquez, Barletti Pasquall, & Del Castillo Torres, 2002.
18. On the subsistence economy, see Claggett, 1998, p. 1.
19. Claggett, 1998, pp. 9–10.
20. Padoch & de Jong, 1992, pp. 159–160.
21. Pinedo-Vasquez, Zarin, & Jipp, 1995, p. 241.
22. Castonguay, 1990, p. 36; Gow, 1991, p. 73.
23. López Beltrán, 2001, p. 574 nn. 4–5.
24. Stanfield, 1998, p. 23.
25. Lieberei, 2007.
26. Weinstein, 1983, pp. 26–27.
27. Ruiz, 2006, p. 13; Stanfield, 1998, p. 24.
28. Weinstein, 1983, p. 26.
29. Ruiz, 2006, p. 12.
30. Pimenta, 2005.
31. Weinstein, 1983, p. 26.
32. Weinstein, 1983, p. 26.
33. Taussig, 1987, p. 3.
34. Pimenta, 2005.
35. Stanfield, 1998, pp. 24–25.
36. Santos-Granero & Barclay, 2000, p. 37; Cardenas, Ocampo, & Thorp, 2000, p. 172.
37. MacRae, 1992, p. 30; Lumby, 2000.
38. Santos-Granero & Barclay, 2000, p. 162.
39. Stocks, 1984, p. 44.
40. Santos-Granero & Barclay, 2000, p. 37.
41. Santos-Granero & Barclay, 2000, p. 162.
42. Gow, 1996, p. 96.
43. Chaumeil, 1992, p. 102.
44. The term is probably from the Shipibo *cungatuccha* (Luna, 1986c, p. 125 n. 73; Luna & Amaringo, 1993, p. 108 n. 157).

45. Luna & Amaringo, 1993, pp. 108, 110; see Luna, 1986c, pp. 123–125.
46. Luna & Amaringo, 1993, p. 108 n. 157.
47. Weiskopf, 2005, p. 114; Whitten & Whitten, 2008, p. 69.
48. Davis, 1996, p. 175; see also Schultes & Raffauf, 1990, pp. 419–424.
49. Schultes & Raffauf, 1992, pp. 52, 54.
50. Schultes & Raffauf, 1992, p. 52.
51. See Gow, 1991, pp. 77–78.
52. Castonguay, 1990, p. 90.
53. Gow, 1991, p. 82.
54. De la Cadena, 2001, p. 6; Manrique, 1998, p. 217; Taussig, 1980/2004, p. 198.
55. Whitten & Whitten, 2008, p. 151.
56. Castonguay, 1990, p. 114.
57. Pinedo-Vasquez et al., 1995, p. 242.
58. Pinedo-Vasquez et al., 1995, pp. 244–246, Tables 10.3, 10.5.
59. Hiraoka, 1995, pp. 207, 209.
60. Pinedo-Vasquez et al., 1995, p. 245.
61. Hiraoka, 1995, p. 207.
62. Bodmer, 1994, p. 130.
63. Gow, 1996, pp. 105–111.
64. Gow, 1991, p. 83. On the spatial organization of Amazonian towns, see Chevalier, 1982, pp. 215–242; San Roman, 1977.
65. Luna & Amaringo, 1993, p. 22 n. 16.
66. Rengifo, 2001, p. 120.
67. Smithsonian Tropical Research Institute, 2006a, 2006b.
68. Rengifo, 2001, p. 63.
69. Emmons, 1997, p. 168.

CHAPTER 28

1. See generally Dobkin de Ríos, 1970a, 1970b, 1971, 1972b, 1973; Gow, 1991, pp. 235–241; Katz & Dobkin de Ríos, 1971; Luna, 1984a, 1984b, 1986c, 1991a, 1992; Luna & Amaringo, 1993.
2. See also Luna, 1986c, p. 86.
3. Chevalier, 1982, p. 345; Luna & Amaringo, 1993, pp. 15, 58 n. 104.
4. Castonguay, 1990, p. 86.
5. Brown, 1986, p. 60.
6. Harner, 1971, p. 156.
7. Descola, 1993/1996, p. 33.
8. Calvo, 1981/1995b, p. 258.
9. Chevalier, 1982, p. 389.
10. Bear, 2000, pp. 37, 56; Cebrián, 2005, p. 172.
11. Kamppinen, 1997, pp. 13–14.
12. Chevalier, 1982, p. 389; Dobkin de Ríos, 1973, p. 79.
13. Cebrián, 2005, p. 173.
14. Segal, 1999, p. 71.
15. Chevalier, 1982, p. 389.

16. Segal, 1999, p. 72.
17. See generally Chevalier, 1982, pp. 390–391; Luna, 1986c, pp. 74–75; Luna & Amaringo, 1993, p. 122 n. 171. For pictures, see Luna & Amaringo, 1993, pp. 78, 122.
18. Calvo, 1981/1995b, p. 243.
19. Calvo, 1981/1995b, pp. 10–12, 22–23.
20. Calvo, 1981/1995b, p. 13.
21. Luna, 1986c, p. 75.
22. Calvo, 1981/1995b, p. 13; Luna, 1986c, p. 76.
23. Chevalier, 1982, p. 391.
24. Velásquez Zea, 2006.
25. Ochoa Abaurre, 2002, p. 128; my translation.
26. Velásquez Zea, 2006; my translation.
27. Bear, 2000, pp. 128–130.
28. Calvo, 1981/1995b, pp. 255, 259; Luna, 1986c, pp. 78–79; Luna & Amaringo, 1993, pp. 74 n. 124, 76, 86; Tindall, 2008, pp. 167–168, 209.
29. Bear, 2000, p. 140.
30. See generally Cebrián, 2005, pp. 166–167; Dobkin de Ríos, 1972b, p. 81; Luna, 1986c, p. 80; Luna & Amaringo, 1993, p. 37. Pablo Amaringo has painted a vision he had of what the yacuruna world looks like (Luna & Amaringo, 1993, p. 85).
31. Luna, 1986c, p. 80; Luna & Amaringo, 1993, p. 37.
32. Luna, 1986c, p. 87; Luna & Amaringo, 1993, p. 124.
33. Bear, 2000, p. 26; Cebrián, 2005, pp. 166–167.
34. Tindall, 2008, pp. 210–211.
35. Descola, 1986/1994, p. 124, 1993/1996, p. 323.
36. Harner, 1971, pp. 154–155.
37. Perruchon, 2003, p. 231.
38. Perruchon, 2003, p. 324.
39. Perruchon, 2003, pp. 161, 318.
40. Perruchon, 2003, pp. 317–327.
41. Perruchon, 2003, pp. 324–325.
42. Descola, 1993/1996, p. 325.
43. Descola, 1993/1996, pp. 324–325.
44. Whitten & Whitten, 2008, pp. 35, 49, 76–77, 166, 267.
45. See generally Bear, 2000, p. 26; Cebrián, 2005, p. 166; Dobkin de Ríos, 1972b, pp. 81–82; Luna, 1986c, p. 82; Luna & Amaringo, 1993, pp. 36–37.
46. Luna, 1984b.
47. Luna, 1986c, p. 82.
48. Cebrián, 2005, p. 166; Tindall, 2008, p. 210.
49. Bear, 2000, p. 40.
50. Luna, 1986c, p. 83; Luna & Amaringo, 1993, p. 36.
51. Bear, 2000, pp. 135, 142.
52. Emmons, 1997, pp. 170–171; Luna & Amaringo, 1993, pp. 50–52 n. 87.
53. Emmons, 1997, p. 170.
54. Moran, 1993, pp. 106–107.

55. Nugent, 1994, p. 123.

56. Calvo, 1981/1995b, p. 241; Cebrián, 2005, p. 167; Dobkin de Ríos, 1972b, p. 81; Luna, 1986c, pp. 84–86; Luna & Amaringo, 1993, pp. 37, 74. For legends and stories about dolphins as spirits and lovers, see Slater, 1994.

57. Kricher, 1997, p. 206.

58. Calvo, 1981/1995b, p. 3.

59. Brown, 1986, p. 156.

60. Bear, 2000, p. 42.

61. Kricher, 1997, p. 206.

62. Luna & Amaringo, 1993, pp. 116–118 n. 168; Nugent, 1994, p. 124.

63. Luna, 1986c, p. 86, 1992, p. 241.

64. Cetacean Specialist Group, 1996; Pearson & Beletsky, 2008, p. 227.

CHAPTER 29

1. Trotter & Chavira, 1997, pp. 85–86.
2. For example, see Wisechild, 2001.
3. Trotter & Chavira, 1997, pp. 98–99.
4. Buchanan, 1938/1991, pp. 33–34; Gould, 2000.
5. Quoted in Arber, 1938/1987, pp. 250–251.
6. Crellin & Philpott, 1990, p. 14; Knight, 2002.
7. Knight, 2002, p. 238.
8. Balée, 1994, pp. 102–104.
9. Heaven & Charing, 2006, p. 141.
10. For an extended and illuminating discussion, see Hahn, 1995, pp. 40–56. On Western culture-bound disorders, see Helman, 1990, pp. 235–236; Littlewood & Lipsedge, 1987. For a postmodernist critique of the concept, see Morsy, 1996, p. 23.
11. For example, Kay, 1993; Kiev, 1968; Koss-Chiono, 1993; Logan, 1993; Pachter, 1993; Trotter & Chavira, 1997; Weller, Pachter, Trotter, & Baer, 1993.
12. Compare the lists given for Mexicans along the Texas border by Trotter (1981), for Peruvians by Dobkin de Ríos (1992, p. 48), for urban Mexican Americans by Martinez and Martin (1979), and for Central Americans by Murguia, Peterson, and Zea (2003). For Honduran explanations of diarrhea, see Kendall, 1990; Kendall, Foote, & Martorell, 1983, 1984; Pelto, Bentley, & Pelto, 1990, pp. 260–261.
13. Hill, 1992, pp. 194–198; Wright & Hill, 1992, pp. 281–282. For an Aguaruna parallel syndrome of *ishámkamu*, fright, but probably without soul loss, see Brown, 1986, p. 56.
14. For example, Helman, 1990, pp. 236–237; McElroy & Townsend, 1996, p. 273; O'Nell, 1975; O'Nell & Rubel, 1976; Rubel, 1964; Rubel, O'Nell, & Collado-Ardon, 1984.
15. Luna, 1986c, p. 133.
16. Hahn, 1995, p. 14.
17. Luna, 1986c, p. 133.
18. McElroy & Townsend, 1996, p. 273.
19. Rubel et al., 1984.

20. Calvo, 1981/1995b, p. 201.
21. Good & Kleinman, 1985, p. 315.
22. See Dobkin de Ríos, 1972b, p. 87.
23. Holland & Courtney, 1998, p. 53; McElroy & Townsend, 1996, pp. 104, 352.
24. See generally Kearney, 1976.
25. Kamppinen, 1997, pp. 13–14.
26. Luna & Amaringo, 1993, p. 104.
27. Luna & Amaringo, 1993, pp. 58 n. 103, 74.
28. Good, 1994, pp. 101–102.
29. Browner, 1985; Escobar, Salazar, & Chung, 1983; Graham, 1976; Kay, 1977; Kendall et al., 1983; Nations & Rebhun, 1988; Rubel, 1960, 1966; Scheper-Hughes, 1988; Schreiber & Homiak, 1981.
30. Strathern & Stewart, 1999, p. 16.
31. McElroy & Townsend, 1996, p. 103.
32. Trotter & Chavira, 1997, pp. 16–17.
33. Schultes & Raffauf, 1990, pp. 424–425. Chiricsanango is widely used among indigenous peoples in the Amazon to treat fevers (Schultes & Raffauf, 1990, p. 425), but this is undoubtedly due to the sensation of chills produced by the plant, and I know of no indigenous theorizing about hot and cold qualities of either sicknesses or medicines.
34. Lamb, 1985, pp. 174–175.

CHAPTER 30

1. See also Luna, 1986c, p. 89.
2. The figures for 2003 are Roman Catholic, 81 percent; Seventh Day Adventist, 1.4 percent; other Christian, 0.7 percent; other, 0.6 percent; unspecified or none, 16.3 percent (Central Intelligence Agency, 2006).
3. Chibnik, 1994, p. 90.
4. Gill, 1998, p. 80.
5. Holligan de Diaz-Limaco, 1998, p. 73; see generally Minaya, 1995.
6. Green, 2006, p. 200.
7. Gill, 1998, p. 85.
8. Chibnik, 1994, p. 90.
9. Gill, 1998, p. 88.
10. Whitten & Whitten, 2008, p. 150.
11. Segal, 1999, p. 71.
12. Quoted in Charing, 2007a.
13. Dobkin de Ríos & Rumrrill, 2008, p. 59.
14. Gill, 1998, pp. 68, 208.
15. An excellent review and a discussion of these items are in Yronwrode, 2000, 2003a.
16. *La santa cruz de Caravaca: Tesoro de oraciones*, 2005, pp. 123, 126–127, 129; my translation.
17. Taussig, 1987, p. 259.
18. Taussig, 1987, pp. 146, 259, 261.

19. Perruchon, 2003, p. 243.
20. *El Libro de San Cipriano y Santa Justina*, 2006, p. 37.

CHAPTER 31

1. Comaroff & Comaroff, 1993, p. xi.
2. Luna & Amaringo, 1993.
3. Amos, 1994; Dunn, 1998; Mikewhy, 2000; "Oliver's acid trip down memory lane," 2006; Otis, 2008; Riddle, 1994; Riordan, 1995, p. 429; Sting, 2003, p. 14.
4. Allende, 2008, pp. 210–213; Matthiessen, 1965, pp. 87–104; Theroux, 2005, pp. 77–101; Walker, 2004, pp. 51–53.
5. Simon, 1990, Track 9.
6. Bongie, 1998, p. 12.
7. Starn, 1999, p. 222.
8. Bongie, 1998, p. 26.
9. See Luna & Amaringo, 1993, pp. 34–36, 41.
10. Siskind, 1973a, p. 147.
11. Luna, 1986c, p. 93.
12. Luna & Amaringo, 1993, p. 35.
13. Whitten & Whitten, 2008, p. 77.
14. Bear, 2000, pp. 25, 211.
15. Chevalier, 1982, pp. 370, 373, 398–399, 404.
16. Luna, 1986c, p. 110.
17. Calvo, 1981/1995b, p. 192.
18. Chevalier, 1982, pp. 398, 404.
19. Chevalier, 1982, pp. 352–353, 360, 369.
20. Siskind, 1973a, p. 162.
21. Chaumeil, 1983/2000, pp. 321–324; my translation.
22. Luna & Amaringo, 1993, pp. 72, 78, 82, 96, 98, 102, 122, 124, 128, 130, 132, 140, 142.
23. Luna & Amaringo, 1993, p. 118.
24. Reichel-Dolmatoff, 1975, p. 100.
25. Dobkin de Ríos, 1992.
26. Luna & Amaringo, 1993, pp. 72, 104, 114, 120.
27. Luna & Amaringo, 1993, p. 104. We may also perhaps see the Indic word *kundalini* in the name of the spirit King Kundal and a reference to the Sakya clan, from which the Buddha came, in a "celebrated king of the Sakias" and a "great Chinese guru . . . from the great family of the Sakias" (Luna & Amaringo, 1993, pp. 80, 104).
28. Sinchi Ayahuasca, 2004.
29. Dobkin de Ríos, 1969, 1972b, pp. 88–89, 2006.
30. Perruchon, 2003, p. 255.
31. Luna & Amaringo, 1993; see Santos-Granero & Barclay, 2000, pp. 307–308.
32. Luna & Amaringo, 1993, p. 29.
33. Krippner, 2000, p. 200.
34. Luna, 1991b.

35. Labbé, 1999.
36. Perreault, 1998.
37. Chilvers, 1998, p. 427; Goethals, 1990.
38. Luna & Amaringo, 1993.
39. Rivas, 1998.
40. La Rosa, Pandura, Campos, & Sinuiri, 2003.
41. Charing, 2007b; Del Río, 2005, 2006, 2007. A good example of the style is Del Río, 2003.
42. A good example of the sound is Maestro Ayahuasquero, 2006. It is also possible to compare the same icaro with (Maestro Ayahuasquero, 2007) and without (Flores, 2005b) the instrumental setting. See also Flores, 2005a, 2005c; Flores & Maestro Ayahuasquero, 2007.
43. Cristina & Kopper, 2006.
44. Mahua, 2002, Track 2.
45. See, for example, Perkins, 2005, p. 209.
46. Voget, 1984.
47. Znamenski, 2007, p. 302.
48. Perruchon, 2003, p. 177.
49. Perruchon, 2003, pp. 177–181.
50. Schultes & Raffauf, 1992, pp. 154–157. See generally Glass-Coffin, 1998; Joralemon & Sharon, 1993; Sharon, 1972.
51. On Calderon, see Joralemon, 1990; Joralemon & Sharon, 1993; Sharon, 1972.
52. Quoted in Dobkin de Ríos & Rumrrill, 2008, pp. 48–49.

CHAPTER 32

1. Bhabha, 1994, p. 107.
2. Slater, 1995, p. 118.
3. Kingsolver, 1998, p. 5.
4. Ackerman, 2001, pp. 228–229.
5. Blank & Bogan, 1984, p. 56.
6. Cronon, 1998, p. 486; Denevan, 1992/1998, p. 422.
7. For example, Newman, 2000; Silcock, 1990.
8. Gómez-Pompa & Kaus, 1992/1998, p. 299.
9. Uhl et al., 1998, p. 30.
10. Slater, 1995, p. 127.
11. McGrane, 1989, p. 110.
12. Ramos, 1998, p. 71.
13. For a general review of Amazonian stereotypes, see Nugent, 2007.
14. Errington, 1998, p. 115.
15. Ramos, 1998, p. 16.
16. McGrane, 1989, pp. 25–26.
17. Gandhi, 1998, p. 32.
18. Dubin, 2001, p. 140.
19. Quoted in Sasser, 1983, p. 91.
20. Dilworth, 1996, p. 8.

21. Dubin, 2001, p. 131.
22. McGrane, 1989, p. 108.
23. Slater, 1995, pp. 115, 129.
24. Dobkin de Ríos, 1994; Dobkin de Ríos & Rumrrill, 2008, pp. 69–85; Elton, 1999; Grunwell, 1998; Joralemon, 1990; Luna, 2003; Ott, 1996, pp. 244, 254; Proctor, 2001; Rumrril, 1996; Stuart, 2002. For an excellent description of "mystical tourism" in general, see Znamenski, 2007, pp. 155–164.
25. Puma Shamanic Journeys, 2002.
26. Blue Morpho Tours, 2003.
27. Saldanha, 2007, pp. 6, 12, 14.
28. These terms are quoted from discussions among participants on the Ayahuasca Tribe, http://ayahuasca.tribe.net/, during the first four months of 2008.
29. Winkelman, 2005.
30. Harris, 2008, p. 79.
31. Dobkin de Ríos & Rumrrill, 2008, pp. 73–74.
32. Dobkin de Ríos, 1994; Dobkin de Ríos & Rumrrill, 2008, pp. 70, 74.
33. Luna, 2003.
34. Joralemon, 1990, p. 110.
35. Gómez-Peña, 2000, p. 37; Shoemaker, 1997b, p. 40.
36. Proctor, 2001.
37. In the interests of full disclosure, I point out that Howard Lawler is a good friend of mine and has been a great help to me both personally and in the writing of this book.

CHAPTER 33

1. Controlled Substances Act, 21 USC §812(b)(1), §812(c), Schedule I(c)(6).
2. Controlled Substances Act, 21 USC §841(b)(1)(C).
3. Controlled Substances Act, 21 USC §812(c), Schedule I(c).
4. For example, Drug Enforcement Administration, 1993, p. 4317.
5. Drug Enforcement Administration, 1993.
6. *State v. Big Sheep*, 75 Mont. 219, 243 (1926), p. 1067.
7. *State v. Big Sheep*, p. 1073.
8. *Reynolds v. United States*, 98 U.S. 145 (1878).
9. *Prince v. Massachusetts*, 321 U.S. 158 (1944).
10. *Braunfeld v. Brown*, 366 U.S. 599 (1961).
11. *Sherbert v. Verner*, 374 U.S. 398 (1963), p. 406.
12. *Wisconsin v. Yoder*, 406 U.S. 205 (1972).
13. *People v. Woody*, 61 Cal. 2d 716, 394 P.2d 813, 40 Cal. Rptr. 69 (1964).
14. *United States v. Kuch*, 288 F. Supp. 439 (D.D.C. 1968); *Kennedy v. Bureau of Narcotics and Dangerous Drugs*, 459 F.2d 415 (9th Cir. 1972); *Native American Church of New York v. United States*, 468 F. Supp. 1247 (S.D.N.Y. 1979). For example, in California alone, *People v. Mitchell*, 244 Cal. App. 2d 176, 52 Cal. Rptr 884 (Ct. App. 1966); *People v. Collins*, 273 Cal. App 2d 486, 78 Cal. Rptr. 151 (1969); and *People v. Mullins*, 50 Cal. App. 3d 61, 123 Cal. Rptr. 201 (1975).
15. *State of Oregon v. Soto*, 21 Or. App. 792 (1975), p. 792.

16. *Smith v. Employment Division, Department of Human Resources*, 301 Or. 209 (1986), pp. 217–219.
17. *Employment Division v. Smith*, 494 U.S. 872 (1990), p. 885 (citations omitted).
18. Including me. Ten years before Smith, I had observed the judicial trend toward religious accommodation and predicted—incorrectly—that it would continue (Beyer, 1980).
19. *City of Boerne v. Flores*, 521 U.S. 507 (1997).
20. *State of Kansas v. McBride*, 24 Kan. App. 2d 909 (1998).
21. *O Centro Espirita Beneficiente Uniao do Vegetal v. Ashcroft*, 282 F.Supp.2d 1236 (2002), p. 1240; *O Centro Espirita Beneficiente Uniao do Vegetal v. Ashcroft*, 342 F.3d 1170 (10th Cir. 2003), p. 1174; *Gonzales v. O Centro Espirita Beneficente Uniao do Vegetal*, 546 U.S. 418 (2006), p. 425.
22. Grob, 1999; Grob et al., 1996.
23. Luna, 2003.
24. *O Centro Espirita Beneficiente Uniao do Vegetal v. Ashcroft* (2002); *O Centro Espirita Beneficiente União do Vegetal v. Ashcroft* (2003).
25. *Gonzales v. O Centro Espirita Beneficente Uniao do Vegetal.*
26. *Gonzales v. O Centro Espirita Beneficente Uniao do Vegetal*, p. 439.
27. Mazzetti, 2008.
28. Gorman, 2001.
29. Rumrril, 1996.
30. Rumrril, 1996.
31. Rankin, 2002a, 2002b.
32. Noriega, 2001a.
33. Noriega, 2001b.
34. Noriega, 2001c.
35. Gorman, 2005.
36. Center for Cognitive Liberty and Ethics, 2003; Rankin, 2002a, 2002b.
37. Rankin, 2002a; Shoemaker, 2005a.
38. 42 USC § 2000bb-1; *O Centro Espirita Beneficiente União do Vegetal v. Ashcroft* (2002).
39. *O Centro Espirita Beneficiente União do Vegetal v. Ashcroft* (2003).
40. Rumrril, 1996.
41. *O Centro Espirita Beneficiente União do Vegetal v. Ashcroft* (2002), pp. 1248–1250.
42. Shoemaker, 2005a.
43. Shoemaker, 2005b.
44. Shoemaker, 2006.
45. Shoemaker, 2002.
46. Shoemaker, 2003.
47. Beynon, 1993; Boire, 1994; Dawson, 2007, pp. 70–71; Labrousse & Laniel, 2001, p. 134; Trimble, 2003.
48. Labrousse & Laniel, 2001, pp. 134–135; Trimble, 2003.
49. *In the Matter of Fijneman*, 2001; Labrousse & Laniel, 2001, p. 135; Trimble, 2003.
50. Labrousse & Laniel, 2001, pp. 133–135.
51. *In the Matter of Bauchet*, 2005, pp. 4–8; Labrousse & Laniel, 2001, p. 135.

52. *In the Matter of Bauchet*, 2005, pp. 17–18.
53. Ministère des solidarités, de la santé et de la famille, 2005.
54. U.N. Convention on Psychotropic Substances, 1971, Preamble.
55. U.N. Convention on Psychotropic Substances, 1971, Article 2(4)(b).
56. U.N. Convention on Psychotropic Substances, Status of Treaty Adherence, 2008.
57. U.N. Convention on Psychotropic Substances, 1971, Article 3(1), Article 1(f)(i).
58. U.S. Const. Art. VI ("Treaties made, or which shall be made, under the Authority of the United States, shall be the supreme Law of the Land; and the Judges in every State shall be bound thereby"); *Breard v. Green*, 523 U.S. 371 (1998), p. 376.
59. *O Centro Espirita Beneficiente União do Vegetal v. Ashcroft* (2003), p. 1184.
60. *Breard v. Green*, p. 376; *O Centro Espirita Beneficiente União do Vegetal v. Ashcroft* (2003), pp. 1183–1184.
61. Psychotropic Substances Act, Pub.L. 95-633, November 10, 1978, 92 Stat. 2768; Controlled Substances Act, 21 USC §801a(2).
62. *Gonzales v. O Centro Espirita Beneficente Uniao do Vegetal*, p. 439.
63. *O Centro Espirita Beneficiente União do Vegetal v. Ashcroft* (2002), pp. 1255–1269; *O Centro Espirita Beneficiente União do Vegetal v. Ashcroft* (2003), pp. 1179–1184; *Gonzales v. O Centro Espirita Beneficente Uniao do Vegetal*, pp. 426–427.
64. *Gonzales v. O Centro Espirita Beneficente Uniao do Vegetal*, pp. 437–438.
65. *Gonzales v. O Centro Espirita Beneficente Uniao do Vegetal*, p. 438.
66. *O Centro Espirita Beneficiente União do Vegetal v. Ashcroft* (2003), p. 1184; *Gonzales v. O Centro Espirita Beneficente Uniao do Vegetal*, p. 438.
67. *Gonzales v. O Centro Espirita Beneficente Uniao do Vegetal*, p. 438 n. 2.
68. *Gonzales v. O Centro Espirita Beneficente Uniao do Vegetal*, p. 438.
69. See Controlled Substances Act, 21 USC §812(c), Schedule I(c)(11) (mescaline), Schedule I(c)(12) (peyote); *O Centro Espirita Beneficiente Uniao do Vegetal v. Ashcroft* (2002), p. 1249.
70. Controlled Substances Act, 21 USC §812(c), Schedule I(c).
71. *United States v. Shoemaker*, Case No. 02-CR-46-ALL (N.D.Ga., filed January 22, 2002), quoted in Rankin, 2002b.
72. *O Centro Espirita Beneficiente União do Vegetal v. Ashcroft* (2002), p. 1250.
73. Lande, 1976; Stroup, 2004.
74. Lande, 1976, pp. 385, 387.
75. Lande, 1976, p. 387.
76. See *O Centro Espirita Beneficiente União do Vegetal v. Ashcroft* (2002), p. 1269 n. 13.
77. Lande, 1976, p. 387.
78. Lande, 1976, p. 387 nn. 1227–1228.
79. See *O Centro Espirita Beneficiente União do Vegetal v. Ashcroft* (2002), pp. 1266–1269.
80. Schaepe, 2001.
81. *O Centro Espirita Beneficiente Uniao de Vegetal v. Ashcroft* (2002), pp. 1266–1269; *O Centro Espirita Beneficiente Uniao de Vegetal v. Ashcroft*, 314 F.3d 463 (10th Cir. 2002, emergency motion for stay pending appeal), p. 466; *Gonzales v. O Centro Espirita Beneficente Uniao do Vegetal*, pp. 437–438.
82. U.N. Convention on Psychotropic Substances, 1971, Article 1(e).

83. *O Centro Espirita Beneficiente Uniao de Vegetal v. Ashcroft* (2002, emergency motion for stay pending appeal), p. 466; *O Centro Espirita Beneficiente Uniao de Vegetal v. Ashcroft* (2003), p. 1193 (J. Murphy, dissenting).
84. *O Centro Espirita Beneficiente Uniao de Vegetal v. Ashcroft* (2003), p. 1193 n. 6 (J. Murphy, dissenting).
85. *Zicherman v. Korean Air Lines Co.*, 516 U.S. 217 (1996), p. 226; *O Centro Espirita Beneficiente Uniao de Vegetal v. Ashcroft* (2003), p. 1193 n. 6 (J. Murphy, dissenting).
86. *O Centro Espirita Beneficiente Uniao de Vegetal v. Ashcroft*, 389 F.3d 973 (10th Cir. 2004, rehearing en banc), pp. 989, 990 n. 11 (J. Murphy, concurring in part and dissenting in part).
87. *In the Matter of Fijneman*, 2001.
88. *O Centro Espirita Beneficiente Uniao de Vegetal v. Ashcroft* (2003), p. 1193 n. 6 (J. Murphy, dissenting).
89. *Gonzales v. O Centro Espirita Beneficente Uniao do Vegetal*, p. 438.
90. Instituto Nacional de Cultura, 2008.
91. Instituto Nacional de Cultura, 2008, pp. 376040–376041; my translation.
92. Instituto Nacional de Cultura, 2008, p. 376041; my translation.

CHAPTER 34

1. Muratorio, 1991, p. 222.
2. Muratorio, 1991, p. 213.
3. Whitehead & Wright, 2004, p. 14.
4. Vidal & Whitehead, 2004, p. 62.
5. Whitehead, 2002, p. 250; Whitehead & Wright, 2004, pp. 2, 4, 7.
6. Lee, 2001.
7. Scott, 1990, pp. 143–144.
8. On canaima generally, see Colson, 2001; Gillin, 1936, pp. 149–152; Harvey, 2006, p. 132; Webster, 1948, pp. 425–426; Whitehead, 2001, and especially the extended discussion in 2002. An interview with Whitehead on canaima and dark shamanism is in Tenenbaum, 2003.
9. Whitehead, 2002, p. 5.
10. Whitehead, 2002, p. 250.
11. Colson, 2001, p. 227; Whitehead, 2002, pp. 38–39.
12. Whitehead, 2001, p. 237.
13. Whitehead, 2006, p. 172.
14. Eakin, 2001.
15. Taussig, 1987, p. 216.
16. Taussig, 1987, p. 467.
17. Taussig, 1987, p. 218.
18. Taussig, 1987, p. 328.
19. Taussig, 1987, p. 467.
20. Sahlins, 1993, p. 17.
21. Humphrey & Onon, 1996, p. 320.
22. Brown, 1996, p. 734.
23. Brown, 1991, p. 389, 1994, p. 288.

24. Brown, 1994, p. 288.
25. Ortner, 1995, pp. 176–177; emphasis in original.
26. Jackson, 1994, p. 394.
27. Kleinman, 1992/1995, p. 275 n. 17.
28. Greene, 1998, p. 653.
29. Médicos Indígenas Yageceros de la Amazonía Colombiana, 2000; Zuluage & Díaz, 1999, pp. 105–117.
30. Zuluage & Díaz, 1999.
31. Médicos Indígenas Yageceros de la Amazonía Colombiana, 2000, pp. 7–8.
32. Zuluage & Díaz, 1999, pp. 109–110; my translation.
33. Zuluage & Díaz, 1999, pp. 112–114.
34. Pedersen, 2007.
35. Consejo Nacional de Salud, 2007.
36. Jernigen, 2003; Rengifo, 2001, p. 33.
37. Jernigen, 2003.
38. Dobkin de Ríos & Rumrrill, 2008, p. 101.
39. Cray, 1999; Herman, 2000; Holden, 1999; Knight, 1998a, 1998b; Muscati, 1996; "Planting seeds of malcontent," 1999; "Vine victory," 2000; Woodard, 1999.
40. Center for International Environmental Law, 2003. For an analysis of the 2001 PTO decision, see Wiser, 2001.

CHAPTER 35

1. Luna & Amaringo, 1993, p. 48 n. 81.
2. Perruchon, 2003, p. 243.
3. Quoted in Dobkin de Ríos & Rumrrill, 2008, p. 53.
4. Quoted in Hvalkof, 2004, pp. 212, 214.
5. Quoted in Dobkin de Ríos & Rumrrill, 2008, p. 53.
6. Quoted in Dobkin de Ríos & Rumrrill, 2008, p. 63.
7. Luna, 1984b.
8. Koch, 2000, p. 51.

REFERENCES CITED

Abram, D. (1997). *The spell of the sensuous: Perception and language in a more-than-human world*. New York: Vintage.

Ackerman, D. (2001). Rain forest. In L. Hogan & B. Peterson (Eds.), *The sweet breathing of plants: Women writing on the green world* (pp. 228–230). New York: North Point.

Adams, M. V. (1997). The archetypal school. In P. Young-Eisendrath & T. Dawson (Eds.), *The Cambridge companion to Jung* (pp. 101–118). Cambridge: Cambridge University Press.

Aguiar, C., Rosenfeld, J., Stevens, B., Thanasombat, S., & Masud, H. (2007). *An analysis of malnutrition programming and policies in Peru*. Retrieved from the University of Michigan International Policy Students Association Web site, http://www.umich.edu/~ipolicy/peru/1)%20An%20Analysis%20of%20Malnutrition%20Programming%20and%20Policies%20in%20P.pdf.

Agurell, S., Holmstedt, B., & Lindgren, J.-E. (1968). Alkaloid content of *Banisteriopsis rusbyana*. *American Journal of Pharmacy*, 140(5), 148–151.

Aiken, N. E. (1998). *The biological origins of art*. Westport, CT: Praeger.

Aikhenvald, A. Y. (2004). *Evidentiality*. Oxford: Oxford University Press.

Alarco, R. (1985). Análisis musical de las canciones del ayahuasca usadas por los brujos de le tribu de los orejones del río Napo y por los curanderos de Iquitos [Musical analysis of the ayahuasca songs used by the sorcerers of the Orejone tribe and the healers of Iquitos]. In M. Chiappe, M. Lemli, & L. Millones (Eds.), *Allúcinogenos y shamanismo en el Perú contemporáneo* (pp. 135–136). Lima: Ediciones El Virrey. (Original work published 1965.)

Alexiades, M. N. (1999). Ethnobotany of the Ese Eja: Plants, health, and change in an Amazonian society (Ph.D. dissertation, City University of New York). *Dissertation Abstracts International*, 60(1), 21.

Allende, I. (2008). *The sum of our days*. New York: Harper Collins.

Almenara, R. L. (2008, January 1). La leyenda de cacique [The legend of *cacique*]. *El Comercio*. Retrieved April 25, 2008, from http://www.elcomercio.com.pe/edicionimpresa/Html/2008-01-07/la-leyenda-cacique.html.

Alvarado, C. S. (2000). Out-of-body experiences. In E. Cardeña, S. J. Lynn, & S. Krippner (Eds.), *Varieties of anomalous experience: Examining the scientific evidence* (pp. 183–218). Washington, DC: American Psychological Association.

American Psychiatric Association. (1994). *Diagnostic and statistical manual of mental disorders* (4th ed.). Washington, DC: American Psychiatric Association.

Amos, T. (1994, September 11). Interview with Michael Pearce. Retrieved November 24, 2007, from the Jason Watts Web site, http://jasonrwatts.com/include.php?include=/taart/PearceInternetInterview_091194.txt&.

Andritzky, W. (1989a). Ethnopsychologische Betrachtung des Heilrituals mit Ayahuasca unter besonderer Berücksichtigung der Piros (Ostperu) [An ethnopsychological analysis of ayahuasca healing rituals, with special attention to the Piros of eastern Peru]. *Anthropos*, 84(1–3), 177–201.

Andritzky, W. (1989b). Sociopsychotherapeutic functions of ayahuasca healing in Amazonia. *Journal of Psychoactive Drugs*, 21(1), 77–89.

Anisimov, A. F. (1958). The shaman's tent of the Evenks. In A. F. Anisimov (Ed.), *Religiya Evenkov* (pp. 84–123). Moscow: N.p.

Applegate, R. B. (1978). *Atishwin, the dream helper in south-central California*. Banning: Ballena.

Aquino, R., & Encarnación, F. (1994). *Primates of Peru*. Retrieved May 29, 2008, from the U.N. Food and Agriculture Organization Land and Water Development Division Web site, http://www.fao.org/ag/AGL/agll/rla128/unmsm/unmsm-i2/unmsm-i2–09.htm.

Aranibar, J. (2006). El fulbito. Retrieved August 12, 2008, from the De Perú Web site, http://www.deperu.com/fulbito/.

Araujo-Lima, J. A., & Alvarez-León, R. (2003). Migratory fishes of the Brazilian Amazon. In J. Carolsfeld, B. Harvey, C. Ross, & A. Baer (Eds.), *Migratory fishes of South America: Biology, fisheries and conservation status* (pp. 233–302). Ottawa: International Development Research Centre.

Arber, A. (1987). *Herbals: Their origin and evolution*. Cambridge: Cambridge University Press. (Original work published 1938.)

Arehart-Treichel, J. (2002, December). Symptom relief may keep schizophrenia patients smoking. *Psychiatric News*, 37(24), 22–24. Retrieved February 4, 2007, from http://pn.psychiatryonline.org/cgi/content/full/37/24/22.

Arévalo, G. V. (1986). El ayahuasca y el curandero Shipibo-Conibo del Ucayali (Perú) [Ayahuasca and the Shipibo-Conibo of the Ucayali (Peru)]. *America indígena*, 46(1), 147–161.

Arkenberg, C. (2006). My lovewar with Fox News. In J. Louv (Ed.), *Generation hex* (pp. 203–217). St. Paul, MN: Disinformation.

Armed Forces Pest Management Board. (2008). Living hazards database. Retrieved May 29, 2008, from http://www.afpmb.org/pubs/living_hazards/snakes.html.

Arora, D. (1986). *Mushrooms demystified: A comprehensive guide to the fleshy fungi*. Berkeley: Ten Speed.

Arouko, H., Matray, M. D., Bragança, C., Mpaka, J. P., Chinello, L., Castaing, F., et al. (2003). Voluntary poisoning by ingestion of *Datura stramonium*. Another cause of hospitalization in youth seeking strong sensations. *Annales de Medecine Interne*, 154, 46–50. Retrieved May 6, 2008, from the National Library of Medicine Web site, http://www.ncbi.nlm.nih.gov/pubmed/12910033.

Ashcroft, B., Griffiths, G., & Tiffin, H. (2000). *Post-colonial studies: The key concepts*. London: Routledge.

Badilla, B., Chaves, F., Mora, G., & Poveda, L. J. (2006). Edema induced by *Bothrops asper* (Squamata: Viperidae) snake venom and its inhibition by Costa Rican plant extracts. *Revista de Biologia Tropical*, 54(2), 245–252. Retrieved May 3, 2008, from http://www.biologia.ucr.ac.cr/rbt/attachments/volumes/v0154–2/01-BADILLA-Edema.pdf.

Baer, G. (1969). Eine Ayahuasca-Sitzung unter den Piro (Ost-Perú) [An ayahuasca session among the Piro of eastern Peru]. *Bulletin de la Société Suisse des Americanistes, 33*, 5–8.

Baer, G. (1979). Religión y chamanismo de los Matsigenka [The religion and shamanism of the Matsigenka]. *Amazonía peruana*, 4, 101–138.

Baer, G. (1992). The one intoxicated by tobacco: Matsigenka shamanism. In E. Langdon & G. Baer (Eds.), *Portals of power: Shamanism in South America* (pp. 79–100). Albuquerque: University of New Mexico Press.

Baer, G. (1994). *Cosmología y shamanismo de los Matsiguenga* [Matsiguenga cosmology and shamanism]. Quito: Abya-Yala.

Baer, G., & Snell, W. W. (1974). An ayahuasca ceremony among the Matsigenka (eastern Peru). *Zeitschrift für Ethnologie*, 99(1–2), 63–80.

Balée, W. (1994). *Footprints in the forest: Ka'apor ethnobotany—The historical ecology of plant utilization by an Amazonian people*. New York: Columbia University Press.

Balestrieri, A., & Fontanari, D. (1959). Acquired and cross tolerance to mescaline, LSD-25, and BOL-148. *Archives of General Psychiatry*, 1, 279–282.

Balzer, M. M. (1997). Introduction. In M. M. Balzer (Ed.), *Shamanic worlds: Ritual and lore of Siberia and Central Asia* (pp. xiii–xxxii). Armonk, NY: North Castle.

Bardales, P. (2008a, March 3). Juaneco y Su Combo: Tres al hilo [Juaneco y Su Combo: Three in a row]. *Diario de IQT*. Retrieved April 28, 2008, from http://pakobardales.blogspot.com/2008/03/juaneco-y-su-combo-tres-al-hilo.html.

Bardales, P. (2008b, March 10). Mi rica cumbia Amazonica (globalizada) [My wonderful *cumbia Amazonica* (globalized)]. *Diario de IQT*. Retrieved April 28, 2008, from http://pakobardales.blogspot.com/2008/03/mi-rica-cumbia-amazonica-globalizada.html.

Bartlett, R. D., & Bartlett, P. (2003). *Reptiles and amphibians of the Amazon: An ecotourist's guide*. Gainesville: University Press of Florida.

Bartolomé, M. A. (1979). Shamanism among the Avá-Chiripá. In D. Browman & R. Schwartz (Eds.), *Spirits, shamans, and stars: Perspectives from South America* (pp. 95–148). The Hague: Mouton.

Bear, J. (2000). *Amazon magic: The life story of ayahuasquero and shaman don Agustin Rivas Vasquez*. Taos, NM: Calibri.

Beckerman, S., & Yost, J. (2007). Upper Amazonian warfare. In R. J. Chacon & R. G. Mendoza (Eds.), *Latin American indigenous warfare and ritual violence* (pp. 142–179). Tucson: University of Arizona Press.

Bentall, R. P. (1990). The syndromes and symptoms of psychosis: Or why you can't play 20 questions with the concept of schizophrenia and hope to win. In R. P. Bentall (Ed.), *Reconstructiong schizophrenia* (pp. 23–60). London: Routledge.

Bentall, R. P. (2000). Hallucinatory experiences. In E. Cardeña, S. J. Lynn, & S. Krippner (Eds.), *Varieties of anomalous experience: Examining the scientific evidence* (pp. 85–120). Washington, DC: American Psychological Association.

Bentall, R. P., Baker, G. A., & Havers, S. (1991). Reality monitoring and psychotic hallucinations. *British Journal of Clinical Psychology, 30*, 213–222.

Berlin, I., & Anthenelli, R. M. (2001). Monoamine oxidases and tobacco smoking. *International Journal of Neuropsychopharmacology, 4*(1), 33–42.

Beyer, S. (1973). *The cult of Tārā: Magic and ritual in Tibet.* Berkeley: University of California Press.

Beyer, S. (1980). Brave new world revisited: Fifteen years of chemical sacraments. *Wisconsin Law Review, 1980*, 879–916.

Beynon, R. (1993). The use of ayahuasca in Brazil by the Santo Daime religion. *Newsletter of the Multidisciplinary Association for Psychedelic Studies, 3*(4), 29–30. Retrieved April 10, 2008, from http://www.maps.org/news-letters/v03n4/03429aya.html.

Bhabha, H. (1994). *The location of culture.* London: Routledge.

Bigwood, J., & Ott, J. (1977, November). DMT. *Head Magazine*, 56–61. Retrieved January 13, 2006, from http://jeremybigwood.net/JBsPUBS/DMT/.

Birchwood, M. J., Preston, M., & Hallet, S. (1992). *Schizophrenia: An integrated approach to research and treatment.* New York: New York University Press.

Bird-David, N. (1999). "Animism" revisited: Personhood, environment, and relational epistemology. *Current Anthropology, 40*, 67–79.

Birmes, P., Chounet, V., Mazerolles, M., Cathala, B., Schmitt, L., & Lauque D. (2002). Self-poisoning with *Datura stramonium*. 3 case reports. *Presse Medical, 31*(2), 69–72. Retrieved May 6, 2008, from the National Library of Medicine Web site, http://www.ncbi.nlm.nih.gov/pubmed/11850988.

Bisset, N. G. (1992). War and hunting poisons of the New World. Part I. Notes on the early history of curare. *Journal of Ethnopharmacology, 36*(1), 1–26.

Blackburn, T. C. (Ed.). (1975). *December's child: A book of Chumash oral narratives.* Berkeley: University of California Press.

Blain, J. (2002). *Nine worlds of seid-magic: Ecstasy and neo-shamanism in North European paganism.* London: Routledge.

Blank, L., & Bogan, J. (1984). *Burden of dreams.* Berkeley: North Atlantic.

Blue Morpho Tours. (2003). Ayahuasca shamanism—Shamanic tour/workshop in the Amazon. Retrieved August 6, 2008, from the Blue Morpho Center for Shamanic Studies and Workshops Web site, http://www.bluemorphotours.com/shamanic_tour_info.asp.

Bodmer, R. E. (1994). Managing wildlife with local communities in the Peruvian Amazon: The case of the Reserva Communal Tamshiyacu-Tahuayo. In D. Western, S. C. Strum, & R. M. Wright (Eds.), *Natural connections: Perspectives in community based conservation* (pp. 113–134). Washington, DC: Island.

Boire, R. G. (1994). *Accommodating religious users of controlled substances: Revisioning the Controlled Substances Act to permit the religious use of entheogenic substances.* Retrieved August 19, 2004, from the Spectral Mindustries Web site, http://www.specmind.com/accomodating.htm.

Bongie, C. (1998). *Islands and exiles: The Creole identities of post/colonial literature.* Stanford, CA: Stanford University Press.

Bonson, K. R., & Baggott, M. (2002). Emerging drugs of abuse: Use patterns and clinical toxicity. In E. J. Massaro (Ed.), *Handbook of neurotoxicology, Vol. II* (pp. 223–258). Totowa, NJ: Humana.

Bose, T. K., Basu, R. K., Biswas, B., De, J. N., Majumdar, B. C., & Datta, S. (1999). Cardiovascular effects of yellow oleander ingestion. *Journal of the Indian Medical Association, 97*(10), 407–410.

Bowers, M. A. (2004). *Magic(al) realism*. New York: Routledge.

Bowie, F. (2000). *The anthropology of religion: An introduction*. Oxford: Blackwell.

Bragdon, E. (2004). *Kardec's spiritism: A home for healing and spiritual evolution*. Aptos, CA: Lightening Up.

Brandão, C. R. (1993). Popular faith in Brazil. In G. H. Gossen (Ed.), *South and Meso-American native spirituality: From the cult of the feathered serpent to the theology of liberation* (pp. 436–473). New York: Crossroad.

Briggs, C. (1996). The meaning of nonsense, the poetics of embodiment, and the production of power in Warao healing. In C. Laderman & M. Roseman (Eds.), *The performance of healing* (pp. 185–232). New York: Routledge.

Bristol, M. L. (1966). The psychotropic *Banisteriopsis* among the Sibundoy of Colombia. *Harvard University Botanical Museum Leaflets, 21*, 113–140.

Bristol, M. L., Evans, W. C., & Lampard, J. F. (1969). The alkaloids of the genus Datura, section Brugmansia. VI. Tree Datura drugs (*Datura condida* cvs.) of the Colombian Sibundoy. *Lloydia, 32*(2), 123–130.

Brodwin, P. E. (1992). Symptoms and social performances: The case of Diane Reden. In M. D. Good, P. E. Brodwin, B. J. Good, & A. Kleinman (Eds.), *Pain as human experience: An anthropological perspective* (pp. 77–99). Berkeley: University of California Press.

Brody, H. (1987). *Stories of sickness*. New Haven: Yale University Press.

Bronson, M. (1983). Brazilian spiritist healers. *Shaman's Drum, Journal of Experiential Shamanism, 3*, 23–27.

Brown, D. J. (2007). *Exploring the therapeutic benefits of DMT: An interview with Dr. Rick Strassman*. Petaluma, CA: Smart Publications. Retrieved August 12, 2008, from http://www.smart-publications.com/articles/MOM-strassman.php.

Brown, M. F. (1978). From the hero's bones: Three Aguaruna hallucinogens and their uses. In R. I. Ford (Ed.), *The nature and status of ethnobotany* (pp. 118–136). (Anthropological Papers No. 67). Ann Arbor: University of Michigan Museum of Anthropology.

Brown, M. F. (1985). Individual experience, dreams, and the identification of magical stones in an Amazonian society. In J. W. D. Dougherty (Ed.), *Directions in cognitive anthropology* (pp. 373–387). Urbana: University of Illinois Press.

Brown, M. F. (1986). *Tsewa's gift: Magic and meaning in an Amazonian society*. Washington, DC: Smithsonian Institution Press.

Brown, M. F. (1988). Shamanism and its discontents. *Medical Anthropology Quarterly, 2*, 102–120.

Brown, M. F. (1989, November). Dark side of the shaman: The traditional healer's art has its perils. *Natural History, 98*, 8–10.

Brown, M. F. (1991). Beyond resistance: A comparative study of utopian renewal in Amazonia. *Ethnohistory, 38*(4), 388–413.

Brown, M. F. (1994). Beyond resistance: Comparative study of utopian renewal in

Amazonia. In A. Roosevelt (Ed.), *Amazonian Indians from prehistory to the present: Anthropological perspectives* (pp. 287–311). Tucson: University of Arizona Press.

Brown, M. F. (1996). On resisting resistance. *American Anthropologist, 98*, 729–735.

Brown, R., & Herrnstein, R. (1981). Icons and images. In N. Block (Ed.), *Imagery* (pp. 19–49). Cambridge, MA: MIT Press.

Browner, C. H. (1985). Criteria for selecting herbal remedies. *Ethnology*, 24(1), 13–32.

Brownrigg, L. A. (1996). Categories of faunal and floral economic resources of the native communities of the Peruvian Amazon in 1993. *Journal of Ethnobiology*, 16(2), 185–211. Retrieved December 6, 2006, from the Bureau of the Census Statistical Research Division Report Series Web site, http://www.census.gov/srd/papers/pdf/lab9601.pdf.

Brüzzi, A. da S. (1962). *A civilização indígena do Uaupés* [An indigenous culture of the Vaupés]. São Paolo: Linográfica Editôra Ldta.

Buber, M. (1965). *Between man and man*. New York: Collier. (Original work published 1947.)

Buchanan, S. (1991). *The doctrine of signatures: A defense of theory in medicine*. Urbana: University of Illinois Press. (Original work published 1938.)

Buchillet, D. (1992). Nobody is there to hear: Desana therapeutic incantations. In G. Baer & J. E. Langdon (Eds.), *Portals of power: Shamanism in South America* (pp. 211–230). Albuquerque: University of New Mexico Press.

Buchillet, D. (2004). Sorcery beliefs, transmission of shamanic knowledge, and therapeutic practice among the Desana of the Upper Rio Negro region, Brazil. In N. L. Whitehead & R. Wright (Eds.), *In darkness and secrecy: The anthropology of assault sorcery and witchcraft in Amazonia* (pp. 109–131). Durham: Duke University Press.

Buckholtz, N. S., & Boggan, W. O. (1977). Monoamine oxidase inhibition in brain and liver by b-carbolines: Structure–activity relationships and substrate specificity. *Biochemical Pharmacology, 26*, 1991–1996.

Buckholtz, N. S., Freedman, D. X., & Middaugh, L. D. (1985). Daily LSD administration selectively decreases serotonin2 receptor binding in rat brain. *European Journal of Pharmacology, 109*, 421–425.

Buckholtz, N. S., Zhou, D. F., & Freedman, D. X. (1988). Serotonin2 agonist administration down-regulates rat brain serotonin2 receptors. *Life Sciences, 42*, 2439–2445.

Buckholtz, N. S., Zhou, D. F., Freedman, D. X., & Potter, W. Z. (1990). Lysergic acid diethylamide (LSD) administration selectively downregulates serotonin2 receptors in rat brain. *Neuropsychopharmacology, 3*, 137–148.

Buhner, S. (1996). *Sacred plant medicine: Explorations in the practice of indigenous herbalism*. Coeur d'Alene, ID: Raven Press.

Buhner, S. (2002). *The lost language of plants: The ecological importance of plant medicines to life on Earth*. White River Junction, VT: Chelsea Green.

Burger, E., & Neale, R. E. (1995). *Magic and meaning*. Seattle: Hermetic Press.

Burroughs, W. S. (1977). *Junky*. New York: Penguin. (Original work published 1953.)

Burroughs, W. S., & Ginsberg, A. (1975). *The yagé letters*. San Francisco: City Lights. (Original work published 1963.)

Bussmann, R. W., & Sharon, D. (2007). *Plants of the four winds: The magical and medicina flora of Peru*. Trujillo, Peru: Graficart.

Butt, A. J. (1956). Ritual blowing: *Taling*—A causation and cure of illness among the Akawaio. *Man*, 61, 49–55.

Calderwood, A. (2008). Feature artist: Interview with Pablo Amaringo. *Second Creation*, *3*(1), 18–25.

Callaway, J. C. (1988). A proposed mechanism for the visions of dream sleep. *Medical Hypotheses*, *26*(2), 119–124.

Callaway, J. C. (1999). Phytochemistry and neuropharmacology of ayahuasca. In R. Metzner (Ed.), *Ayahuasca: Hallucinogens, consciousness, and the spirits of nature* (pp. 250–275). New York: Thunder's Mouth Press.

Callaway, J. C. (2005). Various alkaloid profiles in decoctions of *Banisteriopsis caapi*. *Journal of Psychoactive Drugs*, *37*(2), 151–155.

Callaway, J. C., Airaksinen, M. M., McKenna, D. J., Brito, G. S., & Grob, C. S. (1994). Platelet serotonin uptake sites increased in drinkers of ayahuasca. *Psychopharmacology*, *116*(3), 358–387.

Callaway, J. C., Brito, G. S., & Neves, E. S. (2005). Phytochemical analyses of *Banisteriopsis caapi* and *Psychotria viridis*. *Journal of Psychoactive Drugs*, *37*(2), 145–150.

Callaway, J. C., & McKenna, D. J. (1998). Neurochemistry of psychedelic drugs. In S. B. Karch (Ed.), *Drug abuse handbook* (pp. 485–498). Boca Raton: CRC Press.

Callaway, J. C., McKenna, D. J., Grob, C. S., Brito, G. S., Raymon, L. P., Poland, R. E., et al. (1999). Pharmacokinetics of *hoasca* alkaloids in healthy humans. *Journal of Ethnopharmacology*, *65*(3), 243–256.

Callaway, J. C., Raymon, L. P., Hearn, W. L., McKenna, D. J., Grob, C. S., Brito, G. S., et al. (1996). Quantitation of N,N-dimethyltriptamine and harmala alkaloids in human plasma after oral dosing with ayahuasca. *Journal of Analytical Toxicology*, *20*, 492–497.

Calvo, C. (1995a). Maria Lando [Recorded by Baca, S.]. On *Afro-Peruvian classics: The soul of Black Peru* [CD]. New York: Luaka Bop Records.

Calvo, C. (1995b). *The three halves of Ino Moxo* (K. A. Symington, Trans.). Rochester, VT: Inner Traditions International. (Original work published 1981.)

Camp, D. (2008, January 12). Dancerific! Fantastica! Yee haw! [Review of the CD *Roots of chicha: Psychedelic cumbias from Peru*]. Retrieved June 28, 2008, from the Amazon.com Web site, http://www.amazon.com/review/product/B000V8MR7A/ref=cm_cr_dp_synop?%5Fencoding=UTF8&sortBy=bySubmissionDateDescending#R1WP55VEJPWZEI.

Campos, J. (2000). *Icaros from ayahuasca healing rituals* [Audiocassette]. Berkeley: Conference Recording Service.

Cánepa, G. (2008). *The fluidity of ethnic identities in Peru* (CRISE Working Paper No. 46). Oxford: Centre for Research on Inequality, Human Security and Ethnicity. Retrieved July 24, 2008, from http://www.crise.ox.ac.uk/pubs/workingpaper46.pdf.

Caravati, M. E., McCowan, C. L., & Marshall, S. W. (2004). Plants. In R. C. Dart (Ed.), *Medical toxicology* (pp. 1671–1713). Philadelphia: Lippincot Williams & Wilkins.

Cardeña, E., Lynn, S. J., & Krippner, S. (Eds.). (2000). *Varieties of anomalous experience: Examining the scientific evidence*. Washington, DC: American Psychological Association.

Cardenas, E., Ocampo, J. A., & Thorp, R. (2000). *An economic history of twentieth-century Latin America*. Hampshire, England: Palgrave.

Carlson, R., & Shield, B. (Eds.). (1989). *Healers on healing*. Los Angeles: Jeremy P. Tarcher.

Carneiro, R. L. (1964). The Amahuaca and the spirit world. *Ethnology, 3*, 6–11.

Carneiro, R. L. (1977). Recent observations on shamanism and witchcraft among the Kuikuru Indians of Central Brazil. *Annals of the New York Academy of Sciences, 293*, 215–228.

Carneiro, R. L. (1980). Chimera of the Upper Amazon. In R. de Mille (Ed.), *The don Juan papers: Further Castaneda controversies* (pp. 94–98). Santa Barbara: Ross-Erikson.

Carr, S. (1995). Exquisitely simple or incredibly complex: The theory of entoptic phenomena (unpublished M.A. thesis, University of Newcastle upon Tyne, Newcastle upon Tyne. Retrieved December 10, 2005, from http://www.oubliette.org.uk/dissind.html.

Casey, E. (1991). *Spirit and soul: Essays in philosophical psychology*. Dallas: Spring.

Casey, E. (2000). *Imagining: A phenomenological study* (2nd ed.). Bloomington: Indiana University Press.

Cassell, E. J. (1976). *The healer's art: A new approach to the doctor–patient relationship*. Philadelphia: Lippincott.

Castaneda, C. (1968). *The teachings of don Juan: A Yaqui way of knowledge*. Berkeley: University of California Press.

Castaneda, C. (1971). *A separate reality: Further conversations with don Juan*. New York: Simon & Schuster.

Castaneda, C. (1972). *Journey to Ixtlan: The lessons of don Juan*. New York: Simon & Schuster.

Castaneda, C. (1973). Sorcery: A description of the world (Ph.D. dissertation, University of California, Los Angeles). *Dissertation Abstracts International, 33*(12), 5625B.

Castner, J. L., Timme, S. L., & Duke, J. A. (1998). *A field guide to medicinal and useful plants of the Upper Amazon*. Gainesville, FL: Feline Press.

Castonguay, L. (1990). *Vocabulario regional del Oriente Peruana* [Regional dictionary of eastern Peru] (2nd ed.). Iquitos: Centro de Etsudios Teologicos de la Amazonía.

Cebrián, M. (2005). *La clara vision: Chamanismo y ayahuasca*. Buenos Aires: Libros en Red.

Center for Cognitive Liberty and Ethics. (2003, January 17). Alan Shoemaker Ayahuasca Legal Defense Fund needs support. *The Week Online with DRCNet, 272*. Retrieved January 14, 2006, from the Drug War Chronicle Web site, http://stopthedrugwar.org/chronicle/272/shoemakerdefense.shtml.

Center for International Environmental Law. (2003, December 8). *The ayahuasca patent case*. Retrieved April 3, 2007, from http://www.ciel.org/Biodiversity/ayahuasca patentcase.html.

Centers for Disease Control. (1996, June 7). Scopolamine poisoning among heroin users—New York City, Newark, Philadelphia, and Baltimore, 1995 and 1996. *Morbidity and Mortality Weekly Report, 45*(22), 1.

Central Intelligence Agency. (2006). *The world factbook—Peru*. Retrieved November 6, 2006, from https://www.cia.gov/cia/publications/factbook/geos/pe.html.

Cetacean Specialist Group. (1996). *Inia geoffrensis*. In International Union for the Conservation of Nature (Ed.), *2007 IUCN Red List of threatened species*. Retrieved on May 30, 2008, from http://www.iucnredlist.org/search/details.php/10831/summ.

Chacón, O. (2001). Medicina indígena y psiquiatría moderna: Diálogo posible [Indig enous medicine and modern psychiatry: Possible dialogue]. In J. Mabit (Ed.), *Memoria del segundo foro interamericano sobre espiritualidad indígena* (pp. 160–172). Tarapoto, Peru: Consejo Interamericano Sobre Espiritualidad Indígena y Centro de Rehabilitación y de Investigación de las Medicinas Tradicionales Takiwasi.

Chacon, R. J. (2007). Seeking the headhunter's power: The quest for *arutam* among the Achuar of the Ecuádorian Amazon and the development of ranked societies. In R. J. Chacon & D. H. Dye (Eds.), *The taking and displaying of human body parts as trophies by Amerindians*. New York: Springer.

Chan, K. (2002). Jimson weed poisoning—A case report. *Complementary and Alternative Medicine, 6*(4). Retrieved May 6, 2008, from the Permanente Journal Web site, http://xnet.kp.org/permanentejournal/fa1102/jimson.html.

Charing, H. G. (2007a). Ayahuasca shaman—Javier Arevalo interviewed in the Amazon rainforest Peru. *EzineArticles*. Retrieved November 22, 2007, from http://ezinearticles.com/?Ayahuasca-Shaman—Javier-Arevalo-Interviewed-in-the-Amazon-Rainforest-Peru&id=672764.

Charing, H. G. (2007b). Ayahuasca shaman and Peruvian mystic, Alonso Del Rio interviewed. *EzineArticles*. Retrieved November 22, 2007, from http://ezinearticles.com/?Ayahuasca-Shaman-and-Peruvian-Mystic,-Alonso-Del-Rio-Interviewed&id=670705.

Charing, H. G. (2007c). Ayahuasca shamans and the healing plants of the Amazon rainforest—Part 2. *EzineArticles*. Retrieved November 22, 2007, from http://ezinearticles.com/?Ayahuasca-Shamans-and-the-Healing-Plants-of-the-Amazon-Rainforest—Part-2&id=762220.

Charing, H. G. (2007d). Medicine for the soul—Plant spirit shamanism of the Amazonian rainforest. *EzineArticles*. Retrieved November 22, 2007, from http://ezinearticles.com/?Medicine-for-the-Soul—Plant-Spirit-Shamanism-of-the-Amazonian-Rainforest&id=549134.

Charing, H. G. (2007e). Shipibo ayahuasca shaman Leoncio Garcia interviewed. *EzineArticles*. Retrieved November 22, 2007, from http://ezinearticles.com/?Shipibo-Ayahuasca-Shaman-Leoncio-Garcia-Interviewed&id=620018.

Charing, H. G., & Cloudsley, P. (2006). The ayahuasca visions of Pablo Amaringo. *Sacred Hoop*, 53, 16–19.

Chaumeil, J., & Chaumeil, J.-P. (1979). El chamanismo yagua [Yagua shamanism]. *Amazonia peruana*, 4, 35–69.

Chaumeil, J.-P. (1992). Varieties of Amazonian shamanism. *Diogenes*, 20(158), 101–112.

Chaumeil, J.-P. (2000). *Voir savoir pouvoir: Le chamanisme chez les Yagua de l'amazonie péruvienne* [Vision, knowledge, power: Shamanism among the Yagua of the Peruvian Amazon]. Geneva: Georg Editeur. (Original work published 1983.)

Chávez, L. (2001). Arte objectivo en la cultura Shipibo-Coniba [Objective art in Shipibo-Conibo culture]. In J. Mabit (Ed.), *Memoria del segundo foro interamericano sobre espiritualidad indígena* (pp. 134–144). Tarapoto, Peru: Consejo Interamericano Sobre Espiritualidad Indígena y Centro de Rehabilitación y de Investigación de las Medicinas Tradicionales Takiwasi.

Chen, J., & Saunders, S. C. (1999). Microclimate in forest ecosystem and landscape ecology. *Bioscience*, 49(4), 288–297.

Chevalier, J. M. (1982). *Civilization and the stolen gift: Capital, kin and cult in eastern Peru.* Toronto: University of Toronto Press.

Chibnik, M. (1994). *Risky rivers: The economics and politics of floodplain farming in Amazonia.* Tucson: University of Arizona Press.

Chichester, D. (2005). Animism. In B. R. Taylor (Ed.), *Encyclopedia of religion and nature* (pp. 78–81). New York: Continuum.

Chilvers, I. (1998). *A dictionary of twentieth-century art.* Oxford: Oxford University Press.

Cholden, L. S., Kurland, A., & Savage, C. (1955). Clinical reactions and tolerance to LSD in chronic schizophrenia. *Journal of Nervous and Mental Disease, 122,* 211–221.

Christopher, M. (1973). *The illustrated history of magic.* New York: Thomas Y. Crowell.

Claggett, P. R. (1998). The spatial extent and composition of wildlife harvests among three villages in the Peruvian Amazon. Paper presented at the 1998 meeting of the Latin American Studies Association, Chicago, September 24–26, 1998. Retrieved April 13, 2007, from the Consejo Latinoamericano de Ciencias Sociáles Web site, http://168.96.200.17/ar/libros/lasa98/Claggett.pdf.

Classen, C. (1990). Sweet colors, fragrant songs: Sensory models of the Andes and the Amazon. *American Ethnologist, 17*(4), 722–736.

Clastres, P. (1972). *Chronique des Indiens Guayaki* [Chronicle of the Guayaki Indians]. Paris: Plon.

Clastres, P. (1989). *Society against the state: Essays in political anthropology* (R. Hurley, Trans.). Brooklyn: Zone.

Clastres, P. (1994). *Archeology of violence* (J. Herman, Trans.). New York: Semiotext(e).

Clements, J. F., & Shany, N. (2001). *A field guide to the birds of Peru.* Temecula, CA: Ibis.

Cloudsley, P. & Charing, H. G. (2007). Interview with Shipibo shaman Enrique Lopez—Part 1. *Shamanism's Weblog.* Retrieved April 25, 2008, from http://shamanism.wordpress.com/2007/12/24/interview-with-shipibo-shaman-enrique-lopez-part-1/.

Cohen, S. (1985). LSD: The varieties of psychotic experience. *Journal of Psychoactive Drugs, 17*(4), 291–296.

Colson, A. B. (1977). The Akawaio shaman. In E. B. Basso (Ed.), *Carib-speaking Indians* (pp. 43–65). Tucson: University of Arizona Press.

Colson, A. B. (2001). Itoto (kanaima) as death and anti-structure. In L. Rival & N. Whitehead (Eds.), *Beyond the visible and the material: The Amerindianization of society in the work of Peter Rivière* (pp. 221–233). Oxford: Oxford University Press.

Comaroff, J., & Comaroff, J. (1993). Introduction. In J. Comaroff & J. Comaroff (Eds.), *Modernity and its malcontents: Ritual and power in postcolonial Africa* (pp. xi–xxvii). Chicago: University of Chicago Press.

Conan, O. (2007). *Roots of chicha: Psychedelic cumbias from Peru* [CD]. New York: Barbes.

Consejo Nacional de Salud. (2007). Declaracion de Cuenca "Por una salud equitativa, digna y de calidad" [Declaration of Cuenca: Towards fair, decent, and quality health care]. Cuenca, Ecuador: III Congreso por la Salud y la Vida "Dr. César Hermida Piedra." Retrieved April 25, 2008, from the Consejo Nacional de la Mujéres Web site, http://conamu.gov.ec/CONAMU/files/declaraciondecuencaok.pdf.

Coomes, O. T., & Barham, B. L. (1997). Rain forest extraction and conservation in Amazonia. *Geographical Journal, 163*(2), 180–184.

Cooper, J. M. (1944). The shaking tent rite among the plains and forest Algonquians. *Primitive Man*, 17(1), 60–84.

Corbin, A. (1986). *The foul and the fragrant: Odor and the French social imagination.* Cambridge, MA: Harvard University Press.

Corbin, H. (2000). *Mundus imaginalis*: Or the imaginary and the imaginal. In B. Sells (Ed.), *Working with images* (pp. 71–89). Woodstock, CT: Spring Publications. (Original work published 1972.)

Crandon-Malamud, L. (1991). *From the fat of our souls: Social change, political process, and medical pluralism in Bolivia.* Berkeley: University of California Press.

Cray, C. (1999, December). Patent justice. *Multinational Monitor*, 20(12), 4.

Crellin, J. K., & Philpott, J. (1990). *Trying to give ease.* Durham: Duke University Press.

Cristina & Kopper, B. (2006). *La aurora: Icaros from the Amazon* [CD]. Denver: NFA Studio.

Crocker, J. C. (1985). *Vital souls: Bororo cosmology, natural symbolism, and shamanism.* Tucson: University of Arizona Press.

Cronon, W. (1998). The trouble with wilderness, or, getting back to the wrong nature. In J. B. Callicott & M. P. Nelson (Eds.), *The great new wilderness debate* (pp. 471–499). Athens: University of Georgia Press.

Crosby, D. M., & McLaughlin, J. L. (1973). Cactus alkaloids. XIX. Crystallization of mescaline HCl and 3-methoxytyramine HCl from *Trichocereus pachanoi*. *Lloydia*, 36(4), 416–418.

Csordas, T. (2002). *Body/meaning/healing.* Hampshire, England: Palgrave Macmillan.

Currie, G. (2000). Imagination, delusion and hallucinations. In M. Coltheart & M. Davis (Eds.), *Pathologies of belief* (pp. 167–182). Oxford: Blackwell.

Cwik, G. (1995). Active imagination: Synthesis in analysis. In M. Stein (Ed.), *Jungian analysis* (2nd ed., pp. 137–169). Chicago: Open Court.

Dart, R. C., & Gold, B. S. (2004). Crotaline snakebite. In R. C. Dart (Ed.), *Medical toxicology* (pp. 1559–1565). Philadelphia: Lippincott Williams & Wilkins.

Davis, E. W. (1995). Ethnobotany: An old practice, a new discipline. In R. E. Schultes & S. von Reis (Eds.), *Ethnobotany: Evolution of a discipline* (pp. 40–51). Portland, OR: Dioscorides Press.

Davis, E. W., & Yost, J. A. (1983a). Novel hallucinogens from Ecuador. *Harvard University Botanical Museum Leaflets*, 29(3), 291–295.

Davis, E. W., & Yost, J. A. (1983b). The ethnobotany of the Waorani of eastern Ecuador. *Harvard University Botanical Museum Leaflets*, 29(3), 159–218.

Davis, E. W., & Yost, J. A. (1983c). The ethnomedicine of the Waorani of Amazonian Ecuador. *Journal of Ethnopharmacology*, 9(2–3), 273–297.

Davis, W. (1996). *One river: Explorations and discoveries in the Amazon rain forest.* New York: Simon & Schuster.

Davis, W. (1998). *Shadows in the sun: Travels to landscapes of spirit and desire.* Washington, DC: Island.

Dawson, A. (2007). *New era—new religions: Religious transformation in contemporary Brazil.* Hampshire, England: Ashgate.

De Budowski, J., Marini-Bettòlo, G. B., Delle Monache, F., & Ferrari, F. (1974). On the alkaloid composition of the snuff drug yopo from the Upper Orinoco (Venezuela). *Il Farmaco (Edizione Scientifica)*, 29(8), 574–578.

de Calella, P. (1935). Los indios Sionas del Putumayo [The Siona Indians of the Putumayo]. *Boletín de Estudios Históricos, 73–74*, 49–52.

de Calella, P. (1944a). Datos mitológicos de los Huitotos de La Chorrera [Information on the mythology of the Huitotos of La Chorrera]. *Amazonia Colombiana Americanista, 2*(4–8), 33–37.

de Calella, P. (1944b). Breves notas mitológicos de los Huitoto de Santa Clara [Brief notes on the mythology of the Huitots of Santa Clara]. *Amazonia Colombiana Americanista, 2*(4–8), 38–40.

de Civrieux, M. (1980). *Watunna: An Orinoco creation cycle* (D. M. Guss, Ed. & Trans.). San Fancisco: North Point.

DeGrandpre, R. (2006). *The cult of pharmacology*. Durham: Duke University Press.

DeKorne, J. (1994). *Psychedelic shamanism: The cultivation, preparation and shamanic use of psychotropic plants*. Port Townsend, WA: Loompanics.

de la Cadena, M. (2000). *Indigenous mestizos: The politics of race and culture in Cuzco, Peru, 1919–1991*. Durham: Duke University Press.

de la Cadena, M. (2001, September). The racial politics of culture and silent racism in Peru. Paper presented at the 2001 U.N. Research Institute for Social Development Conference on Racism and Public Policy, Durban, September 3–5. Retrieved June 20, 2008, from http://www.unrisd.org/unrisd/website/document.nsf/ab82a6805797760f80256b4f005da1ab/ee7eb1e30a96c11f80256b6d00578643/$file/dcadena.pdf.

Delacroix, J.-M. (2000). *Ainsi parle l'esprit de la plante: Un psychothérapeute français à l'épreuve des therapies ancestrales d'Amazonie*. Berbex-Genève, Switzerland: Editions Jouvence.

Déléage, P. (N.d.). [Review of the book *Koshi shinany ainbo: El testimonio de una mujer shipiba*]. Lima: Universidad Nacional Mayor de San Marcos. Retrieved February 17, 2007, from http://pierredeleage.googlepages.com/cr_valenzuela.pdf.

Del Río, A. (2003). Doctoricito ayahuasca [MP3]. Retrieved May 3, 2008, from the Ayahuasca Wasi Web site, http://www.ayahuasca-wasi.com/songs/Alonso%20del%20Rio/Puerto%20Maldonado,%202003/Doctoricito%20Ayahuasca.mp3.

Del Río, A. (2005). *Canciones de medicina* [CD]. Taray-Cusco, Peru: Ayahuasca-Ayllu.

Del Río, A. (2006). *Canciones de medicina II* [CD]. Taray-Cusco, Peru: Ayahuasca-Ayllu.

Del Río, A. (2007). *Canciones de medicina III* [CD]. Taray-Cusco, Peru: Ayahuasca-Ayllu.

Demange, F. (2002). Amazonian *vegetalismo*: A study of the healing power of chants in Tarapoto, Peru (unpublished M.A. thesis, University of East London, London). Retrieved October 25, 2006, from the Traditional Amazonian Medicines Society Web site, http://www.tamsociety.org/francois_thesis.htm.

de Mille, R. (1976). *Castaneda's journey*. Santa Barbara: Capra Press.

de Mille, R. (Ed.). (1990). *The don Juan papers: Further Castaneda controversies*. Belmont, CA: Wadsworth.

Denevan, W. M. (1998). The pristine myth: The landscape of the Americas in 1492. In J. B. Callicott & M. P. Nelson (Eds.), *The great new wilderness debate* (pp. 414–442). Athens: University of Georgia Press. (Original work published 1992.)

Denno, D. W. (2007). The lethal injection quandary: How medicine has dismantled the death penalty. *Fordham Law Review, 76*, 49–128.

Der Marderosian, A. H., Kensinger, K. M., Chao, J. M., & Goldstein, F. J. (1970). The use and hallucinatory principles of a psychoactive beverage of the Cashinahua tribe (Amazon Basin). *Drug Dependence*, 5, 7–15.

Der Marderosian, A. H., Pinkley, H. V., & Dobbins, M. F. (1968). Native use and occurrence of N,N-dimethyltryptamine in the leaves of *Banisteriopsis rusbyana*. *American Journal of Pharmacy*, 140(5), 137–147.

Descola, P. (1994). *In the society of nature: A native ecology in Amazonia* (N. Scott, Trans.). (Cambridge Studies in Social and Cultural Anthropology 93). Cambridge: Cambridge University Press. (Original work published 1986.)

Descola, P. (1996). *The spears of twilight: Life and death in the Amazon jungle* (J. Lloyd, Trans.). New York: New Press. (Original work published 1993.)

Deshayes, P. (2002). L'ayawaska n'est pas un hallucinogène [Ayawaska is not a hallucinogen]. *Psychotropes*, 8(1), 65–78.

Desjarlais, R. (1996). Presence. In C. Laderman & M. Roseman (Eds.), *The performance of healing* (pp. 143–164). New York: Routledge.

Desmarchelier, C., Gurni, A., Ciccia, G., & Giulietti, A. M. (1996). Ritual and medicinal plants of the Ese'ejas of the Amazonian rainforest (Madre de Dios, Peru). *Journal of Ethnopharmacology*, 52(1), 45–51.

De Smet, P. A. G. M. (1985). A multidisciplinary overview of intoxicating snuff rituals in the Western Hemisphere. *Journal of Ethnopharmacology*, 13(1), 3–49.

Dewick, P. M. (2001). *Medicinal natural products: A biosynthetic approach*. Chichester, England: John Wiley & Sons.

De Wys, M. (2009). *Black smoke: A woman's journey of healing, wild love, and transformation in the Amazon*. New York: Sterling.

D'Haen, T. L. (1995). Magic realism and postmodernism: Decentering privileged centers. In L. P. Zamora & W. B. Faris (Eds.), *Magical realism: Theory, history, community* (pp. 191–208). Durham: Duke University Press.

Dilworth, L. (1996). *Imagining Indians in the Southwest: Persistent visions of a primitive past*. Washington, DC: Smithsonian Institution Press.

Dobkin de Ríos, M. (1969). Fortune's malice: Divination, psychotherapy, and folk medicine in Peru. *Journal of American Folklore*, 82(324), 132–141.

Dobkin de Ríos, M. (1970a). *Banisteriopsis* in witchcraft and healing activities in Iquitos, Peru. *Economic Botany*, 24(3), 296–300.

Dobkin de Ríos, M. (1970b). A note on the use of ayahuasca among urban mestizo populations on the Peruvian Amazon. *American Anthropologist*, 72(6), 1419–1422.

Dobkin de Ríos, M. (1971). Ayahuasca: The healing vine. *International Journal of Social Psychiatry*, 17(4), 256–269.

Dobkin de Ríos, M. (1972a). [Review of the book *Wizard of the Upper Amazon*]. *American Anthropologist*, 74(6), 1423–1424.

Dobkin de Ríos, M. (1972b). *Visionary vine: Psychedelic healing in the Amazon*. San Francisco: Chandler.

Dobkin de Ríos, M. (1973). Curing with ayahuasca in an urban slum. In M. Harner (Ed.), *Hallucinogens and shamanism* (pp. 67–85). London: Oxford University Press.

Dobkin de Ríos, M. (1981). Saladerra: A culture-bound misfortune syndrome in the Peruvian Amazon. *Culture, Medicine, and Psychiatry*, 5(2), 193–213.

Dobkin de Ríos, M. (1990). *Hallucinogens: Cross-cultural perspectives*. Dorset: Prism. (Original work published 1984.)

Dobkin de Ríos, M. (1992). *Amazon healer: The life and times of an urban shaman*. Dorset: Prism.

Dobkin de Ríos, M. (1994, January). Drug tourism in the Amazon: Why Westerners are desperate to find the vanishing primitive. *Omni*, 16(4), 6.

Dobkin de Ríos, M. (2006). Anthropologist as fortuneteller. *Skeptic Magazine*, 12(4). Retrieved February 4, 2007, from the Access My Library Web site, http://www.accessmylibrary.com/coms2/summary_0286–29011877_ITM.

Dobkin de Ríos, M., & Rumrrill, R. (2008). *A hallucinogenic tea laced with controversy: Ayahuasca in the Amazon and the United States*. Westport, CT: Praeger.

Dodds, E. R. (1951). *The Greeks and the irrational*. Berkeley: University of California Press.

Doody, M. A. (1997). *The true story of the novel*. New Brunswick, NJ: Rutgers University Press.

Doore, G. (Ed.). (1988). *Shaman's path: Healing, personal growth and empowerment*. Boston: Shambhala.

Douglas, M. (2005). Witchcraft and leprosy: Two strategies for rejection. In *Risk and blame: Essays in cultural theory* (pp. 83–101). London: Routledge.

Dow, J. (1986). *The shaman's touch: Otomi Indian symbolic healing*. Salt Lake City: University of Utah Press.

Drug Enforcement Administration. (1993, January 14). *Schedules of controlled substances: Placement of cathinone and 2,5-dimethoxy-4-ethylamphetamine into Schedule I*. 58 Fed. Reg. 4316 (amending 21 CFR pt. 1308). Retrieved July 29, 2008, from the Isomer Design Web site, http://www.isomerdesign.com/Cdsa/FR/58FR4316.pdf.

Drug made from Indian plant produces movielike visions. (1932, April 23). *Science News*. Retrieved March 23, 2009, from http://blog.sciencenews.org/view/generic/id/2674/titleScience_Past__From_the_April_23,_1932,_issue.

Drug said to cause clairvoyance. (1932, April). *Modern Mechanics*. Retrieved March 23, 2009, from http://blog.modernmechanix.com/2009/02/02/drug-said-to-cause-clairvoyance/.

Druiddream. (2004, November 23). Experiential differences of rue and caapi [Msg 4]. Message posted to the Ayahuasca Forums Web site. Retrieved May 6, 2008, from http://forums.ayahuasca.com/phpbb/viewtopic.php?t=6886.

Drury, N. (1982). *The shaman and the magician: Journeys between the worlds*. London: Routledge.

Dubé, F. (2003, April 25). Woman dies in healing ritual; shaman guilty. *National Post (Canada)*. Retrieved October 4, 2003, from Religion News Blog, http://www.religionnewsblog.com/archives/00003132.html.

Dubin, M. (2001). *Native America collected: The culture of an art world*. Albuquerque: University of New Mexico Press.

Ducke, A. (1957). Capí, caapi, cabi, ayahuasca e yagé. *Revista da Associação Brasileira de Farmácia*, 38(12), 283–284.

Duellman, W. E. (2005). *Cusco Amazónico: The lives of amphibians and reptiles in an Amazonian forest*. Ithaca, NY: Cornell University Press.

Duke, J. A. (2006). *Amazing Amazon eleven*. Retrieved September 2, 2008, from the Exigo

Preview Web site, http://preview-publish.exigo.com/public/1428/websites/39/images/AmazingAmazon11-JD_1–17–06_.pdf.
Duke, J. A. (2009). *Duke's handbook of medicinal plants of Latin America*. Boca Raton: Taylor & Francis.
Duke, J. A., & Vasquez, R. (1994). *Amazonian ethnobotanical dictionary*. Boca Raton: CRC Press.
Dunn, E. (1973). Russian use of *Amanita muscaria*: A footnote to Wasson's *Soma*. *Current Anthropology*, 14(4), 488–492.
Dunn, J. (1998, February 5). Sting: A hip-hop rebirth? *Rolling Stone*, 779, 26–28.
Dunning, R. W. (1959). *Social and economic change among the Northern Ojibwa*. Toronto: University of Toronto Press.
Duntley, M. (1993). Observing meaning: Ritual criticism, interpretation, and anthropological fieldwork. In P. R. Frese & E. R. Ohnuki-Tierney (Eds.), *Celebrations of identity: Multiple voices in American ritual performance* (pp. 1–10). Westport, CT: Bergin & Garvey.
Eakin, E. (2001, April 21). Anthropology's alternative radical. *New York Times*. Retrieved November 11, 2007, from http://query.nytimes.com/gst/fullpage.html?res=9D01EEd81330F932A15757C0A9679C8B63.
Eisenberg, J. F., & Redford, K. H. (1999). *Mammals of the neotropics, Vol. 3: The central neotropics: Ecuador, Peru, Bolivia, Brazil*. Chicago: University of Chicago Press.
Eisenberg, L. (1981). The physician as interpreter: Ascribing meaning to the illness experience. *Comprehensive Psychiatry*, 22, 239–248.
Eliade, M. (1961). Recent works on shamanism. *History of Religions*, 1, 152–168.
Eliade, M. (1964). *Shamanism: Archaic techniques of ecstacy* (W. R. Trask, Trans.). Princeton: Princeton University Press. (Original work published 1951.)
El Libro de San Cipriano y Santa Justina [The book of St. Cyprian and St. Justine]. (2006). Mexico City: Editores Mexicanos Unidos.
Elliott, C. (2000). A new way to be mad. *Atlantic Monthly*, 286(6), 73–84.
Elton, C. (1999, October). Day trippers: A dubious ecotourist offering aims to take you out of this world. *Outside Magazine*, 24(10), 34.
Emmons, L. H. (1997). *Neotropical rainforest mammals: A field guide* (2nd ed.). Chicago: University of Chicago Press.
Errington, S. (1998). *The death of authentic primitive art and other tales of progress*. Berkeley: University of California Press.
Escobar, G. J., Salazar E., & Chung, M. (1983). Beliefs regarding the etiology and treatment of infantile diarrhea in Lima, Peru. *Social Science and Medicine*, 17, 1257–1269.
Esquirol, J. E. D. (1832). *Aliénation mental: Des illusions chez les aliénés. Question médico-légale sur l'isolement des aliénés* [Insanity: On the illusions of the insane. The medico-legal question of the isolation of the insane]. Paris: Librairie Médicale de Crochard.
Essig, R. (2001). *DMT entity*. Retrieved December 22, 2005, from the deviantART Web site, http://rogdog.deviantart.com/art/DMT-Entity-14046221.
Estrada, Á. (1981). *María Sabina: Her life and chants* (H. Munn, Trans.). Santa Barbara: Ross-Erikson.
Etkin, N. L. (1986). Multidisciplinary perspectives in the interpretation of plants used in indigenous medicine and diet. In N. L. Etkin (Ed.), *Indigenous medicine and diet: Behavioral approaches* (pp. 2–30). Belford Hills, NY: Redgrave.

Everitt, B. J., & Robbins, T. W. (1997). Central cholinergic systems and cognition. *Annual Review of Psychology, 48*, 649–684.

Fabrega, H. (1974). *Disease and social behavior*. Cambridge, MA: MIT Press.

Fan, H. W., & Cardoso, J. L. (1995). Clinical toxicology of snakebite in South America. In J. Meier & J. White (Eds.), *Handbook of clinical toxicology of animal venoms and poisons* (pp. 667–688). Boca Raton: CRC.

Farabee, W. C. (1922). *Indian tribes of eastern Perú* (Papers of the Peabody Museum of American Archeology and Ethnology, Harvard University, Vol. 10). Cambridge, MA: Peabody Museum.

Faust, F. X., & Bianchi, A. (1998). Die mysteriöse cabalonga [The mysterious cabalonga]. *Yearbook for Ethnomedicine and the Study of Consciousness, 5*, 247–251.

Fausto, C. (2004). A blend of blood and tobacco: Shamans and jaguars among the Parakanã of eastern Amazonia. In N. L. Whitehead & R. Wright (Eds.), *In darkness and secrecy: The anthropology of assault sorcery and witchcraft in Amazonia* (pp. 157–178). Durham: Duke University Press.

Feldman, H. (2003). The international soul of black Peru. In S. Loza (Ed.), *Musical cultures of Latin America: Global effects, past and present* (pp. 155–162). Berkeley: University of California Press.

Feldman, H. (2006). *Black rhythms of Peru: Reviving African musical heritage in the black Pacific*. Middletown, CT: Wesleyan University Press.

Feltwell, J. (2005). Regua: Vital conservation area in the southern Atlantic rainforests. *Plant Talk, 42*, 24–27. Retrieved December 6, 2006, from the Reserva Ecologica de Guapi Assu Web site, http://www.regua.co.uk/files/Plant%20Talk%20Article%2005.pdf.

Fenton, J. J. (2001). *Toxicology: A case-oriented approach*. Boca Raton: CRC.

Feraca, S. E. (1998). *Wakinyan: Lakota religion in the twentieth century*. Lincoln: University of Nebraska Press.

Fernandez, A., Lichtshein, G., & Vieweg, W. V. (1997). The Charles Bonnet syndrome: A review. *Journal of Nervous and Mental Disease, 185*(3), 195–200.

Fernandez, J. W. (1972). *Tabernanthe iboga*: Narcotic ecstasis and the work of the ancestors. In P. T. Furst (Ed.), *Flesh of the gods: The ritual use of hallucinogens* (pp. 237–316). New York: Praeger.

Fikes, J. C. (1993). *Carlos Castaneda: Academic opportunism and the psychedelic sixties*. Victoria, BC: Millenia Press.

Findeisen, H. (1957). *Schamanentum* [Shamanism]. Stuttgart: W. Kohlhammer.

Finkler, K. (1994a). Sacred healing and biomedicine compared. *Medical Anthropology Quarterly, 8*(2), 178–197.

Finkler, K. (1994b). *Spiritualist healers in Mexico: Successes and failures of alternative therapeutics*. South Hadley, MA: Bergin & Garvey. (Original work published 1985.)

Fischman, L. G. (1983). Dreams, hallucinogenic drug states, and schizophrenia: A psychological and biological comparison. *Schizophrenia Bulletin, 91*(1), 73–94.

Flannery, R. (1944). The Gros Ventre shaking tent. *Primitive Man, 17*(1), 54–59.

Flomenbaum, N. E. (2002). Rodenticides. In L. R. Goldfrank, N. E. Flomenbaum, N. A. Lewin, M. A. Howland, R. S. Hoffman, & L. S. Nelson (Eds.), *Goldfrank's toxicologic emergencies* (7th ed., pp. 1379–1392). New York: McGraw-Hill.

Flores, F. A., & Lewis, W. H. (1978). Drinking the South American hallucinogenic ayahuasca. *Economic Botany, 32*, 154–156.

Flores, J. (2005a). *Arcana* [Video]. Retrieved November 24, 2007, from the YouTube Web site, http://www.youtube.com/watch?v=1jP5SzG6klY.

Flores, J. (2005b). *Ayahuasca icaro* [Video]. Retrieved November 24, 2007, from the YouTube Web site, http://www.youtube.com/watch?v=QtBJf_pmPtw.

Flores, J. (2005c). *Icaro* [Video]. Retrieved November 24, 2007, from the YouTube Web site, http://www.youtube.com/watch?v=SdhbHROV1JI.

Flores, J., & Maestro Ayahuasquero (2007). *Juan Flores performs at the Harvest Moon Festival, 2006* [Video]. Retrieved November 24, 2007, from the YouTube Web site, http://www.youtube.com/watch?v=VN6p3jopxWE.

Flores Sandoval, J., González Flores, R., & Trujillo Cuéllar, F. (2001). Clasificación de maderas para durmientes en cuatro grupos de calidad sobre la base de su durabilidad natural [Classification of wood for railroad ties in four quality groupings based on natural durability]. *Anales Científicos UNALM, 48*, 1–21. Retrieved December 17, 2005, from the Universidad Nacional Agraria la Molina Web site, http://tumi.lamolina.edu.pe/resumen/anales/mayo_junio_2001.pdf.

Fock, N. (1963). *Waiwai: Religion and society of an Amazonian tribe* (Nationalmuseets Skrifter, Etnografisk Raekke, Vol. 8). Copenhagen: National Museum.

Fontanilla, D., Johannessen, M., Hajipour, A. R., Cozzi, N. V., Jackson, M. B., & Ruoho, A. E. (2009). The hallucinogen N,N-dimethyltryptamine (DMT) is an endogenous sigma-1 receptor regulator. *Science, 323*(5916), 934–937.

Forsström, T., Tuominen, J., & Karkkäinen, J. (2001). Determination of potentially hallucinogenic N-dimethylated indoleamines in human urine by HPLC/ESI-MS-MS. *Scandinavian Journal of Clinical and Laboratory Investigation, 61*(7), 547–556.

Forte, R. (2000a). A conversation with R. Gordon Wasson. In R. Forte (Ed.), *Entheogens and the future of religion* (pp. 67–94). San Francisco: Council on Spiritual Practices.

Forte, R. (Ed.). (2000b). *Entheogens and the future of religion*. San Francisco: Council on Spiritual Practices.

Foster, G., & Anderson, B. (1978). *Medical anthropology*. New York: Wiley.

Fouldes, J., & Toone, B. (1995). A case of nicotine psychosis? *Addiction, 90*(3), 435–437.

Frank, J. (1974). *Persuasion and healing: A comparative study of psychotherapy*. New York: Schocken Books. (Original work published 1961.)

Freedman, D. X. (1968). On the use and abuse of LSD. *Archives of General Psychiatry, 18*, 330–347.

Freedman, F. B. (2000). The jaguar who would not say her prayers: Changing polarities in Upper Amazonian shamanism. In L. E. Luna & S. F. White (Eds.), *Ayahuasca reader: Encounters with the Amazon's sacred vine* (pp. 113–119). Santa Fe, NM: Synergetic.

Frenopoulo, C. (2004). The mechanics of religious synthesis in the Barquinha religion. *Revista de Estudos da Religião, 1*, 19–40. Retrieved April 13, 2008, from the Pontificia Universidade Católica de São Paulo Web site, http://www.pucsp.br/rever/rv1_2004/p_frenopoulo.pdf.

Friedberg, C. (1965). Des *Banisteriopsis* utilisés comme drogue en Amérique du Sud. Essai d'ètude critique [On *Banisteriopsis* used as a drug in South America: Toward

a critical study]. *Journal d'Agriculture Tropicale et de Botanique Appliquée*, 12(9–12), 403–437, 550–594, 729–780.
Friedman, H. (1983). The self-expansiveness level form: A conceptualization and measurement of a transpersonal construct. *Journal of Transpersonal Psychology*, 15, 37–50.
Frison, G., Favretto, D., Zancanaro, F., Fazzin, G., & Ferrara, S. D. (2008). A case of b-carboline alkaloid intoxication following ingestion of *Peganum harmala* seed extract. *Forensic Science International*, 179, 37–43.
Frith, C. D. (1992). *The cognitive neuropsychology of schizophrenia*. Hillsdale, NJ: Erlbaum.
Froese, R., & Pauly, D. (Eds.). (2008). *FishBase*. Retrieved August 2, 2008, from http://www.fishbase.org/.
Frohne, D., & Pfänder, H. J. (2005). *Poisonous plants: A handbook for doctors, pharmacists, toxicologists, biologists and veterinarians* (I. Alford, Trans.). London: Manson.
Fuguet, A. (2001, July–August). Magical neoliberalism. *Foreign Policy*, 125, 66–73.
Fulop, M. (1954). Aspectos de la cultura Tukano: Cosmogonía [Aspects of Tukano culture: Cosmogeny]. *Revista Colombiana de Antropología*, *3*, 99–137.
Furst, P. T. (Ed.). (1972). *Flesh of the gods: The ritual use of hallucinogens*. New York: Praeger.
Galy, S., Rengifo, E., & Olivier Hay, Y. (2000). Factores de la organización del mercado de las plantas medicinales en Iquitos—Amazonía Peruana [Factors in the organization of the medicinal plant market in Iquitos in the Peruvian Amazon]. *Folia Amazónica* 11(1–2), 139–158. Retrieved December 7, 2006, from the Instituto de Investigaciones de la Amazonía Peruana Web site, http://www.iiap.org.pe/publicaciones/folias/folia11/Articulo%207%20Folia%2011.pdf.
Gandhi, L. (1998). *Postcolonial theory: A critical introduction*. New York: Columbia University Press.
García, F. S. (2002). *Formas indígenas de administrar justicia: Estudios de caso de la nacionalidad quichua ecuatoriana*. Quito: Facultad Latinoamericana de Ciencias Sociales Sede Ecuador. Retrieved July 14, 2008, from http://www.flacso.org.ec/docs/saformasindigenas.pdf.
García Barriga, H. (1958). El yagé, caapi o ayahuasca: Un alucinógeno amazónico [Yagé, caapi, or ayahuasca: An Amazonian hallucinogen]. *Revista de la Universidad Nacional de Colombia*, *23*, 59–76.
García Sampaya, L., Montes Shuña, F., Gerena Pinedo, J., & Torres Devila, A. (2003). *Icaros: Magical songs and incantations of the master shamans of Peru* [CD]. London: El Mundo Magico Music.
Garro, L. C., & Mattingly, C. (2000). Narrative as construct and construction. In C. Mattingly & L. Garro (Eds.), *Narrative and the cultural construction of illness and healing* (pp. 1–49). Berkeley: University of California Press.
Gayle. (2007, May 21). Vine/harmala [Msg 2]. Message posted to the Ayahuasca Tribe Web site. Retrieved May 6, 2008, from, http://ayahuasca.tribe.net/thread/c23e198c-4a9a-4697-a007-ff84ad06ab5e.
Gebhart-Sayer, A. (1984). *The cosmos encoiled: Indian art of the Peruvian Amazon*. New York: Center for Inter-American Relations.
Gebhart-Sayer, A. (1985). The geometric designs of the Shipibo-Conibo in ritual context. *Journal of Latin American Lore*, 11(2), 143–176.
Gebhart-Sayer, A. (1986). Una terápia estética. Los diseños visionarios del ayahuasca

entre los Shipibo-Conibo [An aesthetic therapy. Visionary ayahuasca designs among the Shipibo-Conibo]. *América Indígena*, 46(1), 189–218.

Gehr, R. (2008, March 25). Chicha libre and the Brooklyn–Peru connection: Bringing Lima's trippy underground sound to Park Slope. *Village Voice*. Retrieved June 25, 2008, from http://www.villagevoice.com/2008-03-25/music/the-brooklyn-peru-connection/.

Gell, A. (1995). The language of the forest: Landscape and phononological iconism in Umeda. In E. Hirsch & M. O'Hanlon (Eds.), *The anthropology of landscape: Perspectives on place and space* (pp. 232–254). Oxford: Oxford University Press.

Gentry, A. J. (1993). *A field guide to the families and genera of woody plants of northwest South America (Colombia, Ecuador, Peru)*. Chicago: University of Chicago Press.

Geyer, M. A., & Moghaddam, B. (2002). Animal models relevant to schizophrenia disorders. In K. L. Davis, D. Charney, J. T. Coyle, & C. Nemeroff (Eds.), *Neuropsychopharmacology: The fifth generation of progress* (pp. 689–702). New York: Lippincott Williams & Wilkins.

Giese, C. C. (1989). *Curanderos: Traditionelle Heiler in Nord-Peru (Küste und Höchland)* [*Curanderos*: Traditional healers in the North Peru coast and highlands] (Münchner Beiträge zur Amerikanistik, Bd. 20). Hohenschäftlarn, Germany: Klaus Renner.

Gilbert, J., & Pearson, W. (1999). *Discographies: Dance music, culture and the politics of sound*. London: Routledge.

Gill, A. (1998). *Rendering unto Caesar: The Catholic Church and the state in Latin America*. Chicago: University of Chicago Press.

Gillin, J. (1936). *The Barama River Caribs of British Guiana* (Papers of the Peabody Museum of American Archaeology and Ethnology, Harvard University, 14[2]). Cambridge, MA: Peabody Museum of American Archaeology and Ethnology.

Gillin, J. C., Kaplan, J., Stillman, R., & Wyatt, R. J. (1976). The psychedelic model of schizophrenia: The case of N,N-dimethyltryptamine. *American Journal of Psychiatry*, *133*, 203–208.

Ginsberg, A. (1961). *Kaddish, and other poems, 1958–1960*. San Francisco: City Lights Books.

Giove, R. (2001). Warmi kuraini: La mujer-medicina, la espiritualidad y el espíritu de las plantas [*Warmi kuraini*: The medicine woman, spirituality, and the spirit of the plants]. In J. Mabit (Ed.), *Memoria del segundo foro interamericano sobre espiritualidad indígena* (pp. 33–44). Tarapoto, Peru: Consejo Interamericano Sobre Espiritualidad Indígena y Centro de Rehabilitación y de Investigación de las Medicinas Tradicionales Takiwasi.

Glass-Coffin, B. (1998). *The gift of life: Female spirituality and healing in northern Peru*. Albuquerque: University of New Mexico Press.

Glass-Coffin, B. (2001). El shamanismo y el género: Un caso desde la costa norte del Perú [Shamanism and its genus: A case from the north coast of Perú]. In J. Mabit (Ed.), *Memoria del segundo foro interamericano sobre espiritualidad indígena* (pp. 47–57). Tarapoto, Peru: Consejo Interamericano Sobre Espiritualidad Indígena y Centro de Rehabilitación y de Investigación de las Medicinas Tradicionales Takiwasi.

Glennon, R. A. (1990). Do classical hallucinogens act as 5-HT_2 agonists or antagonists? *Neuropsychopharmacology*, *3*, 509.

Glucklich, A. (1997). *The end of magic*. New York: Oxford University Press.

Goethals, H. (1990, September–October). Naive art takes on the world. *Americas, 42*, 3.

Goldberg, R. (2006). *Drugs across the spectrum*. Belmont, CA: Thomson.

Goldman, I. (1979). *The Cubeo: Indians of the northwest Amazon* (2nd ed.). (Illinois Studies in Anthropology No. 2). Urbana: University of Illinois Press.

Goldman, J. (1999). Preface. In A. Polari de Alverga, *Forest of visions: Ayahuasca, Amazonian spirituality, and the Santo Daime tradition* (R. Workman, Trans., pp. xx–xxxiii). Rochester, VT: Park Street. (Original work published 1984.)

Gomez, H. F., & Dart, R. C. (1995). Clinical toxicology of snakebite in North America. In J. Meier & J. White (Eds.), *Handbook of clinical toxicology of animal venoms and poisons* (pp. 619–644). Boca Raton: CRC.

Gómez-Peña, G. (2000). *Dangerous border crossers: The artist talks back*. New York: Routledge.

Gómez-Pompa, A., & Kaus, A. (1998). Taming the wilderness myth. In J. B. Callicott & M. P. Nelson (Eds.), *The great new wilderness debate* (pp. 293–313). Athens: University of Georgia Press. (Original work published 1992.)

Gonzales Ramirez, J. (1998). *Musica amazonica shamanica* [CD]. Tarapoto, Peru: Pedrito Productions.

Good, B. J. (1994). *Medicine, rationality, and experience: An anthropological perspective*. Cambridge: Cambridge University Press.

Good, B. J., & Kleinman, A. M. (1985). Culture and anxiety: Cross-cultural evidence for the patterning of anxiety disorders. In A. H. Tuma & J. Maser (Eds.), *Anxiety and the anxiety disorders* (pp. 297–323). Hillsdale, NJ: Lawrence Erlbaum Associates.

Goodman, F. D. (1990). *Where the spirits ride the wind: Trance journeys and other ecstatic experiences*. Bloomington: Indiana University Press.

Goodman, J. (1994). *Tobacco in history: The cultures of dependence*. London: Routledge.

Gorman, P. (2001, October 24). Aftermath: The jungle bungle. Joint US/Peru report lays blame for shootdown at missionary pilot's feet. *Narco News*. Retrieved January 14, 2006, from http://www.narconews.com/Issue15/junglebungle.html.

Gorman, P. ("pgorman"). (2005, October 1). Alan Shoemaker case [Msg 7]. Message posted to the Ayahuasca Forums Web site. Retrieved January 13, 2006, from http://forums.ayahuasca.com/phpbb/viewtopic.php?t=8833.

Gorman, P. (2006). *A primer on shamanism in northwest Amazonia*. Retrieved April 26, 2008, from the Peter Gorman Archive Web site, http://petergormanarchive.com/A_Primer_on_Shamanism.html.

Gould, S. J. (2000, June). The Jew and the Jew stone. *Natural History, 109*, 26.

Gow, P. (1991). *Of mixed blood: Kinship and history in Peruvian Amazonia*. Oxford: Oxford University Press.

Gow, P. (1995). Land, people, and paper in western Amazonia. In E. Hirsch & M. O'Hanlon (Eds.), *The anthropology of landscape: Perspectives on place and space* (pp. 43–62). Oxford: Oxford University Press.

Gow, P. (1996). River people: Shamanism and history in western Amazonia. In N. Thomas & C. Humphrey (Eds.), *Shamanism, history, and the state* (pp. 90–113). Ann Arbor: University of Michigan Press.

Gow, P. (1999). Piro designs: Painting as meaningful action in an Amazonian lived world. *Journal of the Royal Anthropological Institute*, 5(2), 229–231.

Gow, P. (2001). *An Amazonian myth and its history*. Oxford: Oxford University Press.

Gracie & Zarkov. (1985). DMT: How and why to get off. In *Notes from underground: A "Gracie & Zarkov" reader* (n.p.). Berkeley: Gracie & Zarkov Productions. Retrieved November 14, 2007, from the Erowid Archives Web site, http://www.erowid.org/chemicals/dmt/dmt_info1_bklet.pdf.

Graham, J. S. (1976). The role of *curanderos* in the Mexican-American folk system in West Texas. In W. D. Hand (Ed.), *American folk medicine* (pp. 175–189). Berkeley: University of California Press.

Grauer, N. A. (1994). *Remember laughter: A life of James Thurber*. Lincoln: University of Nebraska Press.

Gray, A. (1997). *The last shaman: Change in an Amazonian community*. New York: Berghahn.

Green, C. (1990). Waking dreams and other metachoric experiences. *Psychiatric Journal of the University of Ottawa*, 15(2), 123–128.

Green, C., & McCreery, C. (1994). *Lucid dreaming: The paradox of consciousness during sleep*. London: Routledge.

Green, D. (2006). *Faces of Latin America* (3rd ed.). New York: Monthly Review.

Greene, S. (1998). The shaman's needle: Development, shamanic agency, and intermedicality in Aguaruna lands, Peru. *American Ethnologist*, 25(4), 634–658.

Grieve, M. (1971). *A modern herbal* (Vol. 2). New York: Dover. (Original work published 1931.)

Grimby, A. (1993). Bereavement among elderly people: Grief reactions, post-bereavement hallucinations and quality of life. *Acta Psychiatrica Scandinavica*, 87, 72–80.

Grob, C. S. (1999). The psychology of ayahuasca. In R. Metzner (Ed.), *Ayahuasca: Hallucinogens, consciousness, and the spirit of nature* (pp. 214–249). New York: Thunder's Mouth.

Grob, C. S. (Ed.). (2002). *Hallucinogens: A reader*. New York: Jeremy P. Tarcher.

Grob, C. S., McKenna, D. J., Callaway, J. C., Brito, G. S., Neves, E. S., Oberlaender, G., et al. (1996). Human psychopharmacology of *hoasca*, a plant hallucinogen used in ritual context in Brazil. *Journal of Nervous and Mental Disease*, 184, 86–94.

Grof, S. (1988). *The adventure of self-discovery: Dimensions of consciousness and new perspectives in psychotherapy and inner exploration*. Albany: State University of New York Press.

Grof, S. (1994, Winter). Alternative cosmologies and altered states. *Noetic Sciences Review*, 32, 21–29.

Groisman, A., & Sell, A. B. (1996). "Healing power": Cultural-neurophenomenological therapy of Santo Daime. In M. Windelman & W. Andritzky (Eds.), *Yearbook of cross-cultural medicine and psychotherapy 1995* (pp. 241–255). Berlin: Verlag für Wissenschaft und Bildung.

Grossman, R. ["Richard G."]. (2006, September 23). Shakapa [Msg 2]. Message posted to the Ayahuasca Tribe Web site. Retrieved June 20, 2008, from http://ayahuasca.tribe.net/thread/b3a3a061-f456-406e-8045-c2c58d9ee7d2.

Grossman, R. ["Richard G."]. (2008, February 9). Brugmansia [Msg 8]. Message posted to the Vegetalismo Tribe Web site. Retrieved May 8, 2008, from http://tribes.tribe.net/vegetalismo/thread/3d6ac2fd-2fed-41ba-a9ef-23999264cd48.

Grunwell, J. N. (1998). Ayahuasca tourism in South America. *Newsletter of the Multidisciplinary Association for Psychedelic Studies, 8*(3), 59–62. Retrieved August 8, 2007, from http://www.maps.org/news-letters/v08n3/08359gru.html.

Guerra Gonzalez, P. (1987). *Songs of the plant spirits* [Videocassette]. Mill Valley, CA: Sound Photosynthesis.

Guerra Gonzales, P. (2001). *Songs of the plant spirits* [CD]. El Prado, NM: Colibri.

Guevara, E., Loveman, B., & Davies, T. M. (1997). *Guerilla warfare.* Lanham, MD: Rowman & Littlefield.

Gupta, R. C. (2007). Rotenone. In R. C. Gupta (Ed.), *Veterinary toxicology: Basic and clinical principles* (pp. 499–501). New York: Academic Press.

Guss, D. M. (1990). *To weave and sing: Art, symbol and narrative in the South American rain forest.* Berkeley: University of California Press.

Hacking, I. (1995). *Rewriting the soul.* Princeton: Princeton University Press.

Hacking, I. (1998). *Mad travelers.* Cambridge, MA: Harvard University Press.

Hahn, R. (1995). *Sickness and healing: An anthropological perspective.* New Haven: Yale University Press.

Hallowell, A. I. (1942). *The role of conjuring in Saulteaux society.* Philadelphia: University of Pennsylvania Press.

Hallowell, A. I. (1975). Ojibwa ontology, behavior, and world view. In D. Tedlock & B. Tedlock (Eds.), *Teachings from the American earth* (pp. 141–178). New York: Liveright.

Hallowell, A. I. (1992). *The Ojibwa of Berens River, Manitoba: Ethnography into history* (J. S. H. Brown, Ed.). New York: Harcourt Brace.

Halpern, L. (1930a). Der Wirkunsgmechanismus des Harmins und der Pathophysiologie der Parkinsonehen Krankheit [The mode of action of harmine and the pathophysiology of Parkinson's disease]. *Deutsche medzinische Wochenschrift, 56*, 651–655.

Halpern, L. (1930b). Über die Harminwirkung im Selbstversuch [On the effect of harmine in a self-experiment]. *Deutsche Medzinische Wochenschrift, 56*, 1252–1254.

Hamsa. (2007, December 4). Comment. Retrieved April 30, 2008, from the Singing to the Plants Web site, http://singingtotheplants.blogspot.com/2007/12/omnipresence-of-spirits.html?showComment=1196791320000#c2014120731383768810.

Hancock, G. (2005). *Interview with Regina Meredith* [Video]. Retrieved November 23, 2007, from the Conscious Media Network Web site, http://consciousmedianetwork.com/members/ghancock.htm.

Hankiss, A. (1981). Ontologies of the self: On the mythological rearranging of one's life-history. In D. Bertaux (Ed.), *Biography and society: The life history approach in the social sciences* (pp. 203–209). Beverly Hills: Sage.

Hanson, B. A. (2005). *Understanding medicinal plants: Their chemistry and therapeutic action.* Binghamton, NY: Haworth.

Harner, M. J. (1971). *The Jívaro: People of the sacred waterfalls.* Berkeley: University of California Press.

Harner, M. J. (1973a). The sound of rushing water. In M. Harner (Ed.), *Hallucinogens and shamanism* (pp. 15–27). London: Oxford University Press.

Harner, M. J. (1973b). Common themes in South American yagé experiences. In M. J. Harner (Ed.), *Hallucinogens and shamanism* (pp. 155–175). London: Oxford University Press.

Harner, M. J. (1973c). In the primitive world: The Upper Amazon. In M. J. Harner (Ed.), *Hallucinogens and shamanism* (pp. 1–7). London: Oxford University Press.

Harner, M. J. (Ed.). (1973d). *Hallucinogens and shamanism*. London: Oxford University Press.

Harner, M. J. (1980). *The way of the shaman: A guide to power and healing*. New York: Bantam Books.

Harner, M. J. (1988a). Shamanic counseling. In G. Doore (Ed.), *Shaman's path: Healing, personal growth and empowerment* (pp. 179–187). Boston: Shambhala.

Harner, M. J. (1988b). What is a Shaman? In G. Doore (Ed.), *Shaman's path: Healing, personal growth and empowerment* (pp. 7–15). Boston: Shambhala.

Harner, M. J. (1989). The hidden universe of the healer. In R. Carlson & B. Shield (Eds.), *Healers on healing* (pp. 135–138). Los Angeles: Jeremy P. Tarcher.

Harner, M. J. (Ed.). (1973e). *Hallucinogens and shamanism*. London: Oxford University Press.

Harris, J. R. (2008). *Journal: Into the heart of the Amazon in search of truth*. No city: Joel R. Harris.

Harris, M. (1979). *Cultural materialism: The struggle for a science of culture*. New York: Random House.

Harris, M. (1992). *Our kind*. New York: Harper & Row.

Harris, R. M. (2007). Strychnine. In R. H. Waring, G. B. Steventon, & S. C. Mitchell (Eds.), *Molecules of death* (pp. 367–386). London: Imperial College Press.

Harvey, G. (2003). General introduction. In G. Harvey (Ed.), *Shamanism: A reader* (pp. 1–23). London: Routledge.

Harvey, G. (2005). Animism—A contemporary perspective. In B. R. Taylor (Ed.), *Encyclopedia of religion and nature* (pp. 81–83). New York: Continuum.

Harvey, G. (2006). *Animism: Respecting the living world*. New York: Columbia University Press.

Harvey, S. A., Olórtequi, M. P., Leontsini, E., Pezo, C. B., Pezantes, L. M., & Winch, P. J. (2008). The whole world will be able to see us: Determining the characteristics of a culturally appropriate bed net among mestizo communities of the Peruvian Amazon. *American Journal of Tropical Medicine and Hygiene, 79*(6), 834–838.

Hashimoto, Y., & Kawanishi, K. (1975). New organic bases from Amazonian *Banisteriopsis caapi*. *Phytochemistry, 14*, 1633–1635.

Heaven, R., & Charing, H. G. (2006). *Plant spirit shamanism: Traditional techniques for healing the soul*. Rochester, VT: Destiny.

Heckenberger, M. (2004). The wars within: Xinguano witchcraft and balance of power. In N. L. Whitehead & R. Wright (Eds.), *In darkness and secrecy: The anthropology of assault sorcery and witchcraft in Amazonia* (pp. 179–201). Durham: Duke University Press.

Heery, M. W. (1989). Inner voice experiences: An exploratory study of thirty cases. *Journal of Transpersonal Psychology, 21*(1), 73–82.

Heinze, R.-I. (1991). *Shamans of the 20th century*. New York: Irvington.

Helman, C. (1981). Disease versus illness in general practice. *Journal of the Royal College of General Practice, 31*, 548–552.

Helman, C. (1985). Disease and pseudo-disease: A case history of pseudo-angina. In

R. A. Hahn & A. D. Gaines (Eds.), *Physicians of Western medicine: Anthropological approaches to theory and practice* (pp. 293–331). Dordrecht, the Netherlands: D. Reidel.

Helman, C. (1990). *Culture, health, and illness: An introduction for health professionals* (2nd ed.). Oxford: Butterworth-Heinemann.

Helmlin, H. J., & Brenneisen, R. J. (1992). Determination of psychotropic phenylalkylamine derivatives in biological matrices by high-performance liquid chromatography with photodiode-array detection. *Chromatography, 593*(1–2), 87–94.

Henderson, A., Galeano, G., & Bernal, R. (1995). *Field guide to the palms of the Americas.* Princeton: Princeton University Press.

Hendricks, J. W. (1993). *To drink of death: The narrative of a Shuar warrior.* Tucson: University of Arizona Press.

Henman, A. R. (1986). Uso del ayahuasca en un contexto autoritario. El caso de la União do Vegetal en Brasil [The use of ayahuasca in an authoritarian context: The case of the União do Vegetal in Brazil]. *América Indígena, 46*(1), 219–234.

Henry, G. L., Little, N., Jagoda, A., & Pellegrino, T. R. (2003). *Neurologic emergencies: A symptom-oriented approach.* New York: McGraw-Hill.

Herman, T. (2000, Fall). Fighting for life. *Alternatives Journal, 26*, 5.

Hermle, L., Funfgeld, M., Oepen, G., Botsch, H., Borchardt, D., Gouzoulis, E., et al. (1992). Mescaline-induced psychopathological, neuropsychological and neurometabolic effects in normal subjects: Experimental psychosis as a tool for psychiatric research. *Biological Psychiatry, 32*, 976–982.

Hill, J. D. (1992). A musical aesthetic of ritual curing in the northwest Amazon. In E. Langdon & G. Baer (Eds.), *Portals of power: Shamanism in South America* (pp. 175–210). Albuquerque: University of New Mexico Press.

Hillard, K., & Kopischke, K. (1992). Resource use, traditional technology, and change among native peoples of lowland South America. In K. H. Redford & C. Padoch (Eds.), *Conservation of neotropical forests: Working from traditional resource use* (pp. 83–107). New York: Columbia University Press.

Hillman, J. (1975). *Re-visioning psychology.* New York: Harper Perennial.

Hillman, J. (1983a). *Archetypal psychology: A brief account.* Woodstock, CT: Spring.

Hillman, J. (1983b). *Healing fictions.* Woodstock, CT: Spring.

Hillman, J. (1988). James Hillman on soul and spirit: An interview with Barbara Dunn. *The Common Boundary, 6*(4), 5–11.

Hillman, J. (1990). *The essential James Hillman* (T. Moore, Ed.). London: Routledge.

Hillman, J. (2000). Peaks and vales: The soul/spirit distinction as basis for the differences between psychotherapy and spiritual discipline. In B. Sells (Ed.), *Working with images: The theoretical base of archetypal psychology* (pp. 112–135). Woodstock, CT: Spring. (Original work published 1976.)

Hilty, S. L., & Boyd, W. L. (1986). *A guide to the birds of Colombia.* Princeton: Princeton University Press.

Hiraoka, M. (1992). *Caboclo* and *ribereño* resource management in Amazonia: A review. In K. H. Redford & C. Padoch (Eds.), *Conservation of neotropical forests: Working from traditional resource use* (pp. 134–157). New York: Columbia University Press.

Hiraoka, M. (1995). Aquatic and land fauna management among the floodplain *ribereños* of the Peruvian Amazon. In T. Nishizawa & J. I. Uitto (Eds.), *The fragile tropics:*

Sustainable management of changing environments (pp. 201–225). Tokyo: United Nations University Press.

Hochstein, F. A., & Paradies, A. M. (1957). Alkaloids of *Banisteria caapi* and *Prestonia amazonicum*. *Journal of the American Chemical Society, 79*, 5735–5736.

Hodgson, D. (2000). Shamanism, phosphenes, and early art: An alternative synthesis. *Current Anthropology, 41*(5), 866, 873.

Hoffman, R. E. (1986). Verbal hallucinations and language production processes in schizophrenia. *Behavior and Brain Sciences, 9*, 503–548.

Hofmann, A. (2001). LSD as a spiritual aid. In T. B. Roberts (Ed.), *Psychoactive sacramentals: Essays on entheogens and religion* (pp. 121–123). San Francisco: Council on Spiritual Practices.

Hogue, C. L. (1993). *Latin American insects and entomology*. Berkeley: University of California Press.

Holden, C. (1999, November). Random samples. *Science, 286*(5445), 1675.

Holland, L., & Courtney, R. (1998). Increasing cultural competence with the Latino community. *Journal of Community Health Nursing, 15*(1), 45–53.

Holligan de Diaz-Limaco, J. (1998). *Peru: A guide to the people, politics and culture*. Brooklyn: Interlink.

Hollister, L. E. (1962). Drug-induced psychoses and schizophrenic reactions, a critical comparison. *Annals of the New York Academy of Sciences, 96*, 80–88.

Holy Bull, G. (2000). *Lakota yuwipi man* (B. Keeney, Ed.). Philadelphia: Ringing Rocks Press.

Hood, R. (Producer & Director). (1996). *Jungle living skills* [Motion picture]. (Available from Hoods Woods Video Productions, P.O. Box 3683, Coeur D'Alene, ID 83816).

Horgan, J. (2006, November 20). The God experiments: Five researchers take science where it's never gone before. *Discover*. Retrieved July 17, 2008, from http://discovermagazine.com/2006/dec/god-experiments/?searchterm=The%20God%20Experiments.

Horowitz, M. (1970). *Image formation and cognition*. New York: Meredith.

Howe, L. (2000). Risk, ritual and performance. *Journal of the Royal Anthropological Institute, 6*(1), 63–87.

Howes, D. (1988). On the odour of the soul: Spatial representation and olfactory classification in eastern Indonesia and western Melanesia. *Bijdragen tot de tall, land en volkenkunde, 144*, 84–113.

Hugh-Jones, S. (1994). Shamans, prophets, priests, and pastors. In N. Thomas & C. Humphrey (Eds.), *Shamanism, history, and the state* (pp. 32–75). Ann Arbor: University of Michigan Press.

Hultkrantz, Å. (1992). *Shamanic healing and ritual drama: Health and medicine in native North American religious traditions*. New York: Crossroad.

Hultkrantz, Å. (1996). Ecological and phenomenological aspects of shamanism. In V. Diószegi & M. Hoppál (Eds.), *Shamanism in Siberia* (pp. 1–32). Budapest: Akadémiai Kiadó.

Humphrey, C., & Onon, U. (1996). *Shamans and elders: Experience, knowledge and power among the Daur Mongols*. Oxford: Oxford University Press.

Hunter, A. F., & Aarssen, L. W. (1988). Plants helping plants. *Bioscience, 38*(1), 34–40.

Hutton, R. (2001). *Shamans: Siberian spirituality and the Western imagination*. London: Hambledon & London.

Huxley, A. (1954). *The doors of perception*. New York: Harper & Row.

Hvalkof, S. (2004). *Dreams coming true . . . An indigenous health programme in the Peruvian Amazon*. Copenhagen: Elise Jensen Foundation and NORDECO.

Ichinen. (2004, November 23). Experiential differences of rue and caapi [Msg 3]. Message posted to the Ayahuasca Forums Web site. Retrieved May 6, 2008, from http://forums.ayahuasca.com/phpbb/viewtopic.php?t=6886.

Iglesias, G. (1989). *Sacha jambi: El uso de las plantas en la medicina tradicional de los Quichua del Napo*. Quito: Abya-Yala.

Illius, B. (1992). The concept of *nihue* among the Shipibo-Conibo of eastern Peru. In E. Langdon & G. Baer (Eds.), *Portals of power: Shamanism in South America* (pp. 63–77). Albuquerque: University of New Mexico Press.

In the Matter of Bauchet. (2005). Case No. 04/01888 (Paris Ct. App.). Retrieved July 21, 2008, from the Santo Daime Online Library Web site, http://www.santodaime.it/Library/LAW/Francia/courdapeldeparis05_france.pdf.

In the Matter of Fijneman. (2001). Case No. 13/067455–99 (Amsterdam Dist. Ct.). Retrieved July 21, 2008, from the Santo Daime Online Library Web site, http://www.santodaime.com/Library/LAW/Olanda/amsterdamcourt01_english.htm.

Instituto Nacional de Cultura. (2008). R. D. No. 836/INC. Declaran patrimonio cultural de la nación a los conocimientos y usos tradicionales del ayahuasca practicados por communidades nativas amazonicas [Declaration that the traditional knowledge and uses of ayahuasca practiced by indigenous Amazonian communities are a national cultural heritage]. *Boletin de Normas Legales del Diario Oficial El Peruana*, 376040–376041. Retrieved July 22, 2008, from the Pontificia Universidad Católica del Perú Web site, http://blog.pucp.edu.pe/media/1991/20080712–12072008.pdf.

Irigaray, L. (1985). *This sex which is not one* (C. Porter, Trans.). Ithaca, NY: Cornell University Press.

Isbell, H., Belleville, R. E., Fraser, H. F., Wikler, A., & Logan, C. R. (1956). Studies on lysergic acid diethylamide (LSD-25): I. Effects in former morphine addicts and development of tolerance during chronic intoxication. *Archives of Neurological Psychiatry*, 76, 468–478.

Isbell, H., Wolbach, A. E., Wikler, A., & Miner, E. J. (1961). Cross tolerance between LSD and psilocybin. *Psychopharmacologia*, 2, 147–159.

Iwokrama International Centre for Rain Forest Conservation and Development. (N.d.). Venomous snakes of Guyana. Retrieved October 24, 2006, from the Iwokrama International Centre for Rain Forest Conservation and Development Web site, http://www.iwokrama.org/forest/snakes.htm.

Jackson, J. E. (1983). *The fish people: Linhuistic exogamy and Tukanoan identity in northwest Amazonia*. Cambridge: Cambridge University Press.

Jackson, J. E. (1994). Becoming Indians: The politics of Tukanoan ethnicity. In A. Roosevelt (Ed.), *Amazonian Indians from prehistory to the present: Anthropological perspectives* (pp. 383–406). Tucson: University of Arizona Press.

Jackson, M. (1989). *Paths toward a clearing*. Bloomington: Indiana University Press.

Jacob, M. S., & Presti, D. E. (2005). Endogenous psychoactive tryptamines reconsidered: An anxiolytic role for dimethyltryptamine. *Medical Hypotheses, 64*(5), 930–937.

Jacob, P., & Shulgin, A. T. (1994). Structure–activity relationships of the classical hallucinogens and their analogs. In G. C. Lin & R. A. Glennon (Eds.), *Hallucinogens: An update* (pp. 74–91). (National Institute on Drug Abuse Research Monograph Series 146). Washington, DC: National Institute on Drug Abuse.

Jaffé, A. (1963). Introduction. In C. Jung, *Memories, dreams, reflections* (R. Winston & C. Winston, Trans., pp. v–xiv). New York: Pantheon Books. (Original work published 1962.)

Jakobsen, M. D. (1999). *Shamanism: Traditional and contemporary approaches to the mastery of spirits and healing*. New York: Berghahn Books.

Janiger, O., & Dobkin de Ríos, M. (1976). Nicotiana an hallucinogen? *Economic Botany, 30*, 149–151.

Jerngian, K. A. (2008). The importance of chemosensory clues in Aguaruna tree classification and identification. *Journal of Ethnobiology and Ethnomedicine, 4*(12). Retrieved July 14, 2008, from http://www.ethnobiomed.com/content/4/1/12.

Jernigen, K. (2003, Spring). An introduction to ASMEVEI, a recently formed group of *vegetalista* healers in the Peruvian Amazon. *Newsletter of the Multidisciplinary Association for Psychedelic Studies, 13*(1), 41–43. Retrieved April 14, 2007, from http://www.maps.org/news-letters/v13n1/13141jer.html.

Jochelson, W. (1908). *The Koryak*. Leiden, the Netherlands: Brill.

Johnson, A. (2003). *Families of the forest: The Matsigenka Indians of the Peruvian Amazon*. Berkeley: University of California Press.

Johnson, D. (1989). Presence. In R. Carlson & B. Shield (Eds.), *Healers on healing* (pp. 131–134). Los Angeles: Jeremy P. Tarcher.

Johnson, M. H., Hashtroudi, S., & Lindsay, D. S. (1993). Source monitoring. *Psychological Bulletin, 114*, 3–28.

Johnson, M. H., & Magaro, P. A. (1987). Effects of mood and severity on memory processes in depression and mania. *Psychological Bulletin, 101*, 28–40.

Jones, D. E. (2007). *Poison arrows: North American Indian hunting and warfare*. Austin: University of Texas Press.

Joralemon, D. (1990). The selling of the shaman and the problem of informant legitimacy. *Journal of Anthropological Research, 46*(2), 105–118.

Joralemon, D., & Sharon, D. (1993). *Sorcery and shamanism: Curanderos and clients in northern Peru*. Salt Lake City: University of Utah Press.

Jung, C. (1953–1977). *Psychological types*. In H. Read, M. Fordham, & G. Adler (Eds.), *Collected works of C. G. Jung* (Vol. 6, R. Hull, Trans.). Princeton: Princeton University Press. (Original work published 1921.)

Jung, C. (1963). *Memories, dreams, reflections* (R. Winston & C. Winston, Trans.). New York: Pantheon Books. (Original work published 1962.)

Jung, C. (1989). *Analytical psychology: Notes of the seminar given in 1925*. Princeton: Princeton University Press.

Jung, C. (1997a). Confrontation with the unconscious. In J. Chodorow (Ed.), *Jung on active imagination* (pp. 21–41). Princeton: Princeton University Press. (Original work published 1962.)

Jung, C. (1997b). *Mysterium Coniunctionis*. In J. Chodorow (Ed.), *Jung on active imagination* (pp. 166–174). Princeton: Princeton University Press. (Original work published 1955.)

Jung, C. (1997c). The Tavistock lectures. In J. Chodorow (Ed.), *Jung on active imagination* (pp. 143–153). Princeton: Princeton University Press. (Original work published 1935.)

Jung, C. (1997d). The transcendent function. In J. Chodorow (Ed.), *Jung on active imagination* (pp. 42–60). Princeton: Princeton University Press. (Original work published 1958.)

Jung, C. (1997e). Three letters to Mr. O. In J. Chodorow (Ed.), *Jung on active imagination* (pp. 163–165). Princeton: Princeton University Press. (Original work published 1947.)

Junquera, C. (1989). *El chamanismo en el Amazonas* [Shamanism in the Amazon]. Barcelona: Editorial Mitre.

Kalweit, H. (1989). When insanity is a blessing: The message of shamanism. In S. Grof & C. Grof (Eds.), *Spiritual emergency: When personal transformation becomes a crisis* (pp. 77–97). Los Angeles: Jeremy P. Tarcher.

Kalweit, H. (1992). *Shamans, healers, and medicine men*. Boston: Shambhala.

Kamppinen, M. (1989). Dialectics of evil: Politics and religion in an Amazon mestizo community. *Dialectical Anthropology*, *13*, 143–155.

Kamppinen, M. (1990). Out of balance: Models of the human body in the medico-religious tradition among the mestizos of the Peruvian Amazon. *Curare* *13*(2), 89–97.

Kamppinen, M. (1997). *Cultural models of risk: The multiple meanings of living in the world of dangerous possibilities*. Turku: Finland Futures Research Centre. Retrieved August 8, 2008, from the Turku School of Economics Web site, http://www.tse.fi/FI/yksikot/erillislaitokset/tutu/Documents/futu/futu_2_97.pdf.

Kandell, J. (2001, April 13). Richard E. Schultes, 86, dies; trailblazing authority on hallucinogenic plants. *New York Times*. Retrieved November 11, 2007, from http://query.nytimes.com/gst/fullpage.html?res=9E04EEDF1231F930A25757C0A9679C8B63&scp=2&sq=Schultes&st=nyt.

Kärkkäinen, J., Forsström, T., Tornaeus, J., Wähälä, K., Kiuru, P., Honkanen, A., et al. (2005). Potentially hallucinogenic 5-hydroxytryptamine receptor ligands bufotenine and dimethyltryptamine in blood and tissues. *Scandinavian Journal of Clinical and Laboratory Investigation*, *65*(3), 189–199.

Kärkkäinen, J., & Räisänen, M. (1992). Nialamide, an MAO inhibitor, increases urinary excretion of endogenously produced bufotenin in man. *Biological Psychiatry*, *32*(11), 1042–1048.

Katz, F., & Dobkin de Ríos, M. (1971). Hallucinogenic music: An analysis of the role of whistling in Peruvian ayahuasca healing sessions. *Journal of American Folklore*, 84(333), 320–327.

Katz, R. (1982). *Boiling energy: Community healing among the Kalahari Kung*. Cambridge, MA: Harvard University Press.

Kay, M. A. (1977). Health and illness in a Mexican American barrio. In E. H. Spicer (Ed.), *Ethnic medicine in the Southwest* (pp. 99–166). Tucson: University of Arizona Press.

Kay, M. A. (1993). Fallen fontanelle: Culture-bound or cross-cultural? *Medical Anthropology*, 15, 137–156.

Kearney, M. (1976). A world-view explanation of the evil eye. In C. Maloney (Ed.), *The evil eye* (pp. 175–192). New York: Columbia University Press.

Kehoe, A. B. (2000). *Shamanism and religion: An anthropological exploration in critical thinking*. Prospect Heights, IL: Waveland Press.

Kelekna, P. (1994). Farming, feuding and female status: The Achuar case. In A. Roosevelt (Ed.), *Amazonian Indians from prehistory to the present: Anthropological perspectives* (pp. 225–248). Tucson: University of Arizona Press.

Kendall, C. (1990). Public health and the domestic domain: Lessons from anthropological research on diarrheal diseases. In J. Coreil & J. D. Mull (Eds.), *Anthropology and primary health care* (pp. 173–195). Boulder: Westview Press.

Kendall, C., Foote, D., & Martorell, R. (1983). Anthropology, communications, and health: The mass media and health practices program in Honduras. *Human Organization*, 42(4), 353–360.

Kendall, C., Foote, D., & Martorell, R. (1984). Ethnomedicine and oral rehydration therapy: A case study of ethnomedical investigation and program planning. *Social Science and Medicine*, 19(3), 253–260.

Kendall, L. (1996). Initiating performance: The story of Chini, a Korean Shaman. In C. Laderman & M. Roseman (Eds.), *The performance of healing* (pp. 17–58). New York: Routledge.

Kensinger, K. M. (1973). *Banisteriopsis* usage among the Peruvian Cashinahua. In M. J. Harner (Ed.), *Hallucinogens and shamanism* (pp. 9–14). New York: Oxford University Press.

Kent. J. (2004). The case against DMT elves. Retrieved December 21, 2005, from the Trip Magazine Web site, http://www.tripzine.com/articles.asp?id=dmt_pickover.

Kent, J. (2007a, March 12). Psychedelics and paranormal experience: An interview with Daniel Luke. Retrieved April 22, 2008, from the DoseNation Web site, http://www.dosenation.com/listing.php?id=1492.

Kent, J. L. (2007b, March 16). To catch a DMT elf. Retrieved November 26, 2007, from the DoseNation Web site, http://www.dosenation.com/listing.php?id=1552.

Kiev, A. (1968). Curanderismo: *Mexican American folk psychiatry*. New York: Free Press.

Kingsolver, B. (1998). *The poisonwood bible*. New York: HarperCollins.

Kirk, G. (1974). *The nature of Greek myths*. Harmondsworth, England: Penguin.

Kirmayer, L. (2000). Broken narratives: Clinical encounters and the poetics of illness experience. In C. Mattingly & L. Garro (Eds.), *Narrative and the cultural construction of illness and healing* (pp. 153–180). Berkeley: University of California Press.

Kleinman, A. (1980). *Patients and healers in the context of culture: An exploration of the borderland between anthropology, medicine, and psychiatry*. Berkeley: University of California Press.

Kleinman, A. (1995). Pain and resistance: The delegitmation and relegitimation of local worlds. In A. Kleinman, *Writing at the margin: Discourse between anthropology and medicine* (pp. 120–146, 271–276). Berkeley: University of California Press. (Original work published 1992.)

Kleinamn, A., & Kleinman, J. (1995). Suffering and its professional transformation:

Toward an ethnography of interpersonal experience. In A. Kleinman, *Writing at the margin: Discourse between anthropology and medicine* (pp. 95–119). Berkeley: University of California Press.

Knight, D. (1998a, May–June). Indigenous groups challenge U.S. drug company. *NACLA Report on the Americas, 31*(6), 1.

Knight, D. (1998b, June). An enemy of indigenous peoples. *Multinational Monitor, 19*(6), 24–26.

Knight, K. (2002, October). A precious medicine: tradition and magic in some seventeenth-century household remedies. *Folklore, 113*(2), 237–247.

Koch, W. (2000). Contemporary shamanism—*Vegetalismo* in the Peruvian Amazon. *Unisa Latin American Report, 16*(2), 42–58. Retrieved February 4, 2007, from the Unisa Centre for Latin American Studies Web site, http://www.unisa.ac.za/contents/publications/docs/latre171.pdf.

Koch-Grünberg, T. (1909–1910). *Zwei Jahre unter den Indianern. Reisen in Nordwest-Brasilien 1903/1905* [Two years among the Indians: Travels in northwest Brazil, 1903–1905] (2 vols.). Stuttgart: Stecker und Schröder.

Koch-Grünberg, T. (1923). *Von Roraima zum Orinoco* [From Roraima to Orinoco]. Stuttgart: Stecker und Schröder.

Kornfield, J. (1989). Obstacles and vicissitudes in spiritual practice. In F. Grof & C. Grof (Eds.), *Spiritual emergency: When personal transformation becomes a crisis* (pp. 137–169). Los Angeles: Jeremy P. Tarcher.

Koss-Chiono, J. D. (1993). The interaction of popular and clinical diagnostic labeling: The case of *embrujado*. *Medical Anthropology*, 15, 171–188.

Koss-Chiono, J. D. (2005). Spirit healing, mental health, and emotion regulation. *Zygon: Journal of Religion and Science, 40*(2), 409–421.

Kosslyn, S. M. (1994). *Image and brain: The resolution of the imagery debate*. Cambridge, MA: MIT Press.

Kracke, W. H. (1992). He who dreams: The nocturnal source of transforming power in Kagwahiv shamanism. In E. Langdon & G. Baer (Eds.), *Portals of power: Shamanism in South America* (pp. 127–148). Albuquerque: University of New Mexico Press.

Krassner, P. (2004). *Magic mushrooms and other highs: From toad slime to Ecstasy*. Berkeley: Ten Speed.

Kricher, J. (1997). *A neotropical companion: An introduction to the animals, plants, and ecosystems of the New World tropics*. Princeton: Princeton University Press.

Krieger, D. (1989). The timeless concept of healing. In R. Carlson & B. Shield (Eds.), *Healers on healing* (pp. 124–126). Los Angeles: Jeremy P. Tarcher.

Krippner, S. (1989). Touchstones of the healing process. In R. Carlson & B. Shield (Eds.), *Healers on healing* (pp. 111–113). Los Angeles: Jeremy P. Tarcher.

Krippner, S. (2000). Altered states of consciousness and shamanic healing rituals. In R. Heinze (Ed.), *The nature and function of rituals: Fire from heaven* (pp. 191–207). Westport, CT: Bergin & Garvey.

Krippner, S., & Sulla, J. (2000). Identifying spiritual content in reports from ayahuasca sessions. *International Journal of Transpersonal Studies*, 19, 59–76.

Kübler-Ross, E. (1989). The four pillars of healing. In R. Carlson & B. Shield (Eds.), *Healers on healing* (pp. 127–130). Los Angeles: Jeremy P. Tarcher.

Kulick, D. (1998). Travesti: *Sex, gender, and culture among Brazilian transgendered prostitutes.* Chicago: University of Chicago Press.

Kusel, H. (1965). Ayahuasca drinkers among the Chama Indians of northeast Peru. *Psychedelic Review, 6*, 58–66.

La Barre, W. (1972). *The Ghost Dance.* New York: Dell.

La Barre, W. (1989). *The peyote cult* (5th ed.). Norman: University of Oklahoma Press.

La Rosa, T., Panduro, A., Campos, J., & Sinuiri, M. (2003). *Iqaro canto shamánico* [Iqaro shamanic song] [CD]. N.p.

Labate, B. C., & Araújo, W. S. (Eds.). (2002). *El uso ritual da ayahuasca* [The ritual use of ayahuasca]. São Paulo: Editora Mercado de Letras.

Labbé, A. J. (1999). *Inner visions: Artists of the Peruvian Amazon.* London: October Gallery.

Laberge, S., & Gackenbach, J. (2000). Lucid dreaming. In E. Cardeña, S. J. Lynn, & S. Krippner (Eds.), *Varieties of anomalous experience: Examining the scientific evidence* (pp. 151–182). Washington, DC: American Psychological Association.

Labrousse, A., & Laniel, L. (2001). *The world geopolitics of drugs, 1998/1999.* Dordrecht, the Netherlands: Kluwer Academic.

Lacaze, D., & Alexiades, M. (1995). *Salud para todos: Plantas medicinales y salud indígena en la cuenca del río Madre de Dios, Perú* [Health for all: Medicinal plants and indigenous health in the Madre de Dios Basin, Peru]. Madre de Dios, Peru: Federación Nativa del Río Madre de Dios y Afluentes.

Laderman, C., & Roseman, M. (Eds). (1996). *The performance of healing.* London: Routledge.

Lagrou, E. (1999). Cashinahua drawings and their role in the vision quest. In L. E. Luna (Ed.), *Visions that the plants gave us.* Canton, NY: St. Lawrence University Richard F. Brush Art Gallery. Retrieved December 17, 2005, from http://web.stlawu.edu/gallery/elagrou.htm.

Lagrou, E. (2000). Homesickness and the Cashinahuan self: A reflection on the embodied condition of relatedness. In J. Overing & A. Passes (Eds.), *The anthropology of love and anger: The aesthetics of conviviality in native Amazonia* (pp. 152–169). London: Routledge.

Lagrou, E. (2004). Sorcery and shamanism in Cashinahua discourse and praxis, Purus River, Brazil. In N. L. Whitehead & R. Wright (Eds.), *In darkness and secrecy: The anthropology of assault sorcery and witchcraft in Amazonia* (pp. 244–271). Durham: Duke University Press.

Laing, R. R. (2003). *Hallucinogens: A forensic drug handbook.* London: Academic.

Lamb, F. B. (1974). *Wizard of the Upper Amazon: The story of Manuel Córdova-Rivas.* Berkeley: North Atlantic Books. (Original work published 1971.)

Lamb, F. B. (1981a). Wizard of the Upper Amazon as ethnography. *Current Anthropology, 22*(5), 577–579.

Lamb, F. B. (1981b). Comment on Bock's review of *The Don Juan Papers. American Anthropologist, 83*(3), 641.

Lamb, F. B. (1985). *Rio Tigre and beyond: The Amazon jungle medicine of Manuel Córdova.* Berkeley: North Atlantic.

Lande, A. (1976). *Commentary on the Convention on Psychotropic Substances, done at Vienna on 21 February 1971* (U.N. Document No. E/CN.7/589). New York: United Nations.

Langdon, E. J. M. (1979). Yagé among the Siona: Cultural patterns in visions. In D. Browman & R. Schwartz (Eds.), *Spirits, shamans, and stars: Perspectives from South America* (pp. 63–80). The Hague: Mouton.

Langdon, E. J. M. (1992a). *Dau*: Shamanic power in Siona religion and medicine. In E. J. M. Langdon & G. Baer (Eds.), *Portals of power: Shamanism in South America* (pp. 41–61). Albuquerque: University of New Mexico Press.

Langdon, E. J. M. (1992b). Introduction: Shamanism and anthropology. In E. Langdon & G. Baer (Eds.), *Portals of power: Shamanism in South America* (pp. 1–21). Albuquerque: University of New Mexico Press.

Langdon, E. J. M. (2004). Commentary. In N. L. Whitehead & R. Wright (Eds.), *In darkness and secrecy: The anthropology of assault sorcery and witchcraft in Amazonia* (pp. 306–313). Durham: Duke University Press.

Larsen, S. (1996). *The mythic imagination: The quest for meaning through personal mythology*. Rochester, VT: Inner Traditions International.

Larsen, S. (2000). Foreword. In A. P. De Alverga, *Forest of visions: Ayahuasca, Amazonian spirituality, and the Santo Daime tradition* (S. Larsen, Ed., & R. Workman, Trans., pp. ix–xix). Rochester, VT: Park Street Station.

La santa cruz de Caravaca: Tesoro de oraciones [The sacred cross of Caravaca: A treasury of prayers]. (2005). Mexico City: Editorial Lectorum.

Lathrap, D. W. (1976). Shipibo tourist art. In N. Graburn (Ed.), *Ethnic and tourist arts* (pp. 197–207). Berkeley: University of California Press.

Lathrap, D. W., Gebhart-Sayer, A., & Mester, A. M. (1984). The roots of the Shipibo art style: Three waves on Imiriacocha or there were "Incas" before the Incas. *Journal of Latin American Lore, 11*(1), 31–119.

Lattin, D. L., & Fifer, E. K. (2002). Drugs affecting cholinergic neurotransmission. In D. A. Williams, W. O. Foye, & T. L. Lemke (Eds.), *Foye's principles of medicinal chemistry* (pp. 264–291). Baltimore: Lippincott Williams & Wilkins.

Lee, M. A. (2001, February 19). Shamanism versus capitalism: The politics of the hallucinogen ayahuasca. *San Francisco Bay Guardian*. Retrieved November 11, 2007, from the Lila Web site, http://www.lila.info/document_view.phtml?document_id=28.

Lenaerts, M. (2006). Substances, relationships and the omnipresence of the body: An overview of Ashéninka ethnomedicine (western Amazonia). *Journal of Ethnobiology and Ethnomedicine, 2*(1), 49. Retrieved from http://www.ethnobiomed.com/content/2/1/49.

Letcher, A. (2007). *Shroom: A cultural history of the magic mushroom*. New York: HarperCollins.

Leudar, I., & Thomas, P. (2000). *Voices of reason, voices of insanity: Studies of verbal hallucinations*. London: Routledge.

Leudar, I., Thomas, P., & Johnston, M. (1992). Self-repair in dialogues of schizophrenics: Effects of hallucinations and negative symptoms. *Brain and Language, 43*, 487–511.

Leudar, I., Thomas, P., & Johnston, M. (1994). Self-monitoring in speech production: Effects of verbal hallucinations and negative symptoms. *Psychological Medicine, 24*, 749–761.

Leudar, I., Thomas, P., McNally, D., & Glinski, A. (1997). What voices can do with words: Pragmatics of verbal hallucinations. *Psychological Medicine*, 27, 885–898.

Leuner, H., & Schlichting, M. (1989). A report on the symposium "On the Current State of Research in the Area of Psychoactive Substances." In C. Rätsch (Ed.), *Gateway to inner space: Sacred plants, mysticism and psychotherapy—A festschrift in honor of Albert Hofmann* (pp. 213–240). Bridport, England: Prism Press.

Lévinas, E., & Kearney, R. (1986). Dialogue with Emmanuel Lévinas. In R. A. Cohen (Ed.), *Face to face with Lévinas* (pp. 13–33). Albany: State University of New York Press.

Lévi-Strauss, C. (1963). The effectiveness of symbols. In *Structural anthropology* (C. Jacobson & B. Schoepf, Trans., pp. 167–185). New York: Basic Books. (Original work published 1958.)

Lewin, L. (1964). *Phantastica: Narcotic and stimulating drugs*. London: Routledge. (Original work published 1931.)

Lewis, G. (1993). Double standards of treatment evaluation. In S. Lindenbaum & M. Lock (Eds.), *Knowledge, power, and practice: The anthropology of medicine and everyday life* (pp. 189–218). Berkeley: University of California Press.

Lewis, R. A. (1998). *Lewis' dictionary of toxicology*. Boca Raton: CRC.

Lewis, T. H. (1992). *The medicine men: Oglala Sioux ceremony and healing*. Lincoln: University of Nebraska Press.

Lewis, W. H., Kennelly, E. J., Bass, G. N., Wedner, H. J., Elvin-Lewis, M. P., & Fast, D. (1991). Ritualistic use of the holly *Ilex guayusa* by Amazonian Jivaro Indians. *Journal of Ethnopharmacology*, *33*(1–2), 25–30.

Leysen, J. E., Janssen, P. F., & Niemegeers, C. J. (1989). Rapid desensitization and down-regulation of 5-HT2 receptors by DOM treatment. *European Journal of Pharmacology*, *163*, 145–149.

Lieberei, R. (2007). South American leaf blight of the rubber tree (*Hevea* spp.): New steps in plant domestication using physiological features and molecular markers. *Annals of Botany*, 100(6), 1125–1142. Retrieved May 16, 2007, from http://aob.oxfordjournals.org/cgi/reprint/mcm133v1.

Liester, M. B. (1996). Inner voices: Distinguishing transcendent and pathological characteristics. *Journal of Transpersonal Psychology*, 28(1), 1–7.

Lindgren, J.-E. (1995). Amazonian psychoactive indoles: A review. In R. E. Schultes & S. von Reis (Eds.), *Ethnobotany: Evolution of a discipline* (pp. 343–348). Portland, OR: Dioscorides.

Ling, N. (2003). *Rotenone—A review of its toxicity and use for fisheries management* (Science for Conservation 211). Wellington: New Zealand Department of Conservation. Retrieved August 22, 2008, from http://www.doc.govt.nz/upload/documents/science-and-technical/SFC211.pdf.

Little, M. (2003, April 26). Healer gets house arrest in Wiki woman's death. *Sudbury Star (Canada)*. Retrieved October 4, 2003, from Religion News Blog, http://www.religionnewsblog.com/archives/00003133.html.

Littlewood, L., & Lipsedge, M. (1987). The butterfly and the serpent: Culture, psychopathology and biomedicine. *Culture, Medicine and Psychiatry*, 11, 289–355.

Liwszyc, G. E., Vuori, E., Rasanen, I., & Issakanen, J. (1992). *Daime*—A ritual herbal potion. *Journal of Ethnopharmacology*, *36*(1), 91–92.

Lock, M. (1988). New Japanese mythologies: Faltering discipline and the ailing housewife. *American Ethnologist*, 15, 43–61.

Lock, M., & Scheper-Hughes, N. (1996). A critical-interpretive approach in medical anthropology: Rituals and routines of discipline and dissent. In C. F. Sargent & T. M. Johnson (Eds.), *Medical anthropology: Contemporary theory and method* (pp. 41–70). Westport, CT: Praeger.

Logan, M. H. (1993). New lines of inquiry on the illness of *susto*. *Medical Anthropology*, 15, 189–200.

López Beltrán, C. (2001). La exploración y ocupación del Acre (1850–1900) [The exploration and occupation of Acre (1850–1990)]. *Revista de Indias*, 61(223), 573–590. Retrieved May 16, 2008, from http://revistadeindias.revistas.csic.es/index.php/revistadeindias/article/viewFile/573/640.

López Vinatea, L. A. (2000). *Plantas usadas por shamanes Amazonicos en el brebaje ayahuasca* [Plants used by shamans in ayahuasca drinks]. Iquitos: Universidad Nacional de la Amazonía Peruana.

Lovera, J. R. (2005). *Food culture in South America*. Westport, CT: Greenwood Press.

Lowie, R. H. (1946). The Indians of eastern Brazil: An introduction. In J. H. Steward (Ed.), *Handbook of South American Indians, Vol. 1* (pp. 381–397). (Smithsonian Bureau of American Ethnology Bulletin No. 143). Washington, DC: U.S. Government Printing Office.

Lowie, R. H. (1948). The tropical forests: An introduction. In J. H. Steward (Ed.), *Handbook of South American Indians, Vol. 3* (pp. 1–56). (Smithsonian Bureau of American Ethnology Bulletin 143). Washington, DC: U.S. Government Printing Office.

Lowy, B. (1987). Caapi revisited—In Christianity. *Economic Botany*, 41(3), 450–452.

Lumby, M. C. Y. (2000). *The realm of visions: Towards an evaluation of the role of near-death experience in ayahuasca psychotherapies*. Retrieved September 21, 2006, from the Multidisciplinary Association for Psychedelic Studies Web site, http://www.maps.org/research/lumbyreports1.html.

Luna, E. (2005). *Artist's comment*. Retrieved April 28, 2007, from the Red Cloud Indian Arts Gallery Web site, http://www.redcloudindianarts.com/e-luna.htm.

Luna, L. E. (1984a). The healing practices of a Peruvian shaman. *Journal of Ethnopharmacology*, 11(2), 123–133.

Luna, L. E. (1984b). The concept of plants as teachers among four mestizo shamans of Iquitos, northeastern Peru. *Journal of Ethnopharmacology*, 11(2), 135–156.

Luna, L. E. (Ed.). (1984c). *Peruvian ayahuasca session* [Audiocassette]. Mill Valley, CA: Sound Photosynthesis.

Luna, L. E. (1986a). Bibliografía sobre el ayahuasca [An ayahuasca bibliography]. *América Indígena*, 46(1), 235–245.

Luna, L. E. (1986b). Apéndices [Appendices]. *América Indígena*, 46(1), 247–251.

Luna, L. E. (1986c). Vegetalismo: *Shamanism among the mestizo population of the Peruvian Amazon* (Stockholm Studies in Comparative Religion 27). Stockholm: Almqvist & Wiksell.

Luna, L. E. (Ed.). (1987). *Songs the plants taught us* [Audiocassette]. Mill Valley, CA: Sound Photosynthesis.

Luna, L. E. (Director). (1991a). . . . *And so I tell them to paint* [Motion picture]. Santa Barbara: Thomas Manning Productions.

Luna, L. E. (1991b). Plant spirits in ayahuasca visions by Peruvian painter, Pablo Amaringo. An iconographic analysis. *Integration: Zeitschrift für Geistbewegende Pflanzen und Kultur, 1*, 18–29.

Luna, L. E. (1992). *Icaros*: Magic melodies among the mestizo shamans of the Peruvian Amazon. In E. Langdon, & G. Baer (Eds.), *Portals of power: Shamanism in South America* (pp. 231–253). Albuquerque: University of New Mexico Press.

Luna, L. E. (2003). Ayahuasca: Shamanism shared across cultures. *Cultural Survival Quarterly, 27*(2), 20.

Luna, L. E., & Amaringo, P. (1993). *Ayahuasca visions: The religious iconography of a Peruvian shaman*. Berkeley: North Atlantic Books.

Luna, L. E., & White, S. F. (Eds.). (2000). *Ayahuasca reader: Encounters with the Amazon's sacred vine*. Santa Fe, NM: Synergetic Press.

Lundstrom, J. (1970). Biosynthesis of mescaline and 3,4-dimethoxyphenethylamine in *Trichocereus pachanoi* Br&R. *Acta Pharmaceutica Suecica, 7*(6), 651–666.

Lyttle, T. (1993). [Review of the book *Ayahuasca visions: The religious iconography of a Peruvian shaman*]. *Psychedelic Monographs and Essays, 6*, 201–202.

Mabit, M. (1996). The Takiwasi patient's journey. *Newsletter of the Multidisciplinary Association for Psychedelic Studies, 6*(3). Retrieved April 23, 2008, from http://www.maps.org/news-letters/v06n3/06327tak.html.

MacRae, E. (1992). *Guiado pela lua: Xamanismo e uso ritual da ayahuasca no culto do Santo Daime* [Guided by the moon: Shamanism and the ritual use of ayahuasca in the Santo Daime cult]. São Paolo: Brasiliense.

MacRae, E. (1998). Santo Daime and Santa Maria—The licit ritual use of ayahuasca and the illicit use of cannabis in a Brazilian Amazonian religion. *International Journal of Drug Policy, 9*(5), 325–337.

MacRae, E. (1999). The ritual and religious use of ayahuasca in contemporary Brazil. In W. Taylor, R. Stewart, K. Hopkins, & S. Ehlers (Eds.), *DPF XII policy manual* (pp. 47–50). Washington, DC: Drug Policy Foundation Press.

MacRae, E. (2000). *El Santo Daime y la espiritualidad Brasileña* [Santo Diame and Brazilian spirituality]. Quito: Editorial Abya-Yala.

MacRae, E. (2004). The ritual use of ayahuasca by three Brazilian religions. In R. Coomber & N. South (Eds.), *Drug use and cultural contexts "beyond the West"* (pp. 27–45). London: Free Association. Retrieved June 18, 2008, from the Santo Daime Online Library Web site, http://www.santodaime.it/Library/ANTROPOLOGY&SOCIOLOGY/macrae04b_english.pdf.

Maddox, J. C. (1923). *The medicine man*. New York: Macmillan.

Maestro Ayahuasquero. (2006). *Mapacho* [MP3]. Retrieved November 24, 2007, from the Dada World Data Web site, http://dwdtv.org/files/mapacho.mp3.

Maestro Ayahuasquero. (2007, February 7). *Ayahuasca* [Video]. Retrieved November 24, 2007, from the YouTube Web site, http://www.youtube.com/wathc?v=rQBRys_77to.

Mahua, B. (2002). Ayahuasca healing [Recorded by Mahua, B., & Tulku]. On *A universe to come* [CD]. Santa Fe, NM: New Earth Records.

Manock, S. R., Suarez, G., Graham, D., Avila-Aguero, M. L., & Warrell, D. A. (2008).

Neurotoxic envenoming by South American coral snake (*Micrurus lemniscatus helleri*): Case report from eastern Ecuador and review. *Transactions of the Royal Society of Tropical Medicine and Hygiene*, 102(11), 1127–1132.

Manrique, N. (1998). The war for the Central Sierra. In S. J. Stern (Ed.), *Shining and other paths: War and society in Peru, 1980–1995* (pp. 193–223). Durham: Duke University Press.

Marc, B., Martis, A., Moreau, C., Arlie, G., Kintz, P., & Leclerc, J. (2007). Acute *Datura stramonium* poisoning in an emergency department. *Presse Medical, 36*(10), 1399–1403. Abstract retrieved May 6, 2008, from the National Library of Medicine Web site, http://www.ncbi.nlm.nih.gov/pubmed/17560071.

Maringhini, G., Notaro, L., Barberi, O., Giubilato, A., Butera, R., & Di Pasquale, P. (2002). Cardiovascular glycoside-like intoxication following ingestion of *Thevetia nereifolia/peruviana* seeds: A case report. *Italian Heart Journal, 3*(2), 137–140.

Marks, L. (2000). Synesthesia. In E. Cardeña, S. J. Lynn, & S. Krippner (Eds.), *Varieties of anomalous experience: Examining the scientific evidence* (pp. 121–149). Washington, DC: American Psychological Association.

Marles, R. J., Neill, D. A., & Farnsworth, N. R. (1988). A contribution to the ethnopharmacology of the lowland Quichua people of Amazonian Ecuador. *Revista de la Academia Colombiana de Ciencias Exactas, Físicas y Naturales*, 16(63), 111–120.

Martin, B. H. (2005). Woven songs of the Amazon: *Icaros* and weavings of the Shipibo shamans. Paper presented at the meeting of the Society for Ethnomusicology, Atlanta, November 17–20. Retrieved November 17, 2007, from http://www.barrettmartin.com/essays/Society%20of%20Ethnomusicology%20Paper.pdf.

Martin, B. H. (2006). *Woven songs of the Amazon: Healing* icaros *of the Shipibo shamans* [CD]. Santa Fe, NM: Fast Horse.

Martinez, C., & Martin, H. W. (1979). Folk diseases among urban Mexican-Americans: Etiology, symptoms, and treatment. In N. Klein (Ed.), *Culture, curers, and contagion: Readings for medical social science* (pp. 188–194). Novato, CA: Chandler & Sharp.

Masterson, D. M. (1991). *Militarism and politics in Latin America: Peru from Sanchez Cerro to Sendero Luminoso*. New York: Greenwood.

Matteson, E. (1954). *The Piro of the Urubamba* (Kroeber Anthropological Society, Paper 10). Berkeley: University of California Press.

Matthiessen, P. (1965). *At play in the fields of the Lord*. New York: Vintage Books.

Mattingly, C. (2000). Emergent narratives. In C. Mattingly & L. Garro (Eds.), *Narrative and the cultural construction of illness and healing* (pp. 181–211). Berkeley: University of California Press.

Maxim, N. (2007, May). The quarter-ton fish. *Gourmet*, 67(5), 106.

May, R. (1989). The empathic relationship: A foundation of healing. In R. Carlson & B. Shield (Eds.), *Healers on healing* (pp. 108–110). Los Angeles: Jeremy P. Tarcher.

Mazzetti, M. (2008, November 21). C.I.A. withheld data in Peru plane crash inquiry. *New York Times*, p. A6.

McCreery, C. (2006). Perception and hallucination: The case for continuity (Oxford Forum Philosophical Paper No. 2006–1). Retrieved May 2, 2008, from the Celia Green Web site, http://www.celiagreen.com/charlesmccreery/perception.pdf.

McElroy, A., & Townsend, P. K. (1996). *Medical anthropology in ecological perspective*. Boulder: Westview Press.

McGrane, B. (1989). *Beyond anthropology: Society and the Other*. New York: Columbia University Press.

McHale, B. (1987). *Postmodernist fiction*. London: Routledge.

McKenna, D. J. (1999). Ayahuasca: An ethnopharmacologic history. In R. Metzner (Ed.), *Ayahuasca: Hallucinogens, consciousness and the spirits of nature* (pp. 187–213). New York: Thunder's Mouth Press.

McKenna, D. J., Callaway, J. C., & Grob, C. S. (1998). The scientific investigation of ayahuasca: A review of past and current research. *Heffter Review of Psychedelic Research*, 1, 65–76. Retrieved November 13, 2007, from the Heffter Research Institute Web site, http://www.heffter.org/review/chapter10.pdf.

McKenna, D. J., Luna, L. E., & Towers, G. N. (1995). Biodynamic constituents in ayahuasca admixture plants: An uninvestigated folk pharmacopeia. In R. E. Schultes & S. von Reis (Eds.), *Ethnobotany: Evolution of a discipline* (pp. 349–361). Portland, OR: Dioscorides.

McKenna, D. J., Nazarali, A. J., Himeno, A., & Saavedra, J. M. (1989). Chronic treatment with (F)DOI, a psychotomimetic 5-HT2 agonist, downregulates 5-HT2 receptors in rat brain. *Neuropsychopharmacology*, 2, 81–87.

McKenna, D. J., & Towers, G. H. N. (1985). On the comparative ethnopharmacology of the malpighiaceous and myristicaceous hallucinogens. *Journal of Psychoactive Drugs*, 17, 35–39.

McKenna, D. J., Towers, G. H. N., & Abbott, F. S. (1984). Monoamine oxidase inhibitors in South American hallucinogenic plants: Tryptamine and b-carboline constituents of ayahuasca. *Journal of Ethnopharmacology*, 10(2), 195–223.

McKenna, T. (1989). Among *ayahuasquera*. In C. Rätsch (Ed.), *The gateway to inner space: A festschrift in honor of Albert Hofmann* (J. Baker, Trans., pp. 179–211). Dorset: Prism.

McKenna, T. (1990). Time and mind—The tykes. Partial transcription of a taped workshop, New Mexico, May 26–27. Retrieved December 23, 2005, from the Vaults of Erowid Web site, http://www.erowid.org/chemicals/dmt/dmt_writings3.shtml.

McKenna, T. (1991). *The archaic revival: Speculations on psychedelic mushrooms, the Amazon, virtual reality, UFOs, evolution, shamanism, the rebirth of the goddess, and the end of history*. New York: Harper.

Médicos Indígenas Yageceros de la Amazonía Colombiana. (2000). *El pensamiento de los mayores: Código de ética de la medicina indígena del piedemonte Amazónico Colombiano* [The beliefs of the elders: A code of ethics for indigenous medicine in the Colombian Amazonian plateau]. Bogotá: Unión de Médicos Indígenas Yageceros de la Amazonía Colombiana.

Mejia, K., & Rengifo, E. (2000). *Plantas medicinales de uso popular en la Amazonía Peruana* [Medicinal plants in common use in the Peruvian Amazon] (2nd ed.). Iquitos: Agencia Española de Cooperación Internacional y el Instituto de Investigaciónes de la Amazonía Peruana.

Mentore, G. (2004). The glorious tyranny of silence and the resonance of shamanic breath. In N. L. Whitehead & R. Wright (Eds.), *In darkness and secrecy: The anthropology of assault sorcery and witchcraft in Amazonia* (pp. 132–156). Durham: Duke University Press.

Mercier, J. M. H. (1979). *Nosotros los Napu-Runas, Napu runa rimay: Mitos y historia* [We the Napu-Runas, *Napu runa rimay*: Myths and history]. Iquitos: Centro de Estudios Teológicos de la Amazonia.

Merwin, W. S. (1994). The real world of Manuel Córdova. In *Travels* (pp. 96–114). New York: Knopf.

Métraux, A. (1944). Le shamanisme chez les Indiens de l'Amérique du Sud tropicales [Shamanism among the tropical South American Indians]. *Acta Americana (Mexico)*, 2(3–4), 197–219, 320–341.

Métraux, A. (1949). Religion and shamanism. In *Handbook of South American Indians, Vol.* 5 (pp. 559–599). Washington, DC: Smithsonian Institution.

Métraux, A. (1967). *Religions et magies indiennes d'Amérique du Sud* [Indian religions and magic in South America]. Paris: Éditions Gallimard.

Metzner, R. (1971). Mushrooms and the mind. In B. Aaronson & H. Osmond (Eds.), *Psychedelics: The uses and implications of hallucinogenic drugs* (pp. 90–107). London: Hogarth.

Metzner, R. (Ed.). (1999). *Ayahuasca: Hallucinogens, consciousness, and the spirits of nature.* New York: Thunder's Mouth Press.

Meyer, P. (1994). Apparent communication with discarnate entities induced by dimethyltryptamine (DMT). In T. Lyttle (Ed.), *Psychedelics* (pp. 161–204). New York: Barricade.

Mikewhy. (2000, December 29). *Q Magazine (U.K.)*, February 2001. Retrieved November 23, 2007, from the Dent Web site, http://thedent.com/qmag0201.html.

Mikics, D. (1995). Derek Walcott and Alejo Carpintier: Nature, history, and the Caribbean writer. In L. P. Zamora & W. B. Faris (Eds.), *Magical realism: Theory, history, community* (pp. 371–404). Durham: Duke University Press.

Miles, B. (2000). *Ginsberg: A biography* (Rev. ed.). London: Virgin.

Miles, B. (2002). *William Burroughs: El hombre invisible.* London: Virgin.

Miller, R. B. (1999). Characteristics and availability of commercially important woods. In Forest Products Laboratory, *Wood handbook—Wood as an engineering material* (pp. 1–34). (Gen. Tech. Rep. FPL-GTR-113). Madison, WI: U.S. Department of Agriculture, Forest Service, Forest Products Laboratory. Retrieved December 6, 2006, from http://www.fpl.fs.fed.us/documnts/fplgtr/fplgtr113/ch01.pdf.

Minaya, L. (1995). Is Peru turning Protestant? In O. Starn, C. I. Degregori, & R. Kirk (Eds.), *The Peru reader: History, culture, politics* (pp. 471–476). Durham: Duke University Press.

Ministère des solidarités, de la santé et de la famille. (2005, May 3). Arrêté du 20 avril 2005 modifiant l'arrêté du 22 février 1990 fixant la liste des substances classes comme stupéfiants [Order of April 20, 2005, amending the Order of February 22, 1990, establishing the list of substances classified as narcotic drugs]. *Journal Officiel de la République Française*, 102, 7636, text no. 18. Retrieved July 28, 2008, from the Legifrance Web site, http://www.legifrance.gouv.fr/jopdf//jopdf/2005/0503/joe_20050503_0102_0018.pdf.

Ministerio de Salud del Perú. (2002). *Análisis de la situacion de salud del pueblo Shipibo-*

Conivo [Analysis of the health situation of the Shipibo-Conibo people]. Lima: Officina General de Epidemiología.

Minton, S. A., & Norris, R. L. (1995). Non–North American venomous reptile bites. In P. S. Auerbach (Ed.), *Wilderness medicine: Management of wilderness and environmental emergencies* (3rd ed., pp. 710–730). St. Louis, MO: Mosby.

Mirante, D. (2008a, February 28). Safety for the solitary drinker. Retrieved May 6, 2008, from the Ayahuasca Web site, http://www.ayahuasca.com/?p=11.

Mirante, D. (2008b, April 27). What are ayahuasca analogues? Retrieved May 6, 2008, from the Ayahuasca Web site, http://www.ayahuasca.com/?p=148.

Moerman, D. (1997). Physiology and symbols: The anthropological implications of the placebo effect. In L. Romanucci, D. Moerman, & L. Tancredi (Eds.), *The anthropology of medicine: From culture to method* (3rd ed., pp. 240–253). Westport, CT: Bergin & Garvey.

Mogk, L. G., Riddering, A., Dahl, D., Bruce, C., & Brafford, S. (2000). Charles Bonnet syndrome in adults with visual impairments from age-related macular degeneration. In C. Stuen, A. Arditi, A. Horowitz, M. A. Lang, B. Rosenthal, & K. R. Seidman (Eds.), *Visual rehabilitation: Assessment, intervention and outcomes* (pp. 117–119). Lisse, the Netherlands: Swets & Zeitlinger.

Montes Shuña, F., Laiche Celis, F., Coral, J., & Peña Shuña, R. (2001). Icaros: *Magical melodies* [CD]. London: El Mundo Magico Music.

Moore, T. (1989). The salt of soul, the sulfur of spirit. In T. Moore (Ed.), *A blue fire: Selected writings of James Hillman* (pp. 112–114). New York: Harper Perennial.

Moran, E. F. (1993). *Through Amazonian eyes: The human ecology of Amazonian populations.* Iowa City: University of Iowa Press.

Morrison, K. (2000). The cosmos as intersubjective: Native American other-than-human persons. In G. Harvey (Ed.), *Indigenous religions: A companion* (pp. 23–36). London: Cassell.

Morrison, N. K. (1998). Behavioral pharmacology of hallucinogens. In R. E. Tarter, R. T. Ammerman, & P. J. Ott (Eds.), *Handbook of substance abuse: Neurobehavioral pharmacology* (pp. 229–240). New York: Plenum.

Morsy, S. A. (1996). Political economy in medical anthropology. In C. F. Sargent & T. M. Johnson (Eds.), *Medical anthropology: Contemporary theory and method* (pp. 21–36). Westport, CT: Praeger Paperback.

Morton, C. V. (1931). Notes on yagé, a drug-plant of southeastern Colombia. *Journal of the Washington Academy of Sciences, 21*, 485–488.

Mossembite, F. (1983). *Ayahuasca songs of Peru* [Audiocassette]. Mill Valley, CA: Sound Photosynthesis.

Muratorio, B. (1991). *The life and times of Grandfather Alonso: Culture and history in the Upper Amazon.* New Brunswick, NJ: Rutgers University Press.

Murayay, E. (2007). *El canto del tiempo: Ayahuasca icaros* [CD]. New York: Above Love Records.

Murguia, A., Peterson, R. A., & Zea, M. C. (2003, February). Use and implications of ethnomedical health care approaches among Central American immigrants. *Health and Social Work, 28*(1), 43–51.

Muscati, S. (1996). Hemispheric digest: Patenting of traditional plant sacrilegious to indigenous communities. *Native Americas: Hemispheric Journal of Indigenous Issues, 13*(4), 8.

Napoleon Blownapart. (2004, November 24). Experiential differences of rue and caapi [Msg 5]. Message posted to the Ayahuasca Forums Web site. Retrieved May 6, 2008, from http://forums.ayahuasca.com/phpbb/viewtopic.php?t=6886.

Naranjo, C. (1967). Psychotropic properties of the harmala alkaloids. In D. H. Efron, B. Holmstedt, & N. S. Kline (Eds.), *Ethnopharmacologic search for psychoactive drugs* (pp. 385–391). (Public Health Service Publication No. 1645). Washington, DC: U.S. Department of Health, Education, and Welfare.

Naranjo, C. (1973a). *The healing journey: New approaches to consciousness*. New York: Pantheon.

Naranjo, C. (1973b). Psychological aspects of the yagé experience in an experimental setting. In M. J. Harner (Ed.), *Hallucinogens and shamanism* (pp. 176–190). New York: Oxford University Press.

Naranjo, C. (1987). Ayahuasca imagery and the therapeutic property of the harmala alkaloids. *Journal of Mental Imagery, 11*(2), 131–136.

Naranjo, P. (1975). Drogas psiquedélicas en medicina mágica [Psychotropic drugs in magical medicine]. *Cuadernos Científicos CEMEF, 4*, 73–92.

Naranjo, P. (1979). Hallucinogenic plant use and related indigenous belief systems in the Ecuadorian Amazon. *Journal of Ethnopharmacology, 1*(2), 121–145.

Naranjo, P. (1983). *Ayahuasca: Etnomedicina y mitología* [Ayahuasca: Ethnomedicine and mythology]. Quito: Ediciones Libri Mundi.

Narby, J. (1999). *The cosmic serpent: DNA and the origins of knowledge*. New York: Jeremy P. Tarcher.

Nations, M. K., & Rebhun, L. A. (1988). Angels with wet wings won't fly: Maternal sentiment in Brazil and the image of neglect. *Culture, Medicine and Psychiatry, 12*(2), 141–200.

Needham, W. E., & Taylor, R. E. (2000). Atypical Charles Bonnet hallucinations: An elf in the woodshed, a spirit of evil, and the cowboy malefactors. *Journal of Nervous and Mental Disease, 188*(2), 108–115.

Nellis, D. W. (1997). *Poisonous plants and animals of Florida and the Caribbean*. Sarasota: Pineapple.

Neuwinger, H. D. (1998). Alkaloids in arrow poison. In M. F. Roberts & M. Wink (Eds.), *Alkaloids: Biochemistry, ecology, and medicinal applications* (pp. 45–86). New York: Plenum.

Newman, A. (2000). *The tropical rainforest: A world survey of our most valuable endangered habitat* (Rev. ed.). New York: Facts on File.

New York Times. (2004). Peru. Retrieved November 6, 2006, from the New York Times Travel Almanac Web site, http://travel2.nytimes.com/2004/07/15/travel/NYT_ALMANAC_WORLD_PERU.html?ei=5070&en=41a0548306d79c73&ex=1163048400&adxnnl=1&adxnnlx=1162907305–1bxVtRYb/ZEihoqAFOS+ZQ.

Nichols, D. E. (2004). Hallucinogens. *Pharmacology and Therapeutics, 101*, 131–181.

Nichols, D. E., Oberlender, R., & McKenna, D. J. (1991). Stereochemical aspects of hallucinogenesis. In R. R. Watson (Ed.), *Biochemistry and physiology of substance abuse* (pp. 1–39). Boca Raton: CRC Press.

Noë, A. (2002). Is the visual world a grand illusion? *Journal of Consciousness Studies, 9*(5–6), 1–12.

Noel, D. (1976). *Seeing Castaneda: Reactions to the "don Juan" writings of Carlos Castaneda.* New York: Perigee.

Noel, D. (1997). *The soul of shamanism: Western fantasies, imaginal realities.* New York: Continuum.

Noriega, M. ("chinchilejo"). (2001a, May 25). Forming a church: "Soga del Alma" (Vine of the Soul) [Msg 10]. Message posted to the Ayahuasca Forums Web site. Retrieved January 13, 2006, from http://forums.ayahuasca.com/phpbb/viewtopic.php?t=4243.

Noriega, M. ("chinchilejo"). (2001b, May 27). Forming a church: "Soga del Alma" (Vine of the Soul) [Msg 23]. Message posted to the Ayahuasca Forums Web site. Retrieved January 13, 2006, from http://forums.ayahuasca.com/phpbb/viewtopic.php?t=4243.

Noriega, M. ("chinchilejo"). (2001c, June 6). Forming a church: "Soga del Alma" (Vine of the Soul) [Msg 36]. Message posted to the Ayahuasca Forums Web site. Retrieved January 13, 2006, from http://forums.ayahuasca.com/phpbb/viewtopic.php?t=4243.

Novartis Consumer Health, Inc. (1998). Transderm Scōp® scopolamine 15 mg. Retrieved August 19, 2004, from the U.S. Food and Drug Administration Web site, http://www.fda.gov/cder/foi/label/2001/17874s27lbl.pdf.

Nugent, S. (1994). *Big mouth: The Amazon speaks.* San Francisco: BrownTrout.

Nugent, S. (2007). *Scoping the Amazon: Image, icon, ethnography.* Walnut Creek, CA: Left Coast.

O'Nell, C. W. (1975). An investigation of reported "fright" as a factor in the etiology of *susto*, "magical fright." *Ethos, 3*, 268–283.

O'Nell, C. W., & Rubel, A. (1976). The meaning of *susto* (magical fright). *Actas del XLI Congresso Internacional de Americanistas, 3*, 342–349.

Oberem, U. (1974). Trade and trade goods in the Ecuadorian *montaña*. In P. J. Lyon (Ed.), *Native South Americans: Ethnology of the least known continent* (pp. 347–357). Boston: Little, Brown.

Ochoa Abaurre, J. C. (2002). *Mito y chamanismo: El mito de la tierra sin malen los tupí-cocama de la Amazonía Peruana* [Myth and shamanism: The myth of the land without evil among the Tupí-Cocama of the Peruvian Amazon] (unpublished Ph.D. dissertation, University of Barcelona, Barcelona). Retrieved September 19, 2006, from the Tesis Doctorals en Xarxa Web site, http://www.tdx.cesca.es/TESIS_UB/AVAILABLE/TDX-0204103-123631//TESISOCHOA.pdf.

Oliver's acid trip down memory lane. (2006, July 18). *New York Daily News.* Retrieved November 24, 2007, from http://www.nydailynews.com/gossip/2006/07/18/2006-07-18_olivers_acid_trip_down_memory_lane.html.

Onnie-Hay, J. (2006, Autumn). Toward light in the darkness: A review of the SheShamans-MagicMamas and 2nd Amazonian Shamanism Conferences. *Newsletter of the Multidisciplinary Association for Psychedelic Studies, 16*(2). Retrieved March 2, 2007, from http://www.maps.org/news-letters/v16n2-html/toward_light_in_the_darkness.html.

Oppitz, M. (1981). *Shamanen in Blinden Land* [Shamans in a blind land]. Frankfurt-am-Main: Syndikat.

Ortega, H., & Vari, R. P. (1986). *Annotated checklist of the freshwater fish of Peru* (Smithsonian Contributions to Zoology No. 437). Washington, DC: Smithsonian Institution Press. Retrieved August 23, 2008, from http://www.sil.si.edu/smithsoniancontributions/Zoology/pdf_hi/SCTZ-0437.pdf.

Ortner, S. (1995). Resistance and the problem of ethnographic refusal. *Comparative Studies in Society and History, 37*(1), 173–193.

Otis, J. (2008, May 1). Reactions to the use of ayahuasca. *Houston Chronicle*. Retrieved May 3, 2008, from http://www.chron.com/disp/story.mpl/travel/5746132.html.

Ott, J. (1994). *Ayahuasca analogues: Pangaean entheogens*. Kennewick, WA: Natural Products.

Ott, J. (1995). *The age of entheogens and the angel's dictionary*. Kennewick, WA: Natural Products. Retrieved January 12, 2006, from the Entheogen Dot Com Web site, http://www.entheogen.com/News/article/sid=72.html.

Ott, J. (1996). *Pharmacotheon: Entheogenic drugs, their plant sources and history* (2nd ed.). Kennewick, WA: Natural Products.

Ott, J. (1997). *Pharmacophilia or the natural paradises*. Kennewick, WA: Natural Products.

Ott, J. (2001). Pharmañopo-psychonautics: Human intranasal, sublingual, intrarectal, pulmonary and oral pharmacology of bufotenine. *Journal of Psychoactive Drugs 33*(3), 273–281.

Pachter, L. M. (1993). Latino folk illnesses: Methodological considerations. *Medical Anthropology*, 15, 103–108.

Padilla, A. (1984). The *icaros* of Don Emilio Andrade Gómez: Appendix to the concept of plants as teachers among four mestizo shamans of Iquitos, northeastern Peru. *Journal of Ethnopharmacology*, 11(2), 147–156.

Padoch, C., & de Jong, W. (1987). Traditional agroforestry practices of native and *ribereño* farmers in the lowland Peruvian Amazon. In H. L. Gholz (Ed.), *Agroforestry: Realities, possibilities, and potentials* (pp. 179–194). Dordrecht, the Netherlands: Martinus Nijhoff.

Padoch, C., & de Jong, W. (1992). Diversity, variation, and change in *ribereño* agriculture. In K. H. Redford & C. Padoch (Eds.), *Conservation of neotropical forests: Working from traditional resource use* (pp. 158–174). New York: Columbia University Press.

Paerregaard, K. (1997). *Linking separate worlds: Urban migrants and rural lives in Peru*. Oxford: Berg.

Paicheler, A. (2007). Initiation—The mechanics from a clinical perspective. In V. Ravalec, Mallendi, & A. Paicheler, Iboga: *The visionary roots of African shamanism* (J. Cain, Trans., pp. 61–70). Rochester, VT: Park Street. (Original work published 2004.)

Paicheler, A., & Ravalec, V. (2007). The sacred root, *bwiti*, and *ngenza*. In V. Ravalec, Mallendi, & A. Paicheler, Iboga: *The visionary roots of African shamanism* (J. Cain, Trans., pp. 6–13). Rochester, VT: Park Street. (Original work published 2004.)

Panduro Vasquez, L. (2000). *Ayahusca songs from the Peruvian Amazon* [CD]. El Prado, NM: Colibri.

Patai, D. (1988). *Brazilian women speak: Contemporary life stories*. New Brunswick, NJ: Rutgers University Press.

Patai, D. (2001). Whose truth? Iconicity and accuracy in the world of testimonial literature. In A. Arias (Ed.), *The Rigoberta Menchú controversy* (pp. 270–287). Minneapolis: University of Minnesota Press.

Patkar, A. A., Gopalakrishnan, R., Lundy, A., Leone, F. T., Certa, K. M., & Weinstein, S. P. (2002). Relationship between tobacco smoking and positive and negative symptoms in schizophrenia. *Journal of Nervous and Mental Disorders, 190*(9), 604–610.

Payaguaje, F. (2001) A shaman endures the temptation of sorcery (and publishes a book). In J. Narby & F. Huxley (Eds.), *Shamans through time: 500 years on the path to knowledge* (pp. 230–233). New York: Jeremy P. Tarcher. (Original work published 1990.)

Pearson, D. L., & Beletsky, L. (2008). *Peru* (Travelers' Wildlife Guides). Northampton, MA: Interlink.

Pedersen, M. (2007). Interview with a *yachak*. Retrieved April 25, 2008, from the Colonos—Amazonia por la Vida Web site, http://colonos.wordpress.com/2007/04/16/interview-with-a-yachak/.

Pelto, P. J., Bentley, M. E., & Pelto, G. H. (1990). Applied anthropological research methods: Diarrhea studies as an example. In J. Coreil & J. D. Mull (Eds.), *Anthropology and primary health care* (pp. 253–277). Boulder: Westview.

Pendell, D. (2005). Pharmako Gnosis: *Plant teachers and the poison path*. San Francisco: Mercury House.

Perkins, J. (2005). *Confessions of an economic hit man*. New York: Plume.

Perreault, J. (1998, Summer). Self-taught artists of the 20th century. *Artforum International, 36*, 126–127.

Perrine, D. (1996). *The chemistry of mind-altering drugs: History, pharmacology, and cultural context*. Washington, DC: American Chemical Society.

Perruchon, M. (2003). *I am Tsunki: Gender and shamanism among the Shuar of western Amazonia*. Uppsala: Uppsala University Press.

Peters, L. (1994). The internal mystery plays: The role and physiology of the visual system in contemplative practices. *ReVision*, 17(1), 3–13.

Piccalo, G. (2008, February 2). Ayahuasca: A strange brew. *Los Angeles Times Magazine*. Retrieved May 2, 2008, from http://www.latimes.com/features/magazine/la-tm-ayahuasca.02feb3,1,6118145.story?ctrack=3&cset=true.

Pickover, C. A. (2005). *Sex, drugs, Einstein, and elves: Sushi, psychedelics, parallel universes, and the quest for transcendence*. Petaluma, CA: Smart.

Pimenta, A. (2005). Ashaninka. History in Peru. In *Encyclopedia of indigenous people in Brazil*. Retrieved June 18, 2008, from the Instituto Socioambiental Web site, http://www.socioambiental.org.br/pib/epienglish/ashaninka/hperu.html.

Pinchbeck, D. (2002). *Breaking open the head: A psychedelic journey into the heart of contemporary shamanism*. New York: Broadway.

Pinedo, M., Rengifo, E., & Cerruti, T. (1997). *Plantas medicinales de la Amazonía Peruana: Estudio de su uso y cultivo* [Medicinal plants of the Peruvian Amazon: A study in their use and cultivation]. Iquitos: Instituto de Investigaciónes de la Amazonía Peruana.

Pinedo-Vasquez, M., Barletti Pasquall, J., & Del Castillo Torres, D. (2002). A tradition of change: The dynamic relationship between biodiversity and society in Sector Muyuy, Peru. *Environmental Science and Policy*, 5(1), 43–53.

Pinedo-Vasquez, M., Zarin, D., & Jipp, P. (1995). Local management of forest resources in a rural community in north-east Peru. In T. Nishizawa & J. I. Uitto (Eds.), *The fragile tropics: Sustainable management of changing environments* (pp. 238–252). Tokyo: United Nations University Press.

Pinkley, H. V. (1969). Plant mixtures of ayahuasca, the South American hallucinogenic drink. *Lloydia, 32*, 305–314.

Planting seeds of malcontent. (1999). *Environment, 41*(5), 21.

Plotkin, M. J. (1993). *Tales of a shaman's apprentice: An ethnobotanist searches for new medicines*. New York: Viking.

Plowman, T. (1977, December). *Brunfelsia* in ethnomedicine. *Harvard University Botanical Museum Leaflets, 25*(10), 289–320.

Poisson, J. (1960). The presence of mescaline in a Peruvian cactus. *Annales Pharmaceutiques Françaises, 18*, 764–765.

Poisson, J. (1965). Note sur le "Natem," boisson toxíque péruvienne et ses alcoïdes [A note on "natem," a Peruvian toxic drink and its alkaloids]. *Annales Pharemaceutiques Françaises, 23*(4), 241–244.

Polari de Alverga, A. (1999). *Forest of visions: Ayahuasca, Amazonian spirituality, and the Santo Daime tradition* (R. Workman, Trans.). Rochester, VT: Park Street. (Original work published 1984.)

Pollock, D. (1992). Culina shamanism: Gender, power, and knowledge. In E. Langdon & G. Baer (Eds.), *Portals of power: Shamanism in South America* (pp. 25–40). Albuquerque: University of New Mexico Press.

Pollock, D. (2004). Siblings and sorcerers: The paradox of kinship among the Kulina. In N. L. Whitehead & R. Wright (Eds.), *In darkness and secrecy: The anthropology of assault sorcery and witchcraft in Amazonia* (pp. 202–214). Durham: Duke University Press.

Powers, W. K. (1984). Yuwipi: *Vision and experience in Oglala ritual*. Lincoln, NE: Bison Books.

Prance, G. T. (1970). Notes on the use of plant hallucinogens in Amazonian Brazil. *Economic Botany*, 24(1), 62–68.

Prance, G. T. (2005). Ethnobotany and ethnomedicine of the Amazonian Indians. In Z. Yaniv & V. Bachrach (Eds.), *Handbook of medicinal plants* (pp. 139–154). Binghamton, NY: Haworth.

Prance, G. T., & Prance, A. E. (1970). Hallucinations in Amazonia. *Garden Journal*, 20, 102–107.

Prance, G. T., Campbell, D. G., & Nelson, B. W. (1977). The ethnobotany of the Paumarí Indians. *Economic Botany, 31*, 129–139.

Pratt, M. L. (1992). *Imperial eyes: Travel writing and transculturation*. London: Routledge.

Proctor, R. (2001). Tourism opens new doors, creates new challenges, for traditional healers in Peru. *Cultural Survival Quarterly*, 24(4), 14.

Puma Shamanic Journeys. (2002). Schedule for journeys: Peruvian Amazon jungle with shaman and *ayahuasquero* don Agustin Rivas Vasquez. July 22, 2002. Retrieved October 30, 2006, from http://web.archive.org/web/20020802141109/www.spiritjourney.net/journey.html.

Quinlan, M. (2001). Healing from the gods: Ayahuasca and the curing of disease states

(Brazil) (Ph.D. dissertation, California Institute of Integral Studies). *Dissertation Abstracts International*, 62(2), 654.

Radin, P. (1983). *Crashing Thunder: The autobiography of an American Indian*. Lincoln: University of Nebraska Press. (Original work published 1926.)

Räisänen, M. J. (1984). The presence of free and conjugated bufotenin in normal human urine. *Life Sciences*, 34(21), 2041–2045.

Ramachandran, V. S. (1991). Perceptual filling in of artificially induced scotomas in human vision. *Nature*, 350(632), 699–702.

Ramachandran, V. S. (1992). Filling in gaps in perception: I. *Current Directions in Psychological Science*, 1(6), 199–205.

Ramachandran, V. S. (1993). Filling in gaps in perception: II. Scotomas and phantom limbs. *Current Directions in Psychological Science*, 2(2), 56–65.

Ramachandran, V. S. (1998). *Phantoms in the brain*. New York: Harper Collins.

Ramachandran, V. S., & Hirstein, W. (1999). Three laws of qualia: What neurology tells us about the biological functions of consciousness, qualia and the self. In S. Gallagher & J. Shear (Eds.), *Models of the self* (pp. 83–112). Charlottesville, VA: Imprint Academic.

Ramírez de Jara, M. C., & Pinzón Castaño, C. E. (1992). Sibundoy shamanism and popular culture in Colombia. In E. J. Langdon & G. Baer (Eds.), *Portals of power: Shamanism in South America* (pp. 287–303). Albuquerque: University of New Mexico Press.

Ramos, A. R. (1998). *Indigenism: Ethnic politics in Brazil*. Madison: University of Wisconsin Press.

Ramos, C. A. (2004). Bailando la neurótica danza de la realidad nacional: De huayno, chicha y tecnocumbia, modernidades populares finiseculares [Dancing the neurotic dance of national reality: On *huayno*, *chicha*, *tecnocumbia*, and popular modernity at the end of the century]. *Interculturidad*. Retrieved April 28, 2008, from http://interculturalidad.org/numero01/e/arti/e_son_030404.htm.

Rankin, B. (2002a, October 14). Man in legal wrangle over hallucinogenic tea. *Seattle Post-Intelligencer*. Retrieved January 14, 2006, from http://seattlepi.nwsource.com/national/91091_drug14.shtml.

Rankin, B. (2002b, October 24). Trial ordered in case of hallucinogenic plants. *Atlanta Journal-Constitution*. Retrieved January 14, 2006, from the Cognitive Liberty Web site, http://www.cognitiveliberty.org/dll/shoemaker1.htm.

Rätsch, C. (2007). *Enzyklopädie der psychoaktiven Pflanzen* [Encyclopedia of psychoactive plants]. Munich: AT Verlag.

Reese, W. D. (1971). The hallucinations of widowhood. *British Medical Journal*, 210, 37–41.

Reichel-Dolmatoff, G. (1944). La cultura material de los Indios Guahibo [The material culture of the Guahibo Indians]. *Revista del Instituto Etnológoco Nacional*, 1(1), 437–506.

Reichel-Dolmatoff, G. (1960). Notas etnográficas sobre los Indios del Chocó [Ethnographic notes on the Chocó Indians]. *Revista Colombiana de Antropología*, 2, 75–158.

Reichel-Dolmatoff, G. (1969). El contexto cultural de un alucinógeno aborígen [The cultural context of an aboriginal hallucinogen]. *Revista de la Academia Colombiana de Ciencias Exactas, Físicas y Naturales*, 13(51), 327–345.

Reichel-Dolmatoff, G. (1970). Notes on the cultural extent of the use of yajé (*Banisteriopsis caapi*) among the Indians of the Vaupés, Colombia. *Economic Botany*, 24(1), 32–33.
Reichel-Dolmatoff, G. (1971). *Amazonian cosmos: The sexual and religious symbolism of the Tukano Indians* (G. Reichel-Dolmatoff, Trans.). Chicago: University of Chicago Press. (Original work published 1968.)
Reichel-Dolmatoff, G. (1972). The cultural context of an aboriginal hallucinogen: *Banisteriopsis caapi*. In P. T. Furst (Ed.), *Flesh of the gods: The ritual use of hallucinogens* (pp. 84–113). New York: Praeger.
Reichel-Dolmatoff, G. (1975). *The shaman and the jaguar: A study of narcotic drugs among the Indians of Colombia*. Philadelphia: Temple University Press.
Reichel-Dolmatoff, G. (1997a). Desana shamans' rock crystals and the hexagonal universe. In *Rainforest shamans: Essays on the Tukano Indians of the northwest Amazon* (pp. 149–160). Devon, England: Themis Books. (Original work published 1979.)
Reichel-Dolmatoff, G. (1997b). Drug-induced optical sensations and their relationship to applied art among some Colombian Indians. In *Rainforest shamans: Essays on the Tukano Indians of the northwest Amazon* (pp. 243–259). Devon, England: Themis Books. (Original work published 1978.)
Reinhard, J. (1976). Shamanism and spirit possession: The definitional problem. In J. T. Hitchcock & R. T. Jones (Eds.), *Spirit possession* (pp. 12–22). Warminster, England: Aries & Phillips.
Reis, R. E., Kullander, S. O., & Ferraris, C. J. (2003). *Check list of the freshwater fishes of South and Central America*. Porto Alegre, Brazil: Editora Universitária da PUCRS.
Reisberg, D., & Leak, S. (1987). Visual imagery and memory for appearance: Does Clark Gable or George C. Scott have bushier eyebrows? *Canadian Journal of Psychology*, 41, 521–526.
Rengifo, E. (2001). *Plantas medicinales y biocidas de la Amazonía Peruana* [Medicinal and biocidal plants of the Peruvian Amazon]. Iquitos: Instituto de Investigaciónes de la Amazonía Peruana.
Richards, R. A. (1978). Mystical and archetypal experiences of terminal patients in DPT-assisted psychotherapy. *Journal of Religion and Health*, 17, 117–126.
Richards, W. A., Rhead, J. C., DiLeo, F. B., Yensen, R., & Kurland, A. A. (1977). The peak experience variable in DPT-assisted psychotherapy with cancer patients. *Journal of Psychedelic Drugs*, 9, 1–10.
Richman, G. D. (1990–1991, Winter). The Santo Daime doctrine. *Shaman's Drum: Journal of Experiential Shamanism*, 30–41.
Ricoeur, P. (1981). *Hermeneutics and the human sciences* (J. Thompson, Ed. & Trans.). Cambridge: Cambridge University Press.
Ricoeur, P. (1983). On interpretation. In A. Montefiore (Ed.), *Philosophy in France today* (pp. 175–197). Cambridge: Cambridge University Press.
Ricoeur, P. (1984). *Time and narrative, Vol. 1* (K. McLaughlin & D. Pellauer, Trans.). Chicago: University of Chicago Press. (Original work published 1983.)
Ricoeur, P. (1985). *Time and narrative, Vol. 2* (K. McLaughlin & D. Pellauer, Trans.). Chicago: University of Chicago Press. (Original work published 1984.)
Riddle, S. (1994, July). The deeper you listen. *Nuvo*. Retrieved November 24, 2007, from the Jason Watts Web site, http://www.stuff.to/include.php?=/taart/NUVO_94.txt&.

Ridgely, R. S., & Greenfield, P. J. (2001). *The birds of Ecuador. Vol. II. Field guide.* Ithaca, NY: Cornell University Press.

Riordan, J. (1995). *Stone: The controversies, excesses, and exploits of a radical filmmaker.* New York: Hyperion.

Ríos, M., Dourojeanni, M. J., & Tovar, A. (1975). La fauna y su aprovechamiento en Jenaro Herrera (Requena, Perú) [Animals and their use in Jenaro Herrera (Requena, Peru)]. *Revista Forestal de Perú, 5*(1–2), 73–92. Retrieved May 29, 2008, from the Centro de Documentación e Información Forestal Web site, http://cedinfor.lamolina.edu.pe/Articulos_RFP/V0105_n01–2_Ene71-Dic74_(08)/v015_art7.pdf.

Ríos Zañartu, M. C. (1999). *Historia de la Amazonía Peruana—1. Período autóctono* [History of the Peruvian Amazon—1. Indigenous period]. Iquitos: Impresiones CETA.

Ritzenthaler, R. (1963). Primitive therapeutic practices among the Wisconsin Chippewa. In I. Galdston (Ed.), *Man's image in medicine and anthropology* (pp. 321–322). New York: International Universities Press.

Rivas, A. (1988). *Canto musica ayahuasca en la selva de Peru* [Audiocassette]. Mill Valley, CA: Sound Photosynthesis.

Rivas, A. (1998). La magia: *Music of don Agustin Rivas* [CD]. Denton, TX: RudraRuna Music.

Rivier, L., & Lindgren, J.-E. (1972). "Ayahuasca," the South American hallucinogenic drink: An ethnobotanical and chemical investigation. *Economic Botany, 26*(1), 101.

Rivière, P. (1994). WYSINWYG in Amazonia. *Journal of the Anthropological Society of Oxford, 25*(3), 255–262.

Roberts, T. B. (Ed.). (2001). *Psychoactive sacramentals: Essays on entheogens and religion.* San Francisco: Council on Spiritual Practices.

Rodd, R. (2008). Reassessing the cultural and psychopharmacological significance of *Banisteriopsis caapi*: Preparation, classification and use among the Piaroa of southern Venezuela. *Journal of Psychoactive Drugs, 40*(3), 301–307.

Rodríguez, E., & Cavin, J. C. (1982). The possible role of Amazonian psychoactive plants in the chemotherapy of parasitic worms—A hypothesis. *Journal of Ethnopharmacology, 6*, 302–309.

Rodríguez, J. (1999). Medicina Andina-Amazónica los Quijos [Andean-Amazonian medicine of the Quijos]. In V. Serrano, R. Gordillo, S. Guerra, M. Naranjo, P. Costales, A. Costales, et al., *Ciencia Andina* (pp. 251–322). Quitos: Abya-Yala.

Rodriguez, M. A. (2007). A methodology for studying various interpretations of the n,n-dimethyltryptamine-induced alternate reality. *Journal of Scientific Exploration, 21*(1), 67–84. Retrieved November 26, 2007, from http://www.soe.ucsc.edu/~okram/papers/paralleldmt.pdf.

Roe, P. G. (2004). At play in the fields of symmetry: Design structure and shamanic therapy in the Upper Amazon. In D. K. Washburn & D. W. Crowe (Eds.), *Symmetry comes of age: The role of pattern in culture* (pp. 232–303). Seattle: University of Washington Press.

Romero, R. R. (2002). Popular music and the global city: *Huayno, chicha,* and *technocumbia* in Lima. In W. A. Clark (Ed.), *From tejano to tango: American popular music* (pp. 217–239). New York: Routledge.

Roque, J., & León, B. (2006, December). Orchidaceae endémicas del Perú. *Revista*

Peruana de Biología, 13(2), 759–878. Retrieved August 6, 2008, from the Universidad Nacional Mayor de San Marcos Sistema de Bibliotecas Web site, http://sisbib.unmsm.edu.pe/BVRevistas/biologia/v13n2/pdf/a145.pdf.

Rosenberg, D. E., Isbell, H., Miner, E. J., & Logan, C. R. (1964). The effect of N,N-dimethyltryptamine in human subjects tolerant to lysergic acid diethylamide. *Psychopharmacology*, 5, 217–227.

Rosengren, D. (2000). The delicacy of community: On *kisagantsi* in Matsigenka narrative discourse. In J. Overing & A. Passes (Eds.), *The anthropology of love and anger: The aesthetics of conviviality in Native Amazonia* (pp. 221–234). London: Routledge.

Rothenberg, J. (1968). *Technicians of the sacred*. New York: Doubleday.

Rothenberg, J. (1976). Pre-face to a symposium on ethnopoetics. *Alcheringa: Ethnopoetics*, 2(2), 6–12.

Rothenberg, J. (1981a). The poetics of shamanism. In *Pre-faces and other writings* (pp. 186–189). New York: New Directions.

Rothenberg, J. (1981b). Pre-face to a symposium on ethnopoetics. In *Pre-faces and other writings* (pp. 129–136). New York: New Directions.

Rouget, G. (1985). *Music and trance: A theory of the relations between music and possession* (B. Biebuyck, Trans.). Chicago: University of Chicago Press. (Original work published 1980.)

Rouhier, A. (1924). Le yajé: Plante télépathique [Yagé: A telepathic plant]. *Paris Médical*, 15, 341–346.

Rowan, J. (1993). *The transpersonal: Psychotherapy and counselling*. London: Routledge.

Rubel, A. J. (1960). Concepts of disease in Mexican-American culture. *American Anthropologist*, 62, 795–814.

Rubel, A. J. (1964). The epidemiology of a folk illness: *Susto* in Hispanic America. *Ethnology*, 3, 268–283.

Rubel, A. J. (1966). *Across the tracks: Mexican-Americans in a Texas city*. Austin: University of Texas Press.

Rubel, A. J., O'Nell, C. W., & Collado-Ardon, R. (1984). Susto: *A folk illness*. Berkeley: University of California Press.

Rubenstein, S. (2002). *Alejando Tsakimp: A Shuar healer in the margins of history*. Lincoln: University of Nebraska Press.

Ruck, C. A., Bigwood, J., Staples, D., Ott, J., & Wasson, R. G. (1979). Entheogens. *Journal of Psychedelic Drugs*, 11, 145–146.

Ruiz, J. L. (2006). Civilized people in uncivilized places: Rubber, race, and civilization during the Amazonian rubber boom. Unpublished M.A. thesis, University of Saskatchewan, Saskatoon, Alberta, Canada. Retrieved June 12, 2008, from http://library2.usask.ca/theses/available/etd-05202006–230338/unrestricted/Thesis_Jean_Ruiz.pdf.

Rumrrill, R. (1996, December 5). Pelados alterados: Turistas místicos se entregan al alucinante ritual del ayahuasca en cuerpo y alma [Kids getting high: Mystical tourists give themselves over, body and soul, to the hallucinatory ayahuasca ritual]. *Caretas*, 1443, 34–37. Retrieved January 14, 2006, from http://www.caretas.com.pe/1443/indios/indios.htm.

Rusby, H. H. (1923). The aboriginal uses of caapi. *Journal of the American Pharmaceutical Association*, 12, 1123.

Russell, M. (N.d.). Looking for reptiles in the Amazon. Retrieved May 28, 2008, from the Reptile Channel Web site, http://www.reptilechannel.com/snakes/wild-snakes/looking-reptiles-amazon.aspx?cm_sp=InternalClicks-_-RelatedArticles-_-snakes/wild-snakes/looking-reptiles-amazon.

Sá, L. (2004). *Rain forest literatures*. Minneapolis: University of Minnesota Press.

Saar, M. (1991). Ethnomycological data from Siberia and north-east Asia on the effect of *Amanita muscaria*. *Journal of Ethnopharmacology*, 31, 157–173.

Sahlins, M. (1993). *Waiting for Foucault*. Cambridge, MA: Prickly Pear Press.

Saladin d'Anglure, B., & Morin, F. (1998). Mariage mystique et pouvoir chamanique chez les Shipibo d'amazonie péruvienne et les Inuit du Nunavut canadien [Mystical marriage and shamanic power among the Shipibo of the Peruvian Amazon and the Inuit of the Canadian Nunavut]. *Anthropologie et Sociétés*, 22(2), 49–74.

Salak, K. (2005). The vision seekers. In J. Kincaid & J. Wilson (Eds.), *The best American travel writing 2005* (pp. 308–313). New York: Houghton Mifflin.

Saldaña, J., & Rojas, T. (2004). Consumo de carne de monte y su importancia en la alimentación del poblador de Jenaro Herrera, Loreto—Perú [The consumption of wild game and its importance in the diet of the inhabitants of Jenaro Herrara, Loreto—Peru]. Paper presented at the Congreso Internacional sobre Manejo de Fauna Silvestre en la Amazonía y Latinoamérica. Retrieved May 30, 2008, from the Revista Electronica Manejo de Fauna Silvestre en Latinoamérica Web site, http://www.revistafauna.com.pe/memo/602–609.pdf.

Saldanha, A. (2007). *Psychedelic white: Goa trance and the viscosity of race*. Minneapolis: University of Minnesota Press.

Saler, B., Horton, R., & Lothrop, S. K. (1970). Sorcery in Santiago El Palmar. In D. E. Walker (Ed.), *Systems of North American witchcraft and sorcery* (pp. 125–146). Moscow: University of Idaho Press.

Salmón, E. (2000). Kincentric ecology: Indigenous perceptions of the human–nature relationship. *Ecological Applications*, 10(5), 1327–1332.

Salzman, E., Salzman, J., Salzman, J., & Lincoff, G. (1996). In search of *mukhomor*, the mushroom of immortality. *Shaman's Drum*, 41, 36–47.

Sammarco, F., & Palazzolo, D. (2002). *Conversations with Sachamama. Amazonian vegetalismo in the words of don Francisco Montes Shuña*. Retrieved October 25, 2006, from the El Mundo Magico Web site, http://www.ayahuasca-shamanism.co.uk/InterviewFM.htm.

San Roman, J. V. (1977). Pautas de asentamiento en la selva [Patterns of settlement in the jungle]. *Amazonía peruana*, 1/2, 29–52.

Santhouse, A. M., Howard, R. J., & ffytche, D. H. (2000). Visual hallucinatory syndromes and the anatomy of the visual brain. *Brain*, 123(10), 2055–2076.

Santos-Granero, F., & Barclay, F. (2000). *Tamed frontiers: Economy, society, and civil rights in the Upper Amazon*. Boulder: Westview.

Sarbin, T. R. (1986). The narrative as a root metaphor for psychology. In T. R. Sarbin (Ed.), *Narrative psychology: The storied nature of human conduct* (pp. 3–21). New York: Praeger.

Sass, L. A. (1994). *The paradoxes of delusion: Wittgenstein, Schreber, and the schizophrenic mind.* Ithaca, NY: Cornell University Press.

Sasser, E. (1983). A room with a view. *Southwest Art, 13*(7), 86–91.

Schaepe, H. (2001, January 17). Facsimile sent to Inspectorate for Health Care, Ministry of Public Health, the Netherlands. Retrieved May 14, 2008, from the Erowid Ayahuasca Vault Web site, http://www.erowid.org/chemicals/ayahuasca/images/archive/ayahuasca_law_undcp_fax1.jpg.

Schechner, R. (1971, April). Actuals: Primitive ritual and performance theory. *Theatre Quarterly,* 2, 49–66.

Schechner, R. (1985). *Between theatre and anthropology.* Philadelphia: University of Pennsylvania Press.

Schechner, R. (1988). *Performance theory* (2nd ed.). New York: Routledge.

Schechner, R. (1994). *Environmental theater* (Expanded ed.). New York: Applause Books.

Scheper-Hughes, N. (1988). The madness of hunger. Sickness, delirium and human needs. *Culture, Medicine and Psychiatry* 12(4), 429–458.

Schiller, L. (1994). *The quiet room.* New York: Warner Books.

Schinzinger, A. (2001). Mysterious tea. In T. B. Roberts (Ed.), *Psychoactive sacramentals: Essays on entheogens and religion* (pp. 103–110). San Francisco: Council on Spiritual Practices.

Schreiber, J. M., & Homiak, J. P. (1981). Mexican Americans. In A. Harwood (Ed.), *Ethnicity and medical care* (pp. 264–336). Cambridge, MA: Harvard University Press.

Schulenberg, T. S., Stotz, D. F., Lane, D. F., O'Neill, J. P., & Parker, T. A. (2007). *Birds of Peru.* Princeton: Princeton University Press.

Schultes, R. E. (1954). A new narcotic snuff from the northwest Amazon. *Harvard University Botanical Museum Leaflets,* 16(9), 241–260.

Schultes, R. E. (1957). The identity of malpighiaceous narcotics of South America. *Harvard University Botanical Museum Leaflets,* 18, 1–56.

Schultes, R. E. (1972). Ethnotoxicological significance of additives to New World hallucinogens. *Plant Science Bulletin,* 18, 34–41.

Schultes, R. E. (1989). Reasons for ethnobotanical conservation. In R. E. Johannes (Ed.), *Traditional ecological knowledge: A collection of essays* (pp. 31–38). Gland, Switzerland: IUCN.

Schultes, R. E., & Hofmann, A. (1980). *The botany and chemistry of hallucinogens* (2nd ed.). Springfield, IL: C. Thomas.

Schultes, R. E., & Hofmann, A. (1992). *Plants of the gods: Their sacred, healing and hallucinogenic powers.* Rochester, VT: Healing Arts.

Schultes, R. E., Holmstedt, B., & Lindgren, J.-E. (1969). De plantis toxicariis e mundo novo tropicale commentationes III [Notes on neotropical toxic plants III]. Phytochemical examination of Spruce's original collection of *Banisteriopsis caapi. Harvard University Botanical Museum Leaflets,* 22(4), 121–132.

Schultes, R. E., & Raffauf, R. F. (1990). *The healing forest: Medicinal and toxic plants of the northwest Amazonia.* Portland, OR: Dioscorides Press.

Schultes, R. E., & Raffauf, R. F. (1992). *Vine of the soul: Medicine men, their plants and rituals in the Colombian Amazonia.* Oracle, AZ: Synergetic Press.

Schultz, G., Needham, W., Taylor, R., & Shindell, S. (1996). Properties of complex hallucinations associated with deficits in vision. *Perception*, 25(6), 715–726.

Scott, J. (1985). *The weapons of the weak*. New Haven: Yale University Press.

Scott, J. (1990). *Domination and the arts of resistance: Hidden transcripts*. New Haven: Yale University Press.

Scotto & Kent, J. (2001). Rick Strassman interview: DMT research, elves, aliens, and more. Retrieved January 8, 2006, from the Trip Magazine Web site, http://www.tripzine.com/listing.php?smlid=166.

Scurlock, H., & Lucas, P. (1996). Another case of nicotine psychosis? *Addiction*, 91(9), 1388.

Seeger, A. (2004). *Why Suyá sing: A musical anthropology of an Amazonian people*. Urbana: University of Illinois Press.

Segal, A. (1999). *Jews of the Amazon: Self-exile in paradise*. Philadelphia: Jewish Publication Society.

Seit, G. J. (1967). *Epéna*, the intoxicating snuff powder of the Waika Indians and the Tucano medicine man, Agostino. In D. H. Efron, B. Holmstedt, & N. S. Kline (Eds.), *Ethnopharmacologic search for psychoactive drugs* (pp. 315–338). (Public Health Service Publication No. 1645). Washington, DC: U.S. Department of Health, Education, and Welfare.

SensIR Technologies. (2000). *Agricultural applications of the TravelIR microanalysis of nicotine in tobacco leaf by Diamond ATR*. Danbury, CT: SensIR Technologies. Retrieved February 2, 2007, from http://www.sensir.com/newsensir/AppNotes/app030.pdf.

Shafton, A. (1995). *Dream reader: Contemporary approaches to the understanding of dreams*. Albany: State University of New York Press.

Shanon, B. (2000). Ayahuasca and creativity. *Newsletter of the Multidisciplinary Association for Psychedelic Studies*, 10(3), 18–19. Retrieved July 10, 2008, from http://www.maps.org/news-letters/v10n3/v10n3.pdf.

Shanon, B. (2001). Altered temporality. *Journal of Consciousness Studies*, 8(1), 35–58.

Shanon, B. (2002). *The antipodes of the mind: Charting the phenomenology of the ayahuasca experience*. Oxford: Oxford University Press.

Sharon, D. (1972). The San Pedro cactus in Peruvian folk healing. In P. T. Furst (Ed.), *Flesh of the gods: The ritual use of hallucinogens* (pp. 114–135). New York: Praeger.

Shaw, G. B. (1931). Saint Joan. In *The Complete Plays of Bernard Shaw* (pp. 963–1009). London: Constable. (Original work published 1924.)

Sheldon, J. W., & Balick, M. J. (1995). Ethnobotany and the search for balance between use and conservation. In T. Swanson (Ed.), *Intellectual property rights and biodiversity conservation: An interdisciplinary analysis of the values of medicinal plants* (pp. 45–64). Cambridge: Cambridge University Press.

Shepard, G. H. (1998). Psychoactive plants and ethnopsychiatric medicines of the Matsigenka. *Journal of Psychoactive Drugs*, 30(4), 321–332.

Shepherd, J. (1992). Music as cultural text. In J. Paynter, J. Howell, R. Orton, & P. Seymour (Eds.), *Companion to contemporary musical thought* (pp. 145–162). London: Routledge.

Shimojo, S., Kamitani, Y., & Nishida, S. (2001). Afterimage of perceptually filled-in surface. *Science*, 293, 1677–1680.

Shirokogoroff, S. M. (1982). *The psychomental complex of the Tungus*. London: Kegan Paul, Trench, Trubner. (Original work published 1935.)

Shneerson, J. M. (2005). *Sleep medicine: A guide to sleep and its disorders*. Malden, MA: Blackwell.

Shoemaker, A. (1997a). *Grace and madness:* Curanderismo—*Mestizo ayahuasca*. Retrieved February 10, 2007, from the Council on Spiritual Practices Web site, http://www.csp.org/nicholas/A12.html.

Shoemaker, A. (1997b). The magic of *curanderismo*: Lessons in mestizo ayahuasca healing. *Shaman's Drum*, *46*, 39–42.

Shoemaker, A. ("shoemaker"). (2002, December 7). Church, religion, and truth . . . , Speaking one's mind [Msg 55]. Message posted to the Ayahuasca Forums Web site. Retrieved January 13, 2006, from http://forums.ayahuasca.com/phpbb/viewtopic.php?t=3203.

Shoemaker, A. ("shoemaker"). (2003, March 12) The "Drug War?," God help Peter Gorman [Msg 1]. Message posted to the Ayahuasca Forums Web site. Retrieved January 13, 2006, from http://forums.ayahuasca.com/phpbb/viewtopic.php?t=2082&highlight=.

Shoemaker, A. ("shoemaker"). (2005a, September 29). Alan Shoemaker case [Msg 14]. Message posted to the Ayahuasca Forums Web site. Retrieved January 13, 2006, from http://forums.ayahuasca.com/phpbb/viewtopic.php?t=8833.

Shoemaker, A. ("shoemaker"). (2005b, October 1). Alan Shoemaker case [Msg 46]. Message posted to the Ayahuasca Forums Web site. Retrieved January 13, 2006, from http://forums.ayahuasca.com/phpbb/viewtopic.php?t=8833.

Shoemaker, A. ("shoemaker"). (2006, March 5). 2nd Amazonian Shamanism Conference [Msg 97]. Retrieved October 24, 2006, from the Ayahuasca Forums Web site, http://forums.ayahuasca.com/phpbb/viewtopic.php?t=9458.

Shulgin, A. T. (1978). Psychotomimetic drugs: Structure–activity relationships. In L. L. Iversen, S. D. Iversen, & S. H. Snyder (Eds.), *Handbook of psychopharmacology, Vol. 11* (pp. 243–333). New York: Plenum.

Shulgin, A., & Shulgin, A. (1991). *PIHKAL: A chemical love story*. Berkeley: Transform.

Shulgin, A., & Shulgin, A. (1997). *TIHKAL: The continuation*. Berkeley: Transform.

Shweder, R. A. (1991). *Thinking through culture: Expeditions in cultural psychology*. Cambridge, MA: Harvard University Press.

Siikala, A.-L. (1992). The interpretation of Siberian and inner Asian shamanism. In A.-L. Siikala & M. Hoppál (Eds.), *Studies in shamanism* (pp. 15–25). Budapest: Akadémiai Kiadó.

Silcock, L. (Ed.) (1990). *The rainforests: A celebration*. San Francisco: Chronicle Books.

Silva, J. R. (2004). Shamanism. In S. Hvalkof (Ed.), *Dreams coming true. . . . An indigenous health programme in the Peruvian Amazon* (pp. 190–199). Copenhagen: Elise Jensen Foundation and NORDECO.

Simms, K. (2003). *Paul Ricoeur*. London: Routledge.

Simon, P. (1990). Spirit voices. On *The rhythm of the saints* [CD]. New York: Warner Brother Records.

Sinchi Ayahuasca. (2004). *Amazonian shamanism with* ayahuasquero *don Antonio*

Barrera Banda. May 21, 2004. Retrieved April 14, 2007, from http://web.archive.org/web/20040521053246/http://antoniobarrera.tripod.com/.

Singer, P. (1990). "Psychic surgery": Close observation of a popular healing practice. *Medical Anthropology Quarterly*, 4(4), 443–451.

Siskind, J. (1973a). *To hunt in the morning*. London: Oxford University Press.

Siskind, J. (1973b). Tropical forest hunters and the economy of sex. In D. Gross (Ed.), *Peoples and cultures of native South America* (pp. 226–240). Garden City, NY: Natural History Press.

Siskind, J. (1973c). Visions and cures among the Sharanahua. In M. J. Harner (Ed.), *Hallucinogens and shamanism* (pp. 28–39). New York: Oxford University Press.

Skillman, R. D. (1990). *Huachumero* (Ethnic Technology Notes No. 22). San Diego: San Diego Museum of Man.

Slade, P., & Bentall, R. (1988). *Sensory deception: A scientific analysis of hallucination*. London: Croom Helm.

Slater, C. (1994). *Dance of the dolphin: Transformation and disenchantment in the Amazonian imagination*. Chicago: University of Chicago Press.

Slater, C. (1995). Amazonia as Edenic narrative. In W. Cronon (Ed.), *Uncommon ground: Toward reinventing nature* (pp. 114–131). New York: W. W. Norton.

Slater, C. (2002). *Entangled Edens: Visions of the Amazon*. Berkeley: University of California Press.

Slawek, C. L. (2007). Interview with Juan Curico, Medical Director of Sacharuna Clinic. Retrieved May 1, 2007, from the Sacharuna Clinic Web site, http://www.sacharuna.net/ayahuasca/english/documents-juancurico-interview.html.

Slotkin, T. A., DiStefano, V., & Au, W. Y. (1970). Blood levels and urinary excretion of harmine and its metabolites in man and rats. *Journal of Pharmacology and Experimental Therapeutics*, 173(1), 26–30.

Smith, J. Z. (1987). *To take place: Toward theory in ritual*. Chicago: University of Chicago Press.

Smith, M. L. (2005, November 16). Peruvian football. Retrieved August 18, 2008, from the Peruvian Graffiti Web site, http://www.gci275.com/peru/football.shtml.

Smith, R. L., Barrett, R. J., & Sanders-Bush, E. (1999). Mechanism of tolerance development to 2,5-dimethoxy-4-iodoamphetamine in rats: Down-regulation of the 5-HT2A, but not 5-HT2C, receptor. *Psychopharmacology*, 144, 248–254.

Smithsonian Tropical Research Institute. (2006a). *Ormosia amazonica*. Retrieved October 16, 2006, from the Discover Life Web site, http://stri.discoverlife.org/mp/20q?search=Ormosia+amazonica.

Smithsonian Tropical Research Institute. (2006b). *Ormosia macrocalyx*. Retrieved October 16, 2006, from the Discover Life Web site, http://stri.discoverlife.org/mp/20q?search=Ormosia+macrocalyx.

Snyder, G. (1969). Poetry and the primitive: Notes on poetry as an ecological survival technique. In *Earth house hold: Technical notes and queries to fellow dharma revolutionaries* (pp. 117–130). New York: New Directions.

Snyder, G. (1973). Poetry and the primitive: Notes on poetry as an ecological survival technique. In D. Allen & W. Tallman (Eds.), *The poetics of the new American poetry* (pp. 395–415). New York: Grove Press.

Snyder, G. (1975). The yogin and the philosopher. *Alcheringa: Ethnopoetics*, *1*(2), 2–3.

Snyder, G. (1976). The politics of ethnopoetics. *Alcheringa: Ethnopoetics*, *2*(2), 13–22.

Snyder, G. (1977a). The politics of ethnopoetics. In *The old ways: Six essays* (pp. 15–43). San Francisco: City Lights.

Snyder, G. (1977b). The yogin and the philosopher. In *The old ways: Six essays* (pp. 9–14). San Francisco: City Lights.

Snyder, G. (1980). Poetry, community and climax. In W. McLean (Ed.), *The real work: Interviews and talks 1964–1979* (pp. 159–174). New York: New Directions. (Original work published 1979.)

Snyder, G. (1983). Poetry and the primitive: Notes on poetry as an ecological survival technique. In J. Rothenberg & D. Rothenberg (Eds.), *Symposium of the whole: A range of discourse toward an ethnopoetics* (pp. 90–98). Berkeley: University of California Press.

Soibelman, T. (1996). "My father and my mother, show me your beauty": Ritual use of ayahuasca in Rio de Janeiro (Brazil) (M.A. thesis, California Institute of Integral Studies, 1995). *Masters Abstracts International*, *34*(5), 1783.

Soini, P. (1972) The capture and commerce of live monkeys in the Amazonian region of Peru. *International Zoo Yearbook*, *12*(1), 26–36.

Spinella, M. (2001). *The psychopharmacology of herbal medicine: Plant drugs that alter mind, brain, and behavior*. Cambridge, MA: MIT.

Stafford, P. (1992). *Psychedelics encyclopedia* (3rd ed.). Berkeley: Ronin.

Stanfield, M. E. (1998). *Red rubber, bleeding trees: Violence, slavery, and empire in northwest Amazonia, 1850–1933*. Albuquerque: University of New Mexico Press.

Starn, O. (1999). *Nightwatch: The politics of protest in the Andes*. Durham: Duke University Press.

Stevens, J. (1987). *Storming heaven: LSD and the American dream*. New York: Harper & Row.

Stewart, P. J., & Strathern, A. (2004). *Witchcraft, sorcery, rumors and gossip*. Cambridge: Cambridge University Press.

Sting. (2003). *Broken music*. New York: Dial.

Stocks, A. W. (1979). Tendiendo un puente entre el cielo y la tierra en alas de la canción (el uso de la música en un ritual alucinógeno de curación en el bajo Huallaga) [Building a bridge between heaven and earth on the wings of song (the use of music in hallucinogenic healing rituals in the Bajo Huallaga)]. *Amazonía peruana*, *2*(4), 71–100.

Stocks, A. (1984). Indian policy in eastern Peru. In M. Schmink & C. H. Wood (Eds.), *Frontier expansion in Amazonia* (pp. 33–61). Gainesville: University Press of Florida.

Stoller, P. (1989). *The taste of ethnographic things: The senses in anthropology*. Philadelphia: University of Pennsylvania Press.

Stoller, P. (1996). Sounds and things: Pulsations of power in Songhay. In C. Laderman & M. Roseman (Eds.), *The performance of healing* (pp. 165–184). New York: Routledge.

Stone, A. (2003). *Explore shamanism*. Loughborough, England: Heart of Albion.

Strassman, R. J. (1991). A report on FDA approved human studies with DMT. *Newsletter of the Multidisciplinary Association for Psychedelic Studies*, *3*(1), 7–8.

Strassman, R. J. (1992). Subjective effects of DMT and the development of the Hallucinogen Rating Scale. *Newsletter of the Multidisciplinary Association for Psychedelic Studies*, *3*(2), 8–12.

Strassman, R. J. (1994). Human hallucinogenic drug research: Regulatory, clinical, and scientific issues. In G. C. Lin & R. A. Glennon (Eds.), *Hallucinogens: An update* (pp. 92–123). (NIDA Research Monograph 146). Rockville, MD: National Institute on Drug Abuse.

Strassman, R. J. (1996). Human psychopharmacology of N,N-dimethyltryptamine. *Behavioral Brain Research*, 73, 121–124.

Strassman, R. J. (2000). Biomedical research with psychedelics: Current models and future prospects. In R. Forte (Ed.), *Entheogens and the future of religion* (pp. 153–162). San Francisco: Council on Spiritual Practices.

Strassman, R. J. (2001). *DMT: The spirit molecule: A doctor's revolutionary research into the biology of near-death and mystical experiences*. Rochester, VT: Park Street Press.

Strassman, R. J. (2007a). Comment: "A methodology for studying various interpretations of the n,n-dimethyltryptamine-induced alternate reality." *Journal of Scientific Exploration*, 21(1), 85–87. Retrieved May 17, 2008, from the Marko Rodriguez Web site, http://www.soe.ucsc.edu/~okram/papers/strassman-comment.pdf.

Strassman, R. J. (2007b). Research projects and symposia at the Cottonwood Research Foundation. Retrieved May 5, 2008, from http://cottonwoodresearch.org/Ongoing_Projects.html.

Strassman, R. J. (2008) The varieties of the DMT experience. In R. Strassman, S. Wojtowica, L. E. Luna, & E. Frecska, *Inner paths to outer space: Journeys to alien worlds through psychedelics and other spiritual technologies* (pp. 51–80). Rochester, VT: Park Street.

Strassman, R. J., & Qualls, C. R. (1994). Dose-response study of N,N-dimethyltryptamine in humans: I. Neuroendocrine, autonomic, and cardiovascular effects. *Archives of General Psychiatry*, 51, 85–97.

Strassman, R. J., Qualls, C. R., & Berg, L. M. (1996). Differential tolerance to biological and subjective effects of four closely spaced doses of N,Ndimethyltryptamine in humans. *Biological Psychiatry*, 39, 784–795.

Strassman, R. J., Qualls, C. R., Uhlenhuth, E. H., & Kellner, R. (1994). Dose-response study of N,N-dimethyltryptamine in humans: II. Subjective effects and preliminary results of a new rating scale. *Archives of General Psychiatry*, 51, 98–108.

Strathern, A. (1995). Trance and the theory of healing: Sociogenic and psychogenic components of consciousness. In A. P. Cohen & N. Rapport (Eds.), *Questions of consciousness* (pp. 117–133). (ASA Monographs 33). London: Routledge.

Strathern, A., & Stewart, P. J. (1999). *Curing and healing: Medical anthropology in global perspective*. Durham: Carolina Academic Press.

Strathern, A., & Stewart, P. J. (2004). Afterword: Substances, powers, cosmos, and history. In N. L. Whitehead & R. Wright (Eds.), *In darkness and secrecy: The anthropology of assault sorcery and witchcraft in Amazonia* (pp. 314–320). Durham: Duke University Press.

Streatfeild, D. (2007). *Brainwash: The secret history of mind control*. New York: Picador.

Stroup, R. K. (2004, May 8). Statement of R. Keith Stroup, Esq., Executive Director, National Organization for the Reform of Marijuana Laws (NORML). Paper presented at the 2004 British Columbia Civil Liberties Association conference "Beyond Prohibition: Legal Cannabis in Canada," Vancouver, May 8. Retrieved July 28, 2008, from the British Columbia Civil Liberties Association Web site, http://www.bccla.org/prohibition/Vancouver%20statement.htm.

Stuart, R. (2002). Ayahuasca tourism: A cautionary tale. *Newsletter of the Multidisciplinary Association for Psychedelic Studies*, 12(2), 36–38. Retrieved August 8, 2007, from http://www.maps.org/news-letters/v12n2/12236stu.pdf.

Stuller, J. (1995, December). Climate is often a matter of inches and a little water. *Smithsonian*, 6(9), 102–110.

Sullivan, J. B., Wingert, W. A., & Norris, R. L. (1995). North American venomous reptiles bites. In P. S. Auerbach (Ed.), *Wilderness medicine: Management of wilderness and environmental emergencies* (3rd ed., pp. 680–709). St. Louis, MO: Mosby.

Sullivan, L. E. (1988). *Icanchu's drum: An orientation to meaning in South American religions*. New York: Macmillan.

Sullivan, L. E. (1994). The attributes and power of the shaman: A general description of the ecstatic care of the soul. In G. Seaman & J. S. Day (Eds.), *Ancient traditions: Shamanism in Central Asia and the Americas* (pp. 29–39). Niwot: University Press of Colorado and Denver Museum of Natural History.

Swerdlow, J. (2000). *Nature's medicine: Plants that heal*. Washington, DC: National Geographic.

Szára, S. (1994). Are hallucinogens psychoheuristic? In G. C. Lin & R. A. Glennon (Eds.), *Hallucinogens: An update* (pp. 33–50). (NIDA Research Monograph 146). Rockville, MD: National Institute on Drug Abuse.

Tacker, J. R., & Ferm, R. P. (2002). Lysergic acid diethylamide and other hallucinogens. In L. Goldfrank, N. Flomenbaum, N. Lewin, M. A. Howland, R. Hoffman, & L. Nelson (Eds.), *Goldfrank's toxicologic emergencies* (7th ed., pp. 1046–1053). New York: McGraw-Hill.

Tangoa Paima, J. (2004). Icaros: *Ancient songs from an ayahuasca ceremony, Parts 1–3* [3 CDs]. Worcester, MA: Ayahuayra Project.

Tanner, C. (2007). *Ayahuayra: Spirit of the wind*. Retrieved April 21, 2008, from the Ayahuayra Web site, http://www.iganicsoundsystem.com/Audio/Ayahuayra/main.htm.

Tart, C. (2001). Psychoactive sacramentals: What must be said. In T. B. Roberts (Ed.), *Psychoactive sacramentals: Essays on entheogens and religion* (pp. 47–56). San Francisco: Council on Spiritual Practices.

Taussig, M. (1987). *Shamanism, colonialism, and the wild man*. Chicago: University of Chicago Press.

Taussig, M. (2004). Folk healing and the structure of conquest in southwest Colombia. In A. A. Znamenski (Ed.), *Shamanism: Critical concepts in sociology, Vol. II* (pp. 189–218). London: Routledge Curzon. (Original work published 1980.)

Taylor, A. C., & Chau, E. (1983). Jivaroan magical songs. *Amerindia*, 8, 87–127. Retrieved August 22, 2008, from the Centre d'Etudes des Langues Indigènes d'Amérique Web site, http://celia.cnrs.fr/FichExt/Am/A_08_04.pdf.

Taylor, L. (1998). *Herbal secrets of the rainforest*. Rocklin, CA: Prima Health.

Taylor, L. (2006a). Database file for *ajos-sacha* (*Mansoa alliacea*). Retrieved June 30, 2007, from the Raintree Nutrition Tropical Plant Database Web site, http://www.rain-tree.com/mansoa.htm.

Taylor, L. (2006b). Database file for *piri-piri* (*Cyperus articulatus*). Retrieved December 8,

2006, from the Raintree Nutrition Tropical Plant Database Web site, http://www.rain-tree.com/piri-piri.htm.

Teixeira-Pinto, M. (2004). Being alone amid others: Sorcery and morality among the Arara, Carib, Brazil. In N. L. Whitehead & R. Wright (Eds.), *In darkness and secrecy: The anthropology of assault sorcery and witchcraft in Amazonia* (pp. 215–243). Durham: Duke University Press.

Tenenbaum, D. (2003, Fall). Unintended consequences [Interview with Neil L. Whitehead]. *On Wisconsin*. Retrieved May 13, 2008, from the Wisconsin Alumni Association Web site, http://www.uwalumni.com/home/alumniandfriends/onwisconsin/archives/2003Fall/unintended.aspx.

Teunisse, R. J., Cruysberg, J. R., Hoefnagels, W. H. Verbeek, A. L., & Zitman, F. G. (1996). Visual hallucinations in psychologically normal people: Charles Bonnet's syndrome: CBS. *The Lancet, 347*, 794–797.

Theroux, P. (2005). *Blinding light*. New York: Mariner.

Thomas, O. (1997). *The dialectics of schizophrenia*. Bristol, England: Free Association Books.

Thurber, J. (1945). The admiral on the wheel. In *A Thurber carnival* (pp. 107–110). New York: Harper Perennial. (Original work published 1937.)

Tindall, R. (2008). *The jaguar that roams the mind*. Rochester, VT: Park Street.

Todorov, T. (1981). *Introduction to poetics* (R. Howard, Trans.). Minneapolis: University of Minnesota Press. (Original work published 1968.)

Topping, D. M. (1999). Ayahuasca and cancer: A postscript. *Bulletin of the Multidisciplinary Association for Psychedelic Studies, 9*(2), 22–25. Retrieved August 8, 2008, from http://www.maps.org/news-letters/v09n2/09222top.html.

Torres, W. (2000). Jaguar-becoming. In L. E. Luna & S. F. White (Eds.), *Ayahuasca reader: Encounters with the Amazon's sacred vine* (pp. 107–112). Santa Fe, NM: Synergetic.

Tournon, J. (1991). Medicina y visiones: Canto de un curandero Shipibo-Conibo, texto y contexto [Medicine and visions: The song of a Shipibo-Conibo healer, text and context]. *Amerindia, 16*(6), 181–212. Retrieved February 19, 2007, from the Centre d'Etudes des Langues Indigènes d'Amerique Web site, http://celia.cnrs.fr/FichExt/Am/A_16_06.htm.

Townsley, G. (2001). "Twisted language," a technique for knowing. In J. Narby & F. Huxley (Eds.), *Shamans through time: 500 years on the path to knowledge* (pp. 263–271). New York: Jeremy P. Tarcher.

Tramacchi, D. (2006). Entheogens, elves and other entities: Encountering the spirits of shamanic plants and substances. In L. Hume & K. McPhillips (Eds.), *Popular spiritualities: The politics of contemporary enchantment* (pp. 91–104). Burlington, VT: Ashgate.

Trimble, D. R. (2003). Disarming the dream police: The case of the Santo Daime. Paper presented at the International Conference of the Center for Religious Studies and Research, Vilnius, Lithuania, April 9–12. Retrieved June 10, 2008, from the Center for Religious Studies and Research Web site, http://www.cesnur.org/2003/vi12003_trimble.htm.

Trotter, R. (1981). Folk remedies as indicators of common illnesses: Examples from the United States–Mexico border. *Journal of Ethnopharmacology, 4*(2), 207–221.

Trotter, R. T., & Chavira, J. A. (1997). Curanderismo: *Mexican American folk healing*. Athens: University of Georgia Press.

Tsemberis, S., & Stefancic, A. (2000). The role of an *espiritista* in the treatment of a homeless, mentally ill Hispanic man. *Psychiatric Services*, 51, 1572–1574.

Tupper, K. W. (2006). The globalization of ayahuasca: Harm reduction or benefit maximization? *International Journal of Drug Policy*. Retrieved May 28, 2008, from http://www.kentupper.com/resources/Globalization+of+Ayahuasca—IJDP+pre-print.pdf.

Turner, B. S. (1984). *The body and society: Explorations in social theory*. Oxford: Blackwell.

Turner, E. (1992). The reality of spirits. *ReVision*, 15(1), 28–32.

Turner, E., Blodgett, W., Kahona, S., & Benwa, F. (1992). *Experiencing ritual: A new interpretation of African healing*. Philadelphia: University of Pennsylvania Press.

Turner, K. (1999). *Beautiful necessity: The art and meaning of women's altars*. New York: Thames & Hudson.

Turner, V. (1969). *The ritual process: Structure and anti-structure*. Chicago: Aldine.

Turner, W. J., & Heyman, J. J. (1961). The presence of mescaline in *Opuntia cylindrica* (*Trichocereus pachanoi*). *Journal of Organic Chemistry*, 25, 2250.

Turner, W. J., Merlis, S., & Carl, A. (1955). Concerning theories of indoles in schizophrenigenesis. *American Journal of Psychiatry*, 112, 466–467.

Udenfriend, S., Witkop, B., Redfield, B., & Weissbach, H. (1958). Studies with the reversible inhibitors of monamine oxidase: Harmaline and related compounds. *Biochemical Pharmacology*, 1, 160–165.

Uhl, C., Nepstad, D., Buschbacher, R., Clark, K., Kauffman, B., & Subler, S. (1998). Studies of ecosystem response to natural and anthropogenic disturbances provide guidelines for designing sustainable land-use systems in Amazonia. In A. B. Anderson (Ed.), *Alternatives to deforestation: Steps toward sustainable use of the Amazon rain forest* (pp. 24–42). New York: Columbia University Press.

Ulanov, A., & Ulanov, B. (1999). *The healing imagination: The meeting of psyche and soul*. Einsiedlen, Switzerland: Daimon Verlag.

U.N. Convention on Psychotropic Substances. (1971, February 21). 32 U.S.T. 543, 1019 U.N.T.S. 175. Retrieved July 25, 2008, from the U.N. Office on Drugs and Crime Web site, http://www.unodc.org/pdf/convention_1971_en.pdf.

U.N. Convention on Psychotropic Substances, Status of Treaty Adherence. (2008, March 14). Retrieved July 25, 2008, from the U.N. Office on Drugs and Crime Web site, http://www.unodc.org/documents/treaties/treaty_adherence_convention_1971.pdf.

U.N. Environment Programme. (1987). *Minimum conflict: Guidelines for planning the use of American humid tropic environments*. Washington, DC: Organization of American States. Retrieved August 12, 2008, from http://www.oas.org/dsd/publications/Unit/oea37e/ch15.htm.

University of Iowa Hospitals and Clinics. (N.d.). Tobacco: *Nicotiana rustica*. Retrieved February 2, 2007, from the Medical Museum Web site, http://www.uihealthcare.com/depts/medmuseum/galleryexhibits/naturespharmacy/tobaccoplant/tobacco.html.

Uscátagui, M. N. (1959). The present distribution of narcotics and stimulants amongst the Indian tribes of Colombia. *Harvard University Botanical Museum Leaflets*, 18(6), 273–304.

U.S. Department of Agriculture, National Resources Conservation Service. (2007). *Capsicum pubescens* Ruiz & Pavón. Baton Rouge, LA: National Plant Data Center. Retrieved April 17, 2007, from the PLANTS Database Web site, http://plants.usda.gov/java/profile?symbol=CAPU38.

Uzendoski, M. (2005). *The Napo Runa of Amazonian Ecuador*. Urbana: University of Illinois Press.

Valenti, F. M. (2000). *More than a movie: Ethics in entertainment*. Boulder: Westview Press.

Valenzuela, P. (2003). Evidentiality in Shipibo-Konibo, with a comparative overview of the category in Panoan. In A. Y. Aikhenvald & R. M. Dixon (Eds.), *Studies in evidentiality* (pp. 33–62). (Typological Studies in Language 64). Amsterdam: John Benjamins.

Valenzuela, P., & Valera Rojas, A. (2005). *Koshi shinany ainbo: El testimonio de una mujer shipiba*. Lima: Universidad Nacional Mayor de San Marcos.

Van Beek, T. A., Verpoorte, R., Svendsen, A. B., Leeuwenberg, A. J. M., & Bisset, N. G. (1984). *Tabernaemontana* L. (Apocynaceae): A review of its taxonomy, phytochemistry, ethnobotany and pharmacology. *Journal of Ethnopharmacology*, 10(1), 1–156. Retrieved May 8, 2008, from the Puzzle Piece Web site, http://www.puzzlepiece.org/ibogaine/literature/vanbeek1984.pdf.

Varese, S. (2002). *Salt of the mountain: Campa Asháninka history and resistance in the Peruvian jungle*. Norman: University of Oklahoma Press. (Original work published 1973.)

Vargas Llosa, M. (1963). *La ciudad y los perros*. Barcelona: Seix Barral.

Vargas Llosa, M. (1990, December). Questions of conquest: What Columbus wrought, and what he did not. *Harper's Magaine*, 281, 45–53.

Vargas Llosa, M. (2001). *The storyteller: A novel* (H. Lane, Trans.). New York: Picador. (Original work published 1987).

Velásquez Zea, V. (2006). *El Duende del Bosque y la cosmovisión forestal del poblador rural amazónico* [The Spirit of the Woods and the forest cosmovision of rural Amazonian inhabitants]. Madre de Dios, Peru: Universidad Amazónica de Madre de Dios. Retrieved October 20, 2006, from the Monografias Web site, http://www.monografias.com/trabajos31/chuyachaqui/chuyachaqui.shtml.

Vidal, S., & Whitehead, N. L. (2004). Dark shamans and the shamanic state: Sorcery and witchcraft as political process in Guyana and the Venezuelan Amazon. In N. L. Whitehead & R. Wright (Eds.), *In darkness and secrecy: The anthropology of assault sorcery and witchcraft in Amazonia* (pp. 51–81). Durham: Duke University Press.

Vine victory. (2000, March). *New Internationalist*, 321, 6.

Vitebsky, P. (1995). *The shaman*. Boston: Little, Brown.

Vitebsky, P. (2000). Shamanism. In G. Harvey (Ed.), *Indigenous religions: A companion* (pp. 55–67). London: Cassell.

Viveiros de Castro, E. B. (1979, May). A fabricação do corpo na sociedade xinguana [On constructing the body in Xingua society]. *Boletin do Museu Nacional (São Paolo)*, 32, 40–49.

Viveiros de Castro, E. B. (1994). *From the enemy's point of view: Humanity and divinity in an Amazonian society* (C. V. Howard, Trans.). Chicago: University of Chicago Press.

Viveiros de Castro, E. B. (1996). Images of nature and society in Amazonian ethnology. *Annual Review of Anthropology*, 25, 179–200.

Viveiros de Castro, E. B. (2002). Cosmological deixis and Amerindian perspectivism. In M. Lambek (Ed.), *A reader in the anthropology of religion* (pp. 306–326). Malden, MA: Blackwell. (Original work published 1998.)

Viveiros de Castro, E. B. (2005). Perspectivism and multinaturalism in indigenous America. In A. Surrallés & P. García Hierro (Eds.), *The land within: Indigenous territory and the perception of the environment* (pp. 36–74). Copenhagen: International Work Group for Indigenous Affairs.

Vizenor, G. (1997). *Hotline healers: An Almost Browne novel*. Hanover, NH: Wesleyan University Press.

Voget, F. W. (1984). *The Shoshone-Crow Sun Dance* (Civilization of the American Indian Series, Vol. 170). Norman: University of Oklahoma Press.

Walden, J. B. (1995). Jungle travel and survival. In P. S. Auerbach (Ed.), *Wilderness medicine: Management of wilderness and environmental emergencies* (3rd ed., pp. 393–412). St. Louis, MO: Mosby.

Walker, A. (2004). *Now is the time to open your heart*. New York: Random House.

Wallach, J. V. (2009). Endogenous hallucinogens as ligands of the trace amine receptors: A possible role in sensory perception. *Medical Hypotheses*, 72(1), 91–94.

Wasson, R. G. (1957, May 13). Great adventures III: The discovery of mushrooms that cause strange visions. Vision-giving mushrooms are discovered in a remote Mexican village by a U.S. banker who describes the strange ritual and effects of eating them. *Life Magazine*. Retrieved August 19, 2004, from the Psychedelic Library Web site, http://www.psychedelic-library.org/life.htm.

Wasson, R. G. (1972a). [Review of the book *A separate reality*]. *Economic Botany*, 26(1), 98–99.

Wasson, R. G. (1972b). The divine mushroom of immortality. In P. T. Furst (Ed.), *Flesh of the gods: The ritual use of hallucinogens* (pp. 185–200). New York: Praeger.

Wasson, R. G. (1980). *The wondrous mushroom: Mycolatry in Mesoamerica*. New York: McGraw-Hill.

Wasson, V. P., & Wasson, R. G. (1957). *Mushrooms, Russia, and history*. New York: Pantheon.

Watkins, M. (1976). *Waking dreams*. New York: Harper Colophon.

Waymire, J. (N.d.). *Plants used for craftwork in the Peruvian Amazon*. Retrieved November 10, 2006, from the Amazon River Cruise and Karakoram Highway Adventure Web site, http://www.biobio.com/Articles/craftplants.html.

Webster, H. (1948). *Magic, a sociological study*. Stanford, CA: Stanford University Press.

Weil, A. (1974). Introduction. In F. B. Lamb, *Wizard of the Upper Amazon: The story of Manuel Córdova-Rivas* (pp. v–xii). Berkeley: North Atlantic Books.

Weil, A. (1986). *The natural mind: An investigation of drugs and the higher consciousness*. New York: Houghton Mifflin. (Original work published 1972.)

Weil, A. (1998). *The marriage of the sun and moon: Dispatches from the frontiers of consciousness*. New York: Houghton Mifflin. (Original work published 1980.)

Weil, A. (2002). The psychedelic vision at the turn of the millennium. In C. S. Grob (Ed.), *Hallucinogens: A reader* (pp. 122–137). New York: Jeremy P. Tarcher.

Weinstein, B. (1983). *The Amazon rubber boom 1850–1920*. Stanford, CA: Stanford University Press.

Weiskopf, J. (1995, Fall). From agony to ecstacy: The transformative spirit of yaje. *Shaman's Drum: Journal of Experiential Shamanism*. Retrieved November 27, 2007, from the Disembodied Eyes Web site, http://diseyes.lycaeum.org/fresh/yagmree.htm.

Weiskopf, J. (2005). *Yajé, the new purgatory: Encounters with ayahuasca*. Bogotá: Villegas Editores.

Weiskopf, J. (2006). Review of *O Uso Ritual da Ayahuasca*. Retrieved May 6, 2008, from the Erowid Review Web site, http://www.erowid.org/library/review/review.php?p=191.

Weiss, G. (1973). Shamanism and priesthood in light of the Campa ayahuasca ceremony. In M. J. Harner (Ed.), *Hallucinogens and shamanism* (pp. 40–47). New York: Oxford University Press.

Weiss, G. (1975). *Campa cosmology: The world of a forest tribe in South America* (Anthropological Papers of the American Museum of Natural History, 52/5). New York: American Museum of Natural History.

Weller, S. C., Pachter, L. M., Trotter, R. T., & Baer, R. D. (1993). *Empacho* in four Latino groups: A study of intra- and intercultural variations in beliefs. *Medical Anthropology*, 15, 109–136.

Welwood, J. (2000). *Toward a psychology of awakening: Buddhism, psychotherapy, and the path of personal and spiritual transformation*. Boston: Shambhala.

Werlich, D. P. (1978). *Peru: A short history*. Carbondale: Southern Illinois University Press.

Wesnes, K., & Revell, A. (1984). The separate and combined effects of scopolamine and nicotine on human information processing. *Psychopharmacology Series (Berlin)*, 84(1), 5–11.

Wesnes, K., & Warburton, D. M. (1984). Effects of scopolamine and nicotine on human rapid information processing performance. *Psychopharmacology (Berlin)*, 82(3), 147–150.

White, O. E. (1922). Botanical exploration in Bolivia. *Brooklyn Botanical Garden Record*, 11(3), 93–105.

Whitehead, N. R. (2001). *Kanaimà*: Shamanism and ritual death in the Pakaraima Mountains, Guyana. In L. Rival & N. Whitehead (Eds.), *Beyond the visible and the material: The Amerindianization of society in the work of Peter Rivière* (pp. 235–245). Oxford: Oxford University Press.

Whitehead, N. L. (2002). *Dark shamans:* Kanaimà *and the poetics of violent death*. Durham: Duke University Press.

Whitehead, N. L. (2006). The sign of *kanaimã*, the space of Guyana and the demonology of development. In A. Strathern, P. J. Stewart, & N. L. Whitehead (Eds.), *Terror and violence: Imagination and the unimaginable* (pp. 171–191). Ann Arbor: Pluto.

Whitehead, N. R., & Wright, R. (2004). Introduction: Dark shamanism. In N. L. Whitehead & R. Wright (Eds.), *In darkness and secrecy: The anthropology of assault sorcery and witchcraft in Amazonia* (pp. 1–19). Durham: Duke University Press.

Whiting, B. (1950). *Paiute sorcery*. New York: Viking Fund Publications in Anthropology.

Whitten, N. E. (1976). *Sacha Runa: Ethnicity and adaptation of Ecuadorian jungle Quichua*. Urbana: University of Illinois Press.

Whitten, N. E. (1985). *Sicuanga Runa: The other side of development in Amazonian Ecuador.* Urbana: University of Illinois Press.

Whitten, N. E., & Whitten, D. S. (2008). *Puyo runa: Imagery and power in modern Amazonia.* Urbana: University of Illinois Press.

Whyte, P. D. (2005). Negotiation and hostage taking: The 1996 Japanese experience in Lima, Peru. Retrieved August 22, 2008, from the Canadian Forum on Civil Justice Web site, http://cfcj-fcjc.org/clearinghouse/drpapers/2005-dra/whyte.pdf.

Wiersema, J. H., & Léon, B. (1999). *World economic plants: A standard reference.* Boca Raton: CRC.

Wilbert, J. (1987). *Tobacco and shamanism in South America.* New Haven: Yale University Press.

Wilbert, J. (1991). Does pharmacology corroborate the nicotine therapy and practices of South American shamanism? *Journal of Ethnopharmacology, 32*(1–3), 179–186.

Wilbert, J. (2004). The order of dark shamans among the Warao. In N. L. Whitehead & R. Wright (Eds.), *In darkness and secrecy: The anthropology of assault sorcery and witchcraft in Amazonia* (pp. 21–50). Durham: Duke University Press.

Wilcox, J. P. (2003). *Ayahuasca: The visionary and healing powers of the vine of the soul.* Rochester, VT: Park Street.

Williams, S. R. (2004). Strychnine. In K. R. Olson (Ed.), *Poisoning and drug overdose* (pp. 348–350). New York: McGraw-Hill.

Winkelman, M. (2000). *Shamanism: The neural ecology of consciousness and healing.* Westport, CT: Bergin & Garvey.

Winkelman, M. (2005). Drug tourism or spiritual healing? Ayahuasca seekers in Amazonia. *Journal of Psychoactive Drugs, 37*(20), 209–218.

Wisechild, L. M. (2001). *La limpia* [The bath]. In L. Hogan & B. Peterson (Eds.), *The sweet breathing of plants: Women writing on the green world* (pp. 93–100). New York: North Point Press.

Wiser, G. (2001). U.S. Patent and Trademark Office reinstates ayahuasca patent: Flawed decision declares open season on resources of indigenous peoples. Retrieved April 3, 2007, from the Center for International Environmental Law Web site, http://www.ciel.org/Publications/PTODecisionAnalysis.pdf.

Witzig, R. (2006). *The global art of soccer.* Harahan, LA: CusiBoy.

Wong, F. M. (2007, December 22). Legado musical con sabor nacional [Musical legacy with a national flavor]. *El Comercio.* Retrieved April 25, 2008, from http://www.elcomercio.com.pe/edicionimpresa/Html/2007–12–22/legado-musical-sabor-nacional.html.

Woodard, C. (1999, July 28). Patent a plant? Americans do, irking shamans. *Christian Science Monitor, 91*(69), 1.

World Music News Wire. (2008, October 21). Amazonian hallucinogens, wah-wah guitar, a plane crash: Juaneco y Su Combo kicks off the Masters of Chicha Series. Retrieved December 20, 2008, from http://www.worldmusicwire.com/2008/10/amazonian-hallu.html.

Wright, P. G. (1992). Dream, shamanism, and power among the Toba of Formosa Province. In E. Langdon & G. Baer (Eds.), *Portals of power: Shamanism in South America* (pp. 149–172). Albuquerque: University of New Mexico Press.

Wright, R. (2004). The wicked and the wise men: Witches and prophets in the history of the northwest Amazon. In N. L. Whitehead & R. Wright (Eds.), *In darkness and secrecy: The anthropology of assault sorcery and witchcraft in Amazonia* (pp. 82–108). Durham: Duke University Press.

Wright, R. M., & Hill, J. D. (1992). Venancio Kamiko: Wakuénai shaman and messiah. In E. Langdon & G. Baer (Eds.), *Portals of power: Shamanism in South America* (pp. 257–286). Albuquerque: University of New Mexico Press.

Yasumoto, M. (1996). The psychotropic *kiéri* in Huichol culture. In S. B. Schaefer & P. T. Furst (Eds.), *People of the peyote: Huichol Indian history, religion and survival* (pp. 235–263). Albuquerque: University of New Mexico Press.

Yerba Mala. (2008, June 10). *Cumbia* old school. Retrieved July 1, 2008, from http://yerbamala-nuncamuere.blogspot.com/2008/06/cumbia-old-school.html.

Young, A. (1983). The relevance of traditional medical cultures to modern primary health care. *Social Science and Medicine*, 17, 1205–1211.

Yronwrode, C. (2000). A Peruvian package amulet: Collage of magical items. Retrieved April 3, 2007, from the Lucky Mojo Web site, http://www.luckymojo.com/packagecollage.html.

Yronwrode, C. (2003a). Charm vials and charm flasks. Retrieved April 3, 2007, from http://www.luckymojo.com/charmvial.html.

Yronwrode, C. (2003b). *Florida* water and *kananga* water. Retrieved April 23, 2004, from the Lucky Mojo Web site, http://www.luckymojo.com/floridakanangawater.html.

Zamora, L. P., & Faris, W. B. (1995). Introduction: Daiquiri birds and Flaubertian parrot(ie)s. In L. P. Zamora & W. B. Faris (Eds.), *Magical realism: Theory, history, community* (pp. 1–11). Durham: Duke University Press.

Zavala, E. (2001). Mujeres indígenas: La dimensión femenina en la medicina tradicional Amazónica [Indigenous women: The feminine dimension in traditional Amazonian medicine]. In J. Mabit (Ed.), *Memoria del segundo foro interamericano sobre espiritualidad indígena* (pp. 213–214). Tarapoto, Peru: Consejo Interamericano Sobre Espiritualidad Indígena y Centro de Rehabilitación y de Investigación de las Medicinas Tradicionales Takiwasi.

Ziegler, B., & Tonjes, W. (1991, January). Scopolamine poisoning as a cause of acute paranoid hallucinatory psychoses [Abstract]. *Psychiatrische Praxis*, 18(1), 21–24.

Znamenski, A. A. (2007). *The beauty of the primitive: Shamanism and the Western imagination*. New York: Oxford University Press.

Zuluage, G., & Díaz, R. (1999). *Encuentro de taitas en la Amazonía Colombiana: Ceremonias y Reflexiones* [Conference of shamans in the Colombian Amazon: Ceremonies and reflections]. Bogotá: Unión de Médicos Indígenas Yageceros de la Amazonía Colombiana.

Zur, D., & Ullman, S. (2003). Filling-in of retinal scotomas. *Vision Research*, 43(9), 971–982.

INDEX

Page numbers in **bold** type indicate photographs or illustrations.

A

B

D

E

F

G

K

L

M

N

O

P

T

U

V

W

X

Y

Z